TWO DOZEN (OR SO) ARGUMENTS FOR GOD

Two Dozen (or so) Arguments for God

THE PLANTINGA PROJECT

Edited by Jerry L. Walls and Trent Dougherty

OXFORD

UNIVERSITY PRESS

Oxford University Press is a department of the University of Oxford. It furthers
the University's objective of excellence in research, scholarship, and education
by publishing worldwide. Oxford is a registered trade mark of Oxford University
Press in the UK and certain other countries.

Published in the United States of America by Oxford University Press
198 Madison Avenue, New York, NY 10016, United States of America.

© Oxford University Press 2018

CIP data is on file at the Library of Congress
ISBN 978-0-19-084222-2 (pbk.)
ISBN 978-0-19-084221-5 (hbk.)

Contents

Acknowledgments ix

List of Contributors xi

Introduction 1
   Jerry L. Walls and Trent Dougherty

I | HALF A DOZEN (OR SO) ONTOLOGICAL (OR METAPHYSICAL) ARGUMENTS

(A) The Argument from Intentionality (or Aboutness): Propositions Supernaturalized 11
   Lorraine Juliano Keller

(B) The Argument from Collections 29
   Christopher Menzel

(C) The Argument from (Natural) Numbers 59
   Tyron Goldschmidt

(D) The Argument from Counterfactuals: Counterfactuals, Vagueness, and God 76
   Alexander R. Pruss

(E) The Argument from Physical Constants: The Fine-Tuning for Discoverability 89
   Robin Collins

(F) The Naïve Teleological Argument: An Argument from Design for Ordinary People 108
   C. Stephen Evans

(H) The Ontological Argument: Patching Plantinga's Ontological Argument by Making the Murdoch Move 123
   Elizabeth D. Burns

(I) *Why Is There Anything at All?* 137
    Joshua Rasmussen and Christopher Gregory Weaver

II | HALF A DOZEN EPISTEMOLOGICAL ARGUMENTS

(J) *The Argument from Positive Epistemic Status: Evolutionary Psychology
and the Argument from Positive Epistemic Status* 159
    Justin L. Barrett

(K) *The Argument from the Confluence of Proper Function and Reliability:
Is God the Designer of Our Cognitive Faculties? Evaluating
Plantinga's Argument* 170
    Alexander Arnold

(L) *The Argument from Simplicity and* (M) *The Argument from Induction:
Atheistic Induction by Boltzmann Brains* 184
    Bradley Monton

(N) *The Putnamian Argument (the Argument from the Rejection of Global Skepticism)
[also, (O) The Argument from Reference, and (K) The Argument from the
Confluence of Proper Function and Reliability]: Putnam's Semantic Skepticism
and the Epistemic Melt-Down of Naturalism: How Defeat of Putnam's
Puzzle Provides a Defeater for Plantinga's Self-Defeat Argument
Against Naturalism* 198
    Evan Fales

(N) *The Putnamian Argument,* (O) *The Argument from Reference, and* (P)
*The Kripke-Wittgenstein Argument from Plus and Quus: Arguments from
Knowledge, Reference, and Content* 214
    Daniel Bonevac

(Q) *The General Argument from Intuition* 238
    Robert C. Koons

III | MORAL ARGUMENTS

(R) *Moral Arguments (actually R1 to Rn): An Abductive Moral Argument
for God* 261
    David Baggett

(R*) *The Argument from Evil: Felix Culpa!* 277
    Hud Hudson

IV | OTHER ARGUMENTS

(S) *The Argument from Colors and Flavors: The Argument from Consciousness* 293
   Richard Swinburne

(T) *The Argument from Love and (Y) The Argument from the Meaning of Life:*
   The God of Love and the Meaning of Life 304
   Jerry L. Walls

(U) *The Mozart Argument and (V) The Argument from Play and Enjoyment:*
   The Theistic Argument from Beauty and Play 321
   Philip Tallon

(W) *Arguments from Providence and from Miracles: Of Miracles:*
   The State of the Art and the Uses of History 341
   Timothy McGrew

(X) *C.S. Lewis's Argument from Nostalgia: A New Argument from Desire* 356
   Todd Buras and Michael Cantrell

(Z) *The Argument from (A) to (Y): The Argument from So Many Arguments* 372
   Ted Poston

V | "OR SO": THREE MORE ARGUMENTS
The Kalam *Cosmological Argument* 389
   William Lane Craig

The Argument from Possibility 406
   Brian Leftow

The Necessity of Sufficiency: The Argument from the Incompleteness of Nature 417
   Bruce L. Gordon

Afterword: Trent Dougherty and Alvin Plantinga: An Interview on Faith and
   Reason 446

APPENDIX: PLANTINGA'S ORIGINAL "TWO DOZEN (OR SO)
   THEISTIC ARGUMENTS" 461

INDEX 481

Acknowledgments

I (JERRY) WANT to thank my former student and close friend Brian Marshall for suggesting to me the idea for this book several years ago. I immediately thought it was a great idea and was amazed no one had ever done it. I was gratified later to learn that Alvin Plantinga himself had expressed the hope that others would develop in more detail the arguments he had sketched in his paper that inspired this volume (see Introduction). Plantinga is not only one of my former teachers, but is one of my heroes and I am deeply grateful that I had the good fortune to play a part in making his hope a reality.

Many thanks to Baylor University's Program for Philosophical Studies of Religion, Institute for Studies of Religion, co-directed by Trent Dougherty and Francis Beckwith, for hosting a conference for the purpose of reading preliminary drafts of several of these papers on November 6–8, 2014. Thanks also to Andrew Bailey, who was instrumental in getting this project up and running at the outset.

It has been a pleasure, as usual, to work with Cynthia Read and Oxford University Press, and we appreciate their enthusiasm for this project from the beginning.

As always, I am grateful to my family: Tim and Angela Amos, Madalyn Rose, Mackenzie Grace, and Abigail Joy; and Jonathan and Emily Walls. Your love and support is an inspiration for everything worthwhile I do.

I (Trent) wish to thank Byron Johnson, director of the Institute for Studies of Religion, and Mike Beaty, chair of the department of philosophy, for their visionary leadership, which created an environment that encouraged me to dream big, and for backing that up with the funding to turn dreams into reality.

Thanks to my family, Sarah, Fiona, Annabelle, Jeep, and Sam for loaning me out so often for conferences and other academic activities and for picking up the slack at home when I'm pursuing these academic pursuits.

Thanks to the contributors for doing such a good job staying on task and making this one of those rare projects where people actually write helpfully on what they were asked to do. Y'all are great!

Finally, thanks to Al Plantinga, for twenty-seven years of inspiration, friendship, and support. I am honored to have taken a part in bringing this project to fruition.

Contributors

Alexander Arnold, John Templeton Foundation

David Baggett, Liberty University

Justin L. Barrett, Fuller Seminary

Daniel Bonevac, University of Texas

Todd Buras, Baylor University

Elizabeth D. Burns, University of London

Michael Cantrell, John Brown University and William H. Bowen School of Law, University of Arkansas at Little Rock

Robin Collins, Messiah College

William Lane Craig, Houston Baptist University

Trent Dougherty, Baylor University

C. Stephen Evans, Baylor University

Evan Fales, University of Iowa

Tyron Goldschmidt, Wake Forest

Bruce L. Gordon, Houston Baptist University

Hud Hudson, Western Washington University

Lorraine Juliano Keller, Niagara University

Robert C. Koons, University of Texas at Austin

Brian Leftow, Rutgers University

Timothy McGrew, Western Michigan University

Christopher Menzel, Texas A&M

Bradley Monton, Wuhan University

Alvin Plantinga, University of Notre Dame

Ted Poston, University of Alabama

Alexander R. Pruss, Baylor University

Joshua Rasmussen, Azusa Pacific

Richard Swinburne, Oxford University

Philip Tallon, Houston Baptist University

Jerry L. Walls, Houston Baptist University

Christopher Gregory Weaver, University of Illinois at Urbana-Champaign

xi

TWO DOZEN (OR SO) ARGUMENTS FOR GOD

Introduction

Jerry L. Walls and Trent Dougherty

THERE IS NO small irony in the fact that the philosopher who gave us the Two Dozen Arguments that inspired this book is Alvin Plantinga. One of Plantinga's most distinctive and important contributions to the philosophy of religion is, of course, his carefully articulated defense of the claim that belief in God can be properly basic. His position here represents a radical response to the modern insistence that belief in God is not justified without explicit argument. The typical response to this challenge is to agree with the demand, and to try to produce the required arguments, which traditionally includes various arguments for God's existence. Plantinga's bold alternative insists not only that belief in God, but full-blown Christian belief, can be fully justified, rational, and warranted without the support of such explicit arguments.

An early foreshadow of this idea appeared in his first monograph, *God and Other Minds,* in which he explored in great detail the rationality of theistic belief. The positive argument he advanced in that book is that belief in God is epistemically on par with belief in other minds; if one belief is rational, so is the other. But what is also telling is his assessment of the traditional theistic arguments, and what it suggests about the status of such arguments in the 1960s, when that book was written. Part One of that book examines the cosmological, ontological, and teleological arguments—the only three arguments for God that Kant famously insisted were even possible—and contends that none of them are successful as items of natural theology (by the standards he then set for it).

It is striking not only that Plantinga judged none of those arguments successful, but that those arguments were the only ones he apparently thought worthy of serious consideration. The moral argument, for instance, which has been defended by a number of notable proponents, and can claim a respectable pedigree as a traditional theistic argument, did not even merit discussion.

By the early 1980s, Plantinga was developing in several essays the idea that belief in God can be properly basic. Arguments for God's existence accordingly remained somewhat, if not altogether, irrelevant for this project. If belief in God can be perfectly justified or epistemically upright, or appropriate, or "warranted" without these arguments, one might think they have little value or significance.

Meanwhile, on the other side of the Atlantic, Richard Swinburne was defending the rationality of belief in God along somewhat more traditional lines. Having already argued at length that the traditional theistic notion of God is at least coherent, Swinburne took on the more interesting question of whether there is good reason to believe that God actually exists. In the introduction to *The Existence of God*, he wrote: "The book is written in deep conviction of the possibility of reaching fairly well justified conclusions by rational argument on this issue, perhaps the most important of all deep issues which stir the human mind."[1]

While Swinburne's project was traditional in the broad sense of relying on arguments from propositional evidence to defend the rationality of belief in God, it was also innovative in the way he deployed those arguments. In particular, he used confirmation theory, especially Bayes's theorem, to argue that the most relevant set of evidence, taken together, shows God's existence to be more probable than not. The evidence Swinburne mustered went well beyond the traditional theistic arguments, and included such matters as human consciousness and the beauty of our world, items that have received less attention in the case for theism. All in all, Swinburne considered some eleven arguments (including the problem of evil, the main argument against God) in his overall assessment.

Notably, Swinburne focused exclusively on arguments that are empirical in nature—broadly speaking, arguments that appeal to evident facts about the world or private human experience. Ontological arguments and other arguments that start from conceptual truths or that depend on a highly abstract metaphysical thesis were dismissed as having little to commend them. In summing up the arguments he would consider, Swinburne wrote: "In reaching my final conclusion about how probable it is that there is a God, I assume that no a priori arguments . . .and no a posteriori arguments other than those which I discuss, have any significant force."[2]

This was the larger context in philosophy of religion when Plantinga first gave his lecture on "Two Dozen (or so) Theistic Arguments," in a summer seminar in Bellingham, Washington, in 1986. The notes for this talk were never expanded into a fully developed work, and were not published until 2007, when they appeared as an appendix of a volume devoted to Plantinga's work edited by Deane-Peter Baker.[3] However, long before they were ever published, these notes were passed around for years as a sort of underground document and read and discussed by graduate students and others, for whom they generated considerable interest.[4]

Plantinga repeated the lecture in the fall of 1986 in a larger and more public venue when he was the main speaker at the Wheaton College Philosophy Conference, held on October 23–25. It was the third of three talks he gave for that event, the first two of which were entitled "On Taking Belief in God as Properly Basic" and "On Working Properly."[5] It is more than a little intriguing that talks preceding the Two Dozen Arguments were devoted to explicating Plantinga's notion that belief in God can be properly basic, and therefore does not in any way require the support of such arguments in order to be justified, rational, or warranted.

Stephen Evans, one of the contributors to this volume, attended that conference, and remembers well that Plantinga's Two Dozen Arguments generated "tremendous excitement." As he recalls, "the talk helped people see that the point of Reformed Epistemology was not that there were no good arguments for God's existence, but that such arguments are not necessary for reasonable belief."[6]

This is an important point, because Plantinga has insisted not only that belief in God can be fully rational for persons who lack any sort of discursive propositional evidence as that represented by the theistic arguments, but even if there simply are no such arguments. So even if there were no good theistic argument available for anyone, belief in God could be fully justified, rational, and warranted.

Now it may be tempting for critics to suspect that Plantinga's bold maneuver is actually making the best of a bad situation. Since the traditional theistic arguments have been widely attacked, and often judged to be unsuccessful (as Plantinga himself concluded in *God and Other Minds*), and since there seem to be no other good arguments available, well, here is an account of belief in God that renders it fully rational without any sort of reliance on such arguments. Reformed epistemology, in other words, is a clever ploy to rescue religious belief from the desperate situation it faced after all the arguments for God had been discredited.

As Plantinga has pointed out, however, and as Evans rightly recognized, it does not follow from the claim that rational belief in God in no way *requires* good theistic arguments, that none are in fact *available*. And indeed, Plantinga's lecture can be seen as a virtuoso performance demonstrating and refuting that non sequitur. Somewhat ironically, the fact that these arguments are available, even if they are not needed, bolsters the credibility of the claim that belief in God can be properly basic. For the main task of *Warranted Christian Belief* was to show that if God exists, belief in God is probably properly basic.

Nor does it follow, moreover, from the claim that the arguments are not needed for rational belief in God that they do not serve other valuable or useful purposes. Plantinga himself has pointed out that there are at least four such purposes.

First, [theistic arguments] can move someone closer to theism—by showing, for example, that theism is a legitimate intellectual option. Second, they reveal interesting and important connections between various elements of a theist's set of beliefs.

For example, a good theistic argument reveals connections between premises and conclusions, connections that in some cases can also contribute to the broader project of Christian philosophy by showing good ways to think about a certain topic or area from a theistic perspective. Examples would be the arguments from counterfactuals, numbers, propositions, sets, and properties. Third, the arguments can strengthen and confirm theistic belief. Not nearly all believers hold theistic belief in serene and uninterrupted certainty; most are at least occasionally subject to doubts. Here these arguments can be useful. Finally, and connected with the last, these arguments can increase the warrant of theistic belief. For me as for most, belief in God, while accepted in the basic way, isn't maximally firm and unwavering; perhaps it isn't nearly as firm as my belief in other minds. Then perhaps good theistic arguments could play the role of confirming and strengthening belief in God; in that way, they might increase the degree of warrant belief in God has for me.[8]

Now here it is essential to highlight one little word that makes an enormous difference for this whole project, namely, the word "good." It is no great feat, obviously, to construct any number of theistic arguments, if they do not need to be good ones. Noting this, however, raises an issue of enormous difficulty that we cannot adequately consider, let alone resolve, in this Introduction.

Indeed, this issue is far more complicated than was widely assumed when Plantinga wrote *God and Other Minds*. As he acknowledges, he was, like most everyone else at the time, in the grip of classical foundationalism, and evaluated all arguments by that standard. Here is his account of what this required for an argument to be a good one: "It must take as premises propositions that are properly basic for all or most people, and proceed via self-evidently valid deductive steps to the conclusion, or else it must make it evident that the conclusion is sufficiently probable with respect to all or most people's foundations."[9]

We can readily admit the appeal of this sort of criterion, and also grant that these are sufficient conditions for an argument to be a good one. But unless one subscribes to an extreme version of classical foundationalism, there is no convincing reason to think these conditions are necessary. Again, there is a certain irony in the fact that the collapse of classical foundationalism, which is part of the narrative for Plantinga's claim that belief in God can be properly basic, also makes room for good theistic arguments to flourish. Good arguments need not meet the stringent demands of classical foundationalism.

We are still left, however, without an answer to the question of which conditions *are* necessary for an argument to be a good one. Plantinga himself takes several stabs at providing an answer, but finally concludes by simply noting "that it is difficult indeed to give a good criterion for argumentative goodness."[10] We shall rest content with this, and not assume in the pages that follow either that there exists such a criterion, or that such a criterion can be identified, that must be met for any or all of the Two Dozen (or so) Arguments to be good ones.

However, there is one standard Plantinga has discussed, mostly in connection with the ontological argument (specifically, the "possibility premise," which asserts that it is possible that there is a maximally great being). We might apply this more widely and suggest that, except in extraordinary circumstances, if the conjunction of the premises of a valid argument is rationally permissible for one, so is the conclusion.[11] It is very plausible indeed that most of these arguments are valid and that most of them are such that (the conjunction of) their premises is rationally permissible. We add further that insofar as the arguments are independent, whatever modicum of epistemic support they render to theism is cumulative.[12]

Plantinga's Two Dozen Arguments are a rather diverse lot, and cover a much broader and more interesting terrain than theistic arguments have usually explored. They range over arguments from collections to counterfactuals, from modality to the meaning of life, from *plus* and *quus* to play. This dazzling variety, moreover, makes it even more difficult to identify a necessary condition for argumentative goodness that would apply to all of them. Several of these arguments are metaphysical or ontological in nature; a number of others are epistemological; a few are moral; and the remaining cluster is a miscellaneous group simply labelled "other" by Plantinga. In the spirit of his parenthetical "(or so)," we have also included a handful of additional arguments that are not among his original Two Dozen. Some of the arguments are fairly traditional, but many are novel and have never been developed before, so far as we know. Many are a priori (in contrast to Swinburne's exclusive focus on a posteriori arguments) and are inspired by relatively new work on the nature of necessity; several more are inspired by recent scientific discoveries.

While most of the arguments are treated separately, we have grouped some of them together where they seemed to be closely related or to overlap. A few are discussed by more than one author in cases of overlap. Each of Plantinga's original arguments except one is developed by our authors. The single exception is the one Plantinga named "Tony Kenny's style of teleological argument." We originally planned to include it, and approached Kenny himself in hopes that he would author that chapter (appropriately enough, since it is named after him). But, alas, neither he nor anyone else could recall enough about the details of the argument, or track them down, so that argument had to be omitted.

In publishing these essays, we hope to provide for a new generation a significant advance on the project Plantinga initiated when he first delivered his lecture on the Two Dozen Arguments a few decades ago. In 2006, twenty years after that first lecture, he reflected on what he had hoped to do with those arguments.

My intention had always been to write a small book based on these arguments, with perhaps a chapter on each of the main kinds. Time has never permitted, however, and now the chances of my writing such a book are small and dwindling. Nevertheless, each, I think, deserves loving attention and development. . . . I hope others will be moved to work them out and develop them in detail. . . . I hasten to add that the arguments as stated in the notes aren't really good arguments; they are merely argument sketches, or maybe only pointers to good arguments. They await that loving development to become genuinely good.[13]

As will be apparent in the pages that follow, most of the authors of these essays believe the arguments they were assigned are indeed, in their developed form, "genuinely good." We are grateful to the contributors for their "loving development."

This is not to say that any of us imagine we have given the last word on any of these arguments—quite the contrary. In the spirit of what Plantinga originally intended, it is our hope that this book will provide a stimulus for further development of these arguments, and indeed, for formulating still others that have yet to be discovered.

We are also happy to say that there has been great enthusiasm for this project ever since its inception, not only on the part of the contributors, but also from many persons who anticipate the final product. Baylor University's Program for Philosophical Studies of Religion, Institute for Studies of Religion, co-directed by Trent Dougherty and Francis Beckwith, hosted a conference for the purpose of reading preliminary drafts of several of the papers on November 6–8, 2014, and this enthusiasm was reflected by the many attendees and participants in that conference. It is our hope that this volume will generate for a new generation some of the same "tremendous excitement" that Plantinga's initial presentation of his Two Dozen Arguments sparked some thirty years ago.

In any case, the authors of these essays have taken great satisfaction in giving these arguments the "loving attention and development" Plantinga hoped they would receive. And while this is not another Festschrift for him, the authors are surely united in sharing great affection and admiration for Alvin Plantinga. In that spirit, we are reminded that philosophy is driven most deeply, not by the cleverness of argument, but by the love of what really matters. And there is no issue that matters more than the one at the heart of this book.

NOTES

1. Richard Swinburne, *The Existence of God* (Oxford: Clarendon, 1979), 1.

2. Ibid., 10.

3. Deane-Peter Baker, ed., *Alvin Plantinga* (Cambridge: Cambridge University Press, 2007).

4. I (Jerry) had the good fortune to be a graduate student at Notre Dame from 1984 to 1987, an extremely exciting period in the philosophy of religion, in large part due to the very different projects that Plantinga and Swinburne were developing. We read Swinburne's *The Existence of God* as a text in one of the courses I took from Plantinga. I had already read that book, and had considerable sympathy for Swinburne's novel approach to the theistic arguments, and it was fascinating indeed to hear Plantinga's critique and his defense of his alternative account of the rationality of theistic belief. I was very happy to come to see that Plantinga still saw significant value

in theistic arguments, and respected their force, even as he insisted they were not necessary for justified belief.

5. Thanks to Steve Evans, who attended that conference, for this information.

6. Personal email, April 26, 2016.

7. Oxford University Press, 2000.

8. Alvin Plantinga, "Preface to the Appendix," in Alvin Plantinga, 209.

9. Ibid., 206.

10. Ibid., 208.

11. There is, of course, an important difference between metaphysical possibility and epistemic possibility. Plantinga's ontological argument appeals to what is metaphysically possible. However, even the premise that God's existence is metaphysically possible, which is either necessarily true or necessarily false, may also be judged to have varying degrees of epistemic probability between 0 and 1.

12. On this point, see the chapter by Ted Poston in this book.

13. Plantinga, "Preface," 203.

I

Half a Dozen (or so) Ontological
(or Metaphysical) Arguments

If there were no eternal substance, there would be no eternal truths; and from this too GOD can be proved, who is the root of possibility, for his mind is the very region of ideas or truths.

(LEIBNIZ, G VII, 311/1973: 77)

(A)

The Argument from Intentionality (or Aboutness)

PROPOSITIONS SUPERNATURALIZED

Lorraine Juliano Keller

∿ ──────────────────────────────

INTRODUCTION

THERE IS A venerable argument, going back at least to Augustine, for the existence of God from the existence of eternal truths.[1] The argument targets the *intentional* or *representational* character of truth; hence, it has come to be known as the "Theistic Argument from Intentionality" (hereafter, "TAI"). The rough idea is this:

> Truth involves representation—something is true only if it represents reality as being a certain way, and reality *is* that way. But representation is a function of minds. So, truth is mind-dependent. Yet there are truths that transcend the human mind, e.g. eternal truths. So, there must be a supreme mind with the representational capacity to "think" these transcendent truths. Therefore, a supreme mind (viz., God) exists.

This argument rests on a conception of truth that is widely rejected today. Most philosophers writing in the wake of Gottlob Frege's influential assault on psychologism hold that truth is mind-*in*dependent: even if there were no minds, some things would be true and others false (Frege 1884). Let's use the term "proposition" for the non-linguistic entities that are fundamentally true or false in virtue of their representational properties, whatever their nature.[2] The TAI can then be formulated as follows:

(TAI-1)

(1) There are propositions: non-linguistic entities that are fundamentally true or false in virtue of their representational properties. [Premise]

(2) Only thoughts are fundamentally true or false due to their representational properties.[3] [Premise]

(3) So, propositions are thoughts. [from 1, 2]

(4) If propositions are thoughts, they are either human or divine thoughts. [Premise]

(5) But there are not enough human thoughts to play the role of propositions. [Premise]

(6) So, propositions are not human thoughts. [from 5]

(7) Propositions are divine thoughts. [from 3, 4, 6]

(8) If there are divine thoughts, then there is a unique divine thinker. [Premise]

(9) Therefore, there is a unique divine thinker (God).

Since it makes fairly minimal assumptions about the nature of propositions, premise (1) will simply be assumed without question. This chapter will focus on premises (2) and (5). Since I will not be discussing premises (4) and (8), I want to briefly flag and set aside some worries about them now.

One might have the following concerns about (4): (i) Why think the disjuncts (in the consequent) are exhaustive? Couldn't propositions be the thoughts of other cognitive beings, for example, intelligent aliens? (ii) Why take the disjunction to be exclusive?[4] Couldn't the propositional roles be played by both human and divine thoughts, as some medieval philosophers seem to have held?

I think (i) can be set aside as not having enough intrinsic plausibility to be taken seriously. For simplicity's sake, I'm going to neglect (ii), but note that it does not affect the outcome of the argument even if it is correct. Given the other premises, if at least some proposition is not a human thought, then it is a divine thought; so there are some divine thoughts, etc.

Regarding premise (8), why think that the existence of divine thoughts entails the existence of a *unique* divine thinker? Why not a collection of divine thinkers? Leibniz considers this objection to his version of the TAI and addresses it by invoking a somewhat radical view of relations. But it seems that a simple appeal to Ockham's razor would favor a unique thinker over a posse of thinkers (cf. Adams 1994: 181). So this premise does not seem particularly problematic.

The argument is directed at propositionalists; however, most contemporary propositionalists would reject premise (2) because they hold that propositions are mind-independent entities that represent and have truth conditions essentially and intrinsically. Call this the "traditional conception." If most propositionalists hold the traditional conception and hence reject premise (2), then the TAI will fail to convince its intended audience—a depressing result.

However, as Alvin Plantinga notes, "Many have thought it incredible that propositions should exist apart from the activity of minds" (2007: 211). Indeed, this was the dominant position in the history of philosophy before the twentieth century, when it was widely rejected.

But the tides have started to turn: in recent work, Jeffrey King, Scott Soames, and Peter Hanks defend views of propositions committed to premise (2), but with the aim of presenting a *naturalistic* conception of propositions—hence, rejecting premise (5). Call this trio of philosophers "propositional naturalists" and their view "propositional naturalism."

In this chapter, I will try to show that propositional naturalists cannot avoid premise (5), thus their view suffers from a problem of scarcity: there are propositions it leaves out. However, this problem would be remedied if they became propositional *super*naturalists. In particular, I will argue that they need to invoke an infinite agent to account for all of the propositions there are. Propositional naturalists make a strong case for (2).[5] If I can make a strong case for (5), then the prospects for a convincing TAI will be greatly improved.

The chapter will proceed as follows. In the first section, I give a fuller explanation of the traditional conception of propositional naturalism and lay out some important terminology. I then present the case against the traditional conception and briefly explain the naturalistic conceptions that are offered as superior alternatives. In the second section, I present what I call the "Scarcity Objection" to propositional naturalism. In a nutshell, the objection is that there are propositions for which propositional naturalism cannot account; thus, the need for propositional *super*naturalism. In the final section, I present a revised TAI.

THE TRADITIONAL CONCEPTION AND PROPOSITIONAL NATURALISM

What are propositions? It's helpful to delineate them in terms of their roles. The following list is fairly representative: the primary bearers of truth and falsity (and the modes thereof: necessary and contingent truth and falsity), contents of the attitudes, what is asserted in contexts of utterance, the semantic values of sentences (in context), and the relata of logical relations.

Plantinga explains what propositions must be like in order to play these roles:

Propositions are *claims* or *assertions*; they *attribute* or *predicate* properties to or of objects; they represent reality or some part of it as having a certain character (1987: 193).

As Michael Jubien puts it, "The essence of a proposition is to represent" (2001: 50).[6] Propositions do not *just* represent, however; they represent in a way that determines *truth-conditions*. Maps and pictures represent, for example, but do not have truth-conditions. Let's call the property of representing in a way that determines truth-conditions "truth-apt representation," and use "represent$_t$" and its subscripted cognates to abbreviate this term (and its cognates).

Not only propositions, but also sentences and certain cognitive states, represent$_t$: members of all three kinds determine truth-conditions and, hence, have truth-values, in virtue of representing reality as being a certain way.[7] On what I am calling the traditional conception of propositions, all other truth-bearers, including beliefs and sentences, represent$_t$ *because* of their relation to propositions: only propositions represent$_t$ fundamentally. Let's define derivative and fundamental representation$_t$ as follows:

$(x)(y)(x$ DERIVATIVELY REPRESENTS$_t y$ iff x represents$_t y$ & $(\exists z)(\sim z=x$ & x represents$_t y$ in virtue of z's representing$_t y)$

$(x)(y)(x$ FUNDAMENTALLY REPRESENTS$_t y$ iff x represents$_t y$ & $\sim(x$ derivatively represents$_t y))$[8]

We can now define the traditional conception more precisely:

(TC) Propositions are abstract, mind- and language-independent entities that are the only fundamental bearers of truth-apt representation. Propositions represent$_t$ absolutely, essentially, and intrinsically.[9] All other truth-bearers represent$_t$ derivatively, in virtue of their relation to propositions.

Consider the following sentence:

1. Mars is a planet.

On TC, both the sentence "Mars is a planet" and David's judgment that Mars is a planet represent Mars as being a planet and are true iff Mars is a planet in virtue of their relation to the proposition <Mars is a planet>: the sentence *expresses* that proposition (in a context of utterance), and David's judgment has that proposition as its *content*. <Mars is a planet> represents Mars as being a planet *absolutely*, unlike the sentence-type "Mars is a planet," which only has this property relative to a language. Also, whereas 1 might have expressed a different proposition and thus had different representational properties, <Mars is a planet> has its representational$_t$ properties *essentially*. Finally, <Mars is a planet> has its representational$_t$ properties *intrinsically*, unlike 1 (at least, on standard views of individuating sentences), which might have expressed a different proposition from <Mars is a planet>.

Before I present propositional naturalism, it will be helpful to contrast TC with the conception of the fundamental bearers of truth-value that it replaced. The analytic tradition in philosophy—at least, its beginnings in the work of Frege, Russell, and Moore—might be defined by its rejection of a historically prominent view that came to be called "psychologism." According to psychologism, the primary bearers of truth-value are mental states or acts of some sort, paradigmatically, judgments. Consider the following account from the influential Port Royal Logic:

> In judging, the mind not only conceives two ideas but also unites or separates them. The result of this activity of the mind is a proposition. . . .A proposition is a judgment we make about things (Arnauld and Nicole 1662: 111).

Psychologism is often associated with modern philosophy, but it is also prominent in the medieval and ancient periods. For example, in his seminal work on truth, Aquinas claims that "truth is found primarily in the joining and separating by the intellect . . ." (*Questiones Disputatae de Veritate*, Article III, Reply). Boethius assigns the role of fundamental bearers of truth and falsity to *propositiones mentales,* sentences in the mind that are composed of mental words.[10]

The medievals were influenced by Aristotle, who, in the *De Interpretatione*, identifies the fundamental bearers of truth and falsity, which "spoken sounds" express, with "affections (*pathemata*) of the soul" (1, 16a). Even Plato distinguishes between the outer and the inner *logos* (something like a judgment or mental sentence), identifying the latter with the fundamental bearer of truth and falsity (see *Theaetetus* and *Sophist*).[11]

On psychologism, it is something mental that plays the fundamental truth-bearer role *because* mental states are the fundamental bearers of *representational* properties. That is, *because* judgments or mental sentences represent things as being thus-and-so by virtue of their intrinsic properties, rather than by their relation to some other representational entities, they are qualified to be the non-derivative bearers of truth and falsity. So, on psychologism, mental states play what we would now think of as the *propositional* roles— they are the primary bearers of truth-value and thus are the things believed, denied, and doubted, and the fundamental relata of logical relations.[12]

One standard argument for rejecting psychologism in favor of TC appeals to the fact that the propositional role-players stand in logical relations. If Maggie believes that Mars is a planet and David believes its denial, then Maggie's belief contradicts David's. Similarly, if Maggie and John both believe that Mars is a planet, then they share a belief. However, token mental states are private and particular: they cannot be shared, nor can they stand in logical relations. Hence, token mental entities do not seem suited to play the propositional roles.

The proponents of psychologism among the pre-analytic philosophers did not make the type/token distinction (at least not explicitly, regularly, or consistently). But suppose one had this distinction at one's disposal: then why not let mental state- or act-*types* play the propositional roles? Since types are abstract, they are appropriately public and share-able and arguably suited to stand in logical relations. However, importantly, types cannot be the fundamental bearers of representational$_r$ properties: this distinction must be reserved for their tokens. For suppose that mental act-types had representational$_r$ properties on their own, independent of their being tokened. Then the view would end up being a version of TC.

Indeed, propositional naturalists reject TC precisely because they find the view that there are abstract objects that represent$_r$ on their own, independent of minds and languages, "unintelligible" (King 2013: 31). So, mental *types* cannot represent$_r$ fundamentally. Rather, their tokens do, while the types represent$_r$ derivatively.

On propositional naturalism, like psychologism, the fundamental representers$_r$ are *agents*. It is agents that are in token mental states in virtue of the way they represent the world. The *types* of these states play the role of propositions.[13] Of course, the only agents countenanced by propositional naturalism are naturalistically acceptable ones—at the very least, it's plausible that a naturalistic view can only countenance the representational$_r$ powers and states of *finite* agents.[14] With this in mind, we can now define propositional naturalism as follows:

(PN) Propositions represent$_r$ because agents represent$_r$. Finite agents are the only fundamental representers$_r$.[15]

This formulation helpfully captures what is common among the otherwise very different conceptions of Hanks, King, and Soames: there is no primitive representation$_r$ by abstract objects; rather, all representation$_r$ is grounded in the powers of finite agents.

Below, we will examine the arguments against TC put forth by the proponents of PN and, thus, get a better idea of the motivation for PN.

An Objection to the Traditional Conception

Propositional naturalists reject TC because, they claim, it suffers from three related defects, a metaphysical, an explanatory, and an epistemological defect:

(D1) TC is committed to the "unintelligible" clam that propositions represent$_r$ on their own, independently of minds and languages (King 2013: 31).

(D2) On TC, that propositions represent$_r$ is a brute fact, with the result that it is a mystery how they do so.

(D3) TC offers "no explanation of how we come to bear attitudes to [propositions], as well as how we are acquainted with, and come to know things about, them" (King et al. 2014: 6).

On TC, propositions are abstract objects that have intentional properties *essentially*, apart from their relation to minds or languages (indeed, all such relations are contingent, since propositions exist in mind-less and language-less worlds).[16] However, it's problematic to think that abstract objects, apart from our stipulation, are "about" anything. Consider, for example, properties: the property *horse* has instances, but is not "about" its instances. Hence, TC suffers from (D1). As Michael Jubien puts it,

> It borders on the absurd to suppose that any inert, non-spatiotemporal entity could have a part that, in itself, plays any . . . referential or quasi-referential role. . . . Representation is ultimately the business of beings with intentional capacities, in short, thinkers (2001: 54).[17]

We can take it as a datum that minds represent, but there's no good reason to think that abstracta have this power, nor that positing intrinsically representational$_t$ abstracta will help explain mental representation. A fortiori, this seems like an explanatory dead end: minds represent$_t$ by standing in a mysterious grasping relation to Platonic entities that themselves represent$_t$ in some unanalyzable way.

As Jeff King contends, "taking any kind of representation as primitive is a paradigm example of misplacing one's primitives" (2009: 260). But this seems to be precisely the strategy of TC: the representation$_t$ of minds and languages is explained in terms of the representation$_t$ of their propositional contents. But the representation$_t$ of propositions is taken as brute. This blocks the development of a naturalistic explanation of mental representation$_t$, since the properties of abstracta are not amenable to such explanation. Thus, TC suffers from (D2).

Finally, TC leaves us with a picture on which there's no explanation of our cognitive access to these abstract, primitively representational$_t$ entities. Rather, it looks as if the proponent of TC has to posit a primitive "grasping" relation in her account of how it is that we entertain these primitively representational$_t$ propositions (see Hanks 2015: 45). So, TC suffers from (D3) as well.[18]

Where to go from here? Soames points the way:

> The key is to reverse our explanatory priorities. Propositions, properly conceived, are not an *independent* source of that which is representational in mind and language; rather, propositions are representational *because* of their intrinsic connection to inherently representational cognitive events. . . . (Soames 2010: 106–107).

PN reverses the explanatory strategy of TC: mental representation$_t$ explains propositional representation$_t$. This leaves the door open to a naturalistic strategy for explaining the sense in which both mental states and propositions represent$_t$.

Recall that propositions are the primary bearers of truth. On the propositional naturalist's strategy, then, the explanation of truth is ultimately in terms of minds and their powers. So, if the propositional naturalists' objection to TC is on target, this lends substantial support to premise (2) of the TAI.

Soames's Theory of Naturalized Cognitive Propositions

In this section, I briefly present Scott Soames's version of PN, which I call "the theory of naturalized cognitive propositions." Then I present the Scarcity Objection: first I apply the objection to Soames's theory, and then I argue that the objection can be generalized to all versions of PN.

The reason for focusing on Soames is that he considers and responds to a version of the Scarcity Objection, offering intricate existence conditions for his propositions. Thus, his theory arguably presents the most formidable challenge to the type of objection I want to raise against PN.

On Soames's theory of naturalized cognitive propositions (hereafter "NCP"), it is agents' acts of predication that represent$_r$ fundamentally. Propositions, the types of such acts, represent$_r$ derivatively. So, <Mars is a planet> represents Mars as being a planet, and is true iff Mars is a planet, because it is a type every conceivable token of which is a fundamentally representational$_r$ act of predicating *being a planet* of Mars. Thus, the central thesis of NCP is that propositions are repeatable, purely representational cognitive acts (Soames 2013: 2). As Soames puts it, "Since entertaining a proposition is performing it, the intentionality of the act of entertaining it is the intentionality of the proposition itself" (2015: 28). However, because token acts are not repeatable and cannot be shared contents of the attitudes, they cannot play the role of propositions. Hence, it is cognitive act-*types* that are propositions. But in what sense do act-types represent$_r$?

According to Soames, agents represent$_r$ in a *primary* sense by predicating properties of objects, whereas cognitive act-types represent$_r$ in an extended or derivative sense. So, for example, the proposition that *b* is red represents$_r$ *b* as being red (in a derivative sense) because every possible token act in which an agent predicates redness of *b* is one in which an agent represents$_r$ *b* as being red (in a primary sense). In a nutshell, propositions (cognitive act-*types*) represent$_r$ because the agents that perform them do.

The fundamental attitude that grounds the representation$_r$ of propositions is *entertaining*, where one entertains the proposition that *a* is *F* iff one predicates *F* of *a*.[19] Other attitudes, such as judging, knowing, and asserting, are defined in terms of the "fundamental ur-attitude" of entertaining (2015: 27–28). For example, to judge that *a* is *F* is to predicate *F* of *a* while affirming that predication and using it as a basis for possible future action (2013: 3).

Soames promotes NCP because it provides "the basis of a plausible naturalistic epistemology and metaphysics of propositions" (2015: 28). It's obvious that human agents judge, believe, desire, and doubt, and it's obvious that these cognitive acts are representational$_r$, but if so, then propositions exist and represent$_t$. Thus, we need not appeal to brute representation$_t$ by abstract objects. Indeed, Soames et al. reject TC precisely for failing to be naturalistic in this sense. This is an important point to bear in mind: for a response to the Scarcity Objection to be successful, it must satisfy this desideratum.

THE SCARCITY OBJECTION TO PROPOSITIONAL NATURALISM

Let's say that a theory T suffers from a problem of scarcity if there *are* propositions that T entails do not exist. For example, there are false propositions. If T entails that there are no false propositions, as did Bertrand Russell's initial formulation of his theory of propositions in *Principles of Mathematics,* then T suffers from a problem of scarcity and must be either revised or abandoned.

I will argue that propositional naturalism, insofar as it excludes the possibility of an infinite agent, suffers from the Scarcity Objection. The general idea is this:

(1) On PN, (i) propositions represent$_t$ essentially, and (ii) all representation$_t$ has a naturalistic basis in the cognitive activities of finite agents.

(2) There are propositions that finite agents cannot entertain (call them "transcendent").

(3) So, there is representation$_t$ that does not have a naturalistic basis in the cognitive lives of finite agents.

(4) Therefore, there are propositions that PN entails do not exist (viz., transcendent propositions).

(1) follows from PN. The burden of the rest of this section will be to clarify exactly what it is to be a transcendent proposition and to argue for (2). The argument will go a follows: since there are transcendent propositions, but PN entails that there are not, PN must be revised or abandoned.

Since Soames has addressed this sort of objection and gives intricate existence conditions for his propositions, I will first apply the Scarcity Objection to his theory, before arguing that it also afflicts any version of PN.

It might seem easy to come up with examples of transcendent propositions. First, there are propositions no (finite) agent ever entertains—doesn't NCP entail that they do not exist? It doesn't: Soames accounts for never-entertained propositions by appeal to systematicity—if any n-place property R and objects $o_1 \ldots o_n$ have been cognized in a world w, this is sufficient for the existence in w of propositions that have any of R and $o_1 \ldots o_n$ (and nothing else) as constituents, even if these propositions are not entertained in w (King et al. 2014: 102). Suppose no one in w ever entertains the proposition that Socrates texted Archimedes. So long as some agents in w have cognized Socrates, Archimedes and the texting relation, this proposition exists in w.

Second, there are *objects* that no agent ever cognizes. Consider a singular proposition about such an object, for example, an un-cognized molecule, m. Since m is un-cognized, no agent predicates being a molecule of m; hence, no agent entertains the proposition that m is a molecule. But then this proposition does not exist, even by appeal to systematicity, since the representation of one of its constituents is missing.

Soames claims that this proposition represents$_t$ because, in some possible world, an agent predicates being a molecule of m. Soames can say this because he embraces the view that a proposition need not exist at a world w in order to have properties (such as truth) at w.[20] So, a proposition p may not exist at α, but nonetheless represent$_t$ at α. However, there must be some world possible with respect to α in which p is entertained. So, if there is no possible world in which p is entertained by a (finite) agent, then p does not represent$_t$ in *any* world. This is why a transcendent proposition must be a proposition that is not entertained by any *possible* finite agent.

Again, it might seem obvious that there are such propositions: consider an infinitely *complex* proposition, say, an infinite conjunction, or a proposition about a number too large for a finite agent to grasp. Soames also has a response to these potential counterexamples: he argues that an appeal to systematicity can ground the representation$_t$ of these propositions. Regarding numerical propositions that no (finite) agent can entertain, Soames cites the fact that "we have a systematic linguistic means—the numeral system—mastery of which allows us to directly designate each number" (King et al. 2014: 232). So, even though some numbers are not cognized by any agent in a world w, the contents of numerals are compositionally generated out of constituents that are cognized in w.[21]

Call an object "linguistically inaccessible" if it is not designatable with the resources of a finitely learnable language. We also need a term for objects that not only are not linguistically accessible, but are not cognizable in some other way: call such objects "inaccessible."[22] We can now say that a singular proposition that has an inaccessible constituent constitutes an example of a transcendent proposition and, hence, a counterexample to NCP.

I cannot directly give an example of a proposition with an inaccessible constituent—if I could, then it wouldn't be inaccessible. However, I will give an argument that there *are* inaccessible objects, hence, singular propositions about them exist.

Choice Propositions

It is a result of the standard axiomatization of set theory (ZFC) that there are certain sets that, I will argue, are inaccessible. According to the Axiom of Choice (hereafter, "AC"), given any collection of mutually disjoint, non-empty sets, there is a *choice set* containing exactly one element from each member of the collection.[23]

Finite choice sets are not beyond our cognitive reach, since their elements can be enumerated. And even in the infinite case, we can sometimes specify a choice set by re-cursive enumeration. Importantly, we do not *need* AC to generate these sets—they can be generated in other ways (e.g., by recourse to the relevant (non-choice) functions).

However, some of the sets that AC generates are sets that finite thinkers cannot cog-nize. I will call these sets "choice-only (relative to ZF)," where a set S is choice-only rela-tive to ZF iff (i) S is a set of kind K and (ii) the existence of K-sets can be proven in ZFC, but not in ZF.[24] If there are choice-only sets, then NCP is false. And there are: Giuseppe Vitali proved in ZFC that there are sets of real numbers in the interval $[0,1]$ that are not Lebesgue-measurable—so-called "Vitali sets" (see Vitali 1905).[25] The details are beyond the scope of this chapter, but suffice it to say that there are such sets (uncountably many) and that the existence of sets of this type is provable in ZFC, but *not* in ZF.[26] ZFC entails that there are Vitali sets. So, by ZFC, there are uncountably many choice-only sets.

I will now argue that choice-only sets are inaccessible.[27] Since these sets exist, there are true singular propositions of the form "S is a set," where S is a set that is not cognized by any possible finite agent. These propositions have constituents that are inaccessible. So their existence is ruled out by NCP.

Since the argument that choice-only sets are un-cognizable relies on the notion of what it is to cognize a set, let me present some conditions for the cognizability of sets by finite agents. It's plausible that a finite agent A is in a position to cognize a set S only if A satisfies at least one of the following three Conditions:

(i) A cognizes all of the members of S.
(ii) A cognizes a rule that generates all and only the members of S recursively from a base of elements cognized by A.
(iii) A cognizes a predicate under which all and only the members of S fall.

Satisfying Condition (i) works only for (relatively small) finite sets. Satisfying Condition (ii) works for infinite sets provided that one grasps the base and the relevant rule: for ex-ample, finite agents are able to cognize the set $\mathbb{N}$ because we cognize the successor function, which generates all and only the members of $\mathbb{N}$ recursively from zero, which we cognize. Finally, finite agents are able to cognize the set of primes by satisfying Condition (iii)—we cognize a predicate ("is prime") under which all and only the prime numbers fall.

I will now argue that finite agents cannot satisfy any of the above three Conditions for choice-only sets. We cannot designate one of these sets by methods (ii) or (iii), since they resist generation by functions we can cognize and are not uniquely specified by any finitely graspable predicates. Though such sets may fall under some such predicates—for example, the predicate "set of real numbers"—those predicates will not *uniquely* specify those sets, and so we won't be able to single them out. Presumably, the only way that one *could* cognize a choice-only set would be by method (i). But because such sets are uncountable, only an infinite intellect could satisfy this Condition. So choice-only sets exist (hence, there are true singular propositions about them), but—if we assume infinite intellects are impossible—they cannot be cognized.

So, Vitali sets exist, but we cannot single one out and have singular thoughts about it. Though we know such singular propositions exist as the proposition <V is a set> (for some Vitali set, V), they are inaccessible to us. The only access we *could* have to Vitali sets would be via language, but we lack any systematic linguistic means for uniquely designating them.

Now consider singular propositions of the form "S is a set," where S is a choice-only set. Call them "choice propositions." Relying on the claim that choice-only sets are un-cognizable by finite beings, my claim now is that no possible finite agent can grasp a choice proposition. This argument can be summed up as follows:

The Choice Argument:

(1) It's necessary that an agent satisfy one of the Conditions to cognize a choice-only set. [premise]
(2) No possible finite agent satisfies any of the Conditions with respect to choice-only sets. [premise—see argument above]
(3) So, no possible finite agent cognizes a choice-only set. [from 1, 2]
(4) If no possible finite agent cognizes choice-only sets, then no possible finite agent is in a position to entertain singular propositions about them. [by the following weak condition on grasping singular propositions about sets: cognizing a set S is necessary for entertaining singular propositions about S]
(5) So, no possible finite agent entertains a choice proposition. [from 3, 4]

Note that if the Choice Argument is sound, it furnishes us with the following reductio of NCP:

Against NCP:

(6) NCP is true. [assume for reductio]
(7) There are true choice propositions. [ZFC plus propositionalism]
(8) But no possible finite agent entertains a choice proposition. [by the Choice Argument][28]
(9) So it's false that there are true choice propositions. [from 6, 8]
(10) So NCP is false. [by reductio ad absurdum, from 7, 9]

To sum up, my claim is that there are transcendent propositions: choice propositions are an example. But NCP entails that there are no transcendent propositions. So NCP is false.[29] This argument applies not just to NCP, but to PN in general, as I argue in the next section.

Recall that on PN, propositional representation$_t$ is grounded in the representation$_t$ of finite agents. The proponent of PN can avail herself of Soames's strategies to avoid the initial objections to her view. Those strategies were (i) widening the net to include *possible* finite agents, thus accounting for propositions that are not entertained by any actual finite agent; and (ii) appealing to compositionality and systematicity to "generate" propositions out of *constituents* that are entertained or possibly entertained by finite agents, but are not "glued together" by acts of predication. I think that both of these strategies are dubious, but have let that pass for the sake of argument. I have tried to show that, even allowing these strategies, Soames's view still suffers from a problem of scarcity. My argument involved providing an example of a class of singular propositions that contain *constituents* that are not entertained by any possible finite agent. Hence, my example, if successful, circumvents strategies (i) and (ii).

I focused my objection on a specific version of PN; however, it seems to me that *any* version is vulnerable to the objection, since PN entails the following thesis:

> (Dependency) A proposition p represents$_t$ only if, for some possible finite agent A, the representation$_t$ of p is derived from the representation$_t$ of (some act or state of) A.[30]

To see why PN entails Dependency, consider its denial: suppose there is some proposition p, but its representation$_t$ is not derived from a (possible) finite agent: i.e., there is no finite agent in the relevant act or state to ground the representational$_t$ properties of p. Then there would be a proposition that represents$_t$ independently of finite agents, which contradicts PN.

But if my argument for transcendent propositions is sound, then there are propositions the representation$_t$ of which is independent of the representation$_t$ of any possible finite agent. This contradicts Dependency. So, if the argument for transcendent propositions is sound, and if PN entails Dependency, then the existence of transcendent propositions entails the falsity of PN. The only other option would be to drop the restriction to *finite* agents; but then this would not be propositional *naturalism* anymore. . . .

A REVISED TAI

The Scarcity Objection can be taken further than just furnishing a reductio of PN—it can provide support for the move from PN to propositional *super*naturalism. The main difference between the two views is that the propositional *super*naturalist can avail herself of the cognitive powers of an *infinite* intellect. The view is no longer naturalist, of course, but it retains the spirit of the original insofar as all representation$_r$ is traceable to agents. So, the Scarcity Objection can be used to provide a revised TAI:

(TAI-2)

   (1) Propositions represent$_r$ essentially. [premise]
   (2) Only agents represent$_r$ fundamentally. [premise]
   (3) So propositions depend for their existence on agents. [from 1, 2]
   (4) There are propositions that no finite agent entertains (transcendent propositions). [choice argument]
   (5) The representation$_r$ of transcendent propositions is independent of the representation$_r$ of finite agents. [from 4]
   (6) So, transcendent propositions cannot depend on finite agents. [from 3, 5]
   (7) Therefore, there's an infinite agent.

(1) is an assumption about the nature of propositions that is widely held and has been invoked throughout this chapter. (2) and (3) are entailed by PN, but, as we noted, PN only countenances finite agents. (4) is supported by the arguments of the previous section, and (5) follows from (4). Given (1), if transcendent propositions represent$_r$ independently of finite agents, then they must exist independently of them. So, an infinite agent is needed to ground the representation$_r$ of transcendent (and perhaps all) propositions.

Let me briefly address one significant objection to this argument: can't the propositional naturalist account for transcendent propositions by invoking a merely *possible* infinite agent? As Soames explains, it's sufficient on his view for a proposition to be entertained by some possible agent in order for it to represent$_r$.

Two quick rejoinders: (i) I'm not sure what merely possible agents are, but I assume they are abstract. If a merely possible agent's cognitive acts ground the representation$_r$ of a proposition, then it looks like we have primitive representation$_r$ by abstract objects, which is what PN was seeking to avoid. (ii) Merely possible infinite agents do not seem naturalistically acceptable. First, the account will still be invoking the cognitive powers of an infinite being (only, now, a non-existent infinite being) to explain the representation$_r$ of propositions, which does not seem like much progress over invoking the powers of an *actual* infinite being. Second, invoking a possible infinite agent, along with other plausible premises, opens the door to the modal ontological argument, which one can safely assume that naturalists would rather leave closed.[31]

Of course, TAI-2 is not yet an argument for theism—just as Aquinas's Five Ways work together to support the claim that an omniscient, omnibenevolent, supreme Cause exists, so Plantinga's twenty-four (or so) ways can be taken together to support theism. I conclude that an argument for the existence of an agent of infinite cognitive powers—one who can "cognize" choice-only sets—takes us *part* of the way toward the conclusion that there exists a Being whose "understanding has no limit" (Psalm 147: 5).

NOTES

1. See Augustine, *On Free Choice of the Will* (1964); see also Leibniz's *Monadology* (1954) and the collection of his philosophical writings (1973) for an influential version of the argument.

2. By saying "non-linguistic," I am ruling out the view that *natural* language sentences (or classes thereof) can play the role of propositions; however, this broad way of using the term includes the view that propositions are mentalese sentences, which was held by some prominent medieval philosophers (and perhaps by Aristotle). And of course, one might identify thoughts themselves with mentalese sentences.

3. Stating the argument in terms of thoughts is an over-simplification. I modify the argument later in the chapter.

4. Of course, logical disjunction is *in*clusive, but to get (7) from (3), (4), and (6), one would have to assume that there's a suppressed premise to the effect that the consequent of (4) is exclusive.

5. To be honest, I do not find their case for (2) convincing, but I am convinced by (5). So my main argument can be taken as a conditional one: if one is convinced by (2), then one should take the TAI to be a decent argument for (quasi-)theism.

6. But see Robert Stalnaker (2012) and Jeff Speaks's contribution to King et al. (2014) for examples of views on which propositions have (or are) truth-conditions, but do not represent.

7. For simplicity's sake, I'm assuming that there are just two truth-values and that every proposition/belief/sentence has just one of them; but the account could be modified to accommodate views on which, for example, there is more than one truth-value or there are truth-value gaps.

8. Note that there's no attempt to define representation itself here.

9. Cf. Schiffer (2003, 14).

10. See Nuchelmans (1973) and Sullivan (1970) for discussion.

11. Things are *significantly* more complicated than this too-brief (and shamefully over-simplified) historical excursus suggests. I should also note that some important exceptions to the psychologistic trend in ancient and medieval philosophy are the Stoics and philosophers in the medieval dictist tradition. See Keller (2012) for more detailed discussion.

12. Again, this is a wince-worthy over-simplification: these roles were not always grouped together (when they were acknowledged at all) by pre-analytic philosophers (nor are they always grouped together by philosophers writing on this topic today).

13. This may seem to be in conflict with the definition of "proposition" given earlier; however, propositions on this view are still true/false in virtue of their representational properties, only they *derive* those properties from their fundamentally representational$_t$ tokens. So, the roles of fundamental bearer of truth-value and fundamental representer$_t$ are severed on this view, unlike on psychologism and TC.

14. I realize that some might quibble over this point, but since an agent of infinite cognitive powers would either be God or something very god-like, I cannot see how a view could qualify as naturalistic if it countenanced such a being—or even the possibility of one (as I discuss later). Jeff King, however, has said that he does not have any in-principle objection to *possible* infinite intellects, and does not think this conflicts with naturalism (pc). I think this makes his view vulnerable to an argument for quasi-theism, as I'll argue later. Also, I don't want to get bogged down in debates about "naturalism," a vexed term if ever there was one. If such "naturalistic" views lead to quasi-theism, that is an interesting and surprising result.

15. To save space, I leave implicit that there *are* entities that satisfy the definitions of PN and TC.

16. Except, perhaps, for singular propositions about particular minds or languages.

17. Though Jubien is not a propositional naturalist himself (he rejects propositions), his arguments have inspired propositional naturalists. He also admits some affinities between his view and King's (see Jubien (2001), fn. 17).

18. There are rejoinders at the defender of TC's disposal: I discuss them in detail in "A Controversial Premise of the Theistic Argument from Intentionality" (in progress).

19. Soames is using "entertaining" and "predicating" in a technical sense; for example, one need not be conscious of engaging in the act of predication in Soames's sense.

20. Soames also rejects the distinction between truth-in-a-world and truth-at-a-world, preferring the view that there *are* merely possible propositions. So, he rejects not just serious actualism, but actualism itself (see King et al. (2014), 237).

21. I explain Soames's strategy for dealing with large numbers in greater detail in "Against Naturalized Cognitive Propositions" (2017).

22. Isn't being linguistically inaccessible sufficient for being un-cognizable? Not if, as seems likely, young children and some non-human animals can cognize some objects without mastery of language. However, it seems to me very plausible that certain sorts of objects—in particular, the sorts of mathematical objects under discussion in this chapter—are *only* cognizable *via* language. Soames agrees (see Soames (1989)).

23. Thanks to John Keller for suggesting the use of AC as an example.

24. Thanks to Christopher Menzel for suggesting this definition of "choice-only."

25. The construction of Vitali sets is beyond the scope of this chapter, but see Keller 2017 for more details.

26. By Solovay's Theorem, the claim that there is a set of non-Lebesgue-measurable reals is independent of ZF (see Solovay (1970)).

27. If the axiom of constructability, $V = L$, were true, then it could be objected that some of the sets I claim are inaccessible are constructible in L, hence, finitely cognizable. Most set theorists reject this axiom because it conflicts with the maximum iterative conception of a set, and I follow their lead here (see Arrigoni (2011), 337–342).

28. Recall that Soames's view does not *require* that a proposition be possibly entertained in order to exist and have truth-conditions—rather, it's sufficient that the *constituents* of a proposition are cognized. However, I have argued that choice propositions are not entertained by any possible finite agent *by way of* arguing that they have constituents that are not cognized by any possible finite agent. So this condition is covered by my argument. For simplicity of presentation, though, I state the argument Against NCP in terms of entertainment.

29. There is not sufficient space here to discuss the multiple ways that Soames might resist this argument, but I discuss them in Keller 2017.

30. Note that Dependency does not entail the existence of *merely* possible agents: for actualists, possible agents are just actual agents (since everything that actually exists, possibly exists).

31. See, for example, Plantinga (1961) and van Inwagen (1977). To make the argument work, one would need to add a premise to the effect that a being with infinite cognitive capacities is perfect or maximally great.

REFERENCES

Adams, Robert. 1994. *Leibniz: Determinist, Theist, Idealist*. Oxford: Oxford University Press.

Aquinas, Thomas. 1952. *Questiones Disputate de Veritate*. Trans. Robert W. Mulligan, S.J. Chicago: Henry Regnery Company.

Aristotle. 1984. *De Interpretatione*. Trans. Jonathan Barnes, in *The Complete Works of Aristotle: Volumes One and Two*. Princeton, NJ: Princeton University Press.

Arrigoni, Tatiana. 2011. *V = L* and Intuitive Plausibility in Set Theory: A Case Study. *Bulletin of Symbolic Logic* 17, no. 3: 337–360.

Arnauld, Antoine, and Pierre Nicole. 1662. *La Logique, ou L'Art de Penser* (popularly known as *The Port Royal Logic*). Trans. James Dickoff and Patricia James as *The Art of Thinking*. 1964. Indianapolis, IN: The Bobbs-Merrill Company, Inc.

Augustine. 1964. *On Free Choice of the Will*. Trans. Anna S. Benjamin and L.H. Hackstaff. Pearson. Upper Saddle River, NJ: Prentice Hall.

Frege, Gottlob. 1884. *Grundlagen der Arithmetik*. Breslau: Marcus. 1934.

Hanks, Peter. 2015. *Propositional Content*. Oxford: Oxford University Press.

Jubien, Michael. 2001. Propositions and the Objects of Thought. *Philosophical Studies* 104: 47–62.

Keller, Lorraine Juliano. 2012. *Whence Structured Propositions?* Ph.D. dissertation for the University of Notre Dame.

———. 2017. Against Naturalized Cognitive Propositions. *Erkenntnis* 82: 929–946.

King, Jeffrey. 2009. Questions of Unity. *Proceedings of the Aristotelian Society* CIX, part 3: 257–277.

———. 2013. Propositional Unity: What's the Problem, Who Has It, and Who Solves It? *Philosophical Studies* 165 (1): 71–93.

———with Scott Soames and Jeff Speaks. 2014. *New Thinking About Propositions*. Oxford: Oxford University Press.

Leibniz, Gottfried Wilhelm. 1954. *Monadology*, in *Principes de la nature et de la Grace* and *Principes de philosophie ou Monadologie*. Ed. André Robinet. Paris: Presses Universitaires de France.

———. 1973. *Philosophical Writings*. Ed. and trans. by Mary Morris and G.H.R. Parkinson. Everyman's Library.

Nuchelmans, Gabriel. 1973. *Theories of the Proposition: Ancient and Medieval Conceptions of the Bearers of Truth and Falsity*. Amsterdam: North Holland Publishing Company.

Plantinga, Alvin. 1961. A Valid Ontological Argument? *Philosophical Review* 70: 93–101.

———. 1987. Two Concepts of Modality: Modal Realism and Modal Reductionism. *Philosophical Perspectives, I, Metaphysics*, ed. James Tomberlin (1987): 189–231.

———. 2007. Two Dozen (or so) Theistic Arguments. Unpublished manuscript.

Plato 1997. *Sophist*. Trans. N.P. White, in *Complete Works*, ed. J.M. Cooper, Hackett.

———. 1997. *Theaetetus*. Trans. M.J. Levett and M.F. Burnyeat, in *Complete Works* (*op cit.*).

Russell, Bertrand. 1903. *Principles of Mathematics*. Cambridge, UK; Cambridge University Press.

Schiffer, Stephen. 2003. *The Things We Mean*. Oxford: Oxford University Press.

Soames, Scott. 1989. Semantics and Semantic Competence, *Philosophical Perspectives* 3, Philosophy of Mind and Action Theory (1989), 575–596.

———. 2010. *What is Meaning?* Princeton, NJ: Princeton University Press.

———. 2013. Cognitive Propositions. *Philosophical Perspectives: Philosophy of Language* 27 (2013): 1–23.

———. 2015. *Rethinking Language, Mind, and Meaning*. Princeton, NJ: Princeton University Press.

Solovay, Robert. 1970. A Model of Set Theory in Which Every Set of Reals Is Lebesgue Measurable, *Annals of Mathematics*, Second Series 92, no. 1 (July 1970): 1–56.

Stalnaker, Robert. 2012. *Mere Possibilities: Metaphysical Foundations of Modal Semantics*. Princeton, NJ: Princeton University Press.

Sullivan, Mark. 1970. What Was True or False in the Old Logic? *Journal of Philosophy* 67, no. 20, Sixty-Seventh Annual Meeting of the American Philosophical Association Eastern Division, 788–800.

van Inwagen. 1977. Ontological Arguments, *Noûs* 11, no. 4 (November 1977): 375–395.

Vitali, Giuseppe. 1905. *Sul problema della misura dei gruppi di punti di una retta*. Bologna: Tip. Gamberini e Parmeggiani.

(B)

The Argument from Collections

Christopher Menzel

ᴏ᷒ ———

VERY BROADLY, AN argument from collections is an argument that purports to show that our beliefs about sets imply—in some sense—the existence of God. Plantinga (2007) first sketched such an argument in "Two Dozen" and filled it out somewhat in his 2011 monograph *Where the Conflict Really Lies: Religion, Science, and Naturalism*.[1] In this chapter I reconstruct what strikes me as the most plausible version of Plantinga's argument. While it is a good argument in at least a fairly weak sense, it doesn't initially appear to have any explanatory advantages over a non-theistic understanding of sets—what I call set theoretic realism. However, I go on to argue that the theist can avoid an important dilemma faced by the realist and, hence, that Plantinga's argument from collections has explanatory advantages that realism does not have.

PLANTINGA'S ORIGINAL ARGUMENT

The first premise of Plantinga's argument from collections is twofold: first, that there *are* such things as sets[2] and, second, that they have a *nature*, which includes at least the following properties: (i) they are non-self-membered; (ii) they have their members essentially; and (iii) they collectively form an "iterated structure" that, therefore, yields a well-known explanation of Russell's paradox.[3]

The second premise is that the existence of sets with these distinctive properties is explained by the fact that sets are quite naturally thought of as the products of "a certain sort of intellective activity—a collecting or 'thinking together.'" Thus, as Cantor (1932, 282) famously wrote in the *Beiträge*: "By a 'set' we understand any collecting *M* of well-distinguished objects *m* of our intuition or our thought . . . into a whole."[4] Hao Wang (1974, 182) expresses the idea more explicitly still:

> It is a basic feature of reality that there are many things. When a multitude of given objects can be collected together, we arrive at a set. For example, there are two tables in this room. We are ready to view them as given both separately and as a unity, and justify this by pointing to them or looking at them or thinking about them either one after the other or simultaneously. Somehow the viewing of certain given objects together suggests a loose link which ties the objects together in our intuition.[5]

As to how this conception of sets explains their existence and the properties mentioned in the first premise, Plantinga (2011, 290) writes:

> First, if sets were collections, the result of a collecting activity, the elements collected would have to be present before the collecting; hence no set is a member of itself. Second, a collection could not have existed but been a collection of items different from the ones actually collected, and a collection can't exist unless the elements collected exist; hence collections have their members essentially, and can't exist unless those members do. And third, clearly there are noncollections, then first level collections whose only members are noncollections, then second level collections whose members are noncollections or first level collections, et cetera.)

Third premise: obviously, however, there are far too many sets, many with far too many members, for them to be the product of any sort of (finite and limited) human collecting activity; only an infinite mind—for simplicity, let's call it *God*—has the power to collect the vast infinity of sets that exist in the set theoretic universe according to our best theories. Hence, Plantinga appears to conclude, God exists.

Adopting the terminology in Morris and Menzel (1986) for theories that explain abstract entities in terms of divine intellective activity, call this the *activist* conception of sets; and call the view that sets exist independently of any mind *set theoretic realism*, or *realism* for short. On its face, it might appear that Plantinga's activist argument is meant to be of a piece with the classical theistic arguments—a deductive argument to God's existence from clearly true or, at least, plausible, premises. So conceived, however, there is an obvious gap, viz., an intermediate inference from the second premise—that the existence and nature of sets is explained by their being the products of some kind of intellective "collecting" activity—to the proposition that sets *are* indeed the products of such activity. But that follows only if (a) the existence and nature of sets *requires* an explanation and (b) the proposed explanation is the *only* explanation. Some realists might reject (a), but I suspect most would accept (a) and reject (b) on the grounds that the existence of a set is fully explained simply by the existence of its members; a set, that is, exists *because* its members do. The members of a set are thus *logically prior* to the set and, hence, a set cannot contain itself (property (i)). Moreover, the realist can continue, a set has exactly the members it does *essentially* (property (ii)) because that is simply (part of) what it *is* to be a set, viz., a "collective" object whose identity is wholly determined by the things it contains. Finally, membership generally is *well-founded*. Hence, while the existence of every set is explained, in the first instance, by its members, and their existence in turn by their members, and so on, ultimately, it is explained by the existence of the initial non-sets, or *urelements*, from which the set was built up. Well-foundedness is thus simply a reflection, from the top down, so to say, of the structure of the sets that are given from the bottom up in the iterative conception (property (iii)).[6] The metaphor of "collecting" that motivates the argument from collections, realists will insist, is at best just a useful but unnecessary heuristic for describing the well-founded/iterative structure of the sets and is not to be taken literally.

However, I think the appeal to explanation in the second premise is meant to indicate that Plantinga intended his argument to be abductive rather than deductive, that is, to be an argument to the best explanation. So understood, the missing intermediate inference that sets are the products of an intellective collecting activity should be replaced by a further premise: the explanation for the properties of sets noted in premise 1 yielded by the hypothesis of premise 2—that sets are the products of such an intellective activity—is the *best* explanation of their possession of those properties. The former third premise now becomes the fourth: only an infinite mind—which we're calling *God*—is capable of producing *enough* collections to account for the sets that exist according to our best theories. Given that the best explanation of a phenomenon is confirmed by that phenomenon and that God is the best explanation of the existence of sets, the conclusion is now revised accordingly: the existence of God is confirmed by the existence of sets.[7]

Thus the argument. But is it a good one? In the preface to "Two Dozen," Plantinga provides a trenchant exploration of the senses in which a theistic argument can be considered good. And the abductive argument here surely seems to be good in at least one particularly important sense, viz., that the argument "contributes to the broader project of Christian philosophy [and theistic philosophy generally] by showing good ways to think about a certain topic or area from a theistic perspective" (2007, 209).[8] For in shifting the focus to activism as the best explanation for our beliefs rather than a (dubiously derived) consequence of them, the abductive version of the argument, at least, presents "a good way to think about" set theory and the existence of sets from a theistic perspective.[9]

That said, realists will not likely find this abductive version of the argument any more persuasive than the deductive version, and for the same reason: they will claim that the existence of sets is explained at least as well, and with a great deal less ontological commitment, by the existence of its members and, hence, that activism provides no explanatory advantage. However, in the remainder of the chapter I will argue that, in fact, a well-known tension in the conceptual foundations of set theoretic realism puts the realist's explanation of set existence, but not the activist's, in peril and, hence, that activism does enjoy an explanatory advantage over realism. However, the argument requires quite a lot of stage-setting, to which I now turn.

PRELIMINARIES: PLURALS AND PLURAL QUANTIFICATION

It is illuminating to express the issues surrounding the argument from collections in terms of plural quantification. Note that natural language can express quantification in both singular and plural forms. As understood in first-order logic, singular quantifiers range over individuals—when we say "Some F is G," we mean that there is at least one F that is also a G; when we say "every F is G," we mean that each F individually is also G. Typically, of course, propositions of these forms can also be expressed using plurals: "Some/All Fs are Gs." However, the converse does not appear to be true; that is, not all plural quantifications can be equivalently expressed using singular quantifiers. Perhaps the best-known example of this is the so-called *Geach-Kaplan* sentence:

> **GK** Some critics admire only one another.

Kaplan himself (as reported by Quine (1982, 293)) took the existential quantifier here to be ranging over properties of individuals and, hence, took the logical form of **GK** to be second-order:

$$\textbf{GK2} \quad \exists X[\exists y Xy \wedge \forall y(Xy \rightarrow (Cy \wedge \forall z(Ayz \rightarrow (Xz \wedge y \neq z))))], \ ^{10}$$

that is, on the usual semantics of second-order languages, there is a nonempty set (or, perhaps more generally, class) of critics who only admire other critics in the set. Importantly, Kaplan showed **GK2** to be *essentially* second-order.[11] Assuming, therefore, that **GK2** is an accurate representation of **GK**'s logical form, it follows that **GK** itself has no logically equivalent counterpart involving only singular first-order quantifiers.[12]

Now, as is well known, Boolos (1984; 1985) argued persuasively that, while **GK2** is in fact the correct logical form for **GK**, its second-order quantifier—insofar as it is meant to represent plural quantification—should not be understood in terms of the standard semantics of second-order quantification as ranging over sets of individuals.[13] Rather, it should be understood as ranging over exactly the same things as the first-order quantifiers, albeit "plurally":

> It is not as though there were two sorts of things in the world, individuals and collections of them, which our first- and second-order variables, respectively, range over and which our singular and plural forms, respectively, denote. There are, rather, two (at least) different ways of referring to the same things. (1984, 449)

To clarify, Boolos offers up an alternative way of paraphrasing **GK** and its like that spells out its meaning without any obvious reference to sets of individuals: "There are some critics such that each one of them is such that she admires a person only if that person is also one of them (but not her)." And, indeed, taking those plural expressions at face value in this way involves no obvious ontological commitments beyond the critics themselves that, together, make it true.

Although Boolos himself suggested that (monadic) second-order quantification in general can be understood as plural quantification,[14] the view has not found wide acceptance and second-order quantification in most contexts is still given its usual semantics; confusion is inevitable if this ambiguity in second-order languages were to persist. Moreover, the use of the usual syntactic representation of predication "Xy" to indicate that y is *among* the things X is misleading, insofar as it suggests that y and the Xs are of different types instead of simply all being individuals, albeit referred to in different ways. For these reasons, contemporary discussions formalize plural quantification by introducing a new class of variables "xx," "yy," etc that behave much more like ordinary first-order variables. In particular, to express that an individual y is among some things xx, a distinguished 2-place predicate "$\prec$" is introduced, $y \prec xx$, that takes the variable "xx" as an argument. In this framework, then, **GK** is represented as:

GKP $\exists xx [\exists y\, y \prec xx \wedge \forall y (y \prec xx \rightarrow (Cy \wedge \forall z (Ayz \rightarrow (z \prec xx \wedge y \neq z))))].$ [15]

We will follow Boolos in adopting the "ontologically innocent" understanding of plural quantification in this discussion. This understanding is not uncontroversial. However, we do so for convenience only; nothing of substance hangs on it for our purposes here. It simply provides us with a very convenient framework in which to state and discuss the issues. Likewise, as we've already assumed with the plural pronoun "them" in Boolos's take on **GK**, we will take plural demonstrative/anaphoric expressions like "those objects," as well as terms like "plurality," "the plurality of Fs" and "The Fs," to be in themselves ontologically innocent, that is, simply to refer "plurally" to the indicated objects and not to a set or class containing them.

PLURALITIES, SETS, AND RUSSELL'S PARADOX

So-called naive set theory can be traced back to Gottlob Frege, particularly his great 1893 work *Grundgesetze der Arithmetik* (though, strictly speaking, it can only be considered a reconstruction of a fragment of Frege's system). Naive set theory is based on two intuitive principles. The first is that sets are *extensional*, that the identity of a set is *wholly determined by* its members:

Ext Sets a and b are identical if they have the same members. Formally:
$\forall x (x \in a \leftrightarrow x \in b) \rightarrow a = b.$

The second principle is that every plurality constitutes a set, that is, that, for any given things, there is a set containing exactly *them*:

Collapse $\forall xx \exists y \forall z (z \in y \leftrightarrow z \prec xx)$.

In itself, though, **Collapse** tells us nothing about what sets there are until we have some principle that tells more exactly what pluralities there are. And here there is an obvious principle, the principle of Plural Comprehension:

PC For any property P of things, there are exactly the things that have P.

Unfortunately, as it stands, **PC** appeals to properties, which are perhaps even more controversial than sets. Intuitively, however, a property is just the meaning of a description, or predicate, like "is human" or "is a prime number less than 1,000." Thus, a more tractable way of expressing the idea behind **PC** is to say that, for any description, there is a set consisting of exactly the things satisfying that description. So, for example, given the two preceding predicates, by this principle there are all the humans and all the prime numbers less than 1,000. The notion of a predicate is captured formally in first-order logic by means of formulas φ (typically containing free variables) in a given formal language L designed to describe whatever piece of the world we're interested in. Our more tractable take on **PC**, then, is expressed in first-order logic by means of a Plural Comprehension schema that generates a distinct axiom for each predicate φ (of L):

P-Comp For any formula φ containing no free occurrences of the variable 'yy', there are the things satisfying φ; formally: $\exists yy \forall x (x \prec yy \leftrightarrow \varphi(x))$.

Given **Collapse** and **P-Comp**, the more familiar Comprehension schema of naive set theory follows immediately:

Comp For any formula φ of L containing no free occurrences of the variable 'y', there is a set consisting of exactly the things satisfying φ; formally: $\exists y \forall x (x \in y \leftrightarrow \varphi(x))$.

For all its apparent simplicity, naive set theory is extraordinarily powerful and enables one to prove a great many interesting theorems about sets.[16] Alas, as the familiar story goes, while studying Frege's *Grundgesetze*, Russell discovered the famous paradox that showed that naive set theory (more exactly, a basic principle of the *Grundgesetze* that is more or less equivalent to Comprehension) is inconsistent. To see the problem, consider the property non-self-membership, that is, the property expressed by the predicate '$x \notin x$'. By **Comp**, there is a set r consisting of exactly the things satisfying this predicate, that is, the things (in particular, the sets) that are not members of themselves; formally, $\forall x (x \in r \leftrightarrow x \notin x)$. Instantiating to r, we have that $r \in r$ if and only if $r \notin r$, contradiction.

The discovery of Russell's paradox led to the development of much more rigorously conceived set theories, most notably, Ernst Zermelo's set theory Z, most of whose axioms Zermelo initially proposed in a famous 1908 paper. Russell's paradox showed that not all pluralities, in particular, not all those determined by a well-defined predicate, are "safe"; some things, on pain of contradiction, cannot jointly form a mathematically well-behaved set. At the same time, there *are* some pluralities that seem clearly safe, that can clearly be assumed to constitute a set; and, of course, conversely, any plurality we've shown independently to constitute a set is safe. Thus, we need to replace **Collapse** with:

Safe $\forall xx(Safe(xx) \leftrightarrow \exists y \forall z(z \in y \leftrightarrow z \prec xx))$.

The general problem, then, is to distinguish the safe pluralities from those that are not. Zermelo's brilliant—and brilliantly executed—idea was to introduce, via carefully chosen axioms, a well-circumscribed class of intuitively safe pluralities to get things a-going, along with a variety of safe "set-building" operations introduced by further axioms that lead safely from given sets to further sets. In this way, Zermelo hoped to have a theory that was powerful enough to yield the many important results that had already been proved in naive set theory but not so powerful as to collapse into logical contradiction.

ZERMELO'S AXIOMS FOR SAFE PLURALITIES

Although Zermelo himself did not formulate his axioms explicitly in terms of pluralities, it will be useful to do so for our purposes here.[17] Toward that end, note first that, for any expressible condition $\varphi(x)$, our principle **P-Comp** (together with an extensionality principle I'll leave unstated) warrants the introduction of a term $[x : \varphi(x)]$ to refer (plurally, hence innocently) to the things x that satisfy φ. Hence, for something to be among the φs is simply for it to satisfy φ:

P-Abs $z \prec [x : \varphi(x)] \leftrightarrow \varphi(z)$.

Likewise, when a plurality $[x : \varphi]$ has been deemed safe and, hence, constitutes a set containing exactly the things that are φ, we can switch to traditional set abstraction notation $\{x : \varphi\}$. More exactly, and more generally, whenever we can show that the φs constitute a set y (i.e., that $[x : \varphi]$ is safe) and that y satisfies ψ, then we can (by definition) express this as $\psi(\{x : \varphi\})$; formally:

Sets $\psi(\{x : \varphi(x)\}) \equiv_{df} \exists y(\forall x(x \in y \leftrightarrow \varphi(x)) \land \psi(y))$.

Finally, for finitely many terms $t_1, ..., t_n$, the expression $[t_1, ..., t_n]$ will as usual just be shorthand for $[x : x = t_1 \lor ... \lor x = t_n]$; analogously for $\{t_1, ..., t_n\}$.

The most pressing order of business in light of Russell's paradox is a replacement for the set comprehension principle **Comp** which, of course, no longer follows from

P-Comp when **Collapse** is replaced by **Safe**. On reflection, **Comp** makes clear just how wildly profligate **Collapse** is (together with the ontologically innocent **P-Comp**): given *any* description φ whatever, no matter how obscure, complex, or logically dubious, the principle generates *ex nihilo* a new thing, viz., the set of things that satisfy φ. Zermelo tames **Comp** by declaring, not that the plurality of *all* the things satisfying φ is safe but, rather, only those satisfying it that are *already* the members of some antecedently given set s. Since, by **Safe**, the members of a set are jointly safe, any of those members, as part of a larger safe plurality, should be jointly safe as well. This is formalized in the axiom schema of *Separation*:

Sep $Safe([x : x \in s \wedge \varphi(x)])$.

Safe and **Sep** together, then, yield (in place of **Comp**) the more familiar set theoretic form of the principle:

S-Sep For any formula φ containing no free occurrences of the variable 'y', given a set s, there is a set consisting of exactly the members of s satisfying φ; formally: $\exists y \forall x (x \in y \leftrightarrow x \in s \wedge \varphi(x))$.

Thus, given only **S-Sep**, it is no longer possible to generate sets *ex nihilo* from any given plurality; one can only carve them out of sets that one has already proved to exist. One cannot, in particular, prove the existence *ex nihilo* of a set of all non-self-membered sets but, rather, only the set $a = \{x : x \in s \wedge x \notin x\}$ of non-self-membered sets in some *given* set s. Running Russell's argument on a yields only the harmless conclusion that $a \notin s$ (and, moreover, that $a \notin a$); that there is no universal set $\{x : x = x\}$—as there is under **Comp**— is an immediate corollary.[18]

This, of course, leaves the question of what sets we *can* prove to exist—of itself, **Sep** gives us nothing, since we need to have a set in hand to apply it. The simplest safe pluralities that Zermelo postulates—via the axiom of Pairing—are those consisting of one or two antecedently given things. That is, the axiom tells us that, given any (not necessarily distinct) objects a and b, they are (jointly) safe and, hence, by **Safe**, form a set:

Pr $Safe([a,b])$.

Pairing already gives us important insights into Zermelo's conception of set. Note first that we get at least one thing simply by logic alone (as '$\exists x\, x = x$' is a logical truth). This, together with **Sep**, is enough to yield the empty set $\varnothing$ and, hence, an infinite number of "pure" sets built up from it.[19] But, as matters of empirical and, perhaps, mathematical fact, we know that there are urelements, things that are not themselves sets—persons, planets, natural numbers, etc. Hence, we know by Pairing that any pair of (not necessarily distinct) urelements is a safe plurality and hence that, together, they constitute a set. But then, once we know we have a set or two, we can apply the axiom again to these "new" sets and our initial urelements to prove the existence of yet further sets containing them. And, given *those* sets, together with the ones previously shown to exist, along with our urelements, it follows from Pairing that yet further sets exist, and so on. Moreover, given a further Zermelian axiom, Union, which stipulates that the members of the sets in a safe plurality together are a safe plurality, it follows that, not just pairs, but any finite plurality is safe:

Un $Safe([x : \exists y (y \in z \wedge x \in y)])$.[20]

Pairing and Union together thus yield a rudimentary version of the set theoretic universe according to Zermelo's iterative conception: the sets have a cumulative, hierarchical structure, advancing "upwards" in an expanding series of levels. We "begin" at the first level with some urelements. At the next level we have everything in the first level together with all the finite sets that can be formed from them; and at subsequent levels, we have everything in all the preceding levels together with all the finite sets that can be formed from them.

However, three elements of Zermelo's full iterative conception are missing. First, the urelements themselves should be jointly safe.[21] After all, they are all *there* to begin with, "prior" to any sets, and, on the face of it, unlike the problematic principle **Collapse** that any plurality constitutes a corresponding set—the plurality of non-self-membered sets, for example!—there seems to be no reason not to consider just the urelements jointly to be the initial, base level of our hierarchy and, subsequently, to constitute a set U in the next level of the hierarchy, the first level in which sets are formed. Thus, since U is provably not a member of itself,[22] and that fact does not in turn lead to the conclusion that, like the contradictory set r, it also *is* a member of itself, there appears to be no Russell-style paradox looming anywhere in the vicinity. We therefore add the joint safety of the urelements as an explicit axiom, where $Set(x) \equiv_{df} x = \varnothing \vee \exists y \, y \in x$:

Ur $Safe([x : \neg Set(x)])$.

Second, the restriction to finite pluralities in the "construction" of a given level from pluralities of things in the preceding level seems unwarranted. Regardless of how many entities there might be in a given level, whether finite or infinite in number, the next level should include all the sets constituted by *any* plurality of things in the preceding level. Finally, each level after U, consisting of the things in the preceding level and all the sets constituted by any or all of them, should itself be safe and, hence, should itself constitute a set.

The addition of the Powerset axiom enables us to capture these aspects of the iterative conception precisely. Specifically, Powerset says that, given a set s, all of its subsets are jointly safe and, hence, constitute a set $\wp(s)$, the *powerset of s*. Formally, letting "$x \subseteq s$" mean, as usual, that x is a subset of s:

Pow $Safe([x : x \subseteq s])$.

Given the safety of the urelements and our axioms **Un, Ur**, and **Pow**, the iterative conception can be expressed in a very clear, mathematically rigorous way (albeit, for the time being, only in our metalanguage[23]) via an inductive definition on the natural numbers:

D1
$$U_0 = U$$
$$U_{n+1} = U_n \cup \wp(U_n)$$

That is, as depicted in Figure B.1, the first level U_0 of the universe is just the set of urelements U (which exists by **Ur**); and each subsequent level U_{n+1} consists of everything in the preceding level U_n together with all the new sets $\wp(U_n)$ that can be formed from members of U_n (and hence from all preceding levels U_m, for $m \leq n$, since the levels are cumulative). Each "disk" at each level in Figure B.1 thus signifies that all the things in earlier levels plus all the new sets they constitute together constitute a new, determinate set.

As noted in the first section, and as we see clearly here, the iterative conception yields a cumulative hierarchy of *well-founded* sets: the fact that we start with a set of urelements and build each subsequent level only from sets constructed from entities in the preceding level means there are no self-membered sets and, more generally, no infinite descending membership chains of the form: $\ldots \in a_{n+1} \in a_n \in \ldots \in a_2 \in a_1 \in a_0$. As this feature

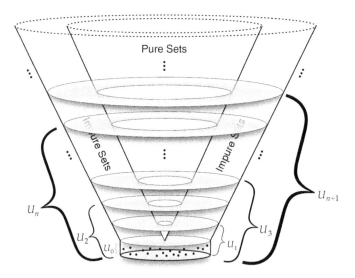

FIGURE B.1 The Cumulative Hierarchy (so far)

of the cumulative hierarchy does not follow from the other axioms, it requires an axiom of its own, the axiom of Foundation. Because this is just a structural axiom about sets, it does not involve the notion of safety:

Fnd $\forall x(x \neq \emptyset \rightarrow \exists y(y \in x \wedge \neg \exists z(z \in y \wedge z \in x)))$.

That is, every non-empty set x contains a member that has no members in common with x.[24]

UNBOUNDED HIERARCHIES: INFINITY AND REPLACEMENT

Note that, while we have shown that the members of each level U_n of the hierarchy are a safe plurality (i.e., each U_n is a set), there is nothing in the axioms thus far to guarantee that the plurality $[x : \exists n\, x \in U_n]$ of *all* the members of *all* the levels is safe. In fact, we need two new principles to guarantee this, both of which are exceptionally important to the modern theory of sets but are also perhaps the most problematic for set theoretic realism, as we'll see.

The first of these is the axiom of Infinity. What is particularly important to note about this axiom is that it is not *merely* the assertion that an infinite set exists. Rather, in addition, it asserts that pluralities with a certain "unbounded" character are safe. To get at the idea, define (recursively) the *rank* $\rho(a)$ of an entity a to be 0 if it has no members (i.e., it is either $\emptyset$ or an urelement) and, otherwise, to be the smallest number n greater than the ranks of its members. Thus, for example, for an urelement a, $\rho(\{\emptyset,a\})=1$, $\rho(\{a,\{\emptyset,a\}\})=2$, and $\rho(\{\{\{\{\emptyset,a\}\}\}\})=4$. Intuitively, the rank of an object is a measure of how "high up" it first occurs in the hierarchy of levels U_n; the two are correlated as follows:

Fact For finite n, a set with rank n will first occur in either U_n or U_{n+1}.[25]

Now, suppose that the objects satisfying a predicate $\varphi(x)$ constitute a (finite or infinite) plurality $[b_0,b_1,b_2,...]$ of objects in the hierarchy of Figure B.1 all of which have ranks $< m$ for some natural number m.[26] Then $[b_0,b_1,b_2,...]$ is obviously in a clear sense "bounded" in the hierarchy—by the preceding **Fact**, each b_i will have first occurred in some level U_j, for $i \leq m$; the plurality, so to say, "runs out" by U_m; U_m thus represents a bound beyond which the plurality does not extend. Moreover, given the cumulative nature of the hierarchy, the b_i will all *exist* in U_m. Hence, $[b_0,b_1,b_2...]$ is just the plurality $[x : x \in U_m \wedge \varphi(x)]$ and so, by **Sep**, it is safe and constitutes a set.

By contrast, consider the plurality $[\emptyset,\{\emptyset\},\{\emptyset,\{\emptyset\}\},\{\emptyset,\{\emptyset\},\{\emptyset,\{\emptyset\}\}\},...]$ given by the following inductive definition:

D2
$$\emptyset_0 = \emptyset$$
$$\emptyset_{n+1} = \emptyset_n \cup \{\emptyset_n\}$$

Then $\rho(\varnothing_0) = \rho(\varnothing) = 0$, $\rho(\varnothing_1) = \rho(\{\varnothing\}) = 1$, $\rho(\varnothing_2) = \rho(\{\varnothing, \{\varnothing\}\}) = 2$, and so on, and each $\varnothing_i \in U_{i+1}$.[27] Hence, the plurality $[\varnothing_0, \varnothing_1, \varnothing_2, \ldots]$ is *unbounded* in the hierarchy of finite levels depicted in Figure B.1: unlike our bounded plurality $[b_0, b_1, b_2, \ldots]$, there is no natural number m such that $[\varnothing_0, \varnothing_1, \varnothing_2, \ldots]$ "runs out" by level U_m; rather, for every number $m > 0$, there is some $c \prec [\varnothing_0, \varnothing_1, \varnothing_2, \ldots]$ such that c first occurs in level U_m. Thus, no proof of its sethood like the one earlier for $[b_0, b_1, b_2, \ldots]$ is forthcoming.

Such unbounded pluralities, then, are of a rather different ilk structurally than any we've seen so far, and the Zermelian axioms laid out to this point do not guarantee their safety. What grounds might there be for trusting them? Pragmatically speaking, we need an infinite set in order to reconstruct classical mathematics in set theory and, ideally, we'd like to be able to do so in the context of pure set theory wherein the set U of urelements is assumed to be empty. But every level U_n of the hierarchy of pure sets that arises under that assumption is finite. Hence, to guarantee the existence of an infinite pure set, the only option is to postulate the safety of some unbounded plurality.

But really, the philosophical justification for the safety of unbounded pluralities ultimately seems no different than when we postulated the safety of our initial plurality of urelements in our axiom **Ur**. Recall there were two aspects to the justification. First, like the urelements, the entities in an unbounded plurality are all *there*—we are not talking about some sort of merely potential plurality; the things in question are fully determinate entities. Second, just as the set U containing the urelements, being a set, is not a member of itself, so too a set s constituted by an unbounded plurality, and hence containing only entities of arbitrarily high finite rank, by definition cannot itself have a finite rank and, hence, cannot be a member of itself; like U, s (if it is to exist) must first occur in a level "above" those of its members. And just as U's non-self-membership does not seem to lead to contradiction, neither, it appears, does s's; even the faintest specter of paradox is nowhere to be seen on the assumption that an unbounded plurality like $[\varnothing_0, \varnothing_1, \varnothing_2, \ldots]$ constitutes a set.

Accordingly, the Infinity axiom simply vouches for the safety of our unbounded plurality $[\varnothing_0, \varnothing_1, \varnothing_2, \ldots]$ the way **Ur** does for the urelements. However, we obviously cannot express this as "$Safe([\varnothing_0, \varnothing_1, \varnothing_2, \ldots])$," since "$[\varnothing_0, \varnothing_1, \varnothing_2, \ldots]$" does not represent a proper term of our language; the ellipsis is shorthand for infinitely many terms, and the terms and formulas of our language are all of finite length. A more promising possibility is "$Safe([x : \exists i (i \in \mathbb{N} \land x = \varnothing_i)])$," where $\mathbb{N}$ is the set of natural numbers. However, while that set is available to us in the metalanguage we are using for our exposition and in which we formulated definition **D2**, we do not yet have it available to us in our theory proper; indeed, as noted earlier, to prove the existence of a set that can serve as the set of natural numbers is exactly why (among other things) we need an axiom of Infinity.

So we need to find some other way to pick out our plurality $[\varnothing_0, \varnothing_1, \varnothing_2, \ldots]$, that is, to recall, the plurality $[\varnothing, \{\varnothing\}, \{\varnothing, \{\varnothing\}\}, \ldots]$. And the key to doing so is to identify the structural property responsible for its unboundedness, namely: the property of being a plurality *yy* of things such that (a) the empty set $\varnothing$ is one of them and (b) $z \cup \{z\}$ is one of them whenever z is; formally, the property (call it *UB*) $\varnothing \prec yy \wedge \forall z(z \prec yy \rightarrow z \cup \{z\} \prec yy)$. Of course, *UB* is true of many other pluralities as well—it's true, in particular, of the Russell plurality of non-self-membered things, $[x:x \notin x]$, so we obviously cannot count on *UB* to guarantee a plurality's safety. However, note that our desired plurality is the *smallest* plurality with *UB*, in the sense that it is made up of exactly the things that are in *every* plurality that has *UB*; that is, it consists of the things x such that $\forall yy(UB(yy) \rightarrow x \prec yy)$. And that is the property we will use in our axiom of Infinity to pick out our chosen plurality (without appealing to an antecedently existing infinite set) and declare it safe:

Inf $Safe([x:\forall yy(\varnothing \prec yy \wedge \forall z(z \prec yy \rightarrow z \cup \{z\} \prec y) \rightarrow x \prec yy)])$. [28]

Hence, by **Safe**, our unbounded plurality constitutes a set $\{\varnothing_0, \varnothing_1, \varnothing_2, ...\}$. This is of course the set ω of *finite von Neumann ordinals* $\varnothing, \{\varnothing\}, \{\varnothing, \{\varnothing\}\}, ...$ which, in modern set theory, are usually identified with the natural numbers. ω thus serves both as a convenient representation of the set of natural numbers and as the first transfinite number, the first (ordinal) number greater than all the natural numbers—we will let it so serve for us henceforth.[29]

Now, the entire iterative hierarchy of finite levels $[U_0, U_1, U_2, ...]$ is of course also an unbounded plurality. However, although obviously structurally similar to $[\varnothing_0, \varnothing_1, \varnothing_2, ...]$, we have as yet nothing to guarantee its safety. A further principle, therefore, is needed, one proposed independently by Thoralf Skolem (1923) and Abraham Fraenkel (1922): the axiom schema of Replacement (the addition of which to Zermelo's set theory Z gives us ZF).[30] The idea is quite simple. As with **Sep**, we need a set s to start with.[31] If you then have some mapping defined on s's members—that is, some description $\psi(x, y)$ that associates each member x of s with a single corresponding entity y—then the range of the mapping, the plurality of things that the members of s are mapped to via $\psi(x, y)$, is safe. (More figuratively put, one can "replace" the members of the original set s with the things they are mapped to in order to derive a new set.) Formally, then (where, as usual, $\exists!x\varphi \equiv_{df} \exists x \forall y(\varphi(y) \leftrightarrow x = y)$):

Rep $\forall x(x \in s \rightarrow \exists!y\,\psi(x, y)) \rightarrow Safe([y:\exists x(x \in s \wedge \psi(x, y))])$.

Taking our von Neumann ordinals to serve as the natural numbers, then, we can show that $[U_0, U_1, U_2, ...]$ is safe by simply mapping each such ordinal n to U_n; that is, we simply let $\psi(x, y)$ be the formula "$x \in \omega \wedge y = U_x$."[32] Since ω is a set, the range of this mapping $[U_0, U_1, U_2, ...]$ is safe and, hence, constitutes a set $\{U_0, U_1, U_2, ...\}$ $(= \{y : \exists x(x \in \omega \wedge y = U_x)\})$. But now that we have shown that the levels constitute a set $\{U_0, U_1, U_2, ...\}$, it follows immediately by the Union axiom **Un** that there is set $U_\omega = \bigcup\{U_0, U_1, U_2, ...\}$ consisting of all of the members of all of the levels.

This is the final critical missing piece from Zermelo's full iterative conception: not only are the pluralities resulting from any finite number of iterations of the Powerset and Union operations safe, as per our definition of the finite levels U_n, so too is the plurality that results from *infinitely many* iterations of those operations. We can, that is, figuratively speaking, put a "disk" at the top of the hierarchy of finite levels depicted in Figure B.1. However, we of course can't leave it at that, as if the hierarchy, so capped off, comes to an end. For once we have determined that all the entities in the finite levels U_n constitute a set U_ω, the iterative construction begins anew, and all the finitely unbounded pluralities drawn from U_ω form the basis of a series of new, transfinite levels $U_{\omega+1}, U_{\omega+2}, U_{\omega+3}, \ldots$ (new members x of which have ranks $\rho(x)$ of $\omega, \omega+1, \omega+2, \ldots$ respectively) as depicted in Figure B.2.

The members of these transfinite levels then constitute further pluralities yy that are also unbounded, albeit in the slightly different sense that there is no natural number n such that, for all $x \prec yy$, $\rho(x) < \omega+n$. Using Replacement once again we can show that $[U_{\omega+1}, U_{\omega+2}, U_{\omega+3}, \ldots]$ is safe and, hence, by the Union axiom, that all of *their* members are jointly safe and, hence, constitute a new "limit" level $U_{\omega+\omega}$, whence the hierarchy begins anew yet again. With the notion of a "limit" level—more exactly, that of a limit

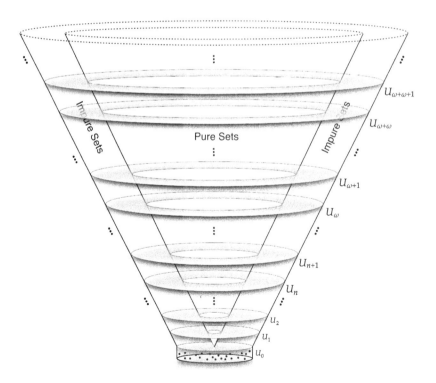

FIGURE B.2 The Cumulative Hierarchy

ordinal—reasonably well in hand, we can state the general definition of Zermelo's full cumulative hierarchy, for all ordinal numbers α:

D3
$$U_0 = U$$
$$U_{\alpha+1} = U_\alpha \cup \wp(U_\alpha)$$
$$U_\lambda = \bigcup_{\beta < \lambda} U_\beta, \text{ for limit ordinals } \lambda$$

It is a fairly straightforward exercise to show that, so long as we choose an ordinal κ that is big enough (at least what set theorists call *inaccessible*[33]) and keep the number of urelements smaller than κ, the set U_κ is a natural model of our ZF axioms.[34]

THE REALIST'S IMPASSE

The cumulative hierarchy is undoubtedly a compelling picture of the set theoretic universe that seems to capture something deep and intuitive about the structure of sets and, moreover, seems to provide a convincing explanation of what goes wrong in Russell's paradox. More specifically, it seems to explain exactly what makes certain pluralities $[x : \varphi(x)]$ unsafe: some predicates $\varphi(x)$ pick out pluralities that are *absolutely* unbounded. That is, some pluralities yy—the Russell plurality $[x : x \notin x]$ in particular—are such that they have no "cap"; that is, for every level U_α of the hierarchy, there are things x among the yy that first appear in levels above U_α; equivalently put, for every ordinal α, there are things x among the yy whose ranks are greater than α.[35] (In particular, since in fact nothing in the cumulative hierarchy is self-membered, the Russell plurality is identical to the entire universe $[x : x = x]$, which is obviously absolutely unbounded.) Hence, there is no level at which such pluralities "run out" and, hence, no level at which they are "available" for collection into a set at the next level.

But here's the problem: the cumulative hierarchy purportedly contains all of the sets there could possibly be that are built up from our initial set U of urelements. But why does the construction of the hierarchy not continue further still? The hierarchy is a definite plurality $[x : x = x]$ containing everything, all the urelements and all the sets that can eventually be constructed from them. Why is *it* not safe? Note, importantly, the question here is *not*: Why is there no universal set? We know from Russell's paradox that there can be no set that contains everything. Rather, the question is why the "process" of constructing new sets does not continue with the sets that, in fact, there are. Why can we not imagine a further "disk" atop the entire hierarchy depicted in Figure B.2—just as we proposed one for the hierarchy of finite levels in Figure B.1—and that the hierarchy continues on with further levels still?[36] For note that it appears we can give precisely the same justification for doing so that we gave for declaring the finitely unbounded plurality $[U_0 \cup U_1 \cup U_2 \cup ...]$ consisting of all of the members of all of the finite levels safe.

First, the things constituting $[x : x = x]$ are all *there*. We are not talking about some sort of merely potential plurality; the things in question—the urelements and all the sets in all the levels—are fully determinate, actually existing entities. Second, just as the set U_ω formed from the plurality $[U_0 \cup U_1 \cup U_2 \cup ...]$ contains entities of arbitrarily high finite rank and, hence, cannot itself have a finite rank and, hence, cannot be a member of itself, so a new set—call it U_Ω—containing the things consituting the (*de facto*) absolutely unbounded plurality $[x : x = x]$ ($= [U_0 \cup U_1 \cup ... \cup U_\alpha \cup U_{\alpha+1} \cup ...]$, for all ordinals α) would exist in a new level "above" those of all of its members and, hence, would not be a member of itself. Hence, for the same reasons again, no paradox appears to be in the offing on these assumptions. And, given U_Ω, the axioms **Pow**, **Un**, and **Safe** together would then seem to yield yet another unbounded extension of the hierarchy.

In a nutshell: For the set theoretic realist for whom (a) all the sets there could possibly be (built up from the actual urelements) are already *there* and (b) the iterative conception is the correct conception of set, there is no clear answer to the question of why the plurality $[x : x = x]$ of everything (i.e., everything that actually exists) is not safe, why the cumulative hierarchy is necessarily only as "high" as it is in fact and could not be extended. Call this the realist's impasse.

Importantly, note also that activism as it stands seems to be at the same impasse: even if we identify sets with products of the divine intellect, so that the cumulative hierarchy necessarily has its existence in the mind of God, the question arises: why has God only collected exactly the sets that God has? The assumption for the activist no less than for the realist is that all the sets there could possibly be (built up from the actual urelements) exist in the divine intellect; they are all *there*. But why, then, is the plurality $[x : x = x]$ not safe? Why can God not turn God's intellect on pluralities like that one that are absolutely unbounded and collect them into further sets?

PLURALITIES, SETS, AND MODALITY

Recent work by Linnebo (2010; 2013) (which, in turn, draws on seminal work by Parsons (1983)) suggests an answer to the realist's impasse, one that I will follow quite closely. The heart of the idea is that the axioms of set theory are implicitly modal; in particular, to say that some things are jointly safe is not to say that they actually constitute a set, but that they *could*. Thus, in the case of the cumulative hierarchy, regardless how "high" the hierarchy actually extends, the process of constructing new sets could always be extended further still; the *actual* absolutely unbounded pluralities there are, while not in fact constituting sets, could constitute sets in a different possible world. Set theory is thus the study, not of the sets there actually are—indeed, how many there are is irrelevant—but, rather, the study of the various set theoretic universes there *could* be.

Now, the actual details involved in working out this deeply interesting and important idea are rather complex (see, in particular, Linnebo 2013). Fortunately, for purpose here, it will suffice only to get a flavor of the broader picture. To begin, the modal operators "□ " and "◊," in the context of set theory, will be interpreted such that $\ulcorner ◊φ \urcorner$, intuitively, means that "it is possible that sets exist that make $φ$ true" and $\ulcorner □φ \urcorner$ means that "no matter what sets come to be (in addition to those there are), it will remain the case that $φ$." The interpretation of "□" here is particularly important. For, expressed in terms of possible worlds, it is not to be thought of as ranging over all worlds absolutely but, rather, at any given world w, over those worlds that include everything in w—all of its urelements and all of its sets. Thus, in particular, at a given world w, the axioms always describe what further sets there could be beyond those there happen to be at w. Hence, the modality characterizes, for any given world w, every possible way the universe of sets that exist in w could be *extended* by sets whose members exist only as mere pluralities in w or in worlds w' accessible from w. As we are thinking about the possibilities of extending the existing sets there might happen in fact to be, this seems like the right modality.[37]

On this understanding, the accessibility relation will be a partial order (reflexive, anti-symmetric, and transitive), since there are many different ways in which the universe of sets in a given world w could be extended to a world w' depending on which unbounded pluralities of w are taken to constitute sets in w'. Hence, our corresponding modal logic will include the system S4.[38] Moreover, when there are alternative possibilities about how the sets in w could be extended (as there always will be), it is reasonable to assume that, regardless of which possibility is chosen, the other alternatives do not go away. In terms of accessibility, this means that for any worlds w_1 and w_2 accessible from a given world w, there will always be a common world w_3 accessible from both w_1 and w_2. This condition, known as *convergence*, when added to our partial order, yields an accessibility relation characteristic of the system known as S4.2, the result of adding the following axiom schema to S4:

4.2 $◊□φ→□◊φ.$[39]

Now, Linnebo (2010, 156ff) goes on to note that the modal character of the sentences of set theory is captured chiefly by analyzing the universal quantifier "∀" as "□∀" and the existential quantifier "∃" as "◊∃"; accordingly for a given sentence $φ$ of our non-modal set theoretic language, let $φ^◊$ be the result of replacing every quantifier occurrence in $φ$ with its modalized counterpart. With this distinction between modal and non-modal readings of the quantifiers in hand, Linnebo points out that Russell's paradox can be given a cogent and compelling analysis. Specifically, the paradox depends on the non-modal readings of the two principles **Collapse** and **P-Comp**, and our initial solution was to accept the latter and place the blame on the former, which led us ultimately to the realist's impasse. However, under our now preferred modal interpretation, the situation is reversed. So interpreted, **Collapse** is true and, indeed, expresses quite precisely the modal intuition underlying the iterative conception that the universe of sets is always extensible:

Collapse$^◊$ $□∀xx◊∃y□∀z(z ∈ y ↔ z ≺ xx).$

That is, necessarily (i.e., in worlds that contain our urelements and sets, and perhaps more sets as well built from them), for any things whatever, it is possible that they be collected into a set; that is, it is possible that there be a set containing (necessarily) exactly them. By contrast, while the principle **P-Comp** is unproblematically true on the non-modal interpretation,[40] its modalized counterpart

P-Comp$^\Diamond$ $\Diamond\exists yy\Box\forall x(x \prec yy \leftrightarrow \varphi(x))$, where φ contains no free occurrences of the variable 'yy'

is false in general. For, while it is trivially the case that there is a world w in which there are the things satisfying φ—the actual world is such a world, for any φ—for some predicates φ, there is not always a world w such that that there are, *in w*, all the things that *could* satisfy φ, that is, all the things that satisfy φ in any accessible world. For, on our understanding of the modalities, for any world w, there are worlds w' accessible from w in which there are sets that don't exist in w—and hence are not among any plurality in w—but that satisfy φ in w'. This is true in particular of the predicate "$x \notin x$" since, on the iterative conception, nothing in any world is a member of itself; necessarily, everything satisfies "$x \notin x$." Hence, the modal interpretation **P-Comp$^\Diamond$** of **P-Comp** for the predicate at issue in Russell's paradox is false, and the paradox dissolves.

Now, as Linnebo (2013) shows, given only the system of quantified S4.2, the iterative principle **Collapse$^\Diamond$**, the axioms of Extensionality and Foundation, and a few other intuitive principles concerning the modal properties of sets and pluralities,[41] it is possible to derive the modalized versions of all of the standard axioms of pure ZF.[42] Indeed, since the notion of a safe plurality reduces to the possibility of a certain set, plurals and the notion of safety can simply drop out of the picture in the statement of the axioms proper. Thus, to get a sense of how things look, instead of **Pr** we have:

Pr$^\Diamond$ $\Box\forall a\forall b\Diamond\exists y\Box\forall z(z \in y \leftrightarrow (z = a \lor z = b))$

That is, for any things a and b, there *could* be a set that (necessarily) contains exactly them. Likewise, instead of **Pow** we have a modalized counterpart telling us that the subsets of any given set s *could* themselves constitute a set:

Pow$^\Diamond$ $\Box\forall s\Diamond\exists y\Box\forall z(z \in y \leftrightarrow z \subseteq s)$.

And Infinity now says that there *could* be a set containing the von Neumann ordinals $\emptyset, \{\emptyset\}, \{\emptyset, \{\emptyset\}\}, ...$:

Inf$^\Diamond$ $\Diamond\exists u(\emptyset \in y \land \Box\forall z(z \in y \rightarrow z \cup \{z\} \in y))]$.[43]

Moreover, Linnebo shows that, in the context of (pure) modal set theory, the modalized quantifiers "$\Box\forall$" and "$\Diamond\exists$" "behave proof-theoretically very much like ordinary quantifiers" (2013, 213) and hence can also largely drop out of the picture—thus explaining why the explicit modalities "do not surface in ordinary set-theoretic practice" (2010, 164).

Succinctly (and somewhat crudely) put, then: Linnebo solves the realist's impasse by proposing that set theory is not the study of the sets there *are*—indeed, it is irrelevant which sets actually exist—but, rather, of what sets there *could be*. Linnebo's solution is thus able to fully embrace what had been an embarrassment for the realist—the fact that the hierarchy of sets must necessarily come to an arbitrary end. But because the hierarchy is always extensible—as embodied in **Collapse**$^\lozenge$—the impasse is resolved.

Note also that the impasse is equally well resolved for the activist: the answer to the question of why absolutely unbounded pluralities like $[x:x = x]$ are not safe, that is, why God could not turn the divine intellect on such pluralities and collect them into further sets, is that God *could* do exactly that. As a matter of contingent fact, God has not; but God could. Understood in activist terms, **Collapse**$^\lozenge$ says that, necessarily, every plurality could be (but might in fact not have been) collected into a set by God. And the impasse again is thereby resolved.

REALISM AND THE SET THEORETIC MODALITY

All in all, this modal take on the nature of sets, especially its analysis of Russell's paradox, seems quite compelling. But a critical question remains for the realist: what, exactly, is the nature of the modality in modal set theory? Linnebo (2013, 207) himself is quite clear that the modality in question

> *is not metaphysical modality in the usual post-Kripkean sense*. Rather, the modality employed in this article is related to that involved in the ancient distinction between a potential and an actual infinity. This modality is tied to a process of building up larger and larger domains of mathematical objects. A claim is possible, in this sense, if it can be made to hold by a permissible extension of the mathematical ontology; and it is necessary if it holds under any permissible such extension. Metaphysical modality would be unsuitable for our present purposes because pure sets are taken to exist of metaphysical necessity if at all.[44]

And here things seem to go a bit off the rails, metaphysically. For it appears that pure sets at least, for Linnebo, exist necessarily after all; the possibility of the modalized ZF axioms are not the possibility of existence but, well, something else—something having to do with "permissible extension(s) of the mathematical ontology." But what is the notion of permissibility here? The questions at issue here are deep and difficult (see, e.g., Rayo and Uzquiano (2006)) but I take it that a permissible extension of a given model of a theory is a further model that (subject to certain constraints, perhaps) preserves all the relations of the original model. So Linnebo (and perhaps even more so, Parsons (1974, 10–11)) seems to have something like the following (semi-fictional) story in mind.[45] Let

κ be the least inaccessible cardinal, i.e., the smallest of the so-called "large" cardinals.[46] Prior to the discovery of inaccessibles, U_κ was our entire set theoretic universe, albeit unrecognized as a set. From our perspective "inside" that universe, κ was unknown and the plurality picked out by "$[x:x=x]$" was unbounded relative to κ and, hence, from our limited perspective, absolutely unbounded. But upon discovering inaccessibles, our conception of the extent of the universe expanded to include a hierarchy of inaccessibles as well. However, suppose next a new large cardinal property is discovered—measurability, say—and it is proved that the smallest cardinal μ with this property is much larger than κ. Then we will have discovered that what we'd thought was the universe prior to this discovery was really U_μ. With each new discovery of a new class of cardinals, our conception of the extent of the set theoretic universe grows. As there seems to be no limit to the new large cardinal properties we could discover, it seems that is it always possible that our conception of the extent of the universe of sets could grow.

It seems clear, however, that this conception of permissible extensibility is not a metaphysical one but an epistemological one; it is not the case that new sets could come to be but, rather, that our *knowledge* of the nature and extent of the universe can grow. If that is right, then indeed, as Linnebo appears to acknowledge, the (pure) sets exist necessarily after all, in the usual post-Kripkean sense—in any world, the sets that could be constructed from the urelements of that world *already exist*; new sets do not really come to be in other worlds that contain the same urelements. If so, however, then it is simply not possible that the universe of sets be extended at all; if a plurality is not a set in a given world, it is not a set in any world.

By my lights, then, if the modal gambit is to be a truly successful way around the realist's impasse, the modality in question has to be the post-Kripkean metaphysical modality and it really does have to be a contingent matter what sets exist. For the impasse is skirted only if there *really could be* more sets than there actually are (constructed from the same urelements), only if there *really could be* sets whose members are, as a matter of contingent fact, mere pluralities of actually existing sets and urelements. If that is not what is meant—if, after all, all the sets there could be already exist—then the impasse recurs: there is no explanation for why the hierarchy is only as high as it is; no explanation for why the plurality $[x:x=x]$ cannot form a further set.

ADVANTAGE: ACTIVISM

But notice that the realist has in fact simply traded one metaphysical problem for another of the same sort and severity. For the contingency of set existence required by the modal gambit entails a sort of vicious metaphysical capriciousness for the realist: it entails that there are possible worlds that are identical in every respect but for the fact that in one, inexplicably, there are sets built up from the urelements of the world that in the other, inexplicably, do not exist, despite the existence of those very same urelements. And this brings us full circle back to the argument from collections. For recall that a critical element of the realist's response to the argument is that the existence of a set needs no more explanation than the existence of its members and hence, ultimately, given the well-foundedness of the membership relation, the existence of the urelements it is built up from. A set exists *because* its members do, and no further explanation is needed. But this explanation is utterly undercut if it's a radically contingent matter which sets exist given the urelements; if a set s exists in one world w but not in another w' despite the existence of its members in w', then its existence in w is metaphysically capricious; since s might not have existed even if its members had, the existence of its members does *not* after all explain its existence in w. Thus what we might call the realist's dilemma: the realist seems forced to choose between the original impasse and the metaphysical capriciousness of the modal gambit. Either way, the realist seems stuck with pluralities that either inexplicably do not form a set or inexplicably do.

The activist, by contrast, happily avoids the realist's impasse by accepting the modal gambit, but avoids capriciousness because she has a satisfying explanation for the existence of the sets in any given world: they are the ones whose members God in fact chose to collect. As the products of the intellective activity of a free agent, there is no mystery whatever as to how it could be that certain pluralities don't form sets and how it could be that an existing set might not have existed even if its members had. It is no more capricious that God in fact chose not to collect certain pluralities than that God chose not to create certain biological species. For it is always possible for God to have created more things, or other kinds of things, than God actually has. It is no knock against God's creative power that God has in fact chosen not to have done so.

But perhaps it isn't quite that easy. Several objections suggest themselves that I will address briefly here but that no doubt deserve further exploration. First, one might question whether it makes sense to hold that God only *could* form a set from a plurality, i.e., whether God's thinking of the plurality *just is* to think of it as a whole. I think that we are misled by language a bit here, specifically, that the use of the substantive "a plurality" (and the singular anaphoric pronoun "it") is misleading. It is less so, I think, if we frame the question using plurals: is it the case that God's thinking (*de re*) of some things *just is* for God to think of them as a whole? So expressed, it is not at all clear on the face of it. Notably, God's thinking of some things does not of itself seem to be sufficient to account for the iterative structure of the cumulative hierarchy. For in thinking of some things xx it does not follow that there is something—namely, the set $\{\, y : \forall z(z \in y \leftrightarrow z \prec xx)\}$ such that something is a member of it just in case it is one of them—that is capable of being a member of further pluralities that, in turn, can be collected in the divine mind. God's simply thinking of some things is not of itself sufficient for that; thinking of them as a whole, collecting those things into a set, has to be a separate intellective act if we are to account for the iterative structure of the sets along activist lines.

But this answer might lead to a related worry about omniscience.[47] If God could collect some things into a set, God knows that this is possible and, hence, knows that there would be such a set. But this, the worrier continues, would seem to entail that God actually know that God could collect that set. For how could God know that he could create a set from some things without God's actually apprehending that very set?

But the preceding reply seems to apply here as well: the move from the *de dicto* to the *de re*, at the least, does not follow. We have just seen that God's thinking of some things as a whole is a separate intellective act and, hence, that his thinking of some things is not of itself to think of them jointly as a set. Hence, when God knows that God *could* collect some things into a set that God has not in fact collected, it neither follows, nor does there seem to be any compelling reason to think, that God must have *de re* knowledge of a set that *would* exist that contains those things—and indeed, as we've gone to some lengths to show, on the activist's account, it cannot always be that such a set would exist; there must *necessarily* be pluralities that are not collected. And, of course, since, there are no such sets for such pluralities, there are no propositions about any such sets and, hence, no true propositions that God fails to know. Hence, there is no clear problem for God's omniscience here.[48]

A further concern is that, while the activist doesn't have the problem of metaphysical capriciousness that the realist seems to have, a vicious sort of capriciousness nonetheless might remain. For if, necessarily, all the existing sets are contingent, then perhaps God chose, capriciously, not to collect, for example, Michelle and Barack Obama into a set $\{m,b\}$. This might seem particularly odd, indeed inexplicable, given that we ourselves seem perfectly able to collect them together in our own intellects.

But it seems the activist, as part of her overall explanation of the connection between God and sets, can reasonably make a case for the actual existence of a very large cumulative hierarchy in the divine intellect. To elaborate, it seems impossible that God, being omniscient, wouldn't know that I, say, had collected the Obamas in my own intellect without God also doing so. Moreover, God knows what finite pluralities we, hence arbitrarily powerful finite minds, are simply *capable* of collecting and, hence, has in fact collected all the finite levels U_n. And, of course, *we* have grasped the idea of levels extending beyond the finite, so it is reasonable to think God has collected all the elements of the finite levels into the first infinite level $U_\omega = \bigcup_{n<\omega} U_n$. Indeed, as God knows how many sets there must be in a cumulative hierarchy to make the axioms of ZF true—the axiom system that most of us think best characterizes the basic structure of the universe of sets—it seems reasonable to think that God in fact collects at least up to the first inaccessible cardinal κ such that the cumulative hierarchy $U_k = \bigcup_{\alpha<k} U_\alpha$ is a model of ZF.[49] And, indeed, since God of course knows what inaccessibles are, it is reasonable to suppose God forms sets of inaccessible size and, hence, collects to the first Mahlo cardinal (the "next smallest" type of large cardinal); however, for the same reason it is reasonable to suppose God collects up to the first weakly compact cardinal; and so on.[50] Indeed, given that God knows all of the large cardinal properties—certainly at least those we are in principle capable of formulating—it is reasonable to suppose that God does enough collecting to satisfy all of them.[51]

Aside from whatever intrinsic philosophical merit it might have, an advantage of this hypothesis is that, if correct, ZF and all conceivable large cardinal extensions of it are all actually true. Hence, the modal axioms of ZF are unnecessary except to characterize possible extensions of the cumulative hierarchy that God could construct beyond the massively large hierarchy that God has actually constructed.

In sum, then. The argument from collections is a good one in at least the sense that it provides an illuminating way of thinking about set theory from a theistic perspective. Additionally, however, activism fills a rather dramatic—arguably irresolvable—explanatory gap in set theoretic realism and, hence, provides a significantly better explanation than realism for the existence and nature of sets. To that extent, at least, then, insofar as one wishes to hold on to the idea that the axioms of ZF (at least in their modal guises) tell us something robustly true about the sets and what they are like, the argument from collections provides positive grounds for believing that God exists.

NOTES

My deep appreciation goes to the Notre Dame Center for the Philosophy of Religion, where I served as the 2016–17 Alvin Plantinga Fellow, and where this essay was written. I am greatly indebted to the attendees of the September 9, 2016 meeting of the CPR Friday seminar for their challenging questions and insightful comments on an earlier draft, which led to a complete reconstruction (and, I believe, a far better version) of my account of the argument from collections. Thanks in particular to Michelle Panchuk, Nevin Climenhaga, Brain Cutter, Sam Newlands, Rebecca Chan, Mike Rea, John Keller, Lorraine Juliano Keller, Andrew Moon, and Malte Bischof. I am also very thankful to Trent Dougherty and Jerry Walls for their extraordinary patience; I made them wait a very long time for a paper they had graciously (if perhaps unwisely) asked me to write. Finally, my greatest debts are to Al himself and to Pen Maddy, both of whom, as my teachers and dissertation advisors, inspired my interest in the metaphysics of mathematics and (more importantly), through their kind encouragement, generosity, and great good humor, taught me that one can be both a good philosopher and a good person.

1. I developed a *model* on which sets, together with numbers, properties, and propositions, are the products of God's intellective activity in Menzel 1987 but did not attempt to turn it into a positive theistic *argument*.

2. Plantinga doesn't emphasize this first part of the premise, but it is of course implicit and I believe it enhances the argument if it is drawn out explicitly.

3. The so-called iterative conception of the set theoretic universe will be discussed in some detail in the fourth section. The explanation it yields of Russell's paradox is spelled out in the first paragraph of the fifth section.

4. The German: "Unter einer 'Menge' verstehen wir jede Zusammenfassung M von bestimmten wohlunterschienden Objekten m unsrer Anshauung oder unseres Denkens . . . zu einem Ganzen." "Zusammenfassung . . . zu einem Ganzen" is usually translated "collection into a whole" (as in Cantor 1915), but the use of the present participle "collecting" seems to me to better convey the active connotation of the phrase, that it is something *done* by an agent. Wang also translates "Zusammenfassung" as a "collecting together" in a 1967 letter to Gödel; see Gödel 2003, 401–2.

5. In Menzel (1987, 370) I attempted to illustrate Wang's idea in a way that might be helpful: Consider the following array:

$$\begin{matrix} * & * & * \\ * & * & * \\ * & * & * \end{matrix}$$

Think of the asterisks as being numbered left to right from 1 to 9, beginning at the upper lefthand corner. While focusing on the middle dot 5, it is possible to vary at will which dots in the array stand out in one's visual field (with perhaps the exception of 5 itself), for example, [1,5,9], [2,4,5,6,8], or even [1,5,8,9]. The dots thus picked out, I take Wang to be saying, are to be understood as the elements of a small "set" existing in the mind of the perceiver.

6. More exactly, well-foundedness rules out the possibility of infinite descending membership chains, so that every set "bottoms out" in some initial (possibly empty) set of urelements. See the discussion of the Foundation axiom **Fnd** in the section on Zermelo's axioms.

7. My thanks to Nevin Climenhaga for this sentence, which he rightly suggested is a better expression of the argument's conclusion. I should note that he has mild reservations about the conclusion even in this improved form.

8. Plantinga in fact specifically identifies the argument from collections as a good one in this sense.

9. The argument also seems to be good in the other two senses that Plantinga mentions (2007, 209): it might move some people closer to theism, and it might have the consequence of strengthening and confirming some theists' beliefs.

10. Boolos's (1984, 432) formalization of **GK** differs from **GK2** because he assumes a domain containing only critics.

11. The simple, elegant proof is that, if one substitutes $y = y$ for Cy and $(y = 0 \vee y = z + 1)$ for Ayz in **GK2**, the resulting sentence—expressing (in the language of arithmetic) essentially "Some positive natural numbers succeed only one another"—is true in all and only nonstandard models of arithmetic, a property that no sentence of first-order arithmetic can have (lest it be possible to construct a categorical axiomatization of first-order arithmetic, contrary to Gödel's incompleteness theorem). See Boolos 1984, 432–433, especially note 7.

12. Strictly speaking, as Yi (2002, 5) points out, this only follows on the assumption that we are restricting ourselves to sentences containing identity and the predicates C and A. Thus Quine (1982, 293) argued that one could formalize **GK** just as well in the first-order language of set theory (hence with the addition of the membership predicate $\in$) if we simply replace $\exists X$ with $\exists x$, Xy with $y \in x$, and Xz with $z \in x$ in **GK2**. However, Yi (2005, 470) argues convincingly that the English rendering of the result of doing so is not logically equivalent to **GK** and, hence, that Quine's first-order formalization is inadequate. See also Yi's note 29 for more on **GK** and some of the surrounding issues.

13. Or, for that matter, in terms of so-called general, or "Henkin," semantics, on which the range of the second-order quantifiers needn't include all sets of individuals. See Enderton 2001, chapter 4, especially sections 1 and 4.

14. See Boolos 1984, 449: "The lesson to be drawn from the foregoing reflections . . . is that neither the use of plurals nor the employment of second-order logic commits us to the existence

of extra items beyond those to which we are already committed. We need not construe second-order quantifiers as ranging over anything than the objects over which our first-order quantifiers range."

15. In many plural logics, it is a logical truth that there are no empty pluralities, that $\forall xx \exists y(y \prec xx)$ (see, e.g., Linnebo 2014, section 1.2). In such contexts, the first conjunct inside the plural quantifier of **GKP** is superfluous. However, for purposes here, it is convenient to allow for empty pluralities (following Burgess 2004 and Linnebo 2013).

16. Without, of course, simply exploiting its inconsistency and proving anything one wants by contradiction. Notably, it is an easy exercise to derive all the axioms of Zermelo-Fraenkel set theory ZF (other than **Ext**) as instances of Comprehension. Hence, every theorem of ZF can be proved in naive set theory exactly as in ZF once the axioms used in the proof are derived.

17. The exposition in this section and portions of the following two sections is similar to that found in Menzel (forthcoming), which was written largely in parallel with the present chapter.

18. In more detail: Suppose s is a set. By **S-Sep**, there is a set a containing all the members of s satisfying the predicate ' $x \notin x$ ', that is, the members of s that are not members of themselves; formally $\forall x(x \in a \leftrightarrow (x \in s \wedge x \notin x))$. Instantiating to a we have that $a \in a$ if and only if $(a \in s \wedge a \notin a)$. Assuming $a \in a$, it follows that $a \notin a$. So $a \notin a$. And assuming $a \notin a$, we have that either $a \notin s$ or $a \in a$. But we already know $a \notin a$. So $a \notin s$. Otherwise put, with **S-Sep**, all we're able to prove is that, for any set s, there is some (non-self-membered) set not in s and, hence, as an immediate corollary, that there is no universal set, no set that contains everything.

19. Specifically, it is a truth of first-order logic that something exists; call it a. Hence, by **Sep** we have that the "empty plurality" $[x : x \in a \wedge x \neq x]$ (see note 15) is safe, and so, by **Safe**, we have the empty *set* $\varnothing = \{x : x \in a \wedge x \neq x\}$. By iterated applications of Pairing, then, we also have, for example, the series of singletons $\{\varnothing\}$, $\{\{\varnothing\}\}$, $\{\{\{\varnothing\}\}\}$, . . . , which are all distinct from one another by the extensionality axiom **Ext**.

20. This is an easy induction: The case $n = 0$ is given by **Sep**, as seen in note 19. Suppose then that any n things are a safe plurality and that we have a plurality $[a_1, \ldots, a_n, a_{n+1}]$ of $n + 1$ things. By our induction hypothesis, $[a_1, \ldots, a_n]$ is safe and hence, by **Safe**, constitutes a set $\{a_1, \ldots, a_n\}$. By **Pr**, $\{a_{n+1}\}$ is a set and hence also $\{\{a_1, \ldots, a_n\}, \{a_{n+1}\}\}$. By **Un**, the plurality $[a_1, \ldots, a_n, a_{n+1}]$ is safe and, hence, constitutes a set $\{a_1, \ldots, a_n, a_{n+1}\}$. We conclude by induction that any finite plurality constitutes a set.

21. It's actually not clear that Zermelo thought that absolutely all urelements form a set, though he is clear in his later works (notably Zermelo 1930) that one needs to assume they do in any particular application of the theory (though it is consistent with his theory that they do not—see, e.g., Friedman 2004). Several recent papers (notably, Nolan 1996 and Sider 2009) have argued that (especially in certain modal metaphysical frameworks) there might well be "too many" urelements to constitute a set and that, under certain assumptions, assuming there is a set U of urelements leads to contradiction. But (as argued in Menzel 2014) these arguments depend on theoretically unnecessary restrictions built into the axiom schema of Replacement (discussed briefly in the next section), not on the assumption *per se* that the urelements constitute a set.

22. That U is not a member of itself follows formally from **Sep**. For, since no urelement has any members, the predicate " $x \notin x$ " is true of all of them. Hence, the set y such that

$\forall x (x \in y \leftrightarrow x \in U \wedge x \notin x\}$ that we get from **Sep** is exactly U. Instantiating to U, following the reasoning detailed in note 18, it follows directly that $U \notin U$.

23. The reason for this is that the existence of inductively defined functions like this one here in general require both the axioms of Infinity and Replacement, which are only first introduced in the following section.

24. It's not obvious how Foundation rules out infinite descending membership chains, because it in fact does so only given some of the other axioms of set theory—in particular, the axioms of Infinity and Replacement, which are discussed in the following section.

25. In particular, every urelement has a rank of 0 and first occurs in U_0. By contrast, $\rho(\varnothing) = 0$ but $\varnothing$ first occurs in U_1. (By the definition of the hierarchy above, $U_1 = U_0 \cup \wp(U_0)$; since $\varnothing$ is not an urelement, $\varnothing \in U_0$. But $\varnothing \subseteq U_0$ and hence, $\varnothing \in \wp(U_0)$). More generally, let a be a set of rank n. If a is pure, that is, "built up" solely from the empty set, and, hence, contains no urelements in its transitive closure (i.e., it has no urelement as a member, or a member of a member, or a member of a member of a member, . . .) then it first occurs in U_{n+1}. If, by contrast, a is built up solely from urelements and does not contain the empty set in its transitive closure, then it first occurs in U_n. If a is of "mixed" origins, that is, if it is built up from both urelements and the empty set, then whether it first occurs in U_n or U_{n+1} will depend upon the exact manner in which it is constructed.

26. The discerning reader will note that such a plurality could be infinite only if there are infinitely many urelements.

27. See note 25.

28. The usual ZF Infinity axiom **Inf′**, expressed in terms of plurals, says only that *some* plurality with UB—hence some plurality containing all of the $\varnothing_i$ —is safe. Hence, by **Safe**, there is a set s containing all of the $\varnothing_i$. Hence, our unbounded plurality $[\varnothing_0, \varnothing_1, \varnothing_2, \ldots]$ is exactly those members of s that are in every plurality that has UB and, hence, it can be declared safe by means of an instance of **S-Sep**: $Safe([x : x \in s \wedge \forall yy(UB(yy) \rightarrow x \prec yy)])$. So **Inf′** implies **Inf**. But **Inf** obviously implies **Inf′**—if $[\varnothing_0, \varnothing_1, \varnothing_2, \ldots]$ is safe, then some plurality with UB is safe—so, in the context of the other axioms, the two axioms are equivalent.

29. Zermelo's own axiom of infinity postulates a set that includes the somewhat different unbounded plurality $[\varnothing, \{\varnothing\}, \{\{\varnothing\}\}, \{\{\{\varnothing\}\}\}, \ldots]$. These are often referred to as the *Zermelo numbers* because they were the surrogates that Zermelo used to represent the natural numbers.

30. Skolem 1923 is translated as Skolem 1967. Both Skolem and Fraenkel point to powerset constructions like our plurality $[U_0, U_1, U_2, \ldots]$ as examples of sets whose existence is unprovable in Z. Skolem provides a proof by constructing a model of Z in which all the sets in his plurality exist but fail to constitute a set.

31. Separation can in fact be derived from Replacement in ZF but set theorists often appreciate knowing what can be proved in Zermelo's original set theory Z, so most presentations of ZF include both schemas.

32. Note that at this point, with both Infinity and Replacement at our disposal, the existence of the inductively defined function U_x in Definition **D1** can be demonstrated *within* our theory, so the proof sketch here is legitimate. However, it is also redundant, as it will follow simply from the existence of the function U_x that its range $\{U_0, U_1, U_2, \ldots\}$ exists as a set. The point of the example here, of course, is simply to illustrate how the axiom works. In fact, however, it is possible to define the plurality of finite levels $[U_0, U_1, U_2, \ldots]$, and hence an appropriate mapping $\psi(x, y)$ on ω, without any appeal to the function U_x. For note that this plurality has the

following structural property P: (a) the set U of urelements is one of them and (b) $z \cup \wp(z)$ is one of them if z is; formally: $U \in xx \wedge \forall y(y \prec xx \to y \cup \wp(y) \prec xx)$. Similar to how we defined $[\varnothing_0, \varnothing_1, \varnothing_2, \ldots]$ without any appeal to the natural numbers, then, we can define our desired plurality $[U_0, U_1, U_2, \ldots]$ of finite levels of the hierarchy without any appeal to the function U_x as the *smallest* plurality with property P, that is, as the sets s such that, for *every* plurality with P, s is one of them. And that in turn enables us to define the mapping $\psi(x, y)$ on ω "$x \in \omega \wedge \theta(x, y)$", where $\theta(x, y)$ expresses "y is the set in the smallest plurality with P such that $x \in y$ and, if $z \subset y$ is also in that plurality, then $x \notin z$"; that is, roughly put, "y is the first level of the hierarchy in which x occurs." This maps each $i \in \omega$ to U_{i+1} and, hence, by **Rep**, the plurality $[U_1, U_2, \ldots]$ (i.e., $[y : \exists x(x \in \omega \wedge \theta(x, y))]$) is safe and, hence, constitutes a set $\{U_1, U_2, \ldots\}$. Our desired set U_ω of all the members of all the levels, of course, is now simply $U \cup \bigcup \{U_1, U_2, \ldots\}$.

33. Inaccessibility is usually ascribed to *cardinal* numbers, which, in set theory, are identified with certain ordinals, viz., those that are larger in size than any of their predecessors. ω, being the first infinite ordinal, is a paradigm here; in its cardinal guise it is known as $\aleph_0$. A cardinal κ is *inaccessible* if (a) it is uncountable (i.e., it is $> \aleph_0$), (b) it is not the sum of fewer than κ smaller cardinals, and, (c) for cardinals $\lambda < \kappa$, $2^\lambda < \kappa$. Thus, if s is an uncountable set of size κ where κ is inaccessible, by property (b) it will not be possible to partition s (i.e., divide it up into subsets such that no two of them have a common member) into fewer than κ cells all of which are smaller in size than s; otherwise put, there either have to be as many cells in the partition as there are members of s, or one of the cells must already be as large as s. And by property (c), the powerset of any set smaller than s will also be smaller than s. To get a sense of how big inaccessibles are, note that $\aleph_0$ has properties (b) and (c). So the jump from the "accessible" infinite cardinals to the first inaccessible is, in a sense, as enormous as that from the natural numbers to $\aleph_0$. For a bit more on inaccessibles and "large" cardinals generally, see notes 46 and 50.

34. Zermelo (1930) himself was the first to define the cumulative hierarchy as in **D3** and prove that U_κ was a model of ZF (formulated to allow urelements) for κ inaccessible. For a good introduction to ZF set theory and the cumulative hierarchy, see Devlin 1991, chapter 2, especially section 2.3. For a philosophically rich, illuminating study that axiomatizes the cumulative hierarchy directly, see Potter 2004.

35. The correlation between ranks and levels once we move into the transfinite is more definite: for infinite ordinals α and sets x, $\rho(x) = \alpha$ if and only if x first occurs in $U_{\alpha+1}$.

36. It is important to emphasize that the term "$[x : x = x]$" is being used "non-rigidly" here to pick out whatever happens to exist. If (*per impossibile*, according to the realist) the plurality of *actually existing* things (that is, the things *actually* picked out by "$[x : x = x]$") were safe, then they would constitute a set and, hence, the plurality that *would be* picked out by "$[x : x = x]$" would properly include the plurality that is *in fact* picked out by "$[x : x = x]$".

37. Studd (2013) develops an alternative bi-modal theory that builds instead on a linear temporal metaphor on which (roughly) the stages of the iterative hierarchy are constructed through time; one modality thus can "look ahead" to future (hence, larger) stages and the other can "look back" at past (hence, smaller) stages. This makes for a rather more elegant axiomatization than on Linnebo's approach.

38. That is, the system of propositional modal logic whose axioms are **K** ($\square(\varphi \to \psi) \to (\square\varphi \to \square\psi)$), **T** ($\square\varphi \to \varphi$), and **4** ($\square\varphi \to \square\square\varphi$).

39. S4.2 is sound and complete for convergent partially ordered frames. See Hughes and Cresswell 1996, 134–136 for more on S4.2.

40. But see Yablo 2006.

41. Particularly important among these are the principles $\exists yy \Box \forall u(u \prec yy \leftrightarrow u \in x)$ and $\exists yy \Box \forall u(u \prec yy \leftrightarrow u \subseteq x)$, expressing that sets have their members and their subsets essentially. See Linnebo 2013, § section 6.

42. ZF with urelements would simply be a somewhat fussier affair that would call for a few further principles.

43. We use (the modalization of) the weaker but equivalent form **Inf′** of the Infinity axiom (see note 28), as the modalized version of **Inf** is needlessly complicated. We also assume for convenience (apparently along with Linnebo (2013, 223–224)) that ∅ exists (and hence exists in all accessible worlds). Without this assumption we would either have to adopt some variant of free logic (in which constants might not denote) or complicate the Infinity axiom considerably.

44. See also Linnebo 2010, section § V, where he spells this idea out in a bit more detail.

45. The rest of this paragraph assumes a bit more set theory than has been assumed hitherto, but the details are not essential to the argument.

46. Large cardinals are so-called because they are provably larger than any cardinal whose existence can be proved in ZF. The reason such cardinals cannot be proved to exist is that they are all inaccessible and, as just noted, for inaccessible κ, U_κ is a model of ZF. By Gödel's second incompleteness theorem, ZF (if consistent) cannot prove its own consistency and, hence (by the soundness theorem for first-order logic), cannot prove that it has any models; so it can't prove the existence of an inaccessible.

47. Versions of which are due to Michelle Panchuk and Mike Rea.

48. Thanks to Brian Cutter for making this point in discussion. There is perhaps an inkling of a difficulty here, though. For, insofar as what is *possible* is determinate, one might argue that there have to be propositions that *actually* have an internal structure that corresponds to all the collecting God could possibly do beginning with a certain plurality of urelements. To make things simple, suppose we just have the single urelement a. Then, as a is a plurality of one, God knows there could be a set s_0 containing just a; and hence that there could be a set s_1 containing a and s_0 and all the sets that can be formed from them; and hence that there could be a set s_2 containing all those things and all the sets that can be formed from them; and hence . . . ; and at limit stages, that there could be a set s_λ containing a and, for $\beta < \lambda$, and all the sets that can be built up from the members of all the s_β; and so on. But it seems that there can't really *be* any such proposition, for any initial plurality xx, since it would *actually* have to include embedded conjuncts for all the collecting that is *possible* for God to do beginning with xx. And the resulting structured proposition would seem to be as problematic as the realist's assumption that all the sets there could be are already actual.

I will leave this objection unanswered, except for noting that it seems open to the activist to reject the idea that propositions have the sort of "internal structure" that would seem to be required to get this objection off the ground. That said, I am not confident that there aren't other cardinality worries along these lines lurking in the nearby bushes (as Plantinga might put it).

49. This reasoning is actually a bit quick. For by a remarkable theorem of Montague and Vaught (1959), if κ is the smallest inaccessible, there is a cardinal $\mu < \kappa$ (hence, "small") such that U_μ is a model of ZF. By Gödel's second theorem, once again, the existence of μ cannot be

proved in ZF alone, even though it is provably "accessible." So, assuming the existence of an inaccessible, the smallest inaccessible is not actually the first cardinal κ such that U_κ is a model of ZF.

50. The intuitive idea behind the postulation of this hierarchy of ever larger large cardinals, on the realist's picture of the cumulative hierarchy, at least, is that the universe of sets is so rich that any property of it that we can think of must already be "reflected" in some set. Large cardinal axioms typically arise, therefore, through the identification of some interesting property of the universe that is not true of any set whose existence can be proved in ZF (perhaps supplemented by existing large cardinal axioms) and postulating the existence of a set with that property. For an excellent discussion of the ZF axioms, the iterative conception, and large cardinals, see Maddy 1988, especially 501–508.

51. This is a bit simplistic as, currently, the known large cardinal properties, ordered by strength, do not quite form a linear hierarchy (see Kanamori 2003, 472), so some of those properties might not actually be true of any genuinely possible set.

REFERENCES

Boolos, George. 1984. To be is to be the value of a variable (or to be some values of some variables). *Journal of Philosophy* 81: 430–449.

———. 1985. Nominalist platonism. *The Philosophical Review*, 94 (3):327–344.

Burgess, John P. 2004. *E Pluribus Unum*: Plural logic and set theory. *Philosophia Mathematica*, 3 (12): 192–221.

Cantor, Georg. 1915. *Contributions to the Founding of the Theory of Transfinite Numbers*. New York: Dover Publications.

———. 1932. *Gesammelte Abhandlungen mathematischen und philosophischen Inhalts*. Berlin: Springer-Verlag.

Cresswell, M.J., and G.E. Hughes. 1996. *A New Introduction to Modal Logic*. London and New York: Routledge.

Devlin, Keith. 1991. *The Joy of Sets*. New York: Springer-Verlag, second edition.

Enderton, Herbert. 2001. *A Mathematical Introduction to Logic*. San Diego, CA: Academic Press,, 2nd edition.

Fraenkel, Adolf. 1922. Zu den Grundlagen der Cantor-Zermeloschen Mengenlehre. *Mathematische Annalen*, 86: 230–237.

Frege, Gottlob. 1893. *Grundgesetze der Arithmetik, Band I*. Jena: Verlag Hermann Pohle.

Friedman, Harvey. 2004. Faithful representation in set theory with atoms. http://www.cs.nyu.edu/pipermail/fom/2004-January/007845.html, January. URL http://www.cs.nyu.edu/pipermail/fom/2004-January/007845.html.

Gödel, Kurt. 2003. *Collected Works, volume V: Correspondence, H-Z*. Solomon Feferman, John W. Dawson, Warren Goldfarb, Charles Parsons, and Wilfred Sieg, editors. Oxford: Clarendon Press.

Kanamori, Akihiro. 2003. *The Higher Infinite: Large Cardinals in Set Theory from Their Beginnings*. Berlin: Springer-Verlag, 2nd edition.

Linnebo, Øystein. 2010. Pluralities and sets. *The Journal of Philosophy* 107(3):144–164.

———. 2013. The potential hierarchy of sets. *The Review of Symbolic Logic* 6, no. 2: 205–228.

———. 2014. Plural quantification. In Edward N. Zalta, editor, *Stanford Encyclopedia of Philosophy* (Fall 2014 Edition). Stanford, CA: Stanford University.

Maddy, Penelope. 1988. Believing the axioms. I. *The Journal of Symbolic Logic* 53, no. 2: 481–511.

Menzel, Christopher. 1987. Theism, platonism, and the metaphysics of mathematics. *Faith and Philosophy* 4(4): 365–382.

———. 2014. Wide sets, ZFCU, and the iterative conception. *Journal of Philosophy* 111, no. 2: 57–83.

———. Forthcoming. Modal Set Theory. In Otávio Bueno and Scott Sturgeon, editors, *The Routledge Companion to Modality*. New York: Routledge.

Montague, Richard, and R.L. Vaught. 1959. Natural models of set theory. *Fundamenta Mathematicaea* 47: 219–242.

Morris, Thomas V., and Christopher Menzel. 1986. Absolute creation. *American Philosophical Quarterly* 23(4): 353–362.

Nolan, Danial. 1996. Recombination unbound. *Philosophical Studies* 84, no. 2/3: 239–262.

Parsons, Charles. 1974. Sets and classes. *Nous* 8, no. 1: 1–12.

———. 1983. Sets and modality. In *Mathematics in Philosophy: Selected Essays*, pages 298–341. Ithaca, NY: Cornell University Press.

Plantinga, Alvin. 2007. Two dozen (or so) theistic arguments. In Dean-Peter Baker, editor, *Alvin Plantinga*, pages 203–227. Cambridge: Cambridge University Press.

———. 2011. *Where the Conflict Really Lies: Science, Religion, and Naturalism*. Oxford: Oxford University Press.

Potter, Michael. 2004. *Set Theory and Its Philosophy*. Oxford University Press.

Quine, W.V. 1982. *Methods of Logic*. Cambridge, MA: Harvard University Press, 4th edition.

Rayo, Augustín, and Gabriel Uzquiano, editors. 2006. *Absolute Generality*. Oxford: Clarendon Press, Oxford.

Sider, Theodore. 2009. Williamson's many necessary existents. *Analysis* 69(21): 250 -258.

Skolem, Thoralf. 1923. Einige Bemerkungen zur axiomatischen Begrundung der Mengenlehre. In *Matematikerkongressen I Helsingfors den 4-7 Juli 1922, Den femte skandinaviska mathematiker- kongressen, Redogörelse*, pages 217–232. Helsinki: Akademiska Bokhandeln.

———. 1967. Some remarks on axiomatized set theory. In Jean van Heijenoort, editor, *from Frege to Godel: A Source Book in Mathematical Logic, 1879–1931*, pages 290–301. Cambridge, MA: Harvard University Press.

Studd, J.P. 2013. The iterative conception of set: A (bi-)modal axiomatisation. *Journal of Philosophical Logic* 42: 697–725.

Wang, Hao. 1974. *From Mathematics to Philosophy*. New York: Humanities Press.

Yablo, Steven. 2006. Circularity and paradox. In T. Bolander, V.F. Hendricks, and S.A. Pedersen, editors, *Self-Reference*, pages 139–157. Stanford, CA: CSLI Publications.

Yi, Byeong-Uk. 2002. *Understanding the Many*. New York: Routledge.

———. 2005. The logic and meaning of plurals. Part I. *Journal of Philosophical Logic* 34: 459–506.

Zermelo, Ernst. 1908. Untersuchungen über die Grundlagen der Mengenlehre, I. *Mathematische Annalen* 65: 261–281.

———. 1930. Über Grenzzahlen und Mengenbereiche. *Fundamenta Mathematicae* 16: 29–47.

(C)

The Argument from (Natural) Numbers

Tyron Goldschmidt

THE PREFACE TO Alvin Plantinga's "Two Dozen (or so) Theistic Arguments" warns that as the arguments are set out there they "aren't really good arguments; they are merely argument sketches, or maybe only pointers to good arguments. They await that loving development to become genuinely good" (2007a, 203). I'm going to give one of these arguments—the argument from numbers—some loving development, but I do not know whether the argument will become genuinely good. I don't know whether there's a genuinely good argument to be had.

Anyone who has been rightly taught—that is, anyone who has read van Inwagen—will know that there are virtually no good arguments for substantive philosophical conclusions (see van Inwagen 2006, Lecture 3). The problem, in part, is that it's hard to know what makes for a good argument. Plantinga implies that van Inwagen's own standards for a good argument are, at least in some cases, *too* liberal (see Plantinga 2007a, 207–208; so far as the success of our argument is concerned, they'd better be too strict). I'll be keeping in mind the numbers: how much of an audience Plantinga's argument will appeal to.

Tyron Goldschmidt

THE ARGUMENT FROM NUMBERS

Alvin Plantinga sketches the following argument for the existence of God:

> *(C) The Argument from (Natural) Numbers.* (I once heard Tony Kenny attribute a particularly elegant version of this argument to Bob Adams.) It also seems plausible to think of *numbers* as dependent upon or even constituted by intellectual activity; indeed, students always seem to think of them as "ideas" or "concepts," as dependent, somehow, upon our intellectual activity. So if there were no minds, there would be no numbers. (According to Kronecker, God made the natural numbers and man made the rest—not quite right if the argument from sets is correct.) But again, there are too many of them for them to arise as a result of human intellectual activity. We should therefore think of them as among God's ideas. Perhaps, as Christopher Menzel suggests (special issue of *Faith and Philosophy*), they are properties of equinumerous sets, where properties are God's concepts. (2007, 213)

The argument is limited both in its conclusion and in its appeal. It's limited in its conclusion since it points only to the existence of infinite intellectual activity. As it stands, the argument doesn't point toward infinite power, infinite goodness or any other divine attributes. It doesn't even show that that the intellectual activity is that of a single intellect rather than spread out among two or more intellects: maybe there are infinitely many, infinitely puny intellects each devoted to thinking just of its own special number.

It's limited in appeal since it depends on a very specific view about the nature of numbers as dependent on intellectual activity. When prompted, students do tend to describe numbers as "ideas" or "concepts." But then students aren't usually prompted and tend not to think about such things. I went through years of math class without stopping at all to ask what kind of things numbers are, if they are so much as things at all. And those most devoted to such questions tend not to think that numbers are ideas, though maybe that has something to do with their neglecting the divine alternative. The argument will have a quite narrow *thinking* audience.

Even so, demonstrating any divine attribute would be quite something. But it would be better if the argument could show a little more. Showing more usually requires assuming more, which means more that can be disputed—which means an even narrower audience. Ambition is traded for audience, or audience for ambition. Still, the trade might be worth it. I'll try to develop the argument so that it shows more about the divine attributes, though my ultimate conclusion will be agnostic about the argument from numbers.

But now for something not entirely different. Immediately after presenting the argument from numbers, Plantinga mentions a similar argument about properties:

> There is also a similar argument re *properties*. Properties seem very similar to *concepts*. (Is there really a difference between thinking of the things that fall under the concept

horse and considering the things that have the property of being a horse?) In fact many have found it natural to think of properties as reified concepts. But again, there are properties, one wants to say, that have never been entertained by any human being; and it also seems wrong to think that properties do not exist before human beings conceive them. But then (with respect to these considerations) it seems likely that properties are the concepts of an unlimited mind: a divine mind. (Ibid)

This isn't at all as natural to me as to those many others. The bar isn't very high. I don't have any inclination to think of properties as concepts. The features of things are out there in the world with those things. Horsiness is in the horse, not in our minds. That's why there can be properties we've never thought of and that existed long before us. I don't know what to say about properties that have never been instantiated, though. I'm not so confident that there are any. In any case, if horsiness isn't a concept, then they aren't concepts either.

The argument from properties also faces a bootstrapping objection: while properties would depend on God, God would seem to depend upon properties, such as omnipotence and omniscience; if there are no such properties, then there can be no God. This threatens to impose an impossible circle of dependence (for a possible answer to the problem see Menzel 2016; and for Plantinga's own view on the relationship between God and his properties see Plantinga 1980). The argument from numbers might face a similar objection: Numbers would depend upon God, even while God would depend on numbers, such as the number one; God is one, an absolute unity and unique. This threatens to impose an impossible circle.

I'll drop this problem, though I will address another vicious circle of dependence—in another argument to be had from properties, an argument that needn't take properties to be concepts. I can't promise it will appeal to a wider audience, since it assumes some principles of its own. I think these principles have more to be said for them than the idea that properties are concepts. The bar isn't very high. If the audience is widened, then it's just by relinquishing the assumption that properties are concepts. Without that, there's less at my disposal to work with in one way—which means reaching less interesting conclusions. Ambition is traded for audience, or audience for ambition.

THE ARGUMENT FROM PROPERTIES

The other argument from properties has its origins in Jonathan Lowe (1996; 1998, Chapter 12; 2012). Strictly speaking, Lowe has in mind *kinds* rather than *properties*. Both kinds and properties are taken to be universals and abstract. The difference is that kinds (e.g., appleness) have their instances in objects (an apple), whereas properties (e.g., redness) have their instances in qualities of objects (the particular redness of the apple). The example Plantinga gives—horsiness—is in fact what Lowe would count as a kind. The argument is very connected to the argument from numbers: the universals Lowe has in mind *are* the numbers, and some of the moves made in the argument will end up informing the argument from numbers.

The broad outline of the argument runs something like this: some abstract beings necessarily exist; abstract beings necessarily depend on concrete beings; so, there must be some concrete beings. Universals enter the scene in the first premise. Numbers are supposed to be the necessary ingredients of the necessary truths of mathematics, and Lowe takes numbers *to be* universals, in particular kinds of sets: single-membered sets instantiate the number 1; double-membered sets instantiate 2, etc. There are some advantages over the more traditional position that numbers are sets (see Lowe 1998, 220–227; Maddy 1990, Chapter 3). But it wouldn't matter if we took numbers to be sets instead.

Which brings us to the second premise. This is based on three principles: that the only possible abstract beings are sets and universals; that sets must depend on non-sets (as their ur-elements); and that universals must depend on non-universals (as their ur-instantiations). Forget how these principles are supported; you won't be convinced— so long as you think other kinds of abstract beings, or the empty set, or uninstantiated universals are so much as *possible*.

The rest of the story: assume sets or universals could have existed alone; then the sets would depend on the universals (for their ur-elements) and the universals on the sets (for their ur-instantiations); which is an impossible circle of dependence; so sets or universals could not have existed alone. Since sets and universals are the only possible kinds of abstract beings, there could not only be abstract beings. Which is to say that abstract beings depend on concrete beings.

Abstract beings, whether construed as universals or sets, are not possible without concrete beings. Since some abstract beings are necessary beings there must be some concrete being or other. Some concrete being *or other*. The abstract beings might depend on cats; but, if cats never existed, they'd depend on dogs. As it stands, the argument does not point toward any single necessary concrete being.

As it turned out, Lowe was also keen about the ontological argument, and subsequently reworked his argument into what he called "a modal ontological argument," though it is not very much like Plantinga's version. Just reject the option that the necessary abstract beings could depend on contingent concrete beings. The idea that necessary beings could depend on contingent beings is weird:

> to contend that the existence of a necessary being, N, is explained in different possible worlds by different contingent beings in those worlds threatens to undermine the very *necessity* of N's existence. For then it appears to be a mere cosmic accident that every possible world happens to contain something that is, allegedly, able to explain the existence of N in that world. (2012, 185)

An accident in the cosmoi of possible worlds is less likely than any ordinary cosmic accident. But why would it be a cosmic accident that every world contains a concrete being?

I suspect: because nothing is preventing the non-existence of all concrete beings. We can't explain why there had to be contingent beings in terms of contingent beings, and we can't explain it in terms of the necessary beings either—since the necessary beings are supposed to depend on the contingent beings in turn.

There's a similar problem with the original argumentative context: Lowe (1996, 1998, Chapter 12) was trying to explain why there is something rather than nothing—something concrete rather than nothing concrete. Lowe answered that there had to have existed some concrete being or other, even while there might not have been any necessary concrete being. However, we can't explain concrete beings in terms of abstract beings if those abstract beings depend on the concrete beings in turn. That's an impossible circle of explanation and dependence. There being necessary abstract beings might entail there necessarily being concrete beings, which entails there being concrete beings in turn. Entailment isn't explanation, though.

Settle with a necessary concrete being instead. And, it turns out, a necessary intellect. Lowe ends up taking abstract beings to depend on intellectual activity. Just like Plantinga does. Here's the relevant part from Lowe:

> A clue here, however, is provided by the very expression "abstract". An abstract being . . . is one which, by its very nature, is in some sense *abstracted* [from]— literally, "drawn out of, or away from"—something else . . . any such being may reasonably be supposed to *depend for its existence* on that *from* which it is "abstracted". All the most plausible examples of abstract beings are, interestingly enough, entities which are, in a broad sense, *objects of reason*—such entities as *numbers, sets* and *propositions*. . . . But then we have a very good candidate for the *sort* of being "from" which such entities may be supposed to be somehow "abstracted": namely, a *mind* of some kind. . . . Putting these thoughts together—(1) that necessary abstract beings, insofar as they are objects of reason, are "mind-dependent" beings, and (2) that they are dependent for their existence on a necessary concrete being—we are led to the conclusion that the being in question must be a *rational being with a mind* and, indeed, with a mind so powerful that it can comprehend all of mathematics and logic. (2012, 189)

Lowe's argument is connected to the argument from numbers in more ways than one. But the argument need not depend on the existence of numbers, let alone their necessary existence: the necessary existence of any abstract being—any universal or set—would do.

Lowe doesn't say much more than Plantinga does about how abstract beings depend on intellectual activity. Let's see how this can be worked out, moving on to the argument from numbers. I promised that I'd develop the argument so that it shows more about the divine attributes.

DEVELOPING THE ARGUMENT

To remind ourselves, here's the argument from Plantinga:

> It . . . seems plausible to think of *numbers* as dependent upon or even constituted by intellectual activity; indeed, students always seem to think of them as "ideas" or "concepts," as dependent, somehow, upon our intellectual activity. So if there were no minds, there would be no numbers. . . . But again, there are too many of them for them to arise as a result of human intellectual activity.

Plantinga's argument for the existence of God is reminiscent of Berkeley's. Just as the phenomenal world outstrips our perceptual capacities (where does it go to when we aren't looking?), so too does the mathematical world outstrip out intellectual capacities. In both cases, an infinite intellect is invoked to do the work. Gödel too might have reasoned something like this from our inability to grasp the set theoretic hierarchy to the existence of superior immaterial minds—monads. Since Gödel believed in God, he could presumably have had recourse to the divine mind too. The details about Gödel's views on monads are obscure (see Maddy 1990, 78–79).

Let's assume that numbers do depend on intellectual activity: no intellectual activity, no numbers. Let's also assume that there are too many numbers for any finite intellectual activity to do the work: no infinite intellectual activity, no numbers. If there are numbers then, there must be infinite intellectual activity. Quite some assumptions, and quite some conclusion. Still, it doesn't give us a very religious conclusion: the infinite intellectual activity may be done by something or some things less than God. I want to take things further, and push for a necessary being and a single being.

First, a necessary being. Let's assume that numbers are the ingredients or truth-makers for mathematical truths—they're what mathematical truths are about. In fact, let's assume that they're necessarily the ingredients. It's not just that they happen to be the ingredients. However things had turned out, nothing else could've done the job; for example, rocks couldn't have had much more to do with the fact that $1 + 1 = 2$. Let's also assume that mathematical truths are necessarily true. But if numbers are the essential ingredients of mathematical truths that are necessarily true, then numbers exist necessarily. Given our assumptions, then, numbers necessarily exist.

So we already have some necessary beings on the scene. But from here we can get to necessary intellectual activity easily. Let's assume that numbers not only depend on intellectual activity, but that they necessarily so depend. It's not just that they happen to depend on intellectual activity. However things had turned out, nothing else could have done the job; rocks couldn't have had much more to do with numbers. Numbers would depend on something tamer if they could. But if numbers necessarily depend on intellectual activity and necessarily exist, then intellectual activity necessarily exists.

Now we have necessary intellectual activity. And where there's intellectual activity there's an intellect. For all that's been said, though, the intellectual activity need not be the intellectual activity of a necessary intellect. However things had turned out, there had to be intellectual activity, and so there had to be some intellect or other, but maybe no particular intellect had to exist. If things had turned out one way, then there'd be a certain intellect, *Barry*, but if things had turned out another way, there'd be another intellect, *Mandy*, without *Barry* at all.

We can push further for a necessary intellect. If there were no necessary intellect, the numbers could depend on different intellects: possibly on *Barry*, possibly on *Mandy*. But numbers are necessary beings while the intellects are contingent beings, and so that would mean that necessary beings depend on contingent beings. As we've seen, that's puzzling. Suppose the relevant contingent intellect, say *Barry*, didn't exist. Then, to secure the necessary existence of the numbers, *Mandy* would exist in his place. The necessary existence of numbers would be preventing the non-existence of intellects; the numbers would be forcing, so to speak, some intellect or other into being. So the intellect would depend on the numbers even while the numbers depend on the intellect, which is an impossible circle of dependence.

Now we have necessary intellect—and intellect infinite enough to generate the infinity of numbers, though not necessarily all-knowing. It might be natural to think that such a powerful intellect would know of other things. After all, punier intellects do have knowledge of various categories (and come along with other things besides, from will to spatiotemporality). However, the analogy would be pathetic, and not entirely wanted. So far as the argument from numbers goes, I see no way to bridge the gap from knowledge of numbers to knowledge of any other things, let alone omniscience.

Nevertheless, I do think that we can push a little further toward another divine attribute—unity. For all that's been said so far, the intellectual activity could be spread among many intellects. There might be infinitely many intellects each housing its own special number. The move toward a single intellect won't be as smooth as any of the moves so far. The argument will now lose adherents. Again: the more that's said, the more room for error. But, as speculative as the following ruminations are, they strike me as having a little plausibility.

The first thought is that a single intellect that is big enough could do all the work. The view that there is a single intellect containing all the numbers is simpler than the view that there are many intellects. On both views, there are as many numbers, but on the first view there are fewer intellects. Ockham's razor slices away all the other intellects. Once we're already this far gone, however, considerations of simplicity might not have so much pull.

The second thought is that numbers are related to each other. I don't just mean that they come together to form sums and products. How they could come together if they are spread among various intellects would be mysterious enough; but then how they come together at all is mysterious. What I have in mind though is the notion that bigger numbers include or contain littler numbers. Think: babushka doll. The number 3 in some way includes 2 and 1; 2 in some way includes 1. This quite different thought might help us understand how numbers come together in other ways.

The thought is captured by set theoretic constructions of the natural numbers—whether we prefer to say, with Zermelo, that $3 = \{\{\{\emptyset\}\}\}$, $2 = \{\{\emptyset\}\}$, $1 = \{\emptyset\}$, and $0 = \emptyset$, or, with von Neumann, that $3 = \{\emptyset,\{\emptyset\},\{\emptyset,\{\emptyset\}\}\}$, $2 = \{\emptyset,\{\emptyset\}\}$, $1 = \{\emptyset\}$, and $0 = \emptyset$. I don't know how seriously to take such constructions, and I don't know how seriously someone who takes numbers to be ideas or concepts should. But being able to do something like this is an advantage of a theory. The thought is also captured by Leibniz's definitions: 2 is 1 and 1; 3 is 2 and 1; 4 is 3 and 1; etc. When I learned how to count, I was given little colored blocks: the first one for 1, and then another one for 2. The first one remained a part of the scene.

If the intellect generates or contains the big number, and the big number includes the little number, then the intellect must contain the little number too. It's not just that an intellect generating a bigger number can do all the work of many intellects each generating littler numbers; it's that the intellect generating a bigger number *will* do all that work. If there are littler intellects, they're redundant, generating many identical or at least indistinguishable number-ish ideas. We'd be stuck with way too much intellectual activity. Now if there were a biggest number, then we could easily move to an intellect that generates all the other, littler numbers. (The little-held view of ultrafinitism would seem to entail their being a biggest number, though it's probably best not to rely on that view here—or anywhere.) However, as it is, if we posit any intellect that does not generate all the numbers, there will always be too much intellectual activity. Ockham's razor cuts again.

Another point in the same direction: Plantinga actually calls the argument from numbers "The Argument from (Natural) Numbers." But why focus on natural numbers? Maybe we do better by focusing on irrational numbers. After all, it would take a much more impressive intellect to house non-repeating decimals that never end. And it would have to contain all the decimals. We can think about pi: but our incomplete knowledge isn't enough to encompass its full and determinate nature. Maybe all we need is 22/7, though. Or better yet, π. (And maybe Euler thought pi could prove that God exists in another way.) Similarly, we can think of a big number without thinking, at least at all explicitly, about littler numbers. But then our thinking hardly constitutes the very being of these numbers.

Leibniz anticipates some of these moves, but in no way drawing from his definitions of numbers. Leibniz argues not from the existence of numbers, but from the existence of necessary truths to the existence of God—including necessary truths beyond the truths of arithmetic and mathematics.

Leibniz construes necessary truths to be dependent beings, only abstracted in the intellect. This is quite like the way Lowe ultimately construes numbers. And just as the truths are necessarily true, there had to exist some intellect. But the truths can't depend on just some intellect or other, without any being necessary. Leibniz insists that necessary beings can't depend on contingent intellects. Again, like Lowe. But Leibniz doesn't explain why.

The argument from numbers that Plantinga attributes to Adams via Kenny is in fact Leibniz's argument, as developed in Adams's book *Leibniz* (see Adams 1994, Chapter 7). At this point in the argument, Adams finds recourse to the Principle of Sufficient Reason: "it is hard to see what the sufficient reason would be that would determine *which* of those individually contingent beings would exist, if there is not one of them that necessarily exists with the power to decide which contingent beings shall exist" (1994, 183). So they must depend on a *necessary* intellect. And, since the necessary truths are logically related, that must be a single intellect.

That last part about the relations between necessary truths is especially complicated, and not especially related to the argument from numbers. The argument we've been developing doesn't depend on these very tricky thoughts or on the PSR. While Leibniz was committed to that principle, we might not be. The argument we've been developing is easier than Leibniz's. Easier. But that doesn't mean better, all things considered.

So we've pushed toward an infinite, necessary, and unified intellect. Not yet God, but not bad company either. After all, more famous arguments for the existence of God show no more than this or that divine attribute, and practically a lot less. Compare the cosmological argument from contingency. If it worked, it would show that there is a necessary being on which contingent beings depend. That points to quite robust power, though not to anything at all intellectual. The argument from numbers would show that there is a necessary being on which other necessary beings depend. It points toward an infinite intellect, though not to anything at all powerful.

Now that I've extended the argument, answering a few potential objections along the way, let's turn to the main advantages of the view, and what I take to be the main problems.

VERSUS PSYCHOLOGISM

Adams, following Leibniz, sees the argument for what we might call divine psychologism in its advantages over the alternatives of run-of-the-mill psychologism and Platonism. As I've noted, the Adams-Leibniz argument differs from Plantinga's in focusing on the necessary truths of logic and mathematics, rather than the existence of numbers. The points apply equally to both. Plantinga's main focus is against human psychologism, which construes numbers as human ideas. Adams calls such a view the "anthropological" theory (1994, 178).

Divine psychologism certainly has various advantages over human psychologism. Human psychologism just won't do for reasons owing ultimately to Frege (1960). If numbers are human ideas, then there'll be too few of them since each of us is finite and there aren't enough of us. If numbers are human ideas, then there won't be any number greater than the greatest number we've thought up. Here's another problem at least close to one put forward by Leibniz about necessary truths generally: if numbers are human ideas, then numbers—and mathematics which has numbers as its essential ingredients—would be just as contingent as we are. But there are enough numbers, and numbers greater than any we've had, and they're not contingent. These points are at work in the argument for divine psychologism developed earlier. Avoid them with an infinite, necessary intellect.

But there are two problems raised by Frege I'm not so sure of: I'm not so sure how serious the problems are, or whether divine psychologism avoids them. The first is about privacy: if numbers are ideas, and ideas are private to thinkers, then we will each have our own numbers: "We should have to speak of my two and your two, of one two and all twos" (1960, Section 27; if only Dr. Seuss wrote the whole book).

If the number 2 is a divine idea, is it any less private than if it is a human idea? Maybe. If 2 is a human idea, then presumably it's as much my idea as yours, so that we have to speak of my 2 and your 2; you're not especially privileged such that we're all talking about *your* idea. However, if it's a divine idea, then we could all be talking about the same idea, God's idea. Divine ideas would have to be relevantly different from our own. They're at least different in that they can secure the infinity and necessity of numbers. But maybe the big difference is that our ideas are confined to our respective minds, so that the best we can do is to sincerely tell each other about our ideas, whereas God has the power to somehow give all of us more direct psychological access to his own ideas. (This might connect with a point later about how divine psychologism helps secure our cognitive contact with numbers.)

The second problem from Frege is more serious. This is a kind of contingency problem. It's not about the numbers being contingent, but about the mathematical truths that result from them being contingent: "As new generations of children grew up, new generations of twos would continually be being born, and in the course of millennia these might evolve, for all we could tell, to such a pitch that two of them would make five" (Ibid; see also Frege 1960, xvii–xix). If numbers are human ideas, then mathematics is as contingent as we are and as our thinking is. Now 2 + 2 happens to equal 4, but if we come to think differently, 2 + 2 will equal 5—and if we had thought differently, it would have equaled 5. This is absurd.

We might think that divine psychologism can answer the problem as easily as it can answer the earlier problem about the contingency of numbers themselves: the necessary nature of the numbers as well as their necessary existence could be secured by the necessity of the divine intellect. And we might be right. But it's not clear that either problem is solved. It could be that God would always have had the ideas of 2 and 4, and it could be that God would always have had the idea that 2 + 2 = 4, no matter what. But perhaps it could be that God would not necessarily have the ideas. Why should he have them? If God could have had quite different ideas (or none at all), it would be a cosmic coincidence for him to choose just those ideas, no matter what.

Let's focus on the main subject of Leibniz's argument first: the necessary truths of mathematics. Whenever we try to ground some domain in the divine, there's a Euthyphro-style dilemma lurking. A comparison here between morality and mathematics might be illuminating. The traditional Euthyphro dilemma: Does God command it because it's obligatory? Or is it obligatory because He commands it? If the former, then there's some morality independent of God's say-so. If the latter, then God could with as much reason command murder as He could forbid it. Does God think that $2 + 2 = 4$ because $2 + 2 = 4$? Or does $2 + 2 = 4$ because He thinks it? If the former, then the truth is independent of God's say-so. If the latter, then God could with as much reason have decided that $2 + 2 = 5$. Descartes was happy enough with such prospects. A bonus: God could have solved Christian theologians a good deal of puzzlement by simply thinking that $1 = 3$.

Leibniz rejected the divine command theory for a couple of reasons, including this: "it seems that all acts of will presuppose a reason for willing and that this reason is naturally prior to the act of will" (1991, 2). What God wills must be guided by reason, and so whatever God wills about morality must be guided by reason, and it's in that reason, rather than God's will, where morality ultimately lies. Similarly, should Leibniz not have seen that what God wills about mathematics must be guided by reasons, and mathematics is ultimately to be found in those reasons?

Return to the main subject of Plantinga's argument: not the necessary truths of mathematics, but the numbers. Draw the parallel conclusion: Does God have the idea of 2 because it exists? Or does it exist because He has the idea? If the former, then the number is independent of God's intellect. If the latter, then God could with as much reason never have had the idea of 2, so that it never existed. Assuming that the numbers necessarily exist, that won't do.

In a way, though, it's less immediately problematic than the implication that God could have decided that $2 + 2 = 5$. If the essential ingredients for $2 + 2 = 4$ did not exist, then it wouldn't have been the case that $2 + 2 = 4$. But it wouldn't have been the case that $2 + 2 = 5$ either, because the essential ingredients for that wouldn't have existed either. The view that it could have been that it is not true that $2 + 2 = 4$ is weird, but the view that it could have been that $2 + 2 = 5$ is even weirder. So the problem might not be as pressing for Plantinga's argument—which is not to say that it won't be pressing.

There might be a way out of the problem altogether. The Euthyphro-style dilemmas trade on the subject (whether morality or mathematics) depending on God's "commands" or "say-so" or "will," as I've variously put it—something that's supposed to be to some extent contingent. And that's a natural way to construe ideas. They're things subjects come up with and are free to play around with. God can then come up with and play around with his ideas about numbers as much as we can with our idea of a friendly mouse who wears red pants, yellow shoes and white gloves. That might be the wrong way to think about God's ideas.

Adams (1979) and Alston (2002) try to avoid the Euthyphro dilemma for morality by invoking a *loving* will: a loving will won't command murder. We might avoid the

Euthyphro dilemma for mathematics by invoking what we might call a *rational* will: a rational will won't lack the idea of 2 and won't think that 2 + 2 = 5 either. If the will is as necessary as necessarily loving and rational, then morality and mathematics couldn't have gone awry. God's ideas about numbers are then necessitated by his rational nature, and are not so much a matter of will (as that term is usually understood) at all.

But I wonder: Why would God's rational nature ensure that 2 + 2 = 4? Unless there's something intrinsically rational about 2 + 2 = 4, unless there's something about the numbers that God's rationality is tracking and that isn't up to anyone, God could have dreamt up something else. But, if God's rational nature is tracking something, then that is what mathematics is about. *That* is where the numbers live. It might be a luminous Platonic realm. It might be next to nothing at all. There might even be something divine about it.

In a similar connection, Alston answers that God's commands are tracking his loving nature. This good nature is in a way prior to the divine commands. There is then value independent of the divine commands. Yet, a Euthyphro-style dilemma need not arise again here. For the fundamental ingredients of morality and value need not be anything independent of God. God can be taken to play the same role a Platonic form of goodness is supposed to. We might try a similar solution to the Euthyphro-style dilemma about mathematics: God's rational will could be tracking something about God. Then the metaphysics for mathematics need not be anything independent of God.

Unfortunately, I don't know how to fill this picture out any further; I don't know what exactly it is about God's nature that's doing the work in our case. The hypothesis that there is a relevant something-we-know-not-what might indeed be the start of an answer to the Euthyphro-style dilemma about mathematics. But don't then be too hard on Platonist opponents of divine psychologism should they appeal to their own we-know-not-whats in defense of Platonism.

My main worry is that leaving things at a mystery comes at a particular cost in the context of the argument from numbers—again a problem about how much of an audience the argument might attract. Even if the maneuver has the benefit of answering the Euthyphro-style dilemma, it costs a premise of the argument from numbers in plausibility. The premise is that numbers depend on intellectual activity, that they are ideas. But, in order to avoid the Euthyphro dilemma, it turns out that the intellectual activity and the ideas are very far from what was originally imagined, and indeed that the numbers are not so much ideas as something quite unknown that the ideas track.

What attracts Plantinga's students to psychologism in the first place? I don't really know. Here's a little speculation: numbers are elusive things. They strike some of us at first as not quite real, but not quite unreal either—"real" and "unreal" in the metaphysical, not the mathematical, sense! They strike some of us as neither the inhabitants of the material realm, nor the inhabitants of a Platonic realm. But the mind lies somewhere between these realms: our ideas and thoughts aren't as heavy and thick as material beings, but aren't as light and thin and distant as Platonic beings. The intellect promises to be the perfect environment for numbers.

As we've seen, though, not just any intellect will do: we need something like a divine intellect. However, once we've reached divine psychologism, the original appeal of psychologism is risked. The divine intellect might not be much more down to earth than the Platonic realm. If the appeal for psychologism was to avoid the mysteries of Platonism, then the divine intellect, with its own mysteries, might not do much better. Is there enough resemblance between God's ideas and our own ideas to secure whatever was originally attractive about identifying numbers with ideas? "For my thoughts are not your thoughts" (Is. 55: 8).

VERSUS PLATONISM

So much for the advantages of divine psychologism over human psychologism. Adams says less of Leibniz's rejection of Platonism. But it has to do with his conception of the objects of logic and mathematics not being the kinds of beings the Platonist construes them as—beings that could subsist independently in a Platonic heaven. They are instead for Leibniz "modes": "the basic idea is that impossibilities, truths, natures and essences, and other objects of logic are abstract objects in the original sense; that is, they can be conceived only by abstractions from a richer, more complete being or 'subject'" (cited in Adams 1994, 180). Recall Lowe. Logical and mathematical beings are dependent beings—dependent on the divine mind.

Plantinga makes the point in a more recent statement of the argument from numbers:

> Now there are two quite different but widely shared intuitions about the nature of numbers and sets. First, we think of numbers and sets as abstract objects. . . . On the other hand, there is another equally widely shared intuition about these things: most people who have thought about the question, think it incredible that these objects should just exist, just *be* there, whether or not they are thought of by anyone. Platonism with respect to these objects is the position that they do exist in that way. . . It is therefore extremely tempting to think of abstract objects as ontologically dependent upon mental or intellectual activity in such a way that either they just are thoughts, or else at any rate couldn't exist if not thought of. (2011, 288)

Again, numbers can't have an independent being, and can't have being independent of thought in particular. Once we've ruled out Platonism, the rest of the story is familiar. We rule out human psychologism in favor of divine psychologism: "if it is *human* thinkers that are at issue then there are far too many abstract objects. . . . On the other hand, if abstract objects were divine thoughts, there would be no problem here. So perhaps the most natural way to think of abstract objects, including numbers, is as divine thoughts" (ibid). All I can say is that I don't have the intuition or face the temptation Plantinga mentions. The term *abstract* did originally have connotations of something abstracted in thought. But now it means something else: now it means non-spatiotemporal or non-causal. So far as I can tell, neither Leibniz nor Adams nor Plantinga nor Lowe provide a real reason here for thinking that such beings must depend on minds.

However, Leibniz, Adams, and Plantinga have another reason—not so metaphysical as epistemological. The most famous problem for Platonism is about our knowledge of mathematics (see Benaceraff 1965). The problem is really tricky when we have a Platonic heaven of impotent numbers: how do we make cognitive contact with such things? It might be a little less tricky if the numbers are in actual heaven. God could be powerful enough to forge the connection that allows us to talk about his ideas. Adams cites Leibniz approvingly: "just as God is the original source of all things, so also is all fundamental knowledge to be derived from God's knowledge, and in his light we see light" (1994, 187).

Plantinga similarly sees the solution to the problem of cognitive contact in theism. According to divine psychologism, numbers:

> stand to God in the relation in which a thought stands to a thinker. This is presumably a productive relation: the thinker produces his thoughts. It is therefore also a causal relation. If so, then numbers . . . stand in causal relation to us. For we too stand in a causal relation to God; but then anything else that stands in a causal relation to God stands in a causal relation to us. (2011, 291)

The earlier worry about the contingency of the divine thoughts about numbers emerges again with the idea that God causally produces thoughts. That looks like contingency. But there is, again, another worry about whether we make any progress with divine psychologism. If it's hard to see how we make contact with transcendent numbers, then will there not be the same problem about how we make contact with a transcendent God or his thoughts?

However, I do not think the problems are the same. The problem about abstract beings, as usually conceived, is that they are not causal. But God, as usually conceived, is causal par excellence: God is supposed to be able to do anything. There may be other relevant differences. Abstract beings are supposed to be perfectly spaceless and timeless. God's relation to space and time is a matter of philosophical controversy; many contend that God exists in time, and some even contend that he exists in space. If absolute transcendence is what makes for the impotence of abstract beings, then God might have an advantage so long as he is not so absolutely transcendent.

The usual objections against substance dualism—that it's hard to see how an immaterial mind could interact with a material body—are usually no more than mere assertions. Exercise: pull a philosophy of mind book off the shelf, and check whether the rejection of interaction on substance dualism is anything more than a mere expression of puzzlement. The critics do well to stick to mere puzzlement; whenever an argument is given it is extremely weak (see Lycan 2009; Plantinga 2007b, 124–33; Hoffman & Rosenkrantz 1994, Chapter 5; Foster 1991, Chapter 6). As much was to be predicted: there is no plausible theory of causation that rules out causal interaction on substance dualism—and not the least because there is no plausible theory of causation.

Furthermore, some of the more serious problems for such interaction—problems about our minds puncturing the causal closure of the physical realm—do not begin to apply to a divine mind who would have brought about and would sustain the entire physical realm. While finite immaterial minds might be constrained by the tight network of physical causes and laws, an infinite immaterial mind would not be so constrained.

But is there really a problem with Platonism to begin with? Platonists have put forward answers, answers that do not invoke God (see Balaguer 1998, Chapters 1 & 2). Nominalists aren't convinced. Perhaps they could find resources in divine psychologism. Then again, the motivations for nominalism might tell against divine psychologism too. These motivations include a more generally naturalistic or materialistic philosophical conscience. Naturalism and materialism rule out God just as much as they do Platonic numbers. Thus James Brown's friends tease him for being both a Platonist and an atheist:

> along the lines that being a Platonist is really no different from believing in God. I'm kidded about being soft on superstition, a closet religionist, and so on. While I enjoy the kidding I've actually never seen the slightest connection between religion and mathematical Platonism. . . . Polkinghorne favorably cites a number of prominent mathematicians who are also Platonists (Gödel, Hardy, Connes) in support of the notion that mathematics is transcendent. God, of course, is transcendent, too, so, Polkinghorne seems to suggest, there is a kind of mutual support—Platonists should believe in God. (2012, 161)

Polkinghorne's idea, apparently, is that once you've let in one kind of transcendent being, you might as well let in another. And Brown's friends agree on that point. "But," answers Brown, "aside from transcendence, there is no real connection between belief in God and belief in a Platonic realm" (ibid). Divine psychologism would provide another connection in answering the problem of cognitive contact. But Brown would not be moved. He doesn't think there is any epistemological problem for Platonism to begin with: he rejects the very premise of the problem, that knowledge requires causal contact.

Others might find the problem of cognitive contact more pressing for Platonism, and make recourse to divine psychologism. However, as we have seen, not many naturalists can consistently do so, and it's naturalists who find the problem most pressing. Again, the audience for Plantinga's argument will dwindle. But here it need not be entirely lost: if they are naturalists because of the problem of cognitive contact with the transcendent, they might be convinced that there is less of a problem about contact with a divine realm than about contact with a Platonic realm; and Platonists who see some problem with cognitive contact might come to see less of a problem on theism. Theism could become an option. Insofar as naturalists are naturalists because they have trouble understanding causal contact between the natural and the transcendent, they should not be naturalists. That is no real support for naturalism. But naturalists tend to have other reasons besides.

CONCLUSION

Plantinga (and Adams and others) see divine psychologism as having advantages over both human psychologism and Platonism. Human psychologism can be ruled out completely as a contender. However, what rules it out might rule out divine psychologism too. Platonism is still a contender. There is a similar worry that the main problem with Platonism will also be a problem with divine psychologism; however, it will, at the least, be less of a problem. Of course, psychologism and Platonism are not the only alternatives. There are views that have not been addressed here at all. For example, there is the fictionalist view that numbers do not exist at all. Within the scope of an essay, I've just been able to touch on the main points raised by Plantinga.

Finally, so far as I can see, none of this touches other arguments about numbers for the existence of God—arguments not from the existence of numbers, but from their applicability to science or from our ability to do really hard math (see Plantinga 2011, 284–291; Steiner 1998). Even if the existence of numbers has nothing to do with God, it still might be that "[t]he miracle of the appropriateness of the language of mathematics for the formulation of the laws of physics is a wonderful gift which we neither understand nor deserve" (Wigner 1960, 14). Well, the main idea here is that on theism it is *not* so hard to understand. The question of God and mathematics in general—quite unlike the question of God and science or the question of God and morality—has not been very much explored. It all needs some more "loving development."

NOTE

Thanks to Robert Adams, John Giannini, Stavroula Glezakos, Hud Hudson, Ralph Kennedy, Sam Lebens, Win-Chiat Lee, Chris Menzel, Christian Miller, Gary Rosenkrantz, Richard Swinburne, and Brandon Warmke for discussion and comments. The relationship between God and abstract objects is debated among the contributors of a recent edited volume (Gould 2014) and is also the subject of a recent monograph (Craig 2016). Unfortunately, I got hold of these books too late to take into consideration for this chapter; Craig's was published after I'd written it. However, I enthusiastically recommend both to readers interested in the topic.

REFERENCES

Adams, R.M. 1994. *Leibniz: Determinist, Theist, Idealist*. Oxford: Oxford University Press.
———. 1979. "Divine Command Theory Modified Again," *Journal of Religious Ethics* 7, no. 1: 66–79.
Alston, W.P. 2002. "What Euthyphro Should Have Said" in W.L. Craig (ed). *Philosophy of Religion: A Reader and Guide*. Edinburgh: Edinburgh University Press, 283–298.

Balaguer, M. 1998. *Platonism and Anti-Platonism in Mathematics*. Oxford: Oxford University Press.

Benaceraff, P. 1965. "What Numbers Could Not Be," *Philosophical Review* 74, no. 1: 47–73.

Brown, J.R. 2012. *Platonism, Naturalism and Mathematical Knowledge*. New York: Routledge.

Craig, W.L. 2016. *God Over All: Divine Aseity and the Challenge of Platonism*. Oxford: Oxford University Press.

Foster, J. 1991. *The Immaterial Self*. London: Routledge.

Frege, G. 1960. *The Foundations of Arithmetic*. J.L. Austin. (trans). New York: Harper.

Gould, P.M. (Ed.) 2014. *Beyond the Control of God: Six Views on the Problem of God and Abstract Objects*. New York: Bloomsbury.

Hoffman, J., and G. Rosenkrantz. 1994. *Substance Among Other Categories*. Cambridge: Cambridge University Press.

Leibniz, G.W. 1991. *Discourse on Metaphysics and Other Essays*. D. Garber and R. Ariew (trans). Indianapolis: Hackett.

Lowe, E.J. 2012. "A New Modal Version of the Ontological Argument" in M. Szatkowski (ed). *Ontological Proofs Today*. Huesenstamm: Ontos Verlag, 179–191.

———. 1998. *The Possibility of Metaphysics*: Oxford: Oxford University Press.

———. 1996. "Why Is There Anything At All?",*Proceedings of the Aristotelian Society*, Supplementary Volume 70: 111–120.

Lycan, W. 2009. "Giving Dualism its Due," *Australasian Journal of Philosophy* 87, no. 4: 551–563.

Maddy, P. 1990. *Realism in Mathematics*. Oxford: Oxford University Press.

Menzel, C. 2016. "Problems with the Bootstrapping Objection to Theistic Activism," *American Philosophical Quarterly* 53, no. 1: 55–68.

Plantinga, A. 2011. *Where the Conflict Really Lies*. Oxford: Oxford University Press.

———. 2007a. "Two Dozen (or so) Theistic Arguments" in D. Baker (ed). *Alvin Plantinga*. Cambridge: Cambridge University Press, 203–228.

———. 2007b. "Materialism and Christian Belief" in P. Van Inwagen and D. Zimmerman (eds). *Persons: Human and Divine*. Oxford: Oxford University Press,

———. 1980. *Does God Have a Nature?* Milwaukee: Marquette University Press.

Steiner, M. 1998. *The Applicability of Mathematics as a Philosophical Problem*. Cambridge, MA: Harvard University Press, 99–141.

Van Inwagen, P. 2006. *The Problem of Evil*. Oxford: Oxford University Press.

Wigner, E. 1960. "The Unreasonable Effectiveness of Mathematics in the Natural Sciences," *Communications in Pure and Applied Mathematics* 13, no.1: 1–14.

(D)

The Argument from Counterfactuals

COUNTERFACTUALS, VAGUENESS, AND GOD

Alexander R. Pruss

﹌ ──

COUNTERFACTUALS

IT CERTAINLY SEEMS as though some counterfactual statements are true. If I dropped the cup I am holding, it would have fallen. If I never turned in this chapter, the editors would have been disappointed. I shall take it for granted that such counterfactuals are simply *true*. This is a controversial claim: I am rejecting accounts on which counterfactuals express, say, a conditional probability (e.g., Edgington 1995) or an inference ticket rather than a proposition (cf. Lance and White 2007). But we treat counterfactual statements like expressions of a proposition. We say "That's true" to the one about the cup, and we would say "That's false" if instead I said that the cup would have sprouted wings and flown away. Counterfactuals embed in complex logical claims just as other bits of propositional talk do. We say that a law of nature entails such-and-such a counterfactual, that a counterfactual conjoined with its antecedent entails the consequent, and so on. We lie with counterfactuals, whereas it is widely taken that to lie one must assert, and only propositions can be asserted. So I will take the controversial claim onboard.

Moreover, we *roughly* know how counterfactuals work. I want to know what would happen if the cup were dropped. I take the truths about how the world actually is, and replace the truth that the cup wasn't dropped with the proposition that the cup was dropped. The result is a mess of logical inconsistency and causal weirdness. For instance, it contains the conjunctive proposition that the cup wasn't dropped and 2 + 2 = 4, as well as perhaps the proposition that it's a law that dropped cups fall, and so on. So then we clean up the inconsistencies and weirdness in a natural way, and see what the resulting propositions entail. And hopefully they end up entailing that the cup falls.

The difficulty is in the details of the cleanup phase, and is twofold. First, there are cases in which we just don't know how to do the cleanup. If Queen Victoria were alive today, would it be true that she never died or would it instead be true that she is clawing on the inside of her coffin?[1] Different cleanup methods yield different answers. Second, we not only can't actually do the cleanup, but we don't have a good account of how the cleanup is to be done. (I can't do the long multiplication of two numbers each with a thousand digits, but at least I have a full account of how it's done.)

There are, of course, theories that attempt to explain how things are cleaned up to get the correct answers. But typically these theories are false or incomplete or both. Take, for instance, the most prominent story in the latter part of the twentieth century: the Lewis-Stalnaker account (Lewis 1973 and 1979). Putting that story in the vocabulary I used and bracketing technicalities, we look for a way of cleaning up the mess that makes for consistency, and prefer those ways of cleaning up that end up describing a possible world more similar to the actual world over those that end up describing one that's less similar.

This theory is both false and incomplete. It is false because of Pollock's coat-thief problem (see Bennett 1984 and Edgington 1995). Suppose at eleven in the morning, you left your coat in a room through which a steady stream of habitual and very similar coat thieves flowed between eleven and noon, and at noon you retrieved your coat, surprisingly unstolen. The truths about the world include truths about each of the coat thieves going through the room and not stealing the coat, and now we replace the truth that the coat was still there at noon with the proposition that it wasn't. The Lewis-Stalnaker account says that we fix the mess in ways that make for a world that is as small a departure from actuality as possible. Having a habitual coat thief who actually went through the room and stole yet another coat is a smaller departure than having someone else take it, or having it turn into a butterfly. But from the time that a coat thief takes the coat, the world is going to be different forever. For instance, the coat thief has an extra coat, and ripples spread in the gravitational field throughout the universe. The later we suppose the thief to take the coat, the smaller the departure from actuality, as the larger the region of space-time that we can make exactly like that of our world. So the Lewis-Stalnaker view indicates that if the coat weren't there, it would have been taken by the last thief.

But surely that's not the right answer. Any one of the thieves might have taken the coat. Probably the right answer is that *some* thief would have taken it, but no counterfactuals of the form "If the coat were not there, thief x would have taken it" is true. So the Lewis-Stalnaker theory is false.

It's also incomplete, because we do not have a complete account of what makes one world closer to actuality than another. Lewis (1979) has a sketch of some conditions, but these conditions are clearly incomplete. For instance, he presupposes the possibility of comparing the size of "miracles," that is, deviations from laws of nature—but how can really one do that in a precise way? Lewis himself thinks that the way that closeness is to be measured depends on context. But we have no account of the function that assigns a measure of closeness to a particular context.

It *is* very plausible to say that the Queen Victoria case shows that counterfactuals are context-dependent. Which features of the world we keep fixed in the counterfactual case depends on context. In some contexts, it is true to say that she would not have died, in others, it is true to say that she would be clawing on the inside of her coffin, and in yet others, it is true to say that the Second Coming would have already come. But positing context-dependence in some set of claims is far from giving a semantic account of those claims.[2] A semantic account would need to tell us *how* it is that context interacts with words and the world to yield a truth-value.

It is tempting at some point to invoke semantic indeterminacy. But that only complicates matters. For not only would we need an account of when a counterfactual is true and when it is false, but we would also need an account of when it is indeterminate.

Furthermore, not only do we not have a complete account of counterfactuals, we have very little hope of ever having a complete account. And that's surprising. After all, it's plausible that the meanings of words and their interactions with contexts are a matter of our conventions, rather than being a function of some alien facts beyond our ken. Consequently, it would seem that the answers to these semantic questions about counterfactuals should be accessible to us.

We seem to have no way to settle questions like whether it is true or false or indeterminate that Queen Victoria would be clawing on the inside of her coffin. We do not even know what facts about the situation we would need to find out to settle the question.

I hypothesize that the following is true: Three different meanings could be attached to "would"-language, fitting our actual usage equally well, such that the sentence "Were Queen Victoria alive today, she'd be clawing on the inside of her coffin is true" would respectively be true, false, and indeterminate. If I'm wrong about this particular case, I am quite confident that something like this is true in some other cases.

The standard thing these days to do in cases like that would be to settle the question by naturalness considerations, asking which way of attaching meaning to the "would"-language better cuts nature at its joints (see, e.g., Sider 2011). Moreover, probably a slight difference in naturalness will not do the job: meaning isn't *that* fragile. So we need to look for a way of attaching meaning that significantly better cuts nature at its joints than competitors. But I suspect that in the end there is going to be no way to do that for counterfactuals: there isn't going to be one of the three meaning-assignments connected with the Queen Victoria case that cuts nature significantly better at its joints than the others do.

Our context-sensitive counterfactuals are a messy beast. They don't cut nature at perfectly natural joints. And it is unlikely that there will be a candidate meaning that settles the question that cuts nature sufficiently more naturally than competitors would.

But if this is how things stand, how can our counterfactual language have a meaning determined by its use?

OTHER CASES

Counterfactuals are far from the only case where such considerations come up. Other cases of messy context-sensitive language will have the same issue. Perhaps the question of what degree of evidence suffices for a belief to count as knowledge depends on the context. But if so, it is unlikely that there is a clear winner among all the functions from contexts to contents that match our usage of "knows."

It is, again, tempting to say that this is just a matter of semantic indeterminacy. No one function from context to content wins out, so it's indeterminate which one gives the meaning of our "knows"-talk when the functions disagree. But that's just another positive proposal about the function from context to content, namely a proposal on which in some cases the content is indeterminate. And that proposal is unlikely to be the unique winner, either, since there are many ways to delineate the region of indeterminacy.

Classic cases of vagueness are another such case. We could respectively assign meanings to "bald" that match our usage in such a way that a person with fifty hairs that are each an inch long (a) counts as bald, (b) counts as non-bald, or (c) counts as indeterminate in respect of baldness. No one of the meaning assignments will be sufficiently more natural than the others to be the unique winner. And yet "bald" is meaningful.

EPISTEMICISM

Counterfactuals and other messy cases all create a problem for the idea that meaning is determined by our use, even when we supplement the considerations of use with naturalness.

One standard solution in the vagueness literature is epistemicism: There is an answer to these questions, but it is beyond our ken. The person with fifty of the inch-long hairs is either bald or non-bald—or, with a higher level epistemicism, bald, non-bald, or indeterminate in baldness—but we don't know which it is. Of the various meanings that could be attached to "bald," one of them is the one that is in fact attached to it, but we are unable to identify it. There are precise transition points between baldness and non-baldness (or between baldness, indeterminacy, and non-baldness), but we don't know where they are.

There is even a well-known argument that there *are* precise transition points in such cases (Sorensen 2001). The premises of the argument are clearly true, and the argument is valid in first-order logic. It's a bit easier to run the argument with a different word than "bald." I will run it with "old." Start with these premises about Elizabeth of Windsor, the Queen of England.

(1) At age one, Elizabeth was wasn't old.
(2) At age eighty-nine, Elizabeth is old.

Consider now this very long sentence:

(3) (Elizabeth wasn't old at age one and she was old at age two) or (Elizabeth wasn't old at age two and she was old at age three) or . . . or (Elizabeth wasn't old at age eighty-eight and she is old at age eighty-nine).

It is just a matter of first-order logic to see that (3) is a logical consequence of (1) and (2). One way is by reductio. If (3) is false, then by De Morgan the following sequence of eighty-eight sentences will be true:

(3i)   Elizabeth was old at age one or she was not old at age two
(3ii) Elizabeth was old at age two or she was not old at age three
(3iii) Elizabeth was old at age three or she was not old at age four.

. . .

But by (1) and (3i) we conclude that Elizabeth wasn't old at age two, and then by (3ii) we conclude that she wasn't old at age three, and so on, so she isn't old at age eighty-nine, which contradicts (2). So (3) must be true if (1) and (2) are. But (3) says that there is an age such that at that age she wasn't old but a year later she was. The conclusion that (3) holds is just a matter of logic. And each disjunct in (3) entails that there is a sharp transition point, that is, an age x at which Elizabeth isn't old but such that she is old at $x + 1$.

This argument for a transition point is classically valid, and the premises are clearly true. What more could one want? The only downside of the argument is its conclusion, that there is a precise transition point between not old and old (perhaps contextual: the premises and conclusion must be all read in a single context).

We thus have a good reason to believe in a sharp transition. Why, then, not be an epistemicist? There are two main reasons. The first is the raw intuition that these kinds of cases are just not cases where there are sharp facts of the matter. Being old or bald should be fuzzy, and likewise counterfactuals shouldn't be perfectly determinate. The second is that epistemicism makes it difficult to see how it is that meanings could be grounded in use. There seems to be nothing in the facts about the use of words that would determine sharp transitions or that would yield precise truth values to counterfactuals.

We thus have an uncomfortable philosophical tension between, on the one hand, a classically valid argument from uncontroversial premises and, on the other hand, a raw intuition and worries about grounding of meaning in use. If we could find a way of assuaging the grounding worries, perhaps that would decrease the force of the raw intuition as well, and allow us a much more comfortable philosophical position: one in which the argument's conclusion is accepted, but is not all that problematic.

Theism allows us to do just that. God could decide on the correct semantics of all the terms. And the availability of a theistic solution to these problems is evidence for theism.

Plantinga (2007) argues in the case of counterfactuals, a theistic solution lets you hold on to both the intuitions that figuring out how to measure the closeness of possible worlds (a) "depend[s] upon mind and (b) there is an "objectively correct" measure of closeness. The point generalizes. We do have the intuition that the semantic facts behind these questions depend on mind, and yet it seems that these facts are genuine objective facts. Theism lets one hold on to both intuitions, and that is evidence for theism.

In fact, there are two theistic ways to resolve the difficulties available. They are analogous to two theistic metaethical theories: divine command theory and natural law.

TWO THEISTIC EPISTEMICISMS
Divine Institution Epistemicism
A Sketch

Divine command theory gets its plausibility from an analogy between divine rules and positive human law. According to divine command theory, we should do what God commands us to do. While one could have a particularist divine command theory on which God issues a separate rule for every particular decision, it is more plausible that God issues general rules. These rules might be simple, such as that the innocent not be killed, but they could also be quite complex, such as that pain not be inflicted unless (a) the patient or a proxy consents and there is proportionate benefit to the patient or (b) the infliction of pain is a just punishment (and there might be lots more disjuncts).

We could similarly suppose that the meanings of language are divinely instituted. Just as we institute meanings in a variety of ways, so too God institutes meanings. It is a commonplace that the layperson's use of technical vocabulary inherits meaning by deferring to experts who instituted that vocabulary sometimes through explicit stipulation and sometimes by ostending to features of the world delineated at natural joints. The lay language user often doesn't know whom she is deferring to, or even that she is deferring. Similarly, we could defer to God in our use of language, even without knowing that we are doing so.

God has an advantage over us in instituting language. For apart from a small handful of terms that can be explicitly stipulated and a probably smaller handful of terms whose meanings cut nature at the most perfectly natural joints, precisely specifying the meaning of a typical term requires making a great number of decisions. This is particularly true when the terms are context sensitive, since then not just a single content must be specified, but a function determining a content in every possible context. But God can make a large number of decisions as easily as a single one.[3] He can specify precisely in which contexts what degree of evidence is needed for a knowledge attribution to be correct; what organisms need to have what age to count as old; how many hairs of what length, thickness, and opacity are needed to rule out baldness; and how it is that the messy mass of truths is to be updated to include the antecedent of a conditional.

A theistic epistemicist, thus, can say that God has instituted human language, and that we defer to God's institution of language, usually unknowingly. God makes sure that we have enough of a picture of how the language works that we can fallibly learn about the use of language by observing how others use them, but neither our understanding of language nor our use of it is sufficient to determine meanings.

Objections to Divine Command Metaethics

Before discussing further details of the theory, it is worth considering some powerful criticisms of divine command metaethics and whether they have analogues for divine institution epistemicism.

The most famous objection to divine command metaethics is the Euthyphro problem. That problem centers on the question of why it is that God commands as he does. The worry is that God either (a) commands the right because it is right, or (b) he does so arbitrarily. If case (a), we have a circle in the order of explanation: God commands something because it's right and it's right because God commands it. But case (b) is unbecoming to a morally perfect being: one needs significant moral reasons to curtail the autonomy of others by commands.

There are, of course, many answers to the Euthyphro problem. But divine institution epistemicism does not need them. Language is conventional. One doesn't need significant moral reasons to institute language in one way or another, when the different ways equally well conduce to communicative goals. It would have been impractical to call a rose an "antidisestablishmentarian" (the word would be too long and the etymology would mislead), but no harm would have been done by calling roses "daisies" and daises "roses." Likewise, there appear to be many different ways of updating counterfactually or dividing up the bald from the non-bald that would be equally useful to us and revelatory of reality, and there is no harm in choosing one over another. This is precisely the sort of situation in which an arbitrary choice would be appropriate.

One may, of course, have general worries that it is impossible for a rationally perfect being to make arbitrary decisions. But while it surely wouldn't do for God to make commands that significantly curtail our autonomy for trivial reasons, there is no problem with trivial reasons driving linguistic choices. Perhaps roses are better fitted for poetry than daisies, because of the literary possibilities implied by thorns, and perhaps the word "rose" has more interesting rhymes than "daisy." That slight consideration would be enough reason to institute "rose" as meaning a rose. There are probably many such incommensurable trivial considerations, and God could choose between them (see Pruss 2016).

The second worry about divine command theories is the possibility of horrendous commands (Morrison 2008 and Wielenberg 2005). If God, perhaps per impossibile, commanded torture of the innocent, would it really be right? That's a hard question for divine command theorists (see Pruss 2009 for discussion). But there does not appear to be a compelling analogy to the problem in the semantic case. Suppose that God instituted an act of torture as a phrase meaning "I love you" in some sign language. Then we could ask whether the torture would mean "I love you?" But there is no harm in biting the bullet and saying that, yes, it would mean that, but it would be a sign we morally ought to avoid using.

There is a disanalogy between positive law and linguistic institution. A law that commands immoral activity has no normative force on an agent, and hence the question of whether torture of the innocent would be right if commanded by God has real bite. But one *can* stipulate words that it would be immoral to use. For instance, one could stipulate a (limited) language that is such that every grammatically correct sentence gravely insults some ethnic group. Perhaps such a language could not be morally spoken, except in cases of dire necessity. But even if the language could not be morally spoken, the institution would be successful. It would just produce a language that could not be morally spoken. Likewise, a sign language all of whose signings involved torturing the interlocutor in different ways could not be morally spoken, but would nonetheless have the thus-stipulated meanings. A perfectly good God presumably would not stipulate such a language, but if per impossibile he did, the language really would have the stipulated meanings.

A third problem for divine command theories is epistemological. How do we know what God has commanded, especially in light of the large variety of religious traditions making different claims about divine commands? This is a serious problem, because moral rules need to be accessible to the agents who are to obey them, and positive laws need to be promulgated. Of course, analogously, speakers also need to grasp meanings. But the phenomenon of deference is available in the case of language. We can sometimes use words we do not understand by deferring to the understanding of others, and we can do so even when we do not know who these others are.

A fourth problem for divine command theories is that of authority. Would God in fact have the authority to issue all of us commands, independently of our relationship to him? (See Murphy 2002.) This is much less of a problem in the case of language. Someone who institutes a language simply has the authority to set meanings. No special authority is needed here, in the way that one needs to have a special authority to constrain others by one's commands.

One may, however, raise an interesting question here. Could someone institute a language that is independent of divine institution? One imagines a group of rebels who believe in God but hate him and who try to institute a completely independent language. I suspect they couldn't. For a language needs to be instituted by symbolic actions—say, pointings. But it is likely that if God has instituted language, he has instituted our symbolic actions. Ultimately, then, all our acts of institution will have to go back to God, whether we like it or not. This need not, however, be because God has a special overriding linguistic authority, but could simply be because he was in fact first in the chain of meaning-institution, and hence we have no symbolic actions independent of divine institution.

The last problem I will consider is the de facto problem. Is there, in fact, a God who has issued the requisite commands? The parallel question is whether there is, in fact, a God who has instituted our language. Here, for once, the answer from the defender of a divine institution view of language can parallel that of the divine command theorist. Both theories solve serious philosophical problems. That they solve these problems is evidence for these theories, and hence for the existence of God.

So, with the exception of the de facto problem, the divine institution theory of language sidesteps major difficulties for divine command metaethics. And the de facto problem is not particularly serious.

Some More Details?

However, there is one place where the divine institution theory has a disadvantage over divine command metaethics. While it is easy to see ways in which God might have issued commands, say, by creating us with a conscience or by revealing commands to prophets, it is more difficult to see *how* he might have instituted language. So for the remainder of this subsection, I will discuss some options.

First, let's consider this possibility. Whenever every bit of language was originated, it was originated first by God, who then communicated it to the person or community to whom the bit of language is normally attributed, and every time semantic shift occurred, God was likewise communicatively behind it. Perhaps in each such case, the individual has some kind of a mental conversation in the language with God, without knowing that it's a conversation with God (she may think she's speaking to herself). Or perhaps God speaks through the individual.

But is this at all plausible? It seems to be an extravagant hypothesis, one making God be communicatively involved in the constant shifting play of meanings. Do I need to have some kind of an inner conversation with God to stipulate that "Smith$_1$" means the actual author of *The Wealth of Nations*? The implausibility here is similar to the implausibility of a particularist divine command theory. God doesn't need to issue a separate prohibition to me each time I'm tempted to lie, say.

Can we say more against this option, besides invoking this intuitive implausibility? Perhaps the existence of slurs and other derogatory terms is evidence against the theory. It is just not plausible that such words were originated by God.

So let's consider an alternative. First, note that language is a special case of communicative behavior. Among the communicative behaviors, there are those that assign meaning to other communicative behaviors. Sometimes this is done by language, as in stipulation, and sometimes through gestures like pointing. We can divide human communicative behaviors into those whose meaning was attached to them through other human communicative behaviors, and those whose meaning was not so attached. On pain of an infinite regress of communications—a regress that certainly did not occur given the finite amount of time humanity has been around—there must be communicative behaviors of the second class. We can then suppose that God instituted the meanings of these "foundational" communicative behaviors.

Perhaps the first time someone pointed to an object while uttering a new word, God communicated with her, giving the human a mental image of pointing as a method of attaching meaning to word. And when God did so, God in turn had in mind a fully precise system of how pointings attach fully precise meanings to words, a system that the first human pointer deferred to. Perhaps there are fundamental grammatical structures of counterfactuals that are built into us, and the first time these structures were tokened, God was communicatively involved in the speaker's mind. The same could be true for other classes of communicative behavior, including those that institute semantic shifts.

Or perhaps the foundational communicative behaviors are at an even higher level of abstraction. Perhaps God was involved when humans started engaging in structured behaviors of the right sort to bear meaning, and God then instituted a particular precise function from patterns of structured behavior to meanings, and did so by some kind of inner communication from himself. Thus our use of counterfactual language, say, does in fact determine the meaning of counterfactual language, but the function from use to meaning is not accessible to us in all its detail. Nonetheless, the function is fully determined by our deference to our linguistic community, since our linguistic community on this picture includes past humans and, eventually, God.

There are, thus, many ways of filling out a theistic institution story. Again, much work would need to be done here. But notice that this work would have payoffs beyond solving the problems of the cases of apparent semantic underdetermination as in cases of vagueness and counterfactuals: it would yield a general theory of how meaning is attached to language.

Finally, the divine institution theorist could even accommodate the intuition that there is real non-epistemic vagueness and semantic indeterminacy. For God could have instituted the foundational meaning-attaching communicative behaviors in such a way that the meanings that are attached to bits of language involve real vagueness. For instance, it could be that there is first-order vagueness, with its being vague whether Elizabeth was old at age seventy, but no higher order vagueness: it could be definitely true that she was definitely not old prior to age sixty-five, and from sixty-six to seventy-one she was vaguely old, and from seventy-two onward she was definitely old. Or it could be that God instituted the meaning-attaching communicative behaviors in such a way that there is vagueness at many finite levels, but the vagueness always disappears at some finite higher level. While such variants have to give up the elegant classical logic argument for epistemicism, they still save the idea that at base there are fully precise semantic facts.

Natural Law

According to theistic natural law ethics, moral facts about human behavior are grounded in human nature. This human nature is irreducibly teleological, and sets the ends and normalcy conditions for our behavior. God is involved in at least two ways. First, God is the final cause of everything and so all teleology ultimately derives from him. Second, God has freely chosen to create these beings with this nature (namely, us) rather than other possible beings with another nature. God is needed for the story, because there is no naturalistic explanation of how creatures with irreducibly teleological natures arose. Let us now consider natural law semantic theories.

If we want to do justice to the intuitions about the conventionality of language, we don't want a particularist natural law semantic theory on which every single bit of language has a meaning directly determined by our nature. Again, it seems to be a better view to say that what our nature determines are the meanings of meaning-instituting behaviors, such as uttering-while-pointing or, more generally, engaging in structured behavior corresponding to a structured world. Similar options as in the divine institution story come up.

How could our nature determine the meanings of foundational communicative behaviors? I see at least two options. The simplest is to say that in addition to there being irreducible normative properties such as teleological ones, there are also irreducible semantic properties.

The more satisfying option, though perhaps it cannot succeed, would be to attempt to reduce semantic properties to normative ones. For instance, one could suppose that a voluntary behavior B of x is an assertion of p just in case it is a normative property of x that B should be voluntarily engaged in only if p is true. In the case of foundational assertion behaviors, if there are such, that normative property would be directly grounded in rock-bottom teleological properties of the speaker. These teleological properties may only in part be accessible to us.

As in the divine institution case, much work would need to be done here to fill out the story. But, just as in that case, the benefits would go far beyond solving the problems of semantic indeterminism that motivate the approach.

EVALUATION

Our linguistic behavior does not appear to determine in a way accessible to us the correct way of cleaning up the mess of propositions one gets when one evaluates a counterfactual. Likewise, it appears to underdetermine what to say about cases of vagueness. We can save the idea that most of our meanings are determined by our behavior by supposing that meanings of foundational communicative behaviors come from God—either by institution or by the intermediary of our nature—and that the other meanings derive from this.

There can be fully precise semantic facts, and classical logic can be maintained. But the details of these facts are not accessible to us.

Of course, a non-theistic epistemicist can make metaphysically or nomically necessary truths of semantics beyond our ken play the role that divine institution or our nature plays in the options I just considered (cf. Hawthorne 2006). Perhaps it is a metaphysically or nomically necessary truth of semantics that pointing by animals with such-and-such a body plan has such-and-such a precise meaning. But this is not an attractive view. These semantic facts seem objectionably brute. There are too many arbitrary details that would have to be necessary if fully precise meanings were of necessity attached to foundational behaviors. The implausibility of such a view would be like the implausibility of thinking that the values had by the constants in the laws of nature are metaphysically necessary. It is just too easy to imagine close alternatives to the constants—and to the ways of evaluating counterfactuals and vague utterances. And in the semantic case at least, a supernatural language-institutor story points neatly to a rational being with an impressive intellect, since it is natural to think of language as originating in minded beings.

NOTES

1. I first heard this joke counterfactual from Richard Gale.
2. This is something I have learned from Jonathan Kvanvig in the case of knowledge claims.
3. There may, however, be special worries with an *infinite* number of decisions. See Pruss 2018.

REFERENCES

Bennett, Jonathan. 1984. "Counterfactuals and Temporal Direction," *Philosophical Review* 95: 509–527.

Edgington, Dorothy. 1995. "On Conditionals," *Mind* 104: 235–329.

Hawthorne, John. 2006. "Epistemicism and Semantic Plasticity," in his *Metaphysical Essays*. New York: Oxford University Press, 186–210.

Lance, Mark and W. Heath White. 2007. "Stereoscopic Vision: Persons, Freedom, and Two Spaces of Material Inference," *Philosophers' Imprint* 7: 1–21.

Lewis, David. 1979. "Counterfactual Dependence and Time's Arrow," *Noûs* 13: 455–476.

———. 1973. *Counterfactuals*. Oxford: Blackwell.

Morrison, Wes. 2008. "What if God Commanded Something Terrible." Paper presented at the University of Texas at San Antonio Philosophy Symposium, San Antonio, Texas.

Murphy, Mark. 2002. *An Essay on Divine Authority*. Ithaca, NY: Cornell.

Plantinga, Alvin. 2007. "Two Dozen (Or So) Theistic Arguments." Unpublished manuscript.

Pruss, Alexander R. *Infinity, Causation and Paradox*. Oxford: Oxford University Press, 2018.

———. "Divine Creative Freedom," in J. Kvanvig (ed.), *Oxford Studies in Philosophy of Religion*, Vol. 7. Oxford: Oxford University Press. 2016, 213–238.

———. 2009. "Another Step in Divine Command Dialectics," *Faith and Philosophy* 26: 432–439.

Sider, Theodore. 2011. *Writing the Book of the World*. New York: Oxford.

Sorensen, Roy. 2001. *Vagueness and Contradiction*. New York: Oxford.

Wielenberg, Erik. 2005. *Virtue and Value in a Godless Universe*. Cambridge: Cambridge.

(E)

The Argument from Physical Constants

THE FINE-TUNING FOR DISCOVERABILITY

Robin Collins

───

INTRODUCTION

IN THIS CHAPTER, I will explicate a new argument for theism, one based on the science-friendly character of the universe; or, more precisely, what I call the fine-tuning of the universe for scientific discovery. To understand the significance of this new argument, it will be helpful briefly to review the argument for theism from the fine-tuning of the universe for life, what is often called the anthropic fine-tuning. This fine-tuning refers to the fact that the laws, initial conditions, and the fundamental parameters of physics must be precisely set for life to exist. The relevant kind of life depends on the hypotheses that the evidence is supposed to support, which in the case of theism is what I call embodied conscious agents (ECAs): namely, embodied conscious beings that interact with each other based on what they perceive as moral criteria. The most commonly cited case of anthropic fine-tuning is that of the cosmological constant.[1] If it were not within an estimated one part in 10^{120} of its theoretical possible range of values, either the universe would expand, or collapse, too quickly for galaxies and stars to form and, hence, ECAs to exist.

A significant number of philosophers and scientists respond to the anthropic fine-tuning evidence by claiming that it is a brute fact that does not need any explanation. I find such a response incredible when one looks at the degree of fine-tuning in some of the cases: for example, one part in 10^{120}—that is, one followed by 120 zeroes—in the case of the cosmological constant and a ridiculous 1 part in $10^{10^{123}}$ for the initial distribution of mass-energy in the universe. Speaking for myself, almost anything is more believable than that this degree of fine-tuning is just a brute fact.[2] Thus, in order to believe this,

I would have to be given an exceedingly strong argument that there is no other remotely plausible alternative than to accept the fine-tuning as just a brute fact, not the kind of arguments typically offered against the theistic explanation. At the very least, such evidence puts a burden on naturalists to provide powerful reasons for rejecting the theistic explanation.

THE MULTIVERSE

A more common response, especially among non-theistic cosmologists, is to invoke a multiverse to explain the fine-tuning. According to this hypothesis, there are a very large, if not infinite, number of regions of space-time with different values of the fundamental parameters of physics, different initial conditions, and perhaps even different laws of nature. Advocates of this response then claim that in a sufficiently varied multiverse, it is no surprise that some universe is structured so that observers will arise in it. Finally, they invoke the so-called observer-selection principle, which is often called the "anthropic principle." This is the tautological claim that embodied observers can only exist in a region of space-time that allows for them to exist. This renders it unsurprising that as observers we find ourselves in an observer-structured region of space-time, since it is impossible for us to exist in any other type of region.

The observer-selection principle is essential to the multiverse explanation because it prevents it from undercutting the need to explain other seemingly surprising events and features of the universe. For example, normally one would think that it is too coincidental for a fair coin to land on heads 100 times in a row just by chance. Yet, in a large enough multiverse, someone will observe this to happen. Nonetheless, it is still enormously improbable that a generic observer in a generic multiverse will see such an occurrence. Thus, under the multiverse hypothesis, the relevant probability for purposes of everyday and scientific inferences is not that of the occurrence of the event itself (e.g., in some universe a fair coin being observed to come up heads 100 times in a row by chance) but rather the probability that a *generic* observer in a *generic* multiverse will observe the event. Given that this is the relevant notion of probability, then arguably the multiverse hypothesis combined with the observer-selection principle can render it unsurprising both that embodied observers exist and that we, considered as generic observers, find ourselves in an observer-structured universe; at the same time it does not undercut ordinary claims of probability.

Various objections can be raised to the multiverse explanation. First, anything that produces such a multiverse itself appears to require significant fine-tuning. Second, it is very difficult to avoid what is called the Boltzmann brain problem. This is the problem that, under naturalistic views of the mind, it is enormously more likely—on the order of $10^{10^{123}}$ times more likely—for observers to exist in the smallest bubble of order required for observers, than in a universe that is ordered throughout. (The order being referred to here is measured by entropy—the lower the entropy, the higher the order.) Yet, we do not exist in a bubble of low entropy, but in a universe with low entropy throughout. Advocates of the multiverse are well aware of this problem, and have been attempting to find acceptable multiverse models that avoid it without the models themselves requiring extensive fine-tuning. So far, no such models have been produced.

Instead of continuing debating the adequacy of the multiverse as an explanation of the anthropic fine-tuning, I present an argument for theism based on another kind of fine-tuning—that for scientific discovery—that cannot be explained by a multiverse, and that also avoids several of the other major objections to the anthropic fine-tuning argument. I believe this adds greatly to the standard anthropic fine-tuning argument for God's existence.

FINE-TUNING FOR DISCOVERY

Many scientists and others have commented on the seemingly "miraculous" intelligibility and discoverability of physical reality, most famously Albert Einstein and Eugene Wigner.[3] Recently, this idea has been developed more carefully by Mark Steiner.[4] Steiner presents an array of examples where, in their attempts to discover the underlying laws of nature, physicists successfully used lines of reasoning that only make sense if they were implicitly assuming that the world is structured for scientific discovery. He concludes that the world "looks 'user friendly.' This is a challenge to naturalism."[5]

Although the authors just mentioned and others present examples in which the universe looks unexpectedly favorable for doing science, they provide no careful method of showing that this really is the case; a person with a more skeptical bent would likely dismiss the claim that this favorability for doing science is more than should be expected by chance as merely based on subjective impressions. What is needed is a way of testing and quantifying this claim. In May 2010, I stumbled on the idea of attempting to quantify and test the claim by examining how our ability to discover the underlying, fundamental physical structure of the universe changes when one varies the values of the fundamental parameters of physics but keeps the mathematical form of the laws of nature the same. These parameters are fundamental numbers in physics that determine such things as the strength of the forces of nature and the masses of particles. An example would be varying Newton's gravitational constant G while holding the mathematical form of Newton's law of gravity, $F = Gm_1m_2/r^2$, the same.[6] (Here F is the force between two mass pairs, m_1 and m_2, a distance r apart.) Roughly, what I found is that insofar as the effects on our ability to discover the universe can be evaluated, the parameters fall into a relatively small range that is much better than average for discovering the universe in the domains for which I was able to reasonably evaluate the level of discoverability;

in fact, they seemed to in some sense be optimal. That is, they seem fine-tuned for discovery.

The most straightforward case of this fine-tuning occurs when the discoverability-optimality range for a parameter p is only a very small subrange of its anthropic range, with the actual value of the parameter falling within that subrange, as shown by the * in Figure E.1.

It is fairly easy to see how this kind of fine-tuning cannot be explained by a multiverse. The observer-selection principle only requires that ECAs find themselves in a universe in which the p falls somewhere in the anthropic region. Suppose we take p itself as a measure of proportion, as is done in the standard anthropic fine-tuning argument. Then, given that the number of observers in a typical universe does not vary across the anthropic range, the vast proportion of observers will find themselves to be in universes in which the value of p falls outside the discoverability-optimality subregion.[7] Hence, even if we know we are in such a multiverse, we should find it highly surprising that the value of the parameter in our universe falls within the discoverability-optimality subregion.

For the technically minded, the reasoning here can be conveniently put in terms of conditional epistemic probability, $P(A|B)$, of one proposition, A, on another B. Following John Maynard Keynes, I define this as the degree to which proposition B of itself rationally supports A.[8] So, for instance, if A is the proposition that it will rain today and B is the proposition that the national weather service predicts that there is a 70 percent chance of rain today, then $P(A|B) = 0.7$ This implies that if all one knows is B, then one's degree of credence in its raining today should be 0.7.

Now, let k be background knowledge consisting of all the laws of physics and the values of all the parameters of physics except for the value of the parameter, p, in question; further, let $p \in DOR$ be the claim that p falls into the discoverability-optimality region (DOR) and let MU be the claim that there exists a multiverse over which the parameter p takes on a wide range of values. Given k includes that we exist, we know that p must fall into the anthropic region. However, k does not tell us anything about where p might fall in that region. Finally, let $\sim T_e$ represent the thesis that the universe is not teleologically structured for ECAs: namely, any apparent teleological structure is either accidental or the result of some selection effect. Assuming an equiprobability distribution over the anthropic region, it follows that $P(p \in DOR|k \& \sim T_e \& MU) =$ (width of discoverability–optimality range)/(width of anthropic range). Therefore, given parameter p is fine-tuned

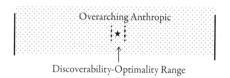

FIGURE E.1 Most straightforward case of fine-tuning.

for discovery, it follows that $P(p \in DOR|k \,\&\, {\sim}T_e \,\&\, MU) \ll 1$, where "$\ll$" means much, much less than. That is, under $k \,\&\, {\sim}T_e \,\&\, MU$, we should find it very surprising that the value of p is in the discoverability-optimality region. Thus, the multiverse cannot explain this kind of fine-tuning.

To make the argument more rigorous, a variety of issues need to be addressed. Here I only briefly sketch how I address some of the major ones. First, in reality, we cannot know for sure that a parameter falls into the discoverability-optimality range. To address this, I define what I call the discernable-discoverability-optimality range (DDOR), which I define as the smallest range for which it is clear that we have more reason than not to believe that discovery-optimality occurs in that range. I then run the same kind of reasoning as above with the DDOR substituted for the DOR. Specifically, what is highly epistemically improbable under the denial of the teleological hypothesis is that, as generic observers, we find ourselves in a universe in which the values of the fundamental parameters fall into their DDORs; and this improbability remains whether or not we live in a multiverse. Because of this problem of knowing for sure the DOR for a parameter, in the rest of the chapter I will refer to the DDOR instead of the DOR.

Second, the idea of the level of discoverability needs to be more carefully defined: specifically, a value v_1 of a parameter is considered better for discovery of a domain D than v_2 if (1) v_1 would likely result in the discovery of D more quickly, with less difficulty, in greater depth or breadth, or greater precision than v_2; and (2), the same cannot be said about v_2 with respect to v_1. Third, it should be noted that discovery in science can be considered to proceed via the use of various tools: for example, discovery in microbiology is via the light microscope and other tools. So the claims regarding the relative discoverability of a domain D for values v_1 and v_2 are based on an assessment of the relative net usefulness of the potential tools that exist at v_1 and at v_2.

Fourth, for the most straightforward cases, the ability of a universe to support ECAs (what I call "livability") is not significantly greater in the DDOR than it is elsewhere in the anthropic range. Otherwise, the typical density of ECAs would be greater in the DDOR than elsewhere in the anthropic range, allowing an advocate of the multiverse to argue that it is more probable for a randomly selected observer to find itself in the DDOR than elsewhere in the anthropic range. This could potentially render it unsurprising that the parameter falls into the DDOR under $k \,\&\, {\sim}T_e$.

Finally, the claim that the parameters are discovery optimal is not essential to the argument, only that many of them have unusually good values for discovery: that is, that the vast majority of values for the parameter in the anthropic range are worse for discovery than the value in our universe. The calculations I have made indicate that the values of the parameters are actually optimal for discovery, so I will assume this in the remainder of the chapter even though it is not essential to my argument.

Next, I will present three examples of this fine-tuning, only the first of which falls into the straightforward pattern discussed earlier in which the DDOR is a very small subregion of the anthropic range.

EXAMPLES

The first example of fine-tuning for discovery is that the universe has relatively low entropy throughout. The existence of ECAs only requires a relatively small region of order, and hence only a relatively small region of low entropy in the universe. Yet, low entropy is required wherever there are stars and galaxies. Consequently, the universe must have relatively low entropy over much vaster regions than what is required for life in order for ECAs to be able to observe other galaxies. The latter is in turn crucial for discovery in astrophysics and cosmology—for example, without other galaxies we would not know that the universe came into existence via a big bang. So, although this large-scale low entropy of the universe is often cited as a case of fine-tuning for life, it is really a case of extreme fine-tuning for discovery. And, although cosmologists have worked on a naturalistic explanation of this low entropy for decades, it still remains a huge puzzle for them.

Our next example is the fine-structure constant, commonly designated by the Greek letter α. This constant governs the strength of the electromagnetic force (a force that manifests itself as a combination of electric and magnetic forces). If α were larger, the electromagnetic force would be stronger; if smaller, it would be weaker. In 2010, I was able to show that a relatively small increase in α would have resulted in all open-wood fires, or that of any other biomass, going out; yet harnessing fire was essential to the development of civilization, technology, and science—for example, the smelting of metals. Why would an increase in α have this result? The reason is that in atomic units (a special system of units often used in physical chemistry), the non-relativistic Schrödinger equation is not dependent on α, and hence everyday chemistry and the size of everyday atoms are not affected by up to a ninefold increase or any decrease in α. In most regards, the world around us would be the same with a change in α within this range. The combustion rate of fires made of wood and other forms of biomass, for example, would remain the same, as would the rate of loss of energy from convection. In these units, however, the rate of output of radiant energy of a fire is proportional to α^2—for example, a twofold increase in α would cause the radiant output of an open fire to be four times as great. (The radiant energy is the reason you can feel a fire's warmth even from relatively far away.) A small increase in α—around 10 percent to 40 percent—would cause the radiant energy loss of open-wood fires to become so great that the energy released by combustion would not be sufficient at any temperature to keep up, thus resulting in the fire going out. Although some biomass is much more combustible than wood—such as oil—and thus would allow for a greater increase in α, these types of biomass either would be less readily available to primitive carbon-based ECAs or they would be less suitable for the size of fires needed for smelting metals; hence it would be far less likely that primitive carbon-based ECAs would have regularly used them, thereby substantially inhibiting the smelting of metals and the consequent development of scientific technology. And even if these were readily available, the amount by which α could be increased before these fires went out would still be very limited.

Going in the other direction, decreasing α would have a variety of negative discoverability effects. First, a small decrease in α would have allowed exposed wood surfaces to keep burning, and hence apart from some special adaption by trees, it would have made it more likely for forest fires to occur and burn up the wood. For example, usually if lightning strikes a tree, it causes a fire on the surface of the wood quickly to go out because the surface emits too much radiant energy to remain on fire; this would not be the case, however, if α were significantly smaller. More forest fires would decrease the amount of available wood and, hence, given our necessary past reliance on wood for smelting metals, they would have inhibited the development of the sort of technological civilization on which science depends.[9] Second, decreasing α has a wide variety of other substantial negative effects on science, without any apparent compensating positive effects: as α is decreased, the resolving power of a light microscope decreases, electric transformers and motors rapidly become less efficient, and the usability of the magnetic compass and paleomagnetic dating rapidly diminishes. Thus, α appears to be fine-tuned to maximize these tools of scientific discovery.[10] This fine-tuning of the fine-structure constant is summarized in Figure E.2.

In January 2012, I found the next major case of fine-tuning for discovery, that of the dependence of the cosmic microwave background radiation (CMB) on the baryon to photon ratio, $\eta_{b\gamma}$. The CMB is a result of radiation emitted in the very early universe, when the matter in the universe was extremely hot. As the universe cooled, the wavelength of this light was stretched, becoming longer and longer until it eventually was in the microwave region. (Microwave radiation has a wavelength around a thousand times longer than visible light.)

Because the CMB was emitted by matter everywhere in the early universe, it comes from all parts of the sky with almost the same intensity and encodes information about the large-scale structure of the early universe and the nature of the big bang. For this reason, it is a key tool of cosmology, with some calling it cosmology's "Rosetta Stone."[11] The CMB is fairly weak, with much of the information in the CMB encoded in variations of its intensity of less than one part in a million. Because tiny variations in the CMB tell us so much about the universe, within reasonable limits, a more intense CMB is better for discovery in cosmology..

Among other factors, the intensity of the CMB depends on the baryon to photon ratio ($\eta_{b\gamma}$), which is just the ratio of the number of baryons (i.e., protons and neutrons) to that of photons (particles of light) per unit volume of space. In our current universe, this ratio is

FIGURE E.2 Discoverability Constraints on α. The star, *, represents the actual value of α ~ 1/137. Upper constraint (thick dashed): no wood fires. Lower constraints (thin dashed lines): much larger risk of forest fires; loss of resolving power of light microscope; major loss of efficiency for electric transformers and motors; major loss of usefulness of paleomagnetic dating and magnetic compass.

approximately one in a billion. Because within limits a more intense CMB would make it a better tool for cosmology, I hypothesized that, neglecting anthropic and unknown discoverability effects of varying $\eta_{b\gamma}$, if the values of the fundamental parameters are optimal for scientific discovery, the value of $\eta_{b\gamma}$ should maximize the intensity of the CMB. In the fall of 2011, I calculated the effect of changing $\eta_{b\gamma}$ on the intensity of the CMB. The result was that the CMB maximized at a value of $\eta_{b\gamma}$ different than the value in our universe, leading me to think that the value of $\eta_{b\gamma}$ disconfirmed the discoverability-optimality hypothesis. However, in January 2012, I returned to my calculation and realized I had made a mistake. When I redid the calculation, it turned out that the value of $\eta_{b\gamma}$ was just right to maximize the intensity of the CMB, at least to within the margin of error of the experimentally determined parameters ($\approx$ 20 percent) used in the calculation. This is shown in the accompanying figure (Figure E.3). These calculations have since been verified by three physicists/cosmologists.[12]

Since the total possible range for $\eta_{b\gamma}$ is at least 0 to 1, and its present value is about one in a billion, neglecting anthropic effects, this constitutes a fine-tuning of at least one in a billion if $\eta_{b\gamma}$ is used as a natural parameter. I found this result very impressive, and hence proceeded to look at other parameters, hoping I could find at least one other case that was as impressive. From the spring of 2012 to the spring of 2014, I checked other fundamental parameters, with all of them being consistent with my thesis and others further confirming it. During that period, I made sure to verify the physical calculations and arguments for these cases with other physicists.[13]

The case of the fine-tuning for entropy falls into the straightforward pattern of the anthropic range being vastly larger than the discoverability-optimality range. On the other hand, although the cases of the fine-structure constant and the baryon to photon ratio suggest a fine-tuning for discovery, they do not fall into such a straightforward pattern. The main problem is that changing the respective parameters has anthropic effects: for example, changing α affects the temperature and stability of stars. This makes it difficult to be sure that the anthropic range is really substantially larger than the discoverability-optimality range. Nonetheless, as long as one can sufficiently conceptually separate the physics giving rise to the discoverability effects from the anthropic effects, one can still

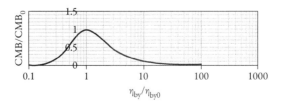

FIGURE E.3 Variation of the intensity of the cosmic microwave background radiation (CMB) observed by a typical observer for various values of the baryon to photon ratio ($\eta_{b\gamma}$). CMB_0 and $\eta_{b\gamma 0}$ are the values of the CMB and $\eta_{b\gamma}$ in our universe. Our universe is at $\eta_{b\gamma}/\eta_{b\gamma 0} = 1$. Notice that the peak intensity for the CMB occurs where the baryon to photon ratio is the same as in our universe—that is, where $\eta_{b\gamma} = \eta_{b\gamma 0}$.

define a discoverability coincidence that the multiverse cannot explain.[14] The most straightforward cases for which this can be done are for the parameters of particle physics. The method for doing this is discussed in the "Unknown Anthropic Range Objection" subsection that follows; I also briefly outline how it could be extended to other cases, such as those already discussed. I next turn to the particle physics cases.

PARTICLE PHYSICS CASES

It was not until the spring of 2014 that I found cases for which the anthropic effects of varying a parameter could, with some qualification, be straightforwardly separated from the discoverability effects. Finding these cases was a result of objections raised to my hypothesis by Caltech cosmologist Sean Carroll at the Greer-Heard point/counter-point forum in February of that year.[15] Carroll presented the mass of the Higgs boson as a counterexample to my thesis. The Higgs boson is a key particle of our most fundamental model of particle physics, called the Standard Model (SM). The SM is the most fundamental physical model regarding the ultimate structure of matter. It is generally thought to be incomplete, a low-energy approximation to a deeper theory; in the forty years since its existence, however, it has withstood every test. It consists of a set of elementary particles and laws governing their interactions. These particles are the quarks and leptons shown in Table E.1; the particles that carry the electromagnetic, weak, and strong forces (called the *gauge bosons*); and the recently discovered *Higgs boson*.

Quarks and leptons come in generations. The particles in a given row are identical except for their mass, with the mass of the particles increasing with each generation: for example, the charm quark is about 500 times more massive than the up quark, and the top quark is about 130 times as massive as the charm quark. Only the first generation plays a direct role in life. Specifically, atoms are composed of electrons orbiting a nucleus composed of protons and neutrons, with the protons being composed of two up quarks and one down quark and the neutron being composed of two down quarks and one up quark. Even though protons and neutrons are made of quarks, most of their mass does not come from the quarks but from the strong force that binds the quarks together.

TABLE E.1

Some of the fundamental particles of the SM

Family	1st Generation	2nd Generation	3rd Generation
Quarks	Up	**Charm**	**Top**
	Down	**Strange**	**Bottom**
Leptons	Electron	**Muon**	**Tau**
	Electron Neutrino	Muon neutrino	Tau neutrino

I estimated the effects on discoverability of varying the masses of the bold-faced particles and the Higgs boson (not shown).

The Higgs boson is the second most massive fundamental particle in the SM, with a mass of around 6000 times that of the up quark. As part of the Greer-Heard forum mentioned previously, Sean Carroll correctly pointed out that if the Higgs boson had a much smaller mass, it would have been much easier to discover; in private email correspondence, he also raised similar objections regarding the mass of the bottom quark, top quark, and so forth. Because of these objections, I became worried that although the discovery-optimality thesis held up for the parameters I had considered up to that point, perhaps the fundamental parameters of particle physics would present the first counterexamples to my thesis. Shortly thereafter, however, I realized the answer to Carroll's objection could be formulated using a distinction made by Abdelhak Djouadi, a leading expert on the physics of the Higgs boson. Djouadi distinguished between two stages of investigation into the Higgs boson: the first stage being the detection of the Higgs boson and the second stage being its use as a tool to probe the SM. He then went on to say that the mass of the Higgs boson was "born under a very lucky star" for using it as tool to probe the SM, and perhaps to detect a deeper physics beyond it.[16] I thus came to realize that as long as the fundamental particles of the SM were detectable within a reasonable timeframe (so that physicists did not lose motivation in searching for them), the most important factor for discoverability in particle physics is whether the values of the parameters of the SM are optimized for further understanding the SM and potentially finding a deeper physics underlying it, a physics most physicists think exists.

Because of the potential for the particle physics cases, I proceeded to consider the effects of changing the parameters of particle physics on our ability to probe key sectors of the SM. With the exception of masses of the muon and strange quark, I chose parameters – such as the mass of the bottom and charm quarks – that pertained to features of particles that were too massive, and lasted for too brief a period, to have any substantial effect on life in our current universe. [17] This led me to focus on the discoverability effects of varying parameters in the SM that meet two criteria: (1) within a well-defined range, they do not have effects on life in the present universe; and (2) we can make reasonable determinations of the discoverability effects of varying these parameters. Such parameters would provide a near-ideal test case of the discoverability-optimality hypothesis. Eight fundamental parameters of the SM met these criteria, such as the mass of the Higgs boson and the masses of the particles in bold in Table E.1. As far as I can tell, each parameter appears to be in its respective discernable-discoverability-optimality range (DDOR), defined above as the range for which it is clear that we have more reason than not to think that some value of the parameter in that range is optimal for scientific discovery.

OBJECTIONS

In this section I will cover some major objections to the claim that the universe is fine-tuned for scientific discovery.

Discoverability Selection Objection

One objection to the claim that there is a fine-tuning for discovery is that it is no surprise that the values of a parameter fall into the range that allow a domain to be discovered, for if they did not, we would not know about the domain.[18] There are several responses to this objection. First, it is possible to know about a domain without being able to discover much about it. Second, the values of the parameters not only fall into the range that allows us to discover a domain, but they fall into their much smaller DDORs. Thus, even if a discoverability selection effect could render it unsurprising that the parameters have values that allow us to discover a domain, it would still be very surprising that the values are seemingly optimal for discovery. For example, even though the CMB would be much weaker if the baryon to photon ratio were increased or decreased by a thousandfold, we would likely still know of the CMB's existence and its dependence on this ratio . This is for two reasons. First, much smaller intensities of the CMB would still be detectable, just not as useful. (For example, with the Planck explorer satellite we can detect variations of better than one part in a million in the CMB.[19]) Second, the CMB is a prediction of the big bang theory, and even though the CMB constitutes our strongest evidence for the big bang, there is a considerable amount of independent evidence for it. Thus, even in a universe with a much different baryon to photon ratio, we would know that the ratio was not as good as it could be for the CMB, as shown in Figure E.4; in fact, as I noted earlier, in 2011, I thought we were in such a universe as a result of a miscalculation. Therefore, a discovery selection effect cannot explain this sort of fine-tuning. Similar things could be said about the cases from particle physics. [20]

Unknown Discoverability Effects

According to this objection, we can only determine for a limited part of physical reality the effects on discoverability of varying a parameter.. For example, even though changing the baryon to photon ratio would make the CMB weaker, and thus less useful as a tool for cosmology, it might have unknown effects elsewhere. Although this is true,

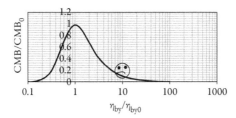

FIGURE E.4 Sad cosmologist in a universe in which the baryon to photon ratio is about ten times the value in our universe. In such a universe, the intensity of the CMB would be about one tenth what it is in our universe, as can be seen in the figure. The cosmologist would know the CMB is an important tool for cosmology, but would be sad that the CMB is not nearly as intense as it could be.

it is still true that, given a parameter is fine-tuned for discovery, the apparent maximization of discoverability for the limited domain and set of tools for which we can make such determinations is not surprising under the hypothesis that the universe is fine-tuned to optimize scientific discovery, but is surprising under the negation of this hypothesis. Consequently, by the likelihood principle of confirmation theory, it confirms the discovery-optimality hypothesis over its negation.

Unknown Anthropic Range Objection

Earlier I claimed that in the Standard Model of particle physics (SM), there is a well-defined anthropic range for the particle physics parameters that we considered. For most of them, this is the range of values that allows the Higgs field to be stable or meta-stable, a range I will call the "Higgs-stability range." However, most particle physicists think the SM is incomplete, and that there is a deeper physics underlying it. Although this deeper physics will not affect the anthropic conditions of the universe after the first several seconds of its existence, it could have effects on the very early universe. Thus, due to the physics of the early universe, it is possible that the actual anthropic range of a parameter is much smaller than the Higgs stability range. In the limiting case, the actual anthropic range might be around the same size as the discoverability-optimality range. In that case, there would be no fine-tuning for discovery in the straightforward sense elaborated earlier since the discoverability-optimality range would not be a relatively small subrange of the actual anthropic range. However, there still would remain the coincidence that the actual anthropic range as determined by early universe physics overlaps the parameter's DDOR as determined by the SM. This is shown in Figure E.5.

This coincidence can be brought out more clearly using the notion of epistemic probability. Let our background information, k, include all the physics we know today, except the actual values of the parameters of particle physics under consideration. Since k also includes the fact that we exist, we know that the value of any parameter, p, must fall into the actual anthropic range shown by the solid rectangle. But, since we do not know what that physics is, we have no reason to believe that, for a given p the actual anthropic range of p is centered at one value instead of another within its Higgs-stability range; hence

FIGURE E.5 Illustration of anthropic-overlap coincidence for a parameter p. The entire scale represents the range of values of p that fall within the anthropic restrictions given by the SM alone—namely, the range that allows the Higgs field to be stable or meta-stable. The left-hand dashed rectangle is the DDOR for parameter p. Given we exist, the actual value p must fall within the actual anthropic range (solid rectangle) determined by the combination of the SM with some unknown early universe physics. The coincidence is that the physics of the early universe is such as to cause the actual anthropic range to overlap the DDOR instead of being centered somewhere else in the Higgs-stability range.

knowing that we exist does not give us any additional reason to think that p is in a particular subrange of its Higgs-stability range. This means that under the denial of the teleological thesis ($\sim T_e$) defined earlier, k of itself gives us no reason to prefer one value of over any other in its Higgs-stability range. Thus the least arbitrary probability distribution for p is an equal probability distribution over that range. Using such a distribution, the probability under k & $\sim T_e$ that p falls into the DDOR is equal to the width, W_{DDOR}, of the DDOR divided by the width, W_{HS}, of the Higgs-stability range: that is, $P(p \in DDOR| \sim T_e \& k) = W_{DDOR}/W_{HS}$, the same as when early universe physics is neglected. Since k already includes that we exist, any observer selection effect is already taken into account, and hence the probability remains the same even if k includes the information that we exist in a multiverse.

This method of taking unknown anthropic effects into account can be generalized to other non–particle physics parameters, though often with more difficulty and ambiguity. This can be done as long as certain conditions are met. Specifically, there must be a well-defined body of physics such that: (1) this physics is conceptually distinct from the rest of physics; (2) it implies substantial discoverability effects of varying p that we can reasonably estimate, thereby allowing us to determine the DDOR of p relative to it; (3) it, along with the requirement that ECAs exist, is compatible with a large range of values of the parameter in question compared to the DDOR of p; (4) it gives us no reason to believe that the density of ECAs is significantly higher in the DDOR than elsewhere in the range specified in (3). Insofar as we can approach these conditions for a non–particle physics parameter, we can define a degree of fine-tuning relative to the specified physics and translate that into an epistemic probability. (To avoid terminological complications, in the rest of the chapter I will refer to range specified in (3) as the specified-physics anthropic range given that condition (4) is also met.)

ARGUMENT FOR THEISM
Outline of Argument

How does the evidence of fine-tuning for discovery provide an argument for theism? We already noted that given the universe is fine-tuned for discovery, the probability that a parameter falls into its DDOR under the background information combined with $\sim T_e$ (that is, the denial of teleology in the universe) is equal to the width of the DDOR divided by the width of the specified-physics anthropic range. That is, $P(p \in DDOR|k \& \sim T_e) = $ [width of DDOR]/[width of specified-physics anthropic range]. Given the parameters are independent in the sense that knowing that one parameter falls into its DDOR does not tell us anything about whether the other parameters fall into their DDORs, these probabilities can be multiplied together. This appears to be largely true in the particle physics cases and some other cases. Hence, the epistemic probability that they all fall into their DDORs will be extremely small—I estimate about one in a billion for the particle physics cases, though this remains to be independently verified.

To complete the argument for theism, let E represent the claim that the values of the parameters fall into their DDORs. I will argue that it is not surprising that God would create a world in which E is the case. Hence by the likelihood principle, since E is not enormously epistemically improbable under theism, but is under $\sim T_e$, it confirms theism over $\sim T_e$. To argue that E is not highly improbable under theism, I first note that since God is perfectly good, we should expect that God would create a universe that positively, if not optimally, realizes moral and aesthetic value. Second, I argue in the next section that we have good reasons for thinking that the successful practice of science is of value. Accordingly, I conclude that it is not surprising that God would create the universe in which the values of the parameters are optimal for doing science, and hence it is not surprising that they fall into their respective DDORs.

At this point, however, it is important to clear up a misunderstanding of what I am claiming. I am *not* claiming that this is the most discoverable possible universe. We can certainly imagine what initially might seem to be more discoverable universes and much less discoverable universes. We cannot draw any conclusions from this, however, unless we know the underlying laws of those universes—for example, an imagined more discoverable universe might require laws that are far more complex or inelegant, thereby taking away from their seeming discoverability. Further, for those who adopt a theistic explanation of discoverability, they should not expect God to create a maximally discoverable universe because there are other tradeoffs—elegance, livability, interestingness, and so forth of the universe—that God must consider.[21] This is why for the most straightforward cases of fine-tuning for discovery, I restrict the evidence to that involving variation of the fundamental parameters within the range that has comparable "livability" to our universe. This keeps the livability the same; and since interestingness and elegance are mostly tied to the mathematical form of the laws, we should expect the level of elegance and interestingness to remain about the same with such variations.

Value of Science

One obvious value of science is the technology resulting from it. The most important cases of discoverability in support of the discoverability-optimality hypothesis, however, are those that are unlikely directly to lead to technology that is of practical benefit. In those cases, one might wonder why the discoverability of the world would be so important. For instance, finding the Higgs boson might be of importance to a few physicists, but for the rest of us, other things—such as world hunger or climate change—are much more important.

In response, I begin by noting that to render the discoverability of the universe unsurprising under theism only requires that we can glimpse some overall value for God's making a highly discoverable world. The value need not be great, unless creating such a world would tend to undermine the realization of some other substantial value.

Further, the value of science extends far beyond those who are directly employed in the scientific enterprise. First, it is difficult to think of a better way to affirm the importance of both reason and faith than to plant a powerful piece of evidence for God's existence at the very base of the citadel of reason itself, science. Second, science has given humans confidence in the power of human reason. Even though skepticism, relativism, and superstition are fairly rampant in today's world, without science, it would likely be far more rampant. For a thinking person, the fact that reason has worked so well in helping us understand the physical world provides a powerful reason to reject skepticism and relativism, and not to fall prey to superstition. Further, this confidence in our use of reason has also motivated us to use reason in other areas, such as in questioning racist attitudes and developing more just and effective political and social systems. I take these to all be good things.

Third, science allows us collectively to express the Image of God, and thereby contributes to human flourishing. Paraphrasing Thomas Aquinas, Alvin Plantinga notes that since God is the ultimate knower, modern science is therefore "a most impressive way in which humankind communally reflects the divine nature, a striking development of the image of God in humanity. Accordingly it is to be prized by Christians and other theists."[22]

Fourth, science allows us to appreciate the glory and ingenuity of God's creation in a way that is not possible without it. Fifth, though often not actually enacted, science at its best exemplifies many ideals of both community and individuality. As for the communal aspect, in today's world progress in fundamental branches of science requires teams of people working together and depending on extensive scientific labors of previous generations. For example, at the Large Hadron Collider (LHC), thousands of physicists and engineers work together from virtually every nation and religion. At the same time, at its best science is not collectivist, but values individual initiative and thought, since these have been central to scientific advancement.

Finally, the findings of science have inspired us with a sense of the elegance of the universe and given us a sense of transcendence via helping us see ourselves in a cosmic context. This, along with our inherent curiosity, is part of the reason so many people are interested in current developments in cosmology and fundamental particle physics, such as exhibited by the widespread interest in the discovery of the Higgs boson.

Of course, one could argue that there are also disvalues associated with science. But, as noted previously, to render it unsurprising that God would create a world that is discovery-friendly, all that is required is that we be able to *glimpse* how such a world could realize values that could not otherwise be realized, or at least realized as well, and that these values could plausibly provide sufficient reason for God to create a science-friendly universe.

CONCLUSION

As presented in this chapter, the argument from the fine-tuning for discovery for theism can be cast into the same quasi-Bayesian probabilistic form as that from the standard anthropic fine-tuning argument. At the same time, it avoids several major objections raised against the latter argument. First, it avoids the multiverse objection, or any other objection that relies on an observer-selection principle, such as Elliot Sober's objection that we should always include the information that observers exist in the background information when evaluating probabilities.[23]

Second, the anthropic fine-tuning argument encounters the problem of old evidence. In standard Bayesian confirmation arguments, one starts with the prior probability that a hypothesis is true. Roughly, this is defined as what one's confidence that the hypothesis is true would be if one did not know the evidence in question. Then one considers how much the evidence in question increases one's confidence in the truth of the hypothesis. In the case of the anthropic fine-tuning, the evidence is standardly taken to be that the universe permits the existence of embodied conscious agents. Since any rational person would know that they exist as an embodied conscious being, however, this could never be new evidence for us, creating a problem in defining, let alone evaluating, the prior probability.[24] The fine-tuning for discovery does not run into this problem, since it is certainly possible for us to fail to know that the fundamental parameters of the universe are optimal for scientific discovery.

Third, the discoverability-optimality hypothesis makes "falsifiable" (i.e., disconfirmable) predictions. In fact, around seven times I thought that I had found a serious counterexample to the idea that the parameters were optimal for scientific discovery This is particularly important, since it shows that the evidence for the hypothesis cannot be accounted for merely via a selection effect.

Finally, many cases of fine-tuning for discovery straightforwardly avoid the problem of determining what I have called the *comparison range*—that is, in the case of the anthropic fine-tuning, the range of possible values of the parameters with respect to which the life-permitting range is very small. (One version of this problem is the normalizability problem for probabilities due to infinite ranges, a problem advanced most forcefully by Timothy and Lydia McGrew, and Eric Vestrup.[25]) For the clearest cases of fine-tuning for discovery—those for which the discovery-optimality range is small compared to the specified-physics anthropic range—the comparison range is the specified-physics anthropic range. In the case of the eight particle physics parameters I consider, this range corresponds to the range over which the Higgs field is stable or meta-stable, which is a well-defined range.

Of course, at present, one of the major weaknesses of the argument from the fine-tuning for discovery is that, unlike many cases of anthropic fine-tuning, the claims regarding this fine-tuning have not been thoroughly vetted. Although I am confident in the existence of this fine-tuning, until they are vetted, the argument for theism from the fine-tuning for scientific discovery should be taken conditionally: given such fine-tuning holds up under careful scrutiny, this is how it provides an argument for the existence of God. Even then, it will have its own weakness that I do not have space here to cover. Thus, it is best to think of this argument as providing a potentially important complement to the anthropic fine-tuning argument.

NOTES

1. More accurately, it is the fine-tuning of the effective dark energy density of the universe, which is the sum of Einstein's original cosmological constant with various energy fields that of themselves would cause an accelerated expansion or contraction of the universe. However, the cosmological literature has typically talked about it in terms of the fine-tuning of the cosmological constant.

2. It is not its mere seeming improbability that makes it cry out for explanation, since there are many occurrences in the world that are enormously improbable. Rather, it is a combination of being seemingly enormously improbable with its being special—in this case, required for the existence of ECAs.

3. Albert Einstein, "Physics and Reality" in *Journal of the Franklin Institute* (March 1936) and Eugene Wigner, "The Unreasonable Effectiveness of Mathematics in the Natural Sciences," *Communications in Pure and Applied Mathematics* 13 (February 1960): 1–14. New York: John Wiley & Sons, Inc.

4. Mark Steiner, *Mathematics as a Philosophical Problem* (Cambridge, MA: Harvard University Press), 1998.

5. Ibid., 176. A recent version of this idea that the universe is optimal for scientific discovery is promoted by Guillermo Gonzales and Jay Richards (*The Privileged Planet: How Our Place in the Cosmos is Designed for Discovery* (Washington DC, Regnery Publishing), 2004.) They cite a significant number of examples where the conditions for a planet being habitable (i.e., allowing for the development of ECAs) appear to coincide with the conditions that optimize the ability to make scientific discoveries. For example, they argue that the region of the galaxy that allows for life-permitting solar systems to develop is also the region that is most favorable for doing astronomy. In their treatment, however, they provide no methodology for determining whether the universe is more discoverable than would be expected by chance.

6. Technically, one should use dimensionless versions of these constants (e.g., $\alpha_G \equiv \dfrac{Gm_p^2}{\hbar c}$), but we will not worry about that here.

7. In an infinite universe, the "number of observers" in the above sentence might need to be replaced by "density of observers."

8. I develop this account of epistemic probability in section 3.2, 228–233 of "The Teleological Argument: An Exploration of the Fine-Tuning of the Universe," in *The Blackwell Companion to*

Natural Theology, William Lane Craig and J. P. Moreland, eds. (Malden, MA: Wiley-Blackwell, 2009), 202–281. Instead of epistemic probability, one could present the argument in terms of logical probability or subjective probability, or use a different definition of conditional epistemic probability such as the rational credence one should have in A given one believes B.

9. Today coal is usually used for the smelting of metals. However, the ability to use coal came only after a long history of perfecting smelting via charcoal produced by wood burning.

10. Changing α would also have astrophysical and cosmological effects on discoverability. However, as far as I can tell, it also seems fine-tuned for maximal discovery in these areas too.

11. See John Barrow and Frank Tipler, *The Anthropic Cosmological Principle* (Oxford: Oxford University Press, 1986), 380.

12. These physicists were Abaz Kryemadhi (Messiah College), Don Page (University of Alberta), and Luke Barnes (University of Sidney).

13. Specifically, these were the same physicists who checked the calculations regarding the CMB.

14. The case of the fine-structure constant is particularly problematic in this regard since the technology arising from our ability to smelt metals allows for a planet to sustain a much larger population. Thus, we would expect universes in which the value of fine-structure constant is favorable for ECAs being able to smelt metals to have a higher density of ECAs. A multiverse advocate could then argue that it is more likely for a typical ECA to find itself in such a universe than one in which the fine-structure constant is less favorable for smelting metals. Despite these weaknesses, I mention the case of the fine-structure constant because it was the first potential case of fine-tuning for discovery I found and it is one of the easiest to understand.

15. http://greerheard.com/wp/past-events/god-cosmology/

16. Abdelhak Djouadi, "Precision Higgs coupling measurements at the LHC through ratios of production cross sections." arXiv:1208.3436v2 [hep-ph] March 26, 2013, 1.

17. Particles with large masses require enormous concentrations of energy to produce; in our current universe, such concentrations exist only in particle accelerators. Further, once produced, they rapidly decay to other particles (e.g., in around a trillionth of a second or less). This means their actual existence will not have any effect on life in our current universe. Consequently, as long as one does not make their masses too small (e.g., less than 100 MeV), they will not have any direct effect on life. However, changing the masses of these particles can have an indirect effect on life since it changes the number of virtual versions of these particles that exist within the proton and neutron, thereby slightly affecting the strength of the strong nuclear force and hence the masses of the proton and neutron; the latter in turn do affect the probability of life existing. However, this effect is small and can be compensated for by slight adjustments to the parameter governing the strength of the strong force. Changing the masses of these particles can also affect the unknown physics in the very early universe, thus having anthropic consequences. We consider this possibility in the "Unknown Anthropic Range Objection" section.

18. This objection is similar to the "weak anthropic principle" response to the anthropic fine-tuning: namely, if the fundamental parameters of physics were not observer-permitting, there would be no one here to observe the fact.

19. See http://sci.esa.int/planck/33333-summary, accessed January 20, 2016.

20. Our third response notes that, for some cases, even if we would not have known the difference it would not affect the claim that it is coincidental that we have the tools to discover the domain in question. To see this, consider the following example. Suppose the government

of a nation of a billion people has what they call a "grace-lottery," which only the highest-level government officials and the past winners know about. Without even buying a ticket, a million dollars is given to one person a year, supposedly chosen at random among the entire population; part of the requirements for receiving the money is that one is to tell no one where the money came from, but offer an official "lie" about its source. Now, suppose some poor farmer—call him Omaz—receives a million dollars from this program. He not only finds out about the program, but when he uses several thousands of dollars of the money to check into his family history, he discovers that he has a half brother who is now a high official in the government and the primary person in control of the lottery.

Omaz now becomes suspicious that the lottery was rigged, reasoning as follows:

> Corruption is rampant in this government, and we are taught from birth that one's happiness in the afterlife depends on taking care of one's closest blood relatives. Consequently, it is not unlikely that my half brother was responsible for me receiving the million dollars through this program. It is very, very unlikely—around one in a twenty million over a fifty-year life span—that I would have received this money by chance. Hence, my receiving the money strongly confirms that my half brother had a role in this over the chance hypothesis.

Certainly Omaz's reasoning seems correct. If Omaz had not been selected, however, he would not have known about the lottery. Yet, this does not take away from the confirmation that receiving the money gives to the hypothesis that his half brother rigged the lottery.

21. By livability I mean the conduciveness of the environment of a typical ECA for living a quality life given some reasonable measure of typicality and quality.

22. Alvin Plantinga, *Where the Conflict Really Lies: Science, Religion, and Naturalism* (Oxford: Oxford University Press, 2011), 5.

23. See Elliot Sober, "Absence of Evidence and Evidence of Absence: Evidential Transitivity in Connection with Fossils, Fishing, Fine-tuning, and Firing Squads," *Philosophical Studies* 143, no. 1 (2009): 63–90.

24. One can also take the fact that life requires that the parameters fall into relatively small ranges as the evidence, but then the argument becomes much trickier to develop adequately.

25. McGrew, Timothy and Lydia McGrew, and Eric Vestrup. "Probabilities and the Fine-tuning Argument: A Skeptical View," *Mind* 110 (October 2001).

(F)

The Naïve Teleological Argument

AN ARGUMENT FROM DESIGN FOR ORDINARY PEOPLE

C. Stephen Evans

⌒ ───────────────────────────────

ARGUMENTS FOR GOD'S existence from the design present in nature, often termed teleological arguments, continue to be presented and have a venerable history. Versions of the argument can be found in Plato and Aristotle, and it is plausible to think that St. Paul has something like this argument in mind in Romans 1:19–20. There, Paul says that the knowledge of God is "plain" or "evident" to people, since God's "eternal power and divine nature" can be seen or understood from what God has created. Paul seems to suggest that there are features of the natural world that make it clear that the world was created by God, and the design that seems present in nature has often been thought to be one of the features of the world that points to God. Other such features might include beauty and order, but these are arguably linked to design as well.

Even during the time of David Hume (late eighteenth century), the design argument was generally regarded as powerful. Hume himself seems to concede this. Although Hume gives several important criticisms of the argument in his *Dialogues Concerning Natural Religion,* in the end the character Philo, usually regarded as Hume's mouthpiece, confesses that the argument has a good deal of force: "In many views of the universe and of its parts, particularly the latter, the beauty and fitness of final causes strike us with such irresistible force that objections appear (what I believe they really are) mere cavils and sophisms; nor can we then imagine how it was ever possible for us to repose any weight on them."[1]

Many philosophers today would argue that Hume only makes this concession because he lived prior to Darwin and therefore had no knowledge of evolution. Natural selection gives an explanation of the apparent design in nature that makes it unnecessary to posit a creator/designer. As Richard Dawkins has famously said, "although atheism might have been *logically* tenable before Darwin, Darwin made it possible to be an intellectually ful-filled atheist."[2] People like Dawkins obviously believe that natural selection provides a rival and superior explanation for the apparent design in nature, making any appeal to God unnecessary. If this is correct, then a successful argument from design will either have to show that Darwinian evolution is false (the strategy of "creation science" and "in-telligent design" advocates) or else show that evolutionary theory, contrary to Dawkins, does not undermine arguments to God's existence from design. The second strategy requires an argument that design and the evolutionary process are compatible, as well as showing that there are aspects of the natural order that has evolved that still require a purposive explanation.[3]

What are the aspects of the natural order that still require a teleological explanation? Richard Swinburne suggests that it is the fact that there are stable laws of nature, which "are such as, under certain circumstances . . . give rise to striking examples of spatial order similar to the machines which men make."[4] A variation on this strategy would be to point to the fact that the laws of nature, as well as the physical constants found in the natural world, which together make evolution possible, seem to be "fine-tuned" so as to make possible the evolution of living creatures.[5] Design arguments that appeal to such scientific truths I shall term sophisticated design arguments. In my view such arguments have great force and do increase the plausibility of God's existence.

In this chapter, however, I want to consider what one might call a "naïve" design ar-gument, an argument whose force does not depend on scientific findings, and which therefore does not require sophisticated scientific knowledge, such as is required for the fine-tuning argument, in order to be convincing. I prefer to call this an argument for or-dinary people rather than a "naïve" argument, since I do not believe that the argument is effective only for those who are naïve in some sense.

My version of this argument interprets the apparent design in nature as a "natural sign" for God's existence. This means that it can produce an awareness of God without any ar-gument or process of inference at all, as Alvin Plantinga himself suggested in the article that became the impetus for this book. Rather, a natural sign can be the means where the *sensus divinitatis* functions to produce a belief in God that is properly basic. However, it is also possible to reflect on a natural sign and make it the basis for an argument. In this case, the belief in God will not be basic in nature. However, the argument in this case will be very simple and easy to understand, and it will be convincing to a wide range of people, regardless of their degree of scientific knowledge.

My "design argument for ordinary people," like contemporary sophisticated design arguments, will require, for some people, an account of how design and natural selec-tion are compatible. This is not, strictly speaking, a necessary feature of the argument itself, but it will be required to answer an objection that claims that the scientific truth of Darwinian evolution constitutes a defeater for the view that there are features of the world that point to a designer. I shall therefore discuss in a later part of this chapter whether evolutionary theory undermines a design argument of the type I want to defend.

NATURAL SIGNS FOR GOD

What is a natural sign for God's existence? The concept is modeled on Thomas Reid's concept of perceptual natural signs.[6] According to Reid, many of our sensations, as well as things like facial expressions, function as natural signs that make it possible for us directly to perceive the world. Although perceptual knowledge is mediated by natural signs, the perceptions those signs make possible are psychologically direct and involve no inference or argument. In order for something like a sensation to function as a natural sign, it must be causally linked both to the objects being perceived by way of the signs, and to the dispositions we have to form conceptions and beliefs about these objects as a result of the perceptions.[7] When, under normal conditions and good lighting, there is a tree in front of me, I acquire sensations that are caused by the tree. These sensations in turn create in me a disposition to form a conception of a tree and a belief that there is a tree in front of me. The causal relations these sensations participate in are crucial to the proper functioning of the sensations. However, the psychological act of perceiving the tree is direct.

Natural signs for God, or what we might call theistic natural signs, must function in a similar way. They must be causally linked "upstream" to God, and they must be causally linked "downstream" to dispositions to form a conception of God and a belief in God's reality. Furthermore, these causal relations must be part of what we might call the proper function of the signs; that they participate in these causal roles cannot be accidental. The former causal relation is easy to satisfy if God exists, since God is the cause of everything that exists other than Himself. All that God would have to do is ensure that some of the aspects of the natural world He creates naturally dispose humans to form an idea of God and believe in Him.

Reid thought that it was a great mistake to take perceptual natural signs as facts from which knowledge of the external world is gained through reasoning or inference. He was well aware that such thinkers as Locke and Descartes had attempted to do this, but he was convinced that this was an error that had led to the idealism of Berkeley and what Reid believed was the skepticism of Hume. However, Reid's view that attempts to use natural signs as the basis of inferences are mistakes is logically distinct from his claim that natural signs can give rise to perceptual experiences that are psychologically direct. It is conceivable that someone might hold that although perceptual knowledge does not require any inference, in some cases it might involve inference. I might, for some reason, direct my psychological attention not to the object perceived by means of the signs, as I normally do, but to the signs themselves. Then, after reflecting on the signs, I might infer something about the external world on the basis of the signs. The plausibility or force of the inference might be derived from the power of the signs themselves.

Even if Reid were right, and this is not possible for perceptual natural signs, it might be the case that it is possible for theistic natural signs. There might well be natural signs that point to God's reality and in some people produce a conception of God and belief in God without any kind of inference. However, there might be other people who make the signs themselves the object of reflection and reason that God must exist as the cause of the signs.

At least this is what I argued in *Natural Signs and Knowledge of God*. What are the natural signs that can function in this way? Some of them lie at the heart of the classical theistic arguments, such as cosmological, teleological, and moral arguments.[8] Let's take moral arguments as an illustration. Our sense that we are under moral obligations that we are rightly held responsible for fulfilling points to a moral legislator who holds us responsible. One individual might take this sense of obligation to be a kind of direct perception of God's call or command on the person. Another individual, however, might take these sensed obligations as data that are best explained by postulating the existence of a transcendent moral legislator and judge.

A second type of moral argument provides yet another example. Our sense that human persons have inherent worth and dignity might function for one individual as a kind of perception of the value humans have by virtue of being made in the image of an infinitely valuable Creator. Such a person, we might say, sees God in other persons. Another person, however, might take human dignity and value as a datum that is best explained by positing that they are created by God in the image of God.

THE PASCALIAN CONSTRAINTS ON KNOWLEDGE OF GOD

Why think that natural signs are one of the ways God might make his reality knowable to humans? One reason is that they satisfy what I call the Pascalian constraints on the knowledge of God. The idea is suggested by a well-known passage from Pascal's *Pensées*.

> If he [God] had wished to overcome the obstinacy of the most hardened, he could have done so by revealing himself to them so plainly that they could not doubt the truth of his essence [. . .] It was therefore not right that he should appear in a manner manifestly divine and absolutely capable of convincing all men, but neither was it right that his coming should be so hidden that he could not be recognized by those who sincerely sought him. He wished to make himself perfectly recognizable to them. Thus wishing to appear openly to those who seek him with all their heart and hidden from those who shun him with all their heart, he has qualified our knowledge of him by giving signs which can be seen by those who seek him and not by those who do not. "There is enough light for those who desire only to see and enough darkness for those of a contrary disposition."[9]

Pascal is here probably thinking about the incarnation of Christ rather than the knowledge of God's existence, but if his reasoning is plausible in the case of the incarnation, it seems equally plausible for belief in God. Pascal seems to think that God has provided enough evidence to make it possible for those who wish to know God to find him, but that this is evidence is not so clear and powerful that everyone will do so. Rather, the evidence is such that those who want to dismiss it will be able to do so.

In my view, someone who shares Pascal's intuitions here will find two principles plausible, which I call the wide accessibility principle (WAP) and the easy resistibility principle (ERP).[10] If there is a God, and God wants humans to have a conscious relationship to God, then WAP seems highly plausible. God would make it possible for ordinary humans who desire a relation to God to know about God. Surely, God would not limit the knowledge of himself to those with very high intelligence, or those who have studied philosophy, or those who understand contemporary physics. ERP seems plausible as well. God does not want humans to serve him out of fear or compulsion, but to do so freely as friends of God. Since God is omnipotent and omniscient, if God's reality were too obvious, then even those who have no sympathy for God's purposes would likely feel coerced into serving God.

Natural signs for God can satisfy these two principles. Things such as a sense of moral obligation are widely shared human experiences that virtually all humans have. For many of those humans, it seems natural to interpret these experiences as pointing to a being who holds one accountable or responsible. Thus, a great many persons, over the centuries, in many cultures and historical periods, have connected their moral experience to God or gods. However, that sense of obligation, though it may point to a God and thus serve as a sign, has to be "read" or interpreted, and it is obvious, as is shown by the fact that most philosophers today reject a divine command account of obligation, that it is possible to resist the sign, by providing an alternative explanation of obligation, or even dismissing moral obligations as objectively unreal.[11]

It thus seems to me that if God exists, natural signs provide a plausible view of how God might make knowledge of himself possible. I shall now proceed to discuss the design we seem to recognize in the natural world as one of the natural signs that points to God's reality.

DESIGN IN NATURE AS A NATURAL SIGN

A classic statement of the argument from design comes from Thomas Aquinas:

> The fifth way is taken from the governance of the world. We see things which lack knowledge, such as natural bodies, act for an end, and this is evident from their acting always, or nearly always, in the same way, so as to obtain the best result. Hence it is plain that they achieve their end, not fortuitously, but designedly. Now whatever lacks knowledge cannot move towards an end, unless it be directed by

some being endowed with knowledge and intelligence; as the arrow is directed by the archer. Therefore some intelligent being exists by whom all natural things are directed to their end; and this being we call God.[12]

It seems to me that Aquinas here directs our attention to two features of the natural world, orderliness and value. We observe natural bodies "acting always, or nearly always, in the same way." We also recognize that by so doing they "obtain the best result." In my view the reference to the "best" here is slightly problematic. To recognize order that leads to some good end as non-accidental, we don't have to postulate that the end is the best possible end. What is important is that we see regularities in the natural world that are beneficial, that are themselves good, or that make possible goods.

What are the "natural bodies" Aquinas refers to here? He does not say, but there are lots of possibilities even in his day, and we are likely aware today of many more. The regular movements of the earth and heavenly bodies make possible the seasons of the years, which make it possible for crops to grow. The heart regularly pumps blood throughout the body, making it possible for the body to receive nourishment and remove waste products. The lungs allow us to inhale fresh air and exhale carbon dioxide.

Notice that Aquinas here makes no essential reference to any kind of analogy between these natural regularities and human artifacts, such as machines. Such analogies are often prominent in later versions of design argument, such as the one famously presented by William Paley, and they also figure importantly in the versions of the argument criticized by Hume. Aquinas does mention the arrow that cannot find its target without an archer to direct it. This, however, is not the basis of the argument but simply an illustration of a principle he finds obviously true: "Whatever lacks knowledge cannot move towards an end, unless it be directed by some being endowed with knowledge and intelligence." This principle obviously is fundamental to the argument, and I shall discuss its plausibility later, particularly in connection with the question as to whether it is undermined by natural selection.

Aside from the key problem of the viability of this principle, there are of course many other objections that are standardly raised against arguments such as Aquinas offers. Frequently, critics point out that the argument does not by itself establish that there is just one intelligent being that is responsible for the ordering. Perhaps the design is due to a group of divine beings. Another standard criticism is that the intelligent designer would not have to be perfectly good and might perhaps lack other attributes of the classical theistic God, such as omnipotence.

It is, however, not clear that these objections have much force against design construed as a natural sign for God. Suppose it is true that there is a God, and that one of the ways God reveals himself to humans is through the experienced design evident in nature. God is responsible for the design and has also given humans a natural disposition to respond to the design by forming the belief that a powerful, intelligent being is responsible for the design. Humans who notice the design (and it is pretty hard not to do so) naturally form such beliefs as "There is an intelligent purpose behind the universe; it is not an accident that things run the way they do." In this case, design could be a feature of the universe that triggers the operation of what Calvin and Plantinga call the sensus divinitatis. The fact that the design in nature does not logically entail that the designer is just one being or is morally perfect does not undermine the claim that the design could function in the way I have suggested.

Interestingly, contemporary psychologists who study the origins of religious belief are increasingly drawn to the claim that something like this picture of religious belief formation is correct.[13] Contrary to the earlier speculations of such thinkers as Freud and Durkheim, these scientists claim that humans are "hard-wired" to believe in God or gods. Religious belief is the result of a cognitive faculty humans have that primes us to respond to nature by believing that there are invisible agents (or one agent) behind nature. Humans have a natural tendency to interpret events in nature as the result of intentional actions.

It is true that the majority of the scientists who claim this is true are themselves atheists who think of this cognitive faculty as one that is not aimed at genuine knowledge.[14] Rather, they think that this faculty is a spandrel, a by-product of a faculty that evolved for some other purpose. For example, a popular theory is that there was an evolutionary penalty for failing to detect the presence of an agent such as a predator, so humans acquired a hyper-sensitive "agent detector." There is doubtless some evolutionary story to be told about this human cognitive faculty. However, this is true for all of our cognitive faculties, such as our ability to learn mathematical truths. The fact that such an evolutionary story can be told about a faculty does not by itself imply that this faculty is untrustworthy and not truth-conducive.

In fact, the claim that this religious cognitive faculty gives us falsehoods rather than truths seems to presuppose the truth of atheism and cannot serve as an independent argument for the truth of atheism. To know that the output of the faculty is mostly falsehoods, we would have to know independently that God does not exist. If there is a God, and if God created us through an evolutionary process, then it seems highly plausible that God is responsible for the fact that humans are hard-wired to be religious, and there would then be no reason to think that the faculty is inherently unreliable. This is particularly true if one takes the aim of the faculty to be modest: not to give us precise and certain knowledge about God and his nature, but rather to give us a natural tendency to believe that there is a supernatural being or beings.

EPISTEMOLOGICAL CONSIDERATIONS: EXTERNALISM AND INTERNALISM

Should we trust this natural tendency to believe that there is a designer behind nature? How can we decide this question? Obviously, the answer will depend on one's general epistemological commitments. One large divide in contemporary epistemology is the disagreement between internalists and externalists. Very roughly and crudely, externalists affirm that knowledge is something that depends on the objective facts about how knowers relate to the world that they know, while internalists think that knowledge must be rooted in evidence that is internally accessible to the knower, a principle that externalists deny. So let me try to sketch an answer to the question from both of these points of view.

An Externalist View

Externalists might say something like this: We can rely on our natural tendency to believe in God or gods if that tendency is one that is on the whole reliable and helps us reach truths. Alternatively, they might say (following Plantinga) that this faculty can be relied upon if it is one that is successfully aimed at truth and is operating properly in the kind of environment in which it was intended to function. Believers in God (such as myself) will likely hold that these conditions are fulfilled and that the faculty is therefore one to which we should accord at least a measure of trust. The externalist may or may not think that the process involves an inference; it may be a more spontaneous and immediate process in which the individual just sees nature as the work of God or gods. However, if there is an inference involved, it is one that would be quite simple and easy to understand. Whether the belief formed be basic or the result of an inference, the cognitive process seems directed at truth if it produces an awareness of God's reality and God does indeed exist.

A critic may object that this verdict is the result of circular reasoning, since it seems to make the judgment that "our beliefs about God are likely true" depend on our judgment that our beliefs about God are true. This objection might be powerful if one took the religious believer to be offering an apologetic argument intended to convince the nonbeliever of the existence of God. However, from the externalist perspective, no such argument is being offered. Rather, the externalist is offering an explanation of how she knows the faculty can be trusted.

It is important to recognize that the alleged flaw in the religious believer's claim stems from the nature of externalism and is not grounded in anything particular to the religious case. On the externalist account of knowledge, as it is typically developed, all of our basic human faculties are justified in this "circular" way and there is no real alternative.[15] We know that memory is reliable because most of the time memory helps us toward the truth, but to learn that this is true we must rely partly on memory. Similarly, we are justified in relying on sense perception, because most of the time sense perception works pretty well, but we know that is the case partly by using sense perception. From an externalist perspective, it would not be surprising, then, that we only can know that our religious faculty is reliable by using that faculty.

An Internalist View

Of course internalists may say that it is just this feature of externalism that makes it objectionable. What then might an internalist say on behalf of our religious faculty that gives us this tendency to believe in God or gods? Recall that the internalist says that what justifies a belief is some feature of the belief to which the believer has mental access. But how do we tell when a feature we are aware of does count as good evidence? The threat of skepticism arises for the internalist at this point, Berkeley's famous skepticism about unperceived material substance being a good illustration of the problem. How can I tell what is true about the objective world on the basis of some feature of my own consciousness?

Many internalists affirm, and I concur, that for internalism to avoid global skepticism, the internalist must affirm what is sometimes called "the principle of credulity." A good example of an internalist who takes this route is provided by Michael Huemer, who defends what he calls "the principle of phenomenal conservatism," stating the principle like this: "If it seems to S as if P, then S thereby has at least *prima facie* justification for believing that P."[16] Huemer's principle seems similar in import to what Richard Swinburne calls the "principle of credulity," though Swinburne states his version in terms of probability rather than justification: "It is a principle of rationality that (in the absence of special considerations) if it seems (epistemically) to a subject that x is present, then probably x is present; what one seems to perceive is probably so."[17] Like Huemer, Swinburne claims that something like this principle must be adopted to avoid a global skepticism.

If this is right, then it looks like there is a way for an internalist to claim that the natural signs for God provide some degree of support for the belief that God exists. (We could describe that support in various ways, by saying it provides prima facie justification, or that it makes the belief probable, or that it raises the probability of the belief, etc.) For what makes some feature F we are consciously aware of evidence for the truth of some belief P is just that when we become aware of F, P seems to be true, or seems more likely to be true. But natural signs for God are precisely features of the natural world that have this function.

The specific feature of the world I want to focus on is its apparent design. As Aquinas notes, the natural world is full of orderly processes involving complex arrangements of parts that act together to make possible results we regard as good or valuable. Human beings, throughout human history and in many different cultures, have noticed these features. Perhaps some of them as a result have spontaneously formed a belief that the natural world must be the result of a God or gods, in much the way Plantinga thinks is the case. In that case, the natural sign would ground a belief that is basic and not based on an argument. However, it also seems possible for some of these humans to reflect on these features, clearly accessible to consciousness, and reflectively try to explain them. The explanation that naturally suggests itself (to many) is that "this is no accident." The best explanation of these features of the natural world is that they are the result of a powerful intelligent agent who aims at the good. The argument gains its force from the power the sign has to "suggest" (using the word of Thomas Reid) that the best explanation for the apparent design in nature is that it is in fact real design.

Notice that there is no need for any sophisticated scientific knowledge for the argument to work. All that is necessary is that humans pay attention to very general and obvious features of the natural world, and pay attention to the natural inference those features suggest to us. I believe that the fact that the argument does not rest on sophisticated scientific knowledge is a virtue and not a weakness. If we believe that God exists and wishes humans to know about him, then we should believe that the wide accessibility principle is true. But if WAP is true, then it seems likely that at least some of the evidence God would provide for his reality would be evidence that humans in every culture and historical period could recognize and understand, evidence that does not require a sophisticated understanding of the laws of physics, for example. It is an argument for ordinary people. The argument can be recognized as one that has genuine force, both from an externalist and an internalist perspective.

A REJOINDER FROM THE NON-BELIEVER

What might a non-believer say in response to the argument? I can imagine three different kinds of responses. The first is to highlight the fact that the argument does not seem to justify anything like the God of orthodox Christianity, Judaism, or Islam. It purports to argue that a powerful, intelligent designer who aims at good ends is responsible for the apparent design in nature. However, the critic may note, we do not know that this designer, even if the designer exists, is omnipotent as opposed to just being very powerful. We do not know whether this designer is perfectly good. We do not even know if there is just one designer, a point that I have implicitly conceded by talking about the belief formed as a result of this natural sign as a belief in "God or gods."

My response to this first rejoinder is to agree with the critic, but to claim that the point made is not a problem. This objection would only be valid if the purpose of the argument was to provide us with accurate complete knowledge about God or the gods. However, in my view, the natural sign of purposive order does not attempt to accomplish this goal, and so its failure to do so is not a problem. The purpose of the argument is to push us toward "anti-naturalism."[18] Natural signs in general, and the arguments they give rise to, are not supposed to give us a full and accurate knowledge of God. Rather, they are supposed to help us see the falsity of naturalism, and to open us to the possibility that there is some kind of personal reality behind the natural order.

A second line of response on the part of the critic might be to concede that the argument from design I have presented does have some force, but that it does not overall make belief in God reasonable because it is defeated by contrary evidence. Such a critic might concede that, taken in isolation, the "simple" design argument raises the probability of God's existence to some degree, but argue that that the evidence against the existence of God, such as the argument from evil, overwhelms this positive evidence.

I agree that this scenario seems possible, and nothing I have said in this chapter rules this out. A comprehensive case for belief in God should look at all the evidence, including evidence that is alleged to be against God's existence, and clearly I have not undertaken this task in this brief chapter. All I will say is that I would be happy if the critic concedes that the argument I have presented has genuine force as evidence for God's existence. The question of the overall reasonableness of belief in God will certainly require a look at the alleged contrary evidence. Though I do not believe the negative evidence is actually strong, I cannot argue for that view here.[19]

The third and final response I can imagine a critic making is one inspired by Dawkins's statement, quoted earlier, that it is Darwin who made it possible to be "an intellectually fulfilled atheist." Such a critic might respond as follows: "Before Darwin, your 'argument for ordinary people' would have made perfect sense. Our natural instinctive tendency to see purposive order as evidence of design seemed plausible enough. However, after Darwin, we now have an alternative explanation that is empirically stronger. Contemporary people who are aware of evolutionary theory and accept the theory as true should not see the apparent design in nature as the result of any kind of intentional purposiveness." Perhaps another way to put the critic's point would be to say that Darwinian evolution provides a defeater for the claim that the beneficial order in nature is evidence for design. It shows that the apparent design in nature is only apparent, the work of a "blind watchmaker" (to use Dawkins's expression), and thus it falsifies the claim that the beneficial order is the result of a purposive agent.

It is clear that someone who replies in this vein is thinking of divine purposiveness as if it were a scientific, empirical hypothesis. The reply supposes that evolutionary theory provides a rival, superior explanation to the hypothesis that the apparent design in nature is the work of God. It looks like God and the evolutionary process are seen as competing explanations. My response is that this reply completely misunderstands the relationship between God and the created order if it is indeed true that God exists and has created the natural universe. If God has created the natural order, he is responsible for the existence of everything in that order, including the natural regularities (laws of nature) that order exhibits. If this is true, then it is a mistake to see God as simply one more cause *within* the natural order. Furthermore, it is in principle not possible for any natural explanation that employs natural entities and natural laws to falsify the claim that God is the ultimate cause of some event or state of affairs. The fact that some event or state of affairs is the result of a natural causal process cannot possibly show that it is not ultimately due to God, if it is true that God has created all natural entities and is the reason why the natural world follows the natural laws it does follow.

To see that this is so, think for example of a devout farmer who thanks God that his crops have received some much-needed rain. Suppose someone says to the farmer: "You should not thank God for the rain; it was caused by a temperature change that caused the water vapor in the clouds to condense." The farmer might well answer that he knows very well that rain comes from clouds and that there are natural explanations for rain. Still, he thinks it is proper to be thankful to God, who made the clouds and is responsible for the natural order that produces the rain. Similarly, someone who accepts evolutionary theory (as I do), may still believe that the apparent design in nature is real and not merely apparent. Evolutionary theory tells us something about how God acted so as to produce a beautiful and orderly world with value. It cannot tell us that the value and order we see in the world is an illusion.

One might think that my argument here proves too much. After all, there have been many people, both religious believers and unbelievers, who think that a good God would not use a process such as evolution to realize his purposes. Some people think that the process of Darwinian evolution is too slow, or too wasteful, or involves too much pain or death. Such arguments are perfectly intelligible. However, the first thing to notice about such arguments is that in the end they are rooted in theological premises. The person who does not think God would use evolution has certain convictions about the means a good God would and would not use to create the universe, convictions that are grounded in their beliefs about God. The arguments are no better than these theological convictions.

Giving a full response to arguments such as this are beyond the scope of this chapter, but it is easy to see how a response might go. Why should we think that our intuitions about the means God would employ to create the world are trustworthy? What do we know about creating universes anyway? Do we fully understand God's purposes in creation? In any case, it is obvious that the theological intuitions that drive this argument—that God would not employ a Darwinian process—are not shared by many thoughtful religious believers. Many Christians who are great scientists, such as Francis Collins and John Polkinghorne, believe that an evolutionary process is one that is quite fitting for God to employ.[20] Far from undermining our belief in God's power and goodness, they hold that a deep understanding of science just increases our awe at what God can do.

There is one other characteristic of evolution that is sometimes thought to be incompatible with a belief that the natural order reflects divine purposiveness, and that is that Darwinian evolution involves randomness. Surely, one might think, a process that is the result of chance cannot be one that is guided by intelligence. Since evolutionary theory posits that the genetic mutations that are "selected for" in the evolutionary process are random, then this might seem to rule out any purposiveness. However, this objection rests on a misunderstanding of Darwinian theory. When scientists say that the genetic mutations are random, they are not saying that the mutations do not have causes, or even that they are completely unpredictable from the point of view of biochemistry. Rather, they mean that the mutations do not happen in response to the needs of organisms. Most mutations are not beneficial to the organism at all. However, this kind of "randomness" is completely compatible with the claim that the whole of the natural order is under God's control. Even if there are real indeterminacies involved in the generation of mutations, traceable to quantum effects, there is no problem for the claim that God is guiding the process. In fact, quantum indeterminacy simply offers a way that God can shape the process without doing anything miraculous, without violating the natural processes he maintains.

To summarize, many ordinary people notice that the natural world is orderly, and that the order makes possible states of affairs that are good. To such people, it appears that the world is designed. However, if the world appears to us to have a certain characteristic, then that is a reason to think it has that characteristic. The beneficial order that we see in the world thus looks like a natural sign for God, one that may produce belief in God in a direct way, for people who perceive the world *as* divinely shaped. For those who reflect on this beneficial order, this same natural sign may make plausible an inferential argument, positing God as the explanation for the apparent design.

Suppose this "ordinary" person learns some science and discovers that what we might call the "surface order" he or she has observed is the result of a deeper, hidden order. There are laws of nature and "physical constants" that make the whole show possible, including the evolutionary process. The discovery that the manifest order is the result of a deeper, more complex order gives this person no reason to think that the beneficial order observed is an illusion, nor any reason to think that God is not responsible for the manifest order. If anything, this scientific knowledge might give rise to a different type of theistic argument, such as the "fine-tuning argument." However, the fact that there are arguments for God's existence that are rooted in sophisticated scientific discoveries is no reason to think God would not also provide evidence for his reality that would be accessible to ordinary people over many different historical eras and in many different cultures. Such an argument satisfies both the wide accessibility principle and the easy resistibility principle. It provides evidence that is accessible to ordinary people, but it does not force those who do not want to believe in God to accept God's reality.

NOTES

1. David Hume, *Dialogues Concerning Natural Religion*, ed. Richard H. Popkin (Indianapolis, IN: Hackett, 1980), 66.

2. Richard Dawkins, *The Blind Watchmaker: Why the Evidence of Evolution Reveals a Universe without Design* (New York: Norton, 1996), 6.

3. See Richard Swinburne, *The Existence of God*, 2nd ed. (Oxford: Oxford University Press, 2004).

4. Ibid., 135.

5. For an example of a "fine-tuning" argument for God's existence, see Robin Collins, "Evidence for Fine-Tuning," *God and Design: The Teleological Argument and Modern Science,* edited by Neil A. Manson (New York: Routledge, 2003), 178–199.

6. For a more developed account of Reid's view of perceptual natural signs that serve as my model, see C. Stephen Evans, *Natural Signs and Knowledge of God: A New Look at Theistic Arguments* (Oxford: Oxford University Press, 2010), 26–34.

7. I am not using the term "causal" here in the technical and precise sense of Reid's own view of causality, but rather to designate what he would have termed causality in a loose and popular sense.

8. Chapters 3–5 of *Natural Signs and Knowledge of God* attempt to defend this claim for these three types of theistic arguments. However, there is no reason to think that theistic signs are only to be found in those classical arguments; things like a sense of gratitude or a sense that one is forgiven for evil might also function as natural signs for God.

9. Blaise Pascal, *Pensées* (New York: E.P. Dutton, 1958), 118.

10. See *Natural Signs and Knowledge of God*, 12–17, for a fuller account and defense of these principles.

11. Of course, it does not follow from the fact that most philosophers reject a divine command account of moral obligation that they are reasonable in doing so, or that the alternative explanations of obligation offered really work. I defend these claims in *God and Moral Obligation* (Oxford: Oxford University Press, 2013).

12. Thomas Aquinas, *Summa Theologica* (Part I, Question 2, Article 3).

13. For examples, see Pascal Boyer, *The Naturalness of Religious Ideas: A Cognitive Theory of Religion* (Berkeley: University of California Press, 1994); Scott Atran, *In Gods We Trust: The Evolutionary Landscape of Religion* (Oxford: Oxford University Press, 2002); S.E. Guthrie, *Faces in the Clouds: A New Theory of Religion* (New York: Oxford University Press, 1993); Dean Hamer, *The God Gene: How Faith is Hardwired into our Genes* (New York: Doubleday, 2004). This is just a fraction of the new books that have appeared in this area, and does not include the large number of articles that have appeared in scholarly journals.

14. For an exception, see Justin L. Barrett, *Why Would Anyone Believe in God?* (Walnut Creek, CA: Altamira, 2004). Barrett argues that God may have intended humans to come to believe in him through this cognitive faculty.

15. For a good defense of this point, see William Alston, "Knowledge of God," in *Faith, Reason, and Skepticism*, edited by Marcus Hester (Philadelphia, PA: Temple University Press, 1992), 6–49.

16. See Michael Huemer, *Skepticism and the Veil of Perception* (Lanham, MD: Rowman & Littlefield, 2001), 98.

17. Swinburne, *The Existence of God,* 303.

18. For a discussion of this concept and how theistic arguments can be construed as supporting it, see C. Stephen Evans, *Why Christian Faith Still Makes Sense: A Response to Contemporary Challenges* (Grand Rapids, MI: Baker Academic Books, 2015), 19–38.

19. Anyone who wants to know how I would personally respond to the problem of evil is welcome to consult C. Stephen Evans, *Faith Beyond Reason: A Kierkegaardian Account* (Edinburgh: Edinburgh University Press, 1998; and Grand Rapids, MI: Wm. B. Eerdmans, 1998), 126–137.

20. See Francis Collins, *The Language of God: A Scientist Presents Evidence for Belief* (New York: Free Press, 2006), and John Polkinghorne, *Belief in God in an Age of Science* (New Haven, CT: Yale University Press, 1998).

(H)

The Ontological Argument

PATCHING PLANTINGA'S ONTOLOGICAL

ARGUMENT BY MAKING THE MURDOCH MOVE

Elizabeth D. Burns

INTRODUCTION

WILLIAM ROWE SUGGESTS that "there is no presentation of the ontological argument that is as carefully developed, forceful, and clear as Plantinga's formulation and discussion of the argument on pp. 198–202 in *The Nature of Necessity* (1974a), and his defense of a modal version of that argument on pp. 213–221" (2009, 90–91).[1] Rowe goes on to argue, however, that Anselm's argument (1962a (1077–1078)), as restated by Plantinga, begs the question because, in order to know the truth of the key premise—"It is possible that God exists in reality"—we must know, independently of the argument, that God does exist in reality. In this chapter, I argue that Rowe focuses on Plantinga's restatement of Anselm's argument at the expense of Plantinga's own influential version of the argument, and that, in fact, Plantinga anticipates and addresses Rowe's objection. Although I acknowledge that Plantinga's response is not entirely satisfactory, I suggest that it might be possible to build on Plantinga's work by adding a further step to the argument derived from the work of Iris Murdoch (1919–1999), which shows that the existence of God is not only possible but necessary, and therefore actual.

THE ONTOLOGICAL ARGUMENT IN ANSELM AND PLANTINGA

In *God, Freedom and Evil* (1974b), Plantinga endeavors to present a version of his argument which may be understood by "the philosophical novice and . . . the fabled general reader" (1974b, 4).

In outline, the argument goes as follows:

1. "There is a possible world in which maximal greatness is instantiated" [29].
2. "Necessarily, a being is maximally great only if it has maximal excellence in every world" [30].
3. "Necessarily, a being has maximal excellence in every world only if it has omniscience, omnipotence, and moral perfection in every world" [31].
4. If 1. is true, there is a possible world, W, in which, if it had been actual, there would have existed an omniscient, omnipotent, morally perfect being which had these qualities in every possible world.
5. If the non-existence of an omniscient, omnipotent, morally perfect being is impossible in at least one possible world, then it is impossible in every possible world, since what is possible does not vary from one world to another.
6. Therefore, the non-existence of an omniscient, omnipotent, morally perfect being is impossible in our actual world and in every possible world (1974b, 111–112).

In short, what the argument amounts to is this:

i. It is possible that there is a being with maximal greatness—that is, one which has maximal excellence in every possible world.
ii. Since our world is a possible world, it must contain a being with maximal greatness.

Alternatively:

There is no conceivable world in which there is no conceivable maximally great being.

The Nature of Necessity, published in the same year as *God, Freedom and Evil*, contains much of the material of the later book in a "more rigorous and complete form" (1974b, 4), and an argument which replaces "maximal greatness" with "unsurpassable greatness." Plantinga argues that, while there are some properties (e.g., "is a human person") that are instantiated only in some worlds, there are other properties (e.g., "is a person in every world") that cannot be instantiated only in some worlds. Such a property is a "universal property"—that is, one that is instantiated either in every world or in no world. Plantinga claims that "unsurpassable greatness" is a property of this kind because "possesses unsurpassable greatness" is equivalent to the universal property of "having maximal excellence in every world," and that unsurpassable greatness is therefore instantiated in this world (1974a, 216).

Despite the title of his article—"Alvin Plantinga on the Ontological Argument"—Rowe's focus is actually Plantinga's restatement of Anselm's version of the argument. This matters because, as Plantinga himself notes, "the existence of many importantly different versions makes most of the 'refutations' one finds in textbooks look pretty silly" (1974a, 212).

A version of Plantinga's restatement of Anselm's argument that incorporates later amendments goes as follows:

1. God exists in the understanding but not in reality.
2. Existence in reality is greater than existence in the understanding alone.
3. It is possible that God exists in reality.
4. If God did exist in reality, then God would be greater than God is (from 1. and 2.).
5. It is possible that there is a being greater than God is (from 3. and 4.).
6. It is possible that there is a being greater than the being than which nothing greater is possible (from 5., by the definition of "God").

But:

7. It is not possible that there is a being greater than the being than which it is not possible that there be a greater.

Therefore, since 6. and 7. are contradictory:

8. It is false that God exists in the understanding but not in reality (1974a, 198–199).[2]

Rowe rejects premise 3. of this argument on the grounds that "[i]t begs the question epistemically because in order to *know* that the crucial premise 'It is possible that God exists in reality' is true, we have to know that God does in fact exist in reality" (2009, 91). If God's existence is possible only in the sense that God might exist in reality but might not, God is not the greatest possible being, because the greatness of such a God would be superseded by the greatness of one whose actual existence could not be doubted. Rowe's switch to epistemology here could, perhaps, be avoided by claiming that the argument depends upon the truth of the crucial premise, for which a further argument would be required. Thus Rowe suggests that we should accept "Anselm's *idea* of God as an omnipotent, omniscient, perfectly good being who exists, not contingently, but necessarily," but argues that the question of whether such a being exists remains unanswered (2009, 92).

Rowe's objection is, however, anticipated by Plantinga both in *God, Freedom and Evil* and in *The Nature of Necessity*, where he considers the application of such an objection to his own argument. In the penultimate paragraph of *God, Freedom and Evil*, Plantinga observes that, insofar as the conclusion of his version of the argument follows from its central premise ("that maximal greatness is possibly instantiated" (1974b, 112)), the argument is valid, but he concedes that, although he himself accepts the truth of this premise, and thus holds that the argument is sound, not everyone will do so (112). For Plantinga it is, nonetheless, evident that "there is nothing *contrary to reason* or *irrational* in accepting this premise" (112). He therefore claims that the argument "establishes, not the *truth* of theism, but its rational acceptability" (112), thereby accomplishing "at least one of the aims of the tradition of natural theology" (112).

In *The Nature of Necessity*, Plantinga explores further his claim that his argument, here referred to as "Argument A," is not only valid but sound. He anticipates Rowe's objection to his formulation of Anselm's version of the argument, noting the objection of some philosophers that, while his own Argument A is valid, it is "clearly *circular* or *question-begging*" (1974a, 217). On some occasions, Plantinga observes, "this *caveat* has no more substance than the recognition that . . . its premiss could not be true unless its conclusion were" (217). This, Plantinga suggests, "does not come to much as an objection" (217)—and yet, surely, this is precisely the objection formulated thirty-five years later by Rowe. Plantinga claims that his argument is not circular, on the grounds that its conclusion—*Unsurpassable greatness* is instantiated in every world—does not constitute an argument for its main premise—"Unsurpassable greatness is possibly exemplified." He also rejects the claim that his argument is question-begging, on the grounds that, while it clearly is possible to construct an argument that *is* question-begging,[3] with regard to Argument A, "[i]t is by no means obvious that anyone who accepts its main premiss does so only because he infers it from the conclusion" (218). Plantinga concedes, however, "that Argument A is not a successful piece of natural theology" (219), since the premises of the latter are usually drawn from propositions accepted by nearly every sane or rational person (219–220). He cites Aquinas's Five Ways, each of which begins with a premise that few would contest, such as that some things are in motion, that things change, or that there are contingent beings (220). Plantinga acknowledges that the central premise of Argument A, "*Maximal greatness* is possibly exemplified" (214), is not of this kind, since a sane and rational person could reject it, remain agnostic, or accept instead the possibility of no-maximality (220)—that is, the possibility that maximal greatness does not exist in any possible world. Plantinga goes on to suggest, however, that if, as Hilary Putnam has argued (1969), it is permissible to give up certain laws of logic, such as the Principle of Distribution (which requires that every proposition is either true or false), in the interests of simplifying physical theory, it is reasonable to accept the premise "Maximal greatness is possibly exemplified" in order to do the same for Theology (220). In fact, it would appear that Putnam's suggestion has not been widely accepted, but Plantinga offers for our consideration two analogous situations:

1. "There are or could be possible but unactual objects."
2. "For any objects x and y and property P, if $x = y$, then x has P if and only if y has P" (Leibniz's Law) (220).

In both cases, Plantinga suggests, although there are no compelling arguments either for the proposition or for its negation, in neither case is it philosophically improper to accept it or to use it as a premise. Plantinga claims that this applies to most philosophical claims and that, if we were "to believe only what is uncontested or for which there are incontestable arguments from uncontested premises, we should find ourselves with a pretty slim and pretty dull philosophy" (221). Indeed, Plantinga argues, in such a situation we would have little more than modus ponens.[4] Therefore, he concludes, the same must be said of the premise "Maximal greatness is possibly exemplified." Thus, while his reformulations of Anselm's argument cannot be said to prove or establish their conclusion, "since it is rational to accept their central premise, they do show that it is rational to accept that conclusion" (221). And, Plantinga suggests, "perhaps that is all that can be expected of any such argument" (221).

I would suggest, however, that Plantinga concedes too much. He argues that his first analogous situation—"There are or could be possible but unactual objects"—resembles "Maximal greatness is possibly exemplified" insofar as "if it is *possible*, it is true and indeed necessarily true" (220). Rowe objects to Plantinga's version of Anselm's argument that, if God's existence is possible only in the sense that God might exist in reality but might not, God is not the greatest possible being, because the greatness of such a God would be superseded by the greatness of one who could not fail to exist. Thus, the greatest possible being is not one who might exist in reality but might not, but rather one who cannot fail to exist—that is, who exists necessarily—and it is this point that Plantinga attempts to bring to the fore in his own version of the argument. Plantinga does not, however, show us how we might construct an argument for belief in a God who exists necessarily, and this, I would suggest, is where a further step of the argument, supplied by Murdoch, might assist us.

THE ONTOLOGICAL ARGUMENT IN ANSELM AND MURDOCH

Murdoch's ontological proof[5] moves on from the claim of Norman Malcolm (1911–1990) that Kant was mistaken to think that the proposition "God is a necessary being" is equivalent to the conditional proposition "If God exists then he necessarily exists" (Malcolm 2003 (1960), 278, quoted in Murdoch 1992, 409),[6] and that of Charles Hartshorne

(1897–2000) that "We should, instead, say 'If the phrase "necessary being" has meaning, then what it means exists necessarily and if it exists necessarily then *a fortiori* it exists'" (Hartshorne 1941, 312–313, quoted in Murdoch 1992, 409). For both scholars, the existence of God is not like that of Kant's triangle, the possible existence of which we can deny without contradiction. The property of necessary existence belongs uniquely to God, which means that it is irrelevant to point out that "in other cases (triangles or islands) existence is not a predicate" (Murdoch 1992, 409).

Thus, Murdoch argues, Anselm's argument from necessary existence is not of the form "if God exists then he necessarily exists"; rather, Anselm argues that "if the concept of God is meaningful (not self-contradictory) God must necessarily exist" (410). This raises the question of what counts as meaning. Although the word "God" clearly has meaning in the sentences that contain it, and a history that is accessible to both believers and unbelievers, Murdoch rejects the view—allegedly held by Malcolm—that the concept has meaning only within the language-game of religious belief. Such an interpretation is, she thinks, "a wrong turning" (1992, 413); it may rescue the ontological argument from Kant's criticisms, but the argument that is rescued is "an empty one with merely grammatical merits" (412).

Murdoch therefore seeks elucidation in Anselm's supplementary argument,[7] his "degrees of goodness argument" from chapter 8 of his reply to Gaunilo:

> Everything that is less good, insofar as it is good, is like the greater good. It is therefore evident to any rational mind that by ascending from the lesser good to the greater we can form a considerable notion of a being than which a greater is inconceivable (Anselm 1962b (1077–1078), 325, quoted in Murdoch 1992, 394).

In short, we can deduce from our experience of different degrees of goodness the existence of a goodness than which none greater can be conceived.[8]

Murdoch's own version of this argument is an argument from moral experience that is characterized as the "ubiquity of goodness argument" because it appeals to "our sense of God (Good) as discovered everywhere in the world" (1992, 404–405). According to this argument, in the experiences of everyday life,

> [w]e are continually shown the reality of what is better and the illusory nature of what is worse. We learn of perfection and imperfection through our ability to understand what we see as an image or shadow of something better which we cannot yet see (405).

Murdoch suggests that our consciousness of failure can also serve as a source of knowledge:

> We are constantly in the process of recognising the falseness of our 'goods', and the unimportance of what we deem important. . . . We find out in the most minute details of our lives that the good is the real (430).[9]

Thus, the ontological argument may enable us to claim "a uniquely necessary status for moral value as something (uniquely) impossible to be thought away from human experience, and as in a special sense, if conceived of, known as real" (396).

For Murdoch, however, the ontological argument proves not the existence of the God of classical theism, but the Good, defined as "an active principle of truthful cognition and moral understanding in the soul . . . a 'reality principle' whereby we find our way about the world" (474). But the Good does have some attributes in common with the God of classical theism, which she defines as a "single perfect transcendent non-representable and necessarily real object of attention" (1985, 55). Although Murdoch argues that the Good is not "God in disguise," it is, nonetheless, "what the old God symbolised" (1992, 428). And since even the Good is, ultimately, a metaphor (1985, 93), this means that, for Murdoch, both the Good and God are metaphors for the same noumenal reality, the true nature of which it is impossible for humankind to understand.

THE ONTOLOGICAL ARGUMENT RECONSTRUCTED

Thus, both Plantinga and Murdoch argue that the nature of God/Good entails that God/Good cannot fail to exist—that is, that God/Good exists necessarily. Plantinga is left with the difficulty, however, that one could simply reject the notion of a God who cannot fail to exist. Although Plantinga characterizes Aquinas's Fourth Way (2008 (1920) (1265–1274), I; 2:3), an argument not dissimilar from Murdoch's "ubiquity of goodness argument," as "much less impressive" than his Third Way (1974a, 217–218), I would suggest that Murdoch's argument represents a bold attempt to address this problem. Murdoch argues that our ability to identify the many examples of goodness that are a common feature of our experience of the world can be explained only by the necessary existence of a perfect standard of goodness and that this, or the noumenal reality that lies behind it, is that for which the God of classical theism is also a symbol.

A two-part reconstructed argument that draws on the strongest elements of the work of Anselm, Plantinga, and Murdoch may therefore be set out as follows:

The Primary Argument:

1. Unsurpassable Greatness possesses Maximal Excellence (all the good qualities that it can logically possess to the maximal extent) in every possible world.
2. It is possible that Unsurpassable Greatness exists.

The Supporting Argument: The "Murdoch Move":

i. Necessarily, Maximal Excellence exists in any world that contains degrees of goodness.
ii. Goodness of varying degrees is ubiquitous in our world.[10]
iii. Necessarily, Maximal Excellence exists in our world.

Clearly, however, even if this two-part argument is both valid and sound, at best it gets us no further than the possible existence of Unsurpassable Greatness, belief in the actuality of which is supported to a limited degree by a Murdochian argument for the necessary existence of Maximal Excellence in our world. Thus, just as some (e.g., Brian Davies 2004, 99–100) have argued that Anselm's arguments of *Proslogion* 2 and 3 are not, as others (e.g., Hartshorne 1941 and Malcolm 2003 (1960)) have suggested, two different forms of the ontological argument but two parts of the same argument, we need a further reconstruction of the Anselm/Plantinga/Murdoch argument such that it forms a single argument.

This argument might run as follows:

a. It is possible that there is Unsurpassable Greatness—that is, Maximal Excellence in every possible world.
b. Necessarily, Maximal Excellence exists in any world that contains degrees of goodness.
c. Goodness of varying degrees is ubiquitous in our world.
d. If c., necessarily, Maximal Excellence exists in our world.
e. If c., it is reasonable to presume that every possible world contains degrees of goodness.
f. If e., necessarily, Maximal Excellence exists in every possible world.
g. If f., Unsurpassable Greatness actually exists.

OBJECTIONS TO THE RECONSTRUCTED ARGUMENT

In this section, I consider four possible objections to the reconstructed argument:

1. The argument is not sound because the first two premises (a. and b.) may be rejected.

This objection might, at first sight, appear to parallel Rowe's objection to Plantinga's interpretation of Anselm's argument—that is, that the premise "It is possible that God exists in reality" begs the question. But the first two premises of the reconstructed argument are supported not by appeals to concealed prior knowledge, but by abductive reasoning from phenomena (premise c.) to a hypothesis that, in the absence of reasonable alternatives, seems plausible. Gene Fendt, developing an argument first put forward by Plato, claims that it is Justice itself that enables us to rank the justice of five men. Furthermore, he suggests, the existence of Justice is different in kind from that of the justice exhibited by the five just men, and, if we deny the essence of that through which any scale of greatness exists, we cannot make any judgements at all (2005, 161). Thus, Justice and Goodness are the conditions for our ability to place varieties of justice and goodness on a scale. Disagreements do not nullify the argument, since if we disagree about where to place examples of justice or goodness on the relevant scales, this might be taken to imply either that our opponent has misunderstood the nature of the perfect standard in question, or that we disagree with regard to the extent to which the perfect standard is instantiated.

2. Even if it is necessary that Maximal Excellence exists in our world, it does not follow that every world contains degrees of goodness and thus that every world contains Maximal Excellence.

One might, for example, wonder whether, on a planet in another universe, it would be generally regarded as good to provide another sentient being with the means of sustenance, but good to a much greater degree to sacrifice one's own life in order to preserve the life of another. The thrust of the argument, however, is that there is no conceivable set of circumstances in which some things are not regarded as better than others, even if the nature of the goods in a hierarchy may differ between one world and another as a consequence of differences in the natures of those worlds.

3. If Unsurpassable Greatness exists, is it not possible to use the same argument to prove the existence of Unsurpassable Evil?

A version of this "Evil God" argument is used by Stephen Law (2010) to suggest that, since the "Evil God" hypothesis is untenable, the "Good God" hypothesis is equally implausible. For example, Law argues that we might reasonably expect Evil God to create a world in which some people experience some happiness in order to create feelings of jealousy in others and loss in those who were formerly happy. Since such an argument is not widely accepted, Law claims that we cannot reasonably argue for its parallel—that Good God creates a world in which people experience varying degrees of suffering in order to provide an environment in which we can display virtues such as kindness, courage, fortitude, and so on.

This objection was, however, anticipated by Kant over 200 years ago. In *Religion Within the Boundaries of Mere Reason* (1996 (1793)), he argues that humankind are obliged to live their lives under attack from "the evil principle," but that they should submit to "the leadership of the good principle" in order to obtain "freedom from the *dominion* of evil." The evil principle does, indeed, exist in some sense, but "to live for righteousness" is the highest prize that a person can win (1996 (1793), 129).

4. The argument is not an ontological argument.

Finally, it might reasonably be objected that this is not a genuine form of the ontological argument, because the reasoning it utilizes is not entirely a priori; since it depends heavily upon human experience of the ubiquity of degrees of goodness, its reasoning is predominantly a posteriori and its membership of the set of ontological arguments must therefore be revoked. But the "degrees of goodness element" is derived from Anselm's "degrees of goodness argument," a version of which is also found two centuries earlier in the work of al-Fârâbî. Thus even Anselm, commonly regarded as the originator of the ontological argument, saw the need to produce a supporting argument by way of a response to Gaunilo's objection that he is unable to think of "that than which a greater cannot be thought." Anselm argues that, if the concept of "that than which a greater cannot be thought" is meaningful, God necessarily exists, and the supporting argument shows that the concept of "that than which a greater cannot be thought" is, indeed, meaningful. It is only by supporting the argument by means of an appeal to moral experience that we can reasonably claim that the concept of God is instantiated; it is human experience that strengthens the a priori part of the argument. As Fendt suggests, Anselm understood that the significance of "than which nothing greater" can be grasped only "by inferring that than which a greater cannot be thought on the basis of those things than which a greater can be thought" (Fendt 2005, 162–163). Since the true nature of the divine cannot be completely understood or directly perceived by humankind (except, perhaps, by those who are able to attain mystical insights into the nature of ultimate reality), the best we may hope for is that some element of that which we are able to understand or perceive might enable us to catch occasional glimpses of that which is concealed from us by the limitations of our humanity. As Murdoch suggests, human moral experience can plausibly provide this helpful insight.

This argument, then, is primarily an ontological argument because it draws on the notion of a perfect being from Anselm's *Proslogion* 2 (premise a.) and the notion of necessary existence from *Proslogion* 3 (premise d., from c.), but it also contains elements of both an argument from religious experience (premise c.) and a moral argument (premise d.). Arguably, insofar as it depends upon "a consideration of the contingent universe or . . . part of it" (Fakhry 1986, 15)—that part being, of course, instances of goodness— then it also contains elements of a cosmological argument; God is the source of the sequence of good things. Indeed, one might say that the ontological argument requires the support of a cosmological argument[11]—as opposed to Kant's claim that the cosmological argument requires the support of the ontological argument on the grounds that only the latter can supply a completely determinate concept of a necessary being (1929, 523–524). But perhaps it would be more accurate to say that these arguments are interdependent. For Kant, a defective a posteriori argument depends upon a defective a priori argument, but the reconstructed ontological argument claims that the defective a priori version of the argument may be repaired by means of a supporting argument that is derived from our moral experience.

The cosmological argument also appeals to experience to claim that the divine is the Ultimate Explanation of the existence of everything that we experience within the universe. This may be understood as personal in a metaphorical sense (see Burns 2015), and thus we may be drawn beyond the non-personal Good advocated by Murdoch and closer to the theism for which Plantinga argues. It is this Ultimate Explanation that determines what is good for the universe, including its sentient beings, of which human-kind forms a subset—that is, it is the nature of our created humanity that determines what is and is not good for human beings, both as individuals and as a species. Thus the divine might be regarded as both the creative process and the Good that it determines, and the cosmological argument supports belief in the existence of the reality to which the ontological argument points.

CONCLUSION

I have argued that, despite the title of his article—"Alvin Plantinga on the Ontological Argument"—what Rowe objects to is, in fact, Plantinga's interpretation of Anselm's on-tological argument. It could, nonetheless, be argued that Rowe's objection also applies to Plantinga's own version of the ontological argument, and thus that Plantinga's argument fails because the premise "It is possible that a maximally great being exists in reality" holds only if one already accepts the argument's conclusion. Plantinga himself anticipates and responds to this objection, but concedes that a sane and rational person could legit-imately reject the central premise of his argument—that "Maximal greatness is possibly exemplified"—because there are no compelling arguments either for or against it.

I have suggested that Plantinga concedes too much. He notes that one may say of his central premise that "if it is *possible*, it is true and indeed necessarily true" (1974a, 220). But if it is possible only in the sense that God might exist in reality but might not, then the greatness of such a being is superseded by that of a being who cannot fail to exist. I have argued that it is Murdoch who extracts from the work of Anselm a further step in the argument—that is, one that supports belief in the necessary existence of the nou-menal reality for which both God and the Good are metaphors—which brings us closer to a fully functioning version of the ontological argument.

I have offered a reconstructed version of the argument, using elements from the work of Anselm, Plantinga, and Murdoch. I have argued, first, that Unsurpassable Greatness possesses all the good qualities that it can logically possess in every possible world and that, secondly, the existence of this Unsurpassable Greatness is necessary in order to ex-plain our human experience of degrees of goodness.

Finally, despite my claim that Plantinga concedes too much, I must conclude with my own concession—that my reconstructed argument is not, perhaps, an ontological argu-ment in its purest form, since it includes an a posteriori element that has something in common with both moral and cosmological arguments for the existence of God. But the ontological, moral, and cosmological elements are tightly interwoven; thus, this is not a cumulative case, a collection of independent arguments, each of which supports belief in a God with some of the divine attributes, but an integrated or fusion argument for the existence of God—that is, an argument that contains features of several arguments in a single argument. Majid Fakhry suggests that al-Fârâbî vacillates between ontological and cosmological arguments without realizing the inconsistency of these two lines of reasoning (1986, 16–17), but I would suggest that, long before Anselm and Murdoch, al-Fârâbî may have been aware that it is only by assimilating elements of other arguments for the existence of God that the ontological—or fusion—argument can prove the existence of God. Thus, the difficulty encountered by Plantinga's version of the ontological argument—along with many previous and subsequent versions—is that possible existence does not entail actual existence. With the help of Murdoch's version of the argument, I have attempted to reconstruct an integrated or fusion version of the ontological argument that endeavors to show that, in the case of Unsurpassable Greatness, possible existence entails necessary, and therefore actual, existence.

NOTES

I am grateful to the Baylor Institute for Studies of Religion for funding my attendance at the conference at which a first draft of this chapter was presented, and to Trent Dougherty for his detailed comments on subsequent drafts.

1. The ontological argument is commonly said to have originated with Anselm of Canterbury (d. 1108), although some have suggested that versions of the argument may be found in Plato (b. 429/423 BCE) (e.g., 1945, 509d–511e, 221–226 (see Johnson 1963 and Murdoch 1992, 392 and Chapter 13 passim); Chrysippus (280–207 BCE), Cicero (106–43 BCE), and Augustine (354–430 CE) (Vergnes 1924, 576–579, quoted in Fakhry 1986, 6); and the ninth-century Neo-Platonist John Scotus Eriugena (d. c. 877 CE) (Draesseke 1907, 326ff, quoted in Fakhry, 7). Majid Fakhry notes that all of these converge on the Platonic tradition, which had a profound influence on the development of Arabic philosophy, and thus that we should not be surprised to find a well-developed parallel to Anselm's argument in the writings of Abû Nasr al-Fârâbî (d. 950) (Fakhry, 7).

2. Unlike Charles Hartshorne (1941) and Norman Malcolm (2003 (1960)), Plantinga does not appear to distinguish between two versions of Anselm's argument. For Plantinga, "necessary existence is a great-making quality . . . one of the qualities that must be considered in comparing a pair of beings with respect to greatness." (1974a, 212).

3. Plantinga gives as an example Argument B, which runs as follows: 1. Either $7 + 5 = 13$ or God exists; 2. $7+5 \neq 13$, therefore 3. God exists (1974a, 217).

4. An argument of the form "If P then Q; P; therefore Q."

5. If a proof is "an argument which all rational or properly disposed subjects *ought* to find cogent or convincing whether they in fact do so or not" (Wainwright 2012, 20), Murdoch makes a surprisingly strong claim on behalf of her argument.

6. Plantinga offers a similar interpretation of Kant at 1974a, 212.

7. The argument that supplements and supports Anselm's first or logical argument of *Proslogion* 2 and 3 in which Anselm argues that that which is perfect, the "object" of our best thoughts, must, in some sense, exist (Murdoch 1992, 404).

8. This, it might be noted, has much in common with al-Fârâbî's earlier version of the argument. From Aristotle's argument that immaterial entities are of varying degrees of perfection (*Metaphysics*, XII, 8), al-Fârâbî draws the conclusion that "despite their multiplicity they (that is, the immaterial entities) rise from the lowest thereof to the higher, and then the highest, until

they terminate ultimately in a perfect being (kāmil), nothing more perfect than which can exist; nor can anything be of equal rank in point of being with it" (1953, 89, quoted in Fakhry 1986, 12). This being is (i) pre-eternal, since it precedes all other entities, (ii) the one, because it imparts unity to everything else, and (iii) the true or real, because it has imparted reality to everything else (Fakhry, 12). Al-Fârâbî concludes that "the being who possesses these attributes is the being who ought to be believed to be God Almighty" (1953, 90, quoted in Fakhry, 12). This argument also has much in common with the Fourth Way of Aquinas (1225–1274) (2008 (1920) (1265–1274), I; 2: 3), and some similarities with the "degrees of Reality" argument in the work of Muhammad Iqbal (1877–1938) (2012 (1934), 57–58).

9. Malcolm argues that God is a concept the necessity of which is supported by the human experience of overwhelming guilt and the need for forgiveness. Murdoch responds that this is not a sufficiently common experience, whereas everyone has the experience of making moral judgments—of seeing that some things are more or less good than others, and inferring from this that there must be some kind of ultimate moral standard (Murdoch 1992, 408). But perhaps Malcolm and Murdoch are not so far apart as Murdoch claims. If, as Murdoch suggests, all human beings are able to make moral judgments, and no human being is capable of perfection (Murdoch suggests that Sigmund Freud (1856–1939) offers us an updated version of the doctrine of original sin (1985, 51)), then every human being must be at some level conscious of failure to live up to the moral standards he/she perceives. The difference between Malcolm and Murdoch might therefore be merely one of degree.

10. It might be argued that, in saying that goodness cannot be "thought away," Murdoch is claiming that belief in goodness may be regarded as a kind of basic or warranted belief that is prompted by human experience of an ultimate reality—that is, as something analogous to Plantinga's properly basic or warranted beliefs, which are the product of a sensus divinitatits (Plantinga 2000: 437–457).

11. Another version of an "onto-cosmological argument" may be found in Vallicella (2000).

REFERENCES

Al-Farabi. 1953 (10th century CE). *Cata'logo de los ciencias*, ed. Angel Gonzalez Palencia, second edition (Madrid).

Anselm. 1962a (1077–1078). *Proslogium*, in S.N. Deane (trans.) *St Anselm: Basic Writings*, tr. La Salle, IL: Open Court Publishing Company, 47–80.

———. 1962b (1077–1078). *Anselm's Apologetic: In Reply to Gaunilon's Answer in Behalf of the Fool*, in S.N. Deane (trans.), *St Anselm: Basic Writings*, tr. La Salle, IL: Open Court Publishing Company, 311–328.

Aquinas, Thomas. 2008 (1920) (1265–1274). *The Summa Theologica of St Thomas Aquinas*, tr. Fathers of the English Dominican Province, http://www.newadvent.org/summa/ Part I, Question 2, Article 3.

Burns, Elizabeth D. 2015. "Classical and Revisionary Theism on the Divine as Personal: A Rapprochement?" *International Journal for Philosophy of Religion* 78, no. 2: 151–165. DOI 10.1007/s11153-014-9500-3.

Davies, Brian. 2004. *An Introduction to the Philosophy of Religion*. Oxford: Oxford University Press.

Draesseke, J. 1907. "Zur Frage nach dem Einfluss des Johannes Scotus Eriugena," *Zeitschrift für Wissenschaftliche Theologie* 50: 326ff.

Fakhry, Majid. 1986. "The Ontological Argument in the Arabic Tradition: The Case of Al-Farabi," *Studia Islamica* 64: 5–17.

Fendt, Gene. 2005. "The Relation of *Monologion* and *Proslogion*," *The Heythrop Journal* 46: 149–166.

Hartshorne, Charles. 1941. *Man's Vision of God*. New York: Harper and Row.

Iqbal, Muhammad. 2012 (1934). *The Reconstruction of Religious Thought in Islam,* ed. M. Saeed Sheikh. Stanford, CA: Stanford University Press.

Johnson, J. Prescott. 1963. "The Ontological Argument in Plato," *The Personalist* 44: 24–34.

Kant, Immanuel. 1996 (1793). *Religion Within the Boundaries of Mere Reason*, in *Religion and Rational Theology*, trans. Allen W. Wood and George Di Giovanni. Cambridge: Cambridge University Press, 39–215.

———. 1929 (1787) (1781). *Immanuel Kant's Critique of Pure Reason*, trans. Norman Kemp Smith. London: Macmillan.

Law, Stephen. 2010. "The Evil-God Challenge," *Religious Studies* 46, no. 3: 353–373.

Malcolm, Norman. 2003 (1960). "Anselm's Ontological Arguments," *The Philosophical Review* 69: 41–62, reprinted in C. Taliaferro and P. Griffiths (eds.), 2003, *Philosophy of Religion: An Anthology* Oxford: Blackwell, 271–281.

Murdoch, Iris. 1985. *The Sovereignty of Good*. London: ARK.

———. 1992. *Metaphysics as a Guide to Morals*. London: Chatto and Windus.

Plantinga, Alvin. 1974a. *The Nature of Necessity*. Oxford: Oxford University Press.

———. 1974b. *God, Freedom and Evil*. London: George, Allen and Unwin.

———. 2000. *Warranted Christian Belief*. Oxford: OUP.

Plato. 1945 (c 380 BCE). *Republic*, trans. Francis MacDonald Cornford. Oxford: Oxford University Press.

Putnam, Hilary. 1969. "Is Logic Empirical?" *Boston Studies in Philosophy of Science* 5. Dordrecht: D. Riedel, 216–241.

Vallicella, William F. 2000. "From Facts to God: An Onto-cosmological Argument," *International Journal for Philosophy of Religion* 48: 157–181.

Vergnes, Jules. 1924. "Les sources de l'argument de Saint Anselme," *Revue des Sciences Religieuses* 4: 576–579.

Wainwright, William J. 2012. "Assessing Ontological Arguments," *European Journal for Philosophy of Religion* 4, no. 2: 19–39.

(I)

Why Is There Anything at All?

Joshua Rasmussen and Christopher Gregory Weaver

INTRODUCTION

THERE ARE CONCRETE things: atoms, antelopes, and armchairs, for example. But why? Why isn't the world instead empty of all concrete things? Imagine a reality that fundamentally consists of nothing but empty space—or for that matter no space at all. Why isn't reality like *that*?

We are intrigued by a simple answer: there is something concrete because there must be. Yet this answer inspires a further question: why must there be something concrete? The traditional answer is that there is a necessarily existing concrete thing or things capable of causing or grounding everything else. Call this theory "Necessary Foundation."

Necessary Foundation is certainly a significant theory. It provides a framework for thinking about cosmogonic theories, since it implies that there is a necessary foundation capable of causing or grounding the cosmos. Moreover, the theory contradicts a version of metaphysical nihilism (according to which there could fail to be concrete things), since Necessary Foundation implies that there must be at least one concrete thing. Third, the theory has this theological ramification: it implies that God, if God exists, would be a necessary being (assuming that no foundation could cause or ground the existence of God). Fourth, and perhaps most significantly, Necessary Foundation answers one of the deepest "why" questions humans have asked—why is there anything at all?

But is Necessary Foundation true?

We will develop a new pathway toward Necessary Foundation. The steps along the way are inspired by developments in the literature on modality and causation, and the resulting argument builds upon recent work on causal-based arguments for a necessary being.[1] Although our investigation is exploratory, we believe that the pathway we mark out provides a means by which someone could become rationally inclined to think, or at least strongly suspect, that Necessary Foundation is true.

Even more speculatively, we will propose a way to extend the pathway from Necessary Foundation all the way to theism. We will again rely on recent developments in modality and causation.[2] The result is a pathway of reason that, in effect, begins with an ultimate "why" question and ends with a broadly theistic explanation of contingent reality.

CAUSE AND EFFECT

Ordinary language includes talk of things causing things. We say such things as "a fire caused their house to fall down," or "his smoking was a cause of his lung cancer," or "the political speech caused riots in the streets." And so on. Let us assume that at least some of these things we say are true. Then some things, at least, are caused by other things.

Which things are caused? Here is the simplest answer: any. If "things" includes pluralities, then the answer amounts to this:

(C1) $\forall xs \, (\exists ys \, (ys \triangleright xs))$, where "$ys \triangleright xs$" reads "the ys are the causes of the xs."

Principle (C1) says that each and every thing and things has a cause. There is much to like about this principle. It has the widest possible explanatory scope. It thus accounts for every single case of cause and effect in our world. Moreover, the principle enjoys theoretical simplicity, where simplicity is measured in terms of the number of basic, primitive terms required to express the principle. Finally, the principle is consistent with everything we can justify on solely empirical grounds.[3]

Sadly, however, (C1) is marred by a fatal vice: falsehood. The principle is false because there are no causes of *all* things together (where the xs occupy the entire domain: everything). For suppose there are causes, Cs, of all things. Then the Cs are among the very things they are causes of, which results in causal circularity. Genuine causation cannot run in a circle, we say.[4] Therefore, there is no cause of all things. Therefore, (C1) is false: some things lack a cause.

If the argument against (C1) is sound, then, although some things (plural) have a cause, others do not. What might account for the difference between the caused and the uncaused?

There are many proposals, but perhaps the most famous is the proposal that the division between the caused and the uncaused coincides with the division between the contingent and the necessary. A motivation for this proposal is that contingent realities might not have obtained, and one might expect that there needs to be an explanation, then, of why they in fact obtain rather than not. A cause of their reality would enable that explanation (cf. Pruss 2006). Necessary realities, by contrast, cannot have been otherwise, and in fact, it is not so clear how necessary realities even *could* be caused to exist.[5] Therefore, a necessary reality is a good candidate for an uncaused reality. We may state the resulting causal principle as follows:

(C2) $\forall xs\,(C(xs) \rightarrow \exists ys\,(ys \rhd xs))$, where "$C(xs)$" reads "x exists or obtains, and it is not necessary that *x* exists or obtains."

This principle restricts the scope to contingent things, and it says that any and all of them have at least one cause. Unfortunately, there are challenging objections to this principle. Perhaps the most important is the Rowe-Ross-van Inwagen objection, which is basically that there can't be a cause of the totality of contingent things, since any external cause would be non-contingent and would thus have only non-contingent effects.[6] Moreover, one may object that certain contingent things aren't of the right category to be caused: for example, one might think that contingent events have a cause but that contingent substances do not. Although the objections are by no means decisive, we prefer to use a less contentious principle to build an argument for a Necessary Foundation.

The logically weakest causal principles in the literature on arguments for a necessary being take the following form (or something in the neighborhood):

Possibly, some reality (entity or entities) of type T has a cause.

For example, we could conceive of the argument by Gale & Pruss (1999) as an argument for the principle that, possibly, there is a cause of a reality of the following type: a contingent fact consisting of the actual world's contingent facts.[7] Rasmussen (2010a) argues for the principle that, possibly, there is a cause of a thing of the type "maximal contingent state of existence." Elsewhere, Rasmussen (2011) argues for the principle that possibly, there is a cause of a thing of the type, "a beginning of an exemplification of contingency." Turri (2011) gives a related argument with the premise that, possibly, there is a cause of a thing of the type, "the first contingent causal power." These causal principles may seem easier to accept than the causal principles in traditional cosmological arguments.

We will offer an argument whose causal principle has the same weakened form, but which is even more restricted than each of the examples just outlined. An initial statement of the principle is as follows:

(C3) $\Diamond \exists x \exists y\,((y \rhd x)\, \&\, T(x))$, where "$T(x)$" reads "x is a totality event consisting of all purely contingent events."

The principle says that it is possible that there is a cause of a totality of purely contingent events. To be clear, the possibility in question is one in which the effect is a totality of purely contingent events, where the cause is not included within the effect. In the next section, we will give a more precise metaphysical account of purely contingent events. But a rough idea suffices for now. Think of events that contain only contingent things. So, for example, a tree falling, star exploding, and car coming into being count as purely contingent events (assuming trees, stars, and cars are not necessary beings).

The term "possibility" expresses metaphysical possibility, which we understand as consistency with the absolutely necessary truths. Absolutely necessary truths are what Alvin Plantinga calls "broadly logically necessary": they include truths of logic and also necessary non-logical truths, such as that no odd number is capable of sneezing (see Plantinga 1974, 2). We take it that metaphysical necessity and possibility are characterized by certain key axioms of S5 quantified modal logic.[8] (If there are doubts here, let us stipulate that the notions of "necessity" and "possibility" we shall be working with are implicitly defined by those axioms. It will be interesting enough if there is a necessary being, where such a being exists no matter what possible situation obtains, and where "possibility" is understood in terms of those axioms.)

So (C3) says it is possible for there to be a cause of a certain totality of events. Why believe that?

We will sketch three reasons in support of (C3). First, (C3) follows from a more general, independently supported principle of causation:

$$(C4) \quad \forall x \big(C(x) \rightarrow \Diamond \exists y \, (y \triangleright x) \big)$$

This principle says that every contingently existing or obtaining thing possibly has a cause.

Some philosophers may wish to adjust the principle to suit their preferred theory of causation. For example, if you think only events are the proper relata of causation, then translate "$y \triangleright x$" so it reads "y causes an event whose occurrence entails that x exists or obtains."[9] Or you might prefer to restrict the quantifier to contingent states of affairs, or to purely contingent states, or to some similar category. There is a variety of options consistent with the spirit of (C4).

Principle (C4) fits with a wide range of data, including (i) our experience with contingent things (states, events, etc.) having a cause, and (ii) our lack of experience with uncaused contingent things.[10] Moreover, it makes modest demands: it only requires the possibility of a cause. If there are counterexamples, they are few and far between.[11] Thus, we propose that (C4) is at least a good rule of thumb: that is, for any given case of a contingent thing, its contingency provides defeasible evidence for its causability.

From (C4), we may deduce (C3) as follows. Let "E" be a totality event consisting of purely contingent events in our world. Then let S be the state of affairs of E's occurring while in a world where E is the totality of purely contingent events. S obtains contingently, since E occurs contingently. So S is causable, given (C4). But causing S requires causing a totality of purely contingent events. Therefore, (C4) implies (C3). As a result, our support for (C4) may contribute to our support for (C3).[12] (This argument may be weakened somewhat by the worry that S is a prime candidate for being a counterexample to (C4), but the next consideration mitigates that worry.)

A second reason in support of (C3) is based upon causal relevance. Suppose some things are caused, while others are not. What relevant difference might there be between the caused and uncaused things? We suggested earlier that a difference between necessity and contingency may seem to be causally relevant. But there is a more modest way to proceed. Take any arbitrary contingent thing and consider whether there is a reason to think that the thing in question differs in a causally relevant way from things that are known to have a cause. In cases in which one lacks such a reason, one lacks a reason to make an exception to the rule of thumb expressed by (C4). And, in cases in which one has a reason to think the differences are not causally relevant, one has an additional "causal uniformity" reason to think that the contingent thing in question is causable.[13]

Does a totality of purely contingent events differ from other purely contingent events in a way that is causally relevant? We'll give one reason to think not. To begin, consider the following states of affairs:

s1: *there being exactly 1 purely contingent event*
s2: *there being exactly 2 purely contingent events*
s3: *there being exactly 3 purely contingent events*

Notice that these states differ by a mere *quantity* of events. You might think mere quantitative differences aren't normally relevant to causal possibility. That is, if there could be a cause of s3, then there could be a cause of s2, and if there could be a cause of s2, then there could be a cause of the smaller state, s1. This inference is supported by what Rasmussen (2014) calls "modal continuity." Rasmussen argues that situations that differ by a mere quantitative term are normally modally unified: if the one is possible, then we have a defeasible reason to expect its neighbors are also possible. We should emphasize that the reason is defeasible, since there are plenty of breaks in modal continuity. The point is just that modal breaks are surprising in arbitrary cases. The idea, then, is that if there could be a cause of s3, then we have a defeasible reason to expect that there could be a cause of s1. The states are causally uniform.

From the causal uniformity of these states, we may extract a reason in support of (C3). To do this, observe first that causal uniformity implies that s1 is causable if s3 is causable. We don't expect it to be controversial that there could be a cause of s3 (where a cause of s3 could be analyzed as a cause of something in virtue of which s3 obtains).[14] For example, there could be two purely contingent events that give rise to a third. In this situation, the two events jointly cause s3 to obtain. So, by causal uniformity, we have some reason to expect that it is possible that there is a cause of s1. What could cause s1? No purely contingent event can cause there to be exactly one purely contingent event, since that would require that an event cause its own existence.[15] So, a cause of s1 must instead be external to the single-member totality of purely contingent events. (C3) follows.

Note here that we leave open whether there may be causally relevant differences between events that are purely contingent and those that are not. We focus on purely contingent events if only to restrict our focus on cases where causal relevance appears clearer. Yet, we do not make any claim about whether causal irrelevance also extends beyond our scope. It may.[16]

Third, the main modal epistemologies on offer provide some epistemic justification for (C3).[17] We will focus on just one such epistemology: Chalmers's conceivability tests (2002).

Chalmers develops various notions of conceivability and shows how they may guide us into reliable judgments about metaphysical possibilities. The most reliable guide packs into the notion of conceivability two great-making properties: being positive and being ideal.[18] Conceiving a situation S is positive when one is able to coherently imagine a situation in which S obtains. For example, I can positively conceive of there being a regular polyhedron with fewer than ten sides by imagining a cube. Or, I can positively conceive of there being more than twenty animals in my coat closet by imagining twenty turtles stacked on top of each other. Chalmers understands "imagination" as broader than visual imaging (like in a vivid dream), since an imagination can include a conceptual or intuitive representation, such as when one brings to mind the details of a logic or math proof. Although one may further scrutinize the notion of coherent imagination, we believe it is a familiar enough notion to give us some grip on the concept of positive conceivability.[19]

Conceivability comes in degrees of epistemic strength. In its strongest form, it is ideal. Conceivability is ideal if no amount of further scrutinizing would or could reveal incoherence in what one is imagining. We could think of this in terms of an ideal rational agent: if a perfect cognizer is able to (positively) conceive the situation in question, then the situation is ideally (positively) conceivable. Or, we could think of ideal conceivability in terms of indefeasible conceivability: as far as one can tell, one can (positively) conceive of S, and there is nothing one could learn that would reveal incoherence in one's conception.[20] In either case, ideal (positive) conceivability is strong evidence of possibility—and may even entail possibility. But even without ideal conceivability, one can enjoy prima facie (upon initial inspection) or secunda (upon further inspection) conceivability. These notions provide varying degrees of justification for modal judgments, where the more we inspect, the more justification our modal judgments may enjoy.

For our purposes, it will be useful to bring in one more notion: primary conceivability. Chalmers introduces this notion to deal with cases involving opaque contexts, as in "Hesperus is not Phosphorus." In these cases, it may seem that conceivability is unreliable: for example, we can easily imagine a world where the star that rises in the evening is not the same as the star that rises in the morning, even though such a world is impossible (since the actual evening star cannot fail to be the actual morning star). There are different ways one might deal with these cases. Chalmers proposes that in such contexts there are actually two importantly different modal statements with two corresponding senses of conceivability. Without going into all the details, the basic distinction is between the purely a priori elements of (say) "Hesperus is not Phosphorus," on the one hand, and a posteriori–sensitive elements (like that Hesperus *is* Phosphorus), on the other. Primary conceivability doesn't turn on a posteriori truths—it's entirely a priori. Fortunately, in our argument we may restrict ourselves to statements that don't admit of opaque contexts, and so we may work entirely with a priori (primary) conceivability.

With Chalmers's conceivability tests in hand, let us now return to our causal principle, (C3), which says that, possibly, there is a cause of a purely contingent totality event. Does conceivability justify (C3)? According to Chalmers, it does to the extent that we can imagine a situation in which a totality event has a cause. So consider the following scenario. There is a supremely powerful entity E (whose nature we leave unspecified), which is capable of causing any and every purely contingent event, including a totality event. We may imagine, for example, that whatever event can occur could be caused by E. Or if that is too much to imagine, then imagine merely that E causes whatever purely contingent events happen to occur. Or if even that is too much, then imagine a particularly big contingent event, which is known to be causable, like a galaxy forming, and then imagine that E causes that event. Now add to your imagination empty space around the caused event so that there are no other purely contingent events. The imagined galaxy is now a totality of purely contingent events, and no incoherence is revealed by supposing that it still has a cause. These imaginations are prima facie and secunda coherent, and thus, by Chalmers's lights, they provide prima facie and secunda evidence for the metaphysical possibility of the imagined situation. We have thus identified a third line of potential support for our causal principle. (In our "Objections" section, we will address the worry that conceivability considerations may cut against our argument from another direction.)

FROM CAUSATION TO NECESSARY EXISTENCE

We are now ready to put together our argument for a necessarily existent, causally potent foundation of reality. The argument is as follows:

(P1) It is possible that there is a purely contingent totality event that has a cause.

(P2) It is impossible that a cause of a purely contingent totality event is purely contingent.

(P3) If, (a) it is possible that there is a purely contingent totality event that has a cause and (b) it is impossible that a cause of a purely contingent totality event is purely contingent, then (c) it is possible that there is a cause that isn't purely contingent.

∴ Therefore, (c) it is possible that there is a cause that isn't purely contingent.

(P4) If (c) it is possible that there is a cause that isn't purely contingent, then (d) there is a necessary thing that can be a cause.

∴ Therefore, (d) there is a necessary thing that can be a cause.

Let us have a closer look at the premises. (P1) simply expresses the causal principle we motivated in the previous section. Recall we gave three independent reasons for the principle: from causal relevance, from inductive generalization, and from conceivability. We'll examine potential defeaters in the objections section.

We add here just that (P1)'s modesty is hardly diminished by Kripke's (1980, 110–115) doctrine that a thing's origin is essential to it. For suppose there can be a contingent totality that lacks a cause. Then, assuming Kripke's origin thesis, there can be a contingent totality that cannot have a cause. But it doesn't follow that there cannot be a contingent totality that can have a cause. There are presumably infinitely many possible contingent totalities, and the claim that possibly some of them cannot have a cause is far away from the claim that, necessarily, none of them can have a cause.

Turn next to (P2), which says that a purely contingent totality event can't have a purely contingent cause. The motivation for this premise is a "no circularity" condition on causation. More exactly, we will assume that a cause cannot be identical to or wholly included within its effect. On this conception, a cause of a purely contingent totality event must itself be an event that is not purely contingent. We intend this assumption to be stipulative: it orients us to the concept of the causation at work in (P2). (The arguments given in support of (P2) lose nothing on this conception of causation.)

Premise (P3) records the inference from the premises just stated to the conclusion that it is possible that there is a cause that isn't purely contingent. This inference is justified by the following schema:

Possibly, there is an F.
Necessarily, no F is a G.

∴ Therefore, possibly, there is an F that is not a G. To see the inference in (P3), let F = "a cause of a purely contingent totality event," and G = "a purely contingent cause."

The final premise is (P4), which links the possibility of a non-purely-contingent cause with an actually existing Necessary Foundation. The inference here takes two steps: a metaphsics-y one, and a logic-y one. Start with metaphysics. Let us suppose that an event is any complex consisting of a substance or mereological fusion of two or more substances contingently exemplifying a universal at a time. This account may remind you of other contemporary accounts of events, such as property exemplification, fact (in the truth-maker sense), concrete states of affairs, change, and property instance theories.[21] Fortunately, we may run our argument in terms of most of these theories, but for presentation sake, we'll focus on just one theory. We may now understand a purely contingent event as follows: "x is a purely contingent event" = "x is an event, and every substance or mereological fusion of two or more substances that is a constituent of x is contingent."

Purely contingent events are different from merely contingent events. An event may be merely contingent and yet fail to be purely contingent by having as a constituent a necessarily existing substance though the event itself could have failed to occur. Purely contingent events only ever involve contingent substances or fusions of such contingent substances. We are now ready to precisely characterize a purely contingent totality event: it's a purely contingent event that includes all contingent substances that there are (relative to some possible world).

Now for the logic-y part. Go to a possible world at which a purely contingent totality event E has a cause C. (P1) tells us there is such a world. Since E exhausts the world's purely contingent profile, C must either be a purely necessary event, or a barely necessary event, assuming the no circularity condition expressed by (P2). Now a purely necessary event's substance-constituents are necessary substances solely, and such an event itself is necessary. A barely necessary event is one that features at least one necessary being as a substance-constituent. If either type of event is the relevant cause, then there could be an entity that is both necessarily existent and such that it can be a cause (in the sense that it is a substance-constituent of a cause). So, in either case, Necessary Foundation is possibly true. Then, given our S5 axioms, Necessary Foundation follows.[22]

OBJECTIONS AND REPLIES

We will consider a couple objections to the causal principle in our argument.

Objection 1. The conceivability test used in support of the causal principle equally supports the possibility of there being a world in which there fails to exist a causally potent being (i.e., a being with causal powers). Thus, we have the following counterargument:

(1) Possibly, there is no causally potent being.[23]

(2) If (1), then it is not the case that there is a necessary (essentially) causally potent being.

(3) Therefore, it is not the case that there is a necessary (essentially) causally potent being.

Reply. The argument isn't parallel. Consider that positive conceivability of an absence of a causally potent being is only possible if we can successfully and coherently imagine a situation in which there is an absence of any and all causally potent beings. Perhaps we can imagine an empty space in which all actual contingent things are subtracted. But what if there could be a necessarily existent, non-spatial thing? Are we able to imagine or conceptually represent its absence? Can we imagine or conceptually represent the absence of the number 9? Answers are far from obvious. Furthermore, it is far from obvious that we can imagine or conceptually represent the absence of a necessary entity that can cause something to exist. Such imagining is modally complex in a way that parallels the modal complexity of Necessary Foundation itself. It seems to us, therefore, that Chalmers's conceivability tests do not justify (1). Or, to be a bit more modest, we suggest that the conceivability test provides no more justification for the possibility of no Necessary Foundation than for the possibility of Necessary Foundation, and that, therefore, the conceivability test doesn't directly favor one possibility over the other. Meanwhile, the conceivability-based support for the causal principle remains undefeated (not to mention the other lines of support).

Objection 2. Our argument will not run if an especially strong version of causal reductionism is true. The causal reductionism we have in mind says that causal properties logically supervene on non-causal properties. Michael Tooley nicely explicates the basic idea as follows:

> Any two worlds that agree with respect to all of the non-causal properties of, and relations between, particulars, must also agree with respect to all of the causal relations between . . . [events]. Causal relations are, in short, logically supervenient upon non-causal properties and relations.[24]

We should add that the causal reductionism (CR) we have in mind goes further. It says that the non-causal properties in the subvenient base have strictly to do with those properties that build up law-governed physical history (and where the laws doing the governing are non-causal natural or physical laws). Thus, CR asserts that causal relations logically supervene upon law-governed physical history. Importantly, though, supervenience relations are ordinarily superdupervenience relations, since such relations require explanation.[25] There are a number of potential explanations available to reductionists. To illustrate by means of just one example, contemporary metaphysics has been enthralled by the idea of grounding, and one might insist that, necessarily, history and natural nomicity ground obtaining causal relations and that that is why causation logically supervenes upon the grounding base.[26] Given, in particular, Jonathan Schaffer's (2009) theory of grounding, an entity x is grounded by another entity y, just in case, x depends for its positive ontological status, and nature, on y. In order to deliver an appropriate explanation in this context, the proponent of a causal reductionism that explains logical supervenience via grounding should add that law-governed physical history grounds causation at every world at which there exist obtaining causal relations. Let us call this distinctive brand of causal reductionism CR*.

If one does not see the problem CR* poses for our argument, then consider the following: If CR* holds, then causation is necessarily grounded in the natural or physical. Presumably, a necessary causally potent being is neither natural nor physical, since a possible world with no space-time manifold is presumably a real metaphysical possibility. A necessary causally potent entity seems to be one that is not grounded by the physical. Its positive ontological status and nature does not depend upon the physical law-governed cosmos. Thus, if CR* holds, then it is difficult to see how a necessary causally potent being could causally produce anything.

The committed naturalist might see no problem at all with the conjunction that is our conclusion and CR*. Such a naturalist may align themselves with Graham Oppy's recent work, for Oppy (2015) maintains that the naturalist is within her epistemic rights in claiming that there exists a necessary causally potent entity that is itself the physical and natural universe, or perhaps the initial state of that universe (call this Oppy's Thesis, or OT).

We do not recommend Oppy's response to the objection at hand. There are two reasons for this. First, OT rests upon an idiosyncratic conception of the natural. Consider the fact that, according to Oppy, a "natural entity cannot exist except as an occupant of a location in the manifold of natural reality."[27] But one of the leading canonical quantization approaches to quantum gravity (loop quantum gravity, or LQG) suggests that the correct geometry of space at the Planck scale is a quantized discrete geometry revealed in s-knot states (for the diffeomorphism invariant level) and a veritable tapestry of weaved spin networks (or states) of the background metric known as weave states (for the non-diffeomorphism invariant level).[28] Importantly, though, these s-knot and spin networks build the very structure of space, and they are not themselves spatially located. Thus, by Oppy's lights, the s-knot and spin states of LQG are not natural. Next, suppose that a space-time substantivalism motivated by the approximate truth of the orthodox interpretation of the general theory of relativity holds.[29] On such a view, space-time is an eternal four-dimensional differentiable manifold. Space-time, in other words, is an entity. However, it does not itself occupy "a location in the manifold"; it is itself the manifold. Should we really regard general relativistic space-times as supernatural entities? The suggestion strains credulity.

These complications arise only if OT rests upon Oppy's particular conception of the natural. Put them aside for now and assume they can be resolved. What is wrong with regarding the universe as a necessary causally potent entity? Well, a lot depends on what's meant by "universe." Is "universe" being regarded in this context as a rigid designator (Kripke 1980), a proper name of sorts for all of physical or natural reality? If so, then we must return again to properly informatively analyzing "natural" or "physical." One way of cashing out that notion is in terms of what's indispensable to our best scientific theories, or else that which can be explained by our best scientific theories. The challenge here, however, is that there's no evidence that any of our best scientific theories has need of a necessary causally potent being; nor is there evidence for the claim that a necessary causally potent being of some variety is actually explained by any of our best scientific theories. But what if the term "universe" is not a rigid term, but is instead a way of flaccidly designating the sum or arrangement of all of the actual natural entities? On such a supposition, Oppy's necessary causally potent universe does not exist. We are not necessary causally potent beings.[30]

Moreover, even if one can overcome these difficulties (maintaining, perhaps, that an initial state of our universe could somehow be constituted by a necessary, natural causally potent being), CR* is in conflict with arguments we give in the final section, according to which the causal foundation would be an immaterial God. We will therefore grant the objector's premise that a necessary causally potent foundation cannot be part of a purely physical causal base.

Reply. Note, first, that if one's reductionism about causation were significantly weaker than CR*, such that it was motivated by the Humean supervenience thesis (HST), for example, then our argument would be unscathed. This is because the HST asserts that the fundamental level (FL) is comprised of local categorical, qualitative, and intrinsic properties and spatio-temporal relations of such properties (particularly their instantiations), and that all else globally supervenes upon FL.[31] In other words, FL is "a vast mosaic of local matters of particular fact, just one little thing and then another . . . an arrangement of qualities. And that is all."[32] But the HST is a contingent truth, if true. Some possible worlds may feature different derivative structures though their fundamental structures match exactly. So, according to the HST, there can be worlds at which causal properties are not determined by non-causal properties that are constitutive of law governed physical or natural history, and that is all our argument will require.[33]

There are theoreticians whose theories of causation do not pretend to inform us about the nature of causation at distant metaphysically possible worlds.[34] Ignoring for now the question of whether or not one should be in the business of merely providing an empirically adequate theory of causation that at best holds at the actual world and worlds very much akin to it (cf. Collins, Hall, and Paul 2004, 14), we stress that the argument of this section goes through given any of the merely empirically adequate reductive theories of causation, since they are at best contingent truths if true.

But, again, what of the stronger form of causal reductionism, specifically CR* mentioned earlier? Against these stronger (in terms of modal force) reductive theories, we advance a report: there is widespread consensus that all such theories fail, and fail miserably. As two foremost experts on causation noted:

> After surveying the literature in some depth, we conclude that, as yet, there is no reasonably successful reduction of the causal relation. And correspondingly, there is no reasonably successful conceptual analysis of a philosophical causal concept. No extant approach seems able to incorporate all of our desiderata for the causal relation, nor to capture the wide range of our causal judgments and applications of our causal concept. Barring a fundamental change in approach, the prospects of a relatively simple, elegant and intuitively attractive, unified theory of causation, whether ontological reduction or conceptual analysis, are dim.[35]

Given our contemporary philosophical milieu, we believe it is safe to shift the burden of proof onto the proponent of CR*. If one would like to resist our argument in this section by defending one's favorite strong reductionist theory of causation, one is entitled to travel that road. But be warned: there are multifarious cases of preemption and/or overdetermination, and not a few strong reductionist theories have fallen victim to them.[36]

FROM NECESSARY EXISTENCE TO MAXIMAL GREATNESS

The greatest conceivable causal foundation would, intuitively, enjoy the most robust form of existence—necessary existence. But would a necessary causal foundation be the greatest conceivable?

We'll build a tentative bridge from necessary existence to maximal greatness using materials from the previous sections. We will proceed by considering what kind of thing a necessary causal foundation might plausibly be. In particular, we will show that, given our principle of modal continuity, there is a defeasible reason to think that a necessary foundation would be great to a maximal degree.

The thrust of our argument is that the totality of necessary concrete reality cannot have arbitrary non-maximal limits with respect to its basic, uncaused attributes. We will begin by applying our strategy to the attributes of causal power and geometric form. Then we will see how the argument may work for degrees of greatness.

Causal Power

Let "N" refer to the totality of the necessary causal foundation. (We leave open whether "N" picks out a single thing, sum of things, or a plural of things.) Assume there is such a thing (or things) as N.

How much causal power does N have in total? N has at least some causal power, if our previous arguments go through. For example, N could cause a purely contingent totality event. To pick just one measure of power, we may consider how many bosons, fermions, and/or fields (BForFs) it can produce within (say) one second. If N can produce all of the BForFs, then we may say that it has at least ten units of causal power. Accordingly, N's causal power is no less than the most amount of BForFs it can produce. How much is that?

Suppose there is an upper limit m, such that N cannot produce more than m units of BForFs. So, for example, say that N can produce at most one trillion units. In that case, the following two propositions are both true:

1. There *can* be a purely contingent totality involving one trillion units of BForFs.
2. There *cannot* be a purely contingent totality involving one trillion and one unit of BForFs.

These propositions mark a break in modal continuity. This break is unexpected, however. We have no reason, as far as we are aware, to think there must be an upper bound with respect to how many units of BForFs are metaphysically possible. We have no reason to think that, for example, there couldn't be a contingent totality of (say) one quadrillion units of BForFs. And we doubt that one could in principle attain such a reason. But if we lack a reason to expect an upper limit, then by the principle of modal continuity, we have an undefeated reason to think that there would be no such upper bound. Thus, we may suppose, instead, that if there can be a beginning of m units of BForFs, then there can be a beginning of m + 1 units of BForFs, for any *m*. If that's right, then we have a reason to infer that there is no upper limit to the amount of units of BForFs that N can produce. In other words, we have a reason to infer that there is no upper limit to N's causal power, if N's causal power is measured in terms of what N can produce.

Our conclusion so far is just that N in total has unlimited causal power. But modal continuity equally applies to causally potent members or parts of N (if there are any). An upper bound on their powers would be arbitrary, and modal continuity leads us to expect that there is no such boundary.

There is a corollary. Modal continuity gives us a reason to think that every conceivable degree of causal power alike can be instantiated. Suppose there is a greatest conceivable degree of causal power—omnipotence suitably defined.[37] Then modal continuity gives us a reason to think a greatest conceivable degree of causal power can be instantiated. What could instantiate such a power? Clearly, if anything can, N can, since N is a source of all possible causal powers. Moreover, unless there is some reason to think that N's unlimited degree of causal power is non-maximal, then modal continuity gives us an undefeated reason to think that N has the greatest conceivable causal power.

There is another corollary. N's causal power is essential to N. This follows from our measure of "causal power" in terms of what N can produce. We are thinking of "can" in the sense of metaphysical possibility. So, if N can produce X, then necessarily, N can produce X—given our modal axioms. (We leave open whether there may be other important senses in which N's causal power "could" vary.)

The argument isn't unassailable. As we see it, the most promising way to block this argument from modal continuity would be to show why there is a break in modal continuity: for example, one may find some reason to think there is an upper limit to the amount of causal power it could take for N to produce a purely contingent totality event. Whether such a reason is available we leave for further inquiry.

Geometry

Modal continuity suggests that N cannot have an essential geometry. To see this, imagine that N, in total, instantiates a certain space-time geometry (or topological and metric structure), G. Let G* be a geometry that would result from offsetting two instances of G. To give a simple illustration, if G were a square, like □, then G* might be two overlapping squares, like ⊓⊔. Of course, in reality G is enormously more complex than a square; it may even be infinitely complex. But in any case, G is not the same as G*. More to the point, the differences between G and G* are accounted for solely in terms of degreed differences in offsets of various shapes. Therefore, by modal continuity, we have a reason to think that N could instead have geometry G*. In other words, we have reason to think that if N has a geometry, it could have had a different one.

This result is especially significant if N's contingent states can be caused. For then N can be an ultimate cause of geometric reality. Moreover, to avoid causal circularity, N can lack a geometry altogether—prior to its causing there to be a geometric reality. There is more. Suppose one thinks that whatever has a geometry must have a geometry. Then one may infer that N is essentially geometric-less and thus immaterial. That's a startling result, though there are multiple places where one might get off before reaching it.

Greatness

The route to unlimited greatness is like the route to unlimited causal power. We observe that N has some extent of greatness (awesomeness, praiseworthiness, value) in virtue of having unlimited power, assuming that unlimited power is itself a great-making attribute. Then we follow modal continuity along the path to unlimited greatness—and perhaps even to maximal conceivable greatness.

What is greatness? We think there is an intuitive, pre-philosophical notion of greatness that is grasped when considering examples of great-making attributes. To illustrate, suppose we praise a being by saying, "you are so great: you have so much power, so much knowledge, and you are terribly wicked." We suspect you'll intuitively see that two of the three attributes are great-making. The third—being terribly wicked—is out of step with the others, precisely because it doesn't contribute to the greatness of a being. If that seems right to you, then you have some grip on what we mean by "greatness."

We should be clear that we have in mind absolute greatness, not relative greatness. Perhaps there could be a greatest lion, or a greatest knife. These are notions of greatness with respect to a specific kind of thing. We have in mind greatness with respect to the most general kind of thing (or more cautiously the most general kind of concrete thing). That is to say, we are interested in the greatness of a thing simpliciter.

We believe that it is possible to see a priori that unlimited causal power is a great-making attribute. Thus, we believe that it is possible to see a priori that N, which has unlimited causal power, has a great-making attribute. Thus, we believe that it is possible to see a priori that N is great to some extent.

The pathway from "N is great to some extent" to "N is great to a maximally conceivable extent" is guided by modal continuity in the usual way. To get us along the path, suppose there is a non-maximal degree of greatness d, such that N can be great to degree d but not to degree $d+1$. Then there is an arbitrary, unexplained modal break in N's potential degree of greatness. To avoid the modal break, we should suppose that N *can* have a maximal degree of greatness (both maximally possible and maximally conceivable). From here, we reach the conclusion that N *is* maximally great if maximal greatness entails essential maximal greatness. The supposition is plausible: maximal greatness intuitively entails essential maximal greatness, for intuitively, the greatest being is the one that has no possibility of falling from greatness. We have thus marked out a pathway to a grand conclusion: there is a causal foundation, such that none greater can be conceived. That is the ultimate reason there is anything.

NOTES

We would like to thank Daniel Z. Korman, Jonathan Livengood, Graham Oppy, Jonathan Schaffer, and Dean Zimmerman for their comments on the chapter. Any mistakes that remain are ours.

1. See Rasmussen (2010a) and Weaver (2016).

2. Cf. Rasmussen (2009).

3. What about so-called virtual particles? Don't they come into being without a cause? We answer that they come into being (apparently) without a logically sufficient cause. But there cannot be an empirical reason to think that causes must be sufficient for their effects. Moreover, on an ordinary use of the term "cause," we may say that Eric's desire to check his email again caused him to refresh his Internet browser even if it was possible for other factors to have prevented him from satisfying that desire in that way.

4. We recognize that causal-loops may be compatible with physical laws, even if they are metaphysically problematic. But in case there are doubts about the impossibility of causal loops, replace occurrences of "cause" with "external cause," where external causes are causes that can't run in a circle (by stipulation). We are interested here in principles of external causation.

5. Someone might think, for example, that causes can exist ontologically prior to—and without—their effects, whereas there cannot be anything that exists prior to—or without—a necessary reality. For our purposes, however, we will leave open whether or not some necessary realities may be caused to exist by a more fundamental necessary reality.

6. Ross, (1969, 295–304); Rowe (1975); van Inwagen (1983, 202–204); cf. the discussion in Pruss (2006, 97–125).

7. Their argument, more exactly, was expressed in terms of a principle of explanation applied to propositions. So, even while their principle is in the neighborhood, there are some important differences.

8. Specifically, we assume the following axioms plus the axioms of classical first-order logic:

$$\textbf{M}: \Box p \rightarrow p$$
$$\textbf{K}: \Box(p \rightarrow q) \rightarrow (\Box p \rightarrow \Box q)$$
$$\textbf{4}: \Box p \rightarrow \Box\Box p$$
$$\textbf{5}: \Diamond p \rightarrow \Box\Diamond p$$

We would like to note that our argument doesn't require **N** (the necessitation rule). We mention this because **N**, together with standard logic, implies that the theorem, $\exists x(x=x)$, is necessary, and thus that there must be something. One may wish to avoid building into the meaning of 'necessity' anything that strictly implies the controversial metaphysical hypothesis that there must be something. In any case, those who wish to preserve the full S5 system may still include **N**. We should add that the statement "$\Box\exists x(x=x)$" is in important respects far from our conclusion.

9. To be a bit more precise: "x causes state of affairs s" = "there is a y, such that (i) x causes y, (ii) necessarily if y exists, then s obtains, and (iii) possibly x exists prior to (or without) the obtaining

of *s*." The last condition accounts for the idea that causes may exist prior to—and so without—their effects.

10. Jonathan Schaffer (among others) have suggested to us that we have exactly parallel support for the thesis that all causes are contingent—which contradicts the conclusion of our argument. The suggestion is reminiscent of a worry Jordan Howard Sobel (2004, 236–237) had for Robert Koons's (1997) cosmological argument.

We see an important difference, however. Let us grant that all the causes we observe are contingent. Still, would our observations be any different if there *were* necessary causes? Consider that if we did glimpse a necessary thing, we would not see that it *is* a necessary reality. How could we? Even if we discover something that we cannot create or destroy, we do not thereby observe that something exists in all possible worlds. We have reason, therefore, to expect our observations to be as they are even if there are necessary causes. By contrast, we have no reason to expect our observations to be as they are if (C_4) is false. On the contrary, if some contingent things can exist without any cause or any possibility of cause, then we might well witness arbitrary and completely disjoint combinations of contingent things entering reality at any moment. Yet we never do. (For a point similar to the last one made, see Craig and Sinclair (2012, 186–187)).

11. There is an objection that (C_4)-like principles ultimately entail a stronger principle that falls prey to the Rowe-Ross–van Inwagen objection mentioned earlier. Here is one way one might attempt to deduce the stronger principle. Suppose every contingent reality is causable. Then if there were an uncaused contingent reality C, then the fact that C is uncaused would itself be causable. But something's being uncaused cannot itself be caused. Therefore, every contingent reality is causable only if every contingent reality actually has a cause. Cf. Oppy (2000, 347–348) and Gale and Pruss (2002, 90).

We make two replies. First, the entailment isn't uncontroversial (for example: maybe something's lacking a cause could be caused by there being a lack of available causes). Second, and more importantly, even if the objection is successful, that is consistent with our observation that counterexamples are rare, at best.

12. See a more complicated argument of the same type (with stronger premises) in Weaver (2016, reply to objection #5).

13. To be clear, we do not claim that one has a defeasible reason to expect that something is causable in cases where one lacks reason to think that the thing in question is contingent. We focus on contingent things because the clearest cases of causable things are all contingent.

14. For more on causing states of affairs, see note 9.

15. We are assuming the "prior cause" condition given in note 9.

16. We thank Dean Zimmerman for asking us whether our restriction to purely contingent events may be artificial and overly restricted. Our answer is that it may be—which is no reason to doubt the principle.

17. We have in mind the theories of modal knowledge in Bealer (2002); Chalmers (2002); Geirrson (2005); Gregory (2004); Jenkins (2010); Williamson (2007); and Yablo (1993).

18. A statement *q* is ideally, positively and primarily conceivable for *C*, just in case, *C* can imagine a circumstance in which *q* is verified, *C* can conceive that *q* is actually true, and *q* "is conceivable on ideal rational reflection." Chalmers (2002, 147). Cf. Chalmers (2002, 150, 157).

19. See Chalmers (2002, 150); see also Yablo (1993).

20. Chalmers (2002, 147).

21. For discussion of these views, see Ehring (2009) and the literature cited therein.

22. Here is one way to show the inference:
Let 'N' abbreviate '∃x (N(x))', where 'N(x)' reads '□ (∃!(x) & ◊ (∃y (x causes y)))'.

    1. Assume ◊N.

    2. Then: ◊□N. (□(N → □N), by axioms **4** & **5**)

    3. Now suppose (for the sake of argument) that ◊~N.

    4. Then: □◊~N. (by axiom **5**)

    5. Then: ~◊~◊~N. (by substituting '~◊~' for '□')

    6. Then: ~◊~~□~~N. (by substituting '~□~' for the second '◊')

    7. Then: ~◊□N. (because '~~X' is equivalent to 'X')

    8. But (7) contradicts (2).

    9. So: (3) is not true. ((3) → (8))

    10. So: ~◊~N.

    11. So: □N. (by substituting '□' for '~◊~')

    12. So: N. (□X → X, by axiom **M**)

    13. So: if ◊N, then N.

23. Alternatively: possibly, there are no necessary causally potent beings.

24. Tooley (2003, 388). Tooley originally expressed this type of "[s]*trong reductionism with respect to causal relations*" (ibid) in terms of states of affairs rather than events.

25. The term "superdupervenience" comes from William Lycan (according to McLaughlin and Bennett (2014, sect. 3.7)), but see also McLaughlin and Bennett (2014, sect. 3.7).

26. See a related but weaker idea in Schaffer (2008).

27. Oppy (2015, sect. 3).

28. Rovelli (2004, 268).

29. As Lawrence Sklar remarked:

> "the theory [i.e., GTR] treats . . . spacetime as substantival in its surface presentation, just as do Newtonian, neo-Newtonian, and Minkowski spacetime theories. Any claim that the theory really affirms spacetime to exist solely as a set of relations among ordinary material things requires, as usual, an argument." Sklar (1974, 214)

30. In fact, such a conclusion is entailed by contingentism, the denial of necessitism (the idea that necessarily every entity is necessarily some entity). Necessitism is defended in Williamson (2013), but I doubt that Oppy wants to rest his thesis upon necessitism.

31. See Lewis (1986, ix–x); cf. Lewis's comments on supervenience in Lewis (1999, 29).

32. Lewis (1986, ix–x).

33. See Weaver (draft).

34. See, e.g., the comments in Aronson (1982, 302); Dowe (2000, 6–12); Kutach (2013, 1–50, see particularly the comments on page 5); and perhaps Salmon (1984).

35. Paul and Hall (2013, 249).

36. See the discussion in Carroll (2009, 287–290); and Schaffer (2000).

37. Flint and Freddoso (1983); cf. Leftow (2009).

REFERENCES

Aronson, J.L. 1982. "Untangling Ontology from Epistemology in Causation" *Erkenntnis* 18: 293–305.

Bealer, G. 2002. "Modal Epistemology and the Rationalist Renaissance," in Tamar Szabó Gendler and John Hawthorne (eds.), *Conceivability and Possibility*. Oxford: Clarendon Press, 71–125.

Carroll, J.W. 2009. "Anti-Reductionism," in Helen Beebee, Christopher Hitchcock, and Peter Menzies (eds.), *The Oxford Handbook of Causation*. New York,: Oxford University Press, 279–298.

Chalmers, D.J. 2002. "Does Conceivability Entail Possibility?," in Tamar Szabó Gendler and John Hawthorne (eds.), *Conceivability and Possibility*. New York: Oxford University Press, 145–200.

Collins, J., N. Hall, and L.A. Paul. 2004. "Counterfactuals and Causation: History, Problems, and Prospects," in John Collins, Ned Hall, and L.A. Paul, *Causation and Counterfactuals*. Cambridge, MA: MIT Press, 1–57.

Craig, W.L., and J.D. Sinclair. 2012. "The *Kalam* Cosmological Argument," in William Lane Craig and J.P. Moreland (eds.), *The Blackwell Companion to Natural Theology*. Malden, MA: Blackwell Publishing, 101–201.

Dowe, P. 2000. *Physical Causation* (Cambridge Studies in Probability, Induction, and Decision Theory). New York: Cambridge University Press.

Ehring, D. 2009. "Causal Relata," in Helen Beebee, Christopher Hitchcock, and Peter Menzies (eds.), *The Oxford Handbook of Causation*. New York: Oxford University Press, 387–413.

Flint, T.P., and A.J. Freddoso. 1983. "Maximal Power," in Alfred J. Freddoso (ed.), *The Existence and Nature of God*. Notre Dame, IN: University of Notre Dame Press, 81–113.

Gale, R., and A.R. Pruss. 1999. "A New Cosmological Argument," *Religious Studies* 35: 461–476.

———. 2002. "A Response to Oppy and to Davey and Clifton," *Religious Studies* 38: 89–99.

Geirsson, H. 2005. "Conceivability and Defeasible Modal Justification," *Philosophical Studies* 122: 279–304.

Gregory, D. 2004. "Imagining Possibilities," *Philosophy and Phenomenological Research* 69: 327–348.

Jenkins, C.S. 2010. "Concepts, Experience and Modal Knowledge," in John Hawthorne and Jason Turner (eds.), *Philosophical Perspectives 24, 2010 Epistemology*. Malden, MA: Wiley Periodicals, Inc, 255–279.

Koons, R.C. 1997. "A New Look at the Cosmological Argument," *American Philosophical Quarterly* 34: 193–211.

Kripke, S.A. 1980. *Naming and Necessity*. Cambridge, MA: Harvard University Press.

Kutach, D. 2013. *Causation and its Basis in Fundamental Physics* New York: Oxford University Press.

Leftow, B. 2009. "Omnipotence," in Thomas P. Flint and Michael Rea (eds.), *The Oxford Handbook of Philosophical Theology*. New York: Oxford University Press, 2009, 167–198.

Lewis, D. 1986. *Philosophical Papers, Volume II*. New York: Oxford University Press.

———. 1999. *Papers in Metaphysics and Epistemology* (Cambridge Studies in Philosophy). New York: Cambridge University Press.

McLaughlin, B., and K. Bennett. 2014. "Supervenience," in Edward N. Zalta, *The Stanford Encyclopedia of Philosophy* Spring 2014 Edition), http://plato.stanford.edu/archives/spr2014/entries/supervenience/.

Oppy, G. 2000. "On 'A New Cosmological Argument,'" *Religious Studies* 36: 345–353.

———. 2015. ""Uncaused Beginnings" Revisited," *Faith and Philosophy* 32: 205–210.

Paul, L.A., and N. Hall. 2013. *Causation: A User's Guide*. Oxford: Oxford University Press.

Plantinga, A. 1974. *The Nature of Necessity*. (Clarendon Library of Logic and Philosophy). New York: Oxford University Press.

Pruss, A.R. 2006. *The Principle of Sufficient Reason: A Reassessment*. (Cambridge Studies in Philosophy). Cambridge: Cambridge University Press.

Rasmussen, J. 2009. "From a Necessary Being to God," *International Journal for Philosophy of Religion* 66: 1–13.

———. 2010a. "From States of Affairs to a Necessary Being," *Philosophical Studies* 148: 183–200.

———. 2011. "A New Argument for a Necessary Being," *Australasian Journal of Philosophy* 89: 351–356.

———. 2014. "Continuity as a Guide to Possibility," *Australasian Journal of Philosophy* 92: 525–538.

Ross, J.F. 1969. *Philosophical Theology*. Indianapolis, IN: Bobbs-Merrill.

Rovelli, C. 2004. *Quantum Gravity* (Cambridge Monographs on Mathematical Physics). New York: Cambridge University Press.

Rowe, W.L. 1975. *The Cosmological Argument*. Princeton, NJ: Princeton University Press.

Salmon, W.C. 1984. *Scientific Explanation and the Causal Structure of the World*. Princeton, NJ: Princeton University Press.

Schaffer, J. 2000. "Trumping Preemption," *The Journal of Philosophy*. (Special Issue). 97: 165–181.

———. 2008. "Causation and Laws of Nature: Reductionism," in Theodore Sider, John Hawthorne, and Dean W. Zimmerman (eds.), *Contemporary Debates in Metaphysics*. (Contemporary Debates in Philosophy). Malden, MA: Blackwell Publishing, 82–107.

———. 2009. "On What Grounds What," in David J. Chalmers, David Manley, and Ryan Wasserman (eds.), *Metametaphysics: New Essays on the Foundations of Ontology*. New York: Oxford University Press, 347–383.

Sklar, L. 1974. *Space, Time, and Spacetime*. Berkeley and Los Angeles: University of California Press.

Sobel, J.H. 2004. *Logic and Theism: Arguments For and Against Beliefs in God*. New York: Cambridge University Press.

Tooley, M. 2003. "Causation and Supervenience," in Michael J. Loux and Dean W. Zimmerman (eds.), *The Oxford Handbook of Metaphysics*. New York: Oxford University Press, 386–434.

Turri, J. 2011. "A New and Improved Argument for a Necessary Being," *Australasian Journal of Philosophy* 89: 357–359.

Van Inwagen, P. 1983. *An Essay on Free Will*. Oxford: Oxford University Press.

Weaver, C.G. (draft). Against Causal Reductionism. Unpublished Paper.

———. 2016. "Yet another New Cosmological Argument" *International Journal for Philosophy of Religion* 80:11–32.

Williamson, T. 2007. *The Philosophy of Philosophy*. Malden, MA: Blackwell Publishers.

———. 2013. *Modal Logic as Metaphysics*. New York: Oxford University Press.

Yablo, S. 1993. "Is Conceivability a Guide to Possibility?," *Philosophy and Phenomenological Research* 53: 1–42.

I I

Half a Dozen Epistemological Arguments

(J)

The Argument from Positive Epistemic Status

EVOLUTIONARY PSYCHOLOGY AND THE ARGUMENT

FROM POSITIVE EPISTEMIC STATUS

Justin L. Barrett

———————————————————————————————————

THE SECOND SECTION of Plantinga's "Two Dozen Theistic Arguments," "Half a Dozen Epistemological Arguments," begins with "(J) The Argument from Positive Epistemic Status." It reads:

> Clearly many of our beliefs do have positive epistemic status for us (at any rate most of us think so, most of us accept this premise). As we have seen, positive epistemic status is best thought of as a matter of a belief's being produced by cognitive faculties that are functioning properly in the sort of environment that is appropriate for them. The easiest and most natural way to think of proper functioning, however, is in terms of design: a machine or an organism is working properly when it is working in the way it was designed to work by the being that designed it. But clearly the best candidate for being the being who has designed our cognitive faculties would be God.

In this chapter, rather than develop and defend such an argument in any thorough way, I will offer a sketch of what such an argument might be and primarily focus on scientific research that bears upon this sort of argument and challenges to it.

For linguistic economy and to aid in capturing the attention of millennials, I will use some abbreviations in my consideration of Plantinga's argument. "Positive epistemic status" will be abbreviated "Pos-Es" (pronounced "PAW-seez," as in *posses*). Cognitive faculties that produce beliefs will be "BFFs" for "belief forming faculties." (They are, at least, among our best friends forever when functioning properly.) The qualifying phrase "functioning properly in the sort of environment that is appropriate for them" will be represented by + and its negation by -. Hence, one simplified version of the argument suggested by Plantinga is:

1) Our best understanding is that only BFFs+ create Pos-Es.[1]
2) We have beliefs with Pos-Es.
3) Therefore, our best understanding is that we have BFFs+.
4) BFFs+ give evidence for design.
5) Design gives evidence for a designer.
6) The most likely candidate for a designer for our BFFs+ is God.
7) Therefore, BFFs+ give evidence for God.
8) Therefore, beliefs with Pos-Es give evidence for God.

That is, BFFs functioning properly (i.e., BFFs+) looks like an intelligently designed state. BFFs+ give evidence for design in the sense that, when in appropriate contexts, they give the appearance of doing particular jobs that arrive at good and useful information. BFFs aptly solve epistemic problems much like tools such as screwdrivers, cars, and microwave ovens can be used to ably solve practical problems. Analogously to accounting for the utility of wheels, hammers, and clothing in particular contexts by appealing to human intelligence that has developed these tools for specific purposes, it appears that the best way to account for BFFs+ is an intelligent designer interested in the good of truth seeking and finding, a designer that sounds a bit like God of classical theism. Therefore, having Pos-Es is evidence for God. Or, if one is inclined to believe that we do have Pos-Es, one should be inclined to believe that there is a God that accounts for the BFFs+ and, hence, the Pos-Es.

Plantinga identifies this argument as falling in the genus of design arguments:

> This premise of this argument is only a special case of a much broader premise: there are many natural (nonartifactual) things in the world besides our cognitive faculties such that they function properly or improperly: organs of our bodies and of other organisms, for example.

As a design argument, this argument immediately provokes the objection that the apparent design in belief-forming cognitive faculties functioning properly in their appropriate environments (BFFs+) is adequately accounted for by evolution by natural selection; God is thus not an uncontested most likely candidate for "designer." I will call this Objection 1 and consider it in the next section. I will also consider three other, less obvious objections, all related to findings from cognitive developmental psychology showing that humans have a natural tendency to see design and purpose in the natural world and that this teleofunctional reasoning may bias us to see BFFs+ (among other natural states of affairs) as the product of a designer. I conclude that analysis of relevant scientific evidence does not obviously support these objections.

For the sake of this chapter, I accept that "positive epistemic status is best thought of as a matter of a belief's being produced by cognitive faculties that are functioning properly in the sort of environment that is appropriate for them." I will also provisionally grant Plantinga the following claim: "The easiest and most natural way to think of proper functioning, however, is in terms of design: a machine or an organism is working properly when it is working in the way it was designed to work by the being that designed it." Why would we trust the deliverances of our BFFs if they are not doing what they are supposed to do when they are supposed to be doing it (i.e., BFFs-)? Conversely, why wouldn't we give our BFFs the benefit of the doubt when they are working properly in the context in which they are "designed" to work (i.e., BFFs+)? Rather than challenge this supposition, at issue here is whether adequate "design" can be derived from a naturalistic source to guarantee the reliability or trustworthiness of our BFFs such that they can create or form Pos-Es.

OBJECTION 1

Plantinga puts the objection this way:

> Objection: perhaps there is indeed this initial tendency to see these things as the product of intelligent design; but there is a powerful defeater in evolutionary theory, which shows us a perfectly natural way in which all of these things might have come about without design.

That is, it may look as though the best way to account for BFFs+ is God, but naturalistic evolution—evolution without God—is an adequate alternative. Hence, Pos-Es are not evidence for God. Does this proposed defeater, Objection 1, succeed? Importantly, at issue here is not whether evolution is a fair account of how human life evolved. Let us grant that it is. Rather, does evolutionary theory of a naturalistic sort—unguided by any divine hand, either at the initial tuning or in sustaining and shaping the process—suffice to plausibly account for BFFs+? That is, granted that evolution is a fair account of how life evolved, is naturalistic evolution sufficient to plausibly account for BFFs+? I offer two replies to Objection 1.

First Reply to Objection 1

Many reasons for doubting Objection 1 appear in Plantinga's defense of his evolutionary argument against naturalism (2011, Chapter 10), and I will only quickly summarize those here. Plantinga argues that various versions of materialist naturalism (the predominant sort of naturalism) presume that beliefs are either reducible to or wholly caused by neurophysical states. Neural systems that support beliefs have evolved from simpler systems that presumably perform detections (e.g., is a signal absent or present?), calculations (e.g., what distance is for the next safe footing?), and indications (e.g., is a temperature suitable or not?), but do not support belief formation. Organisms with these simpler systems have demonstrated their fitness much longer than those we might be confident of having beliefs proper, which illustrates that beliefs and other such higher-order states are not required for evolutionary fitness.

Furthermore, under this view, as behaviors are caused by neurophysical states and not belief contents, there is no good a priori reason to suppose that the belief contents must be generally accurate to motivate fitness-enhancing behaviors. Suppose one adopts the common materialist assumptions that beliefs are either epiphenomenal of neurophysical states or equivalent to such states and it is those states, and not the belief content, that cause behaviors that have been subject to selection pressure (particularly in ancestral species). The content of beliefs are causally impotent under such materialist views and so natural selection does not act upon belief content in any direct fashion. Unguided, naturalistic evolutionary processes may accidentally supply us with truth-tracking, reliable BFFs, but they give us no strong reason to think that they would do so. Plantinga explains:

> Fleeing predators, finding food and mates—these things require cognitive devices that in some way track crucial features of the environment, and are appropriately connected with muscles; but they do not require true belief, or even belief at all. (329)

It is not clear that naturalistic evolution would be expected to produce BFFs, let alone reliable ones, and so evolution does not serve as the alleged designer of BFFs+ as satisfactorily as God.

Second Reply to Objection 1

For naturalistic evolution to compete with God as a plausible designer of BFFs+ that can be counted on to produce Pos-Es, we need some reason to think that if naturalistic evolution did happen to produce BFFs at all, it would produce BFFs+ that are generally reliable. Even if one may reasonably assume that, under naturalism, belief contents are causally potent to produce behaviors that would then be subject to selective pressure, we would need reason to think that the winnowing effect of natural selection would favor BFFs that provide true beliefs the preponderance of the time. On one level, it seems obvious that it must: if you can't reliably tell the difference between something that is food and something that is poison, for instance, you won't be around to reproduce. Initial appearances aside, however, the situation may be far less straightforward.

In the case of determining what to eat, humans do not typically form beliefs consciously about whether something is a poison or not. More often, human minds generate action impulses to eat directed at particular objects in the environment. Something like the formation of a propositional representation that something is food, is likely unnecessary in most cases, just as other animals (chickens, for instance) presumably do not form propositions about an object being food or not, but just form an action decision. In those rare(r) cases in which humans do form propositional beliefs about whether something is "food" or not, evolutionary theory does not provide any strong reason to think that the error rate associated with these propositional beliefs may actually exceed any threshold we would accept as reliable.[2] A hungry person walking through the forest may erroneously label thousands of potential food items "not food" that are food (such as mushrooms, berries, leafy plants, grubs, and the like), and only correctly label a tiny fraction "food" that are good and nutritious to eat, and not necessarily just because of a lack of pertinent information.

Under the label "error-management" it has been argued by Ryan McKay and Daniel Dennett (yes, *that* Daniel Dennett), in their article "The Evolution of Misbelief" (2009), that cognitive systems—including BFFs—may be tuned away from simply tracking truth. Because some costs or benefits of getting things right or wrong are not equal, the cognitive system will become biased toward certain outputs that reduce risk and maximize reward at the expense of accuracy. Being poisoned by one bad mushroom is too great a cost to make a single mistake compared to the benefits of eating many thousands of good ones, so perfectly edible mushrooms may be passed by in error. Scientific evidence seems to bear this out. For instance, if the cost of failing to detect a venomous snake is greater than the cost of falsely detecting an object as a dangerous snake when there is not one, then the snake detection sub-system will err in the direction of false-positive: and it does. Humans readily fear snakes (and animals and inanimate objects that resemble snakes)—regarding them as dangerous—even in places in which there are few or no dangerous snakes (Öhman and Mineka, 2003). If the rewards of thinking a potential mate finds one attractive are great enough in fitness terms to risk dozens of humiliating rejections, then the cognitive system that says "you've got a real shot here" will be tuned to unrealistic optimism (and it is, as noted by Perilloux, Easton, and Buss 2012). Selection demands necessitate that cognitive systems evolve with bias toward some percepts, thoughts, and beliefs over others based upon costs and benefits of accuracy and not on accuracy alone. Naturalistic evolutionary theory alone, then, provides reasons to be cautious concerning the reliability of our BFFs: depending upon the role that they play, some BFFs may be generally reliable, whereas others may not be in terms of truth-tracking accuracy. Fitness enhancement does not necessarily equal reliability.

Furthermore, even if the contents of beliefs could be argued to be causally potent from a naturalistic evolutionary perspective and the feature of being largely reliable in appropriate environmental contexts would be selected for, it does not follow that naturalistic evolutionary theory provides strong reason to expect reliable BFFs in many current environmental contexts. Consider snakes again. It may be that human ancestral species interacted with many more venomous snakes than the bulk of today's humans, and their developmental environment properly tuned up their snake-detecting BFFs. The snake-detecting BFF may have been fairly accurate and reliable for producing Pos-Es in that environment, but be entirely mistuned in many of today's relatively snake-free environments. Similarly, our system for attributing mental states to others, often called the theory of mind, is frequently tripped up by computers that mimic the right input conditions, thereby giving the appearances of having mental states. As the environment in which the BFF is used has changed from its ancestral environment, its reliability may well have decreased. The same could be argued of any number of other BFFs. As evolutionary psychologists have emphasized, contemporary humans carry around stone-aged minds with some BFFs that have likely seen very little important evolution in hundreds of thousands of years (Cosmides and Tooby 1997; Tooby and Cosmides 1992). The selective pressures under which they evolved—that is, the problems they helped ancestors address—may be very different than contemporary conditions. Hence, even BFFs that once were BFFs+ leading to Pos-Es may not be BFFs+ anymore. In many cases we cannot be certain and, in some, we may have reason to doubt their reliability.

Let's suppose, however, that belief contents about snakes and foods are causally potent in a way that they could be expected to be shaped by naturalistic evolution, and that evolutionary theory did require such fitness-essential beliefs to be right the vast majority of the time to be selected for, and that contemporary environments are not so dissimilar from the environment in which these BFFs were shaped as to make their reliability either suspect or inscrutable. Even granting these controversial assumptions, naturalistic evolution still faces a challenge when trying to serve as a substitute for God in guaranteeing our Pos-Es via BFFs+. The challenge is that the critical BFFs for the sorts of higher-order problems that concern philosophers and scientists—including belief in naturalistic evolution—may not be simple products of fitness-essential BFFs (e.g., concerning food procurement, predator detection, and the like) operating in the proper environments. For instance, the Wason card selection task, developed as a test of logical reasoning with problems of the form *If P then Q*, has repeatedly shown that adults exhibit rather poor performance in simple syllogistic reasoning (Johnson-Laird and Wason 1970). Leda Cosmides (1989), however, has shown that when the syllogisms relate to social exchange rules and the detection of defectors, performance becomes very strong. Beliefs formed by higher-order, reflective cognition appear to be produced by a more general sort of reasoning system that would not have particular, focused proper domains of functioning. Such findings concerning the widespread evidence that even college-educated adults are rather clumsy at reasoning has led to speculation that our "reasoning" faculties did not evolve to help our ancestors reason, but rather to solve social problems such as being able to persuade others (Mercier and Sperber 2011). Whether this hypothesis is true or not is not the point. The point is that we have reasonable grounds for suspicion that naturalistic evolution led to the development of BFFs+, including our higher-order reasoning, for ends that did not primarily concern their ability to generate true beliefs.

All of these considerations suggest that the trustworthiness of our BFFs is often inscrutable given naturalistic evolution, and in some cases may even be suspect. Because we have no very good reason to think that naturalistic evolution gives us BFFs+ leading to Pos-Es, it does not appear that naturalistic evolution is a strong candidate to take God's place as the "designer" in question.

Rather than accept that BFFs+ producing Pos-Es looks like a case of design and then arguing that naturalistic evolution will serve as a suitable designer, however, one could object that it is unreasonable to see BFFs+ producing Pos-Es as a case of apparent design. Objections 2 and 3 attempt to challenge the strength of the analogy between BFFs+ and designed tools.[3]

OBJECTION 2

Perhaps one only sees "design" if one already has theological reasons to see it. The strength of Plantinga's suggested Argument from Positive Epistemic Status derives largely from the degree to which our BFFs+ appear designed. That a series of natural processes would give rise to reliable BFFs+ and consequent Pos-Es looks surprising if there is no design behind the natural processes. Or does it? One person's design is another person's dumb luck. Perhaps, those who see design do so because they are already theists and so they expect to see design, purpose, and intention behind and through the natural order, and if they were not theists, they would not perceive design in the emergence of BFFs+.[4]

Reply to Objection 2

The tendency to see design and purpose in features of the natural world, a Design Stance (Dennett), is widespread. Scientific research from cognitive developmental psychology suggests that humans have natural dispositions to see design and purpose in the natural world that arise as a normal part of child development and persists into adulthood unless overridden by cultural structures such as formal education systems that disabuse children of this teleofunctional reasoning. Psychologist Deborah Kelemen has demonstrated what she once dubbed "promiscuous teleology" in children and adults across cultures (Kelemen 2004; D. Kelemen, J. Rottman, and R. Seston 2013; J. Rottman et al. 2017). Given this research, if one detects design in the fact that we have reliable BFFs+ leading to Pos-Es, that detection may be partly or largely due to a natural tendency to see design in natural systems. It is design deniers who are overriding natural intuitions (e.g., because they are naturalists) and not design affirmers attributing design only because they already believe in a divine designer.

OBJECTION 3

Doesn't the fact that humans have documented natural predispositions to think teleofunctionally about the natural world undercut any perceived design as the cause of BFFs+? After all, Kelemen referred to this tendency as "promiscuous teleology" for a reason: humans see design where there isn't any. This cognitive system is error-prone and, hence, beliefs that are a product of this system are suspect.

Reply to Objection 3

The cognitive system responsible for teleological reasoning in humans almost certainly makes mistakes, but it is not clear that we can judge it error-prone or unreliable in this context without question-begging. If design does lie behind the natural world, then the system seems to be largely accurate. Only if one already rejects the possibility of a creator/designer, does the system seem error-prone.

Furthermore, this cognitive system that produces teleological reasoning about plants, animals, mountains, and rivers is thought (by Kelemen and others) to be the same faculty that produces teleological reasoning about artifacts and other human innovations. Surely its reliability must be judged based upon its total body of work and not only the contentious cases.

OBJECTION 4

We may perceive design behind our BFFs+ but we should not do so because that perceived design is itself produced by a BFF-. That is, whatever cognitive system that generates teleological beliefs about natural processes pertaining to human cognitive evolution is, when generating these beliefs, operating outside its proper domain. It is not functioning properly in the sort of environment that is appropriate for it. Like a person trying to identify a small object from a great distance under poor lighting conditions, this BFF may get things right or wrong, but we should mistrust its deliverances regardless. This teleological reasoning system's appropriate or "proper domain" of functioning is human-made objects and systems.

Reply to Objection 4

The distinction made by evolutionary psychologists and anthropologists between proper and actual domain is a useful heuristic for considering the functional dynamics of some cognitive systems and making predictions and explanations about the system's properties. Take, for instance, the human face detection system. If it has evolved to detect and process human faces because rapid detection and thorough processing of visual information about humans around us was adaptive for our ancestors, then its "proper domain" of activation is other human faces. When the same system is activated by face-like bumps and ridges on a rock formation, we recognize that it is operating outside its proper domain. The rock formation's shape falls into the actual domain but is not part of the proper domain for this cognitive system. The distinction between proper and actual domains is useful because it helps scientific researchers generate hypotheses and explanations concerning patterns of data: essentially all human faces will activate the face detection system, whereas only some rock formations will, and those that do will do so because they approximate the input features of stimuli in the proper domain.

It does not follow from this scientifically useful distinction that the distinction between proper and actual domain carries much epistemological utility. A complete exploration of the epistemological utility of this distinction from evolutionary psychology is beyond the scope of this chapter, but applied to teleofunctional reasoning, one concern in particular makes Objection 4 suspect. The proper-actual domain distinction in evolved cognitive systems can be somewhat speculative, and the teleofunctional reasoning system is a case in point. It could be that the proper domain of this reasoning predilection is artifacts: teleofunctional reasoning evolved because considering what artifacts might be used for—both intended use and other possible uses—would lead to rapid learning of how to use and make artifacts and further technological innovations, thereby improving fitness. Perhaps. Alternatively, teleofunctional reasoning might have been a useful way to think about natural objects in terms of what they might be good for, their potential affordances, leading to novel ways to co-opt those natural functions for human ends. Disney's Tarzan saw a rhino gouging a tree with its horn and took that as inspiration to use a horn-shaped stone as a tool. Similarly, seeing purpose, function, and even alleged design in the natural world could have assisted in developing technologies, thereby improving fitness. If so, the proper domain of teleofunctional reasoning is the natural world after all. For many BFFs, it is not clear what the proper domain was or is.[5]

ADDITIONAL OBSERVATIONS

Suppose our BFF that detects design in the fact that we have BFFs+ forming Pos-Es is indeed faulty. Either it is not functioning properly or it is generating beliefs outside of the appropriate environment or domain. Suppose, then, that evolutionary developmental psychology does have a defeater for the perceived design we see in this and other living systems: as Kelemen and others have shown, we have natural cognitive dispositions toward finding design and purpose in the natural world and even accounting for the origins of plants and animals in terms of this purpose. These natural dispositions are the reason that we find some design arguments attractive (De Cruz and De Smedt 2010), including the Argument from Positive Epistemic Status. Suppose that is right. What follows?

If it is true that humans naturally see design and purpose in the natural world unless they learn to override these intuitions through effort and education (Kelemen and Rosset 2009), and these intuitions if unchecked lead to false ideas that there really is intentional design and purpose behind natural states, then we have identified a naturally occurring BFF that is massively error-prone in its typical usage. It is a BFF that, just walking through a forest somewhere, will generate no Pos-Es but lots of beliefs with negative epistemic status. If indeed this is a fact, then evolution has tolerated—or even encouraged—at least this cognitive system that is fundamentally not truth-aimed or reliable in the ordinary lives of people throughout history and around the globe. And, if unreliable BFFs are a demonstrable product of evolution in this case, then how many more are there? Doesn't that mean that it isn't just possible but certain that naturalistic evolution cannot be counted as guarantor of our BFFs producing Pos-Es? At the very least, the vividness of this example should raise the specter that any given BFF is subject to similar undermining.

Note, however, that the theist who regards the ordinary outputs of the teleofunctional reasoning system to be accurate (i.e., there is design and purpose behind the natural world) does not have to accept this same skeptical conclusion. Not only could God, in principle, orchestrate the evolution of the cosmos and living systems such that we have reliable BFFs+ that form Pos-Es, but Kelemen's findings give evidence supporting that possibility. Humans naturally have inchoate but truth-directed intuitions about the design behind the natural world. That is, classical theism, evolution, the scientific findings concerning natural teleofunctional reasoning, and generally reliable belief-forming faculties pose no inconsistencies as a conjunctive set. Naturalism, evolution, the scientific findings concerning natural teleofunctional reasoning, and generally reliable belief-forming faculties produce an inconsistency. It seems, then, that the finding that humans have natural tendencies to find design and purpose in the natural world is no friend to opponents of the Argument from Positive Epistemic Status.

NOTES

1. That is, BFFs doin' how they do form Pos-Es. I will accept this first premise for the sake of this analysis. An alternative, weaker version could be 1) Pos-Es are frequently the consequences of BFFs+, followed by 3) We have evidence for BFFs+. Such an argument, then, would still increase the probability for the final conclusion if the following analysis is sound.

2. It may be that BFFs are reliable in many contexts but calculating accuracy of these systems may be inscrutable in most cases.

3. I do not attempt to specify what an alternative way for conceiving of the Pos-Es independent of BFFs+ might be, because I am not convinced that these objections are successful. If they were, then some alternative grounds for regarding many of our epistemic states as positive would be needed.

4. This objection is inspired by Jennifer Faust (2008).

5. A further complexity concerns when the proper domain changes. A cognitive faculty could initially arise to solve one sort of problem, but then, as selection pressures change, the same cognitive faculty could be encouraged or augmented by natural selection for different aims. Hence, the proper domain could change over the course of evolution.

REFERENCES

Cosmides, L. 1989. "The Logic of Social Exchange: Has Natural Selection Shaped How Humans Reason? Studies with the Wason Selection Task." *Cognition* 31: 187–276.

Cosmides, L., and J. Tooby 1997. *Evolutionary Psychology: A Primer*. http://www.cep.ucsb.edu/primer.html

De Cruz, H., and J. De Smedt. 2010. "Paley's iPod. The Cognitive Basis of the Design Argument Within Natural Theology." *Zygon: Journal of Religion and Science* 45: 665–684.

Faust, J. 2008. "Can Religious Arguments Persuade?" *International Journal for the Philosophy of Religion* 63: 71–86.

Johnson-Laird, P., and P. Wason. 1970. "Insight into a Logical Relation." *Quarterly Journal of Experimental Psychology* 22, no. 1: 49–61.

Kelemen, D. 2004. "Are Children 'intuitive theists'? Reasoning about Purpose and Design in Nature." *Psychological Science* 15: 295–301.

Kelemen, Deborah, and Evelyn Rosset. 2009. "The Human Function Compunction: Teleological Explanation in Adults." *Cognition* 111: 138–143.

Kelemen, D., J. Rottman, and R. Seston. 2013. "Professional Physical Scientists Display Tenacious Teleological Tendencies: Purpose-based Reasoning as a Cognitive Default." *Journal of Experimental Psychology: General* 142: 1074–1083. doi:10.1037/a0030399.

McKay, R.T., and D.C. Dennett. 2009. "The Evolution of Misbelief." *Behavioral and Brain Sciences* 32: 493–561.

Mercier, Hugo, and Dan Sperber. 2011. "Why Do Humans Reason? Arguments for an Argumentative Theory." *Behavioral and Brain Sciences* 34, no. 2:57–74; discussion 74–111. <10.1017/S0140525X10000968>. <hal-00904097>.

Öhman, Arne, and Susan Mineka. 2003. "The Malicious Serpent: Snakes as a Prototypical Stimulus for an Evolved Module of Fear." *Current Directions in Psychological Science* 12, no. 1: 5–9. doi: 10.1111/1467-8721.01211.

Perilloux, Carin, Judith A. Easton, and David M. Buss. 2012. "The Misperception of Sexual Interest." *Psychological Science* 23, no. 2: 146–151. doi: 10.1177/0956797611424162.

Plantinga, Alvin. *Where the Conflict Really Lies: Science, Religion, and Naturalism*. New York: Oxford University Press, 2011.

Rottman, J., L. Zhu, W. Wang, R. Seston Schillaci, K.J. Clark, and D. Kelemen. 2017. "Cultural Influences on the Teleological Stance: Evidence from China." *Religion, Brain and Behavior* 7, no. 1: 17–26. doi: 10.1080/2153599X.2015.1118402.

Tooby, J., and L. Cosmides. 1992. "The Psychological Foundations of Culture," in J. Barkow, L. Cosmides, and J. Tooby (eds.), *The Adapted Mind: Evolutionary Psychology and the Generation of Culture*. New York: Oxford University Press.

(K)

The Argument from the Confluence of Proper

Function and Reliability

IS GOD THE DESIGNER OF OUR COGNITIVE FACULTIES?

EVALUATING PLANTINGA'S ARGUMENT

Alexander Arnold

THE JOHN TEMPLETON FOUNDATION

Let R be the claim that most of the human mind's cognitive powers are reliable—that is, tend to produce more true beliefs than false beliefs—when properly functioning in the right environment. Plantinga's Argument from the Confluence of Proper Function and Reliability (hereafter argument (K)) purports to find support for theism—the thesis that there is an omnipotent, omniscient, morally perfect being—in R. This chapter aims to lay out the best version of the argument and provide (since space is at a premium) an initial evaluation of its prospects. My evaluation is mixed: argument (K) does not, in the end, show that R favors theism over nontheistic evolutionism; but, independently of whether it supports theism, it does highlight in its own way a non-trivial problem for nontheistic evolutionism, the problem of conjuring a naturalist, materialist psychosemantics.

In the first section I reconstruct argument (K) as a likelihood argument; sections 2 and 3 examine the two key premises of that reconstruction. The chapter concludes with some thoughts on the questions raised by argument (K) that may be worthy of further examination.

ARGUMENT (K) AS A LIKELIHOOD ARGUMENT

Argument (K) is a design argument, and so is representable like other design arguments.[1] A good framework for reconstructing them is likelihoodism.[2] Arguments represented in this framework are (i) are comparative—competing hypotheses are evaluated against one another relative to a particular piece or body of evidence; (ii) consequently, their conclusions are comparative—one hypothesis is judged to be better confirmed relative to that body of evidence than another hypothesis; and, (iii) the likelihoods of the two hypotheses being compared, relative to a certain evidence base, are central to the argument, and are themselves compared using the law of likelihood.

"Likelihood" here is not synonymous with "probability" (though in most English contexts the two words are synonymous); it has a technical sense. Let H_1 and H_2 be two hypotheses to be compared relative to evidence E. Sometimes "probability" refers to the posterior probability of a hypothesis given some evidence:

$$Pr(H_1 | E) \text{ and } Pr(H_2 | E).$$

In contrast, the likelihoods of H_1 and H_2 relative to E, in the technical sense intended, are

$$Pr(E | H_1) \text{ and } Pr(E | H_2).$$

The law of likelihood (LoL) is a principle stating a sufficient condition for when a given piece of evidence favors one of two competing hypotheses over the other:

(LoL): If $Pr(E | H_1) \gg Pr(E | H_2)$, then E favors H_1 over H_2.

(LoL) is one way of explicating a comparative concept of confirmation. There are others, but for reasons of space I will not discuss them.[3]

Likelihoodism fits well with Plantinga's formulation of argument (K) in his lecture notes:

> "Theism, with the idea that God has created us in his image and in such a way that we can acquire truth over a wide range of topics and subjects, provides an easy, natural explanation of [the fact that human minds are marvelous]. *The only real competitor here is non-theistic evolutionism.*" (emphasis added)

Talk of theism competing with non-theistic evolutionism suggests the thought that argument (K) is really intended to contrast theism and non-theistic evolutionism with respect to a particular piece of evidence—in our case, R. Likelihoodism enables us to best capture the contrastive aspect of Plantinga's formulation of argument (K).[4]

Moreover, as opposed to a full-blown (objective) Bayesian approach, likelihoodism doesn't require us to speculate about prior probabilities, speculation that is often hard to justify. Substantiating this point would require engagement with far too many thinkers and ideas than space permits here. Let it suffice that I find it hard to justify any assignment of prior probabilities to theism or non-theistic evolutionism, and so likelihoodism is attractive to me, since it doesn't require speculation about prior probabilities.

The reader familiar with the debate between Bayesians (of different stripes), likelihoodists, and others on the foundations of probabilistic inference might ask why I am more confident in my ability to justify speculation about the relative likelihoods of R given theism, and R non-theistic evolutionism. The answer: I am more confident in my ability to discern a priori what theism and non-theistic evolutionism each predict concerning R—generally, we can use judgments about what two competing hypotheses predict concerning a given piece of evidence to form judgments about their relative likelihoods concerning that evidence. As it turns out, even here my confidence isn't that high; but it's higher than my confidence in my ability to say what the prior probabilities of theism or non-theistic evolutionism are. And we can make some progress in evaluating argument (K) even with a hazy understanding of the relative likelihoods of R given theism compared to R given non-theistic evolutionism.

Where T abbreviates theism, and NTE abbreviates non-theistic evolutionism, here is argument (K) in likelihoodist terms:

(K1) $Pr(R|T) \gg$ really small. (Premise)
(K2) $Pr(R|NTE) =$ really small. (Premise)
(K3)   Therefore, $Pr(R|T) \gg Pr(R|NTE)$. (From (K1 & K2).
(K4)   If $Pr(R|T) \gg Pr(R|NTE)$, then R favors T over NTE. (LoL)
(K5)   Therefore, R favors T over NTE.[5]

There are three things I wish to note on this argument.

First, the probabilities involved here are objective, non-frequentist probabilities. One might say they are epistemic probabilities, but my main point here is that they are whatever probabilities are in play when one speculates about to what degree propositions like theism or non-theistic evolutionism make predictions about the truth or falsity of other propositions. A better name for them might be predictive probabilities.

Second, its conclusion (K5) is quite modest. Put in slightly different (and perhaps slightly contentious) terms, (K5) claims that R is evidence that confirms, supports, or indicates theism over atheistic evolutionary theory. (K5) is compatible with our total evidence supporting atheistic evolutionary theory over theism, and even with R favoring bare atheism over theism.

Third, while (K5) is modest, if it's correct, then (modulo some plausible assumptions connecting confirmation with rationality), it tells us M renders theism a bit more rational for us to believe than it does non-theistic evolutionary theory. That is an interesting claim, especially in light of the pronouncements of some atheists to the effect that theism has absolutely nothing going for it.

HOW HIGH IS $Pr(R|T)$?

What reason is there to think that (K1) is true? In this section, I argue that (K1) lacks sufficient support and, furthermore, stands in tension with a popular thesis among theists, namely skeptical theism.

Let's first understand why one might find (K1) prima facie plausible. Given that T is bare theism, we should note that T is compatible with a host of claims about what God's intentions, desires, and plans might be, and so isn't a specific enough hypothesis to generate any predictions about what this being might do. One might simply stop here and say that $Pr(R|T)$ is inscrutable, but this would mean the end of argument (K). So there must be another option.

The most promising option involves identifying some auxiliary claims[6] $A_1 \ldots A_N$ such that

- $Pr(R|T \& A_1 \ldots A_N)$ is high;
- $Pr(A_1 \ldots A_N|T)$ is high; and
- $Pr(R|T \& A_1 \ldots A_N) \approx Pr(R|T)$.[7]

This strategy, in effect, assimilates $Pr(R|T)$ to $Pr(R|T \& A_1 \ldots A_N)$. Importantly, since argument (K) aims to be a piece of natural theology, the auxiliary assumptions invoked must be supported by reasons independent of any antecedent commitment to theism—it cannot be the case that their only support derives from theism.

It is therefore appropriate that Plantinga provides us with some auxiliary claims, courtesy of the doctrine of the *imago dei*. As he elaborates in his book (2011b):

> It is an important part of Christian, Jewish, and some Islamic thought to see human beings *as created in God's image*. This doctrine of the *imago dei*, the thought that we human beings have been created in the image of God has several sides and facets; but there is one aspect of it that is crucially relevant in the present context. This is the thought that God is a knower, and indeed the supreme knower. God is omniscient, that is, such that he knows everything, knows for any proposition p, whether p is true. We human beings, therefore, in being created in his image, can also know much about our world, ourselves, and God himself … Crucial to the thought that we have been created in his image, then, is the idea that he has created both us and our world in such a way that (like him) we are able to know important things about our world and ourselves. (268)[8]

For clarity's sake, the relevant auxiliary claims are:

- that God desired to create human beings in God's image;
- that God intended to create human beings in God's image;
- that part of being made in God's image is having a capacity for knowledge, and therefore possession of at least some reliable cognitive faculties.

Call the conjunction of these three claims the *imago dei* model—*ID* for short. On the basis of what Plantinga says about *ID*, one might think that $Pr(R|T \& ID) = 1$, and that we are therefore justified in thinking that $Pr(R|T) \approx 1$.

One objection to this reasoning comes from reflection on theistic responses to various arguments from evil. By now, theists have learned to be pessimistic about principles of the form:

> For all states of affairs X, if God desires to bring about and intends to bring about X, then X obtains.

For example, the state of affairs *there* not *having been enormous amounts of evil in the world* is a potential counterexample. Surely this is a state of affairs that God both wants and intends to bring about, and yet it nonetheless obtains.[9] One might also substitute in states of affairs like *Curly's freely refusing a bribe* (to use a venerable example) and generate other prima facie counterexamples to principles like that given above. This line of thought gives us reason to doubt that $Pr(R|T \& ID) = 1$, and so reason to doubt that $Pr(R|T) \approx 1$.

That said, the above objection is neither a conclusive nor especially strong reason to reject (K1). It is nonetheless quite plausible that a principle such as "For all states of affairs X, the probability of X obtaining given that God desires X, and intends X," is really high—at least significantly above 0.5,[10] is true. Such a principle would undergird assigning $Pr(R|T \& ID)$ a high value, and so $Pr(R|T)$ a high value.

So far, we have defended (K1) by assuming that we can approximate $Pr(R|T)$ by reckoning what $Pr(R|T \& ID)$ is—that $Pr(R|T) \approx Pr(R|T \& ID)$. By the probability calculus:

$$Pr(R|T) = Pr(R|T \& ID) \times Pr(ID|T) + Pr(R|T \& \neg ID) \times Pr(\neg ID|T).$$

If we assume that $Pr(R|T) \approx Pr(R|T \& ID)$, we must assume that the right-hand summand of the equation just given is very close to 0. This seems a safe assumption. Whatever the value of $Pr(\neg ID|T)$ might be, it is safe to assume that $Pr(R|T \& \neq gID) = 0$ —if there were a God who either did not desire to create humans in the divine image, or did not intend to create humans in the divine image, or were it the case that the divine image did not involve a capacity for knowledge, R would be hugely improbable. Therefore the right-hand summand is basically 0. But note that if $Pr(R|T) \approx Pr(R|T \& ID)$, and if the right-hand summand of the above equation is 0, the value of $Pr(ID|T)$ must be extremely high—close to 1, in fact.

But what reason does Plantinga give us for thinking that $Pr(ID|T) \approx 1$? Consider the just quoted passage's appeal to the importance of the *ID* model in the theologies of the Abrahamic religions—that is a kind of appeal to tradition. But that appeal doesn't warrant ascribing a really high value to $Pr(ID|T)$—certainly not something close to 1. And it presumes that an appeal to a tradition will satisfy the standards in play when doing natural theology—a presumption that isn't justified in this context. What about an appeal to putative divine revelation? For it seems as if some texts that claim the status of divine revelation—for example, Genesis 1:26-27 and Sura 15:26-29—support *ID*. But even if we generously grant some minimal rational force to putative divine revelations, such minimal rational force is hardly going to warrant ascribing a value close to 1 for $Pr(ID|T)$.

Argument (K)'s proponents might draw upon Richard Swinburne's natural theology (2004) to support the claim that $Pr(ID|T)$ is close to 1. Swinburne's idea is that, since we have some grasp of moral goodness, a priori reflection might reveal what kinds of worlds God would create (2004, 114). Maybe such a priori reflection will provide the theist with a relatively strong reason to accept auxiliary assumptions that permit assignment of a relatively high value to $Pr(ID|T)$, and therefore a high value to $Pr(R|T \& ID)$.

The Swinburne-style argument that $Pr(ID|T) \approx 1$ may be stated thusly:[11]

(S1)　Given T, God does an action falling under the best type of action from the set of action-types whose members jointly exhaust the set of possible action-types, each of whose members is within God's power, and each of whose members is incompatible with one another.

(S2)　Given T, the set of action-types whose members jointly exhaust the set of possible action-types, each of whose members is within God's power, and each of whose members is incompatible with one another, has all and only the following elements:(a) bringing about inanimate substances; (b) bringing about animate substances without moral awareness or free will; (c) bringing about animate substances with moral awareness and limited free will, knowledge, and power (Swinburne 2004, 118); or (d) bringing about animate substances with moral awareness and unlimited free will, knowledge, and power.

(S3)　Given T, the action-type of bringing about beings with moral awareness and limited free will, power, and knowledge is the best type of action.

(S4)　Therefore, given T, God brings about beings who have moral awareness and limited free will, power, and knowledge.

(S4) is basically equivalent to the claim that $Pr(ID|T) = 1$.[12]

Despite its ingenuity, this argument is unsound. (S2) is false, at least given the convictions of most orthodox theists who believe that God would be (and was, in fact) free to *refrain* from creating anything at all.[13,14]

In addition to the falsity of (S2), there is another problem for this argument. Both (S2) and (S3) involve value claims about what types of things are good, or better than others. But, if skeptical theism (Bergmann 2001; Bergmann and Rea 2005) is right, then we should be skeptical of a human person's ability to reason a priori about the sorts of value claims involved in (S2) and (S3). Skeptical theism states, among other things, that "[w]e have no good reason for thinking that the possible goods we know of are representative of the possible goods there are" (Bergmann 2001, 279). If this is true, then it undercuts any reason one might have for supposing that the enumeration of act-types given in (S2) is even close to exhaustive, and it also undercuts any reason one might have for believing that (S3) is true. It could be that there are act-types corresponding to goods that we puny humans cannot comprehend that are much better than bringing about beings with moral awareness and limited free will, power, and knowledge.

Moreover, skeptical theism probably gives us reason to doubt any a priori attempt to rationally justify a high-probability attribution to $Pr(ID|T)$ or $Pr(R|T \& ID)$, and therefore any attempt to rationally justify a high-probability attribution to $Pr(R|T)$. This is because any attempt to predict what God would do were God to exist seems to rely on value claims that lie beyond the justificatory ken of mere mortal humans.[15]

Let me conclude this section with a brief summary of its contents. I have been trying to find justification for assigning $Pr(R|T)$ a relatively high value—one greater than very small. Assimilating $Pr(R|T)$ to $Pr(R|T \& ID)$ has been the strategy pursued thus far, but that strategy has foundered upon a seemingly intractable justificatory problem of assigning $Pr(ID|T)$ a relatively high value. Moreover, it seems that skeptical theism, a popular response to various arguments from evil, is in tension with any attempt to justify assigning a high value to $Pr(R|T \& ID)$. Apart from the strategy of assimilating $Pr(R|T)$ to $Pr(R|T \& ID)$ pursued here, it is difficult to see what other strategy might yield justification for assigning a high value to $Pr(R|T)$. Independent of any appeal to divine revelation (which appeal would undercut any need for argument (K) in the first place), it seems that there are no sufficiently strong grounds from which to speculate about what the Deity's purposes, intentions, and designs would be, and so (K1) is not sufficiently supported.

HOW LOW IS $Pr(R|NTE)$?

I now turn to evaluating (K2). At this point we must say more about *NTE*. Nothing Plantinga says in his lecture notes for argument (K) tells us how we ought to conceive of *NTE*. On a weak interpretation, non-theistic evolutionism is just the claim that human organisms arose from a process of natural selection (and other mechanisms studied in evolutionary biology, e.g., genetic drift) operating on heritable trait variations occurring within past populations of living things—in other words, our best theory of evolution, which importantly, remains neutral on whether or not theism is true.[16]

But there are other possible interpretations of *NTE*, and Plantinga's work on the famous (some might say infamous) Evolutionary Argument Against Naturalism (EAAN)[17] indicates an inclination toward something stronger than the weak interpretation of *NTE* just sketched. For instance, in Plantinga (2011b, 320), he says the following about the target of EAAN:

> For present purposes, therefore, I propose to assimilate materialism to naturalism; henceforth, I'll think of naturalism as including materialism, and what I'll be arguing against is the conjunction of current evolutionary theory and naturalism, the latter including materialism.

Plantinga seems to construe *NTE* as the conjunction of current evolutionary theory with naturalism, where naturalism is taken as equivalent to atheism, and also "includes" materialism. This claim, as well as Plantinga's discussion of naturalism and its relationship to materialism (Plantinga 2011b, 318–320), raises many issues. Language of "inclusion" here may indicate that Plantinga thinks that naturalism entails materialism, but Plantinga admits that the reasons for naturalists to be materialists aren't "conclusive" (2011b, 320). Perhaps what he really thinks is that, where N stands for naturalism and M stands for materialism, $Pr(M \mid N)$ is overwhelmingly high, but not 1.

The way forward is to understand M as an auxiliary assumption akin to *ID* in the previous section—M helps us get a grip on what *NTE* predicts concerning R, and moreover, is such that $Pr(M \mid NTE)$ is really high. We can then assimilate $Pr(R \mid NTE)$ to $Pr(R \mid NTE \& M)$—that is, we can assume that $Pr(R \mid NTE) \approx Pr(R \mid NTE \& M)$.

Why think that $Pr(R \mid NTE \& M)$ is really low? We can draw on Plantinga's defense of an identical premise of his EAAN.[18] For reasons of space, I will not engage in detailed exegesis of Plantinga, so here is my best reconstruction of that defense.

(P1) Given *NTE* and *M*, beliefs are neural structures (or events) such that their neurophysiological properties (NP-properties) determine their content properties (C-properties), where content properties are of the form, for some proposition *p*, *representing p*.

(P2) Given *NTE* and *M*, if beliefs are neural structures (or events) such that their NP-properties determine their C-properties, then for every population of organisms *O*, if it was probable that natural selection would result in *O*'s members having reliable belief-forming mechanisms, then it was probable that the NP-properties selected for in *O* would determine mostly true C-properties in *O*.[19]

(P3) Given *NTE* and *M*, for every population of organisms *O* that evolved via natural selection, it was not probable that the NP-properties selected for in *O*
would determine mostly true C-properties in *O*.

(P4) Therefore, given *NTE* and *M*, for the human population (that evolved via
natural selection), it was not likely that selection of reliable belief-forming
mechanisms would occur in the human population.

(P4) is equivalent to saying that $Pr(R \mid NTE \& M)$ is really small, which is the desired
conclusion, (K2).

The obvious premise to attack is (P3), so let's focus our attention on it. The
commonsense response on the part of defenders of *NTE* will be to point out that it
is extremely strange to think that the NP-properties that organisms would exhibit as
a result of natural selection would subserve false beliefs. As Quine memorably puts it,
"[c]reatures inveterately wrong in their inductions have a pathetic but praiseworthy tendency to die before reproducing their kind" (1967). Why does Plantinga think otherwise? The following statements from Plantinga shed some light on why:

> Natural selection selects for adaptive NP properties; those NP properties deter-
> mine content; but natural selection just has to take potluck with respect to the
> propositions or content determined by those adaptive NP properties. It does
> not get to influence or modify the function from NP properties to content
> properties: that's just a matter of logic or causal law, and natural selection can't
> modify either. (Plantinga 2011b, 330)

> More generally, there will have to be a function taking certain kinds of neurophys-
> iology to certain propositions, the ones that constitute the content of the struc-
> ture displaying the physiology in question. But why suppose these propositions, the
> values of that function, are *true*? (Plantinga 2011a, 442)

Both passages advert to the existence of some function or law that determines how various NP-properties map onto C-properties (their representational contents, that is). At
bottom, it seems that Plantinga's main reason in support of (P3) is that, given *NTE* and
M, there is no reason to think that on any feasible materialistically acceptable theory of
mental representation—a theory about how material structures come to represent propositional contents—the NP-properties that organisms exhibit as a result of natural selection will also tend to represent true propositions.

At this juncture, the defender of *NTE* might double down on the commonsense response just given. The caveman who, upon seeing a sharp-toothed tiger, flees in a direction away from the tiger's location *obviously* believes that there is a sharp-toothed
tiger (or something very similar).[20] The NP property (partly) causally responsible for his
fleeing obviously has as its content the proposition that there is a sharp-toothed tiger

over there. More generally, the defender of *NTE* might claim that there is some kind of nomic or causal connection between an NP property's causal profile and its content.[21] This commits the defender of *NTE* to the claim that there is a workable naturalist, materialist psychosemantics.

But Plantinga has a ready reply to anyone who doubles down on the commonsense response: the whole of §III of Plantinga (2011a) is devoted to pointing out significant problems with extant attempts to formulate a naturalist, materialist psychosemantics. The basic argument's structure is one of elimination: here are the live naturalist, materialist psychosemantic theories $T_1 \ldots T_n$; none of them can so much as explain how a material structure could represent a proposition such as "there is no God"; therefore, either no one believes a proposition such as "there is no God," or each of $T_1 \ldots T_n$ is false. But clearly people do believe (some quite vocally and vehemently) that there is no God. More generally, people believe all sorts of complicated propositions that don't seem amenable to the simple analysis presumed by the commonsense response—that "Marcel Proust is more subtle than Louis L'Amour," that "the continuum hypothesis is independent of the axioms of ZFC set theory," and so on. $T_1 \ldots T_n$ are false because they can't account for how material structures might represent such propositions.. And this is some reason—perhaps even really strong reason—to doubt that a naturalist, materialist psychosemantics is forthcoming. If this doubt is correct, then doubling down on the mere commonsense response fails, since the success of this strategy depends on there being a workable, naturalist, materialist psychosemantics.

Fully evaluating the prospects of naturalist, materialist psychosemantics is beyond this chapter's scope.[22] But Plantinga's skepticism concerning the project of naturalist, materialist psychosemantics isn't idiosyncratic. William Lycan, himself a materialist, says:

> in my view, current psychosemantics is feeble: it treats only of concepts tied closely to the thinker's physical environment; it addresses only thoughts and beliefs, and not more exotic propositional attitudes whose functions are not to be correct representations; and it does not apply to any thought that is even partly metaphorical. (2009, note 8)

Taking a similar stance, Tim Crane says (2003, 200–201):

> one of the problems that we postponed earlier still remains: how do we explain the representational powers of concepts other than very simple concepts such as water, food, predator and so on. Reductive theories of representation tend to treat this as largely a matter of detail—their approach is: let's get the simple concepts right before moving on to the complex concepts. But, even if they do get the simple concepts right, how exactly are we supposed to move on to the complex concepts? How are we supposed to explain a concept like (for example) *baroque architecture* in causal or biological terms?

These quotations suggest a different argument within Plantinga's thought for the claim that $Pr(R\,|\,NTE\,\&\,M)$ is low. Let B stand for the thesis that some human beings are capable of having beliefs. The argument would go something like this:

(B1) $\Box\,(R \to B)$.
(B2) $Pr(\neg B\,|\,NTE\,\&\,M)$ is extremely high, perhaps 1.
(B3) Therefore, $Pr(R\,|\,NTE\,\&\,M)$ is really low.[23]

(B3) just is (K2). (B1) should be self-evident—if no human being is capable of believing anything, then naturally it follows that no human being has reliable belief-forming mechanisms. (B2) is a consequence of the failure (in the limit of inquiry, perhaps) of naturalist, materialist psychosemantics. Interestingly, this argument does not seem to involve evolutionary considerations at all—it seems that naturalism and materialism do all the work.

Let me summarize this section. We have been seeking support for premise (K2) of argument (K) reconstructed within the likelihood framework. After some digging, we have identified a promising argument for (K2) in (B1)–(B3). However, a full evaluation of this argument would require canvassing all possible naturalist, materialist psychosemantics and finding them wanting. But if Plantinga, Lycan, and Crane's suspicions are correct, then there might be some reason to suspect that all possible naturalist, materialist psychosemantics will be found wanting.

CONCLUSION

Let us ascend from the details of evaluating the key premises of argument (K) as reconstructed in the likelihood framework, and summarize the main conclusions of this chapter. I have argued that (K1) is not adequately supported, and so argument (K) fails in establishing the conclusion that R is evidence for T just for that reason. But not all is lost for the theist. If (K2) is correct, then it naturalism faces a serious problem independent of whether argument (K) succeeds.

I suggest that a potentially fruitful area of future research might involve examining the prospects of a naturalist, materialist psychosemantics. Doing so would allow philosophers to more thoroughly evaluate the reasons for thinking that (K2) is true. If (K2) is, in fact, true, that should pose a significant challenge to naturalism. And if theism and naturalism are the only live options, that might constitute good reason for theism.

NOTES

I am grateful to Nathan Ballantyne, Trent Dougherty, Andrew Moon, and Jerry Walls for discussion on matters in this chapter. None of the opinions expressed herein reflect those of the John Templeton Foundation, its trustees, or officers, save the author.

1. For extended discussions of this issue, see McGrew (2005) and Sober (2008, 113–122).

2. On likelihoodism, I have learned a great deal from Sober (2008, Chapter 1), whose other work on design arguments is relevant to the discussion of argument (K). See also Hacking (1965) and Royall (1997) for more on likelihoodism.

3. For an overview of the issues, see Fitelson (2007).

4. Compare also how Robin Collins (2009) presents the fine-tuning argument for theism.

5. Here the form of my argument is that of Sober (2008, 141).

6. Duhem (1954) claims that auxiliary claims are always in play when scientists test a theory, and they are probably always in play when scientists extract predictions from a theory. See also Sober (2008, 144), who cites Duhem on this point.

7. These conditions, via the theorem of total probabilities, imply other conditions, some of which I treat below.

8. See also Beilby (2002, 2).

9. Those of a more Reformed persuasion will balk at this reasoning, perhaps citing Matthew 10:29 as a proof text against it. However, to avoid having to impugn God's moral perfection, even Reformed theologians typically distinguish two senses of "want" and "intention" with respect to God (though usually the point is put in terms of God's will or decree). God's *revealed* wants and intentions are resolutely against there being enormous amounts of evil in the world, but God's *hidden* or *decretive* wants and intentions are maybe not so. But this distinction is moot with respect to Plantinga's model. If we understand "want" and "intend" in the model along the lines of God's hidden will, we undercut any reason there might be to accept the model—after all, we don't have access to God's hidden will since it's *hidden*. And if we understand it along the lines of God's revealed will, the Reformed theologian loses any reason to balk at my point in the main text.

10. A principle like this is implicit in probabilistic formulations of the argument from evil, and supports the atheist's contention that evil is unexpected given theism.

11. Here I draw on Swinburne (2004, 114–131, *passim*).

12. This argument is merely Swinburne-*style*, not actually the argument that Swinburne gives. One big difference is that Swinburne assigns $Pr(ID \mid T)$ a probability of 0.5, not 1. This indicates that Swinburne would be less sanguine about the much stronger argument I have given as a defense of (K1). Another big difference is that Swinburne seriously entertains the possibility of God bringing about (note, not creating) other animate substances with moral awareness and unlimited freewill, knowledge, and power—this is Swinburne's way of arguing for the doctrine of the Trinity a priori. The argument I sketch above relies on rejecting this as a possibility for God.

13. Swinburne himself seems to confess the view that God would be compelled to create, that "God must bring about something" (2004, 117). I find this confession puzzling.

14. There is another, more speculative, objection to the Swinburne-style argument, inspired by Johnston (manuscript). The objection first notes that (S1) presumes that the source of God's reasons for action is the divine moral goodness, and that this provides God with morally compelling reasons to improve the world by adding more goodness to it. But, the objection notes, any world where God exists is already, by virtue of including God, *unsurpassably good*, such that nothing God created might add to that world's goodness. Thus, God couldn't have morally compelling reasons to improve the world—no improvement is possible. Therefore, God does not create out of a reason to make more good things. At most, God's moral goodness constrains what God brings about—God cannot bring about really bad things. But God's moral goodness does not require God to bring about the best. So premise (S1) is false.

15. Maybe all design arguments are in serious tension with skeptical theism on this point—for more, see Hudson (2016).

16. This point remains controversial, but I think it's right. On why evolution is compatible with theism—even a quite traditional theism—see Ruse (2004) and Sober (2011, 2014).

17. (K2) is identical to a core premise of EAAN, but I have not discussed any of the literature devoted to expositing, refining, and criticizing this argument, for reasons of space. I will, however, treat some issues raised by EAAN shortly. For Plantinga's various statements of EAAN, see Plantinga (1993, chapter 12), Plantinga (2001, 218–240), Plantinga's opening piece in Beilby (2002), and Plantinga (2011b,a, Chapter 10). For further discussions of EAAN, see Fitelson and Sober (1998), Beilby (2002), and Mirza (2008, 2011).

18. See his (2011a) and (2011b, 320–339, *passim*).

19. A C-property of the form *represents proposition p* iff the proposition *p* is true.

20. Of course, the caveman will also have to believe other things, such as that sharp-toothed tigers tend to pose a risk to his life and limb. He will also have to desire that he not be harmed or eaten. There is a commitment to a kind of holism here, that having one belief depends on having a host of other representational states.

21. This seems to be the move that Boudry and Vlerick (2014, 69) takes.

22. Some of the relevant attempts include Millikan (1987), Fodor (1989), Dretske (1991), and Fodor (1992). Plantinga (2011a) explicitly criticizes Dretske's indicator psychosemantics and Millikan's teleosemantics with arguments of the structure given in the previous paragraph. For problems with Fodor's psychosemantics, see, for example, Seager (1993).

23. By (B1) and the probability calculus, $Pr(R \mid NTE\&M) \leq Pr(B \mid NTE\&M)$. $Pr(B \mid NTE\&M) = 1 - Pr(\neg B \mid NTE\&M)$. Therefore, $Pr(R \mid NTE\&M) \leq 1 - Pr(\neg B \mid NTE\&M)$. If $Pr(\neg B \mid NTE\&M)$ is really high, then $1 - Pr(\neg B \mid NTE\&M)$ is going to be really low. And therefore $Pr(R \mid NTE\&M)$ is going to be really low.

REFERENCES

Beilby, James (ed.). 2002. *Naturalism Defeated?: Essays on Plantinga's Evolutionary Argument Against Naturalism*. Ithaca, NY: Cornell University Press.

Bergmann, Michael. 2001. "Skeptical Theism and Rowe's New Evidential Argument from Evil." *Noûs* 35:278–296.

Bergmann, Michael and Rea, Michael. 2005. "In Defence of Skeptical Theism: A Reply to Almeida and Oppy." *Australasian Journal of Philosophy* 83:241–251.

Boudry, Maarten and Vlerick, Michael. 2014. "Natural Selection Does Care about Truth." *International Studies in the Philosophy of Science* 28:65–77.

Collins, Robin. 2009. "The Teleological Argument: An Exploration of the Fine-Tuning of the Universe." In William Lane Craig and J.P. Moreland (eds.), *The Blackwell Companion to Natural Theology*, 202–281. Malden, MA: Wiley-Blackwell.

Crane, Tim. 2003. *The Mechanical Mind: A Philosophical Introduction to Minds, Machines, and Mental Representation*. New York: Routledge, 2nd edition.

Dretske, Fred. 1991. *Explaining Behavior*. Cambridge, MA: MIT Press.

Duhem, Pierre. 1954. *The Aim and Structure of Physical Theory*. Princeton, NJ: Princeton University Press.

Fitelson, Branden. 2007. "Likelihoodism, Bayesianism, and Relational Confirmation." *Synthese* 156:473–489.

Fitelson, Branden and Sober, Elliot. 1998. "Plantinga's Probability Argument against Naturalism." *Pacific Philosophical Quarterly* 79:115–129.

Fodor, Jerry. 1989. *Psychosemantics: The Problem of Meaning in the Philosophy of Mind.* Cambridge, MA: MIT Press.

———. 1992. *A Theory of Content and Other Essays.* Cambridge, MA: MIT Press.

Hacking, Ian. 1965. *The Logic of Statistical Inference.* Cambridge: Cambridge University Press.

Hudson, Hud. 2016. "Swinburne's Aesthetic Appeal." In Michael Bergmann and Patrick Kain (eds.), *Reason and Faith: Themes from Swinburne,* chapter 4, 64–82. Oxford University Press.

Johnston, Mark. manuscript. "Why Did the One Not Remain Within Itself?"

Lycan, William. 2009. "Giving Dualism Its Due." *Australasian Journal of Philosophy* 87:551–563.

McGrew, Timothy. 2005. "Toward a Rational Reconstruction of Design Inferences." *Philosophia Christi* 7:253–298.

Millikan, Ruth. 1987. *Language, Thought, and Other Biological Categories.* Cambridge, MA: MIT Press.

Mirza, Omar. 2008. "A User's Guide to the Evolutionary Argument against Naturalism." *Philosophical Studies* 141:125–146.

———. 2011. "The Evolutionary Argument against Naturalism." *Philosophy Compass* 6:78–89.

Plantinga, Alvin. 1993. *Warrant and Proper Function.* New York: Oxford University Press.

———. 2001. *Warranted Christian Belief.* New York: Oxford University Press.

———. 2011a. "Content and Natural Selection." *Philosophy and Phenomenological Research* 83:435–458.

———. 2011b. *Where the Conflict Really Lies: Science, Religion, and Naturalism.* New York: Oxford University Press.

Quine, W.V. 1969. "Natural Kinds." In *Ontological Relativity and Other Essays.* Harvard University Press.

Royall, Richard. 1997. *Statistical Evidence: A Likelihood Paradigm.* Boca Raton, FL: Chapman and Hall.

Ruse, Michael. 2004. *Can a Darwinian Be a Christian? The Relationship between Science and Religion.* New York: Cambridge University Press.

Seager, William. 1993. "Fodor's Theory of Content: Problems and Objections." *Philosophy of Science* 60:262–277.

Sober, Elliot. 2008. *Evidence and Evolution.* New York: Cambridge University Press.

———. 2011. "Evolution without Naturalism." *Oxford Studies in Philosophy of Religion* 3:187–221.

———. 2014. "Evolutionary Theory, Causal Completeness, and Theism: The Case of 'Guided' Mutation." In R. Paul Thompson and Denis Walsh (eds.), *Evolutionary Biology: Conceptual, Ethical, and Religious Issues,* 31–44. New York: Cambridge University Press.

Swinburne, Richard. 2004. *The Existence of God.* New York: Oxford University Press, 3rd edition.

(L)

The Argument from Simplicity and (M) The Argument from Induction

ATHEISTIC INDUCTION BY BOLTZMANN BRAINS

Bradley Monton

INTRODUCTION

DOES THE FACT that our inductive practices are successful provide evidence for the existence of God? Do simplicity considerations provide such evidence? I will mostly focus on the argument from induction, and in doing so I will present a new thermodynamic argument for the existence of God. But let's begin with an opening salvo on simplicity.

With regard to the argument from simplicity for the existence of God, here's the natural question to ask: is the hypothesis that God exists a very simple hypothesis (as, for example, Richard Swinburne (1979) claims), or is the hypothesis that God exists a very complex hypothesis (as, for example, Richard Dawkins (2008) claims)? If simplicity is a guide to truth (as both of those Richards think it is), then by Swinburne's lights, the prior probability for the God hypothesis is high, while by Dawkins's lights, the prior probability for the God hypothesis is low. And according to them, after one takes into account all the evidence to get a posterior probability, their posteriors aren't much different than their priors—the simplicity judgments are doing the bulk of the work.

The question of whether simplicity is a guide to truth is a vexing one. It is natural to think that simplicity is a guide to truth in the context of, for example, curve-fitting in physics. Suppose one has a finite set of data points representing the relationship between two parameters in physics, and one wants to draw a curve that projects a relationship from those finite data points to the values of the parameters in-between. The problem is that there are an infinite number of curves that can be drawn that intersect all the data points. Most of these curves are unsimple (in a crazy, all-over-the-place sort of way), and hence are rejected by physicists. And, as more data points are gathered, typically the simpler curves turn out to make the right predictions for those new data points. It sure looks like simplicity is a guide to truth.

But philosophers are sometimes too willing to take these relatively uncontroversial judgements from physics and wildly extrapolate them into controversial judgements in philosophy. For example, consider ontological parsimony (parsimony of objects) versus ideological parsimony (parsimony of concepts). Is it ontological or ideological parsimony that matters for simplicity? While some philosophers attempt to provide an objective answer to this question (see, for example, Cowling (2013)), I am skeptical. Maybe God exists and God has an opinion, but absent God's judgement, I maintain that it's just a matter of personal preference.

My plan in this chapter is to focus on induction, and to bring in simplicity considerations only when they are well-grounded in physics. You might then think that such physics-based simplicity considerations wouldn't come into play in a chapter on God and induction. But you might also recognize that that previous sentence constitutes foreshadowing that they will.

So, back to induction—here is the schedule of this chapter. One can raise worries about the viability of induction generally, as Hume did. My discussion of that will be Preliminary Match #1. One can also raise worries about the viability of induction as applied to a particular philosophical theory. I'll discuss that in the context of David Lewis's modal realism in Preliminary Match #2. Finally, we'll turn to the Main Event, on how naturalistic physics provides positive evidence for the failure of induction, and how to potentially overcome that, whether naturalistically or theistically. (And stick around for the epistemological epilogue, on self-undermining arguments.)

PRELIMINARY MATCH #1: THE GENERAL PROBLEM OF INDUCTION

Hume famously argued that we have no grounds for believing that our inductive practices will be reliable in the future. At least, we have no grounds for thinking this, assuming naturalism. As Descartes, for example, showed, one can get around skeptical worries by establishing (or presupposing) the existence of God, and then pointing out that God is not a deceiver. God wouldn't deceive us, hence our inductive practices will be reliable in the future.

Well, that's nice that believing in God provides a solution to Hume's problem of induction. But wishes aren't horses. Can one turn this into an argument for theism? Let's consider the following transcendental argument:

Premise 1: A precondition for reliable inductive reasoning is the truth of theism.
Premise 2: We do reliably engage in inductive reasoning.
Conclusion: Theism is true.

(Bare theism wouldn't do: it would take something more, like non-deceiver theism. I'll henceforth assume that as built into the theistic hypothesis.)

This argument has the drawback of being unsound. The crucial transcendental premise is false; it's certainly *possible* that we could engage in reliable inductive reasoning in a naturalistic world. All Hume pointed out is that we have no reason to *expect* our inductive reasoning to be reliable.

Perhaps the argument should be put in terms of our justification for inductive reasoning:

> *Premise 1*: A precondition for us being justified in engaging in inductive reasoning is the truth of theism.
> *Premise 2*: We are justified in engaging in inductive reasoning.
> *Conclusion*: Theism is true.

But the (or at least a) problem with this new argument is that Premise 2 is questionable, and question-begging. We don't know that we are justified in engaging in inductive reasoning—we've been successful at it in the past, but it doesn't follow that we are epistemologically justified in that practice.

Instead of giving a transcendental argument for theism, perhaps one can instead give an inductive argument:

> *Premise 1*: Under the assumption of naturalism, we have no reason to expect our inductive practices to be reliable.
> *Premise 2*: Under the assumption of theism, we do have reason to expect our inductive practices to be reliable.
> *Premise 3*: Our inductive practices are reliable.
> *Conclusion*: The reliability of our inductive practices provides evidence for the truth of theism over naturalism.

That argument, admittedly, has some inductive strength—but, I maintain, not much strength. To see why, compare that argument to this one:

> *Premise 1*: Under the assumption of naturalism, we have no reason to expect our next coin flip to land heads (rather than tails).
> *Premise 2*: Under the assumption that a supernatural sprite who loves heads has just popped into existence in the room, we do have reason to expect our next coin flip to land heads.
> *Premise 3*: Our next coin flip lands heads.
> *Conclusion*: That coin flip landing heads provides evidence for the existence of the supernatural sprite and against naturalism.

I am willing to concede that, from a probability theory standpoint, that sprite argument works. But my prior probabilities are such that the level of support the argument provides for the sprite hypothesis is minimal. And the same holds for the previous (inductive) argument for theism. Sometimes, things are the case, even if we have no reason to expect them to be the case, and that shouldn't provide much support for the existence of a supernatural entity. This holds for the coin landing heads, and this also holds for the hypothesis that our inductive practices are reliable.

Here's another way to look at this. There are some things theists can explain that naturalists can't. But naturalists should be comfortable with this. Most naturalists would be happy to concede that they don't have an explanation of why there is something rather than nothing, why the universe has the laws of nature that it does, and so on. Theists have an explanation for all this: God created something, God created the laws, and so on. Similarly, naturalists can't explain why our inductive practices are reliable; theists can. It doesn't follow that the theist's explanation is true.

PRELIMINARY MATCH #2: THE MODAL REALIST'S PROBLEM OF INDUCTION

I earlier discussed a situation in which we have no reason to think that induction is reliable, under the assumption that naturalism is true. But what if we found ourselves in a situation in which we have positive reason to think that induction is unreliable, under the assumption that naturalism is true? I'll now show that there is at least one important philosophical theory that has this consequence. One way to avoid this consequence, of course, is to reject naturalism. My preferred method is to reject the important philosophical theory in question.

The theory I have in mind is David Lewis's modal realism. Lewis (1986) believes that there are an infinite number of physical worlds, spatiotemporally disconnected from each other, representing every possible way that the world could be. Lewis also believes in a principle of recombination, according to which "patching together parts of different possible worlds yields another possible world" (1986, 87–88). Consider all the worlds with a history like ours, up to the present moment. By Lewis's lights, *any* possible future can be patched together with our past, and there is a world in existence with that past and that future.

So think about all the possible worlds with a history like ours, and the wide variety of futures they have. There are, in an intuitive sense at least, a comparatively small number of worlds where things go as expected by the lights of inductive reasoning, and a comparatively large number of worlds that they haywire by the lights of inductive reasoning. So according to Lewis's theory, we should reason counterinductively: we should think it very unlikely that the principle of induction will continue to hold in the future. Just think about all the possible parts of worlds there are: a part of a world with just one electron, a part of a world with just two electrons, a part of a world with just one dragon, et cetera. Any of these parts could be a complete future of our world, by Lewis's lights. So, it's vastly more likely that the future will not line up nicely with the past as that it will.

Interestingly, Plantinga suggests otherwise. He writes:

> there are plenty of possible worlds (worlds run by mischievous Cartesian demons, perhaps) in which things go just as they have up to the present, but then go completely crazy; there are as many worlds like that as worlds in which induction will continue to be a reliable source of belief. (Plantinga 1993, 125)

While Plantinga isn't specifically discussing Lewis in this context, he is discussing a possible-worlds framework that (for our purposes at least) is compatible with Lewis's framework. So in this context, I respectfully maintain that Plantinga is mistaken. I maintain there aren't "as many" worlds where induction is successful as not; I maintain that we're not in a situation like that discussed in the previous section. Instead, I maintain that there are many fewer worlds where induction is successful as not. We have positive reason to think that, by Lewis's lights, the future will most likely go completely crazy.

To really show that Plantinga is mistaken, though, one would have to have a measure over the space of possible worlds, which specifies for any set of worlds how likely they are compared to another set. While we often make intuitive judgements that yield such results, we have no specification of what an overall measure would be. (An example of an intuitive judgement: worlds with a history like ours where every human gets struck by lightning in the next hour are less likely than worlds with a history like ours where some but not all humans get struck by lightning in the next hour.)

Let's assume that I'm correct that there are a comparatively small number of worlds where things go as expected by the lights of inductive reasoning, and a comparatively large number of worlds where they go as unexpected, and let's assume that the measure over the worlds treats all these worlds equiprobably. Then if one believed in modal realism (as some of us do) and found oneself in a world with a particular history (as all of us do) and contemplated whether inductive reasoning is going to hold in the future (as you are so contemplating, now that I've said it), one would recognize that a vast majority of worlds with this history are going to go completely differently in the future, while only rare worlds with this history will have a future that conforms with our inductive reasoning, and one should be incredibly scared. At least, one should be as scared as one would be seeing the rampaging pirate with a sword coming at your neck—in either scenario one is probably not long for this world. The vast majority of possible worlds with a history like ours are ones where the immediate future does not contain you or me or any of the things we care about. Let us contemplate this while we can, for in the next moment we most likely die.

Perhaps you are not happy with this result. How should you reject it? One solution—my favored solution—is to reject modal realism altogether. Another solution is to postulate a theistic version of modal realism: only those possible worlds exist where God exists, and God is not a deceiver, so induction is reliable in all possible worlds. Either move, of course, constitutes a rejection of David Lewis's version of modal realism.

Let's step back. I have been raising the worry of inductive skepticism about the future. But I could have presented a parallel skeptical problem about the past. By the same principle of recombination, one can combine any past history with a present like ours. So just as we should doubt our inductive reasoning about the future given Lewis's modal realism, so we should doubt our memories and inferences about the past.

But let's not harp on modal realism more. Let's move on to the Main Event, in which I'll show that our best physics suggests that in the actual world we are facing just such a skeptical problem, about both the past and the future.

THE MAIN EVENT: THE NATURALISTIC IMPLAUSIBILITY
OF THE PAST HYPOTHESIS
Boltzmann Brains

Consider a regular raw chicken egg, balanced precariously on the edge of a table. The egg eventually falls onto the floor, smashing into many goopy pieces. There is nothing unfamiliar about such an event. But the laws of physics are (as far as physicists can tell) time-reversal invariant (with minor exceptions which, as far as physicists can tell, wouldn't have any relevance to everyday events like egg-fallings; I'll ignore these minor exceptions henceforth). This means that, in principle, the time-reverse of the story I just told is also physically possible. Minor undulations in the floor could congregate on a particular spot, pushing the pieces of the egg up into the air in such a way that the pieces form into a whole egg and the egg lands on the edge of the table. This is—uncontroversially—physically possible. So why do we never see it?

The reason we don't is that it's incredibly unlikely to occur—it's incredibly unlikely that forces would align in just such a way as to reform a broken egg. This incredible improbability is captured in the second law of thermodynamics—that entropy in a closed system never decreases. The broken egg on the floor is a higher-entropy state than the whole egg on the table, so by the second law the broken egg could never reform into the whole egg on the table. But if laws are understood as exceptionless regularities, then the second law isn't really a law; it's just a statistical generalization. The generalization holds because, when considering all the possible states of a system, the low-entropy states are incredibly rare, and high-entropy states are incredibly likely. For a given macro-description of a system (like "broken egg on the floor") the number of ways the system evolves where entropy stays the same or increases vastly outnumbers the number of ways the system evolves where entropy decreases. (To be more precise, we'd want a probability measure over the space, but physicists for the most part agree on what the probability measure is, and it yields the result that the low-entropy states are incredibly unlikely.)

Now let's think about the universe as a whole. I'm going to give an account, based on standard physics, but with an almost unbelievable conclusion. Once I get to the unbelievable conclusion, I'll explain how physicists standardly try to avoid it.

Given the current state of the universe, we expect the universe to evolve toward higher-entropy states, since they are vastly more likely than lower-entropy states. This would culminate in what's called "the heat death" of the universe—particles are spread out throughout the universe (or perhaps clumped due to gravity), but with no structure of the sort that we see in, say, living organisms. Anyway, that's what we expect for the future—the crucial point I want to make is that, given the time-reversal invariance of the laws of physics, *we should expect the same thing for the past*. Higher-entropy states are vastly more likely than lower-entropy states, so, given the current state of the universe, dynamical trajectories for the universe that get to that current state starting from higher-entropy states are vastly more likely than dynamical trajectories that start from lower-entropy states.

But if the universe were in a high-entropy "heat death" state, how could one ever get to the low-entropy order that we see around us? Well, physics allows for random fluctuations out of high-entropy states—on rare occasions, a part of the universe will fluctuate into a lower-entropy state, and then return to the high-entropy state. Perhaps that's what happened to the part that we are in, and we are now on the lower-to-higher entropy trajectory that we expect to be on.

But here's the rub. The larger the size of the part of the universe that fluctuates into a lower-entropy state, the less likely that is to occur. For you to judge a theory to be viable, it minimally needs to be empirically adequate—it needs to account for your observations. Of the various fluctuations out of a high-entropy state that are compatible with your current observations, the most likely ones are where nothing more than a brain-sized region fluctuates out of the high-entropy state, momentarily generating a lower-entropy organized brain that has exactly the experiences you are having now. But moments ago, that brain didn't exist, and moments later, it will have ceased to exist—the momentary fluctuation will be over.

This hypothesis that you are such a brain—a "Boltzmann brain"—is compatible with everything that you currently observe. And, strictly speaking, what you currently observe is the totality of your empirical evidence. We sometimes cite what we remember as evidence, but the hypothesis that you are a Boltzmann brain calls into question the reliability of these memories. And, most importantly for our context, the hypothesis that you are a Boltzmann brain calls into question the reliability of your inductive practices—so many of the beliefs you currently have about the future will (within the next few moments, as the system evolves back to the high-entropy state and your brain ceases to exist) turn out to be *false*.

The Past Hypothesis

Let's step back. In Preliminary Event #1, I reflected on how Hume pointed out that we have no reason to believe that our inductive practices will continue to be successful in the future—but that line of reasoning at least has the happy consequence that we have no reason to believe that they won't. In Preliminary Event #2, I took up modal realism, and argued that, by the lights of that controversial theory, we do have positive reason to believe that our inductive practices won't be successful in the future. Now, in the Main Event, I have argued that contemporary physics provides positive reason to believe that your inductive practices won't continue to be successful—instead you're just a brain that momentarily fluctuated into existence.

So how should we avoid this unhappy conclusion? The theist could say that God exists, and God presumably wouldn't design the world in such a deceptive fashion, and God presumably would value the existence of continuing moral agents, not momentary Boltzmann brains.

Let's grant that this theistic hypothesis is highly implausible. What would the atheist instead say? The standard move that atheists make is to postulate *the past hypothesis*—that the universe started in a low-entropy state (or, if the universe didn't have a temporal beginning, that the past boundary condition of the universe is a low-entropy state).

The past hypothesis is endorsed by many physicists and philosophers of physics (for a nice defense see David Albert (2000, Chapter 4)), but there are dissenters (such as John Earman (2006)). For the purposes of this chapter, I will set aside the dissenters, and examine the justifications philosophers have given for endorsing the past hypothesis.

A problem with the past hypothesis is that it is highly improbable, by the lights of standard physics. It's way more improbable than the broken egg reformulating and soaring up to the table—it's as if improbable things like that have happened, but for the universe as a whole.

Huw Price makes the point vividly:

Suppose . . . physics had discovered that the matter in the universe is collapsing towards a Big Crunch, fifteen billion years or so in our future—and that as it does so, something very, very extraordinary is happening. . . . Somehow, by some unimaginably intricate balancing act, the various forces are balancing out, so that by the time of the Big Crunch, matter will have spread itself out with great uniformity. A butterfly—nay, a molecule—out of place, and the whole house of cards would surely collapse!

As a combination of significance and sheer improbability—the latter judged by well-grounded existing conceptions of how matter might be expected to behave—this discovery would surely trump anything else ever discovered by physics. . . .

In my view, however, this state of affairs is *exactly* what physics has discovered! I have merely described it in unusual language, reversing the usual temporal conventions. . . this redescription has no objective significance. If it is a proper matter for explanation described one way, it is a proper matter for explanation described the other. (Price 2002, 115–116)

I agree with Price—it is very, very extraordinary that everything in the universe is lined up in such a way that the universe started with a low-entropy state. I agree that that state is highly improbable, and that that judgement of improbability is well-grounded in physics. And, I agree (pace, for example, Craig Callender (2004)) that such an improbable state cries out for explanation. So what is Price's explanation? Price (2002, 118) says: "A solution . . . is not yet at hand. Indeed, it is not yet clear what a solution would look like."

One thing bothers me about the approach of Price and all the others who endorse this improbable past hypothesis from within a naturalistic framework. I want to ask them: why reject the Boltzmann brain hypothesis in the first place? The theist has a reason to reject that hypothesis—the theist can point out that God is not a deceiver, and that God values the existence of continuing moral agents. But what reason does the naturalist have, other than wishful thinking that our memories are reliable and our inductive practices will continue to be successful? The naturalist posits the past hypothesis to save those desiderata, but the naturalist should recognize that physics is telling us the hypothesis being postulated to save those desiderata is very, very implausible.

Many naturalistic endorsers of the past hypothesis don't even give a reason for rejecting the Boltzmann brain hypothesis—they just take for granted that the hypothesis should be rejected. David Albert (2000, 93–95), to his credit, gives an argument—but unfortunately, as I'll now show, his argument is flawed.

Albert first points out, as I did earlier, that the hypothesis that you are a Boltzmann brain is compatible with everything you currently observe. Indeed, he goes further, and points out that:

there can be nothing at all about the present macrocondition of the world which can possibly count as evidence that the world's entropy has ever previously been lower. (Albert 2000, 93)

Albert recognizes that you have memories that suggest that entropy was lower—you, for example, looking at the broken egg on the floor, have the memory of it being intact on the table moments before. But, unless we endorse the past hypothesis, physics tells us that it's overwhelmingly likely that the current state of the world is just a fluctuation from a higher-entropy state, and (hence) it's overwhelmingly likely that your current memories are non-veridical.

I agree with all that. But then Albert tries to argue that we do know that the past hypothesis is true:

the fact that the universe came into being in an enormously low-entropy macrocondition cannot possibly be the sort of fact that we know, or ever *will* know, in the way we know of straightforward everyday particular *empirical* facts. We know it *differently*, then. Our grounds for believing it turn out to be more like our grounds for believing general theoretical *laws*. Our grounds (that is) are *inductive*. (Albert 2000, 93–94)

Albert bases his argument on the claim that believing the past hypothesis "turns out to be enormously helpful in making an enormous variety of particular empirical *predictions*." For example, suppose you dig up a boot from the ground. You would predict that it would be reasonably likely that, if you kept digging, you would find a matching boot. We make predictions like this all the time, and they are often verified. Albert argues that the verification of such predictions is to be expected given the past hypothesis, but there's no reason to expect them to be verified given that you are a Boltzmann brain. Thus, he believes the past hypothesis.

The problem with Albert's argument is that when you think you have made a prediction that has been successfully confirmed, that relies on memory. The confirmation cannot come at exactly the same time as the prediction; it's the nature of prediction that the prediction has to be made first, and then confirmation comes later. So when you are thinking at the time of the confirmation, "oh, my prediction has been confirmed," you are relying on the memory that you made such a prediction in the first place. But Boltzmann brains can have such memories, too—it's just that such memories for Boltzmann brains are mostly non-veridical. A Boltzmann brain with such memories would have most likely fluctuated into existence with the false belief that it made such predictions, and the false belief that some of these predictions have been confirmed. (Moreover, Boltzmann brains will most likely fluctuate out of existence before they have the chance to confirm any predictions they do really make about the future.) So you might *think* that you've made predictions that have been confirmed, but Boltzmann brains would think that, too; the fact that you have that thought doesn't provide evidence that you are not a Boltzmann brain.

Thus, Albert's attempt to provide inductive reason that you are not a Boltzmann brain is unsuccessful. Albert has provided no reason for you to think that you really have made successful inductive predictions—and moreover, the evidence from physics is that you are probably a Boltzmann brain and, hence, you haven't made such predictions.

Simplicity

I've shown that Albert's argument for why you should think you're not a Boltzmann brain is unsuccessful. I have a speculative but potentially better argument to offer the naturalist, based on considerations of simplicity, grounded in physics.

We can get a physics-based definition of simplicity, building on an important new paper by Scott Aaronson, Sean Carroll, and Lauren Ouellette (ACO) (2014). (Aaronson and Carroll are physicists at MIT and Caltech, respectively; Ouellette was an MIT student.) They present and defend a formal definition of complexity—and while they never address this in their paper, I think it makes sense for us philosophers to treat complexity as the opposite of simplicity.

Given the past hypothesis, the standard view from physics is that the entropy of our universe increases pretty much monotonically—from a low-entropy state at the beginning of the universe to a high-entropy state at the end. (Picture time on the x-axis and entropy of the y-axis—other than random rare fluctuations, the slope of the line is always flat or positive.) The ACO measure of complexity for the universe, on the other hand, is like an upside-down U—the universe is simple at the initial low-entropy state, and simple at the final high-entropy state, while it is complex in the middle.

ACO write that, before their paper, there was

> no general principle that quantifies and explains the existence of high-complexity states at intermediate times in closed systems. It is the aim of this work to explore such a principle. (2014, 2)

Their paper makes plausible that the universe would have high-complexity states at intermediate times—the time of our existence being such an intermediate time, and the current state of Earth being an example of a high-complexity state. They do not attempt to provide a justification for why the universe started in a low-entropy state—but perhaps here is where philosophical considerations can come into play. Given an account of simplicity that is well-grounded in physics, philosophers can then argue that simple states are likely to exist as the boundary conditions for our universe—that the initial and final conditions of the universe would be simple ones. So this is my tentative proposal for a naturalistic alternative to the theistic hypothesis that avoids the Boltzmann brain problem and saves induction: postulate the past hypothesis, and motivate it not only by pointing out that it saves induction, and the reliability of memory, but also that it is simple, and this gives foundational metaphysical reason to endorse it.

Granted, the naturalistic past hypothesis is implausible—because physics tells us that a low-entropy state for the universe is highly improbable. But by pointing out that the past hypothesis postulates a simple state, and that (perhaps) simplicity is a guide to truth, we can provide some argument that makes the naturalistic past hypothesis more plausible. In doing so, we can make it a more worthy competitor to the theistic hypothesis, with regard to the attempt to account for why our inductive practices will continue to be successful.

This main event doesn't end with a knockout. We're left to judge: which hypothesis is less implausible, the hypothesis that you are a Boltzmann brain, or the naturalistic past hypothesis, or the theistic hypothesis? That will have to be the reader's decision.

EPILOGUE: SELF-UNDERMINING ARGUMENTS

I had coffee with Lily the other day. "Bradley," she said, "I just found out that I have this strange and rare disease. The main symptom is that my memory of phone conversations is highly unreliable."

"Wow," I replied. "How did you find out about this?"

"Well," she said, "my doctor called me the other day and told me so."

There's something funny going on in this story (adapted from Talbott 2002). The funniness can be brought out if we try to convert that conversation into an inductively strong argument:

Premise 1: Doctors reliably tell their patients the truth about what diseases the patients have.

Premise 2: Lily reliably tells me the truth about her diseases.

Premise 3: Lily reliably remembers important phone conversations.

Conclusion: Lily told me the truth about her phone conversation; she does have this disease.

The problem is that, once we accept the truth of the conclusion, we have reason to doubt the truth of one of the premises—we have reason to doubt that Lily's memory of important phone conversations is reliable. But once we reject that premise, we have no reason to accept the truth of the conclusion—the argument is no longer inductively strong. But if we don't accept the truth of the conclusion, then we no longer have any reason to doubt that premise. And if we have no reason to doubt that premise, then the argument is once again inductively strong. And so on. . . .

This is an epistemologically vexing situation, and unfortunately, I don't know of any epistemological literature to which we could turn to definitively resolve it (though for some discussion, see Hume (1738, I, IV, i), Plantinga (1993, 234–235), and Talbott (2002, 157)).

It would be one thing if the vexingness just applied to this artificial Lily example, but it applies to a wide variety of cases. Consider, for example, Michael Huemer's (2005) argument for the claim that when one is not an expert on a topic, one shouldn't engage in critical thinking to decide what to believe; instead, one is better off believing whatever the majority of the experts believe. If a non-philosophy expert reads Huemer's paper and, using her own critical thinking skills, comes to believe the conclusion, she might then decide to survey philosophy experts about Huemer's conclusion. Most of the philosophy experts would reject Huemer's conclusion, so she would be led to reject it, too. But once she rejected it, she'd be back to using her critical thinking skills, and those lead her to accept the conclusion of Huemer's argument, and the circle continues.

The reason I bring all this up is that a key move in the previous section of the paper relies on a self-undermining argument. You have an understanding of the laws of physics, and based on that understanding, you get the result that you are probably a Boltzmann brain. But Boltzmann brains would not be expected to have true beliefs about the physical world—there is no reason to expect a rare random fluctuation out of a high-entropy state to produce a brain that has an understanding of the laws of physics of the world it's appearing in. So if you run through this argument and reach the conclusion that you are probably a Boltzmann brain, you will recognize—now thinking that you are probably a Boltzmann brain—that you have no reason to believe what you thought you initially understood about the laws of physics. But then, you have no reason to believe that you are a Boltzmann brain. But then the circle continues—once you reject that hypothesis that you are a Boltzmann brain, you go back to thinking that you have an understanding of the laws of physics, and based on that understanding, you get the result that you are a Boltzmann brain. . . and so on.

So how should we handle this? Plantinga (1993, 235) briefly suggests that one should recognize that a situation like this is untenable, and hence one should not believe the initial premise. Plantinga admits that the premise might be true, but he says that it is irrational to believe it. His discussion takes place in the context of his Evolutionary Argument Against Naturalism, and he thinks that the key premise one should give up is naturalism. What is the premise that one should give up in the Boltzmann brain situation? Plantinga might be happy to say "again, naturalism." But naturalists would typically say that we should give up the premise that the initial condition of the universe is a high-entropy state, and instead endorse the past hypothesis.

What worries me regarding both of these moves (giving up naturalism, or giving up the premise that the universe starts in a high-entropy state) is that there is no evidence to merit giving up either of those premises. At least, there is no evidence to merit giving them up within the confines of the topic under discussion: the reliability of our inductive practices. Many theists would say that there are other reasons to believe theism (such as religious experience, the ontological argument, or what have you). But are there other, naturalistic, reasons that we should believe something like the past hypothesis, besides that it gets rid of the undesired result that one is probably a Boltzmann brain whose memories are unreliable and whose inductive beliefs about the future are mostly false? I have hope that there are such reasons, based perhaps on the theoretical considerations I raised above regarding simplicity. But it remains to be seen how much value there is in that hope.

REFERENCES

Aaronson, Scott, Sean Carroll, and Lauren Ouellette. 2014. "Quantifying the Rise and Fall of Complexity in Closed Systems: The Coffee Automaton." arXiv:1405.6903.

Albert, David. 2000. *Time and Chance*. Cambridge, MA: Harvard University Press.

Callender, Craig. 2004. "Measures, Explanations and the Past: Should 'Special' Initial Conditions be Explained?" *British Journal for the Philosophy of Science* 55: 195–217.

Cowling, Sam. 2013. "Ideological Parsimony." *Synthese* 190: 3889–3908.

Dawkins, Richard. 2008. *The God Delusion*. Mariner Books.

Earman, John. 2006. "The 'Past Hypothesis': Not Even False." *Studies in History and Philosophy of Modern Physics* 37: 399–430.

Lewis, David. 1986. *On the Plurality of Worlds*. Hoboken, NJ: Blackwell.

Huemer, Michael. 2005. "Is Critical Thinking Epistemically Responsible?" *Metaphilosophy* 36: 522–531.

Hume, David. 1739. *A Treatise of Human Nature*. London: John Noon.

Plantinga, Alvin. 1993. *Warrant and Proper Function*. New York: Oxford University Press.

Price, Huw. 2002. "Boltzmann's Time Bomb." *British Journal for the Philosophy of Science* 53: 83–119.

Swinburne, Richard. 1979. *The Existence of God*. Oxford: Oxford University Press.

Talbott, William. 2002. "The Illusion of Defeat," in James Beilby, ed., *Naturalism Defeated?* Ithaca, NY: Cornell University Press, 153–164.

(N)

The Putnamian Argument (the Argument from the Rejection

of Global Skepticism) [also, (O) The Argument from Reference,

and (K) The Argument from the Confluence of Proper Function

and Reliability]

PUTNAM'S SEMANTIC SKEPTICISM AND THE EPISTEMIC
MELT-DOWN OF NATURALISM: HOW DEFEAT OF PUTNAM'S
PUZZLE PROVIDES A DEFEATER FOR PLANTINGA'S
SELF-DEFEAT ARGUMENT AGAINST NATURALISM

Evan Fales

THE PLAN

IN A SERIES OF three books[1] published between 1978 and 1991, Hilary Putnam chronicled his apostasy from scientific realism. The apostasy appears to have had three primary sources. First, Putnam took from Quine worries about the holistic nature of theory confirmation and about the under-determination of theory by data. Second, he was swayed by Goodman's arguments for conceptual relativism. But thirdly, Putnam's philosophical evolution was driven by an inner dialectic that curiously mirrored, in its own way, the internal dialectic that led logical positivism on its long (and, in retrospect, one might say inevitable) march from an optimistic realism to the coherentism and relativism of the late Carnap and Thomas Kuhn.

Chapters 1–3 of Putnam's *Meaning, Truth, and History* lie at the heart of Putnam's extended argument, and they form the basis of Plantinga's arguments N and O of the "two dozen (or so)." Plantinga's strategy is to throw Putnam a lifeline, a bid to rescue him from the coils of skepticism that seem to have entrapped him. Reformed epistemology, Plantinga (1993) avers, can effect this rescue; and not just Putnam, but all naturalists who find themselves in his predicament will do well to avail themselves of the cure that Calvin's God has on offer.

In order to assess Plantinga's argument N (and, as we will see, closely related arguments O and K), we should ask ourselves both whether Reformed Epistemology really can execute the rescue operation—whether it is immune to the skeptical worries that have ensnared Putnam—and whether naturalistic realism, left to its own resources, is as doomed as Plantinga (and Putnam) aver. I shall proceed as follows. First, we need working definitions of "naturalism" and "(metaphysical) realism." Second, I want to be up-front about some of the resources that I take myself (the naturalist for the moment on call, as it were) to be in a position to avail myself of. Third, I will examine the main lines of argument that led Putnam to the view he calls "internal realism"—a view that seems to collapse, in the end, into idealism or skepticism. We should then be in a position to see whether Putnam has a naturalistic escape—or, for that matter, a theistic one. I shall argue at least for the former. Finally, I aim to show that the naturalistic escape infirms a critical step in Plantinga's argument for the claim that naturalism is epistemically self-defeating.

As it happens, Plantinga and I are in pretty close agreement on the matter of using a minimalist conception of naturalism. Plantinga has suggested that we think of the naturalist as someone who denies the existence of gods, angels, spirits, and the like. In a similar vein but more abstractly, I think of naturalism minimally as the claim that there are no disembodied minds. There are, of course, more robust conceptions. Many, perhaps most, naturalists are materialists. They think that there's nothing but space, time, and matter (if, indeed, those are all distinct); they deny substance dualism. They may also deny, along the same lines, the existence of abstracta: universals, numbers, propositions, and the like. But I'm not such an abstemious naturalist as that. For my money, there are definitely abstracta (including at least those just mentioned), and I find that Cartesian dualism (minus the view that minds can ever "float free" of bodies) has its attractions. In any event, since what is at stake here is the existence of a providential God and of souls that can enjoy an (arguably disembodied) afterlife, I shall stick to minimalist naturalism, and feel free to help myself to embodied minds and abstracta as need be (universals will prove especially helpful).

I am, further, a subscriber to the view that Plantinga calls classical foundationalism (though I deny that it offers a fundamentally deontological conception of epistemic statuses). Thus, I affirm that there are contents of experience—for example, sense experience—that are directly given to us in a concept-independent or pre-conceptual form, and that we can describe those contents by forming and employing concepts tailored to match them. So for my money, concepts fundamentally depend upon contents, not the other way 'round. Putnam has an argument or two for rejecting this sort of foundationalism (Putnam (1981, 54–72), but I expect it will take me too far afield to provide a detailed rebuttal of those arguments. As we will be dealing with brains in vats (BIVs), I shall help myself to what Putnam calls the "notional world" of such creatures, and to their ability to refer directly to the particulars and properties that inhabit their notional world—one that includes their sense experiences, thoughts, emotions, and the like. Such direct acts of reference are a kind of mental ostension that we can think of as attending-to, intending, meaning to single out. I take such attendings to what is directly given in experience to be, in fact, the most fundamental sort of intentional state.

SO I'M NOT A BIV?

Here's a quick argument that shows I'm not a BIV:

1. If I were a BIV, I could not think the proposition: "I am a BIV."
2. I can think the proposition: "I am a BIV."
3. Therefore, I am not a BIV.

Putnam takes this to be a sound argument. On the other hand, as Plantinga notes, Putnam allows that this argument wouldn't offer a defense against BIV skepticism if metaphysical realism were true. According to the metaphysical realist, there is a way the world is, independently of what we think, a way that satisfies some One True and Complete Description. That one true description is what one would know if one had, as it were, a God's-eye view of the world. (From such a perspective as that, it *might* turn out that I am, after all, a BIV. But if I am, then *I* couldn't have the thought that I'm a BIV. To be sure, it would be possible for me to have a thought that is *notionally* the same as the God's-eye thought that I, Evan, am a BIV. But *my* thought wouldn't represent, or express, the same proposition, because, if I am a BIV, I wouldn't be able to think about vats—or brains, for that matter.)

The metaphysical realist believes, however, that we are able, in general, to think about mind-independent states of affairs (even if we are BIVs), and is committed to a correspondence theory of truth; for her money, the truth-maker for the proposition I entertain when I consider *I am a BIV* is—if that proposition is not only possible but true—the mind-independent fact that I am a BIV, and the proposition corresponds to that fact. The question is: how are we to understand this correspondence? What is it for the proposition, or a corresponding belief, to signify or represent the fact that I'm a BIV?

Putnam argues that there's no way that the metaphysical realist can explain what this correspondence relation is; thus metaphysical realism (MR) is dead on arrival. Plantinga demurs. Even if we—we metaphysical realists, that is—can't explain what it is for our beliefs to get into the right sort of correspondence-relation with their external-world truth-makers, God will know what that relation is, and will take care of business for us by insuring, minimally, that we not be in the sort of epistemic predicament that a BIV would find itself in. For, says Alvin, "we can know that God would not deceive us in such a disgustingly wholesale manner." If so, if we can know that, we can all breathe easy and remain the metaphysical realists that we all want, deep down, to be. Here we have Plantinga's argument N.

Now there is some reason to be less sanguine than Plantinga about all this, even granting, for the sake of argument, that God exists. A ground for doubt lies near the familiar problem of evil. Here there be thorns and brambles a-plenty. A good, comprehensive theodicy is hard to find. Defenses argue that *xyz*—which might, for all we know, obtain—would explain God's acquiescence to evils *uvw*. But the defender disclaims knowledge whether *xyz does* obtain (or whether, if it does, it provides God with a morally adequate reason for *uvw*). A defender might go further: she might confess ignorance as to what *xyz* is, or even allow that it may lie beyond her ken. Skeptical theism, unfortunately, plays into the hands of the BIV skeptic. The theist must, to save the day, thread her way between too much ignorance of divine intentions and too little. If she claims to know too much, the dialectical advantages of skeptical theism are lost. If she claims to know too little, then how is she to know that her being a BIV is a "too disgustingly wholesale" form of deception for God to have any justifying reason for allowing it or creating her that way? But let's return to Putnam, because my main aim is to see whether there might be a naturalistic rescue from his predicament.

GERRYMANDERING TRUTH (AND REFERENCE)

Look again at the argument that removes the skeptical threat for the internal realist. Putnam takes his main task to be that of defending the first premise. Why couldn't someone who is a BIV consider the possibility that he is?—or, more precisely, if he represents his thought in exactly the same way that we represent the thought "I am a BIV" (he has the same mental states, internally specified) why wouldn't he succeed in considering the same proposition that we entertain? Why wouldn't it have the same truth-conditions? Suppose we assume a correspondence theory of truth. We can, for present purposes, set aside many complications—for example, those that arise when we consider propositions whose form is logically complex. We have an atomic proposition, S is P. What is it for it to "correspond" to its truth-maker, the state of affairs that S is P? If we think of the state of affairs as a kind of complex containing an individual, a property, and an instantiation "connection," the thought is that "S" refers to S, "P" refers to property P, and the copula indicates instantiation.

Now the question is: how does someone who undertakes to express the proposition S is P get "S" and "P" (or whatever signs or mental representations he uses to express the proposition) to refer to *S* and *P*? Putnam argues—and I shall not dispute—that mere similarity between, for example, a picture or mental image and a referent won't turn the trick. Similarity could be just accidental. More promising is the idea that the right kind of causal connection between S and a subject's deployment of the sign *S* will establish individual reference; similarly, the right kind of causal connection between P and the sign *P* will establish property reference. One may point to the difficulty of specifying what the "right kind" of causal relation is. That's a serious concern—I'll come to it—but that, we will see, isn't the fundamental difficulty in Putnam's list of reasons for rejecting causal accounts.

Let's begin, however, with reference to mental items rather than extra-mental ones. Somewhat surprisingly, Putnam denies the possibility of direct reference even to contents of sense experience; the same problem of how a representation can link up to its referent, except by "magic," is supposed to crop up. Putnam takes up the suggestion that here, at least, similarity between representation and represented item might work, since we are comparing mental items to other mental items. The problem now is supposed to be that of too many similarities between any two items. This, we'll see, ignores the possibility of beginning with simples—simple qualities, in particular. But how is the problem of representation even supposed to arise in this sort of case? If something—a red patch, a pain, shows up in experience, I don't need a representation of it to think about it; I just direct attention to it, and (mentally) ostend it. If I want to refer to it by means of a sign, that is trivial: I pick an arbitrary sign (which itself must be ostended), and stipulate its denotatum to be the content of the experience (there is no question here of the sign having to resemble the referent at all). Given that Putnam says (1981, 32) that "whether or not one is having an experience of a certain kind is something the mind is able to judge," why would Putnam deny this?—unless, perhaps, he has been thoroughly Sellarized.

This tension becomes explicit (1981, 54) when Putnam claims, with some studied vagueness, that "Even our description of our sensations . . . is heavily affected (as are the sensations themselves, for that matter) by a host of conceptual choices." Now suppose one grants, for the sake of argument, that the character of one's sensations is influenced (presumably unconsciously, so one can't pare away that influence) by prior conceptual entrenchments. Why should that matter? Whatever happens pre-consciously or unconsciously during the "processing" of sensory inputs, the phenomenologist's task is simply to describe sensations as they appear in conscious experience. Might phenomenological description, nevertheless, be distorted or biased by prior expectations or conceptual structures? Well, of course it might. But this can't be inevitable: if it were, how could cognitive assessment of experience ever get started? Surely we're not born with a whole mental paraphernalia of conceptual structures.[2] On the contrary: it is fundamental to empirical cognition that we be able to form and fit concepts to experience as we find it. Even the simplest judgments of similarity require that the intrinsic character of the compared items be grasped; absent that, what would the basis for comparison be? We should reject Putnam's apostasy from the given.

So that is a mistake. In this sort of case, the case where I single out some element of sense experience, I am simply doing what consciousness by its very nature does: attend to things, and grasp their character. There is no magic here, though there is mystery—the mystery, at least for the physicalist, of explaining the phenomenon of primitive, or brute (as we might say) intentionality. This I take to be the "hard" part of the mind/body problem. But we all—unless we subscribe to a kind of Rortian agnosia—have to live with that.

Matters are, nevertheless, less straightforward when it comes to extra-mental reference. As Putnam and others have persuasively argued—and I agree—the semantics of ordinary language has an external component. "Water" in English refers to water; "water" in Twin Earth Twinglish refers to XYZ; and that's not because of any difference between what's in our heads and what's in the heads of Twin-Earthers; it's because we live in an aqueous environment, they in an XYZ environment. So the causal route looks like the best game in town.

But first we might ask (and Putnam does ask) whether formal semantics might be able to help us out here. Consider general terms, like "cat," "mat," "cherry," "tree," and "is on." Their extensions will determine the truth-values of such statements as "A cat is on a mat" and "A cherry is on a tree," but will not determine reference (even if all and only mats are puce, "is a mat" and "is puce" are different properties). Nor will intensions—functions from terms to an extension in every possible world—do the trick. Thanks to the Löwenheim-Skolem Theorem and some deft definitional gerrymandering (reminiscent of *grue* and *bleen*), Putnam shows that there are multiple—indeed, indefinitely many—interpretations of a language (with quantifiers) that differ wildly in their assignments of intensions to terms, even while preserving the truth-values of every sentence in the language in every possible world.

Now, someone with robust Platonist proclivities concerning universals might demur. Putnam, for example, suggests that "The cat is on the mat" can be re-interpreted so that it will come to mean "The cat* is on the mat*," which has the same truth-value in every possible world, given that we divide possible worlds into three cases, and define "cat*" and "mat*" by way of these cases:

(a) Some cat is on some mat, and some cherry is on some tree.
(b) Some cat is on some mat, and no cherry is on any tree.
(c) Neither of the foregoing.

Here's the definition of "cat*":
x is a cat* iff case (a) holds and x is a cherry; or case (b) holds and x is a cat; or case (c) holds and x is a cherry.

The realist, I say, will deny that *being a cat** is a real property; and she may place, as an additional constraint on interpretation, that ordinary predicates must denote or aim to denote genuine properties.[3] There are, to be sure, some complexities in the matter of settling what count as real properties (and natural kinds); a foray into that will lead me too far astray here. I am going to assume that the required distinctions exist and can be discovered. But this constraint, though it culls a significant number of formally adequate, truth-value-preserving interpretations, doesn't yet give us any assurance that any remaining interpretations will agree on their assignments of terms to denotata.

So the point of Putnam's exercise, which is to show that formal semantics can't fix the denotata of the terms of a language, remains. This result suggests a further challenge. Suppose we're not brains in vats, but hominins whose ancestors survived the slings and arrows of often-outrageous fortune long enough to beget us. In dodging the arrows, they presumably acted on their beliefs. But what, from a naturalist perspective, does so acting involve? A natural story is this. The beliefs (along with relevant desires) are encoded in neural networks in our brains. The "code" is syntax: physical structures that, on the one hand, have belief contents as their intended interpretations and that, on the other, play central causal roles in controlling those efferent nerve signals that determine the activity of skeletal muscles and get our bodies moving in requisite ways. Natural selection, therefore, will select for advantage-conferring neural syntax, syntax that choreographs survival behaviors. But it won't—at least not directly—select for true beliefs. For fitness-conferring syntax (indeed, *any* neural coding in the brain) can admit of many interpretations—ones that preserve truth-value and ones that don't. Why think, therefore, that there's any likelihood that evolution has conferred upon our species cognitive faculties aimed at truth? I'll presently suggest an answer to that question. First, let's see whether we can help out our BIV cousins.

BIV BLUES

BIVs, it turns out, according to Putnam, can't think that they are in this predicament, even if their notional world—their world of subjective experience with all the extramental facts bracketed off—is indistinguishable from yours or mine. That is because, from the point of view of an external observer (e.g., God), they can't refer to vats (or brains). Suppose they are semantic externalists: they mean for "vat" in BIV-English to refer to things of whatever sort play a certain role in the BIV scenario—the role of containing, and sustaining, their brains in ways causally connected to their use of the term "vat." The trouble is, lots of things causally contribute to a BIV's use of "vat," and the vat it's actually in doesn't appear to play the right sort of causal role to be singled out as the referent. (That honor, if anything, might go to the code in the computer that sends vat-image-producing signals to the brain, or to those signals themselves, or some such.) In short, then, a BIV will be unable to refer to—have as an object of thought—the vat it's in (or any vat, or its own brain, for that matter). That secures Premise 1 of the opening argument—or so it seems.

But let's think about the matter from a BIV's point of view. A BIV, by hypothesis, can live in a notional world just like mine. It thinks it's reflecting on the proposition "I am a BIV." If it has a philosophical bent, it might also affirm (or take itself to be affirming) Premise 1. If the argument were sound, wouldn't it have proved that it's no BIV? Not so: for the propositions it affirms aren't the same propositions that we mean to affirm when we express ourselves using these sentences in English. But wait—what if *we're* BIVs? What if our language is actually BIV-English? This—so Putnam argues—is unthinkable. For there actually is no God's-eye perspective to which we can appeal according to which "vat" in English "really" denotes a code in some computer controlling our sensory inputs.

Still, how are we to know what "vat" in English denotes? For some time, Putnam gave essentially a causal-theory-of-reference answer to this question. Complications aside, the idea was that we acquire a term like "vat," in at least one paradigm sort of case, in circumstances in which others point to vats, and use the term "vat" when doing so. The vats are causally responsible for the formation, in us, of a certain concept (including, perhaps, a "vat-stereotype"), and the verbal input causes us to associate that concept with the phoneme-complex "vat." That is, perhaps, *our* understanding of how "vat" means what it does in English. And, from the perspective of what Putnam calls internal realism, that is all there is to be said: viz., that the "right" causal connections between us and vats allow "vat" to refer to vats. Unfortunately, the metaphysical realist can't help herself to this theory. The problem is that the theory itself is expressed in a language that needs interpretation. And, from a God's-eye perspective, many interpretations are possible. So, in particular, consider the term "causation," which plays a crucial role in the CTR. What relation does that term pick out? You cannot, without vicious circularity, specify its denotatum by specifying it as whatever relation stands in the "right" causal relation to our use of the term "causation"—a claim that perhaps doesn't even make sense in any case. As Putnam (1981, 46) says concerning the objective natural reference-relation R (presumably causation or involving causation):

> Given that there are many 'correspondences' between words and things, even many that satisfy our [operational and theoretical] constraints, what *singles out* one particular correspondence R? Not the empirical correctness of [x refers to y iff x bears R to y], for that is a matter of our . . . constraints. Not . . . our intentions (rather R enters into determining what our intentions signify). It seems as if the fact that R *is* reference must be a *metaphysically unexplainable* fact, a kind of primitive, surd, metaphysical truth. (Italics Putnam's; see also Putnam (1978, 40))

But this, as we will see, gets it backwards. Causation, or some relation centrally involving it, *is* determinately picked out by a referential intention; nor is this circular, once we take account of the difference between reference to items with which we are directly acquainted, and reference to items with which we are not.

Furthermore, internal realism is less benign than Putnam imagines it to be. One way to see this, very briefly, is to note that Putnam speaks repeatedly and with some insouciance about the referential strategies available to a linguistic community. For example, he mentions social cooperation in the specification of reference (Putnam 1978, 58), speaks of cultures translating a foreign tongue (Putnam 1978, 45), of convergence of theories over time within a scientific tradition (Putnam 1978, 34–38), et passim. Explaining that, for the internal realist, as for the metaphysical realist, signs do not signify automatically or in virtue of some intrinsic feature, Putnam (1981, 52) indicates how signs *do* signify according to the internal realist:

> But a sign that is actually employed in a particular way by a particular community of users can correspond to particular objects *within the conceptual scheme of those users*. 'Objects' do not exist independently of conceptual schemes. We cut up the world into objects when we introduce one or another scheme of description. Since the objects *and* the signs are alike *internal* to the scheme of description, it is possible to say what matches what. (Putnam's italics)

This looks to be incoherent twice over. First, different conceptual schemes are individuated by way of distinct schemes of description. But how is one to tell whether two "schemes of description" are distinct or equivalent, unless the descriptors used to formulate those schemes have the same meanings in the one scheme as in the other?[4] Second, appeal is made to a community of users and their patterns of use of signs. But how am *I* as an individual "member" of such a "community" to ascertain what the supposedly shared conceptual scheme is? All *I* have to go on is *my* observations of my fellow communicants, and *my* scheme, whatever it is, for describing what I observe. So I can say things about who my community members are, and what they are doing, but everything I say, every sign I use, and every object to which I refer, will be alike internal to *my* scheme of description. Putnam's internal realism collapses, I fear, into solipsism: not only semantic, but ontological and epistemological solipsism.

HOUDINI'S BRAIN AND MAGICAL NOETIC RAYS

I have a friend, Harry, who is an escape artist. Harry believes that he is a BIV—that is, it's part of Harry's notional world that he is (as he would put it in BIV-English) a brain in a vat. Since, unfortunately, Harry *is* a BIV, there's no prospect of his being able to escape from the vat he's in; to do so would, in any case, be suicide. But here's a challenge worthy of Harry: can he discover a way for his mind to wander beyond the confines of his watery prison? Can he at least have thoughts about what might be "on the outside"? Can he, in particular, come to mean what we mean when *we* say that he's a BIV—and can he come to do this "on his own"—that is, without any help from us; that is, without having *his* referential intentions somehow ride piggyback on *ours*?

Well, if he's clever—and he is—I think he can. It will be helpful for Harry to use a strategy of divide-and-conquer. He will want to make use of reference-fixing definite descriptions, and in order to do that, he has to have at his command a supply of predicates that denote properties exemplifiable by extra-mental objects. Some of these he can access directly—that is, they are given to him within his experience. These include temporal and spatial properties. Thus, Harry can reconstruct the idea of a three-dimensional shape from his direct access to diverse partial "viewpoints." In doing this, he relies upon evidence for the truth of a cluster of subjunctive conditionals, conditionals of the form: "If (experienced) circumstances C were to obtain, object-shape S would appear like so in my visual (or tactile) field," where circumstances C will typically involve subjective experiences as of moving around an object or rotating the object. He can also rely, however, upon his innate knowledge of geometry. This permits him to evaluate the truth-values of the conditionals, on the hypothesis that they are caused by a given stable 3-D shape. To be sure, a full reconstruction would require Harry to invoke claims from geometric optics, but Harry begins naively, as do we all.

Fixing reference on other properties of "external" things requires a similar use of subjunctive-conditional clusters, typically bound together by the fact that phenomenally similar antecedents systematically co-vary with phenomenally similar consequents. Thus, to take a mundane example, physical color-properties are identified in terms of phenomenal color-properties by recognizing clusters of conditionals where varying phenomenal illumination conditions can be associated with varying phenomenal hues of some phenomenal object. Such a strategy may seem rather sophisticated, but in my view it describes what is implicitly going on when young children gain recognitional mastery over their physical environment, and a corresponding mastery over the predicates of a public language. It is a strategy that makes (implicit) use of common-cause reasoning: the best explanation for the clustering of a set of conditionals is that there is some common property exemplified by the environments in which evidence for those conditionals is manifest. The strategy is not foolproof, of course: there might not be such a common property in some cases. But fallibility is minimized in two ways: first, by assembly of more complex and varied clusters (to eliminate multiple common causal ancestors), and second, by a principle of charity, which allows for some "misses" in a cluster, most of whose members do reflect a common causal ancestor.[5]

The beauty of this strategy is that it addresses Putnam's objection that there's no way for Harry, even if he relies (implicitly) upon a causal theory of reference, to pick out *which* extra-mental item is the relevant cause of some perceptual experience—as would be the case if all Harry could intend was to refer to whatever in his environment was the thing that was the most "salient" or "important" causal ancestor of some experience, or even, hopelessly, something resembling the content of the experience. Of course, there's no guarantee that Harry will be able to identify all the physical properties he might need to describe his extra-mental environment; but at least he's got a shot. Armed with a set of physical predicates, he can proceed as follows. Suppose he wants to denote the sort of physical objects he will call "brain vats." What is essential to a brain vat is that it is a physical container, capable of containing and sustaining a brain. Containment is partly a geometric property (having the right sort of hollow shape), and partly physical (being impermeable to other matter, which is a question of resisting co-location or penetration—also largely geometric notions). Harry may also develop a primitive—actually rather Cartesian—conception of matter as essentially space-occupying and movable; he can understand brains as chunks of that sort of stuff that cause thought.

All this is a bit crude, but perhaps enough to give us some idea of how Harry might outfox Putnam's skeptical conclusions about what he can and cannot refer to. Moreover, this account is a naturalistic account; it makes no appeal to divine assurances, known or unknown to Harry, of the reliability or proper functioning of his cognitive faculties, or anything of that sort. And so Harry, it seems, will not find in Plantinga's Argument N a motivation for theism—even if he were so repelled by skepticism as to find it a sufficient reason to reject any philosophical view that entailed it. But there is a fly in the ointment.

Putnam himself perceives the fly. Readers will not have failed to notice that the strategy sketched here relies crucially upon the notion of causal connection. It is causal connections that are (in part) the truth-makers for the subjunctive conditionals and for the ways in which they cluster. It is causal processes that are appealed to as the paths along which Harry's "noetic rays" can thread outward from his mind and into the world, there to ensnare determinate properties. It is the phenomenon of causal forks that gives the common-cause strategy its power to identify. So, roughly, Harry can intend that a predicate P in his language denote whatever property Φ it is whose instances lie distinctively in the causal ancestry of the phenomenal referents of the consequents of members of a certain subjunctive conditional cluster.[6] And, given a physical-predicate vocabulary, Harry can go on to fix the reference of terms denoting physical particulars and physical particular-types by making use of further definite descriptions, including ones that employ similar conditional clusters.

Or can he? In order to do so, Harry must be able to pin down the referent of "causes." That is, he must be able to identify the causal relation itself. But how is he to do that? Even if causation itself were a relation whose instances conferred causal powers upon its relata—which seems incoherent—it would be question-begging, as already noted, for Harry to fix reference on the relation by means of a definite description that itself presupposes reference to the relation. Putnam (1981, 45–46) sets out the difficulty more generally, in terms of a reference-fixing relation natural R such that

(1) *x refers to y* if and only if *x bears R to y*

Putnam imagines (1) to be part of what our ideal theory of the world will tell us. But if the methodological constraints upon scientific theorizing are what will yield that theory, then the reference of '*x* bears *R* to *y*' is *itself* indeterminate, and so knowing that (1) is true will not help. Each admissible model of our object language will correspond to a model of our meta-language in which (1) holds; the interpretation of '*x* bears *R* to *y*' will fix the interpretation of '*x* bears *R* to *y*.' But this will only be a relation *in each admissible model.* [italics Putnam's, 1981, 45–46]

If, Putnam goes on to ask, (1) describes some unique, determinate relation between words and their referents, what makes it true, given the many "correspondences"— mappings—between words and things that preserve truth-value? Putnam poses the difficulty in terms of the truth conditions for (1); I have put it in terms of the possibility of reference to causation itself.

Fortunately, I claim, the fly can be plucked from the ointment. We can refer directly to the causal relation, because it is phenomenally given to us in the experience of pushes and pulls. I have elsewhere argued at some length for this minority view, and will not repeat myself here.[7] The upshot of the argument is that (a) the exertion of force just *is* causation, and (b) that this relation is a "primary property," in Locke's terminology—that is, it is given in experience as a phenomenal relation between phenomenally given relata, but can also take phenomenal/extra-mental pairs and extra-mental/extra-mental pairs as relata. If that is correct, Harry has no worries in fixing reference upon causation; his task is to build up the machinery of reference to extra-mental properties not exemplified within subjective experience. But I hope I've given enough indication to show how that might be done. This by no means suffices to show that Harry's skeptical worries are over, but it does, in my opinion, show how Harry can remain a metaphysical realist in good standing— and how he can understand himself to have the sort of connection to his extra-mental circumstances that will allow him, not only to refer to items in that environment, but to discover truths about it.[8] In fact, the conditionals-cluster strategy makes reference-failure harder than it might initially have seemed, though a truly clever demon could, perhaps, thwart it by so arranging Harry's perceptual experiences as to be too helter-skelter to exhibit the sort of clustering of correlations that would provide Harry with evidence for relevant clusters of conditionals. Absent that, not even Harry has, in my view, reason to accept Plantinga's Argument N for the existence of God.[9]

But if I am right so far, then there are two corollaries. For it will be immediately apparent, I think, that this argument undercuts also Argument O, the argument from the alleged problem that we might be unable to think thoughts that we believe we can, in fact, think. It follows directly from what I have said that this argument shouldn't impress Harry, either. Harry can, indeed, have thoughts about vats and correctly have reason to believe that those thoughts have the intended content. Only slightly less obvious is the implication of what has been said for Plantinga's argument K.

Argument K is, in the main, a précis of a much-discussed argument Plantinga mounted against naturalism in the last two chapters of *Warrant and Proper Function*. According to that argument, Darwinian natural selection is "the only game in town" as a naturalistic explanation of the complexities of living organisms, including human organisms. But natural selection selects for fitness, not for the truth-conduciveness of human cognitive faculties. In fact, Plantinga suggests, there are no fewer than five ways in which natural selection could have produced fitness-enhancing cognitive faculties that are not truth-conducive with respect to beliefs. The likelihood of our beliefs being mostly false is high, for each of these ways, and the likelihood, relative to Darwinism, that none would be the evolutionary outcome for us is either low or inscrutable. So if naturalism is correct, the truth-reliability of our cognitive faculties is either low or inscrutable; a belief in Darwinian evolution, and so in naturalism itself, is therefore self-undermining: if true, then it is probably not produced by cognitive processes in which we should repose any faith.

The most straightforward way to challenge this argument is to confront it head-on, by undertaking to show that none of the five supposed ways in which evolutionary processes might deliver belief-forming faculties not reliably aimed at truth has a high enough probability, or one so inscrutable, as to generate the worry that most of our beliefs—including our beliefs respecting naturalism and Darwinism—may well be false. I adopted this strategy in Fales (2002), but was not entirely happy with my formulation of the objection to Plantinga's Third Way, the way of syntax. Here, therefore, I want to atone by providing a fuller presentation of the objection.

Plantinga's Third Way suggests one way in which cognitive faculties acquired by way of Darwinian evolution may be entirely "disconnected" from the truth. This possibility trades on the distinction between the content of a belief—its semantics—and the brain structures or processes that encode the belief—its syntax. Just as a computer memory can store a proposition in the form of some structure that physically encodes it, so, too, can the brain, according to the naturalist. Now what matters to human survival under conditions of natural selection is that the action-generating capabilities of our ancestors managed, enough of the time, to preserve their bodies from peril well enough to permit successful procreation. In short, our ancestors' behavioral responses to their environment had to keep their body parts relatively intact. All of this was managed by control centers in the brain; perhaps those control centers had to make use of stored beliefs. But, just as it is the physical properties of the physical structures in a computer's memory that control the computer's use of a "memory" in computation, it is, according to the naturalist, the neural structures in the human brain's noetic centers that control the brain processes that direct bodily movements in response to the environment. In short, it's the neural syntax, not the mental semantic content, of beliefs that matters for behavioral fitness and survival. Ergo, it's these neural structures—no matter their semantic content—that a competitive environment selects for. What can insure that this neural syntax will, for the most part, encode propositions that are true—since truth is neither here nor there for the purpose of felicitous disposition of bodily parts in space?

My response to this challenge is intimately connected to my response to Putnam's challenge to metaphysical realism. My response proceeds in two stages. First, whatever the neural structures that underwrite introspective awareness, we may be assured of the truth of beliefs concerning what is given in consciousness, including the subjective content of many perceptual states, pains, pleasures, emotional states, beliefs, and memories—and a good thing, too, unless you think that keeping tabs on our own mental states has no survival value. But clearly it does, and we have ample reason to believe that many such internal states evolved as signals of physical danger or felicity and motivators to action. Our challenge is to show, by way of a rational reconstruction, how the resources available to subjective awareness can be used to connect neural syntax to semantics, and hence to truth, in a reliable way, for propositions about the "external" world.

But the response to Putnam shows how this can be done. Among our resources will be the neural structures that encode thoughts concerning phenomenal properties and relations, including the causal relation. Out of this material we can construct reference-fixing definite descriptions that are meant to single out features and particulars in our environment, as the items causally responsible for making true certain subjunctive-conditional clusters concerning phenomenal experience. These intended referents we can denote, stipulatively, by syntactic markers: terms in a natural language or in "mentalese." It doesn't matter, in fact, what the syntactic representors of content are; what matters is whether propositional content can be encoded in such a way that the representors that control behavior can reliably represent the world as it is.

But if we can reliably represent the mental items of which we are directly aware, and then parlay that into reference to things that lie beyond direct awareness, there's no reason to think that the role of neural representation in guiding behavior floats free of true belief-content. Given a stock of physical properties to which we are able to refer by way of subjunctively related clusters of phenomenal properties, we can begin by using definite descriptions to "tag" items in our environment. Some of these definite descriptions serve as reference-fixers, and generate contingent a priori beliefs about their referents. Thus, for example, I may fix the reference of the natural-kind term "durian" as the thing that looks like the brown head of a mace[10] and smells like—well, like *that*. Then it will be an a priori (but contingent) truth that, if there are durians, then they are brown.[11] Once reference is established, ordinary contingent truths about the external world are delivered by the usual inductive methods.

To summarize: according to Plantinga, neural syntax could easily float free of doxastic content, given that natural selection only responds to behaviors. But this supposes that we have no way to insure that semantics aligns with syntax. What I've argued is that we stipulate the representor-represented relation in the process of introducing denoting terms by way of reference-fixing definite descriptions formulated in terms of phenomenal properties. Of course we don't stipulate that certain neural structures denote anything; we think using terms. But those terms are arbitrary, so it doesn't *matter* for semantic content what neural structures encode our reference to them.[12]

My conclusion, then, can be succinctly stated: a rebuttal of Putnam's motivations for internal realism can supply both the materials for a defense of metaphysical realism, and an undermining defeater for Plantinga's argument N and, in its wake, arguments O and K.

NOTES

1. Putnam (1978), (1981), and (1991).

2. Kant famously argued that we're born with *certain* constraints on sense experience—in particular, with an innate framing of those experiences to conform to Euclidean spatial geometry, linear temporal extension, and causal ordering. But no Kantian would be crazy enough to suggest that we're born with, say, color concepts or the concept of a biological kind. I will presently argue that the concept of causation can be acquired through experience.

3. The same constraint knocks out *grue* and *bleen*. There is no question here about which predicates are simple or complex (as Goodman pointed out—and he's echoed by Putnam—they are intertranslatable, so logical form does nothing to settle the question of *ontological* simplicity). More carefully, the constraint should ban mapping terms that in the intended interpretation denote real properties to non-properties in other interpretations. This is but one of the perks of realism.

4. Or there is an unproblematic translation-manual.

5. Ultimately the strategy relies upon the metaphysical claim that instantiations of physical properties confer causal powers upon their instantiators, powers that are individuating. That is, each distinct property confers a distinct suit of powers that constitute, as it were, its fingerprint. Identifying physical properties, therefore, is a matter of making use of causal chains, triggered by the manifestation of such powers, and terminating in perceptual events. *In principle*, therefore, it should be possible to identify what physical properties there are by taking advantage of such causal processes that are sensitive to, or "track" physical changes. Of course, the whole edifice depends upon there being a range of *phenomenal* properties that can be identified and recognized *directly*, that is, in a way not mediated by causal processes and therefore not themselves requiring deployment of the causal-cluster strategy for identification.

6. By *distinctively* I mean: *is a causal factor (or type of factor whose instances are) common to the causal ancestry of the phenomenally described perceptual experiences mentioned in the conditional cluster, and that is not common to all the members of other conditional clusters.*

7. See Fales (1990), Chapters 1 and 2.

8. After all, the primary epistemically relevant difference between Harry and ourselves is not that he's a brain in a vat—we're brains in crania—but that some intelligent beings are, via a computer of some kind, controlling Harry's sensory inputs.

9. And *with* that kind of chaos, even *we* would be at a loss to pin words to stable referents, God or no God.

10. More accurately, the medieval weapon known as the morningstar.

11. Of course, reference might still fail—in a sufficiently diabolical world, it might even fail massively. But I don't see how God can provide any remedy for that: indeed, I don't see what defeater God has, even in a non-diabolical world, for the evil demon argument, deployed against His own cognitive reliability.

12. Neural representation *does* matter for action-guidance, but not in some straight-line fashion, simply mapping this neural structure onto muscular contractions. Rather, it is precisely

by providing a physical substrate for beliefs, and neural input to our decision-making faculties, faculties that take also input representing our desires and aims to run practical syllogisms, that action guidance is achieved. I argued in Fales (2002) that this is, indeed, the *only* plausible story to be told about the way belief-content can play a role in producing survival-conducive behavior.

REFERENCES

Fales, Evan. (1990). *Causation and Universals*. (New York: Routledge).

———. (2002). "Darwin's Doubt, Calvin's Calvary," in Beilby, James (2002) *Naturalism Defeated?: Essays on Plantinga's Evolutionary Argument Against Naturalism*. (Ithaca, NY: Cornell University Press): 43–58.

Kripke, Saul. (1980). *Naming and Necessity*. (Cambridge, MA: Harvard University Press).

Plantinga, Alvin. (1993). *Warrant and Proper Function*. (Oxford: Oxford University Press).

Putnam, Hilary. (1978). *Meaning and the Moral Sciences*. (London: Routledge & Keegan Paul).

———. (1981). *Reason, Truth, and History*. (Cambridge: Cambridge University Press).

———. (1991). *Reason and Representation (Mind and Representation)*. (Boston, MA: Bradford Books).

But the light of the human mind is God. . . . Knowledge of the truth is Divine.
—LACTANTIUS (1885), iii, iii, i.

(N)

The Putnamian Argument, (O) The Argument from Reference,

and (P) The Kripke-Wittgenstein Argument from Plus and Quus

ARGUMENTS FROM KNOWLEDGE, REFERENCE,

AND CONTENT

Daniel Bonevac

IN THIS CHAPTER, I will examine three of Alvin Plantinga's (2007) arguments for the existence of God: (N) the Putnamian argument (or the argument from global skepticism), (O) the argument from reference, and (P) the Kripke-Wittgenstein argument from *plus* and *quus*.[1] I shall refer to these as the argument from knowledge, the argument from reference, and the argument from content. They are in many respects parallel. They begin with skeptical arguments against the possibility of knowledge, reference, or content and convert them into arguments for God's existence.[2]

I shall focus on the skeptical challenges posed by Hilary Putnam (1978, 1981) and by Saul Kripke's (1982) interpretation of Wittgenstein (1953). Putnam's brain-in-a-vat puzzle attacks the possibility of knowledge and of reference, given an assumption of metaphysical realism. Putnam flips the argument, using the possibility of knowledge and reference to undermine realism. Kripke's puzzle raises a skeptical challenge—one variously described as concerning meaning, content, and rule-following—and then offers a skeptical solution. Paul Boghossian (1989, 1990) flips the skeptical puzzle to argue for a realist, non-reductive, and judgment-independent account of content. My goal is to extend the arguments of Putnam and Boghossian to arguments for the existence of God.

The key idea behind these arguments is straightforward. Content and the knowledge of it are, among other things, infinitary and normative. These features of content,

Kripke argues, make it impossible to account for a speaker's content in terms of facts about that speaker's past usage, mental history, or even dispositions, since a finite being's dispositions are finite. I shall go further: The normative character of content transcends any naturalistic relation or set of facts. Its infinitary character transcends any relation to any finite set of finite minds. Content thus requires a non-naturalistic relation to an infinite set of finite minds or to an infinite mind. The only live options for accounting for content are thus pragmatism and theism. If pragmatism fails, then theism is the only remaining option.

SKEPTICAL ARGUMENTS

Skepticism, as generally understood, attacks the possibility of knowledge. But skeptical challenges can extend beyond the theory of knowledge to theories of meaning and reference. W.V. Quine's (1960, 1969) thesis of the indeterminacy of translation is a skeptical challenge, as is the Kripke-Wittgenstein puzzle concerning *plus* and *quus* (Kripke 1982).

Skeptical Arguments about Knowledge

Say that *A* has a belief or perception *s* that portrays the world as being a certain way—that portrays an object or circumstance *o* as having a property *P* (or having an individualized property *Po*, or a trope *P/o*, or being such that *Po* is true; the metaphysical differences are immaterial for our purposes). We can ask whether *A*'s mental state portrays the world as it actually is, at least in this respect. That is, in this case, we can ask whether *o* really does have *P*.

To make this slightly less abstract, imagine that *A* sees a triangle and thinks, "That's a triangle." On what I will call a traditional understanding of meaning—roughly from Plato through Locke—the word "triangle" stands for an idea or concept, which we might designate as *triangle*.

The traditional skeptic challenges the connection between what *A* means, says, or refers to and facts, objects, and properties in the world—in this case, whether that really is a triangle, and whether anyone could know it to be one. The semantic skeptic challenges the connection between a word, thought, or utterance and a content—in this case, whether "triangle" stands for the right concept, whether the concept stands for the right property, whether "that" stands for the right object, and even whether "is a" stands for the right relation between the object and the property. The skeptic in general sees the possibility of a mismatch between mental or linguistic entities and something else—something those entities are meant to portray or represent, such as objects, properties, states of the world, or mental or linguistic contents.

The skeptic may raise either of two possibilities. The metaphysical possibility of mismatch concerns whether the mental or linguistic entity could match what it is supposed to represent, or whether there is any fact of the matter about whether it does so. The epistemic possibility of mismatch concerns whether we could know it to match what it is supposed to represent (Boghossian 1989, Greco 2012):

Traditional Epistemic: Can I know I match the world?
Traditional Metaphysical: Could I match the world?
Semantic Epistemic: Can I know what I mean?
Semantic Metaphysical: Could I mean anything?

Consider the challenge concerning the relation of mental states to the world. Think of A's utterance or thought, "That's a triangle," as portraying an object o as having a property P. We might represent the situation as follows, in which the subscripts indicate that meaning, reference, and in general content may be dependent on A's idiolect or conceptual repertoire:

A: That$_A$ (standing for object$_A$) (isa)$_A$ triangle$_A$ (standing for the concept
   triangle$_A$)
The world: o has property P

We can now ask the epistemic questions, how A or anyone else could know whether "triangle$_A$" or *triangle$_A$* stands in the appropriate relation to P; whether "That$_A$" refers to o; whether "(is a)$_A$" stands in the appropriate relation to the relation of predication (indicated by "has" above); and whether A's thought stands in the appropriate relation to the world. We can also ask the metaphysical questions of whether A's words and concepts could have content, whether A's thoughts could stand in the appropriate relations to the world, and whether there could be any fact of the matter about their having those contents or standing or failing to stand in those relations. The epistemic questions represent the skeptic's familiar challenges to knowledge. The metaphysical questions represent challenges to the possibility of truth, reference, or content.

Skeptical Arguments about Content

Imagine different temporal stages of the same person or counterparts of the same person in different possible worlds. Could I mean or know that I mean the same thing I meant five minutes ago, or might have meant if today were not Saturday, if I had not just blinked my eyes, or if my cat were not about to jump off the table?

The puzzle is not just about modal or temporal parts. Think of B as someone attributing content to A's utterances and concepts. Think, in other words, of "That$_B$" as an articulation of an interpretation of "That$_A$," "triangle$_B$" as an articulation of an interpretation of "triangle$_A$" etc. We can then ask how anyone could know whether "triangle$_A$" means the same as "triangle$_B$," whether *triangle$_A$* = *triangle$_B$*, whether "That$_A$" and "That$_B$" co-refer, whether "(is a)$_A$" means the same as "(is a)$_B$," or whether object$_A$ = object$_B$. In short, we can ask whether the terms in A's utterance mean the same when uttered by B and whether A and B share the same concepts, refer to the same things, or have the same concept of predication. We can ask whether there is any way to know the answer. We can also ask whether it is even possible for any of these things to hold. The epistemic question: How could anyone know what A is referring to or what A means? The metaphysical question: Is there any fact of the matter about what A is referring to or what A means? Are meaning and reference even possible?

This reasoning applies even to A himself. *Triangle$_B$* in that case is not simply *triangle$_A$*, which is of course self-identical, but an account or interpretation of *triangle$_A$*, perhaps A's own account or interpretation. And A's interpretation of his own concepts is not necessarily correct. The same holds of linguistic items, as Plato's early dialogues dramatically illustrate. Socrates shows his interlocutors that their interpretations of their own terms and concepts are inadequate. Content is opaque.

SKEPTICAL SCENARIOS

Let's begin with traditional epistemic skepticism. Classic skeptical arguments typically start from a mental state—typically, a perception or belief—and invoke a skeptical scenario designed to undermine our faith in its veridicality or truth. The mental states in question are intentional; they represent, stand for, or are of or about things, events, properties, or states of affairs. They present them as being a certain way. If they are that way, the mental state is veridical (if it is a perception) or true (if it is a belief). If not, the mental state is illusory or not true.

Call a situation in which an agent has a veridical or true mental state directed at a state of affairs a *match* for that mental state. Putnam is dismissive of this locution: "But the notion of a transcendental match between our representation and the world in itself is nonsense" (1981, 134). In his view, the realism implied by "match" and skeptical scenarios stand or fall together, and he is happy to dismiss the skeptical arguments to be advanced in this section as nonsense. But a match in the sense I am outlining does not have to be "transcendental," whatever that means. You think that Concord is the capital of New Hampshire, and it is; that's a match. I look out the window and see a rock squirrel, and there is one there; that's a match. I go to the eye doctor, look at the astigmatism chart, and see some of the radial lines as darker than others; that's not a match. A variety of authors, including Wittgenstein (1953) and Sellars (1956), find this kind of talk acceptable case-by-case or for a limited portion of discourse, but not globally; they think the skeptic can challenge any given putative item of knowledge, but not all at once. For now, let's table these considerations, to which we will return in the section on pragmatism.

A skeptical scenario for a mental state is a situation, indiscernible from a match for that state from the agent's point of view, in which the same mental state is illusory or not true.[3] Putnam's skeptical scenario is that of a brain in a vat:

> Here is a science fiction possibility discussed by philosophers: imagine that a human being (you can imagine this to be yourself) has been subjected to an operation by an evil scientist. The person's brain (your brain) has been removed from the body and placed in a vat of nutrients which keeps the brain alive. The nerve endings have been connected to a super-scientific computer which causes the person whose brain it is to have the illusion that everything is perfectly normal. There seem to be people, objects, the sky, etc; but really all the person (you) is experiencing is the result of electronic impulses travelling from the computer to the nerve endings. (1981, 5–6)[4]

In a skeptical scenario, the situation is indiscernible from a match, not just given that mental state itself but given the totality of all the agent's possible mental states. Someone seeing what appears to be a puddle on the road ahead may not be able to tell whether this is a mirage or a veridical perception of a puddle, but traveling a bit further will reveal it to be one or the other. People under the influence of Descartes's evil genius, however, may not be able to tell whether any of their experiences are veridical or any of their beliefs are true, no matter how much experience they might accumulate or how much reasoning they do. The same holds of other skeptical scenarios, for example, that I am a brain in a vat or someone trapped in the Matrix.[5]

There is an important question whether all interesting skeptical scenarios are global. Consider Holliday's (2016) definition: "The skeptic describes a scenario v in which all such beliefs (i.e., all beliefs the agent holds in v) are false, but the agent is systematically deceived into holding them anyway." It seems possible that a demon might deceive me on a proper subset of my beliefs while leaving others intact, however; consider a demon who deceives me solely with respect to my perceptual beliefs, for example, or with respect to my beliefs about conscious beings. Indeed, the brain-in-a-vat scenario is of this kind; it is not clear how that scenario threatens my logical or mathematical knowledge, much less my knowledge that I exist. Interesting skeptical scenarios can be and generally are more limited than challenges to all of everyone's beliefs. Hence, skepticism is worth taking seriously even if Wittgenstein and Sellars are right that a truly global skepticism would be unintelligible.

THE KNOWLEDGE CHALLENGE

Given a perception or belief, we can distinguish situations that are matches, in which the perception is veridical or the belief is true, from situations that are not matches, in which the perception is illusory or the belief is not true, and specifically from the subset of those that are skeptical scenarios, in which the agent cannot discover that the perception is illusory or the belief is not true. We begin with a skeptical premise:

(1) Given a state of mind *s*, among our epistemic possibilities are skeptical scenarios for *s*.

To go further, we need to think about what it would take to defeat the skeptic's strategy. There are many options concerning the needed relationship between skeptical scenarios and matches.[6] I will not try to adjudicate them here. I will use "matches are closer than skeptical scenarios," or, turning it around, "skeptical scenarios are more remote than matches," as placeholders for whatever the appropriate condition might be. And I will speak of discounting skeptical scenarios as shorthand for ranking them as more remote than matches.

We can now formulate a second premise, saying that we have no way of ranking skeptical scenarios for *s* as more remote than matches for *s*:

(2) We have no grounds for discounting skeptical scenarios for *s*.

A third premise:

(3) We can know that a state of mind *s* is veridical only if we have grounds for discounting skeptical scenarios for *s*.

The conclusion, of course:

(4) We cannot know that our states of mind are veridical.[7]

PUTNAM'S ARGUMENT FROM REFERENCE

Let's return to Putnam's brain-in-a-vat scenario. Putnam interpretation is notoriously difficult; he tells us that he is going to give an argument of a certain kind, digresses about Turing tests, and then says he has given the argument. No wonder that commentators reconstruct the argument differently! (See, e.g., Brueckner 1992, Forbes 1995, and Warfield 1998.) He begins with the question (1981, 7), "Could we, if we were brains in a vat in this way, *say* or *think* that we were?" No, he answers. We could say or think the words, but they would not have the same contents. "Brain" would not refer to brains; "vat" would not refer to vats. He means his argument to be transcendental in Kant's sense, investigating "the *preconditions* of reference and hence of thought" (1981, 16). But the actual argument is hard to unearth.

Part of the argument is clear:

(5) a. Suppose A, a brain in a vat, were to think, "I am a brain in a vat."
b. For any common noun N, N_A refers to Ns only if A has a relevant causal connection to real Ns.
c. A has no relevant causal connection to real brains or real vats.
d. So, "brain$_A$" does not refer to brains; "vat$_A$" does not refer to vats.

It does not follow immediately that A's thought is false. All the argument so far shows is that A's thought, despite appearances, does not really refer to brains and vats.

This is enough, however, to generate an interesting skeptical puzzle. I have defined a skeptical scenario for a mental state s as a situation, indiscernible from a match for s from the agent's point of view, in which s is illusory or not true. We can extend the idea to linguistic items. Call a situation a match for an expression t iff, in that situation, t succeeds in having its intended content—referring to its intended referent, if t is a referring term, standing for the intended concept or property, if t is a predicate, etc. Say that a skeptical scenario for a term t is a situation that is not a match for t but is indiscernible from one from the agent's point of view. Putnam's brain-in-a-vat scenario is a skeptical scenario for "brain" and "vat," and thus for "I am a brain in a vat" and "We are brains in vats."

We could formulate this referential portion of the argument:

(6) a. Given a term t, among our epistemic possibilities are skeptical scenarios for t.
b. We have no grounds for discounting skeptical scenarios for t.
c. We can know that a term t succeeds in referring only if we have grounds for discounting skeptical scenarios for t.
d. We cannot know that our terms succeed in referring.

The referential argument tempts the thought that, if semantic externalism is correct, then any skeptical scenario for states of mind is also one for certain linguistic expressions: anything that systematically and undetectably disrupts the connection between my states of mind and the world also systematically and undetectably disrupts the connection between terms and their referents. This holds, however, only for a limited range of such scenarios; defining that range lies beyond the scope of this chapter.

Putnam's goal is in any case larger. He wants to show that we are not brains in vats. Putnam claims that if "we are really the brains in a vat, then what we now mean by 'we are brains in a vat' is that we are brains in a vat in the image or something of that kind (if we mean anything at all)" (15).

But part of the hypothesis that we are brains in a vat is that we aren't brains in a vat in the image (i.e., what we are "hallucinating" isn't that we are brains in a vat). So, if we are brains in a vat, then the sentence "We are brains in a vat" says something false (if it says anything). In short, if we are brains in a vat, then "We are brains in a vat" is false. So it is (necessarily) false (15).

Now the moves from "false (if it says anything)" to "false" to "(necessarily) false" are puzzling. Descartes's "I think" is true every time it is thought or uttered, but it is not necessarily true; similarly, Putnam has at best shown that "I am a brain in a vat" is not true any time it is thought or uttered. Even if he succeeds in demonstrating that, he has not reached the conclusion that I am not a brain in a vat (Brueckner 1986, Forbes 1995). Plantinga puts his argument more convincingly:

> So if we were (brains in a vat), we could not so much as think the thought that we were. But clearly we can think that thought (and if we couldn't we couldn't formulate brain-in-vat skepticism); so such skepticism must be mistaken. (2007, 221)

THE CONTENT CHALLENGE

It is easy to turn Putnam's argument into a general argument against the possibility of content. Kripke's skeptical scenario concerns an arithmetical computation I have never performed before—say, 68 + 57. I get the answer "125."

> Now suppose I encounter a bizarre sceptic. This sceptic questions my certainty about my answer. . . . Perhaps, he suggests, as I used the term 'plus' in the past, the answer I intended for '68 + 57' should have been '5'! . . . in this new instance, I should apply the very same function or rule that I applied so many times in the past. But who is to say what function this was? In the past I gave myself only a finite number of examples instantiating this function. . . . So perhaps in the past I used 'plus' and '+' to denote a function which I will call 'quus' and symbolize by '⊕'. It is defined by:

$$x \oplus y = x + y \text{ if } x, y < 57$$
$$= 5 \text{ } otherwise$$

> Who is to say that this is not the function I previously meant by '+'? (1982, 8–9)

Let b be anything thought to have content—a word, a phrase, a sentence, a proposition, a thought, a perception, a concept, etc. Call it a *content bearer*. We can generalize the ideas of matching and skeptical scenarios to all content bearers. Think of a match for a content bearer as a situation in which it succeeds in having its intended content. If it fails, it might have no content at all, or it might have some other content, a counterfeit. A semantic skeptical scenario for a content bearer is not a match for it, but is indiscernible from one from the agent's point of view. We can think of b as "+," for example, and ask whether it is possible for "+" to have any specific content, addition rather than a close counterfeit, quaddition. This is in part a puzzle about meaning: how is it possible for "+" to mean *plus* rather than *quus*?

(7) a. Among our possibilities for "+" are skeptical scenarios for "+," e.g., in which it means *quus* instead of *plus*.
   b. There are no grounds for discounting scenarios in which "+" means *quus*.
   c. "+" can mean *plus* and not *quus* only by virtue of some fact.
   d. If there were a fact by virtue of which "+" mean *plus* and not *quus*, there would be grounds for discounting scenarios in which "+" means *quus*.
   e. It is not true that "+" means *plus* and not *quus*.
   f. So, "+" has no specific content.

More generally, how is it possible for a content bearer to have one content rather than a counterfeit? Here is an argument that it cannot:

(8) a. Given a content bearer *b*, among our possibilities are skeptical scenarios for *b*.
   b. There are no grounds for discounting skeptical scenarios for *b*.
   c. A content bearer *b* can have a specific content only by virtue of some fact.
   d. If there were a fact by virtue of which *b* had a specific content, there would be grounds for discounting skeptical scenarios for *b*.
   e. So, content bearers cannot have any specific content.

But that seems to imply that there are no content bearers. It at least implies that contents are vague; no symbol or thought can have any specific content, but can at best have a certain *kind* of content.

JUDO, ACADEMY-STYLE

The central strategy of the arguments from knowledge, reference, and content is to deny the conclusion of these arguments and thereby argue for the denial of one of the premises. Philosophers in the Platonic tradition flip the epistemological argument sketched earlier on its head:

(9) a. Given a state of mind *s*, among our epistemic possibilities are skeptical scenarios for *s*.
   b. We can know that some of our states of mind are veridical.
   c. We can know that a state of mind *s* is veridical only if we have grounds for discounting skeptical scenarios for *s*.

    d. So, we have grounds for discounting skeptical scenarios for *s*.

The Platonic strategy admits that among our epistemic possibilities are skeptical scenarios. I might be a victim of a Cartesian deceiver. I might be a brain in a vat. I might be in the Matrix. I cannot rule out the possibility of these scenarios. But I can know that some of my states of mind are veridical. I can know that I exist. I can know that this tastes sweet to me. I can know that 7 + 3 = 10. (These examples are Augustine's (1955, 1995).) So, I *must* have ways of discounting skeptical scenarios. I must be able to rank them as more remote than matches, recognizing their possibility while also realizing that they do not prevent me from having knowledge.[8]

It may be worth reflecting on how Plato's judo differs from Putnam's. Putnam argues that if metaphysical realism is true I could not know that I am not a brain in a vat. But I do know that; therefore, metaphysical realism is false.

(10) a. If metaphysical realism were true, then, given a state of mind *s*, among our epistemic possibilities would be skeptical scenarios for *s*.
     b. If metaphysical realism were true, we would have no grounds for discounting skeptical scenarios for *s*.
     c. If metaphysical realism were true, we could know that a state of mind *s* is veridical only if we had grounds for discounting skeptical scenarios for *s*.
     d. So, if metaphysical realism were true, we could not know that our states of mind are veridical.
     e. But we can know that some of our states of mind are veridical.
     f. Therefore, metaphysical realism is false.

From Putnam's point of view, Plato omits a crucial presupposition embodied in talk of matching and thus implicit in the idea of a skeptical scenario itself.

From a Platonic point of view, however, Putnam's argument, too, omits some crucial steps. We might see more clearly how they relate by making things more explicit:

(11) a. If metaphysical realism is true, then, given a state of mind *s*, among our epistemic possibilities are skeptical scenarios for *s*.
     b. We can know that some of our states of mind are veridical.
     c. We can know that a state of mind *s* is veridical only if we have grounds for discounting skeptical scenarios.
     d. So, *either* metaphysical realism is not true *or* we have grounds for discounting skeptical scenarios for *s*.

From this combined perspective, both arguments are too quick. Plato ignores his realist presuppositions. And Putnam ignores the possibility of finding grounds for discounting skeptical scenarios.[9]

In a similar fashion, we can flip the brain-in-a-vat skeptical argument about reference:

(12) a. Given a term t, among our epistemic possibilities are skeptical scenarios for t.
  b. We can know that at least some of our terms succeed in referring.
  c. We can know that a term t succeeds in referring only if we have grounds for discounting skeptical scenarios for t.
  d. We have grounds for discounting skeptical scenarios for t.

Platonists similarly flip the skeptical argument about content:

(13) a. Given a content bearer b, among our possibilities are skeptical scenarios for b.
  b. Content bearers have specific content.
  c. A content bearer b can have a specific content only by virtue of some fact.
  d. If there were a fact by virtue of which b had a specific content, there would be grounds for discounting skeptical scenarios for b.
  e. So, there are grounds for discounting semantic skeptical scenarios.

Once again, Plato admits the possibility of skeptical scenarios, but insists that there must be grounds for discounting them. Notice Kripke's own reaction to the skeptic he describes; he calls the skeptic's claim that "+" means *quus* "obviously insane" (8). Of course "+" means *plus*. If so, there must be grounds for ranking skeptical scenarios as more remote than matches—for declining to allow the possibility that "+" means *quus* to interfere with its possession of a specific content, namely, meaning *plus*.

Putnam once again would object that distinguishing contents and content bearers presupposes realism about content.[10] But Plato would counter by pointing to the possibility of finding grounds for discounting skeptical scenarios. We might expand the argument to incorporate both:

(14) a. If semantic realism is true, then, given a content bearer b, among our possibilities are skeptical scenarios for b.
  b. Content bearers have specific content.
  c. A content bearer b can have a specific content only by virtue of some fact.
  d. If there were a fact by virtue of which b had a specific content, there would be grounds for discounting skeptical scenarios for b.
  e. So, *either* semantic realism is not true *or* there are grounds for discounting semantic skeptical scenarios.

Once again, we seem to have two options: embrace anti-realism or find grounds for discounting skeptical scenarios.

TRANSCENDENT GROUNDS

For the moment, I will set the anti-realist option aside, returning to it in a later section. For now, let's seek grounds for ranking skeptical scenarios more remote than matches. The question in both epistemological and metaphysical contexts is, How? What kinds of grounds could there be for discounting skeptical scenarios? How could we have epistemic access to these grounds? What kind of fact could underlie a content bearer's having its content?

Plato's answer is the theory of forms. But his approach applies more generally. The keys are the following premises. The first is metaphysical, the second, epistemic:

(15) For a content bearer *b*, there could *be* grounds for discounting skeptical scenarios for *b* only if *b* is anchored to something transcendent, the relation to which gives *b* its content.[11]

(16) For a content bearer *b*, we could *have* grounds for discounting skeptical scenarios for *b* only if *b* is anchored to something transcendent and epistemically accessible, the relation to which is also accessible and gives *b* its content.

This is, of course, the crux of the entire strategy. What does "transcendent" mean? *x* is *transcendent* if and only if *x* is

- independent of individual, finite minds,
- temporally and modally stable,
- infinitary,
- normative, and
- objective.

Let's take these in turn to see why Plato and his followers find each aspect of transcendence important to solving skeptical puzzles. These arguments are mostly implicit in Plato, but appear explicitly in certain early Church Fathers, especially Augustine. They constitute a challenge to philosophers such as Sellars and Quine who reject a relational view of meaning by arguing that the only alternative to transcendence is skepticism.

- *Independence from individual, finite minds.* The Platonic worry can be expressed as a thesis: If a content bearer *b* is anchored to something dependent on individual, finite minds, and that anchoring gives *b* its content, then there would be no grounds for ranking skeptical scenarios for *b* as more remote than matches for *b*, and both content and knowledge are impossible. Kripke's skeptic insists that "+" means *quus*; perhaps in his idiolect it does. We presumably cannot assess the truth of "68 + 57 = 125" in absolute terms, for it will be true in my conceptual idiolect and false in his. If there is no absolute truth, there is no absolute knowledge; If we cannot know whether "+" means *plus*, full stop, then we cannot know whether 68 + 57 = 125. But matters are even worse, for, as Kripke's puzzle points out, we cannot identify anything about me that grounds the claim that "+" means *plus* even in my own idiolect.

- *Temporal and modal stability.* How do I know what I meant by "+" yesterday? How do I know what I will mean tomorrow? Is there any determinate answer to what I meant yesterday or will mean tomorrow, quite apart from epistemological considerations? The dangers posed by temporal variation also apply to modal variation. Would I have meant what I do by "+" if it had rained today, or if I were currently standing rather than sitting? If the danger of dependence on individual finite minds is a relativism born of a personal parochialism, then the danger of dependence on particular times and worlds is a structurally similar relativism born of temporal or modal parochialism. I cannot know, in the moment it takes to think a thought, whether my thought has the same content at the end of that moment that it had at the beginning. I cannot know whether the cat's presence on the table is changing the meanings of my words and thoughts. Modal and temporal relativism will apply across the board, even to "7 + 3 = 10" and "The better should be preferred to the worse." If there are such eternal truths, then what anchors content will have to be *maximally* temporally and modally stable: eternal and necessary (Augustine 1955).

- *Infinitary character.* Contents are infinitary. This is obvious in the case of "+" or "number," since there are infinitely many numbers and infinitely many triples x, y, z such that $x + y = z$. But it is true of other contents as well. "Just," "unjust," "courageous," "beautiful," "red," "hungry," and other predicates apply or fail to apply to infinitely many possible objects or situations. The content of a term or concept somehow determines its applicability or lack of applicability in infinitely many possible circumstances. It will not do to point to recursive definitions, for their ability to characterize something infinite in finite terms, while important, presupposes the infinitary character of the contents of the terms appearing in the definitions.

  Normativity. Contents determine correctness conditions. They specify not merely how a term *is* used but how it *ought* to be used. There are, of course, normative terms themselves, which wear their normative character proudly. But every term is normative in the sense that it has accompanying correctness conditions. Kripke's skeptic, who says that 57 + 68 = 5, is wrong; his assertion is incorrect. He ought to get the answer "125." Similarly, a child who calls a baby bear a cat and a beginner in Spanish who calls a dog *el pero* are doing it wrong.[12]

- *Objectivity.* Whatever anchors our concepts must be objective, not only in the sense of being independent of individual, finite minds, but also in the sense of matching the nature of objects. It must solve the problem of truth, providing grounds for our utterances and our thoughts correctly describing the way things are. That means that whatever anchors our contents must match the structure of the world in appropriate ways (Burnyeat 1983). Our concepts must be able to match the properties they are meant to capture—not always, of course, but sometimes, and perhaps even normally. The same is true of our thoughts and utterances, which must be able to match the facts. What anchors content must connect to the world in ways that make these relationships possible.

THE ARGUMENTS FROM CONTENT

We are now in a position to articulate a metaphysical anti-skeptical argument for God's existence. It follows a general strategy, developed by Plato and such early Church Fathers as Justin Martyr, Lactantius, and Augustine, of flipping skeptical arguments into arguments for the forms or for God's existence. How is it possible for our words and thoughts to have content? One simple way to put the argument is that there is no good naturalistic explanation for our ability to refer to things in the world and mean things by what we think and say. Any account of semantic capacities must at some point resort to magic.[13] And the best explanation we have for that magic involves God.

The key premise the early Church Fathers add to the Platonic argument addresses the central weakness of the theory of forms. Within a generation, the Academy had abandoned forms and embraced skepticism—so much so that, even in Augustine's time, "Academic" was synonymous with "skeptic." (Think of the title of his refutation of skepticism: *Contra Academicos.*) The weakness of Plato's theory was epistemic accessibility: How do we know the forms? How can finite minds relate to the transcendent?

The early Church Fathers argued that the only answer is that there is a transcendent causal power making that relation possible. The power cannot be the forms themselves, or the form of the Good, as Plato thought, for our relation to them is precisely the point at issue. Nor can it be generated from finite minds themselves. The best explanation of our relation to the transcendent identifies the transcendent power with God.

(17) a. If realism is true, then, given a content bearer b, among our possibilities are skeptical scenarios for b.

    b. Content bearers have specific contents.

    c. A content bearer b can have a specific content only by virtue of some fact.

    d. If there were a fact by virtue of which b had a specific content, there would be grounds for discounting skeptical scenarios for b.

    e. There could be grounds for discounting skeptical scenarios for b only if b's content is grounded in something transcendent.

    f. Something independent of individual, finite minds can ground content only if there is something with causal power, independent of individual finite minds, that makes such grounding possible.

    g. Only a transcendent causal power could make possible grounding in something transcendent.

    h. Nothing natural is transcendent.

    i. Anti-realism grounds content in some feature of a collection of finite minds.

    j. A finite collection of finite minds does not suffice to explain the grounding of content.

    k. An infinite collection of finite minds does not suffice to explain the grounding of content.

    l. The best explanation for the existence of a supernatural, transcendent causal power grounding content in the transcendent includes an infinite mind and, in particular, the existence of God.

    m. So, there is a God.

Recall the definition of transcendence. The argument establishes the existence of a supernatural, infinite, eternal, necessary, objective, normative, and independent causal power capable of grounding content. That causal power is normative in the sense that it defines standards for correctness and incorrectness, right and wrong, truth and falsehood, virtue and vice.

This argument is abstract, but it expresses a common religious intuition. God alone gives meaning to the world. In relation to God, this world, our words, our thoughts, and our actions have meaning. If there were no God, there would be no meaning. Existentialism notwithstanding, furthermore, there would be no way for us to assign meaning to anything. This is true not only in the cosmic, meaning-of-life sense, but in the mundane sense that "apple" could not mean *apple* if there were no God. The upshot of the rule-following considerations is precisely that we ourselves cannot assign meanings.

The argument from content must have the form of an inference to the best explanation, for there are gaps that it does not by itself address. The argument does not by itself establish that there is a single transcendent causal power. The argument establishes God's transcendence, but it does not by itself establish omnipotence, omniscience, benevolence, or other components of the classical conception of God. The argument by itself does not provide the explanation of content; it points to a *kind* of explanation, the details of which must be filled in theologically.

THE ARGUMENT FROM REFERENCE

The argument from reference is a special case of the argument from content.

(18) a. If realism is true, then, given a term *t*, among our possibilities are skeptical scenarios for *t*.
   b. Terms have specific referents. (E.g., "brain" refers to brains.)
   c. A term *t* can have a specific referent only by virtue of some fact.
   d. If there were a fact by virtue of which *t* had a specific referent, there would be grounds for discounting skeptical scenarios for *t*.
   e. There could be grounds for discounting skeptical scenarios for *t* only if *t*'s reference is grounded in something transcendent.
   f. Something independent of individual, finite minds can ground reference only if there is something with causal power, independent of individual finite minds, that makes such grounding possible.
   g. Only a transcendent causal power could make possible grounding in something transcendent.
   h. Nothing natural is transcendent.
   i. Anti-realism grounds reference in some feature of a collection of finite minds.
   j. A finite collection of finite minds does not suffice to explain the grounding of reference.
   k. An infinite collection of finite minds does not suffice to explain the grounding of reference.
   l. The best explanation for the existence of a supernatural, transcendent causal power grounding reference in the transcendent includes an infinite mind and, in particular, the existence of God.
   m. So, there is a God.

This argument is strongest for terms such as "brain" and "vat" that refer to kinds and have infinitary and normative dimensions. It seems implausible for proper names and demonstratives, apart from a prior argument about the constitution of objects.

FINITE COLLECTIONS OF FINITE MINDS

The argument from content depends on some crucial premises, including a denial that a finite collection of finite minds can ground content. With respect to the key properties involved in transcendence, a finite collection of finite minds is no better than a single finite mind (Blackburn 1984). The skeptical strategy Kripke explores changes the subject, replacing truth with assertibility and normativity with facts of communal agreement, censure, approval, etc. It is hard to assess the importance of the community in this formulation, for communal acceptability seems to depend on individual acceptability (Blackburn 1984, Boghossian 1989).

The skeptical strategy moreover seems to give up on infinitude altogether. If no finite mind can account for the infinitary and normative features of content, then no finite collection of finite minds can, either, for we still have finitely many occasions of use. Such a collection is still, in aggregate, finite; the uses, occurrences, dispositions, or acts of such a collection still form a finite set. It thus cannot account for the infinitary character of content.

Nor can it account for normativity. Those employing a skeptical strategy replace normativity with practice in such a way that to be incorrect is just to deviate from the usage of the group. The skeptical solution thus seems to tell us not what is correct but what is popular. This makes it hard to distinguish a reform from a change in fashion. Sometimes, after all, the deviant usage is right, or at least better, than the common usage. Sometimes, it is worse, even if it ends up winning the day and changing the usage of the group. Sometimes, of course, it is simply wrong.

A finite collection of finite minds moreover cannot explain temporal and modal stability; the group may change its mind or change its usage, sometimes gradually, sometimes quickly.

Finally, such a collection cannot explain objectivity; it replaces the notion with a shared subjectivity.

INFINITE COLLECTIONS OF FINITE MINDS

Pragmatism poses a more serious threat to the argument than the skeptical solution does, for it holds more promise for explaining transcendence. Suppose content were grounded by an infinite collection of finite minds—if it can be defined, for example, in terms of limits approached by the linguistic usages of finite speakers, much as pragmatists define truth in terms of the limits approached by ideal scientific inquirers. We might even coin a slogan: *Meaning is use at the limit.* Then content could be independent of individual, finite minds. It could be infinitary, for the collection of finite minds underlying content is infinite. If contents are understood in terms of limits, they do not have to be reachable at any finite stage. Contents defined in terms of limits could be temporally stable, for limits do not change as we move along a path toward them. They could not be objective or modally stable in the usual, realist sense, but they could be something close to that if we could show that the limits themselves are independent of initial conditions and paths taken to reach them.[14]

The central question is normativity. How would an appeal to an infinite collection of finite minds explain normativity? The thought might be that the infinitary character of content underlies the problem of normativity. Over an infinite set, one might argue, we could identify content with use. Correctness would be a matter of agreement with the consensus at the limit. Whether this strategy could succeed is a complicated question I cannot resolve here. I will rest content with a few reasons for doubting the plausibility of a pragmatist solution.

First, it is not clear that a pragmatist strategy can explain normativity any more than "You might get caught and go to jail" explains what is wrong with burglary. If you call a tomato a vegetable, you *might* face disapproval, but that raises a Euthyphro question: *Is your usage incorrect because you face disapproval, or do you face disapproval because your usage is incorrect?* The skeptical solution implausibly demands the former. That you will diverge from the eventual consensus—that you in effect are standing against the tides of history—does not make you wrong.[15]

Second, Kripke's objections to dispositional accounts appear to apply to accounts appealing to collections of finite minds, whether they are finite or infinite collections and whether they follow a pragmatist strategy or not. The appeal of identifying competence or truth with usage or belief across some infinite set or at an infinite limit inevitably goes beyond our finite evidence: it requires us to ask what would be accepted in some idealized space. In short, this turns every question of content or truth into a counterfactual question. And if the counterfactual holds, it must be in virtue of some fact. But what sort of fact could this be? We are back in the heart of the Kripke-Wittgenstein puzzle.[16]

It may also be destructive of this option, as Stillwell (1989) argues, elaborating Plantinga (1982). Call an ideally rational scientific community an IRS. This might be a community at a Peircean limit; it might be an idealized community somehow capable of surveying an infinite space in some other fashion. Given the pragmatist's understanding of truth,

p is true if and only if, if there were an IRS, it would accept *p*.

Plantinga and Stillwell argue that an IRS would be transparent to some extent:

If there were an IRS, it would accept that there is an IRS.

By the pragmatist's own lights, that entails that there is an IRS. But that is plainly false.[17]

Finally, how will this strategy be able to discount skeptical scenarios? What grounds could we have for treating skeptical scenarios as more remote than matches? Since skeptical scenarios and matches are indiscernible from the agent's point of view, even given unlimited evidence, ideal inquirers at the limit or having access to an infinite space are no better off than we are when it comes to the central problem of this chapter. Indeed, from the perspective of skeptical challenges, there is no decisive difference between the ideal inquirers and us, their far-from-ideal counterparts.

THE ARGUMENT FROM KNOWLEDGE

The argument from knowledge speaks of *having grounds* rather than there *being* grounds for discounting skeptical scenarios.

(19) a. If realism is true, then, given a state of mind *s*, among our epistemic possibilities are skeptical scenarios for *s*.

    b. We can know that some of our states of mind are true or veridical.

    c. We can know that a state of mind *s* is true or veridical only if we have grounds for discounting skeptical scenarios for *s*.

    d. For a state of mind *s*, we could have grounds for discounting skeptical scenarios for *s* only if *s* is grounded in something transcendent and epistemically accessible that connects *s* appropriately to the world, allowing *s* to be true or veridical.

    e. Something independent of individual, finite minds can be epistemically accessible only if there is something with causal power, independent of individual finite minds, that makes such access possible.

    f. Only a transcendent causal power could make possible epistemic access to the transcendent.

    g. Nothing natural is transcendent.

    h. Anti-realism grounds content in some feature of a collection of finite minds.

    i. A finite collection of finite minds does not suffice to explain our access to something transcendent.

    j. An infinite collection of finite minds does not suffice to explain our access to something transcendent.

    k. The best explanation for the existence of a supernatural, transcendent causal power making it possible for us to have veridical perception and true beliefs includes an infinite mind and, in particular, the existence of God.

    l. So, there is a God.

God is part of the best explanation of our knowledge of the world. Apart from God, I cannot understand the contents of my words and thoughts or their connection to the world. I cannot know whether they have any contents at all. I cannot know whether my perceptions are ever veridical. I cannot know whether my statements and beliefs are ever true. I cannot know that any given perception is veridical or any given statement or belief is true.

This, too, reflects a common religious intuition: Without God, I have no reason to think of this world as anything but a hostile environment, a "field of death" (Nishitani 1982) that is ultimately unintelliglble to me. God aligns my mind with the nature of reality, making it possible for me at least sometimes to grasp the world as it is. God is the light of the mind, as Lactantius declares, as well as the light of the world.[18]

NOTES

1. Plantinga's paper, under that latter heading, simply says, "See Supplementary Handout," and I have not been able to track down a copy of that handout. So, I make no guarantee that the argument from content as I develop it corresponds to the argument Plantinga had in mind.

2. These arguments belong to a family of anti-skeptical arguments, including arguments from truth, intersubjectivity, interpretation, and communication, which I term *arguments from intelligibility*. For a discussion of the general kind, see Bonevac (forthcoming).

3. Some writers (e.g., Williamson (2007) and Kung (2011)) include under the heading of skeptical scenarios cases in which a belief is true but unwarranted, so that it does not count as knowledge. On that understanding, Gettier cases, fake barn cases, and the like count as skeptical scenarios. I refrain from doing that here, for two reasons. First, these are not cases that are truly indiscernible from matches from the agent's point of view: The agent could come to learn that the other person also has ten coins in his pocket, that the key is not to Jones's car, that there are many fake barns in the vicinity, etc. Second, the question of warrant pertains to knowledge, and so has bearing only within epistemology, having no obvious correlate in metaphysical skepticism.

4. Putnam embellishes this scenario by imagining that, through "some kind of cosmic chance or coincidence" (12), all of us have jointly been wired to a computer network in this way, and always have been, in order to avoid the objection that your reference to things is parasitic on your earlier contact with them, other people's contact with them, or the evil scientist's contact with them.

5. Note that this is the skeptic's way of understanding skeptical scenarios. Descartes, for example, thinks that he can show that we are not under the sway of an evil deceiver. Putnam thinks he can show that we are not brains in vats. So, it might be more accurate to define a skeptical scenario as a situation that is not a match but is *apparently* indiscernible from one from the agent's point of view.

6. I am simplifying somewhat in thinking solely about possible relationships between skeptical scenarios and matches. One might instead choose to focus on relationships between skeptical scenarios and other scenarios, including corrigible non-veridical states as well as matches. Or, one might choose to focus on relationships between matches and non-matches, which might fit skeptical arguments such as the argument from illusion more faithfully than what appears here in the text.

7. This is one way to think of skeptical arguments; there are many others in the literature (e.g., Schofield, Burnyeat and Barnes (1980), Annas and Barnes (1985), DeRose and Warfield (1999)).

8. From a contemporary point of view, this seems to commit Plato to denying closure. The argument: I know that $7 + 3 = 10$. I do not know that I am not under the spell of Descartes's demon. (Among my epistemic possibilities is such a skeptical scenario.) I know that if I am under the spell of Descartes's demon, then $7 + 3 \neq 10$. By contraposition, I know that if $7 + 3 = 10$, then I am not under the spell of Descartes's demon. By closure, if I know that $7 + 3 = 10$, then I know that I am not under the spell of Descartes's demon. I know that I am not under the spell of Descartes's demon; contradiction. Plato, however, might be willing to allow knowledge even

given epistemically possible skeptical scenarios. There are yet other plausible options. One is denying contraposition. Aristotle and Alexander of Aphrodisias appear at some points to rely on contraposition, but it creates problems for Aristotle's view that true conditionals have possible antecedents, since $A \rightarrow B$ does not guarantee the possibility of $\neg B$, which is a prerequisite, on his view, for the truth of $\neg B \rightarrow \neg A$. Boethius appears to be the first person to state contraposition explicitly (Bonevac and Dever 2012). So, Plato might indeed have objected to the argument at just that stage. The first statement of a closure principle is in Paul of Venice (1369–1429), so Plato may have objected to it as well.

9. In putting it this way, I do not mean to endorse Putnam's allegation that the very idea of a skeptical scenario presupposes metaphysical realism; it seems to me that an inverted spectrum scenario offers grounds for a skeptical argument without any commitment to a metaphysically loaded thesis. But for now I will frame the argument to remain as neutral as possible on the question.

10. Again, I do not mean to endorse this claim. Sellars (1956, 1963), Quine (1969), and Putnam all reject relational theories of meaning, in part for this reason. But Kripke's skeptical scenario does not depend on any particular analysis of statements such as "'+' means *plus*."

11. I use "anchored" advisedly, generalizing the idea in Kamp and Reyle (1993): anchoring is a relation by virtue of which something has the content that it has. It is typically a causal connection, such as the link between Aristotle and the name "Aristotle," or the connection between H_2O and the word "water." Thinking of anchoring in this way explains why virtually every basic term designates rigidly.

12. See Boghossian (1989, 513):

> Suppose the expression "green" means *green*. It follows immediately that the expression "green" applies *correctly* only to *these* things (the green ones) and not to *those* (the non-greens). The fact that the expression means something implies, that is, a whole set of *normative* truths about my behaviour with that expression: namely, that my use of it is correct in application to certain objects and not in application to others.

13. Though the term comes from Putnam (1981), here I mean it to indicate a non-naturalistic element; I do not mean to imply that all semantic relations are in any sense necessary. It is entirely contingent that the name "Winston Churchill" refers to Winston Churchill. More to the point of this discussion, it is entirely contingent that "+" stands for addition and that "triangular" stands for triangularity. Predicates and concepts have meaning by being anchored to something transcendent, but the connection between the predicate and its transcendent anchor is not itself transcendent.

14. This is a tall order. Peirce (1878), for example, gives us no reason to think that the eventual agreement of all who inquire would be path-independent and invariant across initial conditions. In fact, he gives us little reason to think that it could be achieved at all; why think the series of stages of inquiry converges? Still less does he provide a reason to think that the limit approached by scientific inquiry would be path-independent and invariant across initial conditions without making reference to a mind-independent world. But perhaps such an argument is possible.

15. This concern underlies Bertrand Russell's broader objection to pragmatism as a theory of truth. Say that the ideal inquirers would eventually converge on p. Why? The realist would say, *because p is true*. The realist holds that truth explains agreement. The pragmatist reverses the

picture, contending that agreement explains truth; we count *p* as true because the ideal inquirers would eventually converge on it—truth comes to nothing more than belief at the limit. Russell argues that this implausibly makes the world dependent on belief and thus on minds: the pragmatic theory "seems to suggest that if I infer a world, there *is* a world. Yet I am not the Creator. Not all my inferences and explanations could prevent the world from coming to an end to-night, if so it were to happen.... Whatever accusations pragmatists may bring, I shall continue to protest that *it was not I who made the world*" (Russell 1919, 26; emphasis added).

16. This leads to an infinite regress worry: if every question turns into a counterfactual question, then the counterfactual question raises a further counterfactual question, which raises yet another, and so on. This may or may not be vicious, depending on the details:

p   is true if and only if

p   would be accepted throughout a given space *S*, which is true if and only if

'*p*   would be accepted throughout *S*' would be accepted throughout *S*, which is true if and only if

"'*p*   would be accepted throughout *S*' would be accepted throughout *S*" would be accepted throughout *S*,

and so on. The lengthier counterfactuals might follow trivially if acceptance throughout *S* is transparent in *S*. But such transparency is not automatic; it has to be established.

17. The Plantinga-Stillwell argument relies on the principle Bonevac, Dever, and Sosa (2006) call *contraction*: $(A \rightarrow (A \rightarrow B)) \Rightarrow (A \rightarrow B)$, which is in a Lewis-Stalnaker system equivalent to weak centering, that is, to modus ponens. This should not be surprising, for the Plantinga–Stillwell objection in effect argues that pragmatism falls prey to a conditional fallacy analogous to that which Robert Shope (1978, 412–413) finds in the ideal-observer theory. It remains open to the pragmatist to reject contraction.

18. I developed these ideas in a seminar on Natural Theology East and West at the University of Texas at Austin in 2015. I am grateful to my co-instructor, Stephen Phillips, and to our students for their insightful comments and criticisms as well as their enthusiasm and support.

REFERENCES

Annas, J., and J. Barnes. 1985. *The Modes of Scepticism*. Cambridge: Cambridge University Press.

Augustine. 1955. *The Problem of Free Choice (De Libero Arbitrio)*. Westminster, MD: The Newman Press and London: Longmans, Green and Company.

———. 1995. *Against the Academicians and the Teacher*. Indianapolis, IN: Hackett.

Blackburn, S. 1984. "The Individual Strikes Back," *Synthese* 58: 281–302.

Boghossian, P.A. 1989. "The Rule-following Considerations," *Mind*: 507–549.

———. 1990. "The Status of Content," *The Philosophical Review*: 157–184.

Bonevac, D., and J. Dever. 2012. "A History of the Connectives." In Dov Gabbay and John Woods (ed.), *Handbook of the History of Logic*, Volume 11. Amsterdam: Elsevier North Holland, 175–234.

Bonevac, D., J. Dever, and D. Sosa. 2006. "The Conditional Fallacy," *The Philosophical Review* 115, no. 3: 273–316.

Bonevac, D. (Forthcoming). *Light of the Mind: Transcendental Arguments for a Transcendent God.*

Brueckner, A. 1986. "Brains in a Vat," *Journal of Philosophy* 83: 148–167.

———. 1992. "Semantic Answers to Skepticism," *Pacific Philosophical Quarterly* 73, 200–219; reprinted in DeRose and Warfield (1999), 43–60.

Burnyeat, M. 1983. "Can the Sceptic Live His Scepticism?" In Burnyeat (ed.), *The Skeptical Tradition.* Berkeley: University of California Press, 117–148.

DeRose, K., and T. Warfield. 1999. *Skepticism: A Contemporary Reader.* Oxford: Oxford University Press.

Forbes, G. 1995. "Realism and Skepticism: Brains in a Vat Revisited," *Journal of Philosophy* 92: 205–222; reprinted in DeRose and Warfield (1999), 61–75.

Greco, D. 2012. "The Impossibility of Skepticism," *Philosophical Review* 121, no. 3: 317–358.

Holliday, W.H. 2016. "Epistemic Logic and Epistemology." In Hansson, S.O., and V.F. Hendricks (eds.), *Handbook of Formal Philosophy.* Berlin: Springer.

Kamp, H., U. and Reyle. 1993. *From Discourse to Logic.* Dordrecht: Kluwer.

Kripke, S. 1982. *Wittgenstein on Rules and Private Language.* Cambridge, MA: Harvard University Press.

Kung, P. 2011. "On the Possibility of Skeptical Scenarios," *European Journal of Philosophy* 19, no. 3: 387–407.

Lactantius. 1885. *A Treatise on the Anger of God Addressed to Donatus.* In Roberts, A., Donaldson, J., and Coxe, A.C. (eds.), *Ante-Nicene Fathers. Volume 7: Fathers of the Third and Fourth Centuries: Lactantius, Venantius, Asterius, Victorinus, Dionysius, Apostolic Teaching and Constitutions, Homily.* Edinburgh: T&T Clark; Grand Rapids, MI: Wm. B. Eerdmans Publishing Company.

Nishitani Keiji. 1982. "Science and Zen." In Franck, F. (ed.), *The Buddha Eye: An Anthology of the Kyoto School.* New York: Crossroad.

Peirce, C.S. 1878. "How to Make Our Ideas Clear," *Popular Science Monthly* 12, 286–302.

Plantinga, A. 1982. "How To Be an Anti-Realist," *Proceedings of the American Philosophical Association* 56: 57–70.

———. 2007. "Two Dozen (or so) Theistic Arguments." In Baker, D. P. (ed.), *Contemporary Philosophy in Focus.* Cambridge: Cambridge University Press, 203–228.

Putnam, H. 1978. *Meaning and the Moral Sciences.* London: Routledge and Kegan Paul.

———. 1981. *Reason, Truth and History.* New York: Cambridge University Press.

Quine, W.V.O. 1960. *Word and Object.* Cambridge, MA: MIT Press.

———. 1969. *Ontological Relativity.* New York: Columbia University Press.

Russell, B. 1919. "Professor Dewey's Essays in Experimental Logic." *The Journal of Philosophy* 16, no. 1: 5–26.

Schofield, M., M. Burnyeat, and J. Barnes. (eds.) 1980. *Doubt and Dogmatism: Studies in Hellenistic Epistemology.* Oxford: Clarendon Press.

Sellars, W. 1956. "Empiricism and the Philosophy of Mind." In Feigl, H., and M. Scriven (eds.), *Minnesota Studies in the Philosophy of Science.* Volume I. Minneapolis: University of Minnesota Press, 253–329.

———. 1963. "Abstract Entities," *Review of Metaphysics* 16, no. 4:, 627–671.

Shope, R.K. 1978. "The Conditional Fallacy in Contemporary Philosophy," *The Journal of Philosophy* 75, no. 8: 397–413.

Stillwell, S. 1989. "Plantinga and Anti-Realism," *Synthese* 78: 87–115.

Warfield, T.A. 1998. "A Priori Knowledge of the World: Knowing the World by Knowing Our Minds," *Philosophical Studies* 92: 127–147; reprinted in DeRose and Warfield (1999), 76–92.

Williamson, T. 2007. "On Being Justified in One's Head." In Timmons, M., J. Greco, and A.R. Mele (eds.), *Rationality and the Good: Critical Essays on the Ethics and Epistemology of Robert Audi*. Oxford: Oxford University Press, 106–22.

Wittgenstein, L. 1953. *Philosophical Investigations*. London: Blackwell.

(Q)

The General Argument from Intuition

Robert C. Koons

∿ ————————————————————————————————————

INTRODUCTION

ARGUMENT Q, THE seventeenth argument in Plantinga's battery, concerns the problem of explaining how we can take seriously our capacity for intuition in such areas as logic, arithmetic, morality, and philosophy. Like many of the arguments in the series, this argument involves a comparison between theistic and non-theistic accounts of certain cognitive capacities of human beings. These considerations are supposed to favor theism, because theism provides a better explanation of the soundness or reliability of our capacity to know certain things that we appear to know in the way in which we appear to know them.

In this introductory section, I will deal with three preliminary issues: What is intuition? What are the competing accounts of intuition? And, what are the possible forms that the theistic argument could take? I will argue that the argument can take three forms: an inference to the best explanation, an appeal to something like the causal theory of knowledge, and an argument turning on the potential threat of undercutting epistemic defeaters concerning the reliability of intuition. I will then consider each of these arguments in turn in the second, third, and fourth sections, ending with some concluding thoughts in the final section.

In philosophical contexts, we typically speak of "intuitions" (plural) rather than "intuition" (singular), perhaps because we aren't sure that there is a single capacity responsible for all of our so-called intuitions. What, then, is an intuition? It is an instance of knowledge, or at least of apparent true belief. Its justification does not depend on inference, either deductive or inductive, and it is not grounded in an exercise of our sensory capacities or our memory or on testimony. Are intuitive beliefs based on anything at all? Here opinions differ. Some, following George Bealer (1999), take intuitions to be a kind of intellectual seeming, supposed to be similar in some respects to sensory or mnemonic seemings. Others (Williamson 2007) take intuitions to be basic beliefs or inclinations to believe that are simply the immediate output of some capacity for underived knowledge. The contents of intuitions are typically assumed to be necessary truths that are general or at least somewhat generalizable, like the axioms of logic or mathematics or norms of ethics. Although this characterization of intuitions is mostly a case of *via negativa*, and although it is vague, it will do for our present purposes.

Plantinga assumes, and I will also assume, that it is impossible to do math, science, or philosophy without relying (at least implicitly) on intuitions. He assumes, and I will also assume, that our intuitions are for the most part instances of genuine knowledge. This raises the question of how such knowledge is possible. As we shall see in the next section, theism (and especially Christian, or at least Abrahamic, theism) has a plausible explanation ready to hand. What about its competitors?

Plantinga assumes, and once more I will assume right along with him, that there is only one really plausible alternative to theism here: a form of materialism in which evolution, guided only by the "blind watchmaker" of natural selection, is the sole explanation for our cognitive capacities. I will set aside here my own (pretty grave) doubts and grant for the sake of argument that the Darwinian mechanism has all the capacity claimed for it by its most ardent supporters (such as Richard Dawkins or Daniel Dennett).

There have historically been other major contenders, such as the monism of absolute idealists, like F.H. Bradley, or atheistic forms of dualism or subjective idealism. Monistic idealism could probably mimic the explanatory power of theism pretty successfully, but it is perhaps close enough to theism that we could live with a disjunctive conclusion. Atheistic dualists or idealists of a rationalist bent, who posit multiple rational souls as uncaused and fundamental entities, are left with the tremendously difficult problem of explaining how a coherent physical and social universe could arise from the uncoordinated interactions of such immaterial souls, or how such souls could be injected into a pre-existing physical world. Although such alternatives to theism might well warrant further attention, for present purposes I will set them aside.

So, we can assume that there are just two salient hypotheses to consider: theism and evolutionary materialism. How can we use the phenomenon of intuitive knowledge to build an argument for theism and against its competitor? There is a series of three arguments to be made, each one depending on the success (at least partial success) of its predecessors, but each adding considerably to the dialectical force of the whole series.

First, there is an inference to the best explanation of the phenomenon of the reliability of intuition as a source of truth. Theism provides an intelligible and plausible explanation, and any explanation in terms of naturalistic evolution is problematic in various ways, especially in respect of the lack of rigor in deducing reliability from naturalism, even when associated with plausible auxiliary hypotheses. If this is right, then the existence of reliably true intuition confirms the truth of the theistic hypothesis—assuming that that hypothesis has non-zero prior probability. There are, in fact, many reasons for attributing a significant, non-zero prior probability to theism, including some of the arguments discussed in this book. There is also the fact of widespread religious experience, and the fact (emphasized in the work of Richard Swinburne—see, for example, Swinburne 2004, Chapter 5) that theism is an admirably simple hypothesis, positing the existence of a single entity, without parts, and with a nature wholly characterizable in eminently simple terms.

The second argument turns the failure of naturalism to provide a plausible explanation of the reliability of intuition into a deductive proof of the falsity of naturalism, relying on the premise that all knowledge requires some kind of real connection between acts of knowledge and the facts that are known, a connection that can ground a substantive explanation of the reliable correspondence between the two.

The third argument requires only that the first two arguments be at least partially successful, throwing reasonable doubt on the existence of a reliable connection between the output of our intuitive capacities and the relevant facts, given the assumption of naturalism. If naturalism were true, the existence of a salient, epistemic possibility that our faculties of intuition are unreliable would constitute an undercutting defeater of all intuitive knowledge. Knowledge is possible only in the absence of such a defeater; hence, the fact that we have intuitive knowledge at all entails the falsity of naturalism, and so confirms the truth of theism.

INFERENCE TO THE BEST EXPLANATION
OF THE RELIABILITY OF INTUITION
Theism Can Explain the Reliability of Intuition

Christian theism includes the claim that human beings have been created in God's image. This implies our possession of basic capacities for understanding that mirror God's own understanding, although on a limited scale. Therefore theists can confidently predict that our basic cognitive capacities (including intuitive capacities) have an inherent orientation toward the acquisition of true beliefs, at least in certain contexts (i.e., contexts of pure and unhurried inquiry, discussion, and contemplation).[1]

Of course, God can ensure our reliability only if He is also reliable. Hence, the explanation of our reliability depends upon an adequate explanation of God's reliability. Here theists have a number of plausible strategies. First, they can suppose that both God and human beings have a kind of direct (causally unmediated) contact or connection with logical, mathematical, and ontological facts, a connection so intimate as to produce knowledge of those facts by acquaintance. Such a model is not available to the naturalist, for whom all such connections must be mediated by purely physical processes. Second, theists could go further and identify necessary facts with God's awareness of them, building on the sort of fusion of Platonism with theism advocated by Philo of Alexandria, Augustine, and Leibniz. On this view, there is no ontological gap between the truth of the intuitively known propositions and God's knowledge of them: the fact that such a proposition is true is either identical to or at least constituted by the necessary structure of God's intellectual activity. The second model also secures God's infallibility with respect to such matters. We would then participate (in a limited way) in this truth-constituting divine cognition.

Joel Pust (2004) has argued that the theist cannot use God's reliability to explain anything at all, since God's existence and intuitive beliefs are themselves necessary (according to classical theism). Pust claims that explanation is possible only when a corresponding counterfactual conditional is true, one of the form: if the explanans were not the case, then the explanandum would not be the case either. Granting this assumption, it would follow that explanations can be made only in terms of contingent facts. However, Pust is simply mistaken here. Necessary truths can be used to explain contingent facts, as, for example, when we appeal to mathematical facts about the numbers of combinations to explain statistical regularities. In addition, there can be explanatory relations between necessary truths. For example, we can explain the validity of modus ponens in terms of the truth-function associated with the material conditional.

Naturalism Cannot Explain the Reliability of Intuition

Under the assumption of naturalism, natural selection provides the only grounds for explaining any functionality of our cognitive capacities. Natural selection selects for features that promote survival and reproduction. Therefore, it can explain only why our beliefs and other mental states are (jointly) useful or adaptive: it cannot explain directly why our beliefs tend to be true. This is especially true for those of our intuitive beliefs that are far removed from the practicalities of surviving in Paleolithic Africa. Getting such an intuitive belief right does not seem (at least prima facie) to provide a human being with any adaptively useful information about his or her environment. One might speculate that, for all we know, the cognitive mechanisms useful for survival are the very ones needed to get the intuitive beliefs right, but the naturalist has no strong grounds for thinking so.

Does Intuition Require, or Even Admit of, Any Explanation?

David Lewis (1986, pp. 114–115) argued that there is no need to explain the reliability of beliefs whose contents are necessarily true, since there is no principled way to evaluate counterfactual conditionals of the form: if p (the necessary truth) were false, we wouldn't have believed it. (On Lewis's semantics for the conditional, such "counterpossible" conditionals are all vacuously true.) There are several cogent objections to Lewis's position. First, reliability requires more than just sensitivity to falsity (the property corresponding to Lewis's conditional). We also want safety: in any nearby world in which p is true (i.e., in any nearby world), we would still believe p (or something very close to it). Second, as Joshua Schechter (2010, p. 444) points out, it is primarily methods or faculties that we evaluate for reliability, not individual beliefs. It certainly makes sense to ask whether the faculties that generate beliefs intuitively do so in such a way as to generate predominantly true beliefs. Third, we can sometimes interpret counterpossible conditionals non-vacuously, so long as some necessary truths (the ones negated in the antecedents of the conditionals) can be explanatorily prior to contingent facts—something I've already argued for. Consider a conditional like the following one:

(1) If half of all possible poker hands contained four of a kind, such hands would be much more likely than they are.

Finally, as Schechter (2010, p. 447) also points out, explanation is not closed under necessary (or even logical entailment). Even if we explain why we have the intuitive beliefs we do, and even if it is necessary that those beliefs all be true, it doesn't follow that we've explained why our intuitive beliefs are true. We need to explain why, among all the possible capacities we might have had, we've ended with one with the feature of reliability with respect to truth.

Can Conceptual Constraints on Concept Possession Explain the Reliability?

In response to Plantinga's more general Evolutionary Argument against Naturalism (Plantinga 1985, Chapter 12, 1995, 2002, 2003, 2011a, 2011b), Stephen Law (2012) has argued that conceptual constraints (of a sort available to naturalists) on concept possession can explain the general reliability of our cognitive faculties. As Plantinga concedes, natural selection can explain the generation of human brain states that reliably indicate adaptively relevant features of the environment. Law argues that it is plausibly a constraint on our attribution of contents to those brain states (including our characterizing them as constituting beliefs in certain propositions) that the majority of our beliefs in normal circumstances come out with true contents, even if there is no plausible reduction of belief to brain states. Timothy Williamson (2004) has argued convincingly that such conceptual constraints ought to be considered to require the maximization of knowledge, rather than that of true belief, since one's capacity to know truths containing a concept is more plausibly taken as a criterion of one's possession of the concept than is one's merely having (by chance) a large number of true beliefs involving the concept.

Of course, Law's strategy will work, in the first instance, only with respect to beliefs with contingently true contents, since only such contingent contents can be systematically linked to the information carried by "indicator" states in the brain. However, it is not implausible to suppose (as both Miščević 2004 and Williamson 2004 have argued) that reliability with respect to intuitive beliefs is a very probable by-product of reliability with respect to beliefs with contingent contents. Miščević points out that, at least for those necessary truths concerning the modal structure of reality, it is impossible in practice to isolate beliefs about important contingent matters (like dispositions, powers, potentialities, and propensities) from beliefs about the (necessarily true) principles of modal logic. For example, if I have the power to express a falsehood intentionally, and if expressing a falsehood intentionally metaphysically necessitates telling a lie, then I have the power to lie—an inference that requires a principle of modal logic, namely, the weakening of the consequent of a subjunctive conditional. Similarly Williamson argues that knowledge of everyday subjunctive conditionals is of great value in the struggle for existence. The operators of necessity and possibility can be defined in terms of counterfactual conditionals, in such a way that knowledge of counterfactual conditionals will ground inferential knowledge of some necessary truths. For example, a *might* conditional, like "If we were to build a bridge of this kind from inferior materials, it might fall down," entails a proposition about metaphysical possibility: "A bridge of this kind could fall down." This inferential knowledge of necessary truths might constrain our modal intuitions in such a way as to ensure their having some measure of reliability.

Response #1: Four Special Cases Where the Explanation Is Especially Weak

Both Williamson and Miščević have given us some reason to think that our knowledge of facts about *de dicto* metaphysical possibility and necessity might be the expectable by-product of our knowledge of contingent facts about modality, including our knowledge of counterfactual conditionals. However, this account leaves us with no reason to expect our intuitive beliefs to be reliable in other domains. I will discuss four such cases here: moral and epistemic norms, number theory, the a priori likelihood of possible laws of nature, and de re modal facts concerning the composition and persistence of material things.

Moral and Epistemic Norms, Reasons, and Judgments
Moral anti-realists have appealed to evolutionary debunking arguments, based on the assumption of naturalism, quite often over the last fifteen years. Many naturalists are happy to embrace anti-realism about objective moral norms and reasons, based on the impossibility of a naturalistic explanation of the reliability of our moral intuitions (following Harman 1977), but few have recognized that the same considerations tell against our having naturalistically intelligible intuitive knowledge of epistemic norms and reasons (Street 2009 is an exception), such as respect for logical consistency, the principle of total evidence, the avoidance of wishful thinking and other merely emotional responses to epistemic tasks, the importance of empirical testing and confirmation, and so on (see Koons 2010 for the details).

Natural selection might be able to explain our believing in practically useful norms, or in norms that are widely accepted among our peers, but neither of these have any necessary connection with truth. There is a kind of categorical imperative behind moral and epistemic judgments, making their validity insensitive to questions of practical usefulness or social acceptance. If there were a reliable connection between the real existence of such reasons and their practical usefulness or widespread affirmation, this connection would have to be anti-naturalistic in nature: such as the ordering of divine providence.

Unlike in the case of metaphysical modalities, in the case of moral and epistemic norms there is no reason to think that natural selection would make us reliable in making judgments about particular, contingent truths—for example, in judging whether a particular person has many beliefs on a subject that are really justified. In addition, there is no reason to think that evolution would generate reliable, information-carrying indicator states in the brain corresponding to variable normative facts. Therefore, there is no reason to expect there to be pre-cognitive correlations for our interpretive norms to work with, and so no reason to expect those norms to favor the attribution of true beliefs to those brain states.

There is, in the case of our knowledge of epistemic norms, several special difficulties for the naturalist in appealing to interpretive norms like the principle of charity or knowledge maximization to defeat the evolutionary defeater.

First, to appeal to the hermeneutical principle of charity is to attempt to ground our reliability by a mere stipulation. In the context of explaining our reliability, this is clearly question-begging. If we want to know whether naturalism has the resources to explain our having reliable intuitive faculties, it is unsatisfying to be told, "Let's just assume that they are reliable." This is clearly wrong in the case of the pro-and-con epistemic judgments we make about particular concrete acts and beliefs of fellow human beings: there is no way to make these judgments correct by interpretive fiat, assuming that epistemic values and norms are objective, independent of our actual beliefs and dispositions.

Second, the naturalist faces a dilemma: is knowledge-maximization a fundamental semantic law or the by-product of epistemic norms of interpretation? If it is supposed to be a fundamental law, the supposition is a poor fit with the hypothesis of naturalism. What facts about the natural world could make such a generalization law-like? How can such semantic laws fit into the fundamentally physical structure of the world? Moreover, why should we expect naturalistic laws of semantics (if there are such) to respect hermeneutical principles like charity at all?

If naturalists embrace the second horn of the dilemma, then they cannot appeal to *purely* normative facts about interpretation (disjoint from the physical world) as the ultimate ground for the reliability of intuition, since such facts must (for naturalists) be wholly grounded in the physical world, presumably by way of being roughly approximated by actual interpreters in favorable conditions. However, actual interpreters cannot even approximately apply Williamson's knowledge-maximization norm to intuitive states except by having substantial intuitive knowledge themselves. In order to interpret subjects in order to maximize their intuitive knowledge, we would have to be able to recognize possible instances of intuitive knowledge, and this would require that we have a great deal of intuitive knowledge so that we can check when the subjects' intuitive beliefs, as we might interpret them, would match our own instances of intuitive knowledge. After all, in order to count as knowledge the beliefs would have to be true, something we could verify only by means of our own intuitive knowledge. For example, in order to maximize a subject's knowledge of arithmetic, we would have to be able to tell which possible beliefs of that subject would constitute knowledge of arithmetic, a task that is possible only if *we* know something of arithmetic. Since all such knowledge is intuitive, we would ultimately have to appeal to our assumed intuitive knowledge (qua interpreters) in order to explain our own intuitive knowledge (qua interpreted). Hence, the explanation of our reliability would be circular. (See Bonevac, this volume, for more problems with naturalistic accounts of interpretation.)

Could the naturalists simply renounce any interest in categorical epistemic norms and reasons, contenting themselves with following whatever rules or judgments are useful in practice? First, this doesn't solve the problem of accounting for the categorical norms of rationality. We can't help but think that the relevance of those norms (consistency and so on) is not conditional upon their usefulness. Second, if the force of the norms were conditional on their usefulness, we would have to have some evidence for their actual usefulness that is independent of the norms of rationality, which is surely an impossibility.

Number Theory

Another special case concerns our intuitive knowledge of the infinite structure of the natural numbers, namely, our knowledge that every number has a successor, and that the totality of natural numbers satisfies the principle of mathematical induction (i.e., any property that is true of zero and whose extension is closed under succession is true of all numbers).[2] Since our ancestors never encountered infinitely intricate situations in their struggle for existence, and since intuitive knowledge of the abstract numbers or of abstract proof theory by itself offers no selective advantage, natural selection can provide no explanation of our intuitive knowledge of the omega-structure of the numbers. You don't need mathematical induction to count the number of lions in the clearing.

First, this is a case in which an abundant or plenitudinous theory of concepts is quite implausible. There is something objectively special about the concepts of standard number theory. Second, as I argued in Koons 2003, one cannot coherently adopt a fictionalist account of number theory, since a mathematical theory is useful only if it is conservative (that is, only if it does not allow us to infer non-mathematical consequences that we could not infer in its absence), and a theory is conservative only if it is proof-theoretically consistent. As Gödel demonstrated, the fact that number theory (or any other theory) is consistent is itself logically equivalent to a number-theoretic proposition. *Hence, one cannot believe that number theory is consistent without being implicitly committed to the truth of something at least as strong as number theory itself.* In fact, one can be justified in believing that number theory is consistent only by being justified in believing number theory to be *true*, as Frege pointed out. Third, this same problem eliminates the plenitudinous account of mathematics (Balaguer 1995) as a naturalistically acceptable explanation of our reliability with respect to number theory: in order to be confident that there is a mathematical structure (even in a mathematically plenitudinous universe) that satisfies the axioms of number theory, we must first be reliable at detecting the consistency of that theory.

A Priori Likelihood of Laws of Nature

As I have argued elsewhere (Koons 2000b), the reliability of the scientific method depends on the reliability of the a priori component of our theory-choice practices, which is characterized by a pervasive preference for various kinds of simplicity, symmetry, elegance, and other quasi-aesthetic characteristics. Thanks to the inevitable underdetermination of theory by data, if our non-empirical grounds for theory choice are unreliable, we can never collect enough data to have any confidence that we have narrowed down the possible laws of nature to a finite or even relatively compact set. Even if, as Steven Weinberg (1993, pp. 158–159) has argued, Nature herself trains us in what aesthetic qualities to look for, refining our theoretical "tastes" as we progressively uncover her secrets, it remains the case that we can be so trainable only by being pre-disposed to learn the right lessons from the early stages of scientific investigation.

Even more importantly, aesthetic qualities like simplicity can be a reliable guide to true theories about the laws of nature only if there is, objectively speaking, a real bias toward such simplicity in the laws themselves. If what laws nature has is independent of human practices (as any decent naturalist must suppose), then the source of the bias could only be some supernatural cause that is responsible for the pervading shape of those laws or that has supernatural acquaintance with those laws. Therefore, only theism can explain the reliability of the scientific method.

The naturalist cannot renounce knowledge about the objective laws of nature without calling into doubt naturalism itself, thought of as a very abstract, high-level theory about reality.

De Re Modal Facts concerning Material Composition and Persistence

Finally, Michael Rea (2002, p. 86) has argued: "There is no naturalistically acceptable basis for thinking that reflecting upon conceptual or conventional truths is a way of acquiring information about the world's intrinsic modal structure." This is especially clear when considering knowledge of *de re* necessities and possibilities concerning the composition and persistence of material objects (Rea discusses persistence: see Korman 2014 for parallel arguments about synchronic composition). Although there may well be some adaptive advantage to anticipating the counterfactual consequences (described in *de dicto* terms) of various actions, there is no obvious biological payoff to knowing whether *this very thing* has survived this or that change, as opposed to having been destroyed and replaced by something new, assuming that bare facts of identity and distinctness cannot by themselves make any difference to the distribution of physical and biological properties in space and time. To put it metaphorically, natural selection cares about the perpetuation of genetic types: it couldn't care less about whether individual *token* organisms or *token* inorganic entities survive. There may be an advantage to having relatively simple intuitions, but there is no advantage to having true ones.

Why can't the naturalist just include a plenitudinous theory of material objects (e.g., mereological and four-dimensional universalism[3]), thereby securing the reliability of all of our positive ontological intuitions? This can always be added as an auxiliary hypothesis to naturalism, with some loss of prior probability, due to its ad hoc nature. In addition, Dan Korman (2014, pp. 6–10) has put forward a convincing reason why this won't be ultimately satisfactory—at least, not when we reach the section on defeaters. As we shall see, all the theist needs is some reason to believe the plenitude thesis to be false (such as negative intuitions about the non-existence of exotic objects, or a reasonable preference for relatively sparse ontologies). The naturalist will ultimately need *conclusive* grounds for believing in the plenitude thesis itself in order to defeat this defeater, and all of the usual grounds for accepting plenitude are (as Korman argues) undermined once one accepts a purely naturalistic account of our intuitions.

Conventionalism about de re modality (with its assumption of a plenitude of genuine material-object concepts) would give us only mind-dependent material objects.

As Rea argues convincingly, the fact that naturalists can claim no knowledge of the existence or nature of individual material things plays havoc with that philosophy, leaving naturalists without good reason for believing in the existence of any extra-mental reality at all. If I cannot know that any particular material object or any particular kind of material object exists, can I mean anything substantive by (extra-mental) *matter* (as Berkeley long ago questioned)? Ironically, it is their ignorance of the body (rather than of the mind) that prevents naturalists from providing a solution to the mind/body problem.

Response #2: Conceptual Constraints Do Not Ensure Sufficient Reliability

Let's suppose that conceptual constraints are enough to ensure some measure of reliability to our intuitions. Is the resulting reliability great enough for knowledge? To count as knowledge, a belief must be the product of a faculty that is, when functioning normally under normal circumstances, in a context of pure inquiry, with sufficient leisure, and within suitable margins of error, perfectly reliable (or *very* nearly so). This standard of normal infallibility is the upshot of reflecting on the Lottery Paradox: the inherently fallible method of believing that any arbitrary ticket is a loser cannot produce knowledge of that fact, no matter how high the probability that it would, in any case, yield the right answer.

Natural selection prefers "quick and dirty" approximations to principled solutions. Knowledge, in contrast, must be the product of a per se infallible faculty—all error must be the product of interfering factors or abnormal conditions. Compare, for example, two engineers: one who uses an approximation technique that is known to give the right answer 80% of the time, the second who uses a method that is guaranteed to give the right answer every time but who fails to apply that method correctly 25% of the time, due to distractions or confusion. The second engineer knows the exact answer 75% of the time, while the first never knows the exact answer, even though his guesses are right 80% of the time. From the point of view of knowledge, the first is a complete failure, and yet Nature would surely often prefer the first to the second.[4]

How much reliability can we expect to result from the sort of conceptual constraints discussed by Law and Williamson? It is hard to say exactly how much—at most, we can be confident that we will be as reliable *as absolutely necessary* for the attribution to us of the relevant concepts to be reasonable. That is a pretty low standard: we are all familiar with cases of systematic error and confusion that coexist quite happily with the undeniable possession of the relevant concepts. To possess the relevant concepts it is sufficient to be able to apply them in a few clear cases, while being quite unreliable in general.

Can Williamson's suggestion of knowledge maximization as an interpretive standard be of help? Not really, since, as Williamson (2004, pp. 139–140) explains, the maximization norm would lead us to attribute knowledge only in those cases in which the subjects are in appropriate causal contact to the relevant facts. This is why we are not driven to attribute knowledge of quantum mechanics, for example, to people in the Stone Age. However, when it comes to causal contact with the facts of mathematics, morality, or ontology, we are all in the same boat as our Paleolithic ancestors were with respect to quantum phenomenon—indeed, we are worse off with respect to mathematical, moral, and ontological facts than they were with respect to quantum mechanical ones. Given naturalism, our ancestors were at least in some remote causal contact with the latter since they are physical in nature, while we are completely isolated from the former, since they are not. Consequently, Williamson's knowledge maximization standard of interpretation can't by itself ensure any reliability to our intuitive beliefs of necessary truths.

Response #3: Are Concepts Sparse or Abundant?

There are two conceptions of the ontology of simple concepts that are relevant to the idea of constraints on concept possession: a sparse and an abundant conception (corresponding to the well known distinction between sparse and abundant conceptions of properties). On the abundant conception, there is a genuine simple concept that corresponds to every coherent inferential role within a person's cognitive economy. On the sparse conception, in contrast, an inferential role corresponds to a real simple concept only when it effects acquaintance with a real property, presenting that property as it is to the mind—a property that is highly natural, part of the fundamental structure of the world, cuts nature "at its joints." On the sparse view, we can think of unnatural properties only by means of complex concepts. It is then possible for some of our thoughts to include pseudo-concepts (like *phlogiston*), analogous to empty names like "Zeus" or "Santa Claus."

This distinction between two models of concepts sets a dilemma for the naturalists' appeal to standards for concept possession. On the abundant-concepts model, it is relatively easy to see how we could have intuitive knowledge that is grounded in the concepts we possess, but that knowledge is irredeemably anthropocentric and devoid of real significance about the world. (I'm supposing here a plenitude of concepts, not objects, in such a way that the applicability of a set of concepts puts no constraints on the nature of the world.)

If, however, we adopt the sparse-concepts model instead, then we face a new source of skepticism about the reliability of our intuitive beliefs: in order to be reliable, our intuitive beliefs would have to succeed in providing our thoughts with genuine simple concepts. However, naturalists will be unable to explain why nature should care whether our inferential-cognitive roles should hook up with ontologically substantive concepts, especially in those domains (see Response #1) that are unrelated to practical concerns.

THE CAUSAL THEORY OF KNOWLEDGE

We've seen that theism can readily provide a plausible causal connection between necessary facts and human intuitions, while naturalism has no such facility. The majority of post-Gettier epistemologists have come to recognize that in paradigmatic cases of knowledge (perception, memory, testimony), some such causal connection is a necessary condition of knowledge. If we can adopt such a causal condition (or something analogous to it) for knowledge of necessary truths, we will have to conclude that intuitive knowledge is compatible with theism but inconsistent with naturalism.

A Transcendental Argument

Here is a simple version of such an argument:

1. If naturalism is true, our faculties evolved by unguided natural selection.
2. If our faculties evolved by unguided natural selection, then there is no connection (either causal, metaphysical, or constitutive) between our intuitions and the corresponding facts.
3. A connection of this kind is a necessary condition for intuitive knowledge.
4. Consequently, if naturalism is true, then there is no intuitive knowledge.
5. We have intuitive knowledge.
6. So, naturalism is not true.
7. If naturalism is not true, then (probably) God exists.

We must first recognize that this argument proposes only a kind of hypothetical skepticism about intuitions: if naturalism is true, then we have no intuitive knowledge. It does not join the company of "experimental" philosophers who reject intuitive knowledge tout court. Consequently, many dialectically successful attacks on intuition skepticism or experimentalism (such as those of Pust) are irrelevant to this argument.

The only really controversial premises in the argument are 2 and 3, and I have already argued for premise 2 in the section dealing with the inference to the best explanation earlier. So, the only remaining issue to consider is whether the causal condition of knowledge (or something very close to it) also applied in the case of intuition.

An Exception to the Causal Condition?

Edmund Gettier's paper (1963) revealed the bankruptcy of defining knowledge in terms of justified true belief. Post-Gettier reflections on knowledge have revealed that, at least in the paradigmatic cases of perception, memory, and testimony, knowledge requires a real connection of some kind between the mental state of knowledge and the facts so known. I argued in *Realism Regained* (Koons 2000a) that a similar constraint is also required for our knowledge of the laws of nature, mathematics, and logic. The key fact is that our intuitive (justified) true beliefs can also be Gettierized.

Suppose that a drug XYZ produces randomized intellectual seemings (or, if you prefer, causes our ordinary rational faculties to generate beliefs with randomized contents). When administered to a group of subjects, it is predictable that only 1% end up (by sheer chance) with true intuitive beliefs on a particular mathematical or ethical question. Those relying on veridical seemings (or belief-generation) under these circumstances do not gain knowledge, although they may have justified true beliefs (assuming that they don't know about the drug and its effect). Similarly, suppose that only one person out of a million has a veridical reaction to each of 10,000 such drugs, ending up (by chance) with true intuitive beliefs on all 10,000 questions. This is still not sufficient to give those subjects true beliefs on any of the issues.

Does this result depend in any way on contingency—that is, on the possibility of a given subject believing differently? Replace the drug with genetic manipulation of human gametes. Given origins essentialism, the one out of a million that end up by sheer chance with true beliefs on the 10,000 questions might have the disposition toward those beliefs essentially. This is still not good enough for knowledge.

Would it be sufficient if the seemings or dispositions to believe were essential to one's species? I think not: just replace the preceding scenarios with one in which aliens manipulate the evolutionary history of intelligent species on a million planets, with intuitions producing true beliefs occurring (by blind chance, not by design) on just one planet, and with all 1 million species equally adept at reproduction. The one intelligent species with species-wide essential dispositions to true intuitive belief still lack knowledge, because of the lack of a real connection between their seemings and dispositions and the relevant truths (whether those truths are themselves necessary or contingent).

The upshot of these thought experiments is this: knowledge is undermined so long as there are relevantly similar seemings or dispositions that are unreliable with respect to truth, and which had an equal or nearly equal propensity to exist.

What if it were metaphysically impossible for there to exist relevantly similar seemings that are false? I reply: Is this impossibility supposed to be true as a matter of brute necessity? It is hard to believe in such a metaphysical necessity without some ground—a ground that theism can provide, and that naturalism cannot. And, in any case, a merely brute necessity is too accidental to provide the needed connection between beliefs and their objects. Counterpossible scenarios in which the brute necessity was violated would be epistemologically relevant.

Could it be that intellectual seemings count as belief-justifying only when they are true? On this view, their non-veridical counterparts would not result in justified beliefs, so that all really justified intuitive beliefs would be true, and therefore they would all be cases of knowledge, with justification itself providing the link between the belief and its object. This supposition makes the two cases (veridical and non-veridical seemings) relevantly dissimilar. However, this view would make sense only if the order of explanation went from justified belief to true belief, and not vice versa. It would require some non-accidental connection between intellectual seemings and truth, which is precisely what naturalism cannot provide. If the only difference between justified intuitions and unjustified intuitions were that the first are true and the second false, then there would be no distinction between true opinion and knowledge in the intuitive domain, a result that is obviously wrong (as illustrated by the drug XYZ thought experiment above).

HIGHER-ORDER EPISTEMIC DEFEATERS

If the arguments of the second and third sections are even partially successful, they raise real doubts about the compatibility of naturalism and intuitive knowledge. In this section, I will argue that the mere existence of such doubts would constitute, if naturalism were true, a decisive *defeater* of all intuitive knowledge. Hence, the epistemological objection to naturalism can bootstrap itself from the mere epistemic *possibility* of an incompatibility of naturalism with the existence of intuitive knowledge to the *certainty* of such incompatibility.

Objective vs. Subjective Accounts of Defeaters

The theory of defeaters, as developed by John Pollock, Alvin Plantinga, and Michael Bergmann, has supposed that defeaters are beliefs of a certain kind: beliefs whose presence in the mind undermines some other belief's warrant, justification or reasonableness (in the same mind). Let's call this a *subjective* account of defeaters, in the sense that the defeater is always some state of the subject whose belief is defeated. Jonathan

Kvanvig (2007) has argued for an alternative, objective account, on which defeaters are true propositions that stand in a defeating relation to some epistemic relation (like being support or evidence for) between two other propositions or sets of propositions. Jonathan Dancy's work on practical reasons as facts or actual states of affairs to which a rational agent is sensitive or responsive (Dancey (2000)) could also be adapted to an objective theory of defeat.

Since Plantinga has already developed the subjective theory in some detail in connection with his evolutionary argument against naturalism, I think it would be of interest to try out the objective theory here instead. In addition, the objective theory avoids certain tangles and complexities to which the subjective theory is prone, and it has the nice feature of making facts about defeat insensitive to the order in which the subject learns relevant facts.

On Dancy's view, a *reason* for S to believe p is some actual state of affairs that favors S's believing p. We can extend Dancy's picture to *undercutting defeaters* (to use the term from Pollock 1987). An *undercutting defeater* of R as a reason for S to believe p is a state of affairs that grounds the fact that R is not a reason for S to believe p. An undercutting *defeater-defeater* of D (as a defeater of R as a reason for S to believe p) is a state of affairs that grounds the fact that D is *not* a defeater of R as a reason for S to believe p (see Chandler 2013). A *rational* subject is one whose beliefs and non-beliefs are suitably sensitive to the reasons he or she is aware of (i.e., one who responds as the reasons demand). A subject S *knows* that p if and only if (roughly) S believes p, p is true, and S's belief in p is suitably sensitive to the reasons for and against believing p. A defeater of S's knowledge that p is a defeater of S's reasons for believing p.

D is a *potential defeater* of R (as a reason for S to believe p) just in case (roughly) D would be, in the absence of any relevant defeater-defeaters, a defeater of R. D is a *merely potential* defeater of R if D is actually defeated.

We can also distinguish between first-order and second-order undercutters. A defeater D is a *first-order* undercutter of R as a reason for S to believe p if and only if D is a reason for thinking that relying on R would be unreliable with respect to the truth of p. A defeater D is a *second-order undercutter* of R if D is a reason (even a weak reason) for thinking that some first-order undercutter exists. Second-order undercutters are *highly leveraged defeaters*: a very weak reason for thinking that there exists a state of affairs X that is a first-order defeater of R suffices (if not *completely* defeated) to defeat R, even if R would be (in the absence of defeaters) a very strong first-order reason for believing p, and even if there is no X that is in fact a defeater for R.

Second-order defeaters include those cases (discussed by Plantinga) in which the probability that a belief has been reliably formed is "inscrutable." As Plantinga convincingly argues, such predicaments of inscrutability are sufficient to defeat both warrant and rationality with respect to the ground-level belief.

Why is there a no-defeater condition on knowledge? If one's reasons for believing p are defeaters, they are in fact no reason for believing p at all.

Why do undercutters defeat? In particular, why do second-order undercutters defeat? To believe any proposition on the basis of some reason for believing it, one must be nearly perfectly reliable in one's responsiveness to similar reasons for similar propositions. For reasoning subjects as complex as human beings, bombarded as we are by information from many rival claimants to reliability, being nearly perfectly reliable in such responsiveness requires that one *also* be nearly perfectly reliable at distinguishing reliable sources of belief from other sources, and that one respond appropriately to that knowledge. Hence, second-order defeaters demand that the rational agent discount those reasons that would, in the actual presence of the threatened first-order defeaters, be no reasons at all for one's belief.

The EAAN (with Objective Defeaters) Applied to Intuitive Knowledge

Here is a sketch of the argument applied to intuitive knowledge and employing objective, Dancy-style defeaters—specifically, treating the arguments in the sections earlier on the inference to the best explanation and on causal theory as constituting a second-order undercutting defeater.

1. If naturalism is true, our faculties evolved by natural selection. (If N, then E)
2. Necessarily, if N&E, then there is no ironclad explanation of the genesis of reliable intuition in human beings. (From section 2) (Alternatively, from section 3: … then there is reason to think that intuitive beliefs lack the sort of connection to the facts required for knowledge.)
3. Necessarily, if there is no ironclad explanation of the genesis of reliable intuition in human beings, then there is at least some reason to believe that the prior objective probability of human intuition's being reliable (R) is low. (And similarly, there is some reason to believe that intuitive beliefs lack the connection to fact required for knowledge.)
4. Necessarily, there being some reason to believe that the prior objective probability of R is low constitutes a potential second-order undercutting defeater for all intuitive belief. (And, similarly, there being some reason to think that intuitive beliefs lack the connection to fact required for knowledge also constitutes such a potential second-order undercutting defeater.)
5. Consequently, N&E entails the existence of a potential defeater for all intuitive belief. (2–4)
6. The only possible defeater for this defeater of intuitive belief would involve the corroboration of human intuitive beliefs by human intuitive knowledge.
7. Such self-corroboration cannot defeat any defeater. (The No-Self-Corroboration thesis)
8. Consequently, N&E entails the existence of an undefeatable (and therefore actual) undercutting defeater for all intuitive belief. (5–7)

9. If an actual defeater for any case of belief exists, then the corresponding type of knowledge is not instantiated. (The no-defeater condition for knowledge)
10. Consequently, if naturalism is true, then none of our intuitive belief constitutes knowledge. (1, 8, 9)
11. We have intuitive knowledge.
12. So, naturalism is not true. (10, 11)
13. If naturalism is not true, then (probably) God exists.
14. So, probably God exists. (12, 13)

We have discussed premises 1, 2, 9, and 11, so the crucial premises here are 3, 4, 6, and 7. Concerning 3: since natural selection can provide no ironclad explanation for the genesis of reliable intuition, we have to take seriously (as a real epistemic possibility, supported by some reason) that the objective propensity of the process of natural selection to produce such a reliable faculty of intuition was low. But this very fact is (as premise 4 asserts) a potential second-order defeater of any case of intuitive knowledge, since it grounds reasonable doubt in the reliability of the outputs of our intuitive faculties. So far, I think, the argument is relatively uncontroversial. The remaining question is this: is this potential defeater of intuitive knowledge itself defeated (and so, not an actual defeater at all)?

How could this potential defeater be defeated? Not only did we not find any categorical explanation of the reliability of intuition in terms of natural selection that was ironclad, we did not find any prospects for even a conditional explanation of it in those terms. That is, we didn't find any plausible naturalistic mechanism that, when added to natural selection, would predictably produce reliable intuitions. If we had, we could have looked for independent verification of the operation of that mechanism. As it is, the naturalists are stymied. Consequently, the only tack naturalists have taken in response to this task is to claim that we can find evidence that we have "won the cosmic lottery," that is, that despite the possible improbability of its doing so, nature has in fact conferred reliable intuitive faculties upon us.

Where, however, is the evidence that our faculties are in fact reliable? There are only two ways to verify, ex post facto, that we've acquired from evolution reliable intuitive faculties. The first would be to compare the outputs of those faculties with the actual facts. However, it is obvious that we cannot do so, since any such comparison would be guilty of what we might call "the self-corroboration fallacy." Here is a procedure that cannot produce evidence of the accuracy of a ruler: use the ruler to measure a line, and then use the same measurement again to verify the ruler's accuracy. However, any evidence that could be used to defeat the potential defeater of section 2 would be guilty of this very fallacy. Hence, the defeater cannot be defeated, and naturalism is incompatible with intuitive knowledge.

The second way to verify that our intuitive faculties are reliable would be simply to notice that intuition brings us in direct, unmediated contact with the modal, mathematical, or metaphysical facts (that in intuition the intellect is really contains its object, as Aristotle suggests in *De Anima* III). However, such contact implies the causal nonclosure of the natural domain and so is incompatible with naturalism.[5]

Answering Objections
The Perspiration Objection (or The Conditionalization Problem)

Plantinga sets up the EAAN in terms of the rational conditional probability of R on N&E. Instead, I put the argument in terms of the epistemic possibility (by way of the absence of an ironclad naturalistic explanation) of a low objective probability (at the time of the emergence of the human species) of intuitive reliability. My formulation avoids what Plantinga calls "the perspiration objection," and what many others have called "the conditionalization problem." Objective probability is automatically *conditionalized*, in a sense, on all the causal factors present at the moment of genesis. Naturalism cannot exclude the very real possibility that the reliability of human intuition at that point in history was quite low, certainly far below the levels required for knowledge. Omar Mirza (2008) builds the argument in a similar way, focusing on the process P that produced our faculties, and the fact that the naturalist has reasonable grounds for doubting that P "filtered out" unreliable faculties.

Tu Quoque

Hasn't the theist cheated by in effect building into her hypothesis the reliability of human intuition? Couldn't the naturalist do the same thing? No, and no. As I argued in section 2, explaining the reliability of human intuition is a substantive task for theists, but one that they are able to carry out. The auxiliary hypotheses required fit easily into a theistic framework. The naturalist, in contrast, has no compelling reason to believe (as Mirza 2008 points out) that the actual processes responsible for shaping human intuition were likely to produce reliable faculties.

CONCLUSION

Given the power of second-order undercutting defeaters, naturalists who wish to affirm the possibility of intuitive knowledge have the burden of proof of decisively refuting the conditional doubts raised in this chapter's second and third sections. The prospects for their doing so seem very slim. Hence, theists have a powerful argument for the superiority of theism over naturalism.

NOTES

My thanks to Cory Juhl, Dan Korman, Jason Schukraft, Jon Kvanvig, and Tomas Bogardus for their helpful comments on an earlier draft.

1. I'm setting aside the impact of the Christian doctrine of the Fall, partly because it varies widely within the Christian tradition and has no exact counterpart in other theistic religions. Personally, I take it to be a constraint on any acceptable doctrine of the Fall that it not disturb the reliability of our central cognitive faculties (including our moral knowledge—cf. Romans 2:14–15).

2. Nota bene: this requires a great deal more than simply knowing that each number has a successor.

3. A pure form of such universalism would entail that *every* occupied region of spacetime, no matter how gerrymandered or discontinuous, corresponds to a real composite and persisting entity, which has, at each point in time, all of the physical bits in the corresponding time-slice as proper parts. So, for example, there would really exist an entity that consists of the moon in 33 B.C. and the left half of the Eiffel tomorrow afternoon, and nothing else at any other time. This will, of course, entail, as a special case, the existence of all common-sense objects, and their common-sense ways of persisting.

4. Note well that I am not saying that *we* must be infallible in order to have knowledge. We must distinguish between faculties that are intrinsically fallible (and so not knowledge-generating) from those that are intrinsically infallible but fragile—subject to external interference. The latter generate knowledge, when they are free to work properly, but they can fail, when interfered with. I'm also not assuming any kind of luminosity or KK principle, since I'm requiring infallibility only within suitable margins of error.

5. Thanks to Tomas Bogardus for this point.

REFERENCES

Balaguer, Mark. 1995. "A Platonist Epistemology." *Synthese* 103: 303–325.

Bealer, George. 1999. "A Theory of the A Priori." *Philosophical Perspectives* 13: 29–55.

———. 2002. "Modal Epistemology and the Rationalist Renaissance," in *Conceivability and Possibility*, T.S. Gendler and J. Hawthorne (eds.), Oxford: Clarendon Press, 71–125.

Chandler, Jake. 2013. "Defeat Reconsidered." *Analysis* 73, no. 1: 49–51.

Dancy, Jonathan. 2000. *Practical Reality*. Oxford: Oxford University Press.

Gettier, Edmund. 1963. "Is Justified True Belief Knowledge?" *Analysis* 23: 121–123.

Harman, Gilbert. 1977. *The Nature of Morality*. New York: Oxford University Press.

Koons, Robert C. 2000a. *Realism Regained: An Exact Theory of Causation, Teleology, and the Mind*. New York: Oxford University Press, 2000.

———. 2000b. "The Incompatibility of Naturalism and Scientific Realism," in *Naturalism: A Critical Appraisal*, William Lane Craig and J.P. Moreland (eds.), Routledge, London, 2000), pp. 49–63; reprinted in *The Nature of Nature*, Bruce L. Gordon and William A. Dembski (eds.), Wilmington, DE: ISI Books, 2011.

———. 2003. "Review of *Truth and the Absence of Fact*, by Hartry Field." *Mind* 112: 119–126.

———. 2010. "Epistemological Problems with Materialism," in *The Waning of Materialism*, Robert C. Koons and George Bealer (eds.), Oxford: Oxford University Press, pp. 281–308.

Korman, Daniel Z. 2014. "Debunking Perceptual Beliefs about Ordinary Objects." *Philosophers' Imprint* 14, no. 1.

Kvanvig, Jonathan. 2007. "Two Approaches to Epistemic Defeat." in *Alvin Plantinga*, Deane-Peter Baker (ed.), Cambridge University Press, pp. 107–124.

Law, Stephen. 2012. "Naturalism, Evolution, and True Belief." *Analysis* 72, no. 11: 41–48.

Lewis, David K. 1986. *On the Plurality of Worlds*. Oxford: Blackwell.

Mirza, Omar. 2008. "A User's Guide to the Evolutionary Argument Against Naturalism." *Philosophical Studies* 141, no. 2: 125–146.

Miščević, Nenad. 2004. "The Explainability of Intuitions." *Dialectica* 58: 43–70.

Plantinga, Alvin. 1995. "Reliabilism, analyses and defeaters." *Philosophy and Phenomenological Research* 55, no. 2: 427–464.

———. 2002. "Reply to Beilby's Cohorts," in *Naturalism Defeated? Essays on Plantinga's Evolutionary Argument against Naturalism*, James Beilby (ed.). Ithaca, NY: Cornell University Press, pp. 204–276.

———. 2003. "Probability and Defeaters." *Pacific Philosophical Quarterly* 84 (2003): 291–298.

———. 2011a. "Content and Natural Selection." *Philosophy and Phenomenological Research* 83 no. 2: 435–458.

———. 2011b. *Where the Conflict Really Lies: Science, Religion, and Naturalism*. Oxford: Oxford University Press.

Pollock, John. 1987). "Defeasible Reasoning." *Cognitive Science* 11: 481–518.

Pust, Joel. 2004. "On Explaining Knowledge of Necessity." *Dialectica* 58: 71–87.

Rea, Michael. 2002. *World Without Design: The Ontological Implications of Naturalism*. New York: Oxford University Press.

Schechter, Joshua. 2010. "The Reliability Challenge and the Epistemology of Logic." *Philosophical Perspectives* 24: 437–464.

Street, Sharon. 2009. "Evolution and the Normativity of Epistemic Reasons." *Canadian Journal of Philosophy* 39 (sup 1): 213–248.

Swinburne, Richard. 2004. *The Existence of God*. Oxford: Oxford University Press.

Weinberg, Steven. 1993. *Dreams of a Final Theory: The Scientist's Search for the Ultimate Laws of Nature*. New York: Vintage Books.

Williamson, Timothy. 2004. "Philosophical 'Intuitions' and Scepticism about Judgement." *Dialectica* 58: 109–153.

———. 2007. "Philosophical Knowledge and Knowledge of Counterfactuals." *Grazer Philosophische Studien* 74: 89–123.

III

Moral Arguments

(R)

Moral Arguments (actually R1 to Rn)

AN ABDUCTIVE MORAL ARGUMENT FOR GOD

David Baggett

AMONG THE COUPLE dozen arguments (or so) for God's existence from Alvin Plantinga's famous and seminal article is one argument that, in his estimation, may be the best of the lot. The argument in question is one of the moral arguments he adduces, specifically, one that infers God's existence on the basis of moral obligations. In terms of the strength of the premises and the evidential connection between the premises and conclusion, this is the argument from natural theology that he thinks is perhaps second to none.

TWO FORMULATIONS

This chapter will give two versions of the argument and make the case that the second formulation, in particular, constitutes a formidable challenge indeed for the skeptic about God's existence.

The first version of the argument, the deductive version, goes like this:

1. There are objective moral obligations.
2. If there are objective moral obligations, then God exists.
3. So, God exists.

This version of the argument is obviously valid, so the only question that remains is whether the premises are more likely true than not (i.e., whether the argument is likely sound). But the question of "whether the premises are more likely true than not" is ambiguous between an individual and a collective reading. On an individual reading, the question is whether or not each premise is more likely true than not. On the collective reading, the question is whether or not the premise set, taken as a whole, is more likely true than not. These are importantly different. In principle, each premise could be more likely true than not but the likelihood that the conclusion is true be less than fifty percent.

Timothy McGrew gives a helpful illustration here. Consider rolling a single die. Concerning that one roll, consider this argument:

4. The roll will yield a 1, 2, 3, or 4.
5. The roll will yield a 3, 4, 5, or 6.
6. So, the roll will yield a 3 or 4.

Each premise is more likely true than false, and the conclusion follows with certainty from the premises. Nevertheless, the conclusion is less likely true than false. This is good evidence to suggest that what the deductive version requires is a collective reading of the truth of the premises. The conjunction of premises (1) and (2) needs to be more likely true than false. This is what will ensure that the conclusion is likely true.

A second formulation of the moral obligation argument is the abductive version, and it goes like this:

7. There are objective moral obligations.
8. The best explanation of objective moral obligations is God.
9. Therefore, (probably) God exists.

By "God" is meant an Anselmian God—the possessor of the omni-qualities (omnipotence, omniscience, etc.), the God of classical theism.

This abductive sort of argument is an inference to the best explanation (IBE). It begins with certain data to be explained, and, from a list of possible explanations, narrows the list down to the one best explanation by an application of a principled set of criteria, including explanatory scope and power. Explanatory scope pertains to how much of the relevant data is explained, and explanatory power asks how well the facts are explained. Notice, too, that premise (7) is the same as premise (1) in the previous argument, which reveals that both the deductive and abductive arguments from moral obligation are predicated on the existence of objective moral duties.

The salient difference comes next: In the deductive version, a conditional is affirmed, "If there are objective moral obligations, then God exists," whereas the IBE version argues that God is the best explanation of moral obligations. Then, in the deductive version, God's existence is entailed, whereas the abductive version warrants at least tentatively an inference to God's existence as the likely true explanation of moral obligations. Abduction is not a deductive approach, so it does not claim to yield a conclusion entailed by the evidence. The inference rather pertains to what most plausibly best explains the relevant data, in this case the existence of objective moral obligations. A good abductive argument at least tentatively entitles the reasoner to infer that the best explanation—assuming it's a *good enough* explanation, of course—is the true one.

ALVIN PLANTINGA'S FORMULATION

In his original paper, Plantinga wrote this concerning the general structure of the moral argument:

(1) One might find oneself utterly convinced (as I do) that morality is objective, not dependent upon what human beings know or think and that it cannot be explained in terms of any "natural" facts about human beings or other things; that it can't ultimately be explained in terms of physical, chemical, or biological facts. (2) One may also be convinced that there could not be such objective moral facts unless there were such a person as God who, in one way or another, legislates them.

Notice that, in this synopsis, Plantinga makes reference to "morality" per se rather than to moral obligations in particular, but he has confirmed in other contexts that he considers moral obligations to be the moral fact most resistant to naturalistic analysis. The sense of "objectivity" he affirms involves the lack of dependence on what human beings know or think. For example, twice two being four does not depend on any human being thinking it so; at most, what depends on humans are the conventional symbols used to express the proposition, but the existence of the proposition, its truth value, and its modal status do not depend on human beings.

It is interesting that Plantinga included in his first point both the existence of objective morality and the inability of secular accounts to explain or undergird them. His second point, then, pointed to the need for a "such a person as God" to serve as the foundation of morality in some sense. There are a few points to stress here. Plantinga identified three distinct tasks to be completed to flesh this argument out: (a) establishing or assuming moral realism, (b) underscoring the explanatory inadequacy of naturalistic accounts, and (c) defending the superior explanatory account provided by classical theism.

Plantinga tied (a) and (b) together, whereas, more typically, (b) and (c) go together. Nothing much rides on Plantinga having cast the argument this way, except perhaps that it may reveal something about what he considers to be the stiff explanatory challenge posed to naturalists. In light of the distinctive nature of moral facts, particularly of moral obligations—their objectivity, authority, prescriptivity—naturalists and secularists have a hard time accounting for them.

Since the first premise is held in common by both the deductive and abductive versions of the argument, let's first say a few words about realism with respect to moral obligations, before taking a closer look at each version in turn.

OBJECTIVE MORAL OBLIGATIONS

Most people, believers and unbelievers alike, claim to believe that we have moral duties that dictate some of what we ought to do. Not every "ought" is a moral ought or obligation, of course; but moral oughtness/obligation is an important moral category to make room for and sense of in one's worldview. Even plenty of secular thinkers claim to believe in moral obligations and to be able to abide by their dictates without the need for supernatural assistance. One consideration in favor of moral realism with respect to moral obligations is epistemic in nature. In light of the depth and ingression of moral convictions and clarity of certain moral apprehensions, someone might respond to skepticism about moral obligations along these lines:

10. Rational skepticism about moral obligations must depend on reasons.
11. Those reasons are not as obviously true as are moral obligations themselves.
12. So it is not rational to be a skeptic about moral obligations.

What might be one of those reasons for skepticism about moral obligations? A contemporary challenge has come from evolutionary moral psychology. The basic idea behind such a challenge is that moral beliefs, including beliefs about moral obligations, can be explained by appeal to how we as a species have evolved, and explained in a way that makes no essential reference to moral truth itself. And if our moral beliefs about obligations can be explained adequately without reference to moral truth, we have reason to be skeptical about the truth of our moral beliefs. Even if our moral beliefs happen to turn out to be true, we are left without good rational reason to think them true because we lack sufficient grounds to think that our moral beliefs track moral truth.[1] At the least, then, such an argument undermines rational belief in moral obligations, if not moral obligations themselves.

One way to try answering this challenge against moral realism is by providing a straightforward tracking account, and Angus Ritchie is an example of someone who has tried to do this very thing.[2] He argues that, unlike various secular accounts of moral knowledge, the rich teleological framework of a theistic story can better explain the truth-tracking nature of our cognitive apparatus. According to such an account, God's intention for human beings to possess moral knowledge, including knowledge of moral obligations, can provide the needed account for how our moral belief-generating capacities can depend on truth in the right way. On this basis Ritchie provides an epistemic moral argument for God's existence. This is not the version of the moral argument we are considering here, but it's interesting to note that the challenge from evolutionary moral psychology does seem to pose a considerably bigger problem for secular ethicists than for theistic ethicists.

Another way to try answering the evolutionary debunking challenge to moral obligations is by means of a non-tracking account. A non-tracking solution tries to explain the correspondence between moral truth and belief (such as an actual moral obligation and one's belief in it) without a direct causal explanation by appealing to a third factor that accounts for both moral truth and moral belief. This would explain the correlation without having to rely on a direct causal tracking account. Such an approach has appeal especially for those who consider moral truth to be causally inert. Erik Wielenberg, a contemporary secular ethicist, opts for such an approach; David Enoch does the same, although choosing a different "third factor."[3] A brief consideration of Wielenberg's proposal is in order, because it's relevant to understanding moral obligations.

Wielenberg's "third factor" to account for a correspondence between moral belief and moral truth is our set of cognitive faculties, which both generate beliefs and are properly connected with moral truth. The specific moral truth he uses for illustrative purposes is the reality of moral rights. In his recent book, he writes, "My third factor is certain cognitive faculties: the relevant cognitive faculties secure a correlation between moral rights and beliefs about moral rights because they entail the presence of moral rights and generate beliefs about such rights."[4] So the relevant cognitive faculties entail the rights and generate the corresponding beliefs, thus guaranteeing a correlation despite the causal inertness of moral facts.

It seems rather clear why he thinks our relevant cognitive faculties generate beliefs about moral realities, but how is it, on his view, that those faculties entail moral rights? On his view, following Derek Parfit, normative reasons count in favor of having some attitude, or acting in some way.[5] Normative reasons can be connected with claims about what we ought to do as follows: when we have decisive reasons, or most reason, to act in some way, this act is what we should or ought to do. Sometimes we have decisive moral reasons to act in a particular way. In such cases we have moral obligations. Correlative with a (perfect) moral obligation to another person is that other person's right to be treated (or not treated) in a particular way. So, in light of our cognitive faculties that recognize, on occasion, overriding normative reasons to act, rights (and correlative duties) are thereby entailed.

His account of rights here is helpful to grasp his understanding of moral obligations. Wielenberg and a number of other contemporary secular ethicists characterize such obligations as resulting from "overriding normative reasons." When we have enough reasons of a particular type, we have decisive reasons to act, and thus a moral obligation to act. But does this satisfactorily explain the existence of binding moral obligations and inextirpable human rights? Something in the neighborhood of Wielenberg's "third factor" approach may possess potential to avoid the debunking arguments, but Wielenberg's account of moral obligations may leave too many unanswered questions, as will be argued later. A closer look at the logic, language, and phenomenology of moral obligations will clarify why this is so, but first, a few words about the deductive version are in order.

THE DEDUCTIVE VERSION

Recall the deductive variant of the moral obligation argument:

13. There are objective moral obligations.
14. If there are objective moral obligations, then God exists.
15. So, God exists.

This argument has a number of virtues. It's pithy, succinct, and clear. It's potentially persuasive to some, and it's close to the argument that William Lane Craig has used on many college campuses with good success. The difference between this version and Craig's is that the antecedent Craig uses refers both to objective moral values and duties, so the version we're considering is slightly narrower in scope. (Craig also uses the contrapositive of the second premise and constructs a modus tollens argument.) Despite its virtues, though, this version of the argument is susceptible to various telling criticisms. Let's consider just one. Take the second premise: "If there are objective moral obligations, then God exists." The logically equivalent contrapositive of this conditional is (2'): If God doesn't exist, then there are no objective moral obligations.

This is, at least for dialectical reasons, unfortunate. Arguments are aimed, first and foremost, at capturing the truth, but, secondarily, at persuading. Committed, intelligent atheists, on hearing the claim that if God doesn't exist, there are no objective moral obligations, won't process such a conditional as a counterfactual or counteressential, but rather as a straightforward conditional whose antecedent they consider true. If they retain a commitment to moral realism, they will naturally take the consequent to be false, and thus the conditional itself to be false. This is less a logical flaw in the argument than a common dialectical dynamic, but still a relevant consideration.

Plantinga's formulation pushes in the direction of a deductive approach. Recall his words that objective morality "cannot be explained in terms of any 'natural' facts about human beings or other things; that it can't ultimately be explained in terms of physical, chemical, or biological facts." He also says one may be convinced "that there could not be such objective moral facts unless there were such a person as God who, in one way or another, legislates them." This would seem to suggest that God is the *only* explanation of objective moral obligations; and that, if God didn't exist, there would be no moral obligations. But what sort of claim can be made about a world in which God doesn't exist? If God exists necessarily, then there is no possible world in which God doesn't exist, a point of fundamental significance frequently emphasized in Plantinga's work on the metaphysics of modality. So what does a claim amount to that speaks of or gestures at aspects of a world in which God doesn't exist? How is it different from empty conjectures about a world in which twice two is five? On Anselmianism, or classical theism, such a conditional is a counteressential, a particularly intractable one at that: a world in which a necessarily existing being and, indeed, the ground of being does not exist. It would of course be quite true that, in such a world, there would be no moral obligations. There would be nothing at all, because such a world would be metaphysically impossible.[6]

Of course, atheists don't believe God exists, much less exists necessarily, so typically when the moral argument is presented in this form, the counterfactual is not taken or intended to refer to a counteressential. Most usually, it is rather taken to mean something like this: On the assumption that God does not exist in the actual world, no objective moral duties would obtain. To see an example of this, consider Wielenberg's response to Craig's claim that, without God, human beings lack moral rights and duties: "Human beings can reason, suffer, fall in love, set goals for themselves, and so on. God or no God, human beings obviously differ when it comes to their intrinsic properties from dogs and mere lumps of slime."[7] Clearly Wielenberg takes Craig's suggestion to pertain to the actual world and the assumption that, in this modal reality, God doesn't exist. And in such a world, the claim goes, rape isn't wrong, racism isn't wrong, nor was Hitler. Craig writes, "On the atheistic view, there's nothing *really* wrong with your raping someone."[8] Again, this is, at least from a dialectical perspective, unfortunate. It's also arguably needless, because there is a better way to couch the argument that isn't so, frankly, jarring, nor so susceptible to criticism and, arguably, is a more effective way to build a bridge with secular interlocutors. This alternative is an abductive argument, an inference to the best explanation, which need not claim that theism provides the only explanation of moral facts, only that theism provides the *best* explanation. It also need not entertain synthetic counteressentials and involve itself in pontificating about features of what may well turn out to be intractably impossible worlds.

As we will see, however, going the abductive route requires patience, because it means we have to be more painstaking in careful consideration of a range of secular ethical attempts to account for moral obligations. The patience is worth it, though, as this approach allows for the expectation that various naturalistic and secular efforts at moral theory will have something to say and contributions and insights to offer. They can't, therefore, be handily dismissed or responsibly ignored. But through careful analysis, their limitations become increasingly evident. So to an abductive version of the moral obligation argument we turn, first identifying the relevant moral facts in need of explanation, and then in the final two sections embarking on the quest for the best explanation of those facts.

MORAL OBLIGATIONS AND THEIR FEATURES

Deontic ethics involve one important set of moral judgments; they include issues of moral permissibility, moral obligation, and moral forbiddenness, and they often get expressed with such locutions as (morally) "right" and "wrong" used in various ways. An action wrong not to do is a moral obligation; an action not wrong to do is morally permissible; an action wrong to do is forbidden. Although moral duties do not cover the whole moral terrain, they represent, by the lights of many ethicists, an essential part of ethics, and one that cries out for adequate explanation.

It would be an easy task to explain moral obligations if by "obligations" we simply meant feelings of obligation, but the latter are neither necessary nor sufficient for the former. Perhaps someone neglects a particular duty for so long that she has ceased to feel it to be one. Conversely, one can have the feeling he ought to do something, yet have no obligation to do it at all. Consider the punctilious moralist saddled with an overactive superego who feels guilty even for minor infractions of etiquette. More typically, though, it's plausible that feelings of obligations at least roughly correspond to actual obligations.

Moral obligations are not mere suggestions, cautionary ideals, means of avoiding trouble, or sage pieces of advice. Not only are duties not mere suggestions; they are not even merely prescriptions which there are excellent reasons to fulfill. Moral obligations are not just options for us, even options supported by good reasons; they are, to use a characterization of Cornell realist David Brink, inescapable. Another word for "duty" or "obligation" is "imperative," and Immanuel Kant was well known for distinguishing between hypothetical and categorical imperatives. Hypothetical imperatives depend for their legitimacy on some goal desired by the subject of the prescription; for example, to lose weight you *ought* to eat less. The hypothetical prescription to eat less isn't universally applicable, obviously enough; it hardly applies, for example, to an emaciated victim of anorexia. A categorical imperative, though, on a Kantian construal, *is* universally applicable, not dependent at all for its legitimacy on any goal desired by the subject of the prescription. To treat others as ends in themselves and not merely as means, to use Kant's famous example, is a categorical imperative, something everyone has a moral duty to do.

Moral obligations construed as categorical imperatives require more than inescapability. Morality requires an additional vital ingredient that Richard Joyce characterizes as "authority"; and this, he notes, gives us a normative system enjoying both features (inescapability and authority), one that possesses "practical clout."[9] Such practical clout dictates that the obligatory is what we have to do, what we must do—not in the sense of the causal must, but of the moral must. When C.S. Lewis spoke of the moral demand at the beginning of *Mere Christianity*, he referred to it as a "law" but distinguished it from the laws governing the operation of the physical world in just this sense. We can't opt out from being governed by gravity; we can, however, choose to ignore the moral law—and too often we do.

Moral duties give us reasons, indeed compelling and overriding reasons, to act; but Wielenberg and Parfit arguably reverse the order when they say obligations result from enough reasons to act (of a particular sort) adding up. Parfit connects normative reasons with claims about what we ought to do as follows: "When we have decisive reasons, or most reason, to act in some way, this act is what we should or ought to do in what we can call the decisive-reason-implying senses."[10] Wielenberg elaborates, "S ought, must, or is required to do A just in case S has most normative reason to do A. Sometimes we have decisive moral reasons to act in a particular way. In such cases we are morally obligated to act in a certain way."[11] Parfit and Wielenberg seem to endorse a "duty-posterior" analysis, according to which duties *result from* enough reasons of a particular sort to act. More traditionally, moral obligations were analyzed in a "duty-anterior" sense, according to which duties obtained and it was they themselves that provided compelling reasons to act.[12]

As C. Stephen Evans puts it, "People frequently have reasons to perform actions, even powerful and decisive reasons, which they have no moral obligation to do," adding that "although it is certainly true that a moral obligation gives an individual a reason for acting in a certain way, it does not follow that an explanation of a reason for action is *eo ipso* an explanation of a moral obligation."[13] Echoing Evans, Paul Copan and Matthew Flannagan write, "moral obligation is not identical with what one has good reasons to do. Obligations involve a certain type of reason to act: one that involves a demand with which we must comply, one by which others can rationally blame us and reproach us for failing to do so, one for which we can rightly be held accountable and feel guilty for violating, and one that is rational to inculcate into others."[14]

This illustrates the way that language about moral obligations points to the authority of moral requirement, which leads to another characteristic feature of moral duties. We can see this additional feature most clearly when we consider what Lewis says we often do: act in violation of the moral law. One result is the experience of guilt, as discussed before—guilt understood as a moral condition in need of rectification, and not merely a subjective feeling.

Two more features are responsible for much of the human significance of guilt. One is harm caused by one's (wrong) action, and the other and yet more pervasive feature of guilt is alienation from other people, to some degree or other. C. Stephen Evans thinks that, of the various features of moral duty, authority is their most important distinguishing feature. He recognizes that an important task for the moral cognitivist is to explain such authority. The challenge of doing so, along with the epistemic challenges facing the proponent of objectively binding moral obligations, led J.L. Mackie, of course, to reject such obligations as too ontologically odd, leading to his "error theory." What is so special, and potentially strange, about moral obligations? As George Mavrodes has emphasized (in a famous piece that Plantinga also refers to), to have a moral obligation is to have a special reason to act; an obligation conveys the notion of an absolute verdict. This distinguishes moral obligations, thus construed, from a picture of morality like we find in Aristotle. When Aristotle used terms like "should" or "ought," these relate to what is good and bad for something in terms of what is needed for that thing to flourish or achieve its potential. Justice, to use Evans's example, is a virtue needed for human flourishing, and being unjust is therefore harmful to a person.

By contrast, in modern moral philosophy, terms like "should" and "ought" often have a special moral sense, in which they imply some absolute verdict.[15] Anscombe attributed the difference to the intervening influence of Christianity, with its law conception of ethics. But if such a conception of a law-giving God is dominant for many centuries and then given up, it is hardly surprising that the concept of obligation, of being bound or required as by a law, should remain for some time even though it has been cut off from its root. This is just what Anscombe thought had happened, resulting in vestiges of moral language retaining the atmosphere of its more traditional use but its soul gone, its clout removed. This is why Anscombe, writing in the 1950s, thought it might be best to leave the modern conceptions behind and go back to Aristotle's understanding, because she thought the theoretical underpinnings of modern morality were irretrievably lost. As Evans notes, Anscombe, a devout Catholic, may have been pleasantly surprised to live to see the more recent resurgence of interest in theistic ethics, including interest in variants of a divine command account of moral obligations.

What is important for present purposes is to note what Evans dubs the "Anscombe intuition": the idea that moral obligations as experienced have a unique character, and that attempts to explain moral obligations must illuminate that special character. Four features stand out to Evans as comprising moral obligations: (1) A judgment about a moral obligation is a kind of verdict on my action; (2) A moral obligation brings reflection to closure; (3) A moral obligation involves accountability or responsibility; and (4) A moral obligation holds for persons simply as persons.[16]

Interestingly enough, Evans wishes to suggest, contra Anscombe, that Socrates seemed to operate with the concept of moral obligation. In Plato's *Apology*, for instance, all four features are present. Evans thinks this is significant because the notion of moral obligations as verdict-like and rife with authority may not simply be a function of special revelation, but something more generally accessible. This is potentially important for a reason most relevant to this chapter's concern: If the features of moral obligation are defined in a question-begging sort of way, then the failure of a moral theory to satisfy the strictures that emerge as conceptual features of moral obligations may not be seen as a significant failure after all. If, for example, moral obligations construed in such a way as to satisfy the Anscombe intuition came about only or primarily as a result of Jewish and Christian teachings, then a secularist could reply, "That's fine; so much the worse for moral obligations understood along those lines." So recognizing that Socrates himself entertained an understanding of moral obligations in such close proximity to the modern conception is an important point, and one that should discourage us from dismissing modern conceptions too quickly.[17]

Much more could be said to spell out various features of moral obligations, but enough has been said to proceed to the next phase of our argument. To summarize, then, perhaps the most important distinguishing feature of moral obligations, classically construed in the Socratic and theistic traditions, is that they are authoritative, offering us compelling reasons to comply with them. Failure to discharge our moral duties typically results in objective guilt, alienation from others, and, where damage is rendered, even greater guilt.

SURVEYING THE FIELD

Since the moral argument asks us to consider the actual world and attempt to explain moral obligation without appeal to theistic resources, it becomes all the more important to spend the time required to give various secular efforts at moral explanation their due. This can't be done in a single chapter, much less a single section of a chapter—but Jerry Walls and I have just finished a volume in which we give this issue a book-length treatment, which we admitted was still only a start to the project; it's a far more ambitious program than can be done in a book or two.[18] Here it must suffice to gesture in the directions that need to be taken. Again, since secular ethicists have a world like this to work with—a world that, if theists are right, was created by God and inhabited with creatures made in God's image—it would be altogether surprising, from a theistic perspective, if secular ethicists couldn't make any progress in ethical theory, in light of the rich resources of this world at their disposal.

A deductive approach, in a sense, often takes away with one hand what it offers in another. By granting the resources of this world to be used in the formation of a secular ethical theory, the argument gives secularists quite a bit of fodder to work with in their efforts to explain moral obligations. But too often all such secular ethical theories get lumped together and summarily dismissed far too quickly. So, truly granting our secular interlocutors the freedom to use the resources of the world—from the deliverances of intuitions to the satisfactions of morality to the requirements for social harmony, to name just a few—means that we need to take the time to give their proposals adequate consideration and, if need be, credit for their legitimate insight.

What too often suffices in popular apologetics in their treatment of secular ethical theories are a few broad-brush criticisms that fail to do justice to the careful work that's been done by serious thinkers on this issue. What C.S. Lewis tries to do at the beginning of *Mere Christianity*, for instance, may serve the purposes of popular apologetics, but it is much too hasty to serve the purpose of subjecting secular ethical theory to robust critical scrutiny. Often critics of secular ethics settle for a general criticism, like the difficulty naturalists encounter making sense of meaningful moral agency. Specifically, such an argument goes, at most the sense in which people "can do otherwise" in a world determined or "near determined" (at least at the macro level) is in the counterfactual sense: if they had wanted to do differently, and could have, then they would have. But of course such an account leaves much to be desired—like any actual ability to ever do otherwise. If meaningful moral agency and ascriptions of moral responsibility require such freedom, and naturalism encounters a devilishly difficult time furnishing it, we have a general sort of critique of naturalistic ethics.

The problem with such a general critique, despite its potential power, is twofold: First, it opens up a can of worms about how best to understand free will, which introduces a vast literature; very soon, the whole focus of the discussion has shifted from morality to metaphysics. Such discussions are worth having, but in this context it largely functions to change the subject. Second, and more fundamentally, such general critiques fail to engage with any of the specifics of secular ethical theory, which is an odd way to go about subjecting such theories to scrutiny. It's often better, then, and certainly better on an abductive approach, to delve into the specifics of secular ethics, recognizing the variety of views on offer and not only what they share in common, but how they differ.

For example, a full treatment would consider a range of secular ethical and metaethical approaches, both naturalistic and non-naturalistic, ranging from Philippa Foot's natural law view, to Shafer-Landau's non-naturalism, to supervenience accounts like Erik Wielenberg's, to naturalistic ethical accounts like those of the Cornell realists, to various evolutionary approaches, to Korsgaardian constructivism, and more besides, holding off on critiques applicable across the board until after such work is done. Obviously, this chapter can't do all that work in this space, but it can provide one brief example of the sort of work that's called for, an example provided by Plantinga himself.

Take Philip Kitcher, who offers a naturalized virtue ethic. Kitcher is the author of the recent *Life After Faith: The Case for Secular Humanism*. About a decade back, Kitcher sketched a summary of his position at the time. He wrote that the main function of normative guidance was to reinforce the psychological capacities that made sociality possible for us. Such psychological capacities involve an ability to empathize with the needs and interests of others, and, to some extent, they are reinforced by directives to take greater account of other people's plans and projects, even where there is, at least initially, no empathetic response. He thinks the primary function of morality is to extend and amplify those primitive altruistic dispositions through which we became social animals in the first place; this, then, has the secondary effect of promoting social cohesion.

On Kitcher's view, elaborated in his 2011 *The Ethical Project*, evolution has put into place certain capacities to empathize with others, feel their pain, identify with their desires, and the like. But since these imaginative faculties remain limited, morality has for its function to extend such empathy. As moral creatures, our function is to extend our empathetic responses, widen our altruistic tendencies, and by so doing choose an objectively better way of living. One characterization of Kitcher's view is as a pragmatic social contract theory grounded in ethical altruism, which functions in two ways: in seeking altruistic good, we are recapitulating the original human ethical problem and thus working to carry forward the fundamental human ethical project; and in seeking such good, we are contributing to ethical progress. The theory can also be seen as a variant of a naturalized virtue ethic. Such an effort replaces Aristotle's talk of nature with something considered more scientifically respectable; on such a conception, what we ought morally to do follows from the traits we ought to develop, which depend on the sorts of creatures that we are.

For present purposes, it bears emphasis that Kitcher's view is particularly bad at explaining moral obligations. For, rather than trying to explain such obligations, he denies their existence. He acknowledges that we do not have access to ethical truth or the ethically real, but argues that the ethical community can function as an approximate equivalent to ethical truth by forging what is believed to be progressive ethical principles and choices. This becomes quite clear in his latest book, the ethics chapter of which Plantinga describes like this:

> [Kitcher's] aim in this chapter, then, is to give a naturalistic vindication of values; an account of ethics that fits with secularism but doesn't reduce the ethical life to the expression of subjective attitudes. As he notes (p. 28) it is common to think of moral or ethical standards as independent of human desires and aspirations, having a sort of objectivity that fits well with their being divinely commanded. On Kitcher's account, of course, these standards don't originate in anything like a divine command, and Kitcher's account of ethics and morality doesn't give it that sort of objectivity. What status do ethical standards have, according to him? It's not easy to tell. As far as I could make out, Kitcher believes that ethical rules have simply evolved over the centuries as a means to the reduction of "functional conflict" (p. 53) and the promotion of harmony in a society. It's a good idea for us (as members of a society) to follow these rules, and to coerce the unwilling also to follow them, in order to introduce and maintain functional harmony in our society. On this prudential account, of course, there isn't any such thing as objective moral obligation, and there would be nothing wrong, morally speaking, in my flouting current ethical precepts (provided I could escape detection).[19]

Again, this example is not designed to apply to every secular ethical theory. An abductive approach requires patience in applying careful analysis to the full range of secular ethical theories on offer. Once more, an abductive approach needn't conclude that none of the theories, either individually or in various combinations, has anything to offer; rather, all that needs to be argued is that none of the secular and naturalistic approaches provides as good an explanation of moral obligations as does theism.

Finally, then, what sort of case for moral obligations can classical theism provide, and are there reasons to think it's the better explanation?

CLASSICAL THEISM

Theistic ethics can avail itself of features of the physical world—features that have a deeper significance when understood as the product of creation—but in addition, it can tap into distinctively theistic resources, as well. In light of the limitations and deficiencies of naturalistic approaches, both individually and collectively, the explanatory strength and power of theistic ethics seems likely to be stronger. That case can be extended to include explaining a broad array of moral facts and realities—from values to rights to moral transformation to moral knowledge to moral rationality—but for present purposes, we'll continue confining our attention specifically to moral obligations.

Efforts by theistic ethicists to account for moral obligations range from natural law accounts to divine motivation theories; from divine will theories to divine command theories; from divine desire theories to divine attitude theories; and more besides. In light of Plantinga's preference for divine command theory, we will direct our focus there. Divine command theory (DCT) asserts that our moral duties are constituted or caused by the commands of a loving and just God. Since Alston's landmark article on the subject, most divine command theorists have been careful to delimit divine commands to moral rightness (permissibility and mainly obligation), not moral goodness. Robert Adams is probably the most famous thinker in recent years who's developed this line of thought, constructing a theistic adaptation of a social requirement model, according to which our moral duties are constituted by the commands of a loving and just God.[20]

Evans and others have argued at length that DCT is particularly well suited to explain the salient features of moral obligations, including their authority, action-guiding power, reason-giving force, and the Anscombe intuition. Of course, objections against DCT abound, but a number of able defenders have provided excellent responses to such challenges, objections ranging from arbitrary to vacuity to epistemic objections. A series of seven crucial distinctions, when brought to bear on this subject, can enable an effective reply to a variety of Euthyphro-inspired objections to divine command theory, including objections mistakenly depicted by some as intractable.[21]

To illustrate with a few examples, consider the distinction between *difficulty* and *impossibility*. For defenders of divine impeccability who take seriously Old Testament conquest narratives, for example, some would challenge such a view by insisting that such biblical stories are impossible to reconcile with a perfectly good God. Certainly the passages do contain challenges to answer in this regard, but, as Paul Copan and Matt Flannagan have recently argued, it's far from clear the passages, rightly understood, are impossible to square with a perfectly loving God. When enough contextual considerations are brought to bear, much of the challenge seems manageable. In a sense, bringing to bear the difficulty/impossibility distinction here resembles Plantinga's famous defense against the logical problem of evil. If A entails B, and B and C are consistent, then A and C are consistent. Similarly, if the salvation history effected by a perfectly loving God allows, in certain extremely unusual circumstances, for a conquest, then God's perfect goodness and such a conquest are at least in principle possibly consistent.

Or consider this argument against the divine impeccability on which divine command theory is usually predicated:

16. It is conceivable God can sin.
17. If it is conceivable that God can sin, it is possible that God can sin.
18. So, it is possible that God can sin (contra impeccability).

If God by definition is impeccable, then God is impeccable de dicto, but the deeper question is whether God is impeccable de re—whether the person of God himself is essentially morally perfect. This conceivability argument can be directed against impeccability construed de re. But its flaw is in its casual assumption that conceivability entails genuine, broadly logical possibility. All sorts of metaphysically impossible things might be thought to be conceivable in some way—like the falsehood of Goldbach's conjecture. But, of course, in such a case, if it's true, it's necessarily true, and not even possibly false. So either the conceiving, despite its compelling phenomenology, is a pseudo-conceiving, or conceivability does not entail genuine possibility after all. Either way, in the conceivability argument against impeccability, at least one of the premises seems likely false. This of course doesn't establish impeccability, but it's an effective refutation of one important argument against it.

The recent discussion of divine command theory helps show that such an approach is worthy of serious consideration and that it or something in its close proximity arguably may well indeed exhibit superior explanatory scope and power in accounting for moral obligations and their distinctive traits.

CONCLUSION

The image of Russian nesting dolls is a good one when considering the moral argument of this chapter. Confined to an examination of moral obligations in particular, a compelling abductive case can be made that theism provides the best explanation of both moral duty and its various logical, semantic, and phenomenological features. But that argument can fit into the larger and broader moral apologetic, encompassing not just moral duties, but other moral facts like moral agency and moral value, along with moral knowledge, moral transformation, and moral rationality. And even that expansive moral apologetic can fit into the yet larger apologetic that dozens of evidential considerations—such as we see in this book—collectively comprise.[22]

NOTES

1. Plantinga himself uses an argument similar to this in his argument against rational belief in naturalism.

2. Angus Ritchie, *From Morality to Metaphysics: The Theistic Implications of our Ethical Commitments* (Oxford: Oxford University Press, 2012).

3. David Enoch, *Taking Morality Seriously: A Defense of Robust Realism* (Oxford: Oxford University Press, 2011); Erik Wielenberg, *Robust Ethics: The Metaphysics and Epistemology of Godless Normative Realism* (Oxford: Oxford University Press, 2014).

4. Wielenberg, *Robust Ethics*, 145.

5. Derek Parfit, *On What Matters*, 2 vols. (Oxford: Oxford University Press, 2011).

6. One might suggest that such counteressentials aren't particularly problematic, because we can quite meaningfully assert that, say, "If God doesn't exist, then God didn't create the world." That's true, but also arguably merely analytic. Substantive synthetic claims featuring the impossible antecedent of God's non-existence, on the other hand, seem problematic indeed—if the claim involves affirming more than this: nothing exists in a null world.

7. Wielenberg, 51.

8. William Lane Craig and Walter Sinnott-Armstrong, *God? A Debate Between a Christian and an Atheist* (Oxford: Oxford University Press, 2004), 18.

9. Richard Joyce, *The Evolution of Morality* (Cambridge, MA: MIT Press, 2007), 57.

10. Parfit, vol. 1, 33.

11. Wielenberg, 7.

12. David Brink's argument that, on occasion, even strong moral obligations might not provide us compelling enough rational reasons to act shows that he seems to embrace a duty-anterior model.

13. C. Stephen Evans, *God and Moral Obligations* (Oxford: Oxford University Press, 2013), 9.

14. Paul Copan and Matthew Flannagan, *Did God Really Command Genocide? Coming to Terms with the Justice of God* (Grand Rapids, MI: Baker Books, 2014), 165.

15. G.E.M. Anscombe, "Modern Moral Philosophy," reprinted in *The Collected Philosophical Papers of G. E. M. Anscombe, Volume 3: Ethics, Religion, and Politics* (Oxford: Basil Blackwell, 1981), 26–42.

16. Evans, 12–14.

17. Richard Joyce, too, thinks that it is part of the conception of moral judgments generally and moral obligations particularly that they possess moral clout, "oompth," the sort of binding authority to which Anscombe's intuition points.

18. David Baggett and Jerry L. Walls, *God and Cosmos: Moral Truth and Human Meaning* (New York: Oxford University Press, 2016).

19. Alvin Plantinga, review of *Life after Faith*, Notre Dame Philosophical Reviews, https://ndpr.nd.edu/news/54977-life-after-faith-the-case-for-secular-humanism/ (accessed June 18, 2017).

20. Robert Merrihew Adams, *Finite and Infinite Goods: A Framework for Ethics* (Oxford: Oxford University Press, 1999); John E. Hare's recent and remarkable *God's Command* (Oxford: Oxford University Press, 2015) also deserves mention.

21. Here's the full list:

  – A *scope* distinction: definition versus analysis
  – A *semantic* distinction: univocation versus equivocation
  – A *modal* distinction: conceivability versus possibility
  – A *moral* distinction: good versus right
  – An *epistemic* distinction: difficulty versus impossibility
  – A *meta-ethical* distinction: knowing versus being, and
  – An *ontological* distinction: dependence versus control.

For more specific examples, see David Baggett and Jerry L. Walls, *Good God: The Theistic Foundations of Morality* (New York: Oxford University Press, 2011).

22. In *God and Cosmos*, Jerry Walls and I have the chance to flesh out a broader moral apologetic and to incorporate some of the explanatory resources of not just theism, but of Christianity in particular.

(R*)

The Argument from Evil

FELIX CULPA!

Hud Hudson

IN HIS "SUPRALAPSARIANISM, or 'O Felix Culpa,'" Alvin Plantinga proposes to revive and to carefully consider a response to evil that "has been with us for a long time," a response that can help us to achieve "an important goal for Christians"—namely, to understand "the evil our world displays from a Christian perspective." Plantinga does not claim that adopting the proposal he explores in his piece is required in order to respond adequately to those arguments grounded in evil that target theistic and Christian belief—responses featuring soul-making, freewill, multiverse scenarios, the price of regular worlds, and the feebleness of noseeum inferences apparently suffice for that. Rather, he proposes to make progress on a second issue, the question of how Christians in particular should think about "evil and its place in God's world."[1]

And yet, despite emerging from such humble origins, a full-blown theodicy appears halfway through the paper, and this from the man who once offered the following reflection on the promise of theodicy: "And here I must say that most attempts to explain why God permits evil—theodicies, as we may call them—strike me as tepid, shallow, and ultimately frivolous."[2] A change of tune, to be sure! But perhaps the change is (as Plantinga persuasively urges) worth taking very seriously, after all.

I will not comment on the second theme of his paper—the interpretation and adjudication of the debate between supralapsarianism and infralapsarianism on the order of the decrees of God to permit human beings to fall and to save some of the fallen—apart from noting that I think he is correct that if he has presented us with a successful theodicy, "the Supras are right." Instead, I would like to focus on the details of the theodicy itself.

SOME TOOLS

Plantinga articulates and advocates for a number of theses concerning value that are at the heart of his proposal. Here are the opening moves:

1) Among the good-making qualities of worlds we find creaturely happiness, beauty, justice, creaturely goodness, performance of duty, and creatures' conformity to love God above all else and to love their neighbors as themselves.
2) Among the bad-making qualities of worlds we find suffering, pain, creaturely rejection of God, hatred, and sin.

Sensible selections, if you ask me. Those are, indeed, good-making and bad-making features of worlds, respectively. But then we venture out into deeper waters—it turns out that our first list of good-making features omitted the two most important goods:

3) God is good. *Better*—God is the greatest good. *Better yet*—God is infinitely good. *Better still*—God's goodness is unlimited, where unlimited value advances beyond mere infinite value by crediting God with a goodness which is better than *any* quantity, quality, variety, or distribution of creaturely goods. The line is drawn there, however. Plantinga does not insist that God's existence is maximally valuable; there are a few things to add here and there to a world containing God that can make it even better. (Significantly, it is worth noting that as a side benefit, owing to God's tremendous goodness and to God's necessary existence and to the constraints on creation given God's nature, every possible world is a very good world.)
4) The state of affairs consisting of Incarnation-and-Atonement is good and (unlike God's existence) is a contingent good. *Better*—Incarnation-and-Atonement is the second greatest good, an unthinkably magnificent good "that towers enormously above all the rest of the contingent states of affairs." *Better yet*—Incarnation-and-Atonement is infinitely good. *Better still*—the value of Incarnation-and-Atonement (like the value of God himself) is incommensurable with creaturely goods; it is better than *any* quantity, quality, variety, or distribution of creaturely goods—and it is also so splendid that when combined with *any* quantity, quality, variety, or distribution of creaturely evil, sin, and suffering, its presence will still tip the overall balance in favor of a very good world, indeed. As before, though, there is no need to go overboard and call it maximal.[3]

I have to admit that the third and fourth sets of claims aren't as transparent to me as are the lists of good- and bad-making features of worlds; but keep them in mind, since they drive the theodicy to come. Finally, Plantinga introduces three assumptions (all of which he endorses, the strongest of which he employs, but only the weakest of which, he maintains, is required for his argument):

The Strong Value Assumption: Each possible world that contains Incarnation-and-Atonement is better than every possible world that lacks Incarnation-and-Atonement.

The Moderate Value Assumption: For any possible world that contains free creatures who never fall into sin and who live in love and harmony with one another and with God forever, there is a better possible world that contains exactly the same free creatures who fall into sin and wickedness, who bring about great evil and suffering with their rebellion, and who graciously are offered a means of salvation through Incarnation-and-Atonement.

The Weak Value Assumption: At least one possible world of great value contains Incarnation-and-Atonement (a thesis that, unlike the stronger value assumptions, can be supported by appeal to the Christian characterization of the actual world and the principle of reflexivity).

Thus we have on display the claims about value that may provide Plantinga with the tools he needs to articulate a theodicy that manages to avoid the charge of being tepid, shallow, and ultimately frivolous.

THREE VERSIONS OF THE THEODICY PROPER

Since it is not at all clear that they stand or fall together, it is worth disentangling three versions of the theodicy, one corresponding to each of the three value assumptions just noted.

Here, then, is the first version featuring the strong value assumption that Plantinga explicitly acknowledges as operative in his argument: God aims to create a world that rises to a certain magnificent level of value. Given the strong value assumption, that level of value is achieved only by Incarnation-and-Atonement worlds. But Incarnation-and-Atonement worlds are worlds that include the Fall, sin, and the consequences of sin—evil and suffering. Accordingly, Plantinga concludes, "If a theodicy is an attempt to explain why God permits evil, what we have here is a theodicy—and, if I'm right, a successful theodicy."

The second version: God does not merely aim to create a world that rises to a certain magnificent level of value, for, merely given the moderate value assumption, that goal might be achieved without Incarnation-and-Atonement. God also intends to guarantee that the very creatures that inhabit the world are afforded one of the very best worlds they can collectively inhabit. Given the moderate value assumption, that second aim again requires an Incarnation-and-Atonement world. But Incarnation-and-Atonement worlds are worlds that include the Fall, sin, and the consequences of sin—evil and suffering.

The third and considerably weaker version: God aims to create a world of great value. Given the weak value assumption, our world, owing to its inclusion of Incarnation-and-Atonement, is such a world. But Incarnation-and-Atonement worlds are worlds that include the fall, sin, and the consequences of sin—evil and suffering.

Note that the second version of the theodicy (featuring the moderate value assumption) requires that we attribute two rather different goals to God (one quasi-agent-centered— i.e., that *these* very creatures live in a world with a certain level of value, but not quite that these very creatures also enjoy lives that guarantee a certain kind of value to them individually). Note also that if it really is to be weaker than its predecessor, we will need to relinquish many of the claims about the Incarnation-and-Atonement whose introduction and defense occupied most of the first half of Plantinga's paper: namely, that it is the second-best good, which towers enormously above all others save God's existence, which is of infinite and unlimited value, and which is incommensurable with any creaturely goods. Strictly speaking, the moderate value assumption (as formulated) does not contest those verdicts, but to the extent that it is supposed to be more modest by not maintaining that each world with Incarnation-and-Atonement is better than any world without, we are apparently to hear it as including a denial of the strong value assumption—and *that* is inconsistent with those verdicts.

Note also that the third version of the theodicy (featuring the weak value assumption) goes even further when including a denial of its alternatives, for it answers the question "Whence evil and suffering?" with the words "Because they are necessary in a world like ours which features the magnificent good of Incarnation-and-Atonement," only to leave unanswered the question "But why Incarnation-and-Atonement at *that* price for *these* creatures, given that the world could have been just as valuable without that particular good and without denying any of them existence?"

Despite the promise of weaker versions of the theodicy, I think it is fortunate that Plantinga endorses the strong value assumption and chooses to conduct his case with this most robust thesis as his central premise, since the third version strikes me as supplying an explanation that does not in the end help the Christian think about the presence of evil in God's world in a satisfying way, and since the second version effectively abandons the value claims about the good of Incarnation-and-Atonement, which, if true, provide this strategy for theodicy with whatever bite it has.

Accordingly, in the following I will continue to examine only Plantinga's own preferred version of the theodicy, which (once again) can be summarized simply and clearly as follows: God aims to create a world that rises to a certain magnificent level of value. Given the strong value assumption, that level of value is achieved only by

Incarnation-and-Atonement worlds. But Incarnation-and-Atonement worlds are worlds that include the Fall, sin, and the consequences of sin—evil and suffering.

THREE OBJECTIONS AND THREE REPLIES

Before I turn to some powerful critical responses from Kevin Diller and Marilyn McCord Adams, let me briefly note that Plantinga anticipates three objections that are likely to occur to his audience and offers some intriguing reflections designed to blunt their force.

> *The first question*—Why does God permit suffering in addition to sin and evil? *And the outlines of its answer*—Because the permitted sin and evil perpetrated by significantly free creatures causes suffering and because suffering is an important instrumental good in several different respects.
>
> *The second question*—Why does God permit so much suffering and evil? *And the outlines of its answer*—Because, again, even this much may be instrumentally good in a compensating way, or because for all we know the relevant counterfactuals of freedom necessitate just this much and no less, or perhaps because suffering and evil have to reach a certain threshold before Incarnation-and-Atonement is a fitting reaction (rather than a grotesquely excessive response). Moreover, some amount of unnecessary suffering may be unavoidable, if there is a lower bound on how much suffering is required but no precise amount of suffering such that slightly less would not have sufficed for God's purposes.
>
> *The third question*—Why view this whole affair as a great and towering good rather than a nightmarish, cosmic version of Munchausen by Proxy Syndrome, in which God orchestrates the fall of his children and permits astonishing depths of evil and suffering just so that he can leap bravely into view and heroically rescue us in the final reel? *And the outlines of its answer*—Because although this involves treating his creatures as means, unlike standard and genuine instances of the Syndrome, it does not involve any unfair or impermissible treatment of or any instance of imperfect love for his creatures (despite the fact that God allows them to suffer for his own purposes rather than for their own good and despite the fact that God has not secured their permission for this sacrifice in advance). Why? Perhaps because God knows that his creatures would consent if they fully understood and their desires were properly ordered, or perhaps because those creatures are, in fact, compensated directly in some way or other that satisfies many of those plausible agent-centered restrictions that, as it turns out, only appear to be imperiled here.

Again, I think these are genuinely significant and serious opening challenges, but I also think Plantinga has provided genuinely significant and promising initial responses to them. We will return to the force of those responses in a later section. However, even if these first three objections were thus decidedly put to rest, there are a few other theological and philosophical matters worth worrying about before we should be prepared to sign on to this theodicy.

DILLER'S CRITIQUE AND ADAMS'S CRITIQUE

Powerful worries targeting Plantinga's strategy have emerged in recent literature from which I would like to highlight three objections advanced by Kevin Diller and Marilyn McCord Adams.

Diller asks why Plantinga takes the value of the Incarnation-and-Atonement to be so high, and finds in his theodicy this answer: Because Incarnation-and-Atonement yield both the stupendous good of significantly increased intimacy with God and also the exceedingly good display of God's self-sacrificing love for those creatures who have rebelled against him.

To this answer, Diller raises a philosophical objection (later echoed by Adams): The Incarnation and the Atonement are logically independent of one another; we could have Incarnation without Atonement (perhaps even absent suffering of any kind), and (although it is a considerably more controversial claim) we might even have Atonement without Incarnation. Yet it is the precondition of Atonement alone that supplies the present theodicy with its answer to the question "Whence evil and suffering?," whereas it is very probably the Incarnation that primarily generates the great good of increased intimacy.[4]

Further, Diller raises a theological objection: The Felix Culpa approach mis-identifies the relative value of a proper relationship with God in comparison with a demonstration of God's love for us insofar as that theodicy maintains that sacrificing the former relationship (for everyone for a while and for some forever) is an appropriate price to pay in order to be humbled and astonished and benefited by the latter display of love, which, for some peculiar reason, can only be communicated by way of Atonement.[5]

Diller's excellent objections force the proponent of the Felix Culpa theodicy to retreat into a somewhat more precarious position.

The options in response to Diller's first objection are either to argue that every Atonement world is also an Incarnation world so that they cannot come apart after all (but this is a path fraught with philosophical and theological obstacles), or else to argue that the value of the towering and magnificent good of Atonement alone deserves all the accolades earlier bestowed on Incarnation-and-Atonement together so that the revised strong value assumption now reads, "each possible world that contains Atonement is better than every possible world that lacks Atonement." But since some of those non-Atonement worlds will nevertheless contain the Incarnation and the increase in intimacy it brings to our relation with God, the plausibility of the value assumption now operative is seriously diminished.

There are two options in response to Diller's second objection. In the first, one may argue that the magnificent display of God's love really is as good as advertised and that, whereas a proper relationship with God may be the best good in our lives, its temporary interruption for the sake of securing the value of God's great expression of love for his rebellious creatures is a worthwhile exchange. In the second, one can argue that it is not just the display of such divine love that furnishes the Atonement with its supreme value, but the presence of something else tucked in as well (e.g., perhaps the unique kind of intimacy that comes from cooperating with God in effecting our rescue from the consequences of sin). This, like the deep expression of love in question, is obtainable by way of Atonement alone.

In her analysis and critique, Adams adds a third worry to these first two by focusing squarely on agent-centered restrictions. Adams agrees with Plantinga that God would not violate any moral obligations in making use of his creatures to further his aim of increasing global value at the expense of extreme and uncompensated personal disvalue. Their parting of ways turns instead on whether in so doing God would be unloving, unmerciful, or less than perfectly good. And just to be clear—on the theodicy on offer—some of us are not merely being forced to suffer the headache for an hour or two for purposes that do not personally benefit us, but to suffer being wrecked and ruined, damnable and (barring Universalism) damned. In short, Adams charges Plantinga's theodicy with having an "insufficient appreciation of the category of horrors"—evils so ruinous, so detrimental to a person, that any greater good produced thereby would have to be personally compensating in a way that restores individual meaning and value to the life of the horror-participant in order to properly exonerate God from the accusation of being unloving or unmerciful.[6]

As with Diller's critique, Adams's objection also forces the proponent of the Felix Culpa theodicy to take on explicit further philosophical and theological commitments.

The options in response to Adams's objection are either to answer the call at the end of her critique to show just how Atonement worlds nevertheless allow horror-participants to be personally compensated in a way befitting God's perfect love and mercy (with the proviso that mere Universalism isn't individually specific or personally restoring enough to achieve that end), or else to argue that not only are perfect love and mercy compatible with requiring the suffering of a person for ends that are unconnected to her own good but that these traits are also compatible with that suffering extending to being wrecked and ruined, damnable and (maybe in some cases) damned.[7]

If we were to stop the discussion here and were asked to choose sides, I have to admit I could work up some real sympathy toward Plantinga's end of this debate. (Of course, I may not be especially representative, obsessed as I am with the Fall and all things sin!) But I feel the force and deep attraction of the Felix Culpa theodicy and its strong value assumption. I am heartened by Plantinga's promising answers to why it would require evil and suffering in addition to sin, and why it would require as much evil, suffering, and sin as we see in the actual world, and why it can escape the charge of being an objectionable instance of Munchausen by Proxy Syndrome on a cosmic scale. I acknowledge and welcome the need to reformulate the theodicy by making its further commitments explicit in deference to Diller's objections, first by maintaining that Atonement either requires Incarnation or (more plausibly) is equipped with sufficient goods on its own to earn the job, and second, by maintaining that the expression of God's love embodied in the Atonement together with its other unique good-making properties really are as great as advertised. And I recognize and welcome Adams's call to take a stand on the issue of horrors, either by revealing how Atonement furnishes the appropriate level of personal-recompense for horror-participants, or else (and I confess a preference for this option) by explaining why perfect love and mercy require no such thing, after all.

Unfortunately, however, I think we can't just leave the discussion here; it's not yet time to take sides. There is a further problem for Plantinga's Felix Culpa theodicy that strikes me as decisive.

A PROBLEMATIC PASSAGE

The Felix Culpa theodicy (as presented in Plantinga's paper) depends on the revised strong value assumption. This, in turn, depends on Plantinga's claims about comparative value rehearsed in the opening sections of this chapter. Since the worry I will investigate now does not turn on whether the Incarnation is separable from the Atonement, I will continue to treat them (in accordance with Plantinga's own presentation) as a single, unified good.

Recall Plantinga's position:

Incarnation-and-Atonement is good, and (unlike God's existence) is a contingent good. *Better*—Incarnation-and-Atonement is the second greatest good, an unthinkably-magnificent good "that towers enormously above all the rest of the contingent states of affairs." *Better yet*—Incarnation-and-Atonement is infinitely good. *Better still*—the value of Incarnation-and-Atonement (like the value of God himself) is incommensurable with creaturely goods; it is better than *any* quantity, quality, variety, or distribution of creaturely goods—and it is also so splendid that when combined with *any* quantity, quality, variety, or distribution of creaturely evil, sin, and suffering, its presence will still tip the overall balance in favor of a very good world, indeed.

The assertions are clear, but the support is elusive, for in the few paragraphs devoted to establishing the absolutely essential value claims that fuel this theodicy, Plantinga writes:

I believe that any world with Incarnation-and-Atonement is a better world than any without it—or at any rate better than any world in which God does nothing comparable to Incarnation-and-Atonement. It is hard to imagine what God could do that is in fact comparable to Incarnation-and-Atonement; but perhaps this is just a limitation of our imagination. But since this is so hard to imagine, I propose that we ignore those possible worlds, if there are any, in which God does not arrange for Incarnation-and-Atonement, but does something else of comparable excellence.

That's problematic. Of course, any world with Incarnation-and-Atonement is better than any world in which God does nothing comparable in value . . . but rather than hearing a triviality, I detect a rhetorical assertion to the effect that there is in fact nothing comparable in value. But why, precisely, are we to accept this verdict? Because, we are told, it is hard to imagine what it could be. Clearly, it would be uncharitable to hear in this the verdict that we can eventually imagine it although doing so would be a difficult task for us, but exactly what is communicated, then? I suspect nothing more than the observation that we are not in fact aware of anything comparable in value to Incarnation-and-Atonement that we recognize to be comparable in value to Incarnation-and-Atonement. Perhaps that's right—suppose we grant this point. What advice follows upon this observation about our inability? Well, that we ignore all those possible worlds in which such comparable (but unidentified) goods are substituted for Incarnation-and-Atonement. But, of course, without proper assurance that there aren't any, this advice can't really be intended to be taken at face value in this context, for then the theodicy on offer would transparently fail in its goal of offering a genuine and satisfying explanation to Christians of the sin, evil, and suffering in our world, for it would simply propose to ignore those highly eligible worlds God could have created that are every bit as good as ours but that do not contain the sin, evil, or suffering required by the Atonement. Once again, the only plausible reading at hand is one that repeats the position that there is in fact nothing comparable in value.

So, just what line of reasoning emerges from behind the rhetorical flourishes? The answer, I believe, is a simple and straightforward noseeum inference. Nothing stronger is justified, nothing weaker has any chance of supporting the weight placed on it, and (as far as I can see) nothing else can reasonably be extracted from the passage. *The explicit premise*—We are not in fact aware of anything comparable in value to Incarnation-and-Atonement that we recognize as such. *The suppressed premise*—But if there were any such thing, we would be aware of it and recognize it as such. *The conclusion*—Hence, there is nothing comparable in value to Incarnation-and-Atonement.

Thus, in the end, the core claim in the theodicy at issue is a thesis about the relative value of Incarnation-and-Atonement defended by appeal to a noseeum inference.

Noseeum inferences of precisely this sort, however, are vulnerable to so-called skeptical theism considerations. Skeptical theism provides a satisfactory block to one of the most promising arguments for atheism, and this is responsible for much of its appeal, but it is also independently immensely plausible. Skeptical theism can be characterized in a number of ways, but I here will formulate it as a conjunction of three theses.[8]

1) We are in the dark about whether the possible goods and possible evils we are aware of are representative of the possible goods and possible evils that there are, and

2) We are in the dark about whether the necessary connections we know of be-tween the obtaining of possible goods and the obtaining of possible evils are representative of the entailments of this type that there are, and

3) We are in the dark about whether the amount of possible good or possible evil we recognize in a state of affairs is representative of the total amount of possible good or possible evil it manifests.

(Note that "representative" in the present context is elliptical for "representative with re-spect to the property—*figuring in a potentially explanatory reason for God's permitting the sin, evil, and suffering of our world.*")

This seems to me a clear-headed, honest, and humble recognition of our epistemic state, and (more to the point) it seems to me to have a direct and lethal analogue when applied to Plantinga's noseeum inference.

Admittedly, we surely have a fair amount of knowledge about value. Certainly, for ex-ample, we know that Incarnation-and-Atonement is a towering and magnificent good. But given the intellectually modest concessions embodied in skeptical theism, we have no good reason to think that if there were a contingent state of affairs comparable in value to Incarnation-and-Atonement that we would be aware of it, or—if it were somehow an object of mere awareness—that we would recognize its full range of infinite and unlimited value.

That's not to say that Plantinga's strong value assumption is false. Far from it. Rather, it is simply a reminder that if we do know that assumption, it is not by way of a noseeum inference grounded in what is hard to imagine.

Unfortunately, other potential routes to demonstrating the supreme and unique value of Incarnation-and-Atonement do not seem to be very promising, either. It is not espe-cially plausible to maintain that this crucial thesis is available for confirmation through the exercise of our other natural capacities. It is not, for example, a deliverance of some Cartesian faculty of intuition or illuminated by the natural light of reason. It is not a product of memory, sense perception, or introspection. It is not yielded by an employ-ment of Reidian common sense. It is not a self-evident, transparent, or first truth. It is not a celebrated discovery of contemporary axiology.

Moreover, it is worth noting that this crucial thesis is similarly unlikely to be known by us by way of divine revelation. Of course, I fully recognize that my word that this thesis is not a proper subject of revelation may not be very authoritative (despite my having spent minutes and minutes poring over the salient texts and resources in the area), but my the-ological informants have assured me that it would be a decidedly controversial position to insist that we know by way of revelation that Incarnation-and-Atonement is (and is the only) infinite and unlimited and incommensurable, contingent good. Moreover (al-though this is a minority view), the skeptical theism that spells trouble for the noseeum inference detailed earlier also poses considerable problems for any claim to knowledge by revelation alone, so that even if there were no controversy to be had over the view that this crucial value thesis was backed by revelation, still—not all would be well.[9]

Accordingly, I do not see any way to adequately support the central move in the theodicy. Without good reason to accept the thesis on the overwhelming value that Incarnation-and-Atonement contributes to a world (everything considered) and about the uniqueness of this package in this respect among created goods, we would be irresponsible to take the strong value assumption to be true, and without the strong value assumption, the Felix Culpa theodicy (as formulated by Plantinga) is in trouble.

Significantly, however, without good reason to reject that characterization of the value that Incarnation-and-Atonement contributes to a world (everything considered) or to reject the claim of uniqueness, we would be equally irresponsible to take the strong value assumption to be false. Moreover, since both parties to the debate seem to rely on all-in judgments about value, the considerations discussed in this chapter seem as well suited to contest taking the thesis to be false as they are to contest taking it to be true.

SO WHO GETS IT RIGHT?

So who gets it right—Plantinga in his endorsement of the Felix Culpa theodicy and its strong value assumption, or Diller and Adams in their rejection?

Full of doubt—it is Milton's Adam who gets it right in Book XII of *Paradise Lost*:

> *O goodness infinite, goodness immense!*
> *That all this good of evil shall produce,*
> *And evil turn to good; more wonderful*
> *Than that which by creation first brought forth*
> *Light out of darkness! Full of doubt I stand,*
> *Whether I should repent me now of sin*
> *By mee done and occasiond, or rejoyce*
> *Much more, that much more good thereof shall spring.*

Milton's Adam has no idea whether his rebellion was, in the end, a fortunate fall or not—and neither do we.[10]

NOTES

1. Plantinga 2004, 3–5.

2. Plantinga 1985, 35. Perhaps, though, a theodicy may appear tepid and shallow dialectically (from the point of view of the non-Christian theorist) while nevertheless appearing illuminating and comforting (from the perspective of the Christian believer).

3. I will hyphenate the term "Incarnation-and-Atonement" throughout the discussion in order to follow Plantinga in treating the state of affairs that constitutes the Incarnation together with the state of affairs that constitutes the Atonement as a single, unified good. The separability of these states of affairs will be considered later.

4. Diller 2008, 90–91 and Adams 2008, 131–132.

5. Diller 2008, 92–93.

6. Adams 2008, 128–138.

7. This second strategy will face the formidable opposition developed in Stump 2010 and in Adams 1999 and 2006.

8. Compare the formulations in Bergmann 2001 and 2009 and Howard-Snyder 2009, which contain excellent discussions and defenses of skeptical theism. In selecting the phrasing "in the dark about whether," I bracket theism in the interests of not making a dialectically inappropriate move. In other words, whereas the theist may well take herself to have very good reasons to believe that the objects of our awareness are not representative (on the grounds that since God exists, compensating goods or morally justifying reasons also exist—notwithstanding our being unaware of them), the skeptical-theism theses are meant to express the state we are and should be in if we do not presuppose God's existence and then simply infer that some compensating good or morally justifying reason is thereby guaranteed, as well.

9. Hudson 2014.

10. I would like to express appreciation to Trent Dougherty for inviting me to present this paper at the Plantinga Workshop at Baylor University and to thank the fine audience at that gathering for criticism and comments. I also thank Daniel Howard-Snyder, Neal Tognazzini, and Dennis Whitcomb for reading the paper in an earlier draft and for very helpful suggestions.

REFERENCES

Adams, Marilyn McCord. 2008. "Plantinga on 'Felix Culpa': Analysis and Critique." *Faith and Philosophy* 26: 123–140.

———. 1999. *Horrendous Evils and the Goodness of God.* Ithaca, NY: Cornell University Press.

Bergmann, Michael. 2009. "Skeptical Theism and the Problem of Evil," in Thomas Flint and Michael Rea (eds.), *The Oxford Handbook of Philosophical Theology*. Oxford: Oxford University Press, 374–399.

———. 2001. "Skeptical Theism and Rowe's New Evidential Argument from Evil." *Noûs* 35: 278–296.

Diller, Kevin. 2008. "Are Sin and Evil Necessary for a Really Good World? Questions for Alvin Plantinga's *Felix Culpa* Theodicy." *Faith and Philosophy* 25: 87–101.

Howard-Snyder, Daniel. 2009. "Epistemic Humility, Arguments from Evil, and Moral Skepticism," in Jonathan Kvanvig (ed.), *Oxford Studies in Philosophy of Religion*, Vol. 2 (Oxford: Oxford University Press), 17–57.

Hudson, Hud. 2014. "The Father of Lies?" in Jonathan Kvanvig (ed.), *Oxford Studies in Philosophy of Religion*. Vol. 5. Oxford: Oxford University Press, 147–166.

Plantinga, Alvin. 2004. "Supralapsarianism, or 'O Felix Culpa,'" in Peter van Inwagen (ed.), *Christian Faith and the Problem of Evil*. Grand Rapids, MI: Wm. B. Eerdmans, 1–25.

———. 1985. "Self-Profile," in James Tomberlin and Peter van Inwagen (eds.), *Alvin Plantinga*. Dordrecht: D. Reidel, 3–100.

Stump, Eleonore. 2010. *Wandering in Darkness: Narrative and the Problem of Suffering*. Oxford: Oxford University Press.

IV

Other Arguments

(S)

The Argument from Colors and Flavors

THE ARGUMENT FROM CONSCIOUSNESS

Richard Swinburne

∽——————————————————————————————————

I

ALVIN PLANTINGA CALLED the argument that I am going to discuss "The Argument from Colours and Flavours"; but colors and flavors, understood as sensations of color and flavor, are just one kind of pure mental event, and I propose to treat this argument as an argument from (what I call) pure mental events to the existence of God (understood in the traditional sense as omnipotent, omniscient, and perfectly good). I understand by an event the instantiation of a property (intrinsic or relational) in a substance (or substances) at a time. (I understand by a "substance" a constituent of the universe, such as a table, a human being, or a planet; and by a "intrinsic" property a characteristic of one substance such as having a mass of 10gm, and by a "relational" property a relation between two or more substances, such as "being taller than" or "being situated between." One human may be taller than another, and one planet may be situated between the sun and a different planet.) The history of the world (or of some segment of the world) (in an objective sense) is just all the events that have occurred or will occur in the world (or in that segment of it). To know that history, we need to pick out substances and properties (and times—but I ignore these as irrelevant for our present concerns) by what I call "informative designators."

An informative designator, as I define the term, is a rigid designator such that anyone who knows what the designator means (that is, has the linguistic knowledge of how to use it) knows a set of conditions necessary and sufficient for a thing to be the designated thing. To know these conditions is to be able (when favorably positioned, faculties in working order, and not subject to illusion) to recognize where it (or, if it is defined, the words by which it is defined) applies and where it does not, and to be able to make simple inferences from its application. Then I shall say that one event is the same as another event if and only if the substance and properties involved can be picked out by logically equivalent informative designators. If we allow that two events can be the same even if that criterion is not satisfied, there would be more to know about the history of the world than knowing all the events that have occurred, and we should need to use a more complicated system of categories (than that of substances, properties, and times) to provide that description. In future, when I refer to an event by naming the substances and properties involved in it, I am assuming the names of the properties to be informative designators of those properties. Thus by "my pain" or "my belief that today is Saturday," I mean the event of my feeling pain or believing that today is Saturday, pain being the property that I can recognize when I feel it, and the belief being the property that I consider when I reflect on which day of the week it is, not some brain event underlying that feeling or that belief.

Given this criterion of event identity, it follows that the history of the world includes events of two kinds: physical events (including brain events) and mental events. Mental events—as I shall define them—are events to which the subject (the person whose events they are) necessarily has privileged access, that is, a way of knowing about them not available to others, by experiencing them. Physical events—as I shall define them—are such that no one has this sort of privileged access to them; they are public events. Thus my pain is a mental event because whatever ways others can have of discovering whether or not I am in pain, I could also use; if they infer this from my behavior, I could infer it from my behavior—for example, by watching a film of that behavior, and if they infer it from my brain events, I could do the same. But I have an additional way of discovering that I am in pain—by actually experiencing the pain, and *that* no one else can do. By contrast, anyone can discover as well as can anyone else what brain events are happening in me, and so my brain events are physical events.

Among mental events are pure mental events, ones that do not entail any physical event. Thus, my seeing the tree outside the window is a mental event, because I am experiencing it; but its occurrence entails the existence of a tree outside the window, which is a physical event. So, seeing the tree is a mental event but not a pure mental event, whereas "apparently seeing the tree" is a pure mental event. When I mention "mental event" in future I shall understand by that "pure mental event." Among such events are beliefs, occurrent thoughts, intentions, desires, and sensations. These events neither entail nor are entailed by any physical event and so are necessarily distinct from them. Sensations, thoughts, and intentions are occurrences of which necessarily someone who has them at a time must be to some extent conscious at that time of having them. Beliefs and desires, by contrast, are what I call "continuing mental states"; that is, states that may continue to exist while we are quite unconscious of them, but are mental because we can become conscious of them if we choose. The argument that I shall be discussing is an argument from the occurrence of pure mental events, that is, events of which we are or can become conscious; and for that reason I call it "the argument from consciousness."

Fairly evidently sensations, thoughts, beliefs, and desires are all caused, many of them directly and many of them indirectly (via other beliefs, etc.) by brain events. We must suppose that pure mental events often cause other pure mental events. For we often believe propositions because we believe that they are forced upon us by the evidence—that is, our belief that the evidence is so-and-so causes us to hold the belief that such-and-such a hypothesis is true. But if we thought that our beliefs never caused other beliefs, we couldn't hold any scientific theory based on evidence. The extent to which our intentions (the intentions in our movements, guiding them, that is, not intentions for the future) are caused is debatable, but clearly—while I shall assume that they are not always totally caused—brain events have a considerable influence on which intentions we form. Conversely, it seems to us—and so we should assume in the absence of counter-evidence[1]—that our intentions cause our brain events, which in turn cause our bodily movements. So if there is, as we reasonably assume, a scientific explanation of all these causal relations, there must be laws of nature of the form "all brain events of kind B_1 cause mental events of kind M_1," "all mental events of kind M_2 cause brain events of kind B_2," and "all mental events of kind M_1 cause mental events of kind M_2" (or statistical versions thereof). I will call laws of these kinds "psychophysical laws" and a theory containing such laws I will call a "psychophysical theory."

II

Now the argument from the existence of mental events, and so-given their causal relations—from psychophysical laws to the existence of God—is an argument to show that it is much more probable that there would be such laws if there is a God (who therefore causes the operation of the laws) than if there is no God; and so the operation of these laws raises very considerably the probability that there is a God. I shall assume, as background knowledge when assessing the probabilities of there being psychophysical laws, that there are physical laws governing our physical universe of roughly the kind we believe them to be.

What makes a scientific theory such as a theory of mechanics able to explain a diverse set of mechanical phenomena is that the laws of mechanics all deal with the same sort of thing—physical objects—and concern only a few of their properties, such as their mass, shape, size, and position, which differ from each other in measurable ways (for example, one has twice as much mass as another, or is three times as long as another). Because the values of these measurable properties are affected only by the values of a few other such properties, we can have a few general laws that relate two or more such measured properties in all objects by a mathematical formula. We do not merely have to say that, when an inelastic object of 100gm mass and 10m/sec velocity collides with an inelastic object of 200gm mass and 5m/sec velocity, such and such results, with quite unconnected formulae for the results of collisions of innumerable inelastic objects of different masses and velocities. We can have a general formula, a law stating that for every pair of inelastic objects in collision, the quantity of the sum of the mass of the first multiplied by its velocity plus the mass of the second multiplied by its velocity is always conserved. But that can only hold if mass and velocity can be measured on scales—for example, of grams and meters per second. And we can extend mechanics to a general physics, including a few more measurable quantities (charge, spin, color charge, etc.), that interact with mechanical quantities, to construct a theory that makes testable predictions.

A psychophysical theory, however, would need to deal with things of very different kinds. Brain events differ from each other in the chemical elements involved in them (which in turn differ from each other in measurable ways) and in the velocity and direction of the transmission of electric charge. But pure mental events do not have any of these properties. Nor can most of them be analyzed in terms of common elements. Being sweet does not differ from being blue or even from being sour in having more or less of some common element. The intentional or—as I shall call them—"propositional" events (beliefs, desires, etc.), which consist of an attitude to a proposition, are what they are and have the influence they do in virtue of their propositional content. My belief that today is Saturday is what it is in virtue of its content (today is Saturday) and has the influence it does in virtue of that content (for example, when combined with my belief that I have promised to give a lecture in this room on Saturday, and my desire to do what I have promised, it influences me to come to this room on Saturday.) While the content can be expressed in a language and, so, different propositional events do consist of attitudes to things consisting of common elements (the different concepts expressed by the different words of sentences of the language), there are an enormous number of those elements. Consider how few of the words that occur in a dictionary can be defined adequately by other words in the dictionary; the same must hold for the concepts that they express.

Further, there are an enormous number of different ways in which those concepts can be arranged so as to express different propositions. Propositional events have relations of deductive logic to each other; and some of those deductive relations determine in part the identity of the propositional event. My belief that all men are mortal wouldn't be that belief if I also believed that Socrates was an immortal man; and my thought that "$2 = 1+1$, and $3 = 2+1$, and $4 = 3+1$" wouldn't be the thought normally expressed by those equations if I denied that it followed from them that "$2+2 = 4$." So every token belief comes in a package with many other beliefs that it entails. And the same type of belief belongs to many different packages. For consider two beliefs, whose content is expressed in English by "this is square" and "this has four sides"; someone couldn't hold the first belief without holding the second—so the second must belong to any package to which the first belongs. However, it must belong to many other packages as well, for example, the packages containing the belief, "this is a rectangle." And what goes for beliefs goes for the other propositional events. Yet there is no simple general law determining which propositional event expressed by a given sentence belongs to which packages, for example, which belief individuated by a sentence that expresses it entails other beliefs. The rules of a language that relate the concepts of that language to each other cannot be captured by a few "laws of language," because the deductive relations between sentences and so the propositions that they express are so complicated that it needs all the rules contained in a grammar of the language to express them. These rules are independent rules and do not follow from a few more general rules. Consider in how many different ways describable by the grammar of the language words can be put together so as to form sentences with different kinds of meaning, and so the same must hold for the propositions which they express.

Further, a given word or a given sentence form is often understood by different language users in different ways. For some, "table" may mean any flat surface at the waist height of any adult or child on which medium-sized objects can be placed, which has the consequence that desks and sideboards are "tables"; other language users distinguish desks and sideboards from tables. Some language users understand "he never said that" to mean "at no time did he say that," whereas others understand it to mean simply "he did not say that."

At one time a person has many different conscious events and innumerable beliefs and desires; and many of these have the particular character they do because of the other mental events in the package. What I seem to see when I look out of the window or what I seem to hear when I hear you talking depends on how I cut up the whole array of substances into separate substances or sounds, and that depends on what substances I believe to exist and that I believe I can recognize. If I have a belief about what John looks like, I may seem to see John when I look out of the window; otherwise I'll just seem to see some man and not notice what he looks like. If I have beliefs about the meanings of sentences of the foreign language you are speaking, I may seem to hear a proposition you are expressing without noticing the words of the sentence by which you are expressing it; but if I don't have such beliefs I will merely hear a succession of sounds. It follows from these contingent connections between mental events that occur at the same time and from the necessary connections between them described in the previous paragraph, that any laws relating brain events to mental events will have—as connectionism maintains—to relate large brain events to large mental events; there cannot be a one-one correlation between small brain events and small mental events—as supposed by "language of thought" theory. There is no unique type of brain event that causes the belief and only the belief that "today is Saturday." And as sensations are seldom interdefinable, any laws relating brain events to sensations will not follow from any general law about how kinds of brain events relate to kinds of sensations. Also in view of the different life experiences of each of us, no one will ever have exactly the same mental events as anyone else, and fairly rarely exactly the same conscious events (since the way they understand their occurrent thoughts and intentions depends on the beliefs entailed by them). Likewise no one will ever have exactly the same brain events as themselves at any other time or as anyone else ever. So a psychophysical theory would consist of an enormous number of separate laws, not derivable from a few more general laws, relating large brain events (most of which only one person would have) with numerically measurable values of transmission of electric charge in various circuits, to large conscious (and non-conscious) states consisting of beliefs, desires, intentions, etc., with a content individuated by sentences of a language (varying in its words and grammar slightly for different people), and also sensations.

All of the mental events apart from thoughts have different strengths, which, because they are experienced only by one person, cannot be measured on an objective scale; for objective measurement requires a public object, such as a ruler or meter, that can be laid beside or attached to the object. The strength of a mental event can only be measured relative to other mental events of the same kind experienced by the same subject. I can tell the doctor that this pain is more intense than that pain, but it would make no sense to tell him that it was 58.2 percent stronger.[2] And I can tell you or you can reasonably infer from my behavior that this belief (e.g., that Arsenal will win the FA cup) is stronger than that belief (e.g., that Manchester City will win the FA cup), but it would make no sense to ascribe an exact value to that probability.[3] One could perhaps reasonably postulate such absolute values if we could reasonably postulate that the same kind of mental event was always caused by and caused only by the same kind of brain event itself caused by the same kind of external stimulus, and if there was some measurable property of the brain event, the value of which always increased or decreased in line with an increase or decrease of strength of the mental event (as judged by the subject of that event). For example, if eating curry always caused the same brain event that caused a taste to which everyone reacted in the same way, then it would be reasonable to postulate that curry tasted the same to everyone. And then if there was some measurable property of the brain event, the value of which increased as the strength of the taste, as reported by tasters, also increased, one could take the absolute value of the former as the absolute value of the latter. But everyone has brains with different connections, and the same external stimulus causes its mental effects (whether a taste or some other sensation or some kind of propositional event) by different routes in different people, and the mental event causes different reactions in different people. And that makes it impossible to ascribe an absolute value to the strength of a mental event[4].

Natural selection may have eliminated those whose brains caused them to think irrationally (and so for example seemed to perceive tigers in front of them as being behind them), but for this to have happened there must be even more laws connecting brain events with mental events than which currently affect humans. All of this has the consequence that the psychophysical laws will be an enormous set of laws of the following kind, correlating all the different mental and brain events that any human could have, which do not follow from any more general law:

$$\text{Brain events}(B_1, B_2 \,\&\, B_j) + \text{sensations}(M_1 \,\&\, M_i) + \text{Beliefs}(M_j \,\&\, M_k) + \text{Desires}$$
$$(M_k \,\&\, M_l) \rightarrow \text{Intention}(M_n) + \text{Beliefs}(\text{about how to execute the intention})$$
$$(M_p \,\&\, M_q) + \text{Brain events} \rightarrow \text{bodily movements}.$$

(Arrows represent causal influences.)

Since absolute values cannot be attributed to the mental events, the laws could not ascribe precise values to the brain events that they cause and so make precise predictions about the resulting bodily movements. To suppose that a theory of physics with all this added is the ultimate explanation of the data of consciousness is to postulate a very unsimple and so a priori very improbable ultimate theory.

III

Before I move to consider whether such laws are to be expected if there is a God, I need next to draw attention to a further feature of those laws, that they are such that—even given their imprecise nature—it is immensely unlikely that humans will ever be able to discover them, even if they can discover some superficial statistical regularities that are consequences of those laws. For to discover any law we would need to know which mental events someone was having at a given time when certain brain events were occurring, and in order to know this we are crucially dependent on the reports of subjects about their own mental events. Subjects' reports do not, however, suffice to inform us of exactly which sensations they are having, for all one can study is what people say about their sensations and the other effects they produce. But subjects may mean different things by the reports they give of their sensations. Maybe what looks what you call "red" to you looks what I call "green" to me, and what looks what you call "green" looks to me what I call "red"; so long as we discriminate between the colors of public objects in the same way, the difference between the sensations would never be recognized. And it is not a mere implausible philosophical thought experiment to suppose that this might be so; it is plausible that this sometimes happens. For clearly either what others call "red" or what others call "green" looks different to those who are red-green color blind. So plausibly to some such colorblind people everything of these two colors looks the way red things look to others, and to other such people everything of these two colors looks the way green things look to others. So it is not implausible to suppose that in some people both these differences occur— red things look the way green things look to others, and green things look the way red things look to others. But, if so, this would be quite undetectable.[5] True, for propositional events (unlike for sensations) there are logical connections between those events and the public effects they cause—if I intend to get A and I believe that the best way to do this is to get B, (if I have the physical ability to do so) I will get B—which enable us to check on what subjects mean by the words by which they describe those propositional events. Nevertheless, just because words often have slightly different meanings for different people and so each person's event of "seeing a table" will differ slightly for many people, and since it is packages of mental events that are correlated (in accord with a complicated formula of a kind illustrated on the previous page) with large brain events, it will be enormously difficult in practice to get enough examples of some type of mental event occurring when different types of brain events were occurring, to postulate a well-justified generalization of which brain events are necessary and sufficient for its occurrence. And anyway, as I have already noted, no one has exactly the same brain connections and patterns of neural firing as anyone else, and so for this reason also it would be almost impossible to replicate exactly the same brain event of any large size in order to check whether the same mental event predicted by a postulated law in fact occurred.

It follows from all this that it is immensely improbable that humans will be able to discover the (imprecise) psychophysical laws. And from this it follows that we will never be able to discover much of the mental life of others. It is not merely that each person has privileged access to their own mental life, but the access that others have is fairly limited.; our mental life is relatively private. Let me fill out with a simple example of how the nature and undiscoverability of these laws ensures our privacy. Suppose that the public event of smoking cannabis at any time always caused the same brain state (a continuing brain event) in everyone, a state that was never caused in any other way; and that this state caused a strong desire continuing for exactly six months to smoke cannabis again. Then we could discover this fairly easily just from the reports of large numbers of smokers, even without inspecting many brains. Then if the police wanted to know whether someone had been smoking cannabis recently or was subject to a strong temptation to smoke it in the near future when she had the opportunity to do so, they could just scan his brain with a very accurate brain scanner. Now suppose, somewhat more plausibly, that the effect on the brain of smoking cannabis varies with the prior behavior of the individual (e.g., whether and how frequently they have smoked cannabis previously), which causes different states of that individual's brain. Then the relevant laws are going to be much more difficult to discover, because we'd need to inspect the brains and listen to the reports of many different cannabis smokers. But it will be almost impossible to discover any deterministic laws if, as is in fact the case, everyone starts life with brains with different connections between the brain organs. We are each of us unique. So any laws that determine the effect of smoking cannabis at a certain time on a brain and so on the resulting strength of the smoker's desire (if any) to smoke it again will consist of a conjunction of laws for people with brains of different kinds exposed to different past influences. These will be so difficult to discover—in view of the very few individuals (perhaps only one) with each kind of brain subject to sufficiently similar past influences on whom smoking cannabis has exactly the same effect—that inspecting someone's brain would not reveal how often (if at all) they had smoked cannabis in the past, nor whether they would be strongly tempted to smoke it again. And what goes for this very simple example goes of course for any attempt to infer with any very high degree of probability what someone feels or believes or is thinking about from mere observation of their brains, let alone from mere observation of their past behavior.

IV

So how probable is it that God would bring about psychophysical laws of the kind analyzed in this chapter with the limits to their discoverability that I have described?

Humans are good things in virtue of our rationality, the rich mental life connected to our bodies (including the ability to understand the physical world, and to some extent understand other humans), and the choices we can make between good and evil (a good that even God himself who "cannot do evil" does not have), choices that have significant effects on each other and the world. In order to give us a large range of choices and the ability to understand the way the physical world works and (to a limited extent) the way human beings think and act, God needed to provide us with a mental life of the richness and ability to reason that humans in fact have.

In order to interact with others, we must have a location in a public space where others can get hold of us if they want to benefit or harm us, yet such that we can to some extent avoid that influence. To be locatable and influenceable in a public space is to have a body, and to be able to avoid that influence to some extent we need a movable body. In order to understand the physical world, and so to know how we can use it to improve or damage human lives, we need to know both how the physical world works (and having such knowledge is anyway an intrinsic good) and how changes in it would affect us and (to some extent) how they would affect other people. To make it possible for us to discover how the physical world works, God needed to ensure that it is governed by fairly simple natural laws. If the subsequent path of an arrow varied greatly in accord with quite different laws with minute changes in its initial direction and velocity, we wouldn't be able to kill enemies more frequently than to kill allies. In order that our choices may include the choices of whether or not to grow in knowledge and to help others to grow in knowledge, we need to be able to learn from experience and from instruction. Learning from others requires that we improve our concepts, and so do not have identical concepts to begin with. And we wouldn't be able to hurt other humans or give them pleasure, unless we had some idea of how the physical world affects their mental life—for example, that burning humans causes them great pain, and that drinking alcohol or eating when very hungry or having sexual intercourse often gives them great pleasure. In order to enable us to discover how changes in the physical world (including their bodies) affect other people, God needs to make them somewhat like ourselves in their behavior and so the brains through which their mental life is influenced by and influences the world. But in order for us to have significant moral choices of whether and how to hurt or benefit others, we need to be able to work things out for ourselves without being subject to excessive influence from others. There needs to be a limit to the extent to which other people can know what we are thinking and feeling; we need to have a relatively private mental life. If parents or teachers or the police could discover exactly what we were feeling, or believed, or desired, no one would have any serious opportunity even to consider doing any illegal act or an act that society considered grossly immoral. For those even considering behaving in a way of which society disapproved could be segregated and—in a more literal sense than the term is currently used—"brain-washed," long before their rebellious thoughts led to action. So in order to have the privacy needed in order to have serious moral choices, God needs to put a limit on the extent to which others can discover our sensations, beliefs, and desires with any high degree of probability. Hence God has good reason to create humans having the kind of mental life we have, largely but not totally private. For this purpose God needs to give us very complex brains, each of a different construction whose states are influenced by all of a person's past experience and behavior, and to ensure that which mental events are caused by brain events depends in a complicated and not fully discoverable way on the total package to which they belong. I conclude that if there is a God, it would be probable that there would be the enormous number of very complicated psychophysical laws of the kind that are operative in us. (And if God caused present-day humans to exist as a result of natural selection of those who think fairly rationally, he needed to make very many more laws than are now operative in us, so that those whose genes cause the brain states that cause the mental states characteristic of irrational thinking in accord with certain laws not now operative could be eliminated.) I repeat that it would be quite probable that there would be such an enormous number of psychophysical laws if there is a God, but very improbable that there would be such if there is no God. Hence the argument from pure mental events to the existence of God is very strong.

NOTES

1. See my *Mind, Brain and Free Will* (Oxford: Oxford University Press, 2013), chapter 4 for argument that it could not possibly be shown that our intentions do not cause our brain events.

2. Thus D.R.J. Laming in his article "Psychophysics" in Richard L. Gregory (ed.), *The Oxford Companion to the Mind*, second edition (Oxford: Oxford University Press, 2004), writes: "Most people have no idea what 'half as loud' means. In conclusion, there is no way to measure sensation that is distinct from measurement of the physical stimulus."

3. There is a view among probability theorists that we can attribute an exact value to the strength of someone's beliefs by measuring the "subjective probability" that they tacitly ascribe to beliefs. The method that they advocate for ascribing the "subjective probability" originates from the work of F.P. Ramsey ("Truth and Probability" in his *The Foundations of Mathematics and Other Logical Essays*, Routledge and Kegan Paul, 1931.) This method measures the "subjective probability" that someone tacitly ascribes to a belief by the lowest odds at which they would be prepared to bet that that belief was true. If someone is, they believe, prepared to bet £N that q is true at odds of 3-1 (so that they would win £3N if q turned out true, but lose their £N if q turned out false) but not at any lower odds (e.g., 2-1), that—it was claimed—showed that they ascribe to q a probability of ¼ (because then in their view what they would win multiplied by the probability of their winning would equal what they would lose multiplied by the probability of their losing). But that method of assessing subjective probability will give different answers varying with the amount of money bet—someone might be willing to bet £10 at 3-1 but £100 only at odds of 4-1; which shows that people's desire not to lose money on a bet increases more rapidly than does the sum bet. And surely too how it increases varies with the person betting. And most importantly people have desires and moral beliefs that affect whether or not they bet that have nothing to do with the sum of money they might win or lose. In consequence of all this, no information about how subjects have acted in different past situations or even information about

how subjects believe that they would act in different future situations will yield precise numerical values of beliefs, desires, etc., to enable us to calculate how they would act in any still different new situation.

4. Kimble and O'Connor claim that while the "essentially private nature 'of conscious events' may preclude exactitude in measurement, as a practical matter . . . the argument from consciousness concerns the in-principle availability of a scientific explanation of correlations, not the practical feasibility of doing so." (K. Kimble and T. O'Connor, "The Argument from Consciousness Revisited" in J.L. Kvanvig (ed.), *Oxford Studies in the Philosophy of Religion*, vol. 3 (Oxford University Press, 2011), 134. I acknowledge that conscious events can have relations of greater or less extent, intensity, etc., to each other, which can be recognized if the same person has the events, but is otherwise difficult to detect, yet I deny that the intensity can be given a quantitative value. This is because this requires measurement on some sort of public ruler or scale, the tokens of which coincide with each other; and the essential privacy of conscious events makes that impossible—necessarily so, not merely "as a practical matter."

5. We are able to discover from what they say the *pattern* of sensations that they are having, for the reason that patterns of events characterize the physical as well as the mental world. A mental image of a square has the same shape as a public square, and the rhythm of an imagined tune has the same pattern as a sequence of drum beats. Hence neuroscience is on the way to discovering a law-like formula by which it can predict from a subject's brain events both the images caused by the public objects at which she is looking and the images that she is intentionally causing. See K.N. Kay and others, "Identifying Natural Images from Human Brain Activity," *Nature* 452 (March 20, 2008): 352–355.

(T)

The Argument from Love and (Y) The Argument from

the Meaning of Life

THE GOD OF LOVE AND THE MEANING OF LIFE

Jerry L. Walls

IN A LITTLE essay describing the final weeks of his ninety-five-year-old father, Charles Taliaferro recounted their interactions about the nature of mortality as they faced his imminent death. Reflecting on the Christian hope that heaven is our final destiny, he cited the anonymously authored English spiritual manual *The Cloud of Unknowing*, particularly the author's recommendation that when we feel lost in our search for God, we should repeat the words "love" or "God." Both words amount to the same thing, after all, given the axiomatic Christian conviction that "God is love." Taliaferro concludes his essay as follows.

> Two weeks before he died, Dad and I had the following exchange. I said: "I really love you, Daddy." He said: "Don't make me cry." Neither of us cried. We held hands. "You know, Dad, when you get to the other side, there might be lots of questions. I hear that it's a good idea to say the word 'love' a lot." He squeezed my hand three times and said: "Love, Love, Love."[1]

There is a divide of radical proportions between those who believe love is stronger than death, and those who believe death is stronger than love. When I say "stronger than" I do not mean to speak poetically or metaphorically. I do not mean that love is stronger than death only in the sense that it is possible to express love on one's deathbed, or even to say "Father forgive them, they know not what they do" as one is being murdered by his enemies. The notion that love is stronger than death I have in mind is the claim that love is eternal and that the day will come when "death will be no more" and personal relationships of love will last forever, never again to be ripped apart by death's harrowing hand. By contrast, the claim that death is stronger than love is the claim that all loving relationships will eventually end forever when the lovers are inevitably overcome by death, and are no longer alive to share their love with each other.

By sharp contrast with the story I just cited, naturalists hold that death is stronger than love in the sense I am using the terms. Notably, among the things Bertrand Russell famously declared to be "but the outcome of accidental collocations of atoms" was not only man's hopes and fears, but also "his loves." Given this fortuitous origin, it is hardly surprising that Russell insisted that "all the devotion," along with everything else we care about, is "destined to extinction in the vast death of the solar system." No lovers will have the power to sustain their devotion against the invincible forces of death, and they "will inevitably be buried beneath the debris of a universe in ruins." A naturalist might love right up to this last breath, but the final refrain of his view of reality is not love, but death.[2]

This profound difference, I want to argue, has enormous implications for the meaning of life. In Plantinga's "Two Dozen (or so) Good Theistic Arguments," he has both an argument from love, and an argument from the meaning of life. In this chapter, I shall combine the two and consider them as complementary arguments, perhaps even as two aspects of a single argument. I shall proceed first by examining two naturalist accounts of the meaning of life, and probing the points at which they fall short of the meaning we crave, or the most satisfactory kind of meaning.

SARTRE, NAGEL AND THE MEANING OF LIFE

Let us begin with Sartre, whose view of the meaning of life is expressed in his famous lecture "Existentialism Is a Humanism." In this lecture, Sartre defends existentialism against various criticisms and affirms the positive significance of his view of the human situation. Particularly significant for our purposes is his claim that "existentialism is nothing else but an attempt to draw the full conclusions from a consistently atheistic position. Its intention is not in the least that of plunging men into despair."[3] Indeed, Sartre criticizes eighteenth-century atheists for not being fully consistent in their atheism, for while they denied God's existence, they still held to the notion that man possessed a given human nature, and consequently, that "essence preceded existence." Atheistic existentialism, by contrast, held with greater consistency that existence comes before essence in the case of human beings, that we must define our essence by our radically free choices.

Radical freedom is a sword that cuts both ways. On the one hand, since there is no God to whom we are accountable, nor an objective morality, nor a given human nature to which we must be true in order to be human, we are free to create our own morality as well as our own meaning and significance. But on the other hand, since we are limited to our resources and the reach of our freedom, the meaning of our lives runs up against some inevitable limits. While Sartre insists that his view is not one without hope, it is still very much a hope circumscribed by his naturalistic convictions. As he put it, "we seek to base our teaching upon the truth, and not upon a collection of fine theories, full of hope but lacking real foundations."[4]

The stark truth about our situation can be described as "abandonment," which Sartre notes is a favorite word of Heidegger. Again, what makes this an apt word to characterize the human condition is that it underscores the consequences we must face if God does not exist. Sartre sharply criticizes those philosophers who pretended that very little must change if God does not exist, and fondly imagined that traditional morality would remain pretty much in place, perhaps with some minor adjustments. The atheist existentialist is under no such delusion, and faces the hard reality that we are now "abandoned" to create our own values and even our very selves with no a priori good or commands of God to legitimize our choices.

Moreover, Sartre explains that the "despair" for which existentialists are famous is similarly nothing more than a frank recognition that "we limit ourselves to a reliance upon that which is within our wills, or within the sum of probabilities which render our action feasible."[5] So again, our meaning-making resources are limited to the capacities of the human will and our ability to gauge probabilities as we make the choices that define our lives.

These limitations impose some rather severe strictures that Sartre recognizes as simply an inevitable part of the human condition. First, there is the harsh reality that our action and freedom to choose and create is limited by death, and we have no idea whether our efforts will succeed and carry on after we die or whether subsequent events will undermine or destroy everything we worked for or cared about. Those who remain alive after we die are free to create their own meaning, and their choices may be completely at odds with ours. "Tomorrow, after my death, some men may decide to establish Fascism, and the others may be so cowardly or so slack as to let them do so. If so, Fascism will then be the truth of man, and so much the worse for us. In reality, things will be such as men have decided they shall be."[6] And in the final reality, according to naturalism, things will be much worse: a universe that perishes either in fire or in ice, where no man's decisions endure.

There is another hard implication of Sartre's view that the meaning of our lives is limited not only by what human will can muster, but also by the finality of death. In particular, it means that unrealized potentialities shall never be fulfilled. Only the choices actually made in this life count, and indeed, Sartre seems to suggest that there is no such thing as unrealized potentiality.

> But in reality and for the existentialist, there is no love apart from the deeds of love; no potentiality of love other than that which is manifested in loving; there is no genius other than that which is expressed in works of art. . . . No doubt this

may seem comfortless to one who has not made a success of his life. On the other hand it puts everyone in a position to understand that reality alone is reliable; that dreams, expectations, and hopes serve to define a man only as deceptive dreams, abortive hopes, expectations unfulfilled; that is to say, they define him negatively, not positively.[7]

In view of this, Sartre notes that existentialists are criticized not for their pessimism, but rather for the sternness of their optimism. But again, the only hope that is not a "deceptive dream" is one that is proscribed by the obvious limits of human will and the severe limits imposed by death, along with the uncertain course of the future as it will be shaped by the unpredictable human choices that will define "the truth of man."

Let us now turn to contemporary philosopher Thomas Nagel, who has forthrightly addressed the meaning of life and the factors that threaten our lives with absurdity. The heart of his analysis rests on his observation that there is a gaping chasm between how our lives look from an objective perspective, from outside, and how they look from a subjective perspective, from inside. "From far enough outside my birth seems accidental, my life pointless, and my death insignificant, but from inside my never having been born seems nearly unimaginable, my life monstrously important, and my death catastrophic."[8]

Indeed, it can be disorienting to contemplate how improbable it is that we were ever born, and how easily it could have been the case that we had never existed. The odds that all the factors necessary for our birth should converge are vanishingly small, and the same is true for all those we love and care about. Moreover, there is nothing particularly important, objectively speaking, about our birth unless we happen to be a world-class genius or major cultural figure. The world, it seems, would have gotten on pretty much the same even if we had never been born. And yet, this is hardly the whole story. "Subjectively we feel that we and those we love belong here—that nothing could undermine our right of admission to the universe. Whatever others may think, the last thing we expect is that *we* may come to see the world in a way that drains our birth of value."[9]

If we lived only in the subjective world, and saw things only from the inside, we would perhaps be isolated from the problem of meaning. But it is precisely our capacity for self-transcendence, our ability to see ourselves from the outside that generates the problem of meaning. From that perspective, it is hard to take our individual existence all that seriously. Having felt the shudder of our insignificance from that vantage point, we then make a determined effort to reassert the value of our lives by finding a larger meaning that secures our importance. It is this effort, Nagel believes, that leads to absurdity. And this problem, he notes, has nothing to do with the quality of our subjective experience. Even lives that are subjectively satisfying are threatened with insignificance when viewed objectively, from the outside.

Nagel considers three ways we might attempt to close the gap between the inside view and the outside view. First, we might take the drastic measure of simply denying the claims of our subjective view, and concentrate solely on the objective view as the sober truth. While this may sound like nothing more than hardy realism, Nagel thinks it is a measure that exacts far too large a cost to be realistic. Second, we might take the opposite approach and simply deny that our lives are insignificant. We can try to close our eyes and ears to the objective standpoint. This strategy might allow us to close the gap to some degree, but even assigning our lives a significance that is "grotesquely out of line with our objective value" will not be enough to close the gap entirely.[10] The third suggestion is to insist that the problem is an artificial one, and we should simply ignore it. It is not a real problem, so the argument goes, because it is deranged to look at our lives from the outside perspective to the point that we wonder about our own significance. We are first and foremost individual human beings, and the objective standpoint is a development of our very humanity, and must be employed in service to our humanity, not allowed to challenge or undermine it. The problem with this suggestion in Nagel's view is that we cannot tame or domesticate the objective viewpoint that easily. Objectivity simply will not yield to the subjective viewpoint and conform to its wishes and preferences. "The objective self is a vital part of us, and to ignore its quasi-independent operation is to be cut off from oneself as much as if one were to abandon one's subjective individuality."[11]

The upshot of all this is that Nagel believes we simply cannot get around this impasse. We can neither avoid our desire for meaning nor ignore the objective reality that threatens it. We can take small steps in closing the gap between the view from inside and the view from outside, but we fall quite short of closing it altogether. The inner conflict we feel remains very much in force, so we need to come to terms with the reality that the absurd is intrinsic to the human condition. Indeed, it is not to be regretted since it is generated by the very capacities that make us human, particularly our ability to view things both objectively and subjectively.

While we can come to terms with the absurd, even if we cannot escape or evade it, there is another aspect of the problem of meaning that is even more severe and implacable. We face the inevitable prospect of death, and that means the end of my subjective experience, indeed, it is the end of my whole world as an individual subject.

Nagel does not try to soften the blow. For him death is a curse. He wants to go on living, and cannot imagine tiring of life, as many persons claim to do. Unfortunately, however, our first-person subjective desire to go on living clashes ruthlessly with the objective reality that the universe is indifferent to our continued survival. "We are so accustomed to the parallel progress of subjective and objective time that there is some shock in the realization that the world will go calmly on without me after I disappear. It is the ultimate form of abandonment."[12]

Nagel's talk of "abandonment" here is particularly poignant if we recall Sartre's use of this classic existential language, cited earlier. For Sartre, the term "abandonment" simply registers the fact that in a godless universe, we are on our own to create our values, and to define our very selves. There is no given plan or path we can follow to find meaning and truth. For Nagel, "abandonment" signals a further lonely dimension of naturalism. The natural world, of which we are a part, will continue on its way, leaving us forever behind when we fall into our graves.

And yet, despite the fact that the natural world, the ultimate representation of objective reality, is harshly indifferent to individual subjects and will destroy all of them in the end, Nagel insists that some values can transcend death. "Anyone incapable of caring enough about something outside himself to sacrifice his life for it is seriously limited." Indeed, Nagel even suggests that by caring about such things you can "reduce the evil of death by externalizing your interests as it approaches: concentrating on the welfare of those who will survive you and on the success of projects or causes that you care about independently of whether you will be around to see what happens." [13]

But such measures can only take us so far in reducing the evil of death. Nagel concludes his discussion by insisting that the objective self cannot successfully cultivate an attitude of indifference to its own annihilation, and the very attempt to do so will invariably have something inauthentic about it. Our individual attachment to life will inevitably reassert itself. Here is the predicament he leaves us with in the final lines of his discussion: "When we acknowledge our containment in the world, it becomes clear that we are incapable of living in the full light of that acknowledgment. Our problem has in this sense no solution, but to recognize that is to come as near as we can to living in light of the truth." [14]

This is an unfortunate situation indeed if Nagel is right. We are left with a precarious situation in which we are forced to negotiate an uneasy compromise between truth and meaning that can never be resolved in a satisfactory manner.

Before concluding this section, it is worth noting that in his more recent book *Mind and Cosmos*, Nagel has launched a spirited attack on the materialist, Darwinian picture of reality, arguing that it fails to account for the most interesting features of our world such as consciousness, intentionality, and value. While persisting in his atheism, Nagel insists that we must see mind as fundamental to reality, not a mere side effect. He urges us to seek alternatives to reductive materialism "that make mind, meaning, and value as fundamental as matter and space-time in an account of what there is." [15]

His attempt to make meaning fundamental seems to suggest that there may be more to the meaning of life than he thought in his earlier writings. However, his naturalistic assumptions still impose severe limits on what that meaning might be. We shall come back to this when we consider how the problem of meaning can be solved by theism and how this constitutes a good argument for God's existence. But let us turn now to look briefly at the naturalist account of love.

LOVE IN A NATURALISTIC WORLD

Let us consider two forms of love that pose something of a challenge to naturalism, particularly the naturalistic theory of evolution—namely, eros and altruism. Broadly speaking, of course, evolutionary accounts of love will explain it in terms of how it provides an advantage in terms of survival and reproduction. Altruism especially has been recognized as a problem for naturalistic evolution, and Darwin himself opined that it could potentially wreck his theory. More recently, Edward O. Wilson acknowledged on the very first page of his massive work *Sociobiology* what he calls "the central theoretical problem of sociobiology: how can altruism, which by definition reduces personal fitness, possibly evolve by natural selection?"[16]

But eros poses challenges of its own. According to Richard Dawkins, the romantic phenomenon of falling in love must have genetic advantages, but it appears to be rather irrational. "Rather than the fanatically monogamous devotion to which we are susceptible, some sort of 'polyamory' is on the face of it more rational."[17] Dawkins notes, however, that researchers have shown that being in love is accompanied by some distinctive brain states and chemicals. According to evolutionary psychologists, the irrational thunderbolt of erotic love may be a mechanism that ensures loyalty to one co-parent long enough to raise their offspring, or at the very least until the child is weaned.

Interesting for our purposes, Dawkins ventures the suggestion that religion could be a by-product of the irrationality mechanisms built into the brain that cause us to fall in love. Religious faith is similar to falling in love and leads us to the same sort of exclusive loyalty and intense devotion to the object of worship that erotic love does for the beloved. Moreover, religion provides positive reinforcements that are comforting and encouraging in the same sort of ways as the positive reinforcements of erotic love.

Now let us turn to altruism and see how evolution can account for it. One theory suggests that the key to understanding altruism is "kin selection." The basic idea here is that the key to evolutionary success is passing on your genes at a higher rate than other competing organisms. Those who are related to us share genetic material with us, particularly close relatives, most especially our children. So any assistance we give to relatives will further the end of passing on our genes. This explains why we are especially willing to sacrifice for our children, with little or no expectation of return. They are better situated than anyone else to pass on our genes, so to help them is to enhance our reproductive interests.

But what about altruism that extends to others besides our relatives, perhaps even to complete strangers? This may be more difficult to account for, but much of this behavior can be explained in terms of "reciprocal altruism." That is to say, we are inclined to engage in altruistic behavior because we expect to be compensated. So if I help another person in time of need, he may be willing to help me in a similar situation. Moreover, my sacrificial behavior may gain admiration from other observers, who may also be willing to assist me when I am in need. This is all the more likely given that humans for most of their evolutionary history lived in small groups, so such acts would likely be witnessed by others. Thus, altruism is mutually beneficial to those who practice it, so in the end it is not so much of a problem for naturalistic evolution as it first appeared to be.[18]

While naturalistic evolutionary theory has worked hard to accommodate altruism, it is worth pointing out that some naturalists reject the idea altogether. A notable example is Nietzsche, who had disdain for the notion. So-called altruism, in his view, was actually clear evidence of decadence, and the reality was that the alleged altruist simply had no idea how to press his own advantage.[19]

Nietzsche's deepest reason for disdaining altruism is his conviction that the "will to power" is the true driving force of all human actions. In one of his more memorable expressions of this notion, he remarks that there is no reason to blame powerful birds of prey for carrying off little lambs and eating them, for it is just their nature. "To expect that strength will not manifest itself as strength, as the desire to overcome, to appropriate, to have enemies, obstacles, and triumphs, is every bit as absurd as to expect that weakness will manifest itself as strength."[20] It is a popular myth, he believes, to distinguish between strength and the expression of strength. Strength and power necessarily express themselves in the form of conquest and domination. There is no such thing as an agent who has the power to manifest his strength, but may freely choose to refrain from doing so. It is simply not "within the discretion of the strong to be weak, of the bird of prey to be a lamb."[21]

GOD AND THE MEANING OF LIFE

So let us turn now to consider the argument for God's existence from the meaning of life. On this argument, Plantinga is singularly unhelpful in his "Two Dozen" article, where he devotes but a single sentence to the argument, and that sentence is a question: "How does thought about the meaningfulness or meaningless of life fit in?"[22]

Now the obvious first response to this question, and one that has considerable promise, is to show that the existence of God can get us out of the impasse Nagel identified, and resolve the problem for which he thinks there is no solution. If God exists, our lives are not inescapably bound by the sort of absurdity that Nagel thinks they are. Rather than threatening our lives with absurdity, the objective standpoint can enrich our lives with depths of meaning and significance that are out of the question if naturalism is the objective metaphysical truth.

This sort of argument has even more potential in light of the claims Nagel wants to advance in *Mind and Cosmos,* in particular what he insists that we recognize as the truth about our very selves. One of the fundamental themes running through the book is the intelligibility of the world, and his insistence that this is part of the key to understanding why things are the way they are. Nature, he suggests, not only gives rise to minds, but is also such that it is comprehensible to those minds. "Ultimately, therefore, such beings should be comprehensible to themselves."[23]

An underlying assumption is a version of the principle of sufficient reason, which holds that everything can at some level be understood, and nothing is merely arbitrary. Now on this assumption, we can hope that the meaning of our lives can be understood and we should be dubious of any account that leaves us stuck with either absurdity or an inexplicable mystery.

As in *The View from Nowhere*, Nagel insists that we can hardly avoid an objective, transcendent view of ourselves. In seeking a satisfactory transcendent viewpoint, the hope, he says, "is to find a way of understanding ourselves that is not radically self-undermining. The aim would be to offer a plausible picture of how we fit into the world."[24] Now this goal of finding a way of understanding ourselves that is not "radically self-undermining" sounds rather modest in one way. Indeed, one might think it more appropriate to seek a way of self-understanding that is not self-undermining at all, or better yet, one that is radically self-fulfilling. This is all the more so when we take into account the remarkable feature of human beings that Nagel highlights, particularly consciousness and our ability to recognize objective moral truth. What understanding of ourselves can do justice to these extraordinary aspects of human nature?

Nagel considers, but dismisses, theism as an alternative to the materialist-reductionist account of transcendence. As he notes, theism accounts for the intelligibility of reality ultimately in terms of intentionality and purpose, and thereby avoids a purely descriptive end point. Matter is the intentionally created product of mind, rather than mind somehow being generated by matter. But not just any old sort of intentionality will do. Indeed, it would be easy enough to imagine numerous intentions behind our creation that would hardly support the prospect that our lives are meaningful. They might be meaningful in the rather narrow sense that we were *meant* to exist, and to exist for a particular purpose, even for a purpose that we fulfilled rather well, but our lives could still be absurd. Suppose, for instance, that we were created to provide entertainment for a perverse deity, who took a special delight in observing the likes of us puzzling over our existence, dreading the prospect of our eventual annihilation, and fearing that our lives are nothing more than some sort of cosmic joke. The more we wring our hands and fret over our lives, the more amused he is. The more profound, eloquent, and aesthetically pleasing our expressions of absurdity or puzzlement, the more pleasure he takes in them.

Such a scenario, I take it, would hardly make our lives meaningful in any deep or satisfying sense. Nagel observes: "An intentional agent must be thought of as having aims that it sees as good, so the aims cannot be arbitrary; and a particular religion can make this much more specific, though it also poses the famous problem of evil."[25] An arbitrary aim is no better than a perverse one, and Nagel is surely right that any worthy aim must be one the intentional agent sees as good. But of course, a perverse being might see an end as "good" when it really is not. So it is not enough merely for the intentional agent to see the end as good. Rather, it must actually *be* good. And one way to be sure it is good is to specify that the intentional agent not only knows what is good, but only wants what is good.

Here is where the distinctively Christian account of theism is most pertinent, particularly the doctrine "God is love." And here Plantinga is considerably more helpful. For instance, consider his suggestive thoughts on the problem of evil, and one possible reason why our world contains so much of it. Perhaps, Plantinga suggests, God wanted to create, out of all possible worlds, one of outstanding goodness. This, of course, raises the fundamental question of what makes a world a good one, or what are good-making properties for possible worlds, and on this question disagreement will surely arise. Here Plantinga offers us this provocative suggestion: "Among good-making properties for worlds, however, there is one of special, transcendent importance, and it is a property that characterizes our world. For according to the Christian story, God, the almighty first being of the universe and the creator of everything else, was willing to undergo enormous suffering in order to redeem creatures who had turned their backs on him."[26] He goes on to sketch the Christian story of the Fall, the Incarnation and the Atonement, and then remarks: "This overwhelming display of love and mercy is not merely the greatest story ever told; it is the greatest story that *could* be told. No other great-making property of a world can match this one."[27]

Now here we have the makings not only of a deeply satisfying account of the meaning of our lives, but also of an explanation of love that surpasses naturalist accounts. Notice in particular Plantinga's claim that the Christian story is the "greatest story that *could* be told." If this is so, and we play the part in the story that Christianity teaches, then our lives have enormous meaning.

So let us reflect further on Plantinga's claim that the Christian story is the greatest story that could be told. First, note that the central character in the story is the Greatest Possible Being, a God who has every great-making property to the highest possible level. His maximal greatness includes perfect goodness, which for Christianity is rooted in the fact that He is love in his very nature. This is shown particularly in the doctrine of the Trinity, the claim that God is three persons who have existed in a relationship of mutual love and ecstatic delight for all eternity. And it is out of this eternal love that God created human beings in His own image so we could enjoy loving relationships with Him and with each other. When we turned our backs on God, He chose to restore the relationship with us by an act of unsurpassable love as expressed in the incarnation and death of His Son, a death in which He willingly underwent extreme pain, suffering, and humiliation. In short, we are the beloved of the Greatest Possible Being, the Greatest Possible Lover.

Now it is not hard to see how this story, and our part in it, gives enormous meaning to our lives. Indeed, consider in this light the three factors Nagel highlights that threaten our lives with meaninglessness. First, if God is our creator, and the one who is ultimately responsible for our very existence, we should not view our conception and birth as merely a staggeringly improbable event of miniscule significance in an indifferent cosmos. For if God is a loving Father who observes every sparrow that falls,[28] then we can be sure that He knew of our birth, and delighted in it. Recall Nagel's observation earlier that, subjectively, we cannot help but feel that we and those we love belong here, and we resist any thought that drains our birth of value. Well, the Christian theist would say that we do in fact belong here, as beloved creatures of the God of love, and that our birth in fact has great value to Him, so our subjective feelings are in fact true to reality.

Second, the sense of absurdity that is generated by the profound clash between the objective view and the subjective view on Nagel's account is altogether dispelled. The reason is simple. If ultimate reality is the God of love who loves us in the way Christianity teaches, then the objective viewpoint, far from undermining our subjective sense of significance and meaning, actually elevates it to levels not otherwise possible. Once again, the Christian theist will think that our subjective view of things points us in the direction of what is actually true, to a depth of meaning that is greater than anything naturalism can underwrite. For the Christian drama gives our lives significance and meaning that surpasses our wildest imagination. The notion that we are the beloved of the Greatest Possible Lover opens up possibilities for happiness and fulfillment we have yet to conceive. We are not limited to what human will is capable of achieving, as Sartre thought, nor are we "abandoned" or consigned to existentialist despair with its severely circumscribed hopes. Indeed, we can and should aspire to much more.

This brings us to the third factor Nagel cited that threatens the meaningfulness of our lives, namely, the stark reality of our death, the harsh reality of which in his view is the utter end of our subjective world. And here is the most dramatic difference between Nagel's naturalism and Christian theism. For Christian theism, love is stronger than death, so it is not the case that we are "abandoned" at the point of death, while the objective world rolls heedlessly on. To the contrary, our subjective life will not only continue, but ultimately bring us satisfaction and joy far beyond anything we experienced in this life.

Recall Sartre's concession to the fact that on his view, all his efforts for good may come to naught. For all he knows, Fascism will prevail after his death and become "the truth of man," for as he sees it, not only the course of history, but the very essence and truth of man is up to nothing higher than human choice with all its whims and caprice. And the prospect that our good efforts could be utterly undone by those who come after us does threaten the meaning of our lives with a certain sort of futility, for it means we might ultimately have failed to achieve the worthwhile goals for which we worked. Indeed, the author of the book of Ecclesiastes recognized this dismal truth millennia ago when he reflected on the fact that he must leave all he had toiled for to those who followed him: "and who knows whether they will be wise or foolish? Yet they will be masters of all for which I toiled and used my wisdom under the sun. This also is vanity."[29]

This grim realization also puts a check on Nagel's suggestion that we can soften the blow of death by externalizing our interests as it approaches. It is one thing to try to focus on projects we care about whether or not we will be around to see how they turn out, but it is another matter to be indifferent to whether or not they turn out well or not. And if we desire them to turn out well—and they may not—that surely injects a certain futility into our projects, and even more so if they do not.

And indeed, for naturalism, all our projects face the inevitable end of Russell's "universe in ruins." Nagel thinks anyone incapable of caring enough about something outside himself to die for it is "seriously limited," and while this claim will resonate with anyone with a sense of traditional values, it is much less apparent whether this limit should trouble a naturalist. If death is the annihilation of our subjective world in which we are inescapably and profoundly invested, perhaps that is simply a limit that goes with the circumscribed territory naturalism can claim, and Nagel should not cast aspersions on it.

Recall, too, Sartre's claim that there is no love apart from the deeds of love, no such thing as the potential to love that is not actually expressed. Here Sartre aims to bind us to hard reality, and to insist that "hopes serve to define a man only as deceptive dreams, abortive hopes, expectations unfulfilled; that is to say, they define him negatively, not positively." Again, the Christian drama sees things profoundly differently. It nurtures and intensifies the hope that there are indeed vast potentialities for love that have yet to be developed and brought to maturity. Neither the limits of our own powers, nor the limits of this life exhaust the love we may receive, or the love we may yet learn to give. Rather, our potential for love is defined by the resources of the Greatest Possible Lover.

Consider these three passages from the Gospel of John, all spoken by Jesus, and all pertaining to love.

"Father . . . you loved me before the foundation of the world" (17:24)
"As the Father has loved me, so have I loved you; abide in my love" (15:9).
"This is my commandment, that you love one another as I have loved you" (15:12).

These three passages encapsulate the heart of the Christian story as it pertains to love. Notice the extraordinary implications when we think about the connection between these three texts. The first expresses the Christian belief that the love between the Father and Son is primordial reality. Before the world ever existed, there was love in the eternal relationship of mutual giving and receiving between the Persons of the Trinity. The second text states the remarkable claim that the love Christ displayed to His disciples reflects the same sort of love as the Father expressed for Him. In His incarnation, we see Trinitarian love on open display. When we come to the third text, it is amazing enough to think that the Son of God commands His disciples to love one another as He has loved them, but it is even more stunning when we consider this command in light of the previous two verses. Notice: His love for them mirrors the love the Father has for Him, the same love that existed among the Persons of the Trinity from all eternity, and that is the sort of love Jesus's disciples are to share with each other. In other words, their love for each other should in some sense reproduce and reflect eternal Trinitarian love!

Now this is a rather tall order for the likes of ordinary mortals like us. But notice that we are not expected to produce and express this sort of love on our own steam or by our own efforts. Jesus directs His disciples to abide in His love. He is the vine and His disciples are the branches, and only as they abide in Him can they produce the fruits of love that He commands them to produce (John 15:1–17). Again, our potential for love is defined by the resources of the Greatest Possible Lover.

GOD AND THE MEANING OF LOVE

Now all of this has large implications for the argument from love, namely, that God provides a better, and deeper, explanation of love than naturalism does. Recall the evolutionary explanation of eros that sees it as an irrational sort of "fanatically monogamous devotion" that serves the positive purpose of leading us to remain faithful to marriage partners until children are raised. Recall too the suggestion that religion could be a byproduct of this irrational impulse, since religious devotion is a similar sort of passionate commitment.

Here it is ironic to note that while Dawkins intended this suggestion to undermine the credibility of religious belief, a similar point about the similarity between eros and love for God has been made by some noted Christian believers. In his book *The Four Loves,* C.S. Lewis has argued that the natural loves—affection, friendship, and eros—are all images of God, and moreover, that none of the natural loves can remain themselves unless they are rightly related to Love Himself. In other words, all of the natural loves need to be transformed by the fourth love, charity, and become forms of that highest kind of love. What Lewis says about eros is particularly striking in this regard.

> His [eros's] total commitment is a paradigm or example, built into our natures, of the love we ought to exercise toward God and Man. As nature, for the nature lover, gives a content to the word glory, so this gives a content to the word Charity. It is as if Christ said to us through Eros, " 'Thus—just like this—with this prodigality—not counting the cost—you are to love me and the least of my brethren.' "[30]

Notice that eros thus transformed is essentially the same as altruism. Later in his book, Lewis points out that Charity empowers us to love in ways that go far beyond our natural impulses. "But Divine Gift-love in the man enables him to love what is not naturally lovable; lepers, criminals, enemies, morons, the sulky, the superior and the sneering."[31] Love of this sort is not readily explained by either kin selection or the naturalistic notion of reciprocity, but it is entirely in keeping with what we might expect if it is a reflection of a God who gave up His son to die a humiliating death at the hand of the very people for whom He died in order to save them.

Christian theists believe, however, that reciprocity is a larger reality than can be accounted for in terms of naturalism. So the sort of love that is genuinely given to lepers, say, by Mother Teresa, or to enemies by martyrs, is reciprocated ultimately by God. While it is never possible to advance our ultimate well-being and true happiness by acting selfishly, the other side of the coin is that we inevitably promote our true well-being and happiness any time we engage in acts of genuine love, including those acts that are most costly. The economy of love is thus a reflection of the fact that primordial reality is the mutual, reciprocal love of the Persons of the Trinity from all eternity.[32] Indeed, perhaps even the reciprocity observed by naturalistic evolution to explain altruism is a reflection of this same truth.

In any case, notice in the quote earlier that Lewis's suggests that eros is a paradigm "built into our natures, of the love we ought to exercise toward God and man." This explanation, that it is part of the divine design for human nature to reveal how we ought to live, is a very different sort of explanation than the naturalistic evolutionary one we noted earlier. Eros, on this view, is not fundamentally an irrational impulse that serves a positive function for biological survival and that has as a curious by-product that it may also explain the similarly "irrational" nature of religious devotion. Rather, it is a clue that points to the fact that love is at the very heart of ultimate reality.

Most interesting for our purposes, Plantinga has also argued that eros is a sign of deeper truths. First, it points to our love for God, which is the passionately joyful relationship for which we were created. It is a foreshadowing of the yearning love for God we will feel in heaven when we are fully renewed and healed from the sin that presently makes us fall short of the union with God that will completely satisfy us. Second, it is a sign of God's passionate love for us, a love that is like the love a bridegroom has for his beloved bride. Once again, the argument for God's existence that can be proposed is in terms of a satisfactory explanation of something profoundly important to human life and existence. Plantinga comments:

> The fact that human eros is a type of divine love means that this feature of our lives can be explained or understood a certain way. We understand it better, see what it is all about, see what is most important about it when we see that it is a type or sign of divine love. We see how it fits in with the rest of reality, and how it is connected with what is most real.[33]

GOD AND "WHAT IS MOST REAL"

The force of these arguments from the meaning of life, and the nature of love, will depend largely on one's judgements about what sort of questions demand an answer, and finally, what one judges to be "most real." For those who believe that love is one of those things that is most real, and one of those things that lie at the very heart of the meaning of life, these arguments may carry considerable weight.[34] The same is true for those who believe the meaning of life is a question that demands a satisfying answer. On the other hand, these arguments will have less force for those who think the meaning of life is a question we have no right or reason to believe has a satisfactory answer, or who think love is perfectly well explained as a biological phenomenon.[35]

We have noted that for Plantinga, the Christian story of the love of God is not only the greatest story ever told, but the greatest story that could be told. Possibility here has reached its limits. Moreover, the necessary proscribes what is possible, and here it is most interesting to note that Plantinga has employed the language of necessity in describing the love of God. "Human erotic love is a sign of something deeper, something so deep that it is uncreated, an original and permanent and necessarily present feature of the universe."[36]

Plantinga has written much groundbreaking work about necessity, but this is perhaps the most striking claim of all about the nature of necessity: that love is a necessary feature of the universe. The possibilities that arise from this account of necessity are both stunning and profoundly beautiful.

Here it is worth comparing Plantinga's story of the necessity of love with Nietzsche's story of how power necessarily expresses itself. Recall that for Nietzsche, birds of prey who carry off defenseless lambs are a good image of the hard reality that strength must manifest itself as conquest and domination. For him, it is a pious myth that "it is within the discretion of the strong to be weak, of the bird of prey to be a lamb." In sharp contrast to this notion, Christianity teaches that that is exactly what God did when Jesus assumed the role of the Lamb of God who was sacrificed to save us from our sins.

One of the most striking, and paradoxical, images in the New Testament is that of Jesus as the Lamb who was slain but is now at the center of the throne in heaven.[37] What this image underscores is that the Lamb is not weak by nature, but rather, supremely powerful. His "weakness" in being slain was not due to the fact that someone stronger than He overcame and dominated Him, but rather, it was the willing expression of the power of supreme love. As Jesus made clear elsewhere, no one can take his life from Him, and he laid it down of his own accord.[38]

Plantinga's account of the love that is a necessary feature of the universe is a beautiful explanation of why love is stronger than death. It provides an illuminating account not only of why love is more than an ephemeral or merely biological reality that must eventually yield to death, but also of why our lives have a depth of meaning that vastly exceeds the severe limits imposed by naturalism. To quote Plantinga once more, here is what it means to be loved by the Greatest Possible Lover, the "charmed circle" composed of the Father, the Son and the Holy Spirit.

> And God's love for us is manifested in his generously inviting us into this charmed circle (though not, of course, to ontological equality), thus satisfying the deepest longing of our souls. Within this circle, there is mercy, self-sacrifice, overflowing agape; there is also that longing and delight, that yearning and joy that make up eros.[39]

For those who resonate with this account, who believe that love is most real, and that it provides an unsurpassably satisfying answer to why we are here, the arguments of this chapter will prove good reasons to believe in God.[40]

NOTES

1. Charles Taliaferro, *Love, Love, Love and Other Essays* (Cambridge: Cowley Publications, 2006), 175.

2. Bertrand Russell, *Why I Am Not a Christian*, ed. Paul Edwards (New York: Simon and Schuster, 1957), 107.

3. Jean-Paul Sartre, "Existentialism is a Humanism," www.marxists.org/reference/archive/sartre/works/exist/sartre.htm, 21.

4. Ibid., 14.

5. Ibid., 10.

6. Ibid., 11.

7. Ibid., 12.

8. Thomas Nagel, *The View from Nowhere* (New York: Oxford University Press, 1986), 209.

9. Ibid., 213.

10. Ibid., 220.

11. Ibid., 221.

12. Ibid., 226.

13. Ibid., 230.

14. Ibid., 231.

15. Thomas Nagel, *Mind and Cosmos: Why the Materialist Neo-Darwinian Conception of Nature Is Almost Certainly False* (New York: Oxford University Press, 2012), 20.

16. Edward O. Wilson, *Sociobiology: The New Synthesis* (Cambridge, MA: Belknap Press of Harvard University Press, 2000), 3.

17. Richard Dawkins, *The God Delusion* (Boston: Houghton Mifflin, 2006), 184.

18. See Michael Ruse, *Taking Darwin Seriously* (Amherst, MA: Prometheus, 1998), 217–223; Thomas Jay Oord, "Morals, Love and Relations in Evolutionary Theory," in *Evolution and Ethics: Human Morality in Biological & Religious Perspective*, eds. Philip Clayton and Jeffrey Schloss (Grand Rapids, MI: Eerdmans, 2004), 287–291.

19. Friedrich Nietzsche, *Twilight of the Idols* and *The Anti-Christ*, trans. R.J. Hollingdale (London: Penguin, 1990), 98.

20. Friedrich Nietzsche, *The Birth of Tragedy* and *The Genealogy of Morals*, trans. Francis Golfing (New York: Anchor Books, 1956), 178.

21. Ibid., 179.

22. That is not exactly true, as Plantinga does add three names: Sartre, Camus, Nagel.

23. *Mind and Cosmos*, 17.

24. Ibid., 25.

25. Ibid., 25.

26. Alvin Plantinga, *Where the Conflict Really Lies: Science, Religion and Naturalism* (New York: Oxford University Press, 2011), 58.

27. Ibid., 59.

28. Matthew 10:29

29. Ecclesiastes 2:19.

30. C.S. Lewis, *The Four Loves* (New York: Harcourt Brace Jovanovich, 1960), 110.

31. Ibid., 128.

32. See Jerry L. Walls, *Heaven: The Logic of Eternal Joy* (New York: Oxford University Press, 2002), 161–163, 185–193.

33. *Warranted Christian Belief*, 323.

34. For an excellent defense of the claim that love is the meaning of life, see John Cottingham, "Meaningful Life" in *The Wisdom of the Christian Faith*, eds. Paul K. Moser and Michael T. McFall (Cambridge: Cambridge University Press, 2012), 175–196.

35. For an excellent discussion of this issue from the standpoint of probability theory, see Trent Dougherty, "Belief that Life Has Meaning Confirms that Life Has Meaning: A Bayesian Approach," in *God and Meaning*, eds. Joshua W. Seachris and Stewart Goetz (New York: Bloomsbury, 2016), 81–98.

36. *Warranted Christian Belief*, 321.

37. Revelation 5:6; 7:17.

38. John 10:18.

39. *Warranted Christian Belief*, 321.

40. Thanks to Trent Dougherty for helpful comments on an earlier version of this essay.

(U)

The Mozart Argument and (V) The Argument from Play and Enjoyment

THE THEISTIC ARGUMENT FROM BEAUTY AND PLAY

Philip Tallon

INTRODUCTION

BEAUTY IS PLAYFUL. SPEAKING well of beauty, then, often requires the art of improvisation: following the dance of its unconstrained movements, rather than a firm adherence to our initial ideas of what it is and *should be.* Hans Urs von Balthasar captures something of both the charm and challenge of theologizing about beauty when he writes, "Beauty is the last thing which the thinking intellect dares to approach, since only it dances as an uncontained splendor around the double constellation of the true and the good and their inseparable relation to one another."[1] There's no reason to take Nietzsche too seriously when he says that philosophers were bad with truth because truth was a woman and philosophers are awkward around women.[2] But there is some truth in the statement, especially when it comes to courting the figure of beauty. Theologians and philosophers, with our carefully placed steps, often cannot keep up with the light footwork of beauty's playful dance.[3]

Beauty has rarely been the main theme of any major modern theologian's or philosopher's thought.[4] (Or perhaps, even this statement reflects already an implicit bias against aesthetics and aesthetic theology, because, as we might tacitly judge, prolonged focus on aesthetics excludes one from the pantheon of greats.) Balthasar, again, that great contemporary exception that proves the rule, characterizes the modern approach to beauty (through the veiled figure of Kant), when he writes, "[Beauty is] a word with which the philosophical person does not begin, but rather concludes . . . a word from which religion, and theology in particular, have taken their leave and distanced themselves in modern times by a vigorous drawing of the boundaries."[5]

Yet even with these methodological boundaries in place, few thinkers who reflect on the full scope of reality can resist the temptation to scale the walls and at least briefly visit the gilded ghetto into which beauty and her daughters have been quarantined. Even when praise of beauty's significance does not seem to fit with the overall methodology of a theologian, the power of the call is often too great to resist. In the case of Karl Barth, for instance, the majesty of Mozart's music overwhelms his dialectical impulses and he must pause to champion Mozart as one who heard something of creation and eschatology that "neither the real fathers of the Church nor our Reformers, neither the orthodox nor Liberals" heard.[6] More often, however, among theologians who have no deep, underlying reasons for excluding consideration of beauty in theological discourse, we still find the incursions into the gilded ghetto brief, marked by a sudden spurt of rhapsody at their surroundings, followed by a hasty retreat into more familiar territory. There are many examples that might be cited, but perhaps the most vivid instance is the "Argument from Aesthetic Experience" in Kreeft and Tacelli's "Twenty Arguments for the Existence of God."[7] Though the other nineteen arguments are given multi-page treatments, or at least a full paragraph, the argument from beauty is only three lines long: "There is the music of Johann Sebastian Bach. Therefore there must be a God. You either see this one or you don't."[8] Far be it for me to pillory Kreeft and Tacelli for their playful brevity (we all understand their point), but it is telling that in the midst of more robust arguments with lengthier defenses of key premises, they not only omit the major premise that would validate the syllogism, but they also decline to defend it in any way. The implicit assumption the reader is left with is surely that, in the realm of the aesthetic, rational persuasion is well-nigh impossible. This kind of argument, in a sense, assumes a post-Kantian interlocutor, who, like the Sage of Königsberg, would "stop his ears" to any argument for why a thing is beautiful.[9]

This foray into theistic arguments from beauty (and later, play) attempts to reverse some of these trends. Its aim is simple: to argue that beauty and play are deeply significant features of created life that find their deepest fulfillment and best explanation in the Triune God. Though I will discuss arguments for God's existence from beauty and play, my main goal is to show that beauty and play, like loose puzzle pieces, fit naturally into the picture of Christian theology, and do not fit well at all within naturalism. An open-minded investigator, examining the clues within creation regarding beauty and play, should infer that Christian theism provides the best explanation for them, and further that Christianity provides the best hope for satisfying our desire for beauty and play.

There are many arguments, already well articulated, that the experience of beauty counts as evidence (even if mild evidence a la Swinburne) for God's existence. This essay will briefly summarize a few of these, but will move into somewhat new territory as it argues that the problems as well as the pleasures of beauty are the kind we should expect given theism. (In the final section I will offer a much briefer argument from play.)

THREE (OR SO) ARGUMENTS FROM BEAUTY

As I have indicated, the argument from beauty has often appeared as a minor theme in the writings of many philosophers and theologians. Perhaps more interestingly, it has also remained an object of fascination for atheists, who seem willing to grant it prima facie evidential power. In more than one debate between atheists and theists, I have heard unbelievers tip their hat to beauty's power to at least disturb their doubts about God's existence.[10] Anthony O'Hear, an atheist, writes of beauty this way: "Through art, particularly the great masterpieces of the past, we do have intimations of beauty, of order, of divinity . . . in appreciating the beauty of the world . . . we are seeing the world as endowed with value and meaning."[11] Despite thinking that these "intimations" are ultimately illusory, it is clear that O'Hear thinks that beauty suggests a radically different meaning for the world besides the one he believes is ultimately true. Even more strongly, atheist Paul Draper indicates that beauty is *evidence* for God, but thinks that it is dwarfed by the evidential weight of evil against God's existence. He writes:

> I agree that beauty supports theism, but maintain the overall pattern of good and evil in the world is much more probable on naturalism than on theism. . . . So the ability of theism to explain beauty and our enjoyment of it is a relatively small advantage for theism. Arguments from evil against theism are much more powerful than the argument from beauty in favor of theism.[12]

I am inclined to agree with Draper (and have done so elsewhere) that in a simple contest between the prima facie evidence of evil and the evidence of beauty, evil has more evidential weight.[13] But I do not think that the evidence of evil must stand unchallenged. A robust theodicy is able to reduce the weight of the evidence from evil to the point that (taking the two together) beauty contributes to the likelihood of God's existence. The main point, however, to take from this and the other examples just cited, is that even among atheists, the argument from beauty has a persistent persuasive power that remains when more traditional arguments for God's existence falter in the mind. Akin to theists who do not know quite what to do with beauty, yet remain fascinated by its perennial persuasive power, atheists often seem haunted by the theistic argument from beauty.

Beauty as evidence for God has a sort of common-sense appeal. It is a natural inference to move from the beautiful design of creation to the hand of a designer. The Psalmist does this: "The heavens declare the glory of God, and the sky above proclaims his handiwork" (19:1). Many ancient and medieval theologians made this move. Athenagoras wrote in the second century, "Thus if the world is a harmonious . . . instrument rhythmically moved, I worship not the instrument but the one who tuned and strikes the strings and sings to its accompaniment the melodious strain."[14] Likewise, Basil the Great wrote, "the world is a work of art, set before all for contemplation, so that through it the wisdom of him who created it should be known."[15] Thomas Cole, a famous painter in the Hudson River School, in "Essay on American Scenery," wrote this, "Amid [these scenes of nature] the consequent associations are of God the creator—they are his undefiled works, and the mind is cast into contemplation of eternal things."[16]

More recent, and more sophisticated, versions of the argument are too many to list here, but three are worth mention. Richard Swinburne, in *The Existence of God,* offers a range of inductive arguments he thinks have cumulative weight sufficient to make God's existence likely. The component of beauty brings another dimension to the classic argument from design, and adds to the overall case.

> The strength of the argument from the universe and its spatial and temporal order to God is increased when we take into account the beauty of the universe. As we have noted, the universe is beautiful in the plants, rocks, and rivers, and animal and human bodies on Earth, and also in the swirl of the galaxies and the birth and death of stars . . . if God creates a universe, as a good workman he will create a beautiful universe. On the other hand, if the universe came into being without being created by God, there is no reason to suppose it would be a beautiful universe.[17]

It is interesting to note that Swinburne thinks the argument assumes that beauty is an objective matter. If beauty's objectivity is denied, however, Swinburne thinks the argument could be "rephrased" to merely argue from humans having "aesthetic sensibilities that allow them to see the universe as beautiful."[18] Again, having aesthetic sensibilities that are delighted by perceiving particular features of the universe is more likely given theism. However, Swinburne thinks that objective beauty is needed for the argument to have "significant strength."[19] That Swinburne declines to argue for objective aesthetic value leaves the reader wondering just how much he thinks his argument from beauty bolsters his previous arguments, or if, in Plantingan style, he leaves it as "homework" for others to shore up. The latter option seems most likely.

This essay aims to shore up arguments like Swinburne's by arguing for objective beauty. However, this is no small task. As William Davis points out in his essay "Theistic Arguments," arguments from objective, non-utilitarian value are difficult to make because the late twentieth century is "replete with efforts to show that the very idea of objective value of any kind is mistaken, and that all attempts to identify objective value (especially non-utilitarian objective value) are attempts to impose subjective values on others."[20] As Davis intimates, this is especially true of beauty. No doubt this is why the argument from beauty is rarely spelled out despite having intuitive appeal. However, just because something is hard doesn't mean it is not worthwhile. This essay will exert its effort to elevating the argument from beauty from its humble state.

Returning to Swinburne, despite his tentativeness on the theistic argument from beauty, he does point to an argument offered by his student, Mark Wynn, who, in *God and Goodness,* offers an argument to God based on the work of F. R. Tennant. Tennant's argument, as adapted by Wynn, contends that the uniform beauty of nature suggests a designer attuned to aesthetic values.[21] Nature exhibits beauty in its various forms: deserts, savannahs, icy mountains, grand galaxies, sea shells, and even at the microscopic level. Uniform beauty in nature is hard to explain given naturalism. Human creations are rarely beautiful without artistic intent. (And, it should be added, are often not beautiful even *with* artistic intent. Creating beautiful objects often requires careful training.) Wynn does not strongly commit to the notion that the beauty in things is objective. He is inclined to agree with Tennant that the argument works even if nature is simply receptive to aesthetic appreciation.[22] Yet Wynn also notes that certain forms of "projectivism" (the view that we are projecting beauty onto nature) may be more damaging to the argument.[23] Still, unlike Swinburne, he does not think that an objectivist account of beauty is *necessary*. For Wynn, it is sufficient that we can *project* beauty onto nature in all its varieties. That nature is receptive in this way allows us to infer a designer.

Wynn's adaptation of Tennant's argument is helpful on the whole, and his defense against various naturalistic objections is worth discussion. I will revisit his work in a later section but for now, I will note that an objectivist account of beauty seems overall more promising for theists to defend. It matches with the view of moral values most theists have traditionally affirmed, and accords better with our intuitions. Beauty is not simply a way of describing our *response* to our perceptions, but a *property* in the things perceived. This brings me to Alvin Plantinga's version of the argument.

In his famous paper that inspired this book, Plantinga offers what he calls "The Mozart Argument":

> On a naturalistic anthropology, our alleged grasp and appreciation of (alleged) beauty is to be explained in terms of evolution: somehow arose in the course of evolution, and something about its early manifestations had survival value. But miserable and disgusting cacophony (heavy metal rock?) could as well have been what we took to be beautiful. On the theistic view, God recognizes beauty; indeed, it is deeply involved in his very nature. To grasp the beauty of a Mozart's D Minor piano concerto is to grasp something that is objectively there; it is to appreciate what is objectively worthy of appreciation.[24]

Plantinga's argument here is notable for a number of reasons. First, it does not begin with the observation of natural beauty (as do Swinburne's and Wynn's arguments). Rather, it moves from the beauty of a bit of human making, and notes proper appreciation of a Mozart piece entails perceiving that the thing itself is beautiful. Second, Plantinga's argument mirrors much of his other work in focusing on how we can have "warrant" for this knowledge about the beauty in Mozart.

Here, I think Plantinga moves us closer to the heart of the argument. He not only provides the sketch of an argument from beauty, but also situates the argument firmly within a robust Christian theology. In noting that beauty is "involved in" God's nature he evokes a rich tradition which makes beauty a part of being itself, and God's very being to a maximal degree. Further, I take Plantinga to be alluding to passages in scripture which show God appreciating the beauty of creation (e.g., Genesis 1). This move seems right to me. Why argue for a mere designer when one could argue for more than that? Further, Plantinga's embrace of objective beauty fits better with the kind of values-objectivism most theists hold with regard to moral values, and also fits better with our common-sense intuitions about beauty's objectivity.

In the next section, I will give a common-sense case for objective beauty. Not only is objective beauty a natural assumption (perhaps a basic belief?), but denying it leads to philosophical problems. In the section after that, I will discuss a naturalistic counter argument (discussed by Wynn) to shore up Plantinga's case against naturalism as a source of reliable aesthetic judgments. In the final section on beauty, I will offer an account of how to understand aesthetic disputes in a way the fits with objective beauty and Christian theism.

A PRELIMINARY CASE FOR OBJECTIVE BEAUTY

The *theological* case for objective beauty is strong. Genesis 1 tells us that all throughout the process of creation, God not only made the world but "saw that it was good." Both the language of seeing and the judgment of goodness suggest that, even before moral actions by humans were possible, God's perception of creation's value was, in some sense, passive. The goodness was in creation itself. The Hebrew and Septuagint versions of Genesis both use words (*tov* and *kalon*) that imply an element of beauty in the judgment of creation's value.

Because this is an argument *from* beauty and not from scripture, it is necessary to offer good reasons for believing that beauty is an objective matter independent of Christian commitments. So I begin by noting that common English usage of the language of beauty suggests an objective view of beauty. We say, "Grace Kelly was beautiful," or, "Forgiveness is a beautiful act," or "What a beautiful day!" We ascribe beauty as a property of things or actions. Predicating objective value to things is, of course, not specific to English usage. C.S. Lewis, in *The Abolition of Man,* points out that subjectivism about value cuts against the grain of the history of human thought:

Until quite modern times all teachers and even all men believed the universe to be such that certain emotional reactions on our part could be either congruous or incongruous to it—believed, in fact, that objects did not merely receive, but could merit, our approval or disapproval, our reverence or our contempt.[25]

This explains why we often feel offended when others have radically different aesthetic judgments. "What do you mean you didn't think that novel was good? It was the best book I read last year!" "How could *that* movie win an Oscar? It was sentimental garbage!" Without some sense of objective aesthetic value, we have little or no basis for meaningful disagreement.

Of course, it is quite common for many people who believe in objective moral values to reject objective aesthetic values. Sometimes, this is due to a vague sense that moral values eclipse aesthetic ones. Morally sensitive people may feel there is something wrong about evaluating the beauty of different people, or types of bodies for instance, out of a desire to affirm inner, unseen qualities, or out of fear of cultural insensitivity. They *rightly* sense that some standards of beauty may be culturally specific, but *wrongly* conclude that the proper response is to deny any judgments of beauty out of fairness. More often, modern people have uncritically absorbed a strain of thinking that has flowed downstream from Enlightenment philosophy (especially Kant and Hume). Even when people object to nearly every other aspect of Kantian or Humean philosophy, they will sometimes reiterate views about aesthetics that owe their origins to these thinkers.

In practice, most reasonable people find it hard to be consistent in rejecting objective aesthetic values. On hearing that ISIS has destroyed the lovely ruins of temple dedicated to Baalshamin, a Phoenician god of fertility–a deity they will never worship and a temple they will likely never visit–most people experience a sense of outrage. But why? What is lost here? No active religion has been profaned. A cultural artifact is lost, to be sure. But why is it valuable as culture? Most likely the outrage stems from a sense that something *beautiful* has been destroyed. Likewise, when a Rembrandt painting is slashed (as happened at the Rijksmuseum), the moral censure is almost wholly directed at the attempt to damage something beautiful for no good reason.[26] Our deep moral intuitions often "out" themselves in cases like these, and cut against explicitly articulated denials of objective aesthetic value.

Yet, perhaps there is a different way to understand these common-sense statements and emotional reactions of outrage at the destruction of beautiful things. One option is to try to *translate* statements about objective beauty into statements about our subjective internal states without doing damage to the language or our intuitions. But non-objective accounts have a hard time coherently expressing this outrage, because they cannot identify a stable concept that meaningfully refers to aesthetic properties. Even a re-phrased form of outrage, "It makes me feel angry when objects that give experiences of beauty are destroyed," cannot give meaning to the word "beauty" in this statement. Likewise, positive statements like "Grace Kelly is beautiful" trade on an undefined meaning to the predicated attribute.

To wit, the philosopher Eddy Zemach has argued, through detailed analysis of the use of language, that the two leading non-objective accounts of aesthetic predication–emotivist (or non-cognitivist) and subjectivist accounts–both suffer from internal problems of coherence. Non-objective views of beauty cannot alternately account for the common sense way we use language to predicate aesthetic properties. Following Zemach, *emotivists* may attempt to explain the meaning of an aesthetic judgment (e.g., "X is beautiful") by stating that this is merely an attempt to commend or approve it. "X is beautiful" comes to mean, then "I commend X," or "I approve of X."[27] But this raises problems, as there are many instances where we predicate beauty of a thing that we do not "commend" for other reasons. For instance, we may say that a novel is beautiful, but think that it is morally corrupt as well. Thus, I can reasonably say, "The novel is beautiful, but I do not commend it."[28] As Zemach shows, even more sophisticated versions of emotivism suffer from similar problems in coherence.[29]

Subjectivist accounts of aesthetic judgment also suffer from problems of coherence. Subjectivists hold that aesthetic judgments do not refer to properties in the thing itself, but to internal states caused by experience of the thing. Zemach mounts numerous attacks on differing versions of subjectivism, of which I shall focus on only one. Subjectivists offer a relativistic account of aesthetic statements as a way of resolving disputes in judgment. Such disputes are linguistically meaningful but irresolvable, they say, because in the statements "X is A" and "X is not A" (for instance, "This painting is gaudy" versus "This painting is not gaudy") uttered by two different people, A and -A refer not to a quality in X but to two different internal states in the two different people. I have an experience viewing X and you have a different experience viewing X, so the thinking goes. For one viewer, "gaudiness" refers to an internal feeling or "way of seeing" specific to him, and for the second viewer "non-gaudiness" refers to her own feeling or way of seeing.[30] On subjectivism, both viewers can be correct in identifying the "way of seeing" internal to their person. They are predicating something about their internal states, not the object itself. Thus, common linguistic usage could be salvaged while reinterpreting its meaning.

But a problem arises when we examine the stability of the meaning of these predicates. As Zemach writes, "[T]he relativist holds that the apparent controversy between Jones and Smith is resolved by showing that they attribute the same property, gaudiness, to different things."[31] Zemach quickly points out a serious problem with this construal:

> So we must ask the relativist, how is it Jones and Smith both understand the term "gaudy"? If all aesthetic predicates apply to private objects [subjective internal states], then Jones has never seen or otherwise examined any object to which Smith ascribes any predicate "A," and vice versa. No one has ever examined any object to which someone else ascribed an aesthetic predicate. In that case, how can one know which property is being ascribed by others when they use the term "A"?...How can children learn to use aesthetic predicates if it is impossible to show them an example of what an aesthetic predicate applies to?[32]

In other words, relativists attempt to resolve aesthetic disputes by arguing that feelings or ways of seeing are person-specific. But how can these internal perceptions be meaningfully described if there are no objective examples to which we can all meaningfully refer? The relativist has assumed that aesthetic experiences were private and irreconcilably different, but that the meanings of the properties they were describing were public and stable. But this is not the case. In order to make any kind of meaningful, public aesthetic evaluations (even the relativistic kind), we require some kind of common, objective aesthetic properties, which relativism denies. Thus, Zemach concludes, "relativism in aesthetics is self-contradictory."[33]

This is far from a total case for the objectivity of beauty, but given the evidence of standard linguistic usage, common moral intuitions, and the incoherence of alternative theories of aesthetic predication (following Zemach), an objective view of beauty seems vastly preferable to a subjective or emotivist view. This puts the burden of proof on those who would try to deny the objectivity of beauty. Back to Plantinga, the person who denies the objective beauty of a Mozart concerto seems to be "missing something." We may excuse someone for choosing to listen more regularly to the Beatles over Mozart (I know I suffer from this defect in taste). In common life, we find it hard to excuse those who deny the objective beauty of masterpieces of nature or human artistry.

However, there are a number of a posteriori arguments that we must consider if we want to defend objective beauty. If we are able to do so, then the theistic argument from beauty (in its various formulations) will be greatly strengthened. In the next two sections I will address a naturalistic counter argument to objective beauty, and a very prevalent objection to objective beauty from the supposed intractability of aesthetic judgments. In both cases, however, I will seek to go beyond countering the arguments and will attempt to show how Christian theism can gain ground in its response.

NATURALISM AND BEAUTY

One counter-argument to the objectivity of beauty might be called the "biophilia proposal." "Perhaps," a naturalistic counter might go, "it is not that beauty is in things themselves, but we are merely conditioned by evolution to find environments conducive to life—like the African savannah—beautiful?"[34] Certain forms of nature have come to be associated with safety and food and therefore naturally provoke pleasurable responses. Likewise, attentiveness to the shift between day and night serves an evolutionary advantage, so we appreciate sunsets. More examples could be given. This attraction to certain natural phenomena would explain the seemingly universal perception of beauty in nature without the need to argue for beauty as an inherent property or, more specifically, the investment of beauty in nature by God. Evolution has fitted our perceptions of beauty to nature because of some survival benefit.

Of course, we must note that this construal does nothing to explain away the possibility that God used evolution to guide our perception of beauty. To do so would be to commit the genetic fallacy. But it might undermine the perception of beauty as *evidence* for God's existence. If the evidence can be thoroughly explained by naturalistic means, it adds nothing to the explanatory power of theism.

Mark Wynn, in *God and Goodness,* addresses this kind of naturalistic counter-response to the argument from beauty by noting that we also aesthetically value "landscapes which are basically hostile to human well-being, or [are] at any rate far removed qualitatively from the savannah type of natural environment."[35] It is common to view Death Valley, or the Matterhorn, as aesthetically excellent, despite their relative hostility to human life. Likewise, tigers, lions, bears, vast oceans, and supernovas are all seen to be both beautiful and threatening. One never hears people speaking of the ugliness of tigers or snow-capped mountains, which we would expect if we our aesthetic responses were primarily determined by survival mechanisms. Thus, it seems that naturalism cannot adequately explain the wide-ranging perception of beauty even in a subjectivist sense. Further, the fact that we perceive even threatening landscapes and animals as beautiful is evidence for the truth of a theistic explanation.

What's more, naturalism does not seem to be remotely equipped to offer an account of our perception of beauty, even in a *partial way*. Alvin Plantinga points out that, on naturalism, we have no reason to think that evolution would give us trustworthy aesthetic faculties of perception. On naturalism, Plantinga writes, "our alleged grasp and appreciation of (alleged) beauty is to be explained in terms of evolution: somehow arose in the course of evolution, and something about its early manifestations had survival value."[36] But, Plantinga continues, "miserable and disgusting cacophony (heavy metal rock?) could as well have been what we took to be beautiful."[37] Since unguided evolution is not aimed at producing faculties that form true beliefs about beauty, it not only suggests that naturalism gives us no reason for trusting our judgments, but may even give us profound reasons for distrusting our judgments on aesthetic matters. Hence, perceiving objective beauty is warranted on theism and not on atheism. Since the naturalistic counter argument fails to satisfactorily account for our intuitions about beauty, beauty remains evidence for theism.

At this point, a reasonable response to my argument could be something like this: "But aren't humans profoundly confused about beauty? Don't the varying judgments on aesthetic matters lend *support* to the notion that our faculties for perceiving beauty are untrustworthy?" Perhaps the fact that many prefer heavy metal to Mozart undermines the theistic argument from objective beauty. In the next section, I will argue that the diversity of judgments about beauty are not so serious as some might claim, and do not undermine our intuitions about beauty's objectivity. Further, I will argue that the presence of varying tastes can even be seen as further evidence for distinctively Christian theism.

SOME PROBLEMS OF BEAUTY, RECONSIDERED AS STRENGTHS

The default view of aesthetic judgments most contemporary people absorb is a subjective one. Beauty is in the eye of the beholder. *De gustibus non est disputandum*, the Latin saying goes: "In matters of taste, there can be no disputes."[38] Yet, as widely held as this opinion is, as I indicated at the start of this essay, in practice, people do quarrel about aesthetic judgments in a way that belies this common belief. Art lovers often argue about the quality of works with an intensity that undermines the easy presumption of aesthetic subjectivism.

We can clarify some of the tensions between differing views about beauty with two propositions. Either, (a) Judgments of beauty are diverse and divisive, or (b) Judgments of beauty are common and comprehensible. If (a) is more likely to be true, then (b) cannot be. Subjectivists would point to (a) as a key premise in the argument that aesthetic judgments are too varied to fit with an objectivist account. Yet (b) fits better with a number of other factors in the world of aesthetics: (c) Judgments of beauty stem from deeply held beliefs about objective qualities in the works themselves (as I argued above), and (d) There are experts on beauty (such as critics, artists, and professional designers).[39] If (a) is true, then it will be hard to hold to an objective view of aesthetic value, as (a) suggests that objective aesthetic properties either do not exist or cannot be reliably known.

Belief in (a), that judgments of beauty are diverse and divisive, arises naturally enough from the observation that critics and regular folk often disagree about the excellence of aesthetic objects. Yet, these diverse reactions often stem from comprehensible causes. Here are two reasons why divergent opinions do not suggest a radically subjectivist aesthetic, (a), but fit better with (b):

1) Disagreements in aesthetic judgment are often not nearly as radical as they may seem. Very often aesthetic disputes are not about whether a work is on-the-whole good or bad, but exactly how good or bad the work is. Film critics will often argue about what the best movies of the year are, but will not dispute than another critic's top films are aesthetically good in some sense. A vast critical consensus does accrue around clearly great artists: e.g. Stravinsky, Picasso, Shakespeare, Hitchcock, etc., even if these artists are not originally viewed with universal admiration. Thus, there is a broad agreement on the aesthetic excellence of many works.

2) The nature of critical disagreements often have identifiable underlying causes:
   I. *Differing valuation of a particular aesthetic elements* (e.g. originality vs. faithfulness to a tradition; complexity vs. integrity; joyfulness vs. solemnity, ambiguity vs. clarity, etc.). When critics disagree, they often recognize the same elements in a work, yet place higher value on one aspect or another. Goethe, for instance, placed higher value on emotionality and organic structure, rather than the formal unity praised in Continental theater at the time.

II. *Difference of aesthetic training and cultural background.* It is no surprise that common people often find little to appreciate in modern art, as they often lack the knowledge of the surrounding context in which modern works are produced. The originality and references of these works are more apparent to those familiar with the context in which modern art is produced.[40] Likewise, great works of the past are situated in historical contexts unavailable to most modern people, and so proper evaluation is difficult.

III. *Intentional ambiguity in the work itself.* Contemporary fine art in particular is often produced with an explicit or underlying goal of being challenging to the viewer, naturally causing divergent reactions. Such reactions, then, suggest that viewers are responding in a fitting manner when they disagree about the work's value and meaning. Since Kant at least, originality has held a high value in the art world. Works aiming at originality often challenge our pre-existing categories for interpretation.

Thus far I have been referring to works of human making, but about the natural world an even greater consensus exists. As Mark Wynn indicates in *God and Goodness,* almost all people see natural scenes as beautiful.[41] When it comes to natural beauty, (b) is clearly a better fit, as there is a great common consensus on the beauty and ugliness of certain natural phenomena (e.g. spiders are relatively uniformly seen as less beautiful than butterflies).

After examination of the *prima facie* plausibility of (a), (b) seems to fit much better with the nature of aesthetic disagreements. Yet the reality of aesthetic disputes cannot be discounted entirely. However, when comparing our judgments about *objective aesthetic value* with our judgments about *objective moral value*, we will see that the two bear many similarities. This is important. As C. S. Lewis demonstrates in his appendix to *The Abolition of Man*, there is a great common consensus across cultures and time about basic moral values, principles and rules.[42] Yet moral disputes still arise, for reasons similar to aesthetic disputes. People have different contexts, backgrounds and priorities. Disputants often recognize the reasoning behind differing moral judgments, but differ on the weight assigned to certain values, or on the facts involved in making the judgment. However, few people are willing to reject the existence of objective moral values on the basis that people differ in certain moral judgments. Why is this?

Despite the similarity between moral evaluation and aesthetic evaluation (i.e. there is a wide common consensus on basic matters along with disagreement on more specific issues) many modern people treat moral and aesthetic values differently. This is no doubt largely due to the tacit influence of Kant and other Enlightenment thinkers like Hume, who laid the groundwork for a subjectivist understanding of aesthetic value. For Kant, the reasoning behind moral rules was explicable (via the categorical imperative) while the reasoning behind aesthetic judgments was not. Yet, despite the substantial critiques that have been offered against Kant's aesthetics, his basic assumptions remain the default.

AN ALTERNATIVE NARRATIVE

Instead of attempting to provide a more thorough critique of subjectivist aesthetics, I would like to offer a counter narrative, drawing on Christian theology, which will show both the disputes about beauty and our deeply held intuitions about its objectivity are comprehensible, fit naturally into a Christian worldview (like a puzzle piece), and therefore constitute further evidence for theism. In other words, the pieces themselves are made better sense of by being situated in the larger picture, and also thereby filling out the details of the larger whole.

First, since Kant, it has been common in aesthetics to view aesthetic perception as separated from non-aesthetic judgments. The "aesthetic attitude" (so the line of thinking goes) attends only to aesthetic features, without considering other moral, conceptual, or practical considerations.[43] Yet this either/or separation is dubious. As Eddy Zemach points out, all aesthetic perception is already aware of conceptual categories: "No seeing is uncategorized: for aesthetic appreciation one needs to be aware of sizes, shapes, and colors, yet these are categories too."[44]

Likewise, perception of beauty often involves consideration of other practical values. Aesthetic perception of a castle at Disney World is different than the perception of an identical castle dating from the fourteenth-century. The difficulty of the latter project increases aesthetic appreciation. Likewise, a series of accidental paint splatters on a drop cloth must be evaluated differently than those identical splatters on a Jackson Pollack painting. The intentions of the artist shape our perception and understanding of the work itself.[45] Further, as Berys Gaut has pointed out, the moral dimension of a work of art has bearing on its aesthetic effect.[46] A derogatory joke may make us laugh spontaneously, but in morally-astute people, the laughter is accompanied by a sense of revulsion, which is part of the aesthetic effect.

If values cannot be neatly separated out in the way that Kant suggests, this shows us two things: (1) Aesthetic judgments are bound up in host of other moral, conceptual, and practical considerations, and therefore require bringing to bear the sum total of a person's understanding of these values for proper evaluation. This reveals why aesthetic disputes often arise, but also illuminates how they can be resolved: by consideration of the other dimensions at play in the aesthetic object. The interconnectedness of values reveals a further feature, connected to Plantinga's argument: (2) If God, in His very being, is the source of truth, goodness, and beauty (held together in unity), we would expect aesthetic judgments to require considerations of the full range of value. Christian theism readily explains why perception of truth and goodness is essential to sound aesthetic judgment.

Third, like moral judgments, aesthetic judgment requires development over time.[47] Good taste is not our default setting. It seems true that we have basic aesthetic and moral judgments to work with. This explains how there is a basic consensus about morality and beauty. But it also explains how there is divergence of judgment on more complex issues. This fits naturally with Christian theology, as the majority consensus among theologians is that all humans have access to basic evaluative intuitions through the grace of God, even in our fallen state (cf. Rom. 1:20 and Jn. 1:4), yet because of our fallenness we lack a natural understanding of more complex values and have many erroneous beliefs and sinful desires.[48] Even with the aid of divine grace, we often err in our evaluations. For instance, aesthetic judgment involves a moral ability to value things outside ourselves (similar, but not identical to Kant's "disinterestedness," perhaps "agape" is a better word), but (unlike Kant), it is not an attitude one can adopt in the moment.[49] Accurate aesthetic judgment requires, in a sense, a sort of ongoing sanctification of taste.

Fourth (though connected to this previous point), even for Christians who are in the process of developing good taste, the ultimate beauty of God challenges our natural ways of understanding beauty. Hans Urs von Balthasar reflects on how our "this-worldly" categories of beauty must be affirmed, yet at the same time should be expected to break down as we encounter the beauty of God Himself through the forms of His self-revelation.[50] The beauty of the cross seems to defy everything we know to be beautiful, and yet it is. Balthasar writes, "As Karl Barth has rightly seen . . . ['glory'] extends to the inclusion in Christian beauty of even the Cross and everything else which a worldly aesthetics (even of a realistic kind) discards as no longer bearable."[51] Balthasar does not deny that we do perceive this-worldly beauty, but that our judgments of the beautiful must continually be sharpened and revised as we see more of the beauty of God. This "Yes" and "No" about our capacity to perceive beauty affirms, in a sense, the reality of the difficulty of aesthetic judgment (*a la* (a)), but without casting doubt on our ability to perceive objective beauty (*a la* (b)). Perhaps, we might even say, that God's beauty is a bit like the work of the modern artist, whose highest beauty also comes with the greatest challenges.

Because of the interconnectedness of aesthetic judgments with other kinds of moral and conceptual judgments, I think it should be clear that it is unfair to aesthetic judgments to treat them as a separate kind of thing from other judgments. If we are willing to hold on to objective moral values (which most people are), despite differences of opinion at times, then we should be willing to hold on to objective aesthetic values. Returning to William Davis's point about the special prejudice directed at non-utilitarian values such as beauty, this prejudice seems to owe more to habits of thinking in modern thought, than to serious arguments.

My main point here, though, is to address objections to an objectivist view of beauty because of the supposed intractability of aesthetic disputes, and to do it in a way that shows these disputes are what we would expect on Christian theism. To sum up, if the Christian God exists, who is beautiful in His very nature, we would expect there to be objective beauty. Because this God is the creator of the world, and it reflects His nature, we would expect the world to be invested with a great amount of objective beauty. We would also expect, given the claims of Christian theology, that beauty would be integrated with other values in a way that reflects the ultimate union of Beauty with Truth and Goodness in the nature of God. Further, because of both our fallenness and the ongoing grace of God to give access to basic perception of value, we would expect perception of beauty to be difficult-yet-achievable. It would difficult to judge rightly in a fully consistent manner, especially as regards more complex aesthetic objects, yet we should retain a capacity to discern beauty, one that deepens as we grow in our knowledge of God and his revelation in Christ. There *is* a great amount of objective beauty (and it is integrated-and-knowable-yet-difficult), therefore these facts about beauty are evidence, not just for theism, but for Christian theism.

THE ARGUMENT FROM PLAY

Again, is his paper "Two Dozen (or so) Theistic Arguments," Alvin Plantinga suggests a direction that an argument from "play and enjoyment" might take:

> *The Argument from Play and Enjoyment.* Fun, pleasure, humor, play, enjoyment. (Maybe not all to be thought of in the same way.) Playing: evolution: an adaptive means of preparing for adult life (so that engaging in this sort of thing as an adult suggests a case of arrested development). But surely there is more to it than that. The joy one can take in humor, art, poetry, mountaineering, exploring, adventuring (the problem is not to explain how it would come about that human beings enjoyed mountaineering: no doubt evolution can do so. The problem is with its significance. Is it really true that all there is to this is enjoyment? Or is there a deeper significance? The Westminster Shorter Catechism: the chief end of man is to glorify God and enjoy him (and his creation and gifts) forever).[52]

Plantinga ends his notes for a possible argument with a question rather than a conclusion. Is it true that (on a naturalistic explanation) all there is to play is an adaptive mechanism to prepare us for adult life? Or is there something deeper going on? If there is something deeper going on, this would make play (or humor, or mountaineering) evidence for the truth of the Westminster Shorter Catechism's affirmation.

In discussing whether "something deeper" is going on with play (in its various forms), the field is wide open. Almost nothing has been written that bears on this issue directly. This brings all the advantages and disadvantages of an underexplored question. How exactly would one argue that play is "significant?"

One way to make an argument would be to suggest that certain finite and fleeting goods foreshadow ultimate and eternal ones. Perhaps our enjoyment of play gives a foretaste of some deeper satisfaction found in God, in the same way that our desire for love and acceptance can never be satisfied fully in the *here* and *now*, and thus suggests an ultimate satisfaction for this desire we are *there* with God, *later*. Perhaps the satisfaction we receive from play is of this sort: a prefiguring. In order to make the case, we have to first talk about what play is, and why we do it.

Johan Huizinga, in his seminal work, *Homo Ludens: A Study of the Play Element in Culture,* identifies a number of key features that define play. Play is "voluntary," "not 'ordinary,'" "limited" in time and place; both "ordered" and at the same time "enchanting."[53] In other words, play is a finite and free activity, which is both fun and also structured by rules. The fun and rules are connected because a play's rules are not separable from the play itself. The game could not exist without them. Whether playing Monopoly or make-believe, the ludic constraints, if violated, break the spell of the delightful enchantment.[54]

Play is, as Huizinga points out, much like the sacramental rituals of the church, which mark our sacred space, time, and actions for celebration that is distinct from "normal" life.[55] Yet there is still a notable difference, as the sacramental worship of the church is commanded, and therefore in one key sense is not "voluntary." Still, the similarity is telling. Worship and play both pursue an intrinsically delightful goal through ordered means that are inseparable from the goal itself. Likewise the defined actions of worship are not separable from the worship itself (e.g., communion liturgies, baptismal formulae, or creedal affirmations). Christian worship depends on the given forms. We cannot invent our own sacraments or creeds. The nature of communal worship depends on fidelity to a *tradition.*

Returning to a specific discussion of play, Bernard Suits has argued that play (through games, especially) can be seen as the highest human activity, because it is one we would still undertake when all other needs are cared for. As Suits argues, "because in Utopia all instrumental activities have been eliminated. . . .What we need, therefore, is some activity in which what is instrumental is inseparable combined with what is intrinsically valuable."[56] Games, argues Suits, "fit this requirement perfectly."[57] When we are fed, sheltered, have access to all knowledge, and are sexually satisfied (in other words, when there is nothing left to *do*), we would still actively seek out games.[58] Suits's point backs up Huizinga's, in that playing a game is a voluntary attempt to overcome unnecessary obstacles, undertaken freely for the pleasure of the attempt itself.[59]

If offering an account of games as the highest form of activity, because they are ones we would pursue when all other needs have been taken care of, Suits has offered a kind of secular eschatology, a vision for the highest kind of satisfaction. Yet it seems as though Suits has unnecessarily limited his scope for what kinds of satisfaction humans might desire. Though games are, indeed, enjoyable in the sense he indicates, perhaps they are not as satisfying as we might want.

It is worth noting that games, especially competitive ones, can often be frustrating and disappointing to the losers. And we grow bored with games, especially ones we have mastered. It is no fun to lose at competitive games, and it is no fun to continually win at them either. To be sure, of the making of games there can be no end. New sports, new artworks, new kinds of make-believe can continually be invented. But, on a long enough timeline, might we not tire of games themselves, especially if they are our only form of challenge in utopia? This seems quite possible, even likely. The mountaineer can scale higher and higher peaks, just for the sake of it (because it's *there*) and after mastering the highest summits, take on new challenges, such as free climbing, and speed climbing. After mastering all these skills and all possible peaks, she may well grow weary of climbing, and take up another sport. The cycle of growing mastery followed by creeping boredom could follow ad infinitum.

Is there, then, an activity that is delightful-yet-structured, in which the instrumental means are inseparable from the goals, and which will never result in boredom? Christian theism here again has an answer. The worship of God forever, which is constituted by our delight in God, and which continually transforms us from glory into "ever-increasing glory" is one such activity.[60] In fact, is the only candidate for a highest activity which would be perpetually enjoyable. Because God is a perfect reality, and therefore is intrinsically worthy of worship, and whose redemptive love can continually transform us into greater and greater likeness to him, would be, in a sense the enjoyment prefigured by the delight of free-yet-orderly play. The instrumental means of glorifying God (worship) are inseparable combined with what is intrinsically valuable (enjoying Him and his gifts, forever).

Thus, this suggests that desire for the kind of enjoyment we find in play cannot be satisfied *fully* on naturalism, but it can be with a robust Christian theism. This brings us back to the way we framed the argument. The enjoyment of play prefigures the enjoyment of glorifying God. Our desire for enjoyment through play is a foretaste of the ultimate utopia: kingdom come. As Lewis writes in *Mere Christianity,*

> The Christian says, 'Creatures are not born with desires unless satisfaction for those desires exists . . . If I find in myself a desire which no experience in this world can satisfy, the most probable explanation is that I was made for another world. If none of my earthly pleasures satisfy it, that does not prove that the universe is a fraud. Probably earthly pleasures were never meant to satisfy it, but only to arouse it, to suggest the real thing. If that is so, I must take care, on the one hand, never to despise, or be unthankful for, these earthly blessings, and on the other, never to mistake them for the something else of which they are only a kind of copy, or echo, or mirage.[61]

NOTES

1. Hans Urs von Balthasar, *The Glory of the Lord: Volume I: Seeing the Form* (San Francisco: Ignatius, 1982), 18.

2. Friedrich Nietzsche, *Beyond Good & Evil*, Preface.

3. Ibid.

4. There are, of course, exceptions, such as the aforementioned Hans Urs von Balthasar, Jonathan Edwards, and Alfred North Whitehead.

5. Balthasar, *The Glory of the Lord*, 17.

6. Karl Barth, *Church Dogmatics, vol. III, 3, The Doctrine of Creation*, trans. G.W. Bromiley and R.J. Ehrlich (Edinburgh: T&T Clark, 1960), 297–298. I should also mention an interesting quote from an article by Theodore Gill that touches on this interesting role beauty-as-general-revelation can play in the mind of unexpected people: "And with a now not so secret delight, I remember noting as I left Barth's study on a first visit those portraits of Calvin and of Mozart hanging over the adjacent doors. He has written of them: 'There are probably very few theological study rooms in which pictures of Calvin and Mozart are to be seen hanging next to each other and at the same height.' What he does not write is what he said when he noticed how taken I was with the juxtaposition. 'My special revelation,' he smiled, looking at Calvin. 'And my general revelation,' he said, as he beamed at Mozart. Was he smiling because it was a joke? Or because he knew something we didn't?" (Theodore A. Gill, "Editorial," *Theology Today* 43.3 (1986)).

7. Another example is William C. Davis's brief exploration of the possibility of arguments from objective, non-utilitarian value. In his essay "Theistic Arguments" in *Reason for the Hope Within* (ed. Michael J. Murray, Grand Rapids, MI: Eerdmans, 1999), Davis briefly raises the possibility of an argument from beauty, but doesn't press it. This is understandable given the constraints of a short essay. I mention this just as another example of the occasional nods, but scant exploration, of this kind of theistic argument.

8. Peter Kreeft and Ronald K. Tacelli, *Handbook of Christian Apologetic* (Downers Grove, IL: InterVarsity, 1994), 81.

9. For example, here's how Kant deals with aesthetic disputes where proofs are brought to bear on taste: "If a man reads me a poem of his or brings me to a play, which does not after all suit my taste, he may bring forward in proof of the beauty of his poem Batteux or Lessing or still more ancient and famous critics of taste, and all the rules laid down by them; certain passages which displease me may agree very well with rules of beauty (as they have been put forth by these writers and are universally recognised): but I stop my ears, I will listen to no arguments and no reasoning; and I will rather assume that these rules of the critics are false, or at least that they do not apply to the case in question, than admit that my judgement should be determined by grounds of proof a priori. For it is to be a judgement of Taste and not of Understanding or Reason." (Immanuel Kant, *Critique of Judgment*, trans. J.H. Bernard (London: Macmillan, 1914), §33)

10. For instance, in a debate with theist Jerry Walls about the problem of evil, Peter S. Fosl admitted that sometimes, listening to Cat Stevens' "Morning Has Broken," his deep agnosticism becomes much less certain. Likewise, in another video debate, atheist Jamie Kilstein admitted that the last bastion of his belief in God was the abundance of beauty in the world (Kilstein, Jaime. "A Debate between an Atheist and a Christian." April 25, 2015. Accessed February 27, 2016. https://www.facebook.com/jamiekilsteinfanpage/videos/1130691933614763/.)

11. Anthony O'Hear, *After Progress* (London: Bloomsbury, 1999), 199, 201.

12. Paul Draper, "Seeking but not Believing," in *Divine Hiddenness: New Essays*, eds. Daniel Howard-Snyder and Paul K. Moser (Cambridge University Press, 2001), 204.

13. Philip Tallon, *The Poetics of Evil* (New York: Oxford University Press, 2012), 39.

14. Ibid., 99.

15. St. Basil the Great, "Exegetical Works, On the Hexameron (Homily 1)," Cited in *Theological Aesthetics: A Reader*, ed. Gesa Elsbeth Thiessen (Grand Rapids, MI: Eerdmans, 2005), 39.

16. Cited in James F. Cooper, *Knights of the Brush* (New York: Hudson Hills Press, 1999), 45.

17. Richard Swinburne, *The Existence of God*, 2nd ed. (Oxford: Oxford University Press, 2004), 190.

18. Ibid.

19. Ibid.

20. Davis, "Theistic Arguments." 39.

21. Mark Wynn, *God and Goodness: A Natural Theological Perspective* (London: Routledge, 1999), 20.

22. Ibid., 16.

23. Ibid., 17.

24. Alvin Plantinga, "Appendix: Two Dozen (or so) Theistic Arguments," *Alvin Plantinga*, ed Deane-Peter Baker (Cambridge: Cambridge University Press, 2007), 226.

25. C.S. Lewis, *The Abolition of Man* (San Francisco: HarperOne, 2000), 16.

26. Elaine Scarry's book, *On Beauty and Being Just,* helpfully explores the connection between beauty and morality. She writes, "We saw that the fact that a thing is beautiful is bound up with the urge to protect it, or to act on its behalf" (Princeton UP, 1999), 80.

27. Eddy M. Zemach, *Real Beauty* (University Park, PA: Pennsylvania UP, 1997), 6.

28. Ibid., 7.

29. I strongly "commend" Zemach's work for a fuller account, as I can only sketch a few of his many arguments in brief.

30. Eddy M. Zemach, *Real Beauty.*

31. Ibid., 43.

32. Ibid., 42–43.

33. Ibid., 43.

34. For more on this, see Wynn, *God and Goodness,* 27.

35. Ibid., 32.

36. Plantinga, "Two Dozen (or so) Theistic Arguments," 226.

37. Ibid.

38. This view is, of course, not exclusive to everyday folks, and can be found articulated by professional philosophers of art, such as Anne Shephard, in *Aesthetics: An Introduction to the Philosophy of Art* (Oxford: Oxford University Press, 1987), who writes, "We shall see that the nature of critical arguments suggests there is no one correct interpretation or evaluation of a given work" (77).

39. This part of my argument was helpfully shaped by an argument offered by Keith E. Buhler, a PhD candidate at the University of Kentucky on the blog *Mere Orthodoxy.* (https://mereorthodoxy.com/is-beauty-objective/ (Accessed May 26, 2016)).

40. Cf. Daniel A. Siedell, *God in the Gallery: A Christian Embrace of Modern Art* (Grand Rapids, MI: Baker, 2008), 22–24.

41. Wynn, *God and Goodness,* 24.

42. Lewis, *The Abolition of Man,* Appendix.

43. One representative example of a post-Kantian aesthetic is found in Jerome Stolnitz's essay, "The Aesthetic Attitude" (in *Introductory Readings in Aesthetics,* ed. John Hospers (NY: Free Press, 1969). Stolnitz writes, "I will define 'the aesthetic attitude' as 'disinterested and sympathetic attention to and contemplation of any object of awareness whatever, for its own sake alone....For the aesthetic attitude, things are not to be classified or studied or judged" (20).

44. Zemach, *Real Beauty,* 36.

45. For a more thorough response to Kantian separation of aesthetic perception from other kinds of moral, practical, or religious considerations, see Frank Burch Brown's *Religious Aesthetics*

(Princeton UP, 1989), especially pages 16–46. See also Balthasar's *The Glory of the Lord,* page 118, wherein Balthasar makes this profound point, "But a true grasp of . . . [the beautiful] will not be attained unless one brings to bear logical and ethical concepts, concepts of truth and value: in a word, concepts drawn from a comprehensive doctrine of Being."

46. For more on this, see Berys Gaut's discussion of the interconnection of ethics and aesthetics in "The Ethical Criticism of Art" (in *Aesthetics and Ethics: Essays at the Intersection,* ed. Jerrold Levinson (Cambridge: Cambridge University Press, 1998), especially pages 195–196.

47. Frank Burch Brown's book *Good Taste, Bad Taste, and Christian Taste: Aesthetics in Religious Life* (New York: Oxford University Press, 2000) offers a robust examination of the process of developing taste through holistic formation.

48. Cf. St. Augustine, *Confessions,* 4.15. St. Thomas Aquinas, *Summa Theologica,* Ia, Q2, Art. 2. John Calvin, *Institutes of Christian Religion,* I.5.1–2.

49. For more on this, see Frank Burch Brown, *Good Taste, Bad Taste, and Christian Taste: Aesthetics in Religious Life* (Oxford: Oxford University Press, 2000), 172–173.

50. Balthasar writes, "[A]dmittedly the divine principle of form must in many ways stand in sharp contrast to the beauty of this world. This contrast notwithstanding, however, if God's will to give form really aims at man as God truly wants to shape him–aims, that is, at the perfecting of that work begun by God's 'hands' in the Garden of Eden–then it appears impossible to deny that there exists an analogy between God's work of formation and the shaping forces of nature and of man as they generate and give birth. . . .This is why, when we approach God's revelation with the category of the beautiful, we quite spontaneously bring this category with us in its this-worldly form. It is only when such a this-worldly aesthetics does not fit revelation's transcendent form that we suddenly come to an astonished halt." Balthasar, *The Glory of the Lord,* 36–37.

51. Ibid., 124.

52. Plantinga, "Two Dozen (or so) Theistic Arguments," 226–227.

53. Johan Huizinga, *Homo Ludens: A Study of the Play Element in Culture* (Boston: Beacon, 1955),7–10.

54. Huizinga gives one example of a child sitting in the front of a row of four chairs, "playing 'trains,' " and warning his father not to "kiss the engine, Daddy, or the carriages won't think it's 'real' " (ibid., 9). Huizinga goes on, "The inferiority of play is continually being offset by the corresponding superiority of its seriousness. Play turns to seriousness and seriousness to play" (ibid., 10). This element of seriousness leads into the orderliness of play. "Play demands order absolute and supreme. The least deviation from it "spoils the game," robs it of its character and makes it worthless" (ibid., 11).

55. Ibid., 20.

56. Ibid., 154

57. Ibid.

58. Bernard Suits, *The Grasshopper* (Peterborough, Ontario: Broadview, 2005), 149–160, *passim.*

59. Ibid., 10.

60. 2. Cor. 3:18., NIV.

61. C.S. Lewis, *Mere Christianity* (New York: HarperCollins, 2000), 136–137.

(W)

Arguments from Providence and from Miracles

OF MIRACLES: THE STATE OF THE ART
AND THE USES OF HISTORY

Timothy McGrew

IN THE MIDDLE of the twentieth century, most philosophical discussions of the topic began with Hume's famous critique in his essay "Of Miracles." And as a quick trawl through philosophy of religion anthologies will confirm, most discussions ended there, as well, with a bit of haggling over details or perhaps an attempt to reformulate Hume's argument for modern ears.[1] Although as a philosophy student I had more than an average interest in this issue, I cannot recall ever once being told by any of my professors that there was anything else of significance to read on the subject. We were all, no doubt, dimly aware that thinkers like Augustine and Aquinas had written something or other about miracles, but in our post-Humean era, *that* was of no consequence. Why should we clamber back through the dusty volumes of the *Summa* or go on a hunt for even more obscure authors when we possessed a silver bullet, an "everlasting check to all sorts of superstitious delusion"?

How we moved out of this philosophical "steady state" half a century ago into the dynamic and expanding field of inquiry we enjoy today is as interesting a question as how we got stuck in it. At least two factors, I think, are responsible for rousing philosophy from its dogmatic slumber. The first is the modern refinement of probabilistic tools of analysis; the second is the rediscovery of the fact that this subject has a history. The former brings us up to the present. The latter takes us back in time but may, if I am not mistaken, help us to map the future as well.

THE COLLAPSE OF CONSENSUS

Hume's argument against miracles is—must be, because of his empiricism—a non-deductive argument. Beginning in the late 1960s, Bayesian methods of modeling non-deductive arguments found their way into the philosophical mainstream, first in the philosophy of science and shortly thereafter in the philosophy of religion as well.[2] Soon enough, Hume's admirers began to apply those methods to his famous argument, assuming at first that if only a few details about the proper representation of Hume's claim could be tidied up, this procedure would yield a satisfying and rigorous formulation of his objection to reported miracles.[3]

It did not. And as attempt after attempt ended in failure, a horrible suspicion arose that the reason for the failures lay not in a lack of technical ingenuity on the part of Hume's advocates but in the objection itself. By the late 1990s, the suspicion was confirmed by several different authors: Hume's objection, probabilistically formulated, does not work.[4] The "everlasting check" began to look like nothing more than a longstanding urban legend.

The reactions of the Humean faithful have been remarkably varied. Some have urged that Hume's argument *cannot* be reconstructed along Bayesian lines because (strange to relate!) there is no consensus on what Hume's argument is or what he is trying to establish with it.[5] Others have decided that despite what almost everyone had understood since the first publication of his Essay, Hume never was trying to establish an absolute barrier to belief in miracles but was just setting the bar rather high—and anyone who thinks otherwise is a "gross misreader" of Hume.[6] Yet others have proposed that perhaps we can capture Hume's intention best by abandoning ordinary mathematical frameworks and adopting nonstandard analysis or non-Pascalian probability.[7] Such disarray among forces that, within living memory, held essentially unchallenged sway over the field is astonishing. The very fact that someone has, in the twenty-first century, felt it necessary to publish a book with the title *A Defense of Hume on Miracles* is a testament to the magnitude of the revolution. Fifty years ago, the publication of a book with such a title would have been almost as unthinkable as the publication—by an agnostic—of a book on the subject of miracles entitled *Hume's Abject Failure*.

The recognition of the breakdown of Hume's argument under a probabilistic reconstruction has paved the way for several other developments, both critical and constructive. On the critical side, certain other limitative claims regarding probabilistic arguments for reported miracles have been shown wanting. Three of these merit particular mention. First, in the opening chapter of his book *The Miracle of Theism*, J.L. Mackie claims that a reported miracle cannot have evidential force for anyone who does not already believe in the existence of God. His assertion is sufficiently bold to be worth quoting:

[I]t is pretty well impossible that reported miracles should provide a worthwhile argument for theism addressed to those who are initially inclined to atheism or even to agnosticism. Such reports can form no significant part of what, following Aquinas, we might call a *Summa contra Gentiles*, or what, following Descartes, we could describe as being addressed to infidels. Not only are such reports unable to carry any rational conviction on their own, but also they are unable even to contribute independently to the kind of accumulation or battery of arguments referred to in the Introduction. To this extent Hume is right. (27)

Mackie's claim was not original—it can be found in John Stuart Mill[8]—and did not go unchallenged; it was contested on informal grounds several times in the philosophical literature.[9] But as Richard Otte showed in 1996, within a Bayesian framework, which Mackie himself elsewhere adopts, the claim collapses at once: for it is tantamount to saying that where H is the hypothesis of a miracle and E is testimony to the miracle, $P(H|E) > P(H)$ only when $P(H) \geq k$, where k is some substantial value, say 0.5. There is not the slightest Bayesian rationale for this stipulation.[10]

A second technical point is even more striking: under a few fairly weak and general assumptions, Hume's pessimistic conclusion can be shown to be false. The proof of this point was worked out first by Charles Babbage in his *Ninth Bridgewater Treatise*, as Earman notes, but it can be put in a simpler form. Suppose that there are testimonies $T_1, \ldots, T_n$ to a miraculous event M, $P(M) > 0$, such that, for all *i*,

$$\frac{P(T_i|M)}{P(T_i|\sim M)} = k > 1,$$

and suppose that these testimonies are *independent*. Define $T_n = df. (T_1 \, \& \, \ldots \, \& \, T_n)$. Then:

$$\lim_{n \to \infty} \frac{P(M|T_n)}{P(\sim M|T_n)} = \lim_{n \to \infty} \frac{P(M)}{P(\sim M)} \times \frac{P(T_n|M)}{P(T_n|\sim M)} = \lim_{n \to \infty} \frac{P(M)}{P(\sim M)} \times k^n = \infty$$

The cumulative weight of independent testimony can overcome any finite presumption against a miracle. Or, in layman's terms, *Hume is wrong*.

We can even weaken these assumptions. For example, suppose that we dispense with the assumption that all of the testimonies are of equal force. If there exists some $k > 1$ such that, for all *i*,

$$\frac{P(T_i|M)}{P(T_i|\sim M)} \geq k,$$

then, so long as the independence assumption is still in place,

$$\lim_{n \to \infty} \frac{P(M|T_n)}{P(\sim M|T_n)} \geq \lim_{n \to \infty} \frac{P(M)}{P(\sim M)} \times k^n = \infty$$

Even the assumption of independence can be dropped provided that the values of the successive likelihood ratios being multiplied do not converge to 1 too rapidly.[11]

A third technical failure arose from an unexpected quarter. In the third volume of his *Warrant* trilogy, Alvin Plantinga mounts a criticism of the historical case for Christianity, claiming that Swinburne's argument is vulnerable to something that Plantinga calls the Principle of Dwindling Probabilities. This Principle turns out to be closely related to an innocuous bit of mathematics known as the chain rule:

$$P(A \& B \& C \& D \& E) = P(A) \times P(B|A) \times P(C|A \& B) \times P(D|A \& B \& C)$$
$$\times P(E|A \& B \& C \& D)$$

If the numbers on the right side of the equation are only moderately high, then—since all probabilities are normalized between 0 and 1—their product will rapidly diminish toward a disappointingly small number.

How someone technically sophisticated enough to understand the chain rule in probability could have thought that he could give a proper representation of Swinburne's argument without making any use of Bayes's Theorem remains, to this day, an unsolved mystery. But the critique based on the PDP unquestionably collapses, for several reasons.[12] First, if the background information is rich enough (as Swinburne and many others would argue it is) to give a high probability not merely to bare theism but also to specific versions of theism, then numbers such as Plantinga supplies for the relevant conditional probabilities are misleadingly low. Second, and more importantly, the *prior* probability for bare theism (say) does not place an upper bound on the conditional probability of theism together with more specific doctrines, *given additional specific relevant evidence*. There is simply no general rule governing the transition between

P(God exists)

and

P(God exists & Moses parted the waters|specific historical testimony to the latter event).

Everything here depends on the details. There is no legitimate way to escape from the thicket of special questions. There is no silver bullet.

On the constructive side, a number of recent developments deserve special notice. First, there is a renewed interest in the project of ramified natural theology—the extension of the project of natural theology into the specific claims of particular religious traditions. In a striking illustration of this new trend, Richard Swinburne, having meticulously mapped the contours of the traditional arguments for the existence of God, has moved forward to a discussion of the New Testament as a body of evidence, considered against the broader background evidence already covered in his earlier works, for the resurrection of God incarnate.[13]

Second, the question of modern-day miracles, including medical events documented in Western hospitals, has recently been opened in earnest.[14] The very suggestion is staggering. A healthy dose of initial skepticism seems quite warranted. But if we have learned any lesson from the collapse of Hume's "everlasting check," it should be that we have no right to put such claims beyond the reach of evidence.

Third, there are signs of renewed interest in a wider circle of events that might count as special divine action than merely prodigious signs and wonders. The argument from predictive prophecy, for example, which Hume brushed aside as merely a special case of the miraculous, deserves and is beginning to receive analysis in its own right.[15] What used to be called "special providences," in which the extraordinary element lies not in any obvious violation of the causal closure of the physical world but rather in the auspicious timing of apparently independent events, are now on the table for serious discussion.

Fourth, there is an active discussion of alternative models of special divine action. The traditional intervention model remains a major feature of discussion, but recent work has also explored the possibility of non-interventionist models, exploring the intersection of philosophy of religion with quantum theory and chaos theory.[16]

A common theme in all of these developments is that they are intrinsically, intensely interdisciplinary. Each of the fields of study required to move the discussion forward— history, philosophy, mathematics, physics, biblical studies, comparative religion, cultural anthropology, cognitive science, and others—is deep and rich enough to absorb and to reward a lifetime's effort even for individuals of extraordinary talents. We should expect, therefore, that some of the most interesting advances will take place where there is significant collaborative work being done.

THE PRESENT HORIZON

I suggested at the beginning that philosophy was roused out of its twentieth-century complacency on the issue of special divine action by two factors: advances in probabilistic modeling, and the rediscovery of the fact that this issue has a history. That rediscovery can be well traced in four important books appearing over the course of twenty-five years.

In his 1981 study of the deist controversy, *The Great Debate on Miracles from Joseph Glanvill to David Hume*, Robert Burns reveals the sources of many of Hume's objections, demonstrating that Hume was neither the first nor the last word on the subject of miracles even within the eighteenth century.[17] Without making any particularly important advances in argument, Burns's historical work undermines the illusion of Hume's *originality* on this topic.

Joseph Houston's book *Reported Miracles: A Critique of Hume*, which appeared in 1994, has a more polemical tone, but it, too, takes a historical view of the subject, going back to Augustine and Aquinas and Locke, treating Hume—notwithstanding his prominent place in the title—as just one voice in a larger conversation.[18] Simply by doing this, Houston's work subverts the concept of Hume's *centrality* to the discussion.

John Earman's book *Hume's Abject Failure*, which came out in 2000, had, of course, its principal impact on the technical side.[19] But what some reviewers seem to have lost sight of is that Earman devotes more than half of the book to reprinting older sources on the subject of miracles and that he says, quite explicitly, that many of Hume's contemporaries on the Christian side of the debate demonstrated a better grasp of the subtleties of inductive reasoning than Hume himself had. In its own way, this frank admission that Hume's contemporaries actually had the better of the argument is as damaging as the formal critique of that argument itself. The second half of Earman's work undermines Hume's *predominance* over his contemporaries.

Timothy Larsen's brilliant historical study *Crisis of Doubt*, first published in 2006, is not a discussion of Hume at all, though Hume's name crops up about a dozen times in the text.[20] Larsen tells the story of seven reconverts—men who lost their faith and became active in the Victorian freethinking and secularist movement but then reconsidered their doubts, returned to the faith of their youth, and devoted a substantial number of years to preaching, lecturing, or writing on behalf of their recovered faith. Hume was, in many cases, one of the causes of their loss of faith. But after their reconversions, several of them expressly and articulately repudiated Hume's arguments. Larsen's book effectively dispels the myth of Hume's *mastery* over reflective intellects.

BACK TO THE FUTURE

That, in brief, is the story of we came to the state of the art in the philosophical discussion of special divine action. What comes next?

This is the place where telling the story gets tricky, for of course I have no special insight into the future. To see beyond one's own blind spots, one needs eyes that are free from them. But where to find them? Here, I think, C.S. Lewis offers an important clue:

> Every age has its own outlook. It is specially good at seeing certain truths and specially liable to make certain mistakes. We all, therefore, need the books that will correct the characteristic mistakes of our own period. And that means the old books.[21]

Of course older authors have their own blind spots as well. And we have, in some respects, moved on; we know things now that even the best scholars writing in the eighteenth and nineteenth centuries did not know. But they also knew some things that we may have forgotten. If I may appropriate a phrase from T.S. Eliot, the communication of the dead is sometimes tongued with fire beyond the language of the living. Time and again I have approached the threshold of some long-abandoned controversy, expecting to see nothing but cold ashes in the grate, only to discover live coals still smoldering there, wanting only a breath of fresh air to burst into open flame.

I have space here for just a handful of illustrations. There are whole categories of argument currently employed in the investigation of historical claims, including claims of divine action, that cry out for both philosophical and historical analysis. Consider the argument from silence—typically, the argument that because some person or place or event is unmentioned in a particular historical text, or perhaps unmentioned in any text we now possess, that person or place never existed, or the event never transpired. It takes only passing familiarity with scholarship both of the Old and of the New Testament to reveal how pervasive this form of reasoning is. Shouldn't Paul have mentioned more details about Jesus's life, if he actually knew them? Shouldn't the authors of the Synoptic Gospels have mentioned the resurrection of Lazarus, if it had really happened? Shouldn't Josephus have mentioned the slaughter of the innocents in Bethlehem? And for heaven's sake, why doesn't anyone besides Matthew say something about those resurrected saints walking about Jerusalem just after Jesus's resurrection, "seen by many"?

What we need to inform our judgment about arguments from silence is both analytical and historical information. What is the proper way to reconstruct such arguments? And given the reconstruction, what sorts of information might help us to evaluate them? For the reconstruction, modern tools are needed. But buried in the annals of previous centuries of controversy we can find a wealth of examples where the argument from silence fails, and fails *spectacularly*. The existence of the works of Thucydides, for example, is not noted by any author whose works we now possess until two hundred fifty years after they were written. Grafton's *Chronicles*, which embrace the reign of King John, make no reference to *Magna Carta*. In the extensive memoirs of Ulysses Grant, Lincoln's general during the American Civil War, there is no mention of the Emancipation Proclamation. Neither Herodotus nor Thucydides, nor any of their contemporaries mentions Rome, even in passing, a point Josephus brings up in his controversy with Apion.[22] In his sprawling travelogue, Marco Polo never refers to the Great Wall of China, or tea, or printed books. Examples of this sort could be multiplied almost endlessly. At what point is it unreasonable for us, in the face of an avalanche of such examples, to retain our initial confidence regarding what ancient authors *would* have said?[23]

Or take the problem of criteria of historicity, currently a hotly contested issue. Among the criteria commonly employed by historians is the criterion of embarrassment. How shall we construe this criterion? And how much weight will it bear? Contemporary scholars are not unified in their approach, but many of them are unhappy with the present use of such criteria.[24] If we are not too proud, we might travel back nearly three centuries to find insight from the participants in the deist controversy who wrote about the same concept under a different terminology and gave serious thought to the methodological issues surrounding its use. Thus, the dissenting minister James Foster, after having canvassed several instances of the candor of the Gospel authors, acknowledges that this consideration is not by itself a guarantee of truth and concludes: "I shall lay no more stress upon it than it deserves; and consider it not as direct proof, but as a circumstance that looks well, and in conjunction with others, must have its weight."[25] Foster's modesty is becoming, but it should not lead us to overlook the deeper fact that he locates the appeal to this criterion within the framework of a cumulative case. A modern Bayesian will at once recognize how such a consideration might contribute to a likelihood ratio; a modern historian will see a field for the investigation of candor and its counterfeits in both genuine and spurious works.

A vivid awareness of the manner in which diverse pieces of evidence may contribute to a case is a hallmark of some of the best work of the eighteenth and nineteenth centuries. Perhaps that is due to the interest taken in the subject by members, some of them eminent members, of the legal profession—Simon Greenleaf, Edmund Bennett, Benjamin Shaw, Walter M. Chandler, George Griffin, Charles Robert Morrison, and Francis Jones Lamb, to name just a few of the older writers. Such authors have a good deal to say on the subject of weighing evidence. When we find Shaw, for example, speaking of "the manner in which a number of distinct lines of proof converge in a common centre," I suggest that we should sit up and take notice.

Sometimes work done for one purpose may serve us well for another, slightly different one. I mentioned the task of collecting and sifting through the documentation for modern miracle claims. Here we may find guidance in the work of writers like John Douglas who sought to lay out criteria for distinguishing genuine from spurious miracle reports.[26] There are grounds for doubt, Douglas suggests, if the report is first issued long after the purported event, or if it is made only at a great distance from the place where the event is said to have occurred, or if it is made in a context where, if it were false, it might suffer to pass unexamined. Douglas applies these criteria to the examples Hume advances in Part II of his Essay—the cures of Vespasian, the claimed miracle at Saragossa, the recoveries at the tomb of the Abbé Paris in France, and finds those examples wanting. How might such an approach help us with the evaluation both of ancient and of modern-day miracle claims?

What factors are salient in an explanatory argument that a historical event (miraculous or not) has taken place? A reasonable initial response would be that there is no canonical list—the ways that we justify historical claims are multifaceted and cannot be reduced to a simple formula. But let us recast the question: is there a set of criteria modest enough that some events do fulfill them but strong enough that, if they are fulfilled, they create a powerful case that an event really occurred?

Charles Leslie, an Anglican divine who lost his living in the aftermath of the Glorious Revolution, thought he had found a set of four criteria, or "rules" as he calls them, that would justify the conclusion that an event had really happened. His rules are:

1. That the matter of fact be such, that men's outward senses, their eyes and ears may be judges of it.

2. That it be done publicly in the face of the world.
3. That not only public monuments be kept up in memory of it, but some outward actions be performed.
4. That such monuments, and such actions or observances be instituted, and do commence from the time, that the matter of fact was done.[27]

The first two rules, Leslie explains, "make it impossible for any such matter of fact to be imposed upon men at the time, when such fact was said to be done, because every man's eyes and senses would contradict it." The latter two rules assure those of us who come after that the account was not invented subsequent to the time of the purported event. Leslie acknowledges that these criteria are not necessary conditions of factual truth. An event might fail to meet one or more of them and yet really have transpired. But he insists that they are—taken jointly—sufficient. If any reported event meets all four of these criteria, then its historicity is certain.

The public acts of observance Leslie himself notes with regard to Jesus' resurrection are baptism and the Lord's Supper; later writers, some self-consciously following Leslie, make a similar appeal to the transfer of Christian worship from the Sabbath to "the Lord's day" as another public memorial of the resurrection.

Leslie's own way of expressing the strength of the argument from his rules is, taken literally, too strong; impossibility of error is more than we can expect from any non-deductive argument. But setting aside his hyperbolic language, we can see that the satisfaction of his four rules provides the basis for an explanatory argument for Jesus' resurrection, one that is in large measure independent of more specific claims about the historical reliability of the resurrection narratives in the canonical Gospels. We can cast this case in probabilistic terms, using the satisfaction of each rule as a piece of evidence for an event E:

$$P\left(L_1(E)\&L_2(E)\&L_3(E)\&L_4(E)|E\right)\gg P\left(L_1(E)\&L_2(E)\&L_3(E)\&L_4(E)|{\sim}E\right)$$

Hence,

$$\frac{P\left(L_1(E)\&L_2(E)\&L_3(E)\&L_4(E)|E\right)}{P\left(L_1(E)\&L_2(E)\&L_3(E)\&L_4(E)|{\sim}E\right)}\gg 1$$

This inequality measures the shift that the evidence of Leslie's criteria will induce between the prior and the posterior odds for E.

There are, of course, questions left unresolved by the reconstruction of the argument from Leslie's criteria in an explanatory form. How public must an event be in order to meet the standard of his second rule? How certain are we in any given case that all of them are actually satisfied? How should we factor uncertainty regarding their satisfaction into a cumulative argument? Are there parallel criteria of falsehood that might sap the strength of the case for E, setting up a sort of inversion of Leslie's argument? How can we ascertain the proper balance between competing considerations?

But it is no drawback to a non-deductive argument that it does not settle these questions. Leslie's criteria are *prima facie* relevant to the claim that E. It is surprisingly difficult to come up with solid examples of reports that actually satisfy the criteria but are independently known to be historically false.[28]

What of the vexed problem of the prior probability of miracles? As we have already seen, some modern authors (and not merely critics of the miraculous) have fallen into serious errors in handling this question. It is interesting, then, to look back at a venerable work by William Paley, who engages with this problem right at the outset.[29] Paley's language is somewhat difficult for some modern readers, but what follows is a fair paraphrase of the first part of his "Preparatory Considerations."

Suppose (and at the moment this has to be just a supposition, because we are not arguing for it here) that the world we live in had a Creator who had, as at least one of his purposes, the happiness of his conscious, rational creations, creatures who could voluntarily obey him and do what he had designed them to do. And suppose that this Creator had intended that, after their physical death, these people would still exist and would move into a new state of existence, what happens to them in that second state depending on what they had done in their original physical lives here on earth—a supposition that answers the standard objection that bad things sometimes happen to good people here in this life.

Now, if this Creator wanted to tell his creatures what is intended for them and how their lives here and now would affect their lives after their physical death, and yet somehow his initial communication to them had been lost or distorted and unlikely to be recovered, then is it not likely that he would make some kind of a further revelation to them? If he cares about them and the choices they make here, is there anything incredible in the idea that he would make such a revelation? Is not this, in fact, the most natural and obvious conclusion to be drawn from these suppositions?

If God wants to make such a revelation, and he wants to make it in such a way that we cannot mistake it for the mere word of man, there is really no other way to seal it than by a miracle—the guarantee, to us, that this is a genuine word from God and not just someone's fine-sounding philosophy or a well-crafted tale. So if we wish to estimate the initial probability, before looking at the particular evidence, that a miracle would occur, we can approach the question by thinking about the probability that there is a God who would want to give us this kind of revelation. If there is, then a miracle is more or less *guaranteed* to happen. So the probability that somewhere some miracle would happen can be resolved into the probability (whether it is great or small) that such a God exists and wishes to make a revelation to us that we cannot, as reasonable creatures, mistake for the word of man.

Someone might misunderstand what Paley is doing here, thinking that he is just helping himself to the assumption that God exists, or to the immortality of the soul, in order to prove that miracles occur. But that would be getting it backwards. Whether miracles have ever happened is a question that must always be settled by evidence. All that Paley is trying to show is that any initial prejudice against miracles—any assignment of a low initial probability to the claim that a miracle has occurred—cannot be any greater than the rational prejudice (great or small—he does not try to settle that question here) against the conjunction of two claims: that *there is a God who has destined his human creations for a future state of existence*, and that *he wants to tell them about that state in such a way that they can know the message comes from him.*

Someone might complain, in Mackie's vein, that Paley has not offered a proof of these two claims. But that would be missing the point. Most of the evidence he goes on to present in this book is an argument in favor of a much stronger claim, a claim that will, in fact, entail these two claims. What Paley is trying to do at the outset is to answer, head-on, the Humean prejudice that would render this entire enquiry pointless: namely, the prejudice that says that *miracles are so improbable that they should be disbelieved no matter how good the evidence is for them.*

Here, then, is a definite link between natural theology, particularly that form of natural theology that is developed in a cumulative fashion, and the more specific historical investigations that the assessment of miracle claims requires. If natural theology can help us to set even a lower bound on the probability of Paley's conjunction, two lines of inquiry that are at present pursued largely in independence of one another become mathematically interlinked.[30] Their intersection offers a wide field for further study and research.

The same may be said, in fact, for the very idea of a cumulative case in the defense of the Christian faith, an area that deserves far more attention than philosophers have devoted to it heretofore. The external evidence for their traditional authorship of the Gospels, for example, is unanimous, early, and extensive.[31] And the Gospels themselves interlock in ways that cry out for formal investigation and modeling. I do not mean here that they tell some similar stories; that could be explained away easily enough. But frequently one Gospel will supply details that explain puzzling features of another and yet does not appear to have been written for that purpose. These interconnections are extensive, crisscrossing the texts in all directions. The Synoptics explain John; John explains the Synoptics; the Synoptics explain one another.[32]

Or consider the character of Jesus as portrayed in the Gospels. It does not look like something that was developed in the telling and retelling of tales. There is unity in the portrait, particularly when we compare things like Jesus's characteristic methods of teaching in the Synoptics with his method of teaching displayed in separate scenes narrated only in John.[33]

As Sherlock Holmes reminds us, great inferences may depend on small points. So it proves here. Each of the Gospels makes contact with data from archaeology and from non-Christian historical sources.[34] I am not speaking here of broad historical and geographical facts that any writer might pick up from a passing traveler or a glance at the writings of Philo, but of details like the historical background that illuminates Jesus's puzzling words to the Samaritan woman in John 4:22, or the reputation of Archelaus in Matthew 2:22, or the curious presence of Pilate's wife in Matthew 22:19. These details lie unexplained in our narratives, but the comparison of appropriate passages of Tacitus or Josephus or Dio Cassius throws them into sharp relief. Philosophers who are interested in inference to the best explanation will find here a rich field for application and testing.

The book of Acts, a continuation of the Gospel of Luke that describes the growth of Christianity as it spreads out from Judea and across the Roman Empire, covers a wider geographical surface area than the Gospels. Unsurprisingly, is confirmed even in its details by an extensive amount of external evidence. The confirmation it receives is hardly to be equaled by any other work of comparable antiquity—of overland routes, landmarks, cities, political boundaries; sea routes and landmarks; local customs, beliefs, languages, dialects, slang terminology; terms for ethnic identities; religious practices; locations of synagogues; titles of local officials; and numerous other points of detail involving local industries, proper nautical terminology, and the voyage and shipwreck of Paul.[35] The book of Acts displays the life of the Christian community, a life interwoven with institutions that would be inexplicable unless the climactic events of the Gospels had taken place more or less as they are described.[36] That narrative is itself cross confirmed by the major letters of Paul, an active participant in the events narrated—most strikingly in the seven letters acknowledged almost universally to be genuine.[37]

All of these lines of argument, compounding and confirming one another, provide a remarkably strong and resilient case for the truth of Christianity. And as I have tried to point out, they were known to writers of generations past. But through neglect, a vast library of work on this subject has been lost to our view. It is not wise—particularly for those who wish to advance the state of the art—to refuse to study the past. If we choose to neglect it, our condition will be even more pitiable, and less excusable, than that described by Alfred the Great in the preface to his translation of Gregory's *Pastoral Care*:

> Then when I was mindful of all this, then I remembered also how I saw, before that it was all laid waste and burned, how the churches stood throughout all England, filled with treasures and books, and also a great multitude of God's servants, and they knew very little benefit of those books because they might not understand them at all, for they were not written in their own language. Thus they might have spoken: "Our elders, when they formerly held these places, they loved wisdom, and through it they found wealth, and left it to us. Here a man may yet see their footprint, but we may not follow after them." And for this reason we have now lost both the wealth and the wisdom, because we would not incline to the footprint with our mind.[38]

NOTES

1. For example, Antony Flew, "Miracles," in Paul Edwards, ed., *The Encyclopedia of Philosophy*, vol. 5 (New York: Macmillan, 1967), 346–353.

2. See Wesley Salmon, *The Foundations of Scientific Inference* (Pittsburgh, PA: University of Pittsburgh Press, 1966) and "Bayes's Theorem and the History of Science," in R. Stuewer, ed., *Historical and Philosophical Perspectives of Science*, vol. 5, Minnesota Studies in the Philosophy of Science (Minneapolis: University of Minnesota Press, 1970), 68–86, and Richard Swinburne, *An Introduction to Confirmation Theory* (London: Methuen & Co. Ltd., 1973) and *The Existence of God* (Oxford: Oxford University Press, 1979).

3. Jordan Howard Sobel, "On the Evidence of Testimony for Miracles: A Bayesian Interpretation of Hume's Analysis," *Philosophical Quarterly* 37 (1987), 166–186; David Owen, "Hume versus Price on Miracles and Prior Probabilities: Testimony and the Bayesian Calculation," *Philosophical Quarterly* 37 (1987): 187–202; Philip Dawid and Donald Gillies, "A Bayesian Analysis of Hume's Argument Concerning Miracles," *Philosophical Quarterly* 39 (1989): 57–65; Jordan Howard Sobel, "Hume's Theorem on Testimony Sufficient to Establish a Miracle," *Philosophical Quarterly* 41 (1991): 229–237.

4. See John Earman, "Bayes, Hume, and Miracles," *Faith and Philosophy* 10 (1993): 293–310; Rodney Holder, "Hume on Miracles: Bayesian Interpretation, Multiple Testimony, and the Existence of God," *British Journal for the Philosophy of Science* 49 (1998): 49–65; David Johnson, *Hume, Holism, and Miracles* (Ithaca, NY: Cornell University Press, 1999); and most scathingly John Earman, *Hume's Abject Failure* (Oxford: Oxford University Press, 2000).

5. Michael Levine, "Review of John Earman, *Hume's Abject Failure*," *Hume Studies* 28 (2002): 161–167.

6. Robert Fogelin, *A Defense of Hume on Miracles* (Princeton, NJ: Princeton University Press, 2003). See Timothy McGrew, "Review of Robert Fogelin, *A Defense of Hume on Miracles*," *Mind* 114 (2005): 145–149.

7. Jordan Howard Sobel, *Logic and Theism: Arguments for and Against Beliefs in God* (Cambridge: Cambridge University Press, 2004); Dorothy Coleman, "Baconian Probability and Hume's Theory of Testimony," *Hume Studies* 27 (2001): 195–226.

8. See, for example, *A System of Logic* (1843), Book 3, chapter 25, and *Three Essays on Religion* (New York: Henry Holt and Co., 1874), 232.

9. See, for example, Grace Jantzen, "Hume, Miracles and Apologetics," *Christian Scholar's Review* 8 (1979): 318–325; Alvin Plantinga, "Is Theism Really a Miracle?" *Faith and Philosophy* 3 (1986): 109–134.

10. See Richard Otte, "Mackie's Treatment of Miracles," *International Journal for Philosophy of Religion* 39 (1996): 151–158, particularly 156.

11. For instance, if their logs form a harmonic series, then even asymptotic convergence toward 1 will not prevent the sum of the logs—and hence the product of the ratios—from going to infinity.

12. For a detailed discussion of Plantinga's critique and its failure, see Timothy McGrew, "Has Plantinga Refuted the Historical Argument?" *Philosophia Christi* 6 (2004): 7–26, and Timothy and Lydia McGrew, "On the Historical Argument: A Rejoinder to Plantinga," *Philosophia Christi* 8 (2006): 23–38.

13. Richard Swinburne, *The Resurrection of God Incarnate* (Oxford: Oxford University Press, 2003).

14. Craig Keener, *Miracles: The Credibility of the New Testament Accounts* (Grand Rapids, MI: Baker, 2011).

15. See, for example, Lydia McGrew, "Probabilistic Issues Concerning Jesus of Nazareth and Messianic Death Prophecies," *Philosophia Christi* 15 (2013): 311–328.

16. Among many other resources, see Robert J. Russell, Nancey Murphy, and Arthur R. Peacocke, eds., *Chaos and Complexity: Scientific Perspectives on Divine Action* (Vatican City State: Vatican Observatory, and Berkeley, CA: Center for Theology and the Natural Sciences, 1995) and F. LeRon Shults, Nancey C. Murphy, and Robert J. Russell, *Philosophy, Science and Divine Action* (Leiden: Brill, 2009).

17. *The Great Debate on Miracles* (Lewisburg, PA: Bucknell University Press, 1981).

18. Joseph Houston, *Reported Miracles: A Critique of Hume* (Cambridge: Cambridge University Press, 1994).

19. John Earman, *Hume's Abject Failure* (Oxford: Oxford University Press, 2000).

20. Timothy Larsen, *Crisis of Doubt* (New York: Oxford University Press, 2006).

21. From C.S. Lewis's Introduction to Penelope Lawson, trans. and ed., *The Incarnation of the Word of God, Being the Treatise of St. Athanasius, De incarnatione Verbi Dei* (London: Centenary Press, 1944), reprinted as "On the Reading of Old Books" in *God in the Dock* (Grand Rapids, MI: Eerdmans, 1994), 200.

22. *Against Apion* 1.12.

23. See Timothy McGrew, "The Argument from Silence." *Acta Analytica* 29 (2014): 215–228.

24. See, for example, Christ Keith and Anthony Le Donne, eds., *Jesus, Criteria, and the Demise of Authenticity* (Bloomsbury: T. & T. Clark, 2012).

25. James Foster, *The Usefulness, Truth, and Excellency of the Christian Revelation* (London: J. Noon, 1731), 112.

26. John Douglas, *The Criterion*, 4th ed. (Oxford: Oxford University Press, 1832).

27. Charles Leslie, *A Short and Easy Method with the Deists* (London: F.C. and J. Rivington, 1815), 13. Leslie's book was first published in 1697.

28. The Victorian freethinker Evans Bell tries to give a counterexample to Leslie's claim by using the story of the French ship *Vengeur*. But the "monument or memorials" criterion is rather dubiously satisfied here; Bell resorts to *imagining* a French banquet in honor of the valor of the crew. See *The Task of To-day* (London: J. Watson, 1852), 25.

29. William Paley, *A View of the Evidences of Christianity* (London: John W. Parker and Son, 1859), 11ff.

30. Timothy McGrew and John DePoe, "Natural Theology and the Uses of Argument," *Philosophia Christi* 15 (2013): 299–309.

31. It is remarkable that Bart Ehrman in his textbook, *The New Testament: A Historical Introduction to the Early Christian Writings*, 2nd ed. (New York: Oxford University Press, 2000), omits all mention of the patristic testimony to the authorship of the Gospels. It is difficult to imagine someone's omitting the principal external evidence for authorship in an introduction to any other set of ancient writings.

32. Some of this evidence can be found in older works, such as John James Blunt, *Undesigned Coincidences* (New York: Robert Carter & Brothers, 1855). While a few of Blunt's specific

arguments have been superseded by subsequent textual discoveries, and a few others are not as cogent as he thinks, the majority of them are still worth careful examination.

33. This is just one of the numerous subsidiary lines of evidence traced by William Paley in *A View of the Evidences of Christianity* (London: John W. Parker and Son, 1859). See Part 2, chapter 4.

34. I have touched on some of this external evidence in various public lectures; interested readers can easily find them online.

35. In his monumental work *The Book of Acts in the Setting of Hellenistic History*, WUNT 49 (Tübingen: Mohr Siebeck, 1989), Colin Hemer lists about a hundred such points of confirmation for the latter half of the book of Acts.

36. This line of argument is worked out with subtlety and care in Stanley Leathes, *The Religion of the Christ*, 2nd ed. (New York: Pott, Young, and Co., 1876).

37. This argument is developed in great detail in William Paley, *Horae Paulinae* (London: SPCK, 1877), an edition made more valuable by the annotations provided by the editor, John Saul Howson. Like Blunt's work, Paley's requires occasional updating but is substantially sound.

38. My rendering, adapted from the one given in the appendix to Lolah Burford, *The Vision of Stephen* (New York: Ace Publications, 1955).

(X)

C.S. Lewis's Argument from Nostalgia

A NEW ARGUMENT FROM DESIRE

Todd Buras and Michael Cantrell

INTRODUCTION

Recent research on the modal ontological argument has established this much: In S5, if it is possible that there is a God—a maximally great, and therefore necessarily existent, being—then there is a God.[1] Progress has slowed when it comes to establishing the possibility of God's existence.[2] The aim of this chapter is to present a new argument for the possibility premise of the modal ontological argument.

Ours is an argument from desire. Some have looked to the nature and content of human desire, and similar feelings, for evidence of the existence of God.[3] We look to desire only for evidence of the possibility of God's existence. In this respect, ours is a new, more modest, argument from desire. With the modal ontological argument in the background, we need to ask no more of the argument from desire.

We do not claim to demonstrate conclusively that God's existence is possible. We aim to present to anyone who is not antecedently committed to the impossibility of God's existence a reason to accept the possibility premise. Entrenched atheists are, likely, antecedently committed to the falsity of the possibility premise, and to the falsity of any premises that entail the possibility premise. Thus they are likely to reject our premises. But rejecting our premises has a cost. Our argument, therefore, offers evidence for the possibility of God's existence, and adds to the theoretical costs of atheism.

We will show that, under certain conditions, desires are a guide to possibility. We then identify a certain form of happiness, and argue that the existence of God is a necessary condition of this form of happiness. We then argue that this form of happiness is the object of the right sort of desire. It follows that this form of happiness is possible. Since the possibility of any state of affairs implies the possibility of its necessary conditions, and since the existence of God is a necessary condition of this form of happiness, it follows that the existence of a maximally great being is also possible. We will conclude by explaining how our approach to the possibility premise evades what we will call the problem of equipollence, a problem that undermines many attempts to support the possibility premise.

DESIRE AS A GUIDE TO POSSIBILITY

Desires are like beliefs. They are intentional mental states. They represent the world as being a certain way. It is customary to distinguish beliefs and desires in terms of the direction of fit between representation and object.[4] Beliefs are supposed to fit their object; the object is meant to fit desires. A successful belief (one that fits the world) is true. A successful desire (one the world is made fit) is fulfilled.

Some beliefs are not simply false but necessarily so. Similarly, some desires are necessarily unfulfilled. Necessarily false beliefs are absurd. Necessarily unfulfilled desires are vain. An absurd belief can never fit the world. The world can never be made to fit a vain desire. Such desires represent an impossible state of affairs and therefore do not represent a way the world might be. A desire is not vain, then, if it has a possible state of affairs as its object, that is, if the world, in some sense, can come to be as it is represented by the desire. [5]

Desires earn their keep in folk psychology by motivating and explaining action, by making action intelligible as such.[6] Beliefs represent the way the world is. Desires represent the way we want the world to be. Belief-desire pairs constitute reasons for action. Such reasons motivate their subjects to act in ways that change the world from the way it is to the way they want it to be. One who believes that the temperature may be controlled by adjusting a thermostat, and desires to change the temperature, has a reason to move to the thermostat and adjust its settings. The belief-desire pair not only guides the agent's action, the pair also makes the agent's action intelligible as such to others and to the agent herself.

A belief-desire pair guides action and makes action intelligible as such, not just by having some action or other as its causal result. The belief and desire regarding the thermostat may cause fight-or-flight behavior. Even though the belief-desire pair may cause such behavior, it does not constitute a reason for engaging in such behavior; and while it makes such behavior intelligible as an effect, it does not make it intelligible as an action of a rational agent. In order to guide action and make it intelligible as such, the action that follows must be related to the content of the desire in such a way that the action either fulfills the desire or constitutes a step toward the fulfillment of the desire.

Desires with explicitly impossible objects guide no action. They make no action intelligible as such. Imagine setting out to build a round-square artifact. After gathering the requisite supplies and tools—actions explained by non-vain desires—one finally sets to work. What action, exactly, would the desire motivate one to do? What action would the desire make intelligible? No action one could take leads to the fulfillment of the desire, nor constitutes a step toward the fulfillment of the desire. Anything one does to make the artifact round makes it not square, and vice versa. The desire to build the artifact may make some events involving the agent intelligible in the merely causal sense; it may lead one to mutter nervously and wring one's hands. But that is not the same as guiding action or making action intelligible as such. In order to do that, the action must be directed toward the fulfillment of the desire, and no action is so directed. There are, furthermore, no beliefs to which the desire can be paired that changes the situation. If one believes, say, that a certain incantation allows the construction of round-square artifacts, saying the incantation makes sense. But saying the incantation does not fulfill, or constitute a step toward the fulfillment of, the desire to construct a round-square artifact.

If all vain desires had explicitly impossible objects, our argument would be simple. We could define a defective desire as one that can be coupled with no beliefs to guide action or make action intelligible as such—where a desire guides action or makes action intelligible as such, just in case it disposes agents to action that fulfills the desire or constitutes a step toward the fulfillment of the desire. Defective desires, so defined, would have vain objects, while non-defective desires would not. A non-defective desire for a state of affairs would imply the possibility of its object. Experiencing such desires as a subject, being motivated by them, would be a reason for the subject to judge the object possible. Our argument would be off and running. But there is a difficulty to negotiate.

Not all vain desires have explicitly impossible objects. Consider the desire to compile a Russellian reference work, a reference work that cites all and only reference works that do not cite themselves. The object of this desire is a famously impossible state of affairs, but the contradiction is not explicit in the description of the object. It is implicit. The reference work will either cite itself or not. If it does cite itself, it will fail to cite only reference works that do not reference themselves. If it does not cite itself, it will fail to cite all the reference works that do not reference themselves.

The desire to compile a Russellian reference work seems non-defective. A man could spend a lifetime combing libraries and compiling lists of reference works. He could invoke the desire to compile a Russellian reference work, together with his beliefs about how best to do so, to make his life's work intelligible to himself and others. Yet nothing the man can do will fulfill his desire or even constitute a step toward the fulfillment of his desires.

In such cases, a defective desire seems non-defective. Defective desires seem non-defective when the state of affairs that constitutes their object includes other states of affairs that are possible. Anyone who desires the impossible state of affairs desires all the possible states of affairs that it includes as proper parts. The desire for any of the possible parts of the whole will be non-defective. Compiling references is a part of compiling a Russellian reference work. A man who desires to compile a Russellian reference work ipso facto desires to compile references. The desire to compile references is non-defective. Thus a vain desire may, for a while, pass as non-defective. When it, eventually, becomes obvious that the desired state of affairs has an impossible object, it is equally obvious that nothing can be done to bring the desire to fulfillment, and that nothing one has done so far has brought the desire any closer to fulfillment. The subject of such a desire will have to find something better to do, either by giving up on the object altogether or persisting in a closely related desire for a possible part of the original object. Some shadow of the original desire may remain lodged in the subject's psyche in the form of a wish. But wishes do not earn their keep by guiding action and making action intelligible as such.

Seemingly non-defective desires thus fall into two categories: those that are genuinely non-defective, and those that are not. The first sort is indicative of the possibility of the objects of desire. These desires give their subjects a reason to believe the desired states of affairs possible. The second sort does not. Since the role of desire in our cognitive life is to represent possible states of affairs, and since experience indicates that most desires do, it is natural to take desires that seem non-defective to be non-defective unless we have a reason to believe their object is impossible. So, we may say that a seemingly non-defective desire is a prima facie indication of the possibility of its object, and a prima facie reason for the subject of such a desire to believe the desired state of affairs is possible. In the case of the Russellian reference work, the prima facie significance of the desire is overridden. We have explicit reasons to believe the object of this desire is impossible: the reference work would have to cite itself and not cite itself, and it cannot do both. But when there is no reason to consider the object of a seemingly non-defective desire impossible, the desire will constitute a good indication of the possibility of its object and a good reason for the subject of such a desire to believe its object is possible. Under these conditions, non-defective desires are a guide to possibility.

In what follows, we will appeal to seemingly non-defective desires whose objects we know no reason to consider impossible, other than antecedent commitment to atheism. For antecedently committed atheists, our argument will therefore serve only to highlight the consequences of atheism. But for those who are not antecedently committed to atheism, seemingly non-defective desires for the states of affairs we discuss offer a good reason to believe God's existence possible.

HAPPINESS AND GOD

Our strategy for supporting the possibility premise requires a single defensible example of a state of affairs that is both non-defectively desired and possible only if there is a God.[7] In fact, we think there are many. Some examples, like the desire for the beatific vision or for mystical union with God, obviously require the existence of God but are not obviously non-defective. Other cases, like the desire for world peace or for an end to all oppression, are obviously non-defective but less obviously require the existence of God. In this section, we identify a certain form of happiness and argue that the existence of

God is a necessary condition of this form of happiness obtaining. In the next section, we will argue that this form of happiness is the object of the right sort of desire.

Happiness

The concept of happiness we are interested in is probably best thought of as perfect, complete, or absolute happiness. It is a certain stable state of well-being in a person. We concentrate only on the crucial aspects of the concept for our argument.

Well-being, as we use the term, has two dimensions—one having to do with excellence and one having to do with experience. Well-being involves intrinsically desirable states of conscious experience (like satisfaction, joy, and contentment), and objective excellence or virtue. As Aristotle suggested long ago, no one would say that happiness has nothing to do with the quality of one's conscious experience—except to save a theory.[8] On the other hand, not just any intrinsically desirable state of consciousness counts toward happiness. Satisfaction, for example, can always be sustained by lowering one's standards; and pleasure by artificial means. A person in some miserable state of existence who is, nonetheless, incongruously content or artificially pleased is not, in the relevant sense, happy; indeed, such a person is more miserable because of his or her contentment and pleasure. To twist a Kantianism, enjoyment without excellence is blind, excellence without enjoyment is empty. The well-being condition on happiness ensures that happiness is some combination of objective excellence and intrinsically desirable states of consciousness.

But there are many such combinations: chance convergences, brief episodes, and incomplete realizations. The stability condition identifies happiness with the optimal combination of excellence and experience. Human persons are congeries of capacities for excellence—physical, intellectual, affective, and social. Partial realization of these capacities is, at best, partial happiness. Complete happiness, as we think of it, is the enjoyment of the fullest compossible actualization of all one's potentialities for excellence. One who achieves this state literally could not be happier. She enjoys the best possible life for a human being. The stability condition identifies happiness per se—happiness without qualification, either implicit or explicit—with this absolute limit.[9]

Fully realized capacities for excellence are stable across time and circumstance. Partial happiness thus comes in two main varieties: the partly virtuous complete life and the completely virtuous part-life. The completely virtuous part-life enjoys well-being across circumstances but not across time. One may fall short of the ideal of stability across times in two ways: either by achieving complete well-being late in life, or losing it early. The sage may become a slave, and vice versa. In both cases, the sage or slave might have been happier; there are times at which each might have enjoyed well-being, but does not. Their happiness is thus at best qualified and incomplete.[10]

Similarly, the half-virtuous complete life enjoys well-being stably across time but not across circumstances. One may fall short of stability across circumstances of two sorts: actual and possible. Some may be partially virtuous in the sense that there are actual circumstances in which they do, and others in which they do not, exhibit virtue. The man who controls his temper at work but flies into a rage at home is partly virtuous. Others may be partially virtuous in the sense that there are possible circumstances in which they would exhibit virtue, and others in which they would not. The woman who would lose her temper if her first son were to miss curfew but not if her second son were to do the same is partly virtuous in this sense. In both cases, one might be happier; there are circumstances in which one does not or would not exhibit objective excellence. The stability condition counts such examples of partial well-being as, at best, examples of partial or qualified happiness.

Two further comments about happiness are in order. First, our constraints on happiness, together with one plausible assumption, place us on one side of the old debate about the role of external goods and goods of the body in the happy life—goods like wealth, health, friends, a secure and virtuous family and community. The assumption is that there are some potentialities for objective human excellence that require the possession of such external goods. Since our conditions on happiness require the actualization of all one's potentialities, and since we assume external goods and goods of the body to be necessary for the actualization of some potentialities, happiness as we understand it is dependent upon external goods.[11]

Second, according to our constraints, happiness is an extremely stringent ideal—so stringent, in fact, it is not a plausible candidate for the object of a non-defective desire. Most of us miss the mark from the moment of our birth, and every subsequent moment puts the ideal further out of our reach. The desire for unqualified happiness, then, is weakly defective, that is, it is inconsistent with contingent facts. It seems, therefore, the most actual human beings can consistently desire is qualified happiness. Still, at each moment of our lives, there is a fact of the matter about how close to the ideal we may yet come, and it remains consistent to desire the maximum we may achieve by way of happiness. When we say that humans desire happiness, we mean to attribute to them only the desire for this person- and time-relative maximum; that is, the desire to come as close to the ideal of happiness as possible from any given point in their life.

God as a Necessary Condition of Happiness

Imagine a world (call it the happy world) in which a human being achieves happiness (call her Felicity). The possibility of any state of affairs entails the possibility of its necessary conditions. So the necessary conditions of Felicity's happiness—whatever they may be—obtain in the happy world. Felicity's happiness—her enjoyment of the stable and complete realization of all her capacities for objective excellence—requires an ideal exertion of moral effort in an ideal set of circumstances. The ideal circumstances are the external goods necessary for happiness. Call these ideal circumstances the provisions. Call whoever or whatever secures the provisions for happiness, the Provider. The possibility of a happy human being entails the possibility that the provisions are secured. The Provider is whoever or whatever secures the provisions. The existence of the Provider is therefore a necessary condition of human happiness. So the Provider exists in the happy world. Who or what could the Provider be? The stability condition on happiness places stringent demands on the candidates—so stringent, we argue, that only a maximally great being could be the Provider.[12]

Suppose the Provider were not an agent. In that case, the provisions would be secured in the happy world by something like luck or the laws of nature. If so, then Felicity's happiness is hostage to fortune. For there are worlds very near the happy world, indeed worlds that represent possible futures for the happy world itself, in which Felicity's ideal moral effort does not meet with ideal external circumstances. This makes Felicity's happiness modally fragile, that is, not stable across possible circumstances. Modally fragile excellence makes for only imperfect happiness. But Felicity's happiness in the happy world is, by hypothesis, not imperfect. In the happy world, then, the Provider is neither luck nor the laws of nature.

Could the Provider be a human agent, or some collection of human agents? Human beings are better candidates than either luck or laws, since they may be concerned for Felicity's well-being in a way that non-agential candidates are not. But human agents—one or many—are neither powerful nor beneficent enough to be the Provider. Given the limits of human intelligence and beneficence, human beings are not capable of securing the provisions across a broad enough range of circumstances for Felicity's happiness to be sufficiently stable. Any human agent (including Felicity herself) and any group of human agents may simply abandon their interest in her happiness, or, in the case of a group of human agents, they may fall afoul of one another. Alternatively, they might face a threat to their own existence or to Felicity's happiness (e.g., an alien invasion) that they are either not smart enough or not strong enough to repel. If human beings are the Provider, Felicity's happiness is, again, unstable and therefore imperfect. So, in the happy world, the Provider is not a human being or group of human beings. (Virtually identical considerations rule out the possibility that the Provider is a non-divine, non-human agent or group of agents.)

For Felicity's happiness to be sufficiently stable, the Provider must be unfailingly beneficent toward her, the Provider's power to secure the provisions must be unsurpassable, and the Provider's own existence must not be dependent upon other things. This is to say, the Provider must be a maximally great being, that is, a non-human agent, invincibly powerful, unconditionally loving, and necessarily existent—*et hoc dicimus deum*.

One may object at this point that the argument fails to show that the existence of a maximally great being is a necessary condition of human happiness. All the argument shows, the objector may claim, is that the existence of what we might call a humanly great being is necessary—where a humanly great being is a being whose greatness is unsurpassed throughout the range of possible worlds in which human beings exist. Human beings do not exist in every world. Strictly speaking, then, the Provider's existence need not be necessary, nor need the Provider's power be absolutely invincible. The Provider can stably secure the provisions in the happy world, even if in very distant worlds, the Provider fails to exist or is overpowered.

The simplest reply to this objection is to grant its truth, and deny that the result is as significant as it seems. For the argument would still show that there is a being whose greatness is unsurpassed in our neighborhood of logical space. Throughout the range of worlds in which human beings exist, the Provider is an invincibly powerful, unconditionally loving, necessarily existent, non-human agent. Since our world is in this range, a being of unsurpassed greatness in humanly possible worlds exists. So conceding the force of the objection is not exactly a defeat for the theist.

But the truth of the objection may be questioned as well. Many of the worlds in which human beings do not exist represent possible futures of worlds (like the happy world) in which they do. To secure the conditions necessary for happiness, the Provider's power in the happy world must be sufficient to prevent the happy world from succumbing to such inhospitable futures. So there must be nothing about such worlds that is incompatible with the greatness of the Provider, that is, nothing in such worlds that could overpower or outsmart the Provider, or on which the Provider's existence is dependent. Since the Provider's existence is not precluded by such worlds, and since worlds are maximal states of affairs (they include or exclude every state of affairs), the Provider exists in any world that represents a possible future of the happy world. This response does not yet show that the Provider's existence is absolutely necessary, i.e., that the provider exists in every possible world simplicter. But it does show, contrary to the objection, that the Provider is more than merely humanly great.

THE DESIRE FOR HAPPINESS

The next step of our argument is to show that happiness of the sort we have identified is, first, the object of seemingly non-defective desires; and, second, that there is no reason to take the object of the desire to be impossible. What we have to say in support of both steps of the argument at this point is ultimately less significant than what we have to say about the costs of opposing them. And what we have to say about the costs of opposing either part depends on the idea that happiness is an intrinsically desirable state of affairs.[13]

Intrinsically Desirable States of Affairs

Intrinsically desirable states of affairs are best understood as a parallel to a familiar type of belief. Some propositions (like the law of non-contradiction) are self-evident. Simply understanding the terms of a self-evident proposition compels assent. The best reason to believe a self-evident proposition is simply an exposition of the content of the concepts involved. If more of a reason is demanded, it is difficult or impossible to satisfy the demand, since there are no more evident propositions to which we may appeal for support. None of this is to say that belief in self-evident propositions is, strictly speaking, incorrigible. With effort one may withhold assent from self-evident propositions. But such beliefs are intractable. Without constant vigilance, belief in self-evident propositions inevitably insinuates itself in one's noetic structure. Intrinsically desirable states of affairs are the conative counterparts of self-evident propositions. Simply understanding the elements of some states of affairs compels desire. There is nothing more desirable to which we may appeal in order to motivate the desire for an intrinsically desirable state of affairs. Desires for intrinsically desirable states of affairs, while not altogether incorrigible, are intractable; it takes work to banish them from one's motivational structure, and they tend inevitably to creep back in.

Happiness as the Object of Desire

That happiness is desired seems so obvious to us as to require no argument. Indeed we are inclined to ask readers to take our word for it, since we desire it.[14] But since we take happiness to be an intrinsically desirable state of affairs, we can say one thing more. For, if happiness is intrinsically desirable, the only reason to think happiness is not desired is that it is not understood, and the only reason we could offer to desire it is an explication of the content of the concept. Since the concept is easily understood, we have every reason to think it is desired.

The significance of this point lies less in the support it offers for the claim that happiness is desired than in the burden it places on what we call the settler's objection. Settlers deny that they desire happiness, as we have defined it. They settle for less, in the sense that something less than perfect happiness is the object of their desire. Imperfect happiness—for example, as much happiness as is consistent with the provisions secured by human beings, luck and the laws of nature—has no theistic necessary conditions. It is therefore consistent with atheism and sufficient to motivate a truly excellent way of life. The settler is not disputing our argument, but deflecting its force. The argument gives a settler no reason to accept the possibility of God's existence, since it appeals to a desire they disown. Atheists may thus evade our argument by being careful to desire no more by way of happiness than atheism affords.

Since we believe perfect happiness is an intrinsically desirable state of affairs, we believe the cost of settling is high. The cost of settling is an invidious distinction. If the enjoyment of objective excellence across n number of times and circumstances is desirable, then so is the enjoyment of happiness across $n + 1$. For, an increase in the degree of stability of one's happiness does not make happiness less, but more, desirable. Thus anyone who desires the enjoyment of objective excellence stably across any number of times and circumstances has a reason to desire perfect happiness, the enjoyment of objective excellence across the largest possible number of times and circumstances. The settler, of course, desires the enjoyment of objective excellence stably across n number of circumstances. So he has a reason to desire perfect happiness. Yet he does not. He thus makes an invidious distinction, claiming (for some value of n) that the enjoyment of objective excellence stably across n number of times and circumstances is desirable, but not $n + 1$. The distinction is invidious because there is no reason to desire imperfect over perfect happiness, nor is it even clear that there could be a reason.[15]

The Desire as Non-defective

We have not offered a complete analysis of the concept of non-defective desire. So we cannot *prove* that the desire for happiness is non-defective by showing that it satisfies the necessary and sufficient conditions for the application of this concept. Nonetheless, we can offer a reason to think that it is non-defective, and we can identify the costs of denying that it is.

The desire for happiness satisfies at least one necessary condition of a non-defective desire: it seems to guide action and make action intelligible as such. The action to which it guides one is the ideal exertion of moral effort, which, in ideal external circumstances, fully realizes all one's capacities for excellence. Furthermore, the desire for happiness is not like a desire to build a round-square monument. The state of affairs that constitutes the object of the desire is not explicitly contradictory, not obviously impossible. So, the desire for happiness seems non-defective. If it is defective, it must be because it is like the desire to compile a Russellian reference work; its object must be implicitly contradictory. In the case of the Russellian reference work, however, we have a reason to think that the object of the desire is contradictory, and therefore that the desire is vain. (The book would have to cite and not cite itself.) In the case of happiness, we have no such reason—no reason, that is, except an antecedent commitment to the non-existence of a maximally great being. So our argument will not convince an antecedently committed atheist. We acknowledge that from the outset. But our argument does add to the theoretical costs of atheism. If our argument is correct, atheists must not only maintain that God's existence is impossible, they must maintain that human happiness (as we understand it) is, too.

Because we believe happiness is an intrinsically desirable state of affairs, we also believe the cost of this way out of our argument is, also, quite high. For, the desire for intrinsically desirable states of affairs are intractable. In this respect, the desire for happiness differs dramatically from cases in which desires have impossible objects. When one discovers that the desire to author a Russellian reference work is vain, the desire is easily abandoned, and the object immediately ceases to be desirable. When an atheist insists that the desire for happiness (as we understand it) is vain, happiness remains desirable, and the desire for it is only abandoned through great effort. If happiness is impossible, then human beings are absurd in this respect: they are strongly inclined to desire an impossible object.[16]

DESIRE AND THE PROBLEM OF EQUIPOLLENCE

We have argued that in certain circumstances desire is a guide to possibility. We have argued further that human beings desire happiness, and that the existence of God is a necessary condition of happiness. It follows that the existence of God is possible. Efforts to support the possibility premise have gotten this far before. Many guides to possibility show that God's existence is possible. The problem is that many show that the non-existence of God is possible, too. But since God exists necessarily, if at all, our guide to possibility cannot have it both ways. This is what we call the problem of equipollence.[17] To establish that the existence of God is possible, our appeal to desire cannot be equipollent with respect to theistic and atheistic possibilities. To argue that desire evades equipollence, we try to find a desired state of affairs for which the non-existence of God is a necessary condition. The most obvious examples fail, instructively. We conclude by taking the instruction to heart.

Since we derived the possibility of God's existence from the desire for happiness, one might expect a desire for unhappiness to entail atheistic possibilities. Some apparently do desire unhappiness, and the desire certainly seems action guiding. So we do not dispute that unhappy states of affairs are desired, nor that the desire is seemingly non-defective. But the non-existence of God is not a necessary condition of unhappiness. As we have said, happiness requires an ideal exertion of moral effort in an ideal set of external circumstances. God is necessary to secure the external circumstances. But a simple lack of human effort is sufficient to secure unhappiness. Since one can achieve unhappiness in a world in which God exists, unhappiness has no atheistic implications.

Other, more sinister, objects of desire are possible only if God does not exist, but the desire for such objects proves defective. Satan is sometimes represented as desiring to be God. But such a desire is not action guiding, and therefore defective. If you are not God, there is really nothing you can do about it. Facts about identity are necessary, after all. If you are not God, then you are necessarily not God. So however god-like you may become, you will not fulfill the desire to be God. The desire to be God—like the desire to write a Russellian reference work—is therefore doomed from the start. Nothing you can do fulfills the desire or brings it any closer to fulfillment. Less extreme examples succumb to similar difficulties. Consider the desire for cosmic independence, a desire to be beholden to no final and ultimate authority.[18] This desire—like the desire for materialism to be true—pits one against truths that are in no way dependent upon one's actions. Materialism is either true or it is not. You are or are not a creature of God. There is nothing you can do about such truths, one way or the other. So the desire fails to guide action, and thus proves defective.[19]

The only examples that might show desire to be equipollent with respect to theistic and atheistic possibilities are simply too hideous to be desired—like the desire to do wrong and never to be held to account for it—that is, the desire for ultimate injustice. Other examples include: the desire for all suffering to be ultimately unredeemed and meaningless; the desire for all of the bonds of love and friendship to be ultimately broken; the desire for all efforts to achieve happiness to be thwarted in the end; the desire for the destruction of everything beautiful. We could go on. But there is no need. Such states of affairs are inconsistent with the existence of God. The desire for such states of affairs at least appears to guide action, since the object of these desires is at least partly within our power. But we see no reason at all to grant that such states of affairs are the object of any desire, non-defective or otherwise. When we actually consider states of affairs that are at least partly in our power to achieve, and which can be brought about only if God does not exist, they elicit disgust, not desire. The existence of God is simply not a threat to anything we might do that would be worth doing.

Throughout this chapter, we have been working with the thinnest serviceable notion of desire, packing no more into the concept than what is needed to animate our argument. Doing so has kept our theoretical liabilities to a minimum, but it has also involved ignoring the obvious. Reflections on the threat of equipollence highlight what is perhaps the most important difference in taking desires, as opposed to less affective mental states, as our guide to possibility. Purely cognitive mental operations (like conceiving or imagining) are neutral with respect to the value properties of their object. If reality is, as theists believe, morally charged, we should not expect a guide to possibility that ignores these features of reality to be very reliable. The very worst states of affairs are as conceivable or imaginable as the very best. But they are not as desirable. Affective mental operations, like desire, are a response to the goodness of their object. Since desire is not equipollent with respect to good and evil, and since theistic possibilities are on the side of the good, natural desire evades the problem of equipollence.

NOTES

1. Work on the modal ontological argument flowered in the 1970s. Robert Adams, "The Logical Structure of Anselm's Argument," *Philosophical Review* 80 (1971): 28–54, shows that God's existence follows from the possibility premise in S5 and the Brouwersche system (see 40–48). Alvin Plantinga, *The Nature of Necessity* (New York: Oxford University Press, 1974), 197–221, propounds the most widely discussed version of the S5 modal ontological argument. Both Plantinga and Adams acknowledge a debt to Charles Hartshorne's "modal argument," presented, for example, in *The Logic of Perfection* (La Salle, IL: Open Court Publishing Company, 1962). Graham Oppy is an indefatigable guide to recent work on ontological arguments. See his *Ontological Arguments and Belief in God* (New York: Cambridge University Press, 1995), esp. 70–78 and 246–259; updated and expanded in *Arguing about Gods* (New York: Cambridge University Press, 2006), 49–96, and "Ontological Arguments," *The Stanford Encyclopedia of*

Philosophy (Winter 2009 Edition), Edward N. Zalta (ed.), URL = <http://plato.stanford.edu/archives/win2009/entries/ontological-arguments/>.

2. Plantinga, *The Nature of Necessity*, 219–221, grants that the "victorious" version of the argument is not a successful piece of natural theology precisely because the possibility premise is rationally deniable—adding that it is often reasonable to accept rationally deniable premises. In "Has It Been Proved that All Real Existence Is Contingent?" *American Philosophical Quarterly* 8 (1971): 284–291, Robert Adams adds, helpfully, that propositions like the possibility premise are not necessarily false. Adams also criticizes a host of Leibnizian approaches to the possibility premise in *Leibniz: Determinist, Idealist, and Theist* (New York: Oxford University Press, 1994), 135–216. Leibniz's presumption of possibility is also the subject of Adams's "Presumption and the Necessary Existence of God," *Nous* 22 (1988): 19–32. Early on, Peter van Inwagen argued that we can not know, or even rationally accept, the truth of possibility premise; see his "Ontological Arguments," *Nous* 4 (1977): 375–395. His concerns are generalized and entrenched in "Modal Epistemology," *Philosophical Studies* 92 (1998): 67–84. Both Michael Tooley in "Plantinga's Defense of the Ontological Argument," *Mind* 90 (1981): 422–427, and Richard Gale in *The Nature and Existence of God* (New York: Cambridge University Press, 1991), 227, suggest that atheistic modal intuitions are preferable. But see Oppy, *Ontological Arguments*, 74–76 and 255–256. Most recently, Alexander Pruss has explored two very creative approaches to the possibility premise in: "Samkara's Principles and Two Ontomystical Arguments," *International Journal for Philosophy of Religion* 49 (2001): 111–120; and "The Ontological Argument and the Motivational Centres of Lives," *Religious Studies* 46 (2010): 233–249.

3. See, for example, C.S. Lewis, *Mere Christianity* (New York: HarperCollins, 2001), 134–137. Lewis actually argues, more modestly, from the nature and content of desire to the existence of a transcendent good that satisfies it. In doing so, he is echoing a long tradition that characterizes the human heart as harboring desires no earthly good can satisfy—desires, in the final analysis, for God. The most memorable expression of this tradition is surely the opening reflections of St. Augustine's *Confessions*, F.J. Sheed, trans. (Indianapolis, Indiana: Hackett Publishing Company, 1993): "Great art thou, O Lord, and greatly to be praised . . . and man desires to praise Thee. . . . For Thou hast made us for Thyself and our hearts are restless until they rest in Thee." St. Thomas Aquinas also argues that human happiness consists in no created good. See *Summa Theologia*, First Part of the Second Part, Question 2, Article 8 (thanks to Alexander Pruss for this reference). It is worth noting that this tradition is not, in its roots, Christian. It is at least strongly consonant, for example, with Aristotle's claim in *Metaphysics*, Book 12, Chapter 7, that the unmoved mover moves all by being the primary object of all desire and thought.

4. Talbot Brewer, *The Retrieval of Ethics* (New York: Oxford University Press, 2009), 17, n. 4, traces this way of distinguishing beliefs and desires to G.E.M. Anscombe, *Intention* (Oxford: Basil Blackwell, 1957), and catalogues some prominent endorsements for the distinction. Brewer also critiques of this way of characterizing desires as part of an ambitious challenge to modern theories of agency. Space does not permit an engagement with Brewer's critique. Suffice it to say that we accept his point that a full account of desires must accommodate a role—perhaps even a primary role—for belief-like direction of fit. We are simply not offering a complete theory of desire. Rather, we are saying something about desire that any complete theory, at some level, must allow—as Brewer himself does (see 55).

5. We are characterizing vanity in a very strong sense, that is, vain desires are those whose desideratum is broadly logically (or metaphysically) impossible. To this class belongs the desire to

build a round-square artifact, the desire to drink water composed of something other than H_2O, and the desire to convince people by argument that arguments do not convince people. But other desires are vain in a weaker sense: the desideratum is incompatible with contingent truths. It is contingently true that humans cannot breath (unaided) underwater. Yet it is true all the same, and thus absurd for actual humans to desire to breath (unaided) underwater. Such desires are only relatively defective, defective relative to the laws of nature. So there may well be possible circumstances (i.e., worlds with different natural laws) in which such desires would not be vain. An even weaker sense of vanity afflicts desires whose desideratum is preformatively contradictory. Desires of this sort are not inconsistent but self-defeating; they undermine the conditions they presuppose. Lying, for example, undermines the trust it presupposes. So the desire to lie is absurd in this self-defeating sense. Similarly, the desire to starve or to be a glutton undermines the life of the body it presupposes, thus it may be judged weakly vain.

6. See Donald Davidson, *Essays on Actions and Events* (New York: Oxford University Press, 1980).

7. We stake our claim in this chapter on the happiness example. But it is important to note that the argument form may succeed even if our instance fails. Several other candidates deserve serious consideration. Consider, for example, the Kantian desire for the ultimate proportioning of happiness to virtue (see book II of his *Critique of Practical Reason*); and the Nagelian desire for answers to the cosmic question of meaning (see Thomas Nagel, *Secular Philosophy and the Religious Temperament* (New York: Oxford University Press, 2009), 3–19).

8. Aristotle, *Nichomachean Ethics*, 1153b 18–20. Elsewhere in the *Nichomachean Ethics*, Aristotle is concerned not with what we describe, here, as intrinsically desirable states of consciousness but rather with activity of the soul in accord with a rational principle; see, for example, 1098a 8–18.

9. Our notion of an absolute concept is borrowed from Peter Unger, *Ignorance: A Case for Scepticism* (New York: Oxford University Press, 1978), especially 47–49.

10. Hence the Aristotelian dictum: judge no man happy while he yet lives. See *Nichomachean Ethics*, 1100a 1–15.

11. Denying the dependence of happiness on external goods is one way out of our argument—call it the Stoic's way out. The alternative is examined, historically and philosophically, in Julia Annas, *The Morality of Happiness* (New York: Oxford University Press, 1993), 388–411. We doubt modern atheists will find this way out appealing. But more importantly, we doubt that the Stoic's concept of happiness is devoid of theistic implications. As Tad Brennan notes (*The Stoic Life: Emotions, Duties, Fate* (New York: Oxford University Press, 2005), 315), "the question of whether we should really believe what [Stoics] say about ethics has been deferred to the question of whether we should believe what they say about the cosmos." What they say about the cosmos, further, is that it reflects (or is animated by) a preeminently rational order, variously identified as Fate, Providence and Zeus (235–240). Thus, the Stoic's way out may be another way into our argument, that is, it may show, in fact, that our argument can do without the assumption that happiness depends on external goods. But that is too large a topic to address here.

12. Our argument is inspired by such claims as these in Aristotle's *Nichomachean Ethics*: "if there is any gift of the gods to men, it is reasonable that happiness should be god-given" (1099b10); "to entrust to chance what is greatest and most noble would be a very defective arrangement" (1099b20); and happiness is "too high" for man and "it is not insofar as he is man that he will live so, but insofar as something divine is present in him" (1077b25). (We quote here from the W.D. Ross translation.)

13. This is one way of elaborating on Aristotle's observation that happiness is not desired for the sake of anything else (*Nichomachean Ethics* 1097a30–1097b).

14. Such a flat-footed appeal to introspection is actually quite problematic. For we are not the best judges of what it is in the world that we actually desire. This is because desires are, arguably, intensional states. One may desire a state of affairs, S_1, and S_1 may be identical with state of affairs, S_2, and yet one not desire S_2 (at least not under that description). The police chief desires to lock up the villain. His mother is the villain. But the chief does not desire to lock up his mother. While this fact about desire makes it more difficult to establish that we desire happiness, it also makes it harder for the atheist to deny the same. It is no objection to our argument that atheists desire happiness but do not desire God or anything that implies God's existence. Perhaps the atheist desires something that implies the existence of God, but does not recognize it (at least not under that description).

15. The normal reasons for resisting inclinations to desire an object certainly do not apply. We often resist an inclination to desire something (e.g., the desire for fatty food), if the desire is prone to be, in some way, destructive, that is, if the desire guides us to action that is weakly unnatural in the sense described in note 6 earlier. But an unchecked desire for happiness is not, in any way, destructive. Other reasons to resist the inclination are more interesting, but not more convincing. One might claim that happiness is too one-dimensional to be a worthy ideal, as Susan Wolf criticizes the ideal of moral sainthood in "Moral Saints," *The Journal of Philosophy* 79 (1982): 419–439. But happiness, as we describe it, involves the realization of all one's capacities for excellence. So it is not one-dimensional. Nor do we see why happiness should be regarded as either boring or demanding such a radical transformation of our desires that they would no longer be ours— points Bernard Williams makes about immortality in "The Makropulos Case: Reflections on the Tedium of Immortality," in his *Problems of the Self* (New York: Cambridge University Press, 1973), 82–100. We do not even grant that immortality should be regarded this way. Space does not permit a full treatment of these issues; but Shelly Kagan offers the basis of an excellent response in his fascinating essay, "The Grasshopper, Aristotle, Bob Adams, and Me," in *Metaphysics and the Good: Themes from the Philosophy of Robert Merrihew Adams*, Samuel Newlands and Larry M. Jorgensen, eds. (New York: Oxford University Press), 388–404.

16. The consequence is nicely illustrated by Bertrand Russell, "A Free Man's Worship," *Mysticism and Logic and Other Essays* (New York: Barnes & Noble, Inc., 1971), 40–47. He announces that our ideals must, in the age of Science, be built on "the firm foundation of unyielding despair." But he does not think this will not be easy. The despair results from the certainty that we are "the product of causes which had no prevision of the end they were achieving" and that all human aspirations "are destined to extinction in the vast death of the solar system" (41). Yet he urges readers to retain some respect "for the ideal of perfection which life does not permit us to attain" (43). He councils a complicated process of revolt, resignation, and renunciation that allows us to acknowledge, contemplate, and even cherish the real, but unattainable, goods that we can not help but desire (43–44).

17. The case of conceivability is illustrative. It is conceivable that God exists. But it is also conceivable that there is a correct atheist. (The example is taken from Peter van Inwagen, "Ontological Arguments," in *Philosophy of Religion: A Guide to the Subject*, Brian Davies, ed. (Washington, D.C.: Georgetown University Press, 1998), 54–58.) We do not say that *all* other proposed guides to possibility are similarly equipollent with respect to theistic and atheistic possibilities. Alexander Pruss's creative approaches to the possibility premise (see note 2) have,

at least, not been shown to be equipollent. Pruss defends the claim that the appeal to the motivational centers of flourishing ways of life is not equipollent in his "The Ontological Argument and Motivational Centres," 239–246.

18. The example is inspired by Thomas Nagel; in his *The Last Word* (New York: Oxford University Press, 1997), 130–131. After noting that his own world picture is consonant in certain ways with a broadly theistic world picture, he says: "I want atheism to be true and am made uneasy by the fact that some of the most intelligent and well-informed people I know are religious believers. It isn't just that I don't believe in God and, naturally, hope that I'm right in my belief. It's that I hope there is no God! I don't want there to be a God; I don't want the universe to be like that." He diagnoses this "fear of religion," quite earnestly, as a "cosmic authority problem."

19. It is actually a credit to our guide to possibility that it yields no results in cases where there is nothing to be done. Otherwise, the credibility of our guide to possibility would be damaged (as many others are) by cases surrounding a posteriori necessities. Whether water is H_2O, for example, does not depend on any action we take. So a desire for water to be something other than H_2O is not action guiding; therefore, it is defective; therefore, the desire implies nothing about the possibility of water not being H_2O.

There probably is a God. Many things are easier to explain if there is than if there isn't.

—JOHN VON NEUMANN

(Z)

The Argument from (A) to (Y)

THE ARGUMENT FROM SO MANY ARGUMENTS

Ted Poston

⌐⌐ _____

MY GOAL IN this chapter is to offer a Bayesian model of strength of evidence in cases in which there are multiple items of independent evidence. I will use this Bayesian model to evaluate the strength of evidence for theism if, as Plantinga claims, there are two dozen or so arguments for theism.[1] Formal models are justified by their clarity, precision, and usefulness, even though they involve abstractions that do not perfectly fit the phenomena. Many of Plantinga's arguments are metaphysical arguments, involving premises that are necessarily true, if true at all. Applying a Bayesian account of strength of evidence in this case involves reformulating some of the arguments, but, even if a Bayesian shoe doesn't fit perfectly into a Leibnizian foot, Bayesian footwear is much more suitable to certain types of terrain, especially when the landscape requires encompassing the overall effect of multiple vistas. I believe that the Bayesian model I offer has significant utility in assessing strength of evidence in cases of multiple items of evidence. The model turns questions of the overall strength of multiple arguments into a simple addition problem and it provides a clear framework for raising more philosophical questions about the argument. I hope that this chapter provides a model for many fruitful conversations about how to aggregate multiple items of evidence.[2]

A BAYESIAN MODEL OF MULTIPLE ITEMS OF EVIDENCE

Bayesianism is well suited to evaluate the evidential impact of multiple items of evidence. It offers a clear account of evidential relevance and the evidential impact of evidence on theory. I begin by discussing several idealizations in order to offer a tractable Bayesian model of evidential impact. I then offer the results of the model and discuss some questions that arise from the model.

The Bayesian Framework

Bayesian models of the strength of evidence for a hypothesis are quite useful. In the following I discuss some aspects of the particular model I use. These aspects are idealizations, but not every idealization involves a significant departure from reality. The model makes tractable a number of issues with respect to the overall confirmation of theism. Its fruitfulness justifies its use even if it doesn't faithfully capture all of our intuitions about confirmation.

A Bayesian model requires that hypotheses and evidence can be given a prior probability that reflects the plausibility of the hypotheses and evidence prior to learning from experience. A probability is a real number inclusively between 0 and 1 that obeys the axioms of the probability calculus. I will take it for granted that we can make comparative claims about the probability of various competing hypotheses and the probability of some items of evidence on those hypotheses. This does not commit us to thinking that every proposition has a probability nor that the probability is some fixed real number.[3] Moreover, I'll leave open the interpretation of a probability function. Personalists can read the forthcoming results as yielding at most consistency requirements for rationality. Objectivists can read the following results in a more robust sense. My task isn't to wade into these murky waters; rather, I cast my net with an eye to putting on the table a clear model of the confirmation of multiple lines of argument.[4]

The specific probabilistic comparisons I will work with are comparisons of what is known as the *likelihoods*. The likelihood is the probability that some evidential claim is true given a specific hypothesis. If a fair coin is to be flipped, then the probability that it lands heads is .5. The relevant likelihood is Pr(heads | fair). The cases that concern us are assigning comparative likelihoods to an evidential claim given theism and naturalism. Suppose our evidential claim is that there is a physical universe whose natural laws allow for the development of embodied creatures. Call this claim "FT" for fine-tuning. The relevant likelihood ratio is the value of this:

$$\frac{Pr\left(FT|theism\right)}{Pr\left(FT|naturalism\right)}$$

The model I offer later is compatible with any estimate of these likelihoods. When we get to the model I will discuss the results on different assumptions about the values for the relevant likelihoods.

Another assumption I make concerns the number of different hypotheses at issue. I shall work with two: the hypothesis of theism and the hypothesis of naturalism. Theism is the hypothesis that there is an omniscient, omnipotent, and omnibenevolent being. This is the hypothesis that there is a perfect being. I shall refer to the theistic hypothesis as "T." Naturalism is the hypothesis that there is no such being or any similar beings, that Democritus was right when he said that "it's just atoms and the void." For the purposes of the following Bayesian model, I assume the useful falsehood that theism and naturalism are mutually exclusive and exhaustive. Thus, naturalism will be represented as "¬T." Two reasons justify this useful falsehood. First, the confirmation of a hypothesis is a matter of how well it beats its conceived rival hypotheses. Given some evidence and a field of hypotheses, we ask ourselves how much this evidence confirms one hypothesis over its competitors. The problems that arise with the catchall hypothesis are often rightfully ignored in a specific context in which a field of hypotheses are at issue. Second, my overall task is to model the evidential impact of multiple lines of argument. The model I offer is more tractable given the assumption that theism and naturalism are mutually exclusive and exhaustive options.

Evidential Relevance and Strength of Evidence

According to the Bayesian account of evidential relevance, an item of evidence, e, is evidentially relevant to a hypothesis h just in case $Pr(h|e) \neq Pr(h)$. If e raises $Pr(h|e)$ then e is evidence for h, and if e lowers $Pr(h|e)$ then e is evidence against h. Bayes's theorem relates $Pr(h|e)$ to three other probabilities: (i) $Pr(h|e)$, called the "likelihood of the hypothesis"; (ii) $Pr(h)$, the prior probability of the hypothesis; and (iii) $Pr(e)$, the prior probability of the evidence. Bayes's theorem states,

$$Pr(h|e) = \frac{Pr(e|h)Pr(h)}{Pr(e)}$$

In our case we are interested in comparing the confirmation of multiple items of independent evidence to theism and naturalism. Thus we can work with the odds form of Bayes's theorem, which is as follows:

$$\frac{Pr(T|e)}{Pr(\neg T|e)} = \frac{Pr(T)}{Pr(\neg T)} \times \frac{Pr(e|T)}{Pr(e|\neg T)}$$

The odds form follows from Bayes's theorem because both posterior probabilities are divided by the same quantity–$Pr(e)$. This form is useful because it allows us to directly compare their relative confirmation by examining the ratios of the priors and the likelihoods.

The odds form isolates two factors in the judgement over the posterior probabilities: (i) prior belief and (ii) evidential strength. In the following I focus only on the relative strength of evidence, that is, the ratio $\frac{Pr(e|T)}{Pr(e|\neg T)}$. This abstracts away from the influence of prior belief. I am interested in a measure of evidential strength that is not sensitive to differences in prior beliefs. Thus, measuring strength of evidence should only concern the relevant likelihood ratios.

Royall's Case

The statistician Richard Royall defends the claim that a likelihood ratio of 8 is "pretty strong" evidence.[5] Royall provides a natural case to ground the evidential strength of a likelihood ratio of 8. Suppose we have two urns. Urn 1 contains only white balls and urn 2 contains half white and half black balls. We select a ball from an urn, record its color, place it back in the urn, and thoroughly mix the contents of the urn. Suppose you begin to draw balls from the urns and you draw three successive white balls. It is natural that this is pretty strong evidence that the urn contains only white balls. The likelihood ratio in this case is $(\frac{1}{.5})^3 = 2^3 = 8$.

We can use Royall's case to provide a natural anchor for any value to the likelihood ratio. Where b the number of successive white balls, then the likelihood ratio in favor of all white over half white is $(\frac{1}{.5^b}) = 2^b$. Royall provides the following values for b and corresponding likelihood ratios (see table 1).

A nice feature of table 1 is that we can go back and forth between a likelihood ratio and a sequence of white draws. Suppose we find that the evidence has a likelihood ratio of 20. What is the natural understanding of the strength of evidence corresponding to a likelihood ratio of 20? It's strong evidence, but how strong? By inspection the table shows us that a LR of 20 is the equivalent of selecting 4.3 white balls in sequence. If our evidence just consists in the fact that 4 white balls were selected in Royall's setup, then that is significant evidence that we are selecting from the white-only urn.

Royall's case is useful for associating a LR value with a more natural case. But the specific details of his case are not ideal for my purpose since we can get conclusive evidence

TABLE I

Number of successive white
balls (b) corresponding to values
of a likelihood ratio (LR)

LR	10	20	50	100	1000
b	3.3	4.3	5.6	6.6	10

that we are selecting from urn 2 if one black ball is selected. This feature of Royall's orig-inal case is easily avoided by changing the contents of the urn.[6] Instead of urn 1 containing all white balls, let us suppose it contains $\frac{2}{3}$ white and $\frac{1}{3}$ black. Moreover, suppose urn 2 has $\frac{1}{3}$ white and $\frac{2}{3}$ black. Then Pr(white | urn 1)=.66 and Pr(white | urn 2)=.33. The relevant likelihood ratio in this case is 2. All the desirable features of Royall's case are maintained. If we observe 5 white balls in sequence, then the likelihood ratio is $2^5 = 32$. This is very strong evidence that we are selecting from urn 1. In the following I use this modified version of Royall's case.

Suppose that all you learn is that a white ball is selected on two draws, say on the ith and j^{th} draws white was selected. How strong of a case is that for urn 2? The relevant like-lihood ratios are

$$\frac{Pr\left(white_i|urn1\right)}{Pr\left(white_i|urn2\right)} = 2$$

and

$$\frac{Pr\left(white_j|urn1\right)}{Pr\left(white_j|urn2\right)} = 2.$$

It is natural to think that $white_i$ and $white_j$ *independently confirm* that Urn 1 was selected. Since the selections from the urns are not affected by previous draws, we can take multiple white draws as each independent evidence for urn 1. In this case we calculate the cumulative power of multiple white selections according to the following:

$$\frac{Pr\left(White_{(1,2,...,n)}|Urn1\right)}{Pr\left(White_{(1,2,...,n)}|Urn2\right)} = \left(\frac{\frac{2}{3}}{\frac{1}{3}}\right)^n = 2^n$$

This formula tells us that when we have n white draws the power of the evidence is 2^n. Because the likelihood ratio for black balls is the multiplicative inverse of the likelihood ratio for white balls, we can also easily accommodate the number, j, of black balls selected by using 2^{n-j}. Thus where our evidence is that 10 white balls were selected and 5 black balls were selected then the relevant likelihood ratio is 2^5. That is strong evidence that we are selecting from Urn 1.

OTHER FEATURES OF ROYALL'S CASE

Royall's case is useful for introducing a number of probabilistic features pertaining to strength of evidence in cases of multiple items of evidence. Earlier we saw that because a specific draw of a ball from an urn is unaffected by the previous draws, we can easily combine the overall strength of evidence for all the draws. This feature is sometimes described under the heading of "independent evidence." But note that in Royall's case and the modified version, the draws are not unconditionally independent from each other. The probability that white is selected on draw 2 *is* influenced by whether or not white was drawn on the first draw. The reason for this is that white on 1 provides evidence that urn 1 was selected and thus changes the probability that white is selected on draw 2.

Let us put these points using the formal model. Let "W_i" stand of the claim that "a white ball is selected on the ith draw" and "U_j" stand for the claim that "Urn number j was selected." The unconditional probability that white is selected on 1 is

$$Pr(W_1) = Pr(W_1|U_1) \times Pr(U_1) + Pr(W_1|U_2) \times Pr(U_2) = (0.66 \times 0.5) + (0.33 \times 0.5) = 0.5$$

Similarly, the unconditional probability that white is selected on draw 2 is 0.5. But the probability that white is selected on draw 2 given that white was selected on draw 1 is not 0.5. Rather, it is the following:

$$Pr(W_2|W_1) = Pr(U_1|W_1)Pr(W_2|W_1 \& U_1) + Pr(U_2|W_1)Pr(W_2|W_1 \& U_2)$$

We can use Bayes's theorem to determine "$Pr(U_1|W_1)$" and "$Pr(U_2|W_1)$." The values here are $\frac{2}{3}$ and $\frac{1}{3}$ respectively. Next we use the features of the modified version of Royall's case to determine the remaining values. $Pr(W_2|W_1 \& U_1) = \frac{2}{3}$ and $Pr(W_2|W_1 \& U_2) = \frac{1}{3}$. Thus, $Pr(W_2|W_1) = \frac{5}{9}$. The formal model tracks our natural judgement that the selection of white on 1 is evidence that white will be selected on 2.

We noted earlier that in Royall's case we can combine the selections of white balls easily to get the overall evidential strength of n white balls. What probabilistic feature of Royall's case is responsible for the natural judgment that W_i and W_j are confirmationally independent regarding the hypothesis that urn 1 was selected? The key feature is that the selection of an urn screens off the results of previous draws. The screening-off condition is the following, where $j > i$

1. $Pr(w_j|Urn1 \& w_i) = Pr(w_j|Urn1)$
2. $Pr(w_j|Urn2 \& w_i) = Pr(w_j|Urn2)$

Claims (1) and (2) hold in Royall's model because once the urn is selected, the results of previous draws don't change the probability of any subsequent draw.

The key features of Royall's case are the following. First, given a likelihood ratio we can find a corresponding number of white balls. This grounds judgements about the evidential strength of various likelihood values. Second, the individual selections are not unconditionally independent. Third, the individual selections are probabilistically independent regarding U_1 and U_2. The importance of probabilistic independence regarding H is that it ensures that we can combine (in a way to be discussed shortly) multiple items of evidence. It is important to realize that the crucial notion of independence is not unconditional independence but independence regarding H. When it comes to modeling multiple items of evidence, each item of positive evidence for a hypothesis may increase the probability that the hypothesis is true and thus lead us to expect more positive evidence. Even so, if the evidence is independent regarding H, then it does not affect a natural way of combining multiple items of evidence. For reasons that I will not go in to, the second and third features of Royall's case uniquely picks up the log-likelihood ratio.[7]

THE LOG-LIKELIHOOD RATIO AND INDEPENDENT EVIDENCE

Independent evidence for a theory is important, because the confirmatory significance of each item of independent evidence is undiluted when added together in a larger case for the theory. C.S. Pierce remarks on this feature of independent evidence. He writes,

> Two arguments which are entirely independent, neither weakening nor strengthening the other, ought, when they concur, to produce a[n intensity of] belief equal to the sum of the intensities of belief which either would produce separately.[8]

Branden Fitelson provides a nice Bayesian account of the conformational significance of independent evidence.[9] Two items of evidence are confirmationally independent regarding H if and only if the support each provides for H is independent of whether the other piece of evidence is already known. That is,

> *Definition of confirmational independence*: E_1 and E_2 are (mutually) confirmationally independent regarding H according to c if and only if both $c(H, E_1 | E_2) = c(H, E_1)$ and $c(H, E_2 | E_1) = c(H, E_2)$.[10]

$c(H, E_1)$ is the degree of confirmation that E_1 provides for H. $c(H, E_1 | E_2)$ is the degree of confirmation that E_1 provides for H given that E_2 is known. This definition captures the idea that the confirmational significance of independent evidence is unaffected by whether the other evidence is known. Fitelson shows that the log-likelihood measure (or an ordinally equivalent measure) satisfies natural principles about evidential independence such as Pierce's claim that when two arguments are entirely independent, then, when they both occur, they should produce a level of confidence equal to the sum of the levels of confidence each would produce separately.[11] Fitelson interprets this Peircean claim as the following:

($\mathcal{A}$) If E_1 and E_2 are confirmationally independent regarding H according to c,
then $c(H, E_1 \& E_2) = c(H, E_1) + c(H, E_2)$.

This claim allows us to add together the confirmational significance of items of independent evidence. Thus, where E_1 and E_2 are confirmationally independent regarding H according to c, we can determine the total confirmation E_1 and E_2 offer to H by the following:

$$log\left(\frac{E_1 \mid H}{E_1 \mid \neg H}\right) + log\left(\frac{E_2 \mid H}{E_2 \mid \neg H}\right)$$

An attractive feature of using logarithms is that it turns multiplication into addition. Thus, where the evidence meets the screening-off condition, we can simply add together the evidential effect of multiple items of evidence.

MODELS FOR MULTIPLE ITEMS OF EVIDENCE

In the following I provide two models for the evidential strength of multiple items of evidence. The models vary by the relevant likelihood ratio. In the first model I assume that the likelihood ratio for each item of evidence favors theism by a factor of 10. Using base-10 log, this gives us a log likelihood ratio of 1.[12] In the second model I assume that the likelihood ratio for each item favors theism by 10 percent. I also discuss ways in which the models can be used to account for evidence against theism.

Strong Independent Evidence

The initial model is one in which the positive evidence for theism is an order of magnitude greater on theism than on naturalism. For each e_i, $log[\frac{Pr(e_i|T)}{Pr(e_i|\neg T)}] = 1$ In Royall's model this is strong evidence; it is equivalent to the selection of 3.3 white balls.

The assumption that the log-likelihood ratio (LLR) for each item of evidence for theism is 1 is not completely indefensible. Richard Swinburne thinks that if we can determine an agent's beliefs, desires, and goals, then we can determine with significant probability that an agent will do some thing.[13] In the case of theism, Swinburne holds that we can make reasonable determinations of what kinds of action a perfect being will bring about. A morally perfect being will bring about the best action if there is one and it is within the scope of his knowledge and power. An omniscient and omnipotent morally perfect being will therefore bring about the best action if there is one and will not perform a bad action. To the extent there are many different incompatible good actions with no best, we can reasonably determine that a perfect being will bring about one out of those good options. Thus, Swinburne thinks we can assign a probability to the claim that God will bring about some good option such as the creation of other beings of limited knowledge, power, and goodness. Since we are interested in purely comparative probabilities, it is not unreasonable to think that there is an order of magnitude difference with respect to whether there would be finite beings of intentional power and goodness given theism as opposed to given naturalism. Whether this holds for multiple items of independent evidence is an open question, but I shall assume so in this model.

A nice feature of this model is that it is a simple head count to determine the overall strength of evidence for theism. If Plantinga is right that there are twenty-four arguments for theism then, on this model, the overall evidential strength of theism is $c\left(T, e_1, e_2, ..., e_{24}\right) = 24$. Given this value, we can then go back to Royall's case to determine the equivalent number of white balls.

We need to do a bit of work first to find that number. First, consider table 2 , which looks at the strength of evidence provided by the first fifteen white balls (see table 2). We see that 15 white balls in sequence only gives us a LLR of 4.5. In order to find the equivalent number of white balls for a LLR of 24 we have to continue the count. Because the numbers get large fast, I have shortened the results in table 3.

TABLE 2

Comparison of Royall's likelihood ratios with the log-likelihood ratio

# of successive white balls	Likelihood ratio (LR)2^n	Log-likelihood ratio (LLR)
1	2	0.301029995663981
2	4	0.602059991327962
3	8	0.903089986991944
4	16	1.20411998265592
5	32	1.50514997831991
6	64	1.80617997398389
7	128	2.10720996964787
8	256	2.40823996531185
9	512	2.70926996097583
10	1024	3.01029995663981
11	2048	3.31132995230379
12	4096	3.61235994796777
13	8192	3.91338994363176
14	16384	4.21441993929574
15	32768	4.51544993495972

TABLE 3

Comparison of successive white balls
with log-likelihood ratios

# of successive white balls	Log-likelihood ratio
1	0.301029995663981
2	0.602059991327962
3	0.903089986991944
4	1.20411998265592
5	1.50514997831991
10	3.01029995663981
20	6.02059991327962
30	9.03089986991944
40	12.0411998265592
50	15.0514997831991
60	18.0617997398389
70	21.0720996964787
80	24.0823996531185

By inspection on table 3 we can see that the evidential strength of 24 independent arguments of theism each with a LLR of 1 is the equivalent of approximately 80 white balls (see table 3). Thus, A LLR of 24 then tells us that the evidential case for theism is as strong as the case in which we have eighty more white balls than black. That is overpowering evidence that urn 1 is selected.

In general, if there are n independent arguments for theism (where each is favorable to theism by a log-likelihood ratio of 1), then we can determine the corresponding number of successive white balls according to the following equation: $b = \frac{n}{0.30102999566398}$. Table 4 produces the value for b for various determinations of how many independent arguments for theism there are (see table 4).

A fruitful aspect of using this model is that it is easy to determine the evidential strength of multiple arguments. Suppose there are five independent arguments, then the evidential case is the equivalent of the selection of 16.6 white balls. The evidential strength of multiple arguments is directly proportional to the number of independent lines of evidence.

Moreover, we can use the odds form of Bayes's theorem to determine the relevant difference in prior belief that would be required for a person unmoved by the evidential case. To be unmoved by the strength of evidence requires that $\frac{Pr(T)}{Pr(\neg T)}$ must be near the reciprocal of the likelihood ratio. If someone is unmoved by strength of evidence having an LLR of 24 then the difference among the priors must be $\frac{1}{10^{24}}$.

TABLE 4

Comparison of # of independent arguments
for theism with # of successive white balls

# of independent arguments for theism	# of successive white balls
5	16.6096404744368
10	33.2192809488736
15	49.8289214233104
20	66.4385618977472
25	83.0482023721841

This model can also accommodate the evidence against theism. Assuming that each item of negatively relevant evidence has a LLR of 1 in favor of atheism, we simply subtract the number of items of evidence against theism from the number of items of evidence for theism. The final count gives us the new LLR. If, for instance, there are five arguments for theism and two arguments against, then, assuming the LLRs are same, the evidential case as a LLR of 3. Consulting table 3, we see that a LLR of 3 is the equivalent of the selection of ten white balls. That is significant evidence.

The model can also accommodate items of evidence that have different LLRs. Many philosophers hold that the primary item of evidence for theism is facts about the distribution and quality of evils we observe in our world. It is not unreasonable to think of this as very powerful evidence against theism. One can easily express the power of this evidence in terms of some multiple of a LLR of 1. If we assign the problem of evil a LLR of 4, then this expresses the judgement that the strength of evidence that evil has is like the selection of thirteen white balls. The overall tally procedure is the same.

WEAK INDEPENDENT EVIDENCE

Let us examine a model in which the relevant LLRs are only slightly in favor of theism. For each item of evidence, let us suppose that the theist has a slightly more plausible story than the naturalism. How shall we interpret probabilistically the idea that a hypothesis as a slightly more plausible account of the evidence than its competitor? Thinking purely about the likelihood ratio, a favorable ratio of a 10 percent captures the idea that the evidence only weakly favors H over ¬H.

In the following, I work with this ratio: $\frac{Pr(e_i|T)}{Pr(e_i|\neg T)} = \frac{a}{\frac{9}{10}a} = \frac{10}{9}$. A likelihood ratio that favors T over ¬T by 10 percent gives us a LLR of 0.046.[14] At this value it would take approximately twenty-two independent lines of evidence to equal the confirmatory power of one white ball.

What we learn from this is that the values of the LLRs are crucial. We can easily accommodate differing LLRs by thinking about how powerful the evidence is in terms of Royall's model. Does the individual evidence have the power of a selection of one ball, two balls, three balls, and so on? In each case, we find the corresponding LLR and add together the cumulative effect of the evidence. As noted earlier, we can add together different values of the LLRs. If one piece of evidence is weak but another piece is strong, then we simply add the LLRs and find the corresponding number of white balls.

Another fruitful feature of these models is that we can estimate a person's LLRs for the evidence if we know the ratio of their prior beliefs and the ratio of their posterior beliefs. If a person thinks that theism and naturalism have roughly the same prior and yet they remain agnostic given the evidence, then the overall impact of all the evidence has an LLR of o. A different person who thinks that the evidence is ever so slightly in favor of theism and whose difference in prior belief is a wash, may well be in a position to engage in Pascalian reasoning. I find these Bayesianism models fruitful if only for clarifying a person's judgements about the relevant likelihood ratios. In the following I shall examine some other fruitful aspects of these models.

INDEPENDENCE AND EVIDENCE

In this final section I tackle two questions. First, the model that I've used requires that multiple items of evidence meet the screening-off condition. This is the following condition:

$$(S) \quad \frac{Pr(e_i \,|\, T)}{Pr(e_i \,|\, \neg T)} = \frac{Pr(e_i \,|\, T \,\&\, e_j)}{Pr(e_i \,|\, \neg T \,\&\, e_j)}, \text{ for each } e_i, e_j.$$

(S) requires that once we specify the hypotheses and the previous items of evidence the probability for each particular item of evidence is not affected by this specification. As noted in the first section, (S) expresses the idea that the evidence is independent regarding h, and this is different from the idea that the evidence is unconditionally independent. It is crucial for a large evidential case that the evidence is not "double counted." This can happen if once piece of evidence entails the other. For instance, if one argument for theism proceeds from the claim that there is intentionality and another argument proceeds from the claim that there are moral beliefs, then these arguments cannot both be added together because they violate condition (S). Since moral beliefs implies intentionality, the probability of the latter given the former is 1. It is a fruitful project to go through Plantinga's two dozen or so arguments for theism and figure out which arguments violate condition (S). Trent Dougherty and I argued in a previous paper that multiple design arguments violate condition (S) and so the natural theologian cannot offer both in an overall cumulative case argument.[15]

Condition (S) forces the natural theologian to think about independent families of theistic arguments. It is an open question how many of these arguments are independent. The major theistic arguments have natural interpretations in which they are conditionally independent. The ontological, cosmological, teleological, and moral arguments plausibly meet condition (S). The central datum in the ontological argument—it is possible that there is a perfect being—does not entail the central claim in any of the other arguments. The Kalam cosmological argument proceeds on the claims that the universe began to exist and anything that began to exist has a cause. The teleological argument proceeds from the claim that the physical laws and conditions required to permit the existence of embodied creatures are overwhelmingly unlikely to occur by chance. And the moral argument proceeds on the different datum that there are embodied, rational creatures who are sensitive to moral aspects of reality. If these claims are conditionally independent regarding theism and naturalism and the relevant LLR favors theism by a factor of 1, then we have significant evidence for theism. In terms of Royall's case, a LLR of 4 is approximately equal to thirteen white balls.

When we explicitly think about the classic theistic arguments, we meet a difficulty in how these arguments should be captured by a Bayesian model. A crucial problem with the Bayesian model I've used is that it requires that the data be given a non-zero probability on naturalism. This may require some tinkering with the arguments. For instance, on S5 model logic if it is possible that there is a perfect being then this being exists in every world and so naturalism is false. There are a variety of ways to get around this problem. One is to shift the central claim in the ontological to something that may be true on naturalism: it appears to be possible that there is a perfect being. Some of the other arguments rest on metaphysical claims that are either necessarily true or necessarily false and so it may be thought that the Bayesian model is inapt. However, it is not unreasonable to think that evidential probabilities may be assigned to claims that are necessarily true or necessarily false. I do not see these details as reasons to forgo the Bayesian model, since that model provides a clear way to assess overall strength of evidence and raises key questions about whether the arguments are conditionally independent regarding theism.

CONCLUSION

I've argued that a fruitful approach to Plantinga's suggestion that there are two dozen or so arguments for theism is to work with a Bayesian model of the significance of multiple arguments for theism. We've seen that on some defensible assumptions about the relevant likelihood ratios, multiple arguments for theism provide significance evidence for theism. We've also seen that the values of the likelihood ratios are crucial. This requires that one defend not only the claim that the evidence is predicted by theism but that it is also not so strongly predicted by naturalism. Finally, I've looked at the crucial screening-off condition and argued that the evidence needs to meet this condition to be summed. We've also looked at a consequence of this model that the relevant evidence must have a non-zero probability on naturalism.

So, how good is the argument from so many arguments? If each argument is conditionally independent regarding theism and has a LLR of 1, then Table 4 tells us that the argument from so many arguments is very powerful evidence for theism.

NOTES

Thanks to Dan Bonevac, Robin Collins, Tim McGrew, Brad Monton, Alexander Pruss, Bill Roche, and Richard Swinburne for helpful comments on an earlier draft. I am especially grateful to Branden Fitelson for multiple conversations that led to significant improvements in this paper.

1. Plantinga (2007).

2. My attitude to the Bayesian methodology is nicely captured by Paul Horwich's excellent article (Horwich 1993).

3. Keynes, for instance, did not think that all probabilities were numerical. Rather on his view probabilities can be comparative. See Keynes (1921).

4. My argument does assume that the probabilities at issue are not physical propensities. I have in my mind a notion of probability; see Maher (2006, 2010).

5. Royall 1997, 12. Thanks to Branden Fitelson for pointing me to the relevance of Royall's discussion.

6. Thanks to Tim McGrew for pointing this out.

7. See Fitelson (2001).

8. Peirce (1878); quoted in Fitelson (2001,125).

9. Fitelson (2001).

10. Fitelson (2001,125).

11. See Fitelson (2001,125).

12. Natural logs are more prevalent in mathematics, but base-10 logs are easier to work with. Nothing hangs on the choice of a base.

13. Swinburne (2004, 112–123).

14. Again, using log base 10.

15. Dougherty and Poston (2008).

REFERENCES

Dougherty, T. Poston, T. 2008. "A User's Guide to Teleological Arguments." *Religious Studies* 44: 99–110.

Fitelson, B. 2001. "A Bayesian Account of Independent Evidence with Applications." *Philosophy of Science* 68(3): 123–140.

Horwich, P. 1993. "Wittgensteinian Bayesianism." *Midwest Studies in Philosophy* 18(1): 62–75.

Keynes, J. M. 1921. *A Treatise on Probability*. New York: Macmillan.

Maher, P. 2006. "The Concept of Inductive Probability." *Erkenntnis* 65: 185–206.

———. 2010. "Bayesian Probability." *Synthese* 172: 119–127.

Plantinga, A. 2007. "Two Dozen (or so) Theistic Arguments," in B. Deane-Peter (ed.), *Alvin Plantinga* (Cambridge: Cambridge University Press), 203–227.

Royall, R. 1997. *Statistical Evidence: A Likelihood Paradigm*. London: Chapman and Hall.

Swinburne, R. 2004. *The Existence of God*, 2nd ed. Oxford: Oxford University Press.

V

"Or so": Three More Arguments

The *Kalam* Cosmological Argument

William Lane Craig

INTRODUCTION

The *kalam* cosmological argument, largely forgotten since the time of Kant, finds nary a mention in Plantinga's "Two Dozen (or so) Theistic Arguments." Indeed, "benign neglect" best describes Plantinga's treatment of the argument throughout the corpus of his work. Neither supported nor refuted, the argument simply goes almost entirely unremarked. So its inclusion in the present volume can be justified only by taking it to be among the unnamed arguments in the catchall category "or so."

My attempt to resurrect the *kalam* cosmological argument in 1979 was initially no more successful than Stuart Hackett's similar attempt two decades earlier.[1] Today, however, the argument is once again in the spotlight.[2] In a recent philosophical appraisal, the author judges that the argument's proponents have battled its critics to a stalemate,[3] a result with which I as a natural theologian am entirely content. In this brief chapter, I want to reflect on some current developments regarding the argument.

The medieval Muslim theologian al-Ghazali presented the following simple statement of the argument: "Every being which begins has a cause for its beginning; now the world is a being which begins; therefore, it possesses a cause for its beginning."[4]

We shouldn't stumble at Ghazali's deductive formulation of the argument. The evidence needn't render a deductive argument's premises certain in order for the argument to be cogent. But if one prefers, the argument can be formulated inductively as an inference to the best explanation. I myself like to present the argument deductively because of the clarity and simplicity of such a formulation.

FIRST PREMISE

Ghazali's first premise, "Every being which begins has a cause for its beginning," raises a number of questions that limitations of space preclude my discussing. Suffice it to say that I now prefer to reformulate the causal premise: "If the universe began to exist, then the universe has a cause of its beginning."

The most important objection to the causal premise comes from Adolf Grünbaum, who points out that it assumes that in beginning to exist, the universe came into being.[5] The issue Grünbaum raises here is whether time is tensed or tenseless. On a tensed or so-called A-Theory of time, temporal becoming is an objective feature of reality, whereas on a tenseless or B-Theory of time, all events are equally real, and temporal becoming is an illusion. On a B-theory, the universe in beginning to exist does not come into being; rather, the tenselessly existing four-dimensional space-time manifold simply has a front edge, so to speak. I should say that a tensed theory of time is a sufficient, though not a necessary, condition for the truth of the premise, because something cannot come into being from nothing. I have therefore tried to do my philosophical duty by writing a two-volume defense of a tensed as opposed to tenseless theory of time.[6]

SECOND PREMISE

Let's hurry on to the argument's crucial second premise, "The universe began to exist." I've defended two philosophical arguments and two scientific confirmations for this premise. We shall focus here on the philosophical arguments.

First Philosophical Argument

I argue:

1. An actual infinite cannot exist.
2. An infinite temporal regress of events is an actual infinite.
3. Therefore an infinite temporal regress of events cannot exist.

Against (1) it has been objected that the same arguments against the existence of an actually infinite number of concrete objects would apply *mutatis mutandis* to abstract objects, which would destroy classical mathematics. One might respond to this objection by drawing some in-principle distinction that would exempt *abstracta* from the argument. For example, Alexander Pruss and Robert Koons (to be discussed in the sequel) hold that arguments against the actual infinite apply only to causally connected things, thereby exempting *abstracta* from their strictures. This would be a welcome conclusion, indeed, since arguments against an actually infinite regress of concrete things would not imply finitism about abstract objects. But assuming a worst-case scenario, would finitism about *abstracta* destroy classical mathematics?

This allegation is far too hasty. It begs the question against anti-realist views of mathematical objects. The truth of classical mathematics and the ontology of mathematical objects are distinct questions, all too often conflated by recent critics of the argument.[7] Most anti-realists would not go to the intuitionistic extreme of denying mathematical legitimacy to the actual infinite; rather, they would simply insist that acceptance of the mathematical legitimacy of certain notions does not imply an ontological commitment to the reality of various objects. The abundance of nominalist (or anti-realist) alternatives to Platonism (such as neutralism, fictionalism, constructiblism, figuralism, modal structuralism, pretense theory, and so on) renders the issue of the ontological status of mathematical entities a moot question. The realist, then, if he is to maintain that mathematical objects furnish a decisive counterexample to the denial of the existence of the actual infinite, must provide some overriding argument for the reality of mathematical objects, as well as provide rebutting defeaters of all the anti-realist alternatives consistent with classical mathematics—a task whose prospects for success are dim, indeed.[8]

It is sometimes asserted that science requires that an actually infinite number of things exist. But this is in fact false. The notion of the potential infinite is entirely adequate to scientific theorizing. Stanford University mathematician Solomon Feferman, commenting that "the actual infinite is not required for the mathematics of the physical world," explains,

> Infinitary concepts are not essential to the mathematization of science, all appearances to the contrary. And this . . . puts into question the view that higher mathematics is somehow embodied in the world, rather than that it is the conceptual edifice raised by mankind in order to make sense of the world.[9]

The best way to support (1) is by way of thought experiments that illustrate the various absurdities that would result if an actual infinite were to be instantiated in the real world, for example, the famous "Hilbert's Hotel," which is able to accommodate infinitely more guests despite its being fully occupied. José Benardete, who is especially creative and effective at concocting such thought experiments, puts it well: "Viewed *in abstracto*, there is no logical contradiction involved in any of these enormities; but we have only to confront them *in concreto* for their outrageous absurdity to strike us full in the face."[10]

Benardete has especially in mind what he calls paradoxes of the serrated continuum, such as the following:

> Here is a book lying on the table. Open it. Look at the first page. Measure its thickness. It is very thick indeed for a single sheet of paper—1/2 inch thick. Now turn to the second page of the book. How thick is this second sheet of paper? 1/4 inch thick. And the third page of the book, how thick is this third sheet of

paper? 1/8 inch thick, &c. *ad infinitum*. We are to posit not only that each page of the book is followed by an immediate successor the thickness of which is one-half that of the immediately preceding page but also (and this is not unimportant) that each page is separated from page 1 by a finite number of pages. These two conditions are logically compatible: there is no certifiable contradiction in their joint assertion. But they mutually entail that there is no last page in the book. Close the book. Turn it over so that the front cover of the book is now lying face down upon the table. Now—slowly—lift the back cover of the book with the aim of exposing to view the stack of pages lying beneath it. *There is nothing to see.* For there is no last page in the book to meet our gaze.[11]

What makes paradoxes like these especially powerful is that no process or supertask is involved here; each page is an actual entity having a finite thickness (none is a degenerate interval) which could be unbound from the others and all the pages scattered to the four winds, so that an actual infinity of pages would exist throughout space. If such a book cannot exist, therefore, neither can an actual infinite.

At this point the actual infinitist has little choice but, in Oppy's words, simply to "embrace the conclusion of one's opponent's *reductio ad absurdum* argument." Oppy explains, "these allegedly absurd situations are just what one ought to expect if there were . . . physical infinities."[12]

Oppy's response, however, is unavailing: it does nothing to prove that the envisioned situations are not absurd but only serves to reiterate, in effect, that if an actual infinite could exist in reality, then there could be Benardete's Book or Hilbert's Hotel, which is not in dispute. The problem cases would, after all, not be problematic if the alleged consequences would not ensue! Rather, the question is whether these consequences really are absurd.

With respect to premise (2), there has been considerable discussion in recent years whether the argument would, if successful, imply the finitude of the future as well as the finitude of the past.[13] The point of this misgiving is not altogether clear. Since the traditional proponents of the *kalam* cosmological argument believed in life everlasting, this sort of consideration might give the argument's critic a dialectical advantage when directed ad hominem; but it neither undercuts nor rebuts either of the premises of the argument against the infinitude of the past. Physical eschatology is perfectly consistent with the temporal series of events' coming to an end in a terminal cosmological singularity. Philosophical arguments in favor of the temporal series of events' coming to an end would occasion serious theological difficulties for orthodox Christians, Jews, and Muslims, but they would constitute no defeater of the argument for the finitude of the past.

Cohen interprets the argument's critics to hold that since an endless universe certainly seems possible, we should be skeptical of the arguments for the beginning of the universe. The proponent of the *kalam* argument could shrug this claim off by responding that the critic has shown no absurdity in the series of events' having an end as well as a beginning. So the skepticism is groundless.

But is the critic warranted in treating past and future events as completely parallel? Defenders of the *kalam* argument may attempt to defeat the objection by drawing attention to some crucial disanalogy between the past and future that spoils the critics' attempt to demonstrate parallelism. On a tenseless or B-Theory of time, the future is entirely analogous to the past, since all events are equally real, and temporal becoming is an illusion. On a B-Theory of time it is perspicuous why arguments against a beginningless series of earlier events would be equally good arguments against an endless series of later events.

But the *kalam* cosmological argument presupposes from start to finish a tensed or A-Theory of time, according to which temporal becoming is an objective feature of reality. The series of events terminates in the present event, and the terminus is constantly changing as new events occur and are added to the series. There are no events later than the present event and, hence, no future events. So an A-Theory of time entails that an actually infinite number of future events does not exist; indeed, the number of future events is 0. The series of events later than any event in time is always finite and always increasing toward infinity as a limit. In other words, such a series is potentially infinite. This feature of the series elucidates why it seems intuitively obvious that the temporal series of events could go on forever: it endlessly approaches infinity as a limit. By contrast the series of events earlier than any event in time cannot be potentially infinite, for in order to be so, it would have to be finite and yet increasing in the *earlier than* direction, which contradicts the nature of temporal becoming. So a beginningless series of such events must be actually infinite.

Cohen insists that in order to rebut the objection, it is not enough to affirm that only the series of past events, in contrast to the series of future events, is actually infinite. Two points should be made here. First, the proponent of the *kalam* argument need not *rebut* the objection in order to defeat it. He may defeat it by simply *undercutting* the warrant for the objection. It is the objector who has in this case a fairly heavy burden of proof to bear: he needs to prove that arguments for the finitude of the past translate unproblematically into arguments for the finitude of the future.[14] Second, if the argument against the infinitude of the past is based on the paradoxical nature of the actual infinite, then affirming that a beginningless series of past events, in contrast to an endless series of future events, is alone actually infinite does, indeed, provide a defeater of the objection. The objector will have the burden of showing that such an affirmation is untenable.

It has been said that on presentism, past events no more exist than future events, so that the number of past events is likewise 0, even if the series of past events is beginningless.[15] But as I have made clear, my argument against the existence of an actual infinite is intended to show that an actually infinite number of things cannot be instantiated in reality.[16] Given an A-Theory of time, if the series of isochronous events is beginningless, then an actually infinite number of past events has been instantiated in reality. By contrast, if the series of isochronous events is endless, an actually infinite number of future events has not and never will be instantiated in reality. *Pace* Cohen, while an infinite temporal regress of events entails that an actually infinite number of (past) events has occurred, an infinite temporal progress of events does not entail that an actually infinite number of (future) events will occur.[17] There never will occur an actually infinite number of events, since it is impossible to count to infinity. The only sense in which there will be an infinite number of events is that the series of events will increase toward infinity as a limit. Therefore, it is not the case, as Hedrick claims,[18] that the events in an endless future can be put into a 1-1 correlation with the events in an endless past, for the number of future events is 0, while the number of past events is *ex hypothesi* $\aleph_0$.

Hedrick also expresses the reservation that "To claim that the same absurdity [as Hilbert's Hotel] can be generated with an actually infinite number of non-existing things like past events makes it seem like Craig's complaint is with the mathematical legitimacy of infinity, not just the idea that the actual infinite is instantiated in reality."[19] I plead not guilty. As an anti-realist about mathematical objects, I take a pretense theoretical approach to set theory.[20] We are invited to imagine its axioms, in particular the Axiom of Infinity, to be true and then are free to explore the consequences. Within that make-believe realm, we may discourse consistently about actual infinites without any metaphysical qualms of conscience. By contrast, past events are not mere fictions but have actually occurred and so are part of the actual world.

Hedrick offers a congenial reformulation of my argument based on the impossibility of an actual infinite as follows:

(D1) There cannot be a world in which an actually infinite number of things have been actualized.

(D2) If the actual world is one in which the universe is past-eternal, then there is a world in which an actually infinite number of things have been actualized.

(D3) Therefore, the actual world cannot be one in which the universe is past-eternal.[21]

Although Hedrick is dubious as to the relevance of absurdities like Hilbert's Hotel to (D1), it seems to me that the reformulation removes any objection to the illustrative use of Hilbert's Hotel based on the non-simultaneity of the entities being numbered, so long as those entities have—like past events and in contrast to future events—been actualized.

In fact, as Andrew Loke shows, if one denies (D1) on the basis of the possibility of an infinite temporal regress of events, then it is unproblematic to show that a simultaneously existing actually infinite number of things can exist.[22] He imagines that the infinite regress of events comprises events involving the construction of hotel rooms and the generation of customers from eternity past. By the present time we shall have a hotel with an actually infinite number of rooms and an actually infinite number of residents. By contrast, if the construction of such a hotel were to commence at the present time, then it would never have an actually infinite number of rooms, though the construction go on endlessly toward infinity as a limit. Hence, an endless future does not generate the same absurdities as does an infinite past.

While acknowledging the force of Loke's argument, Cohen insists that a parallel argument can be constructed to show that if an endless series of events is possible, then Hilbert's Hotel is metaphysically possible. Cohen claims that the theist who affirms God's omnipotence is committed to the following:

> (b) any object *o* that comes into existence at some past time or future time, God can bring about the existence of *o* at the present time.

Imagine, then, that at some future time construction begins on a Hilbert's Hotel, one occupied room being built every minute without ceasing. Cohen asserts,

> It is certainly true that at no point in time will an actual infinite number of hotel rooms be built. However, given (b), if God exists . . . God can simply declare 'let every occupied hotel room that *will* be built come into being now for one year', and thus instantaneously bring about an actual infinite number of occupied hotel rooms (for one year).[23]

Cohen thinks that the theist who affirms that if a beginningless series of events is possible, then Hilbert's Hotel is metaphysically possible should also affirm that if an endless series of events is possible, then Hilbert's Hotel is metaphysically possible.

Again, this objection is curiously ad hominem. Only theists are said to be obliged to accept the objection's conclusion. Absent God, Cohen's thought experiment would require backward causation of rooms, which the A-Theorist will rightly regard as metaphysically impossible. Loke's thought experiment, by contrast, is based on wholly nontheistic assumptions about things' enduring until the present, not upon miraculous re-creation in the present. Cohen's riposte requires theistic assumptions to get off the ground, assumptions that make the *kalam* cosmological argument superfluous as a piece of natural theology.

But never mind. The more serious failing of Cohen's objection is that it involves an illicit modal operator shift.[24] For from (b) it does not follow that God can bring it about that all future objects *o* exist at the present time. If the future is potentially infinite, it does not follow from God's ability to bring about the present existence of any particular future room that He is able to bring about the present existence of all the future rooms. The number of occupied rooms that God could create at present is potentially infinite, but any number of rooms He actually creates will be finite, as may be seen by taking the number of rooms presently created as a function of the number of rooms that will exist:

$$\lim f(x) = \infty$$
$$x \to \infty.$$

Thus, Loke is quite justified in denying that the possibility of an endless future implies the possibility of the existence of an actually infinite number of things, as does the possibility of a beginningless past.

Second Philosophical Argument

My second philosophical argument for the beginning of the universe runs:

1. A collection formed by successive addition cannot be an actual infinite.
2. The temporal series of events is a collection formed by successive addition.
3. Therefore, the temporal series of events cannot be an actual infinite.

This version of the *kalam* argument eventually became enshrined in the thesis of Kant's First Antinomy concerning time in his *Critique of Pure Reason*.

I was fascinated to find that Plantinga briefly addresses Kant's argument in *Warranted Christian Belief*.[25] Unfortunately, his verdict on Kant's argument is unfavorable, to put it mildly. He says that Kant's argument "is hard to take seriously." Plantinga explains, "It is not as if it is an argument the premises of which have a certain limited amount of intuitive plausibility; it is rather that this transition to the conclusion completely begs the question by assuming what was to be proved." "So the argument really has no force at all."

Well! Does Kant's argument really merit this disapprobation? Pay careful attention to Kant's formulation of the argument:

> If we assume that the world has no beginning in time, then up to every given moment an eternity has elapsed, and there has passed away in the world an infinite series of successive states of things. Now the infinity of a series consists in the fact that it can never be completed through successive synthesis. It thus follows that it is impossible for an infinite world-series to have passed away, and that a beginning of the world is therefore a necessary condition of the world's existence (A426/B454).

Plantinga paraphrases the second sentence of Kant's argument as follows: "According to the second premise . . . it is characteristic of an infinite series that it can't be completed by starting from the beginning . . . and adding things (events, say) one at a time."

Plantinga first raises a cavil about this claim by appealing to the possibility of so-called supertasks. He writes, "According to current lore about the infinite, however, there is no bar . . . to completing the infinite series in a finite time if the time taken for each event diminishes appropriately."

Now I see no reason at all to believe "the current lore about the infinite." The impossibility of the formation of an actual infinite by successive addition seems to me obvious in the case of beginning at some point and trying to reach infinity. For, necessarily, given any finite number n, $n + 1$ equals a finite number. Hence, $\aleph_0$ has no immediate predecessor; it is not the terminus of the natural number series but stands, as it were, outside it and is the number of all the members in the series. This rules out the possibility of supertasks. The fatal flaw in all such scenarios is that the state at $\omega + 1$ is causally unconnected to the successive states in the ω series of states. Since there is no last term in the ω series, the state of reality at $\omega + 1$ appears mysteriously from nowhere. The absurdity of such supertasks merely underlines the metaphysical impossibility of trying to convert a potential into an actual infinite by successive addition.

Moreover, as Plantinga recognizes, this objection is really irrelevant because the series of past events was not formed in the manner of a supertask. The temporal series of past events that the proponent of the *kalam* argument is talking about are events having an arbitrary but constant, non-zero, finite duration. So supertasks don't even come into the picture.

Rather, Plantinga's real problem with Kant's argument is that it is question-begging. He writes,

> Kant points out that an infinite series can't be completed by starting from some point finitely far from the beginning and adding members finitely many at a time at a constant rate. . . . The premise tells us that if you start from some finite point in the series—that is some point finitely far from the *beginning* of the series—and add a finite number per unit time, then you will never complete the series. Fair enough; but if the world has existed for an infinite stretch of time, then there was no first moment, no first event, and no beginning either to the series of moments or the series of events; more generally, at any preceding moment an infinite time would *already* have elapsed.

Plantinga claims that Kant's argument "completely begs the question" because it assumes what was to be proved, namely, "that the series in question has a beginning."

Having read the standard refutations of Kant's argument, I have been tempted for many years to write an article entitled, "Was Kant a *Dummkopf*?" Are we seriously to believe that the titan of Königsberg was so stupid that he argued for the beginning of the universe by assuming that the universe had a beginning? Nothing in Kant's argument says or implies that in an infinite series of past events there was an infinitely distant beginning point, much less the incoherent assumption of a point finitely distant from the infinitely distant beginning point, as Plantinga alleges. An infinite series of past years prior to January 1, 2018 for example, is a series without a beginning that is completed on that date. Such a series is of the ordinal type ω^*, the ordinal type of the negative numbers. We can argue about whether Kant was right that such a series cannot be completed by successive synthesis; or about the tensed theory of time that underlay such an argument; but let's not interpret him uncharitably so as to ascribe to him obvious blunders.

Although the problems will be different, the formation of an actually infinite collection by never beginning and ending at some point seems scarcely less difficult than the formation of such a collection by beginning at some point and never ending. If one cannot count *to* infinity, how can one count down *from* infinity? If one cannot traverse the infinite by moving in one direction, how can one traverse it by moving in the opposite direction?

A typical counterexample lodged against (1) is the alleged actual infinity of sub-intervals traversed in the traversal of any finite interval of time or space. The recent defenses of the Grim Reaper Paradox by Pruss and Koons provide, to my mind, convincing reason to think that spatiotemporal intervals are not, in fact, composed of a dense infinity of points or instants.[26] Pruss and Koons invite us to imagine that there are denumerably infinitely many Grim Reapers (whom we may identify as gods, so as to forestall any kinematic objections). You are alive at midnight. Grim Reaper #1 will strike you dead at 1:00 a.m. if you are still alive at that time. Grim Reaper #2 will strike you dead at 12:30 a.m. if you are still alive then. Grim Reaper #3 will strike you dead at 12:15 a.m., and so on. Such a situation seems clearly conceivable—given the possibility of an actually infinite number of sub-intervals of the hour between midnight and 1:00 a.m.—but leads to an impossibility: you cannot survive past midnight, and yet you cannot be killed by any Grim Reaper at any time.

In the traversal of any finite distance, there is thus no completion of an actual infinite by successive addition. Now the implication of the Grim Reaper Paradox is that space and time are not continua composed of points or instants.[27] The question, then, is how best to understand the structure of time and space.

We might conceive of time and space as discrete, that is, as a composition of atoms or chronons of a certain non-zero, finite extension. Since the advent of quantum theory, philosophers, and physicists as well, have exhibited much greater openness to taking time and space to be discrete rather than dense. In fact, many think that the continuity of spacetime in general relativity is what needs to go if we are to have a unified physical theory of the world.[28]

I myself prefer an Aristotelian view, according to which time as pure duration is logically prior to our mathematical modeling of it as a geometrical line composed of points or intervals. On such a view, time is potentially infinitely divisible in that we can specify intervals and sub-intervals of time with infinity as a limit (∞), but time is not a composition of an actually infinite number ($\aleph_n$) of instants or intervals.

Stephen Puryear has recently argued that the Aristotelian view is not open to the proponent of the *kalam* cosmological argument. Remarkably, Puryear argues that the Aristotelian view of time as potentially infinitely divisible implies: (1) the number of past events in a beginningless universe can be at most finite, not actually infinite; (2) the number of past events in a beginningless universe is at most potentially, but not actually, infinite; and (3) the series of past events is formed by division, not by successive addition.[29] These conclusions are so evidently absurd that Puryear's argument might justifiably be construed as a reductio ad absurdum of the Aristotelian view of time.[30]

I suspect that few philosophers will agree that Aristotelians are committed to such bizarre conclusions. Although Puryear's argument might be challenged at a number of junctures,[31] it seems to me that its central failing involves a misunderstanding inherited by Puryear from Wesley Morriston. Morriston puts the following reply in my mouth: "Any such region is, of course, infinitely divisible—but the 'parts' into which it can be divided are not 'there' until someone (at least in thought) marks them out. And since no one could complete *all* the possible divisions, they are only *potentially* 'there.'"[32] The first sentence accurately captures my Aristotelianism. But the second sentence mistakenly ascribes to me a sort of constructivism according to which actual infinites are impossible because they are humanly non-constructible. Such constructivism underlay intuitionistic denials of the actual infinite, but I have been explicit that my Aristotelian view is not intuitionistic. I actually find myself sympathetic with Morriston's view that "what follows from the lack of natural boundaries within a region of space is not that the infinitely many sub-regions are not actually 'there', but only that they are not 'there' *apart from a specified way of dividing things up*."[33] So while space is not itself a composition of, say, miles, once we have decided to so model space mathematically it seems to me that it will be objectively true or false that there is an actually infinite number of miles in a specified spatial direction, regardless of the fact that no human being could actually carry out such a division of space.

Puryear thinks that the Aristotelian must make the constructivist assumption, lest one similarly be able to divide a finite interval into an actually infinite sequence:

> It might be supposed that the past could be divided into sub-events *en masse* simply by specifying a way of dividing it into events of a certain duration: for instance, we could stipulate that the past divides into consecutive events lasting one second each.... Regardless of what duration we chose, it would follow that, if the universe had no beginning, the past would consist in an actually infinite sequence of such events. This, however, will not work.... the finitist reply advocated by Craig can succeed only if it requires that divisions be individually specified, since otherwise it would be possible to specify an actual infinity of divisions within a finite region of space or time, in the way suggested by Morriston.[34]

Morriston had suggested that we can specify all the sub-regions of a given region *R* according to the following prescription: starting with *R*, divide the results of the previous division by half, ad infinitum. Morriston thinks that we do not need to complete the series of divisions in order to know that, relative to this rule, there is an actual—and not merely a potential—infinity of sub-regions.

What Morriston and Puryear fail to appreciate is that specifications of Morriston's sort are ruled out, not by the assumption of constructivism, but by paradoxes like that of the Grim Reaper, which show that a sequence such as Morriston envisions is metaphysically impossible. By contrast, if we divide time up into one-second intervals, then the number of past seconds in a series of seconds prior to today having no first member would be actually, not merely potentially, infinite. Given a tensed view of time, that sequence of seconds, once specified, has come to be one second after another, so that the entire series was, indeed, formed by successive addition.

Pruss and Koons go on to show how to re-formulate the Grim Reaper Paradox so that the Grim Reapers are spread out over infinite time rather than over a single hour, for example, by having each Grim Reaper swing his scythe on January 1 of each past year if you have managed to live that long. This version of the paradox is thus a form of the *kalam* cosmological argument for the finitude of the past based on the impossibility of the formation of an actual infinite by successive addition.

Cohen has attempted to defeat Pruss and Koons's argument for the past's finitude by constructing a parallel argument aimed at showing the impossibility of the future's finitude.[35] Imagine that every future time t is paired with a Grim Reaper whose task is to swing his scythe at t if and only if no Grim Reaper swings his scythe at some $t^*>t$. Grim Reaper #1 will kill you because no later Grim Reaper does so. But if Grim Reaper #1 kills you, no later Grim Reaper will swing his scythe, and so the conditions are also satisfied for Grim Reaper #2, and so on, which is impossible.

Cohen seems to have fallen into the same trap I did when I first formulated the Tristram Shandy Paradox: the situation he describes is impossible because the task he has set is inherently paradoxical. As Koons points out, each Grim Reaper would have to be able to know whether his intended victim "will be alive at the end of his appointed period, and to kill him if he will, which doesn't make any sense."[36] Cohen insists that in his statement of the paradox "what a Reaper does is sensitive to what other Reapers do, rather than being sensitive to whether or not [someone] is alive at some time."[37] This is a difference that makes no difference. A Reaper's "swinging his scythe" is a metaphor for killing his victim, so being sensitive to whether a later Grim Reaper swings his scythe just is sensitivity to whether the victim is killed at a later time and, hence, alive at the end of the preceding period. The Grim Reapers are being commanded to carry out an incoherent set of instructions.

Scientific Confirmation

Had space permitted, I should like to have discussed the status of the current scientific evidence in support of the universe's beginning. In his *Where the Conflict Really Lies*, Plantinga neglects to discuss this aspect of the contemporary scientific worldview, even as an area of mere consonance between science and theology.

I conclude with a word on quantum cosmology and the beginning of the universe. The Borde-Guth-Vilenkin theorem (2003) proves that classical space-time, under a single, very general condition, cannot be extended to past infinity but must reach a boundary at some time in the finite past. Now, either there was something on the other side of that boundary or not. If not, then that boundary is the beginning of the universe. If there was something on the other side, then it will be a non-classical region described by the yet to be discovered theory of quantum gravity. In that case, Vilenkin says, *it* will be the beginning of the universe.[38]

Both Vilenkin and, more famously, James Hartle and Stephen Hawking, have proposed models of the universe according to which classical space-time emerges from a quantum gravity regime that eliminates the initial singularity by transforming the conical geometry of classical space-time into a smooth, curved geometry having no edge.[39] By positing a finite, if imaginary, time on a closed surface prior to the Planck time rather than an infinite time on an open surface, such models actually support, rather than undercut, the fact that the universe had a beginning. Such theories, if successful, would enable us to model the beginning of the universe without an initial singularity involving infinite density, temperature, pressure, and so on. [40]

If there is such a non-classical region, then it is not past eternal in the classical sense. Hawking describes it as "completely self-contained and not affected by anything outside itself. It would be neither created nor destroyed. It would just BE."[41] But this regime cannot exist literally timelessly, akin to the way in which philosophers consider abstract objects like numbers to be timeless or theologians take God to be timeless. For this region is in a state of constant flux, which, given the Indiscernibility of Identicals, is sufficient for time. Moreover, it is supposed to have existed *before* the classical era, and the classical era is supposed to have *emerged* from it, which seems to posit a temporal relation between the quantum gravity era and the classical era.

(This last mentioned feature of quantum cosmogony, by the way, is very problematic.[42] Emergence can be understood either diachronically or synchronically. But a diachronic emergence of time is obviously incoherent. So how can one make sense of a synchronic emergence of time as a supervenient reality in the context of cosmogony? Quantum cosmologists find themselves at something of a loss here. The best sense I can make of it is to say that the imaginary time description is a lower-level description of classical space-time prior to the Planck time. (One recalls Hawking's remark, "Only if we could picture the universe in terms of imaginary time would there be no singularities. . . . When one goes back to the real time in which we live, however, there will still appear to be singularities."[43]) So the same reality is being described at two levels. That implies that if classical space-time has a beginning, then so does the quantum gravity regime. For they are descriptions of the same reality. In the one, a singularity is part of the description; in the other, it is not. So what is prior to the Planck time is not the quantum gravity era as such; rather, what is prior is the classical period of which the quantum gravitational description is the more fundamental description. If this is correct, then, given the beginning of the classically described universe, it is impossible for the universe as quantum gravitationally described to be without a beginning. For they just are the same universe at different levels of description.)

Be that as it may, it seems that even if time as defined in classical physics does not exist at such a quantum gravity era, some sort of time would. But if the quantum gravity era is in some sense temporal, it cannot be extended infinitely in time, for such a quantum state is not stable and so would either produce the universe from eternity past or not at all. As Anthony Aguirre and John Kehayias argue,

> It is very difficult to devise a system—especially a quantum one—that does nothing "forever," then evolves. A truly stationary or periodic quantum state, which would last forever, would never evolve, whereas one with any instability will not endure for an indefinite time.[44]

Hence, the quantum gravity era would itself have to have had a beginning in order to explain why it transitioned just some 14 billion years ago into classical time and space. Hence, whether at the boundary or at the quantum gravity regime, the universe probably began to exist.

CONCLUSION

Back in 1966, Wallace Matson could quickly dismiss the *kalam* cosmological argument as "the crude cosmological argument."[45] Today so easy a dismissal of the argument is no longer possible nor desirable. For the *kalam* cosmological argument not only raises a host of fascinating questions of philosophical importance, such as the conception of the infinite, the ontology of mathematics, the nature of time and space, the beginning and origin of the universe, and so on, but both its premises have a good claim actually to be true.

NOTES

1. Stuart Hackett, *The Resurrection of Theism* (Chicago: Moody Press, 1957).

2. Quentin Smith, "Kalam Cosmological Arguments for Atheism," in *The Cambridge Companion to Atheism*, ed. M. Martin (Cambridge: University Press, 2007), 183.

3. Stephen Puryear, "Finitism and the Beginning of the Universe," *Australasian Journal of Philosophy* 92 (2014): 619–629.

4. Al-Ghazali, *Kitab al-Iqtisad fi'l-Iqtiqad* (Ankara: University of Ankara Press, 1962), 15–16.

5. Adolf Grünbaum, "A New Critique of Theological Interpretations of Physical Cosmology," *British Journal for the Philosophy of Science* 51 (2000): 16.

6. *The Tensed Theory of Time* (Dordrecht: Kluwer, 2000); *The Tenseless Theory of Time* (Dordrecht: Kluwer, 2000). These books are dedicated to Alvin Plantinga.

7. Jordan Sobel, *Logic and Theism* (Cambridge: Cambridge University Press, 2004), 181–189, 198–199; Graham Oppy, *Philosophical Perspectives on Infinity* (Cambridge: Cambridge University Press, 2006), 291–293.

8. See my *God over All: Divine Aseity and the Challenge of Platonism* (Oxford: Oxford University Press, 2016).

9. Solomon Feferman, *In Light of Logic* (Oxford: Oxford University Press, 1998), 19, 30.

10. José Benardete, *Infinity* (Oxford: Clarendon Press, 1964), 238.

11. Ibid., 236–237.

12. Oppy, *Philosophical Perspectives on Infinity,* 48. Arnold Guminski tries to avoid the absurdities by abandoning certain concepts and principles of Cantorian set theory in order to craft a theory of "real infinites," or infinite collections of concrete entities having a cardinality of $\aleph_0$ (Arnold Guminski, "The Kalam Cosmological Argument: The Question of the Metaphysical Possibility of an Infinite Set of Real Entities," *Philo* 5 [2002]: 196–215). He proposes that no "real" infinite can be put into a 1-1 correspondence with a proper part. Apart from the question of whether this move really avoids the absurdities, the claim is wildly counterintuitive. I can understand why someone might question whether collections that can be placed in a 1-1 correspondence really do have the same number of members, but it seems unquestionable that collections having the same number of members can be related 1-1. An infinite collection will thus have proper parts to which it can be related 1-1. For example, a collection of baseball cards having a cardinality of $\aleph_0$ can be put into a 1-1 correspondence of every card to every other card.

13. Wes Morriston, "Beginningless Past, Endless Future, and the Actual Infinite," *Faith and Philosophy* 27 (2010): 439–450; idem, "Beginningless Past and Endless Future," *Faith and Philosophy* 29 (2012): 444–450; Landon Hedrick, "Heartbreak at Hilbert's Hotel," *Religious Studies* 50 (2014): 27–46; Andrew Loke, "No Heartbreak at Hilbert's Hotel," *Religious Studies* 50 (2014): 47–50; Yishai Cohen, "Endless Future: A Persistent Thorn in the Kalām Cosmological Argument," *Philosophical Papers* 44 (2015): 165–187.

14. Cohen highlights a number of metaphysical theses that I have employed in defense of the *kalam* cosmological argument: (i) The A-Theory of time is true; (ii) Presentism is true; (iii) Unlike the future, the past and the present are actual; (iv) Platonism about propositions is false; and (v) God's knowledge is non-propositional. He charges that (i)-(v) alone cannot establish a relevant difference between the past and the future, such that

5. An infinite temporal regress of events is an actual infinite.

is true and

8. An infinite temporal progress of events is an actual infinite.

is false. This shifts the burden of proof. Cohen complains that (i–v) fail to "render (5) true and (8) false" (Cohen, "Endless Future," 177). But it is the objector's burden to show that if (5) is true, then (8) is true, or that (5) entails or implies (8). That is no easy task! All I need do on the basis of (i–v) is to cast reasonable doubt on that implication. It seems to me that a person who is committed to the tenability of (i–v) has good grounds for doubting that (5) implies (8).

15. Hedrick, "Heartbreak," 35.

16. "Taking Tense Seriously in Differentiating Past and Future," *Faith and Philosophy* 27 (2010): 451–456.

17. Compare Cohen's interpretation of (5) and (8) in note 14 earlier as

5_4. An infinite temporal regress of events entails that there were past events such that the number of them is an actual infinite.

8_4. An infinite temporal progress of events entails that there will be future events such that the number of them is an actual infinite.

Cohen needs to show that (5_4) entails or implies (8_4). But on a tensed theory of time, that is not the case.

18. Hedrick, "Heartbreak," 39.

19. Ibid.

20. "Divine Self-Existence," in *Neo-Aristotelian Perspectives in Metaphysics*, ed. Daniel Novotný and Lukáš Novák (London: Routledge, 2014), 269–295.

21. Hedrick, "Heartbreak," 42–43.

22. Loke, "No Heartbreak," 48–49.

23. Cohen, "Endless Future," 180.

24. Let F=is a future object and G=is presently created by God. Cohen affirms

(b) $(\forall x)(Fx \supset \Diamond Gx)$ Premise

From which it follows that

$Fa \supset \Diamond Ga$ UI

$Fb \supset \Diamond Gb$ UI

$Fc \supset \Diamond Gc$ UI

...

Assuming that

$Fa \,\&\, Fb \,\&\, Fc$ ... Premise

it follows that

$\Diamond\, Ga \,\&\, \Diamond\, Gb \,\&\, \Diamond\, Gc \,\&$ ... MP

But from this Cohen's inference does not follow that

$\Diamond\, (Ga \,\&\, Gb \,\&\, Gc \,\&$ ...) Invalid

(My thanks to Daniel Rubio for this symbolization.)

25. Alvin Plantinga, *Warranted Christian Belief* (Oxford: Oxford University Press, 2000), 24–25.

26. Robert Koons, "A New Kalam Argument: Revenge of the Grim Reaper," *Noûs* 48 (2014): 256–267; Alexander Pruss, "From the Grim Reaper paradox to the Kalam argument," http:// alexanderpruss.blogspot.com/2009/10/from-grim-reaper-paradox-to-kalaam. html, October 2, 2009; idem, "Probability on infinite sets and the Kalaam argument," http:// alexanderpruss.blogspot.com/2010/03/probability-on-infinite-sets-and-kalaam.html/, March 16, 2010. For background, see Benardete, *Infinity*, 259–261.

27. Neither can they be composed of what some philosophers have called "gunk," of which every finite interval is composed of subintervals, though no points or degenerate intervals exist.

28. For instance, Christopher Isham, perhaps Britain's leading quantum cosmologist; see J. Butterfield and C. Isham, "On the Emergence of Time in Quantum Gravity," http://arxiv. org/pdf/gr-qc/9901024v1.pdf, January 8, 1999, rep. in *The Arguments of Time*, ed. J. Butterfield (Oxford: Oxford University Press, 1999), §3.2. In fact, Isham believes that "spacetime points should not be taken as real objects, even in interpreting classical general relativity: rather they are an artefact of the way we have formulated the theory" (30; *cf.* 32–33). See further Nick Huggett and Christian Wüthrich, "Emergent Spacetime and Empirical (in)coherence," *Studies in History and Philosophy of Modern Physics* 44 (2013): 276–285.

29. Puryear, "Finitism and the Beginning of the Universe," 627–628.

30. With respect to (1) there is no finite number of isochronous proper parts into which a beginningless past can be divided. As for (2), in order for a beginningless series of past events to be potentially infinite, the series would have to be finite but growing in a backward direction. (3) presupposes a tenseless theory of time that contradicts the *kalam* cosmological argument's assumption of the objectivity of temporal becoming.

31. For example, his claim that viewing time or events as merely potentially infinitely divisible commits one to the view that there really is only one time and one event in history; also his claim that subintervals of time or space commit one to correlated parts of the occupants of time or space, an assumption that Puryear himself realizes is in trouble and to which he weakly responds (Puryear, "Finitism and the Beginning of the Universe," 627, note 9).

32. Wes Morriston, "Craig on the Actual Infinite," *Religious Studies* 38 (2002): 162.

33. Ibid.

34. Puryear, "Finitism and the Beginning of the Universe," 628.

35. This argument is also ad hominem, targeting the theist who believes in divine foreknowledge. Each Grim Reaper needs to know what the others will do.

36. Koons, "New Kalam Argument," 264–265.

37. Cohen, "Endless Future," 183.

38. "If indeed all past-directed geodesics encounter a quantum spacetime region where the notions of time and causality no longer apply, I would characterize such a region as the beginning of the universe" (A. Vilenkin to William Lane Craig, personal correspondence, December 8, 2013).

39. Christopher Isham observes that although quantum cosmogonies "differ in their details they all agree on the idea that space and time emerge in some way from a purely quantum-mechanical region which can be described in some respects as if it were a classical, imaginary-time four-space" (C. Isham, "Quantum Theories of the Creation of the Universe," in *Quantum Cosmology and the Laws of Nature*, second ed., ed. Robert Russell et al. [Vatican City State: Vatican Observatory, 1996], 75).

40. John Barrow, *Theories of Everything* (Oxford: Clarendon Press, 1991), 68.

41. Stephen Hawking, *A Brief History of Time* (New York: Bantam Books, 1988), 136.

42. See Butterfield and Isham, "Emergence of Time in Quantum Gravity," 111–168; Vincent Lam and Michael Esfeld, "A Dilemma for the Emergence of Spacetime in Canonical Quantum Gravity," *Studies in History and Philosophy of Modern Physics* 44 (2013): 286–293; Reiner Hedrich, "Hat die Raumzeit Quanteneigenschaften?—Emergenztheoretische Ansätze in der Quantengravitation," in *Philosophie der Physik*, ed. M. Esfeld (Berlin: Suhrkamp, forthcoming), 287–305.

43. Hawking, *Brief History of Time*, 138–139.

44. Anthony Aguirre and John Kehayias, "Quantum Instability of the Emergent Universe," arXiv:1306.3232v2 (hep-th), November 19, 2013. They are specifically addressing the Ellis-Maarten model, but their point is generalizable.

45. Wallace I. Matson, *The Existence of God* (Ithaca, NY: Cornell University Press, 1965), 56.

The Argument from Possibility

Brian Leftow

I HAVE ARGUED that the metaphysics of possibility provides a good argument for the existence of something that looks very like God.[1] What follows is just a sketch of this one such argument. The full gruesome details are available elsewhere.[2] I'm hoping to tempt you to look at them. The argument concerns what I call absolute possibility—a sort often called "metaphysical" or "broadly logical." For present purposes, two things about this sort are important.[3]

One is that truths about absolute possibility are objective, rather than dependent on how humans think or speak. If dinosaurs could have avoided extinction, this' being true does not depend on us. It was true when the last dinosaur died, and it would be odd to say that it was true then because millions of years later, we were going to think or speak as we do. Consider another possibility, P: there is a big bang, eons later the dinosaurs die out, but the universe never contains anything smart enough to think about it. Even so, in that universe, at the bang, surely it is possible that the dinosaurs die out. After all, it is going to happen. Yet there never will be human minds there for this possibility to depend on. It would be *very* odd to say that had P been actual, at the bang it would have been possible that the dinosaurs die out because the future might have contained minds to think about it. That would make an actual possibility depend on ways of thinking no one ever is even equipped to use. Further, what possible mind would the possibility of those minds depend on—their own? Some other finite person's? There are more ways to argue the human-independence of absolute possibility, but one must start somewhere, and these claims are intuitive enough to stand on their own for now. The other relevant point is that absolute possibility is the sort of objective possibility with the widest extent. By definition, whatever is objectively possible in any other sense is also absolutely possible.

Whether there are absolute possibilities that are not possible in any other sense—for example, not physically or naturally possible—is a question that becomes important later.

If it is an objective matter that certain claims are absolutely possible, items in the mind-independent world go into making them possible. The interesting philosophical question is: what? What things go into making them possible? What are the ultimate grounds of possibility? This question, I now argue, leads us in the direction of God. I begin by discussing some non-God answers to our question. The problems with them will lead where I want to go.

One family of answers to our question is Platonist. These theories all assign the key role to non-spatial, timeless abstract entities of some sort. One sort of Platonist theory, for instance, says this: there are vast infinities of abstract, timeless propositions—the sort of thing sentences express. (The sentence "Dinosaurs died." expresses the proposition that dinosaurs died.) These are the real grounds of possibility. The reason it was possible that the dinosaurs not die out was that the proposition <the dinosaurs never die out> was possibly true.

One problem with this view is that a proposition seems the wrong sort of thing to be the ultimate ground of possibility. True propositions report how things are. Plausibly what they report explains some of their important properties. <Leftow is human> has the property of truth because Leftow is human. <Leftow is alive> has the property of temporary truth because Leftow's life is temporary. And plausibly <the dinosaurs never die out> was possibly true because something else, the dinosaurs' never dying out, was possible. As actuality explains truth, possibility explains possible truth. Saying that possible truth explains possibility seems to get things backward.

This problem afflicts other Platonist theories, too. Consider another: the ultimate grounds of possibility are another sort of abstract, timeless entity: properties. On this view, what makes it true that possibly dinosaurs never die out is that there is a property for universes to have, the property of coming and never ceasing to contain at least one dinosaur, and this property has the property of being possibly-had. Again, this seems to get things backward. It's not that dinosaurs could have avoided extinction because the property could have been had. Rather, the property could have been had because the dinosaurs could have avoided extinction. The way the world could have been made the property possibly-had. It wasn't the property itself that did so. Facts about ways the world could have been are about something else.

We next ask what something else that is. A third sort of Platonist offers a candidate: "states of affairs." A state of affairs is, well, just a way for the world to be: dinosaurs' being extinct, or four's equaling twice two. A problem emerges when we ask just what these *are*. Dinosaurs' being extinct could be a world-property, <having permanently ceased to contain dinosaurs>. If it is, we've made no progress on the second theory. It could be a structure of properties: the property of being a dinosaur bearing the property of having been had by something and the property of no longer being had by anything. But then for it to be possible that dinosaurs be extinct is for it to be possible that a property have two properties. Again, this seems backward. Surely it should be something about the concrete realm that explains why the property can have the two other properties, rather than the properties dictating to the concrete realm. Surely something about dinosaurs and the world around them should make this possible, not something about properties. Finally, states of affairs might be just sui generis—something, we know not what, crafted for a particular philosophical role. It's best to avoid such mysteries if we can.

States of affairs also seem redundant.[4] We have Fido. If he has the property of being hairy, we have the property, too. Surely that's enough to make it true that Fido is hairy. We do not need another entity, Fido's being hairy. Ockham's razor is a sound maxim. If we don't need it, we have no reason to posit it. So we shouldn't. But if that entity is not there when Fido is hairy, it was not there beforehand, when he was only possibly hairy, to bear the property of possibility. Of course, if we couldn't provide grounds for possibility without states of affairs, that would be need enough, even if they are redundant when Fido actually is hairy. But it remains to be seen whether that is so. If we can find grounds anywhere else, it is not.

Another problem afflicts all Platonist views equally. Accepting that there are propositions, states of affairs or the like vastly inflates our ontology. We start out believing in ordinary concrete things like tables and people. We later expand that inventory to extraordinary concrete things—quarks, singularities. But to add an entirely new basic category of thing—the abstract, with uncountable infinities of members—to our picture of the world is an altogether bigger step. We need a good reason to do it. We don't have one if we can provide grounds for truths of possibility by adding fewer things or only other concrete things. Ockham told us to posit no entity without need. We need not drink the Platonist Kool-Aid if we can provide ultimate grounds for possibility that remain entirely within the concrete. I will argue that we can.

So. We want concreta. The waitress scribbles our order down: "actual, existing concreta, yes. Would you like a side-dish? We have only-actual and only-existing." Those sound exotic. We ask her to describe them, and hear "concreta Meinong-style are actual: they share this world with you. They have properties. They are dogs, cats and comets. But they do not exist. The ones in David Lewis's side-dish exist. They're *just* like you and me. But—wait—actually you can't get them here. They exist only in universes with no spatiotemporal relations to us—which for Lewis makes them non-actual." Both will do for grounds of possibility. What made it true that possibly the dinosaurs never die out, back at the big bang? Meinong can say: there was an actual but non-existent concrete object, a world in which dinosaurs never do, and this had the property of being possible. Lewis can say: possible worlds are existing worlds, just like the actual one. What's different about them is that they are not actual—that is, they are not this one here, where I'm talking to you. Possibly the dinosaurs never die out because there is another universe, as flesh-and-blood as our own, in which they do not.

Lewis's view has provoked incredulous stares for almost fifty years now. Giving Lewis a good kicking is the favorite sport of most metaphysicians who write about the possible. One common reaction, which I share, is that Lewis's other universes, if they exist, are just extensions of what is actual, not alternatives to it. Something doesn't become an alternative to actuality by being in a place we can't get to from here. Lewis's is not a candidate metaphysics of unrealized possibility at all. Another common reaction is that Lewis bloats our census of reality beyond toleration. Is it possible that monkeys sing Verdi? Then according to Lewis, somewhere else, there are opera monkeys. Almost anything you can think of, however outré, exists somewhere—and we know this a priori, without even looking. Lewis is Ockham's nightmare. But Meinong is even worse. Whatever Lewis adds, Meinong adds—opera monkeys, the works—but then he adds further that these are actual but non-existent. They "are" there, but they don't exist. Neither Meinong nor his disciples have ever explained what that "are" means. And how can something that doesn't exist be a monkey? It can't gibber, climb, or howl. No one has ever been bitten by one. It can't do anything monkeys can do.

Let's shun the side-dishes. Good Ockhamists would rather not be bloated. We want ultimate grounds for possibility among the concrete, actual, and existing. We need not look far for some: if actually P, then possibly P, so perhaps in some cases, that actually P makes it true that possibly P. However, even if we accept this, it hasn't a wide enough scope. The real puzzle is what to say when it is *not* the case that actually P. When <P> isn't true, what makes it possible that P?

"Makes it possible" is a common locution. The weakness of their schedule makes it possible that the Giants win their next three games. The hardness of diamonds makes it possible that they scratch glass. Often, what make it possible that so-and-so, intuitively, are the powers of concrete things. As a first rough pass, it's possible that the Giants win their next three because of the following. The Giants' players have certain powers. Their opponents' players have powers that do not quite match up. When these powers act together, one way to manifest their interaction is three Giant wins. And there will be an opportunity for these powers to act together, since the schedule pairs these teams. Powers with the right opportunities ground possibilities.

We might, then, consider looking for a metaphysics of the possible based on powers. This might sound Platonist: powers are a sort of property, after all. If we are to remain entirely with the concrete, we must give some nominalist construal of powers. For present purposes, just spot me this. It can be done, but I do not have the space to show this. Granting nominalism at least arguendo, the waitress has another question for us: "You want just concrete, actual and existing. Fine. The main dish will be natural-flavored. But you still can have a side: how about non-natural?" Again, lured by the exotic sound, we ask her to explain. Here the waitress is a bit flummoxed: "Natural things are, well, things in nature. Things in the universe. The sort of thing physics studies, or could. And non-natural things are not natural." It's not great, but it's hard to do better, so let's just accept this for now.

Natural things' powers can provide natural possibilities. The question is whether we are content to let natural possibility be all of *absolute* possibility—all of what objectively can happen, period. We may not be, for we tend on reflection to believe in possibilities that go beyond what nature allows. Could there have been different natural laws? Sure, we think—why not? That $E = MC^3$ makes perfect sense. There's no contradiction in it. Scientists can reason counterfactually in great detail about how the universe would have been with this law instead of the actual one. Could there have been slightly more mass-energy in the universe than there actually is? Again, it's hard to see why not: science can fill in this supposition in such great detail that scientists can practically see it in their minds' eye. This is the same sort of thinking that leads us to judge certain things to be naturally possible. Could there be a tiger hiding behind that bush? Sure. It makes perfect sense. There's no contradiction in it. We can reason counterfactually about it beautifully and even imagine it. We have found this to be a pretty reliable way of fixing our beliefs about the possible, because very often, natural possibilities we judge possible this way prove themselves to be possible by turning out actual. We can see no good reason that this sort of thinking should suddenly turn deceptive when we go beyond what nature allows. So we have very good reason to think that there are trans-natural absolute possibilities. But here is the crux: natural powers can't ground these, because they can't bring them about. Nothing natural has ever had or will ever have the power to make a different natural law obtain. So we face a decision. If we want an account of the ultimate grounds of possibility, either we give up on the "powers" approach, or we bite the bullet and say that only what is naturally possible is absolutely possible, or we posit non-natural powers.

If we give up on a "powers" account, we must go back to one of the other accounts already discussed. We must massively inflate our ontology. Ockham tells us not to do this if we can at all avoid it. So if Ockham's razor is a sound principle of method, this should really be a last recourse. Biting the bullet requires denying the possibility of infinitely many things that seem intuitively to be possible: consider all the possible alternate natural laws and alternate sums of mass-energy, and you will have barely scratched the surface. We should feel a strong resistance to denying so many intuitions of such strength.

Here I am merely noting points at which pressure arises; elsewhere I show that this pressure is quite strong. So I think there is a decent case that we should instead posit non-natural powers. But this is not a slam-dunk. It is a conclusion many will resist. The reason is this. Non-natural powers cannot be sited within nature. If they were, they would be natural. If there were a power within nature to bring it about that $E = MC^3$, for instance, that this be the law would not be beyond the power of nature. So non-natural powers must be sited in non-natural beings, beings outside the order of nature, and by positing non-natural powers, we posit non-natural beings to host them. (Actually, since we are assuming nominalism, positing the powers must ultimately reduce to positing the beings.) It would take actually applying the pressure I've pointed to, at some length, to push anyone with naturalist leanings toward positing non-natural beings. As I have no space to do that, here (again) I am only sketching the course an argument would take, not pressing it home.

If we want not to bite the bullet, we must introduce powers adequate to the intuitive extension of absolute possibility, powers sufficient to bring about all and only what is intuitively absolutely possible. We must now ask how many and what sort of non-natural powers that requires.

OMNIPOTENCE

The full intuitive extent of absolute possibility is roughly that of what our traditional methods of fixing belief about possibility deliver (roughly only—these methods are reliable but not infallible). I think that we fix such belief roughly this way. We start by according a presumption of possibility to what any grammatical assertion asserts. We then test it. We ask whether what it asserts would violate logic or mathematics, whether we can describe it in full detail without doing so, whether we can imagine it, or how well we can reason about it counterfactually, and whether it conflicts with any non-logical or–mathematical necessities we recognize. If it passes all these tests, the presumption is sustained, and we make a final, ultima facie judgment that what is asserted is possible. The full extension of absolute possibility is roughly that of whatever passes all these tests. We want a metaphysics that provides possibilities roughly wherever these methods say there should be possibilities.

Traditionally, an omnipotent being can bring about all of this (at a rough first pass[5]). So a "powers" approach must introduce powers whose range adds up to omnipotence. It could site these powers in more than one non-natural being; there could be as many as there are powers. Or it could collect them in a single being, which would be omnipotent.

The second alternative is most parsimonious of non-natural beings. It introduces a new property, omnipotence, a power or degree of power not met elsewhere, and this might raise a parsimony worry. But one way or another, we're going to introduce enough powers to add up to omnipotence. So consider the many non-natural beings that might cover the range of possibility, with their individual small sets of powers: omnipotence in a single being is just the conjunction of the small sets' powers. If there is no principled objection to the conjuncts, how can there be one to conjoining them? If the conjuncts don't offend against parsimony, nor does the conjunction. The conjunction is no more powers and no more power than were present in the conjuncts. It simply lets us collect them in one being. We are not introducing powers, and beings, without need. We need these to ground possibilities. But we need no more than one if one will do. So I submit that it is most parsimonious to site all the new powers in a single being. The most parsimonious "powers" view that assigns the possible an intuitively adequate extension, then, will posit one non-natural omnipotent being. Let's call this theory Omnipotence.

On Omnipotence, there will always be some omnipotent being grounding the full range of unrealized possibility. Even if the range of the possible varies a bit, that will just mean that for some reason, this being's powers vary. If our a priori modal methods reliably indicate the broad range of the possible, what is possible will not so vary as to imply that something substantially less than intuitive omnipotence will ever do as a ground. More to the point, even if what is possible varies, we still want there always to be a being able to effect (in some way or other) all that is possible. We could posit many temporary omnipotent beings sharing the duties, each lasting a minute, say. But why? It is simpler to have just one single being that always exists. This is not just a parsimony point; we then also needn't try to explain why one omnipotent being always gives rise to another before expiring (or why omnipotent beings expire at all: they should have power enough to maintain themselves).

Of course, we might then have to say why the single omnipotent being always exists. One answer would be that this is because it exists necessarily—though that property, discussed next, raises its own questions. Again, some might object to a new property, eternal existence. But the temporary beings' lives, fused, would last as long as the life of the one omnipotent being. If there is no problem with the extensions the parts such a life would have, it is hard to see why there would be one with the extent of their fusion. Further, it's not clear that eternal existence is a new property. If it is omnitemporality, space-time (if it exists) already has it. At this point there is no pressure to take eternality as atemporality, so there is no pressure to a new, strange property.

There necessarily are some possibilities or other. So on Omnipotence, there will necessarily be some omnipotent being. If one is necessarily more parsimonious than many, there will necessarily be one omnipotent being—one being eternally doing the duties in each possible world. I think that there will necessarily be the one there actually is. We are power theorists who believe only in actual, existing, concrete things. So for us, if there could be a different one, the ground for this unrealized possibility would lie in some actual power(s). No natural power can bring an omnipotent being to be, bring to be a natural being able to do so, or so on. So no natural power could provide for other omnipotent beings in other worlds. Nor could the actual omnipotent being. For how could any actual thing have the power to bring it about that it itself had never existed and had eternally been supplanted by something(s) else? The only thing that could provide an omnipotent being in other worlds, then, is whatever makes the actual omnipotent being exist necessarily. That the omnipotent being should be necessary is another reason to see it as non-natural. Every indisputably natural actual thing is clearly contingent, and qua natural, an omnipotent being would have to be as contingent as they: things equally natural should exist with the same modal status.

Here one can again raise a parsimony concern: Omnipotence as I have now developed it posits a new property, necessary existence, and says that a concrete thing has it. But I have argued elsewhere that there are no good objections to the claim that necessity and concreteness are compatible.[6] And most of Omnipotence's opponents can't actually push this point. Platonists can't object to necessary beings. They also deal in necessary beings, and abstract necessary beings add two properties, not one, to the common-sense ontology. Nor can Meinongians object. Their non-existent "objects" typically "subsist" necessarily, and so they add at least three properties—not just necessary presence in the ontological census, but subsistence and objecthood. Nor can Lewis object. His ontology has concrete worlds all of which exist necessarily (i.e., from the standpoint of all other worlds): not just one concrete necessary being, but an uncountable infinity of them. Only a naturalist powers theorist would actually be able to claim more parsimony than Omnipotence, and that would be a persuasive point only if he or she could convince us that a slight gain in parsimony is worth a massive amount of bullet-biting plus a number of other problems I have no space to develop here. So while the concrete-necessity concern is genuine, in fact it is clear given only the little I've said here that Omnipotence beats all rivals save its naturalist cousin, and elsewhere I develop a case that on balance, it beats that, too.[7]

IT HAS A MIND

We have, so far, a necessarily existent omnipotent being. It is not natural; natural things all ought to be contingent (which is another strike against Lewis-worlds). But we are not yet all the way to theism. Our posit does not yet look like God: we have not said that it has a mind. Perhaps it is powerful as a machine or an initial singularity are.

Three factors push us to ascribe a mind to this necessary being. One is that this being would be less strange to us if it had a mind. According to current cognitive science, we naturally expect disembodied minds.[8] We do not naturally expect disembodied machines. The latter idea does seem quite odd to us. Avoiding strangeness is a theoretical virtue (though this requires discussion I cannot provide here). So minded Omnipotence scores better for theoretical virtue than "machine" Omnipotence overall, and as overall theoretical virtue is a tie-breaker for theories, we should see the necessary being as having a mind.

The second factor has to do with the adequacy of Omnipotence. We want the powers of our necessary being to ground inter alia all maximal absolute possibilities—the ones called possible worlds. It would be good to provide a distinct ground for each one—something that can do duty for a possible world in a fully developed Kripke-style semantics.[9] So we would like a distinct power or congeries of powers for each possible world. Yet nominalists can't distinguish the powers as different really existing attributes. So we need a way to "construct" powers for possible worlds given only concrete particulars.

One nominalist approach would site each such power in a separate necessary being, each just primitively such that if it acted, the result would be a particular possible world, or all of that world that does not depend on the free or random action of other things. Then one could let each necessary being do duty for one possible world in the semantics because each, if acting, would produce just the one possible world (or relevant portion thereof). This move would scatter the content of omnipotence. It would forfeit Omnipotence's parsimony.

One might instead say that there is one necessary being which is infinitely complex, consisting of many parts, each doing duty for a power. But this would forfeit parsimony of substances, since each part would be a substance. Since the first move's separate necessary beings could also be parts of a "scattered" necessary being, the only distinction between this second move and the first is that only the second asserts that the "small" necessary beings are part of one "big" one. Either way, we have the multitude of small ones, and parsimony is gone.

Here is a third proposal. If our concrete necessary being thinks of a world in which P, perhaps we can let this be the basis for claiming a distinct power. We can suppose that for each possible world, our necessary being thinks of that world and so "readies" itself to produce it. We can add that given this readiness, the concrete necessary being is primitively able to trigger its powers to produce worlds (or its proper share of worlds). The two together make it able to produce (say) a world in which P. So they yield a "power" suitable to ground that possibility. I do not see what else than thinking could be generated purely internally by a non-natural substance, or have the needed intentionality to constitute a power to produce one thing rather than another; it would be simply mysterious to suppose our necessary being to generate something else, of unspecified nature, and would therefore also add strangeness. So here is a second reason to ascribe a mind to our necessary being: it gives us a better overall theory by providing distinct world-substitutes while preserving parsimony.

Whether this brings a further category into the ontology depends on whether a nominalist can talk about thinking without reifying thoughts into mental events. The nominalist need not really commit to events as a new category if they are analyzable in some nominalistically acceptable way: nominalists can relax if (say) an event just is a particular's satisfying a predicate at a particular time, because particulars including token predicates were in their ontology anyway. If a nominalist can do without positing events, we have all we need. If a nominalist can't, this will hold for a nominalist naturalist powers theory, too, and a non-nominalist naturalist powers theory has a parsimony burden beyond admitting events. So one way or the other, events will not constitute a cost that disfavors Omnipotence in the comparison with its naturalist cousin. If there are events, they are concrete actual particulars, so adding them should preserve Omnipotence's parsimony edge against positions that admit the abstract or merely possible, too. It remains to be shown, then, that nominalism pays any costs for talk of the necessary being thinking. If we get thinking for free, this leaves single-being minded Omnipotence our most virtuous theory.

The last reason to ascribe a mind to this being also has to do with the adequacy of Omnipotence. We need our omnipotent being to be able to bring about everything that is possible, in some way or other, for otherwise its powers will not serve as grounds for all possibilities. Libertarian-free acts are possible. Even if we do not have such freedom, some possible beings could. So our omnipotent being must be able to bring these possible beings' free acts about, in some way or other. If the only possible thus-free being were the omnipotent being, that would be enough to show not just that it has a mind, but that it is a rational agent. If we begin by supposing only that other possible beings would be thus-free, our omnipotent being must be able, again, to bring their free acts about.

It cannot do so by simply causing them to happen. This would remove their freedom. On Molinism, perhaps it could do so by causing free agents to be in situations in which counterfactuals of freedom guarantee certain actions. It would not have to intend to do this or know it was doing this; a machine could bring this about. But (so I would argue) Molinism is false. Further, it is pretty clearly false that if A causes it to be the case that P, and P > Q, then A brings it about that Q. If I cause it to be the case that you fly to the moon, and were you to fly to the moon, the earth would have a moon, it does not follow that I bring it about that the earth has a moon.

Thus as far as I can see, there is just one way to bring about others' free actions: the omnipotent being would have to alter their desires and/or beliefs, so that they themselves do the actions, freely acting on these desires and beliefs. It could not so far alter them as to amount to causing the action. That would just cause the action by means of their desires and beliefs. It would be relevantly like brainwashing, and brainwashing does not produce free action. On the other hand, if the omnipotent being did not alter the desires and beliefs enough to make the action probable, it would be a lucky break that the alteration produced the action, and that might well defeat the claim that it had brought the action about. What are needed are alterations that make the action rather more probable than not (thus securing the omnipotent being's credit for producing it) but stop short of causing it, leaving the free agent a significant chance to choose otherwise (thus ensuring freedom). If I give you overwhelmingly good reason to do A, and you accept this, my persuasion can fairly be said to have brought about your action. Yet being persuaded is compatible with being free. So the right sort of desire-belief alterations are clearly possible. But there are constraints on how they can be produced.

If the omnipotent being simply causes the desires and beliefs to change, that seems relevantly like brainwashing, in that it entirely bypasses the rationality, agency, and autonomy of the free agent. To the extent that we are brainwashed toward an action, it ceases to be fully free, autonomous or rational. So our omnipotent being could not produce a fully free, autonomous or rational action by these means. Fully free, etc., actions are possible. So these means alone cannot allow the omnipotent being to produce all possible states of affairs. Rather, it must be able to bring some free actions about by means that respect agents' autonomy and leave their agency and rationality undiminished.

I can see only one way to do this. The omnipotent being must be able to give them sufficiently good reasons, over a long enough period, to alter their beliefs and desires in the required ways. The omnipotent being must be able to dialogue with them and change their minds. Its communication might be literal and verbal, or it might use its powers to alter other states of affairs so as to give them reasons (displaying lessons, providing incentives, etc.), respond to their responses, etc. A theist would say that God speaks to us mostly in the latter way. A machine able to do all that for all possible persons would pass a Turing test—indeed, do so much better than pass it as to display the skill of Socrates.

Turing-capable machines are functionally equivalent to minded beings—to rational agents, in fact. Most naturalists would say that there is no difference at all between the two: that a Turing-capable machine would be a rational agent. (Indeed, most would say that we ourselves are just such machines, albeit made of meat.) Naturalists, then, should grant that Omnipotence requires a being with mind, agency, and rationality enough to do Socratic work. Non-naturalists might well resist the thought that any machine could ever pass a Turing test. If they do resist this, they will grant the conclusion about Omnipotence as well—anything that passes the test is not a machine, but a rational agent. If they allow the possibility of Turing-capable machines and also distinguish between these and genuine rational agents, then still, they will find the notion of a Turing-capable immaterial machine stranger than that of an immaterial mind, and so while they might insist that Turing-capability doesn't suffice for being a rational agent, they will still find rational agent Omnipotence less strange than machine Omnipotence, and so favor it in scoring for theoretical virtue.

The best version of Omnipotence, then, will posit a single necessary eternal non-natural omnipotent rational agent. This, then, is what it takes to have the best account of the ultimate grounds of possibility. This is not yet a description of God—we have said nothing about the extent of this being's knowledge, or its moral character. But it is a significantly God-like being. Aquinas was much further from the full concept of God when he declared "and this all call God."

NOTES

1. See my *God and Necessity* (Oxford: Oxford University Press, 2012).

2. See my *God and Necessity* (Oxford: Oxford University Press, 2012), "A Naturalist Cosmological Argument" *Religious Studies* 53 (2017), 321–38, and "The Nature of Necessity," *Res Philosophica* 94 (2017), 359–83.

3. For a fuller account, see *God and Necessity*, ch. 1.

4. I owe the following to David Lewis.

5. For the needed qualifications, see my "Omnipotence," in Thomas Flint and Michael Rea, eds., *The Oxford Handbook of Philosophical Theology* (Oxford: Oxford University Press, 2009), 167–198.

6. See my "Swinburne on Divine Necessity," *Religious Studies* 46 (2010): 141–162, and "Divine Necessity," in Charles Taliaferro and Chad Meister, eds., *The Cambridge Companion to Christian Philosophical Theology* (Cambridge: Cambridge University Press, 2010), 15–30.

7. See ops. cit. n. 1.

8. See Justin Barrett, *Why Would Anyone Believe in God?* (Plymouth: Alta Mira Press, 2004).

9. For explanation and illustration, see *God and Necessity*, 444ff.

The Necessity of Sufficiency

THE ARGUMENT FROM THE INCOMPLETENESS OF NATURE

Bruce L. Gordon

⁌ ───

INTRODUCTION: PLANTINGA ON THE INADEQUACIES
OF NATURALISM IN SCIENCE

PLANTINGA'S EVOLUTIONARY ARGUMENT against naturalism (Plantinga 1993, 216–237, 2000, 227–240, 2011a, 2011b, 307–350; Beilby 2002) is well known. One might say that the aim of this argument is to show that nature, in itself, manifests a sort of epistemological incompleteness: if God's existence is denied, there is little reason to think that our cognitive faculties, including our faculty of reason, achieve epistemological closure by reliably producing true beliefs. There is another incompleteness argument hovering around the edges of Plantinga's recent work, however. One could gloss this argument as contending that God's existence is necessary to bring causal closure to nature and make it ontologically functional. The first hints of this idea appear in his discussion of divine action in the context of quantum theory (Plantinga 2011, 113–121) and recur in his recent qualified endorsement of occasionalism as a better way to think about the laws of nature from a Christian perspective than secondary causation (Plantinga 2016). Since Plantinga doesn't really pursue a natural-theological argument for God from the causal-ontological incompleteness of nature in quantum physics (see Gordon 1998, 488–497, 2002, 2003, 2011, 2013, 2017a, 2017b, 2018 for related discussions of nature's incompleteness), our purpose will be to present such an argument in rudimentary form, beginning, as we must, with a brief discussion of the phenomena of quantum physics.

417

WHENCE QUANTUM THEORY?

Quantum physics—which, along with Einstein's relativity, is one of the foundations of modern physics—includes basic quantum mechanics and its extension into various quantum field theories. In broadest terms, quantum physics (a term we will use interchangeably with "quantum theory") provides a mathematical description of the behavior of reality at the atomic and sub-atomic levels. At dimensions this small, the world behaves very differently than the world of our ordinary experience. This peculiarity is a consequence of the basic quantum hypothesis: energy does not have a continuous range of values but is absorbed and radiated discontinuously in units (quanta) that are multiples of Planck's constant. While this quantum hypothesis was put forward by Max Planck (1858–1947) in 1900 to explain black body radiation (energy emitted by a non-reflecting body due to its own heat), the work of Albert Einstein (1879–1955), Niels Bohr (1885–1962), and others soon showed it was foundational to the whole of physics (Baggott 1992, 1–74; Crease and Mann 1986; Dickson 2007; Kragh 1999; Kuhn 1978; Mehra and Rechenberg 1982–87; Pais 1986; Polkinghorne 2002; Whitaker 1996).

The peculiarity of the quantum realm is evident in the classic double-slit experiment demonstrating the wave-particle duality of light (Feynman 1965, 1971). To make the example clear, consider two waves of the same size (amplitude) traveling through water in opposite directions. Each wave has a crest (its highest point) and a trough (its lowest point). When they meet, they move through each other in various phases of superposition. Since they have the same size, when a crest meets a crest or a trough meets a trough, it will amplify respectively to twice its height or depth, and when a crest meets a trough, each cancels the other and the water is level. The former behavior is called constructive interference and the latter destructive interference. Light exhibits these kinds of interference—manifested as closely spaced light and dark bands on a projection screen—when passed through two narrow parallel slits. So light has a wave nature. But light also knocks electrons out of a variety of metals and therefore, as Einstein's 1905 explanation of this "photoelectric effect" demonstrated, exists as packets of energy called *photons* that behave like particles. This strange quantum-mechanical wave-particle duality is displayed in the double-slit experiment. When *very* low-intensity light is directed through narrow parallel slits, an interference pattern builds up on a photographic plate one spot at a time, manifesting the wave nature of light in the emerging interference pattern and the particle nature of light in its spotty accumulation. The pattern emerges if only one photon is in the apparatus at a given time and it disappears if one of the slits is covered. So *each* photon behaves as though it passes through *both* slits and interferes with itself, something that, from the standpoint of classical (non-quantum) physics and our ordinary experience of the world, is impossible. What is more, matter particles display this same wave-particle duality under similar experimental conditions, as the Davisson-Germer experiment demonstrated for electrons (Davisson 1928).

The way that quantum mechanics deals with such things is to set aside classical conceptions of motion and the interaction of bodies and introduce acts of measurement and probabilities for observational outcomes in an *irreducible* way, that is, in a way that *cannot* be resolved by an appeal to our inability to observe what is actually happening (in fact, quantum physics shows this peculiarity is *intrinsic* to reality rather than an artifact of our limited knowledge).[1] In classical mechanics, the state of a physical system at a particular time is completely specified by giving the precise position and momentum of all its constituent particles, after which the equations of motion determine the state of the system at all later times. In this sense, classical mechanics is deterministic. But quantum mechanics does *not* describe systems by states in which particle position and momentum, for example, have simultaneously defined values. Instead, the state of the system is described by an abstract mathematical object called a *wavefunction* (Ney and Albert 2013). The wavefunction of a quantum-mechanical system evolves deterministically in time, in accordance with the Schrödinger equation, as a linear superposition of different states. This deterministic evolution is disrupted by the measurement process, which, when the measurement has an actual result, always finds the system in a definite state with a particular value in accordance with a probability specified by the Born rule. After such a measurement, the future development of the quantum-mechanical system is based on the state the system was measured to be in, so measurements change the system in an irreducibly probabilistic way that is *not* a consequence of the deterministic Schrödinger evolution.[2] Furthermore, the Born rule probabilities, given by the square of the amplitude of the statefunction, are such that they cannot all equal zero or one (be representative of impossibility or necessity). This fact is expressed in Heisenberg's indeterminacy (uncertainty) principle: no mathematical description of the state of a quantum system assigns probability 1 (determinateness) to the simultaneous existence of exact values for certain "complementary" pairs of observables. What is more, the particular value resulting from the measurement of a quantum observable is irreducibly probabilistic in the sense that no sufficient condition is provided for *this* value being observed rather than another that is permitted by the wavefunction. This is one sense in which quantum theory is *indeterministic*. Also, since *all* the information about a quantum system is contained in its wavefunction, no measurement of the *current* state of a system suffices to determine the value any *later* measurement of an observable will reveal. This is another (related) sense in which quantum theory is indeterministic. Applied to the double-slit experiment, the quantum wavefunction gives a probability distribution for measurement outcomes associated with a photon being observed to hit the photographic plate in a certain region when a measurement is made. This probability distribution describes the interference pattern on the plate that results when both slits are open, even if just one photon is sent through at a time.

This way of describing physical systems has further paradoxical consequences confirmed by experimental observations. Albert Einstein, Boris Podolsky (1896–1966), and Nathan Rosen (1909–1995) pointed out one of these paradoxes in 1935, arguing that the quantum description of physical systems must be incomplete because there are (they contended) elements of reality that quantum theory does not recognize. To make this case, they considered a situation in which two quantum particles interact so as to "entangle" their spatial coordinates with each other and their linear momenta with each other (Einstein, Podolsky, and Rosen 1935; Fine 2013). As a result of this wavefunction entanglement, measuring either the position or the momentum for one particle instantaneously fixes the value for that same observable for the other particle, no matter how far apart they are. If one then assumes, as the 1935 paper did, that what counts as an element of reality for the second particle is independent of which measurement is performed on the first particle, then reality can be attributed to both the position *and* the momentum of the second particle, since measuring the position or the momentum of the first fixes the position or the momentum of the second without disturbing it and without any signal (subject to the limiting velocity of light) having passed between them. As Einstein, Podolsky, and Rosen (EPR) put it, "[i]f, without in any way disturbing a system, we can predict with certainty (i.e., with probability equal to unity) the value of a physical quantity, then there exists an element of physical reality corresponding to this physical quantity" (1935, 777). Since the simultaneous reality of position and momentum was thereby "shown" to be possible, yet quantum mechanics did not allow for this, EPR concluded that quantum mechanics was incomplete. Of course, this "proof" rested on the assumption that reality was local (faster-than-light correlations didn't really exist), so the outcomes of possible measurements for the two particles could be considered separately and had the values they did independently of whether measurements were actually made. But Bohr (1935) denied that separate measurement contexts could be combined like this, and John Bell (1964, 1966) found a way to distinguish between the EPR assumptions and those of quantum mechanics such that each predicted different experimental results (and the EPR predictions turned out to be false). As will become clear, insofar as there is a consensus that has emerged from the voluminous literature on this subject, it is that quantum mechanics reveals a genuine ontological indeterminacy and incompleteness present in nature, not an incompleteness in quantum descriptions that reflects the epistemic ignorance of physicists.

In his response to EPR, Bohr (1935) argued that they had missed the point of quantum-mechanical descriptions by ignoring the different *contexts* of measurement. He agreed that measuring *either* the position *or* the momentum of one particle would render *either* the position *or* the momentum of the other particle an element of reality, but denied that the results from these separate experimental contexts could be combined. In other words, if we try to make context-independent claims about what is real in a distant system, we will violate quantum-mechanical predictions and run afoul of experiment. This amounts to the claim that measurement of the first particle can determine what is real about the second particle, even when they are separated by a distance that would prohibit any signal (subject to the limiting velocity of light) from passing between them.

While Bohr's attempt to justify these claims generated much confusion (see Halvorson and Clifton 2002b for a very helpful clarification), John Bell's (1928–1990) work on the EPR argument and missing elements of reality (see Bell 1964, 1966),[3] along with subsequent experimental tests (for example, Aspect, Grangier, and Roger 1981, 1982; Aspect, Dalibard, and Roger 1982; Rowe et al 2001), have satisfied most physicists that Bohr was correct and Einstein wrong about the completeness of quantum mechanics. As noted, the wavefunctions of interacting quantum systems can become entangled in such a way that what happens to one of them instantaneously affects the other, no matter how far apart they have separated. Since local phenomena are correlated at speeds less than or equal to that of light, such instantaneous correlations are called *non-local*, and the quantum systems manifesting them are said to exhibit non-locality. What John Bell showed is that, if quantum theory is correct, no hidden variables (empirically undetectable elements of reality) could be added to the description of quantum systems exhibiting non-local behavior that would explain these instantaneous correlations deterministically on the basis of local considerations. Arthur Fine (1982a, 1982b, 1986) extended these results by showing that quantum phenomena have a local stochastic model just in case they have a local deterministic one, so if quantum theory is correct, they have neither. In other words, if we conjecture that quantum systems might objectively possess probabilified dispositions, we find that quantum phenomena can no more be understood in terms of local probabilistic causes than local deterministic ones.[4] So, de Broglie-Bohm theory notwithstanding (and we will deal with this subject momentarily), the vast majority of physicists have concluded that experimental violation of the Bell inequalities has confirmed (insofar as experimentation is capable of confirming something) that quantum theory is correct and complete as it stands. Since all *physical* cause-and-effect relations are local, however, the completeness of quantum theory implies the causal-ontological incompleteness of physical reality: the universe is shot through with mathematically predictable non-local correlations that, on pain of experimental contradiction, have *no* physical explanation (Bell 1981; Bub 1997; Clifton 1996; Cushing and McMullin 1989; Gordon 2011; Halvorson 2001; Herbert 1985; Maudlin 2002; Rae 2004; Redhead 1987; Wheeler 1983).

The radicalness of non-locality is actually deeper than this, because it extends to *isolated* quanta as well in the form of non-localizability.[5] Stated roughly, it has been shown (Hegerfeldt 1974; Malament 1996) that if one makes the reasonable assumptions that an individual quantum can neither serve as an infinite source of energy nor be in two places at once, then that particle has zero probability of being found in any bounded spatial region, no matter how large. In short, unobserved quanta do not exist anywhere in space, and so, to be honest, have no existence at all apart from measurement! Hans Halvorson and Robert Clifton (2002a) closed some minor loopholes and extended this argument by demonstrating that the Hegerfeldt-Malament result holds under even more general conditions—including when the standard relativistic assumption that there is *no* privileged reference frame is dropped. So the proper conclusion seems to be that there is no intelligible notion of microscopic material objects: particle talk has pragmatic utility in relation to measurement results and macroscopic appearances, but no basis in an unobserved and independent microphysical reality.

So how should we understand the relationship and transition between the microscopic and the macroscopic world? This question leads to the second famous paradox of quantum theory, the measurement problem, which was first described in Erwin Schrödinger's (1887–1961) famous "cat paradox" paper (1935). In Schrödinger's iconic example, a radioactive atom with an even chance of decaying in the next hour is enclosed in a chamber containing a cat and a glass vial of poison. If a Geiger counter detects the radioactive decay of the atom in that hour, it triggers a relay that causes a hammer to smash the vial and release the poison, thus killing the cat; otherwise, the cat survives. After an hour, the quantum wavefunction for the whole system (atom + counter + relay + hammer + vial + cat) is in an unresolved superposition that involves the cat being neither dead nor alive. The question of where and how the superpositions in the wavefunction "collapse" into a determinate result is the essence of the measurement problem. Is the determinate result a consequence of some special random process? Is it due to the quantum system's interaction with a macroscopic measurement device? Is it somehow connected to the act of observation itself? Is determinateness perhaps not manifested until the result is recognized by a conscious observer? This issue arises because every quantum wavefunction is expressible as a superposition of different states in which the thing it describes, say an alpha particle that could be ejected from an atomic nucleus, fails to possess the properties specified by those states. At any given time, then, some features of a quantum object occupy an ethereal realm between existence and non-existence. Nothing subject to a quantum description ever has simultaneously determinate values for *all* its associated properties. And these ethereal superpositions percolate upward into the macroscopic realm, because anything composed of quanta is always also intrinsically in a superposition of states, even though destructive interference (what physicists call *environmental decoherence*) may give the appearance that the wavefunction has "collapsed" into the single reality we observe (Bacciagaluppi 2012; Joos et al 2003; Landsman 2007; Schlosshauer 2007; Zurek 1991). What is more, under special conditions in the laboratory, we can create macroscopic superpositions. A clear example is provided by Superconducting Quantum Interference Devices (SQUIDs). SQUID states have been combined in which over a billion electrons move in a clockwise direction around a small superconducting ring, while another billion or more electrons simultaneously move around the ring in an anti-clockwise direction: the two incompatible currents are in superposition (Lambert 2008). With respect to this macroscopic quantum realization superposing classically incompatible states, the pressing question is: in what direction are the electrons *supposed* to be moving? Which of these classically incompatible macroscopic states is supposed to be the *real* one?

So it is that quantum theory raises fundamental questions about the coherence of material identity, individuality, and causality that pose a prima facie problem for naturalistic metaphysics (Castellani 1998): if material reality is sufficient unto itself, as metaphysical naturalists insist, then, provided that quantum theory is correct, in what does the intrinsic substantial nature of material reality consist? What is more, given the irreducibly probabilistic nature of quantum outcomes and their demonstrable non-locality, and given relativistic constraints on material causality, in what does the causal integrity and sufficiency of material reality consist? Why, in naturalistic metaphysics, if quantum outcomes lack any material explanation, does the physical universe cohere at all, let alone in a way that makes science possible? Efforts abound to interpret quantum phenomena in a way consistent with a naturalistic worldview, so we turn now to a consideration of the primary strategies and their inadequacies.

QUANTUM DISCONTENT: THE FAILURE OF NATURALISTIC INTERPRETIVE STRATEGIES

Various solutions have been and continue to be offered to the fundamental puzzle these quantum paradoxes pose: how is it even *possible* for the world to be the way that quantum theory describes? These solutions constitute different interpretations of quantum physics that cannot generally be distinguished from each other on experimental grounds, because they do not have decisively distinct experimental consequences. We will briefly consider six such interpretations—the Copenhagen interpretation, the de Broglie-Bohm non-local hidden variable interpretation, the many worlds interpretation, the Ghirardi-Rimini-Weber spontaneous collapse interpretation, the quantum logical interpretation, and instrumentalism—and, by noting their conceptual shortcomings, show how a theistic variant of the Copenhagen interpretation brings metaphysical completion to quantum theory so as to resolve the fundamental puzzle.

The Copenhagen interpretation of quantum mechanics (so-called because of its association with Niels Bohr's Institute for Theoretical Physics at the University of Copenhagen) has been regarded as the "official" or "orthodox" interpretation since the late 1920s when the consensus formed that Einstein had lost the debate with Bohr (for an overview, see Bub 1997, 189–211; Faye 2014; Murdoch 1987; for firsthand accounts see Bohr 1934, 1958; and Heisenberg 1958, 1967). Nonetheless, the Copenhagen interpretation is hardly uniform: it includes the initial concepts hashed out by Niels Bohr, Werner Heisenberg (1901–1976), Max Born (1882–1970), Wolfgang Pauli (1900–1958), John von Neumann (1903–1957), Paul Dirac (1902–1984), and others, along with their positivistic reconstruals; it includes the observer-centered and consciousness-related interpretations of von Neumann (1932), Wigner (1961), and Wheeler (1983); and it also includes the more recent "modal" interpretations of Healey (1989) and van Fraassen (1991). More often than not, however, its advocates adhere to variations on a set of core ideas: (1) quantum theory provides a *complete* description of physical systems (or what we can know about them) at the atomic and sub-atomic level, thus making nature (or our knowledge of it) irremediably causally *incomplete* and therefore irreducibly indeterministic; (2) the square of the amplitude of the wavefunction gives the probability of associated measurement outcomes (the Born rule); (3) obtaining measurement results presupposes the existence of a classical (non-quantum) world of measurement devices; (4) quantum mechanics should recover the predictions of classical mechanics in the limit where increasingly large numbers of quanta are involved (Bohm 1951: 31)—a modified version of the "correspondence principle" advocated by Bohr (Bokulich 2010); (5) for quantum properties like position and momentum that do not have simultaneous values (Halvorson 2004), the measurement process is contextual, since the classical world of measuring devices requires mutually exclusive (complementary) experimental arrangements (this is Bohr's "principle of complementarity"); and (6) while every physical system can in principle be treated as quantum-mechanical, since quantum measurement requires a classical frame of reference provided by the measurement apparatus, not all systems can be treated as quantum-mechanical simultaneously.

The Copenhagen interpretation, taken as a realistic and purely physical explanation of quantum phenomena, has an intractable difficulty. The completeness of quantum theory entails the causal incompleteness and indeterministic character of physical reality—as evidenced by non-locality and the irreducibly probabilistic results of quantum measurements—and if the physical world is all that is recognized to exist, then the absence of a physical explanation for nonlocal correlations and for irreducibly probabilistic quantum outcomes forces us to conclude that innumerable events in the physical realm happen without a sufficient cause and thus for no reason at all. By some miracle, individual events without a cause occur with a frequency that conforms to a probability distribution. By a similar miracle, events that cannot be causally connected nonetheless exhibit predictable correlated behavior, functioning as random devices in harmony.

Of course, some will object that accounts of probabilistic causation have been offered, so this conclusion is too hasty. And indeed, while there are such accounts (see Hitchcock 2010 for an excellent survey), I think they face an insuperable metaphysical problem when the probability involved is, as in the quantum case, irreducibly insufficient to explain the outcome. Consider the very idea of probabilistic causation: an event C is a probabilistic cause of event E just in case C occurred and E occurred and the occurrence of C raised the probability of the occurrence of E, by which is meant something like $P(E|C) > P(E|{\sim}C)$. Nomenclature aside, this might be true as far as it goes, but while the occurrence of C, *ex hypothesi*, is probabilistically relevant to the occurrence of E in this way, the occurrence of C is still not sufficient for the occurrence of E. More pointedly, if we *only* have C to which to appeal as an explanation of the occurrence of E, we have no explanation of E's occurrence, for it is possible that C could have occurred and E not occurred. When E happens under such conditions, we have no real understanding of why it did, and uttering "irreducible probabilistic causality" as a mantra is really just whistling in the dark. All of this is just another way of saying that the Principle of Sufficient Reason (PSR) should be understood as metaphysically and epistemologically necessary—I will say more momentarily about why this is so—and that causal sufficiency is required before anything can happen. This acknowledgement of the necessity of sufficiency speaks to the explanatory vacuity of irreducibly probabilistic causation. Even when C is a necessary but insufficient condition for E's occurrence (as, for example, having untreated latent syphilis is a necessary but notably insufficient condition for the development of paresis), it quite obviously cannot be a *cause* of E unless it is part of a larger collection of events/conditions that are jointly sufficient to the occurrence of E. So while the subject of probabilistic causality in general is complex and there is a great deal more that could be said, I hope enough has been said to instill the intuition that there is no "causality" present in "*irreducibly* probabilistic causation" in anything but a Pickwickian sense.

Now, in quantum physics we are confronted with a situation in which material causality falls irremediably short of explanatory demand, for there is no collection of physical variables jointly sufficient to the explanation of irreducibly probabilistic quantum outcomes. On pain of postulations to the contrary refuted by experimental violations of Bell inequalities, an ontological gap exists in the causal structure of physical reality that no collection of material causes can be offered to fill. So if a prior commitment to metaphysical naturalism constrains us, no non-naturalistic (transcendent) explanation is available to bridge this gap, and we must embrace the conclusion that innumerable physical events transpire without a sufficient cause, that is, for no explanatorily sufficient reason. In short, Copenhagen orthodoxy, framed in a purely physical context, entails a denial of the principle of sufficient reason (PSR) understood as the general maxim that every contingent event has an explanation.

But denying the PSR, so understood, has consequences that undermine the very possibility of doing science (Pruss 2006, 2009). Why? Suppose, among all of the events that happen in the universe, there are countless many that happen without cause or reason. If this were true, we would have no principled way of telling which events were caused and which were not, for events that *appeared* to have a cause might, in fact, lack one. Our current perceptual states, for example, might have no explanation, in which case they would bear no reliable connection to the way the world is. So if the PSR were false, we could never have any confidence in our cognitive states. In short, we would be saddled with an intractable skepticism. Furthermore, if the PSR failed for some event, there would be no objective probability for the occurrence of that event, because there would be no basis on which to make a calculation of probability. But without an evaluative basis, we could not even claim that violations of the PSR were improbable. Since we decide on the credentials of scientific explanations by comparing them with their competitors, and "no explanation" would then be an inscrutable competitor for *every* proposed explanation, we would be unable to decide whether there is a scientific explanation for *anything* that happens! So denial of the PSR is a science-killer that opens the door to an irremediable skepticism. If we were to accept a version of Copenhagen orthodoxy, then, the absence of a physical explanation for non-local correlations and individual quantum outcomes, especially in light of their occurrence in seemingly miraculous conformity to a probability distribution, should point us to the rational necessity of a non-physical explanation for quantum phenomena. We will return to this theme in due course.

A second interpretation of quantum theory is the de Broglie-Bohm non-local hidden variable theory, sometimes simply called "Bohmian mechanics" (Bell 1984; Bohm 1952, 1980; Bohm and Hiley 1993; Cushing 1994; Cushing, Fine, and Goldstein 1996; Goldstein 2013; Holland 1993; Saunders 1999). Bohmian mechanics attempts to restore causality to quantum phenomena by privileging position as an observable and introducing either a "pilot wave" or a "quantum potential field" that gives determinate trajectories to all of the constituents of a quantum system. While this sounds good in theory, there are intractable problems with the proposal. First of all, the operation of the pilot-wave/potential field is undetectable due to the fact that it does not carry energy-momentum (nor could it, since it acts superluminally) and is not, therefore, something material. So contrary to its billing, Bohmian mechanics does not restore material causality to the quantum realm. The physically non-causal operation—in the configuration space of particle positions!— of the pilot-wave/guidance field is intrinsic to its mysterious nature and no more metaphysically transparent than the non-local action-at-a-distance in orthodox quantum theory (cf. Halvorson 2011, 154). While Bohmians have postulated a kind of occult mathematical determinism in the quantum realm, any claim to have revived material causality is entirely specious. I have never seen a response to this seemingly devastating objection, but there are other problems with Bohmian mechanics to which Bohmians are more sensitive.[6] A Lorentz-invariant formulation of Bohmian mechanics remains elusive and problematic, but even more importantly, the necessary field-theoretic extension of non-relativistic Bohmian particle mechanics is ontologically ambiguous and, even at the admission of its advocates (Goldstein 2013, §15), empirically and technically deficient. The Bell-type quantum field theories that are the basis of much of this research do *not* give an adequate account of particle creation and annihilation compatible with the full range of experimentally confirmed predictions of relativistic quantum field theory, and most especially, Bohmian field theories neither predict nor give an account of antimatter. For these reasons and others, it is quite clear that the de Broglie-Bohm theory is *not* a materialist panacea for what ails orthodox quantum theory. Furthermore, even if you grant the basic Bohmian picture of bare point-particle positions instantaneously sensitive to a non-local and non-material guidance field, this ontology is far too thin to account for the rich qualitative world of our experience (as are the mathematical structures of relativistic quantum field theory, a fact we will revisit in due course because of its metaphysical significance). All things considered, therefore, the Bohmian interpretation must currently be judged a failure.

A third approach is known as the "many worlds interpretation" (MWI) of quantum theory (Albert 1992, 112–133; Baggott 2013, 211–221; Deutsch 1999; de Witt and Graham 1973; Everett 1957; Saunders 2014; Saunders et al 2010; Vaidman 2014; Wallace 2003). Its solution to the measurement problem pursues a drastic course by denying wavefunction collapse and asserting instead that *every* possible quantum outcome in the entire history of the universe has been realized in a different branch of the "universal wavefunction" defining ultimate reality. Everything that could happen, quantum-mechanically speaking, has happened and will happen, but since each of us splits into multiple parallel selves with every branching of the universe catalyzed by different quantum outcome possibilities, we each only ever observe those outcomes in branches of the universal wavefunction that are part of the personal history of that version of ourselves.

Aside from its metaphysical implausibility, the MWI also faces intractable theoretical problems.[7] The first difficulty is that there are infinitely many ways to express the universal wavefunction as a superposition of component waves and the branching that takes place in the universal wavefunction depends on which expression (basis) is chosen. So which way of building the universal wavefunction is to be preferred? This difficulty, known as the "preferred basis problem," reveals that the branching process itself is completely arbitrary from a mathematical standpoint and therefore, from the abstract point of view presupposed by the MWI, not reflective of any physical reality. The second difficulty lies in its treatment of quantum probabilities. Suppose that a quantum event has two possible outcomes with unequal probabilities, say 1/3 and 2/3. Since, according to the MWI, *both outcomes occur* in different branches of the universal wavefunction, how can their probabilities be different? In fact, doesn't *everything* happen with absolute certainty? If we follow the suggestion of Deutsch (1999) and Wallace (2003) and say that quantum probabilities reflect how we should decide to bet about which universe we will find ourselves in, then, as David Baker (2007) has argued, we land in vicious circularity, for talk of probabilities in the many worlds scenario assumes the existence of a preferred basis that *only* comes about through decoherence of the wavefunction, which is *itself* an irreducibly probabilistic phenomenon. Furthermore, to paraphrase David Albert (2010), what needs to be explained about quantum theory is the empirical frequency of the outcomes we actually experience, *not* why, if we held radically different convictions about the nature of the world than we actually do, we would still place bets in accordance with Born's rule. And to this observation we may add that since there are no unrealized outcomes, in innumerable branches of the universal wavefunction we will come to *reject* the Born rule (or never formulate it) as a betting strategy because it conflicts with all our measurements! The MWI thus fails for multiple reasons (but see Saunders et al. 2010 for extensive polemics regarding it).

A fourth interpretation that has been growing in popularity is the spontaneous collapse theory of Ghirardi, Rimini, and Weber (1986), often simply called GRW theory (see Bell 1987; Cordero 1999; Dickson 2007, 376–381; Ghirardi 2011; Ghirardi, Rimini, and Weber 1986; Saunders 2014; Tumulka 2006a, 2006b). The basic idea is that quantum-mechanical descriptions should be supplemented by random, infinitesimally small fluctuations that, with extremely high probability, localize the wavefunction to a specific region. While this postulation is ad hoc, Ghirardi's approach is nonetheless similar to Bohm's in emphasizing the density of matter to make the theory as "physical" as possible. The problem is that it cannot be rendered compatible with relativity theory or extended to the treatment of quantum fields in this form. When the effort is made to extend GRW theory to relativistic quantum fields by replacing matter (mass-density) with "flash events" (Tumulka 2006a, 2006b), the theory remains radically non-local and has the additional drawback of eliminating the possibility of particle interactions and thus any physics of interest (Ryckman 2010). Finally, there are no versions of the theory in which the collapse is complete, with the consequence that all "material" objects have low-density copies at multiple locations, the presence and effect of which linger forever in the GRW wavefunction (Cordero 1999; Dickson 2007: 376–381). In short, GRW theory does not succeed in restoring material causality (locality), physical substantiality, or spatiotemporal uniqueness to quantum phenomena, and thus makes no real progress toward resolving the "paradoxes" of quantum theory.

The quantum-logical interpretation (Birkhoff and von Neumann 1936; Dickson 2001; Gibbins 1987; Hooker 1975, 1979; Putnam 1974, 1979; Quine 1951; Reichenbach 1944) is the fifth attempt at a realistic interpretation of quantum theory. Its fundamental premise is that the paradoxes of quantum theory are resolved if we change the logic we use to analyze the world, for example, by modifying the formal structure of classical logic to conform to the algebra of observables in quantum mechanics, or by introducing a third truth-value that is neither true nor false. Of this proposal only two things need be said. The first is that one does not obviate the paradoxes of quantum mechanics by shifting the venue of discussion from the strangeness of the world to a logical structure that embodies that very strangeness. This is not a solution to the problem; it is a redescription of the problem in a different mathematical vocabulary. The second point that needs to be made is that, even if one were to adopt a non-classical logic to analyze propositions about quantum-mechanical reality, the systemic properties of that non-classical logic could only be explored using the tools of classical logic. And as regards its application, in any given situation, either you use quantum logic or you don't, and if you do, you are either correct or incorrect to do so, and the conclusions you reach will be either true or false. In short, quantum logic can never replace classical logic and, while a useful tool for exploring the logical structure of quantum theory, it's yet another description of the quantum paradoxes, not an explanation of them.

Given the difficulties of interpreting quantum theory realistically, perhaps, as a last resort, we would be better off taking an anti-realist and instrumentalist attitude toward it. This approach treats the theory as a tool for generating predictions about experimental outcomes while denying it tells us anything about the nature of reality. On this view, quantum theory is a mathematical "black box" for successful predictions, but is devoid of any explanatory value. Is this a tenable approach? It is true that, without an interpretation of some sort, the mathematics of quantum theory just describes the behavior of the micro-world without any suggestion of explaining it. But to prescind from the task of interpretation simply because the phenomena the mathematics describes are resistant to coherent *physical* explanation seems mere avoidance behavior. The *facts* of quantum behavior are not and cannot be disputed by instrumentalists: the quantum world exhibits measurable non-local correlations and individual outcomes that lack sufficient physical causes. These facts beg explanation, and the instrumentalist strategy is simply to embrace anti-realism and reject explanatory demand rather than deal with the intractability of physical explanations for quantum phenomena.

Yet, on pain of denying the principle of sufficient reason and putting all of science and human knowledge in jeopardy, *some* explanation for these phenomena must exist in spite of the increasingly clear recognition that no physical explanation, in principle, is possible. To review and expand on the bases for this conclusion, we note that: (1) no physical explanation of non-local quantum correlations is possible under relativistic constraints; (2) the non-localizability of individual particles apart from measurement is incompatible with them having intrinsic substantial existence; (3) quantum fields exhibit states of superposition of contradictory numbers of quanta that make the individual substantiality of these quanta impossible; (4) the stability of macroscopic appearances is an artifact of destructive interference (environmental decoherence) in which still extant yet phenomenologically suppressed macroscopic superpositions persist and for which, given the singular unity of our experience as contrasted with the untenable MWI hypothesis, has material *in*substantiality as a necessary condition; (5) macroscopic superpositions have been and can be created under laboratory conditions (Dunningham et al. 2006; Lambert 2008), thus allowing the aforementioned insubstantiality to be observed directly; (6) mass, which is resistance to acceleration, is not itself intrinsic to matter and indicative of its substantiality, but rather a phenomenological artifact of interactions between fermionic fields and the Higgs field; and (7) in every quantum state, whether for microscopic or macroscopic systems, there will always be some elements that fail to have a determinate value, in other words, there will always be some elements that fail to be real.

To employ an imprecise metaphor, the reality that quantum theory gives us is like a Hollywood set where all the buildings are façades and only one side of a structure is visible at any given time, but when you try to open a door on the side currently visible in order to see inside the structure, you find that there's nothing behind it! In short, what both quantum theory and the observational evidence that gives rise to it tell us is that what we take to be the "material universe" is radically incomplete, both with respect to a material explanation of the constitution of the objects we perceive and with respect to the causal interactions of such objects with each other. The fact that *some* explanation is necessary and *no* material explanation is sufficient shows that the physical universe is neither a self-contained nor a self-sustaining entity. Rather, the universe we experience is dependent on a form of causality that transcends what we take to be physical and completes it, giving integrity to its causal structure.

AFTER MATERIAL CAUSATION: WHENCE THE REGULARITY OF NATURE?

Given the insufficiency of material causation and the metaphysical and epistemic necessity of sufficiency, how is this causal closure achieved, and what does the answer to this question tell us about the nature of those things we commonly call physical "laws"? Could we, for instance, usefully explain macroscopic regularities as emergent properties of quantum interactions in a way that would ground material identity and physical law? It is true that we can understand such emergence in terms of the limit behavior of physical systems in two ways—the classical mechanical (CM) limit and the classical statistical (CS) limit. While these limits are useful in seeing how quantum descriptions can give rise to classical appearances, they are metaphysically unenlightening where relevant, and irrelevant in the case of non-local behavior (Gordon 2002, 2011). Consider first the classical limit in which Maxwell-Boltzmann statistical behavior emerges from quantum (Bose-Einstein or Fermi-Dirac) statistics. With the standard definitions of the Poisson and commutator brackets, the CM limit of a quantum system is defined to be:

$$\lim_{\hbar \to 0} \frac{1}{i\hbar}[\hat{A},\hat{B}] = \left\{A,B\right\}.$$

This limit is fictional, of course, because $\hbar$ is a physical constant; nonetheless, it represents the transition between the quantum and classical descriptions of a system, since classical behavior "emerges" when quantum effects are dampened to the point of negligibility. It is important to note, however, that there are still residual effects (dependent on Planck's constant) even after the classical mechanical limit is taken and the underlying reality is still quantum-mechanical in character. In the second case, that of the CS limit, statistical mechanics mathematically relates the thermodynamic properties of macroscopic objects to the motion of their microscopic constituents. Since the microscopic constituents obey quantum dynamics, the correct description must in principle lie within the domain of quantum statistical mechanics. Under thermodynamic conditions of high temperature (T) and low density (n), however, classical statistical mechanics serves as a useful approximation. With this in mind, the CS limit may be defined as the situation represented by:

$$T \to \infty \text{ and } n \to 0.$$

These are the same conditions as those governing the applicability of the ideal gas law ($pV = nRT$), so the CS limit could equally well be called the *ideal gas limit*. Unlike the CM limit, the conditions governing the CS limit are subject to experimental control. In respect of quantum statistical behavior, both the CM and the CS limits are continuous, so the indistinguishability arising from the permutation symmetry of the quanta is not removed, even though it is dampened. Quantum "particles" retain their indistinguishability even when their aggregate behavior can be approximated by a Maxwell-Boltzmann distribution. These observations reveal why any emergentist account of the dependence or supervenience of the macroscopic realm on the microscopic realm, while perhaps descriptively interesting, will be unenlightening as a metaphysical explanation. It is environmental decoherence (essentially, statistical damping through wave-function orthogonalization) that gives quantum-mechanical ephemera a cloak of macroscopic stability, but decoherence is *not* a real solution to the measurement

problem. The apparent solidity of the world of our experience is a mere epiphenomenon of quantum statistics; the underlying noumena retain their quantum-theoretic
ephemerality while sustaining a classical macroscopic phenomenology (see Gordon 2011,
190–195 for a more complete discussion of the explanatory vacuity of the concepts of
supervenience and emergence in relation to the transition between the microscopic and
macroscopic realms).

So where does this leave us in respect of an analysis of what are commonly called physical "laws"? Plantinga (2016) provides a very cogent philosophical critique of the role
of necessity in accounts of physical law. Though some philosophers (Shoemaker 1980;
Swoyer 1982; Fales 1990; and Bird 2005) have argued that natural laws are broad logical
necessities similar to statements like *no equine mammals are mathematical propositions*,
there seems little to no basis for this claim. If we take Coulomb's Law of electric charges,
for instance, the fact that two like (or different) charges repel (or attract) each other with
a force proportional to the magnitude of the charges and inversely proportional to the
square of the distance between them gives no hint of being metaphysically necessary. We
can easily conceive of a different mathematical relationship holding between the charges.
This has led other philosophers (Armstrong 1983; Dretske 1977; Tooley 1987) to assert
that the laws of nature are *contingently* necessary and to develop an account of natural
laws based on this assumption. But quite apart from the oxymoronic appearance of such
a claim, no coherent account of its substance has ever been put forward. One can't just
call natural laws "contingent necessities" and expect it to be true "any more than one can
have mighty biceps just by being called 'Armstrong,'" as David Lewis (1983, 166) famously
quipped. Finally, other necessitarians have proposed an account of physical laws deriving
from innate causal powers (Harré and Madden 1975; Bigelow and Pargetter 1990): laws of
nature are grounded in the essential natures of things inherent in their material substance
and manifested through forces or fields that express necessary capacities or emanations
from these natures and which then mediate or constrain physical interactions in a way
that also is necessary. But again, it is difficult to see why *this* causal power must necessarily
flow from the essential nature of *that* material substance. Calling it necessary or essential
doesn't make it so; we could easily and coherently imagine it otherwise.

Even if necessitarian accounts of physical law were not philosophically intractable,
however, they would be empirically false on quantum-mechanical grounds. All of them
require that physical systems and material objects objectively possess properties that
are capable of being connected together in a law-like fashion. At a minimum, necessitarian theorists have to maintain that quantum systems, or their components, objectively possess properties prior to measurement, whether these properties are determinate
or indeterminate (probabilified dispositions), and that it is the objective possession of
these properties that necessitates (or renders probable) their specific behavior. But Bell's
theorem demonstrates that this assumption leads to empirically false consequences in
the case of both locally deterministic and locally stochastic models (Bell 1964, 1996;
Fine 1981, 1982a, 1982b; Redhead 1987, 71–118; Cushing and McMullin 1989; Clifton,

Feldman, Halvorson, Redhead, and Wilce 1998). Furthermore, this assumption either leads to an ontological contradiction in the non-local stochastic case (Gordon 1998, 444–451; Gordon 2011, 194–195; Maudlin 2002, 204–212), or if an undetectable privileged reference frame is invoked, succumbs to the non-localizability and insubstantiality of the intended possessors of the requisite properties (Gordon 1998, 452–453; Gordon 2011, 198–201; Halvorson 2001; Halvorson and Clifton 2002a; Malament 1996). What we are left with, therefore, is a situation in which there are no objective physical properties at the quantum level in which to ground necessitarian relations, and no emergentist or supervenience account of material identity that would provide a substantial foundation for macroscopic necessitarianism. So necessitarian theories of natural law cannot gain a purchase point in fundamental physical theory and must be set aside. All that remains are so-called regularist accounts of natural law, which assert that while there are regularities present in the phenomenology of the world on a universal scale, there are no real *laws* of nature, that is, there is no necessity that inheres in the natural relationships among things or in the natural processes involving them. In short, nature behaves in ways we can count on, but it does so for no discernible *physical* reason. How do we make sense of this situation?

In dealing with this conundrum, we must first address the metaphysical coherence of regularist accounts of physical law in the context of naturalistic metaphysics. The patron saint of this approach is David Hume and the most sophisticated modern articulation of it is given by David Lewis (Lewis 1973, 1983, 1994). In describing the regularities of our world, Lewis's theory takes the fundamental relations to be spatiotemporal: relativistic distance relations that are both space-like and time-like, and occupancy relations between point-sized things and space-time points. Fundamental properties are then local qualities—perfectly natural intrinsic properties of points, or of point-sized occupants of points. Everything else supervenes on the spatiotemporal arrangement of local qualities throughout all of history—past, present, and future—hence "Humean supervenience." On this view, natural regularities are simply the theorems of axiomatic deductive systems, and the best system is the one that strikes the optimal balance between simplicity and strength (informativeness). Lewis postulates this "best system" to exist as a brute fact whether we know anything about it or not. As Plantinga (2016, 130) points out, we have little conception of what Lewis's "best system" might look like and even less reason to think that there is a uniquely "best" such system as opposed to "a multitude of such systems each unsurpassed by any other." We may add that Lewis's approach, as it stands, is inadequate to deal with quantal nonlocalizability, physical indeterminism, and the undoing of the causal metric of spacetime in quantum gravity. Furthermore, quantum-theoretic Bell correlations, while non-locally and instantaneously coincident, would have to be understood in Lewis's theory in terms of random independent local properties harmonized at space-like separation with other random independent local properties without *any* ontological connection or explanation, all manifested as part of an overarching system of regularities that is in some sense optimal, but which also lacks any explanation for the ongoing order it displays. In short, embracing Lewis's approach requires rejecting the PSR on a colossal scale, which, as we have seen, has among its consequences both self-defeating skepticism and the utter futility of scientific explanation. When its implications are grasped, Lewis's Humean supervenience serves as a reductio of itself.

Having seen that necessitarianism is untenable for quantum-theoretic reasons and that the regularist account of laws is rationally unsustainable in a naturalistic context, let's begin anew with the eminently reasonable assumption that there is a way that the world is, that we can get it right or wrong, and that science is a useful tool in helping us to get it right. In particular, when physical theory backed by experiment demonstrates that the world of our experience must satisfy certain formal structural constraints—for example, quantizability, non-locality as encapsulated in the Bell theorems, non-localizability as indicated by the Hegerfeldt-Malament and Reeh-Schlieder theorems, Lorentz symmetries in space-time, internal symmetries like isospin, various conserved quantities as implied by Noether's theorem, and so on—then these formal features of the world may be taken as strong evidence for a certain metaphysical state of affairs. At a minimum, such states of affairs entail that the structural constraints empirically observed to hold and represented by a given theory will be preserved (though perhaps in a different representation) in any future theoretical development. This gives expression to a generic structural realism.

Whether this structural realism has further ontological consequences pertaining to the actual furniture of the world (entity realism) is a matter of debate among structural realists. The epistemic structural realist believes that there are epistemically inaccessible material objects forever hidden behind the structures of physical theory and that all we can know are the structures (Worrall 1989; Redhead 1995; Cao 1997, 2003a, 2003b, 2003c). The ontic structural realist eliminates material objects completely—it is not just that we only know structures, but rather that all that exists to be known are the structures (Ladyman 1998; French 1999, 2000, 2003a, 2003b, 2005; French and Ladyman 2003a, 2003b; French and Krause 2006; Ladyman and Ross 2007). Both versions of structural realism are deficient, though in different ways.

We have argued that quantum theory is incompatible with the existence of material substances. Given this conclusion, the epistemic structural realist is just wrong that there is a world of inaccessible material individuals hidden behind the structures that quantum theory imposes upon the world. The situation would therefore seem to default to ontic structural realism. But while the ontic structural realist is correct that there are no material objects behind the structures, his position is deficient, too, because there can be no structures simpliciter without an underlying reality that manifests that structure; we cannot build castles in the air. It would seem, then, that we're in a sort of catch-22 situation. The challenge to making sense of quantum physics is to give an account of what the world is like when it has an objective structure that does *not* depend on material substances. What investigations of the completeness of quantum theory have taught us, therefore, is rather than quantum theory being incomplete, it is material reality (so-called) that is incomplete. The realm that we call the "physical" or "material" or "natural" is not self-sufficient, but dependent upon something more basic.

In light of this realization, the rather startling picture that begins to seem plausible is that preserving and explaining the objective structure of appearances in light of quantum theory requires reviving a type of phenomenalism in which our perception of the physical universe is constituted by sense-data conforming to certain structural constraints, but in which there is no material reality causing these sensory perceptions. What we are left with is an ontology of minds (as immaterial substances) experiencing and generating mental events and processes that, when sensory in nature, have a formal character limned by the fundamental symmetries and structures revealed in "physical" theory. That these structured sensory perceptions are *not* mostly of our own individual or collective human making points to the falsity of any solipsistic or social constructivist conclusion, but it also implies the need for a transcendent source and ground of our experience. As Robert Adams points out, mere formal structure is ontologically incomplete:

> [A] system of spatiotemporal relationships constituted by sizes, shapes, positions, and changes thereof, is too incomplete, too hollow, as it were, to constitute an ultimately real thing or substance. It is a framework that, by its very nature, needs to be filled in by something less purely formal. It can only be a structure *of* something of some not merely structural sort. Formally, rich as such a structure may be, it lacks too much of the reality of material thinghood. By itself, it participates in the incompleteness of abstractions. . . . [T]he reality of a substance must include something intrinsic and *qualitative* over and above any formal or structural features it may possess (Adams 2007, 40).

When we consider the fact that the *structure* of reality in fundamental physical theory is merely phenomenological and that this structure itself is hollow and non-qualitative, whereas our experience is not, the metaphysical objectivity and epistemic intersubjectivity of the enstructured qualitative reality of our experience can be seen to be best explained by an occasionalist idealism of the sort advocated by George Berkeley or Jonathan Edwards. In the metaphysical context of this kind of theistic immaterialism, the *vera causa* that brings coherent closure to the phenomenological reality we inhabit is always and only *agent* causation. The necessity of causal sufficiency is met by divine action. As Plantinga emphasizes (Plantinga 2016, 137):

> [T]he connection between God's willing that there be light and there being light is necessary in the broadly logical sense: it is necessary in that sense that if God wills that p, p occurs. Insofar as we have a grasp of necessity (and we do have a grasp of necessity), we also have a grasp of causality when it is divine causality that is at issue. I take it this is a point in favor of occasionalism, and in fact it constitutes a very powerful advantage of occasionalism.

TRANSCENDENT CAUSATION TRIUMPHANT

But while Plantinga is right to emphasize the virtues of occasionalism, he does not take his argument in the idealist direction that the quantum-theoretic evidence seems to warrant. Clearly, the philosophical and quantum-theoretic problems for necessitarianism also prohibit a secondary causation account of divine action as the metaphysical basis for natural regularities. Secondary causation requires God to have created material substances to possess and exercise, actively or passively, their own intrinsic causal powers. God acts in the *ordinary* course of nature only as a universal or primary cause that sustains the existence of material substances and their properties as secondary causes. On this view, material substances mediate God's ordinary activity in the world and function as secondarily efficient causes in their own right. Plantinga recognizes that secondary causation inherits many of the philosophical problems associated with necessitarian accounts. Beyond this, however, it also inherits the quantum-theoretic problems that render necessitarianism unviable: the inherent insubstantiality of fundamental quantum entities, the inability of emergentist accounts of macroscopic objecthood to generate substantial material individuality and identity, and the operative incompleteness of reality in respect of material causation. In the absence of coherent material substances and physical causality, therefore, secondary causation lacks a purchase point in fundamental physical theory. So regardless of whether God *could* have created a world in which there were secondary material causes, it is evident that He *did not do so*. This leaves us with an occasionalist account of natural regularities, which in its "weak" form, as Plantinga is at pains to argue, fares no worse than secondary causation in respect of allowing for libertarian freedom and a resolution of the problem of evil. In fact, if we take advantage of Alfred Freddoso's (1988, 79–83) approach to occasionalism, we can build the *possibility* of libertarian freedom into its definition:

> God is the sole efficient cause of every state of affairs in the universe that is not subject to the influence of *freely* acting creatures.

In other words, divine action is the only *vera causa* of every state of affairs occurring in "pure" nature, namely, that segment of the universe *not* subject to the causal influence of creatures with libertarian freedom.

We can be more explicit. In giving an account of the ontological basis for natural regularities under occasionalist idealism, the regularities of nature may be formulated as counterfactuals of divine freedom (Ratzsch 1987; Plantinga 2016). Rather than understanding God's activity in terms of the divine production of certain behavior in substantial material objects, however, with the perception of these objects divinely induced and correlated with activity in our material brains, we must think instead in terms of the creaturely experience of mental phenomena divinely induced in our finite immaterial minds. So the natural regularities we interpret as "laws of nature" are just specifications of how God would act to produce the phenomena we experience under different complexes of conditions. More precisely, nature's regular behavior should be understood in the following way: if collective phenomenological conditions C were realized, all other things being equal, God would cause us to experience the phenomenological state of affairs S. On this view, then, what we take to be material objects are mere phenomenological structures lacking independent causal powers that we are nonetheless caused to perceive by God. Furthermore, what we perceive as causal activity in nature is always and only God causing us—as immaterial substantial minds whose bodies are also mere phenomenological constructs—to have appropriate formally structured qualitative sensory perceptions.

CONCLUSION: PLANTINGA ON THE ADEQUACY OF THEISM IN SCIENCE

As we have seen, Plantinga's work provides a catalyst for two powerful philosophical critiques of the completeness and coherence of metaphysical naturalism with respect to scientific explanations. The first is an epistemic critique focused on the cognitive consequences of evolutionary naturalism, and the second is a less-developed argument for the inability of naturalism to account for the ordered structure of nature on which science relies. We extended this second critique, through a consideration of quantum theory and the principle of sufficient reason, into an argument for the irremediable incompleteness of physical explanations and the necessity of transcendent causation, concluding that God's existence and continuous activity is the best explanation for the reality, persistence, and coherence of natural phenomena, and the account of divine action best meeting this explanatory demand is a form of occasionalist idealism. All of this supports Plantinga's contention that, while metaphysical naturalism undermines the practice of science, theism provides its foundations (Plantinga 2011, 193–303, especially 265ff). Fittingly, we give Plantinga (2011, 349–350) the last word:

> [T]here is superficial conflict but deep concord between science and theistic belief, but superficial concord and deep conflict between science and naturalism. Given that naturalism is at least a quasi-religion, there is indeed a science/religion conflict, all right, but it is not between science and theistic religion: it is between science and naturalism. That's where the conflict really lies.

NOTES

My thanks to Trent Dougherty for feedback contributing to the clarity, though not the lack of brevity, of this essay (mea culpa), and to Alvin Plantinga for the outstanding Christian scholarship and good-natured humanity that has transformed philosophy for the better.

1. For those of you inclined to object to this characterization on the basis of de Broglie-Bohm theory (Bohmian mechanics), I address what I regard as the inadequacies of the Bohmian alternative in the third section of this essay.

2. We will discuss non-collapse interpretations of quantum theory in the third section of this essay.

3. In the last decade of his life, Bell developed an interest in Bohmian mechanics as doing a "better job" of explanation than orthodox quantum theory, which he thought had settled for an unsatisfactory "FAPP" (for all practical purposes) attitude toward physical descriptions and explanations (for examples of this, see Bell's 1987 collection of papers, *Speakable and Unspeakable in Quantum Mechanics*. Cambridge: Cambridge University Press). For reasons that will become apparent, I think Bell was deeply mistaken that de Broglie-Bohm theory is in any way explanatorily superior to standard quantum theory.

4. We will briefly critique the idea of irreducible probabilistic causality in the next section.

5. An isolated quantum is an individual quantum considered apart from interaction with any other quanta, that is, a solitary non-interacting quantum. While this is an idealization, it is also essential to evaluating the metaphysical implications of relativistic quantum theory. As Hegerfeldt (1974), Malament (1996), and Halvorson and Clifton (2002a) have convincingly argued, no interpretation of relativistic quantum theory in terms of (unobserved) localizable particles is tenable, which is to say, whatever it is, it's not a theory about particles of the traditional sort. But despite the fact that relativistic quantum theory pushes us to conclude that "particles" only exist when observed, it is worth noting that even if one were inclined to say that what we call "particles" are merely epiphenomenal *properties* of fields, there is a very good argument to be made (Baker 2009) that quantum theory is *not* interpretable as a theory about fields, either. But if matter and radiation cannot readily be conceived in terms of either particle or field ontologies, then it's difficult to see how they can be conceived as something materially substantial at all. We seem pushed in the direction of understanding them as *mere* phenomena lacking material substantiality.

6. The work of Sheldon Goldstein and an international coterie of Bohmian researchers is exemplary in this regard. A nice summary of the state of the art may be found in Goldstein (2013). For a more extensive link to technical research papers attempting to address various issues, see http://www.bohmian-mechanics.net/ research_papers.html (last accessed August 26, 2016).

7. For those of us who feel constrained by a broad Christian orthodoxy, there are other problems, too. Since the MWI is completely deterministic, there is no room for libertarian freewill, and this, in the view of many, does away with moral responsibility. Even more important, when everything that is quantum-mechanically possible happens without external constraint or direction, there are some branches of the universal wavefunction from which the Incarnation is absent, and other branches in which there is an Incarnation event that goes awry because that version of Jesus sins continually or decides not to go to the Cross, and so on. Furthermore, there are versions of you and I that go to heaven, and other versions that go to hell, so are there as many heavens and hells as there are branches of the universal wavefunction in which heaven- or hell-bound people exist, or are they eschatologically consolidated so that we can expect to meet countless versions of ourselves in each locale? But if the Christian who embraces the MWI (see, for example, Page 2008) must prune its branches to render it compatible with orthodoxy, and such pruning eliminates the purely deterministic unfolding of the universal wavefunction, then why not prune the branches all the way down to *one* and give us a unique, God-directed history that accomplishes divine purposes?

REFERENCES AND RECOMMENDED READING

Adams, Robert M. 2007. "Idealism Vindicated." Peter van Inwagen and Dean Zimmerman, eds. *Persons: Human and Divine*. Oxford: Oxford University Press, 35–54.

Albert, David Z. 1992. *Quantum Mechanics and Experience*. Cambridge, MA: Harvard University Press.

———. 2010. "Probability in the Everett Picture." Simon Saunders, Jonathan Barrett, Adrian Kent, and David Wallace, eds. *Many Worlds? Everett, Quantum Theory, & Reality*. Oxford: Oxford University Press, 355–368.

Armstrong, David. 1983. *What Is a Law of Nature?* Cambridge: Cambridge University Press.

Aspect, A., P. Grangier, and G. Roger. 1981. "Experimental Tests of Realistic Theories via Bell's Theorem." *Physical Review Letters* 47: 460–467.

———. 1982. "Experimental Realization of Einstein-Podolsky-Rosen-Bohm *Gedanken-experiment*: A New Violation of Bell's Inequalities." *Physical Review Letters* 48: 91–94.

Aspect, A., J. Dalibard, and G. Roger. 1982. "Experimental Tests of Bell's Inequalities Using Time-Varying Analyzers." *Physical Review Letters* 49: 1804–1807.

Bacciagaluppi, Guido. 2012. "The Role of Decoherence in Quantum Mechanics." *Stanford Encyclopedia of Philosophy*. Available at: http://plato.stanford.edu/entries/qm-decoherence/ (last accessed April 15, 2016).

Baggott, Jim. 1992. *The Meaning of Quantum Theory*. Oxford: Oxford University Press.

———. 2013. *Farewell to Reality: How Modern Physics Has Betrayed the Search for Scientific Truth*. New York: Pegasus Books, 27–80.

Baker, David J. 2007. "Measurement Outcomes and Probability in Everettian Quantum Mechanics." *Studies in History and Philosophy of Modern Physics* 38: 153–169.

———. 2009. "Against Field Interpretations of Quantum Field Theory." *British Journal for the Philosophy of Science* 60: 585–609.

Beilby, James. Ed. 2002 *Naturalism Defeated? Essays on Plantinga's Evolutionary Argument Against Naturalism*. Ithaca, NY: Cornell University Press.

Bell, John S. 1964. "On the Einstein-Podolsky-Rosen Paradox." Reprinted in J.S. Bell (1987) *Speakable and Unspeakable in Quantum Mechanics*. Cambridge: Cambridge University Press, 14–21.

———. (1966. "On the Problem of Hidden Variables in Quantum Mechanics." Reprinted in J.S. Bell (1987), *Speakable and Unspeakable in Quantum Mechanics* Cambridge: Cambridge University Press, 1–13.

———. 1981. "Bertlmann's Socks and the Nature of Reality." Reprinted in J.S. Bell (1987), *Speakable and Unspeakable in Quantum Mechanics*. Cambridge: Cambridge University Press, 139–158.

———. 1984. "Beables for Quantum Field Theory." CERN-TH.4035/84. Reprinted in J.S. Bell (1987), *Speakable and Unspeakable in Quantum Mechanics*. Cambridge: Cambridge University Press, 173–180.

———. 1987 "Are There Quantum Jumps?" J. S. Bell (1987) *Speakable and Unspeakable in Quantum Mechanics*. Cambridge: Cambridge University Press, 201–212.

Bigelow, J., and R. Pargetter. 1990. *Science and Necessity*. Cambridge: Cambridge University Press.

Bird, Alexander. 2005. "The Dispositionalist Conception of Law." *Foundations of Science* 10, no. 4: 353–370.

Birkhoff, G., and J. von Neumann. 1936. "The Logic of Quantum Mechanics." *Annals of Mathematics* 37: 823–843.

Bohm, David. 1951. *Quantum Theory*. New York: Prentice-Hall (reprinted by Dover Publications).

———. 1952. "A Suggested Interpretation of the Quantum Theory in Terms of 'Hidden' Variables, I and II." *Physical Review* 85: 166–193. Reprinted in John A. Wheeler and Wojciech H. Zurek, eds. (1983), *Quantum Theory and Measurement*. Princeton, NJ: Princeton University Press, 369–396.

———. 1980. *Wholeness and the Implicate Order*. London: Routledge.

Bohm, D., and B.J. Hiley. (1993. *The Undivided Universe: An Ontological Interpretation of Quantum Theory*. London: Routledge

Bohr, Niels. 1934. *Atomic Theory and the Description of Nature*. Cambridge: Cambridge University Press.

———. 1935. "Can Quantum-Mechanical Description of Physical Reality Be Considered Complete?" *Physical Review* 48: 696–702. Reprinted in John A. Wheeler and Wojciech H. Zurek, eds. (1983) *Quantum Theory and Measurement*. Princeton, NJ: Princeton University Press, 145–151.

———. 1958. *Essays 1932–1957 on Atomic Physics and Human Knowledge*. Woodbridge, CT: Ox Bow Press.

Bokulich, Alisa. 2010. "Bohr's Correspondence Principle." *Stanford Encyclopedia of Philosophy*. Available at: http://plato.stanford.edu/entries/bohr-correspondence/ #BacSciCon (last accessed April 15, 2016).

Bub, Jeffrey. 1997. *Interpreting the Quantum World*. Cambridge: Cambridge University Press.

Cao, Tian Yu. 1997. *Conceptual Developments of 20th Century Field Theories*. Cambridge: Cambridge University Press.

———. 2003a. "Structural Realism and the Interpretation of Quantum Field Theory." *Synthese* 136: 3–24.

———. 2003b. "Appendix: Ontological Relativity and Fundamentality—Is QFT the Fundamental Theory?" *Synthese* 136: 25–30.

———. 2003c. "Can We Dissolve Physical Entities into Mathematical Structures?" *Synthese* 136: 57–71.

Castellani, Elena, ed. 1998. *Interpreting Bodies: Classical and Quantum Objects in Modern Physics*. Princeton, NJ: Princeton University Press.

Clifton, Robert, ed. 1996. *Perspectives on Quantum Reality: Non-Relativistic, Relativistic, and Field-Theoretic*. Dordrecht: Kluwer Academic Publishers.

Clifton, R., D.V. Feldman, H. Halvorson, M.L.G. Redhead, and A. Wilce. 1998. "Superentangled states." *Physical Review A* 58, no. 1: 135–145.

Cordero, A. 1999. "Are GRW Tails as Bad as They Say?" *Philosophy of Science* S66: S59–S71.

Crease, Robert P., and Charles C. Mann. 1986. *The Second Creation: Makers of the Revolution in 20th Century Physics*. New York: Macmillan Publishing Company.

Cushing, James T. 1994. *Quantum Mechanics: Historical Contingency and the Copenhagen Hegemony*. Chicago: University of Chicago Press.

Cushing, James T., and Ernan McMullin, eds. 1989. *Philosophical Consequences of Quantum Theory: Reflections on Bell's Theorem*. Notre Dame, IN: University of Notre Dame Press.

Cushing, James T., Arthur I. Fine, and Sheldon Goldstein, eds. 1996. *Bohmian Mechanics and Quantum Theory: An Appraisal*. Dordrecht: Kluwer Academic Publishers.

Davisson, C.J. 1928. "Are Electons Waves?" *Journal of the Franklin Institute* 205, no. 5: 597–623.

Deutsch, David. 1999. "Quantum Theory of Probability and Decisions." *Proceedings of the Royal Society of London A* 455: 3129–3137.

DeWitt, B., and N. Graham, eds. 1973. *The Many-Worlds Interpretation of Quantum Mechanics.* Princeton, NJ: Princeton University Press.

Dickson, W. Michael. 2001. "Quantum Logic Is Alive ∧ (It is True ∨ It is False)." *Philosophy of Science* 68: S274–S287.

———. 2007. "Non-Relativistic Quantum Mechanics." Jeremy Butterfield and John Earman, eds. *Handbook of the Philosophy of Physics*, Part A. Amsterdam: Elsevier, 275–415.

Dretske, Fred. 1977. "Laws of Nature." *Philosophy of Science* 44: 248–268.

Dunningham, J.A., K. Burnett, R. Roth, and W.D. Phillips. 2006. "Creation of Macroscopic Superposition States from Arrays of Bose-Einstein Condensates." *New Journal of Physics* 8: 182–188. Available at: http://iopscience.iop.org/1367-2630/8/9/182/fulltext/ (last accessed April 15, 2016).

Einstein, A., B. Podolsky, and N. Rosen. 1935. "Can Quantum-Mechanical Description of Physical Reality Be Considered Complete?" *Physical Review* 47: 777–780. Reprinted in John A. Wheeler and Wojciech H. Zurek, eds. (1983), *Quantum Theory and Measurement.* Princeton, NJ: Princeton University Press, 138–141.

Everett, Hugh, III. (1957. "'Relative State' Formulation of Quantum Mechanics." *Reviews of Modern Physics* 29: 454–462. Reprinted in John A. Wheeler and Wojciech H. Zurek, eds. (1983 *Quantum Theory and Measurement.* Princeton, NJ: Princeton University Press, 315–323.

Fales, Evan. 1990. *Causation and Universals.* London: Routledge.

Faye, Jan. 2014. "Copenhagen Interpretation of Quantum Mechanics." *Stanford Encyclopedia of Philosophy.* Available at: http://plato.stanford.edu/entries/qm-copenhagen/ (last accessed April 15, 2016).

Feynman, Richard P. 1965. "Probability and Uncertainty—The Quantum-Mechanical View of Nature," in *The Character of Physical Law.* Cambridge, MA: The M.I.T. Press, 127–148.

———. 1971. *The Feynman Lectures on Physics, Vol. 3: Quantum Mechanics.* Reading, MA: Addison-Wesley Publishing Company.

Fine, Arthur I. 1981. "Correlations and Physical Locality," in Asquith, P., and R. Giere,eds., *PSA 1980,* vol. 2. East Lansing, MI: Philosophy of Science Association, 535–562.

———. 1982a. "Hidden Variables, Joint Probability, and the Bell Inequalities." *Physical Review Letters* 48: 291–295.

———. 1982b. "Joint Distributions, Quantum Correlations, and Commuting Observables." *Journal of Mathematical Physics* 23: 1306–1310.

———. 1986. *The Shaky Game: Einstein, Realism, and Quantum Theory.* Chicago: University of Chicago Press.

———. 2013. "The Einstein-Podolsky-Rosen Argument in Quantum Theory." *Stanford Encyclopedia of Philosophy.* Available at: http://plato.stanford.edu/entries/qt-epr/ (last accessed April 15, 2016).

Freddoso, Alfred J. 1988. "Medieval Aristotelianism and the Case against Secondary Causation in Nature." Thomas V. Morris, ed. *Divine and Human Action: Essays in the Metaphysics of Theism.* Ithaca, NY: Cornell University Press, 74–118.

French, Steven. "Models and Mathematics in Physics: The Role of Group Theory," in J. Butterfield and C. Pagonis, eds. 1999), *From Physics to Philosophy*. Cambridge: Cambridge University Press, 187–207.

———. 2000. "The Reasonable Effectiveness of Mathematics: Partial Structures and the Application of Group Theory to Physics." *Synthese* 125 103–120.

———. 2003a. "A Model-Theoretic Account of Representation (Or, I Don't Know Much About Art . . . But I Know It Involves Isomorphism." *Philosophy of Science* 70: 1472–1483.

———. 2003b. "Scribbling on the Blank Sheet: Eddington's Structuralist Conception of Objects." *Studies in History and Philosophy of Modern Physics* 34: 227–259.

———. 2005. "Symmetry, Structure and the Constitution of Objects." Available at: http://philsci-archive.pitt.edu/327/1/Symmetry%26Objects_doc.pdf (last accessed April 15, 2016).

French, Steven, and Decio Krause. 2006. *Identity* in *Physics: A Historical, Philosophical, and Formal Analysis*. Oxford: Clarendon Press.

French, Steven, and James Ladyman. 2003a. "The Dissolution of Objects: Between Platonism and Phenomenalism." *Synthese* 136: 73–77.

———. 2003b. "Remodeling Structural Realism: Quantum Physics and the Metaphysics of Structure." *Synthese* 136: 31–56.

Ghirardi, G.C. 2011. "Collapse Theories." *Stanford Encyclopedia of Philosophy*. Available at: http://plato.stanford.edu/entries/qm-collapse/ (last accessed April 15, 2016).

Ghirardi, G.C., A. Rimini, and T. Weber. 1986. "Unified Dynamics for Microscopic and Macroscopic Systems." *Physical Review D* 34: 470–491.

Gibbins, Peter. 1987. *Particles and Paradoxes: The Limits of Quantum Logic*. Cambridge: Cambridge University Press, 126–167.

Goldstein, Sheldon. 2013 "Bohmian Mechanics." *Stanford Encyclopedia of Philosophy*. Available at: http://plato.stanford.edu/entries/qm-bohm/ (last accessed April 15, 2016).

Gordon, Bruce. 1998. *Quantum Statistical Mechanics and the Ghosts of Modality*. Ph.D. Dissertation, Northwestern University, Evanston, Illinois. Ann Arbor: UMI.

———. 2002. "Maxwell-Boltzmann Statistics and the Metaphysics of Modality." *Synthese* 133: 393–417.

———. 2003. "Ontology *Schmontology*? Identity, Individuation, and Fock Space." *Philosophy of Science* 70: 1343–1356.

———. 2011. "A Quantum-Theoretic Argument against Naturalism." Bruce L. Gordon and William A. Dembski, eds. *The Nature of Nature: Examining the Role of Naturalism in Science*. Wilmington, DE: ISI Books, 179–214.

———. 2013. "In Defense of Uniformitarianism." *Perspectives on Science and Christian Faith* 65, no.2:79–86.

———. 2017a. "Quantum Theory, Interpretations of." Paul Copan, Tremper LongmanIII, Christopher Reese, and Michael Strauss, eds. *The Zondervan Dictionary of Christianity and Science*. Grand Rapids, MI: Zondervan, 551–554.

———. 2017b. "Occasionalism." Paul Copan, Tremper LongmanIII, Christopher Reese, and Michael Strauss, eds. *The Zondervan Dictionary of Christianity and Science*. Grand Rapids, MI: Zondervan, 491–493.

———. 2018. "The Incompatibility of Physicalism with Physics." Joshua R. Farris and Keith Loftin, eds. *Christian Physicalism? Philosophical-Theological Criticisms*. New York: Lexington Books, 371–402.

Halvorson, Hans. 2001. "Reeh-Schlieder Defeats Newton-Wigner: On Alternative Localization Schemes in Relativistic Quantum Field Theory." *Philosophy of Science* 68: 111–133.

———. 2004. "Complementarity of Representations in Quantum Mechanics." *Studies in History and Philosophy of Modern Physics* 35: 45–56.

———. 2011. "The Measure of All Things: Quantum Mechanics and the Soul." Mark C. Baker and Stewart Goetz, eds. *The Soul Hypothesis: Investigations into the Existence of the Soul.* New York: Continuum, 138–163.

Halvorson, H. and Clifton, R. 2002a. "No Place for Particles in Relativistic Quantum Theories?" *Philosophy of Science* 69: 1–28.

———. 2002b. "Reconsidering Bohr's Reply to EPR." J. Butterfield and T. Placek, eds. *Non-locality and Modality.* Dordrecht: Kluwer Academic, 3–18.

Harré, R., and E.H. Madden. 1975. *Causal Powers: A Theory of Natural Necessity.* Oxford: Basil Blackwell.

Healey, Richard. 1989. *The Philosophy of Quantum Mechanics.* Cambridge: Cambridge University Press.

Hegerfeldt, G.C. 1974. "Remark on Causality and Particle Localization." *Physical Review D* 10: 3320–3321.

Heisenberg, Werner. 1958. *Physics and Philosophy: The Revolution in Modern Science.* New York: Harper & Row Publishers.

———. 1967. "Quantum Theory and Its Interpretation." S. Rozental, ed. *Niels Bohr: His Life and Work as Seen by his Friends and Colleagues.* New York: Wiley Interscience, 94–108.

Herbert, Nick. 1985. *Quantum Reality: Beyond the New Physics.* New York: Anchor Books.

Hitchcock, Christopher. 2010. "Probabilistic Causation." *Stanford Encyclopedia of Philosophy.* Available at: http://plato.stanford.edu/entries/causation-probabilistic/ (last accessed August 25, 2016).

Holland, Peter R. 1993. *The Quantum Theory of Motion: An Account of the de Broglie-Bohm Causal Interpretation of Quantum Mechanics* (Revised edition). Cambridge: Cambridge University Press.

Hooker, Clifford A., ed. 1975, 1979. *The Logico-Algebraic Approach to Quantum Mechanics,* vols. I and II. Dordrecht: D. Reidel Publishing Company.

Joos, E., H.D. Zeh, C. Kiefer, D. Giulini, J. Kupsch, and I-O Stametescu, ed. 2003. *Decoherence and the Appearance of a Classical World in Quantum Theory,* 2nd edition. Berlin: Springer.

Kragh, Helge. 1999. *Quantum Generations: A History of Physics in the Twentieth Century.* Princeton, NJ: Princeton University Press.

Kuhn, Thomas S. 1978. *Black-Body Theory and the Quantum Discontinuity, 1894–1912.* Chicago: University of Chicago Press.

Ladyman, James. 1998. "What is Structural Realism?" *Studies in the History and Philosophy of Science* 29: 409–424.

Ladyman, James, and Don Ross. 2007. *Everything Must Go: Metaphysics Naturalized.* Oxford: Oxford University Press.

Lambert, Joey. 2008. "The Physics of Superconducting Quantum Interference Devices." Available at: http://www.physics.drexel.edu/~bob/Term_Reports/Joe_Lambert_3.pdf (last accessed April 15, 2016).

Landsman, N.P. 2007. "Between Classical and Quantum." Jeremy Butterfield and John Earman, eds. *Handbook of the Philosophy of Physics,* Part A. Amsterdam: Elsevier, 417–553.

Lewis, David K. 1973. *Counterfactuals*. Cambridge, MA: Harvard University Press.

———. 1983. "New Work for a Theory of Universals." *Australasian Journal of Philosophy* 61: 343–377.

———. 1994. "Humean Supervenience Debugged." *Mind* 103: 473–490.

Malament, David. 1996. "In Defense of Dogma: Why There Cannot Be a Relativistic Quantum Mechanics of (Localizable) Particles." Robert Clifton, ed. *Perspectives on Quantum Reality: Non-Relativistic, Relativistic, and Field-Theoretic*. Dordrecht: Kluwer Academic Publishers.

Maudlin, Tim. 2002. *Quantum Non-Locality and Relativity*, 2nd edition. Oxford: Blackwell Publishers.

Mehra, Jagdish, and Helmut Rechenberg. 1982–1987. *The Historical Development of Quantum Theory* (5 volumes). New York: Springer-Verlag.

Murdoch, Dugald. 1987. *Niels Bohr's Philosophy of Physics*. Cambridge: Cambridge University Press.

Ney, Alyssa, and Albert, David, eds. 2013. *The Wave Function: Essays on the Metaphysics of Quantum Mechanics*. Oxford: Oxford University Press.

Page, Don. 2008. "Does God So Love the Multiverse?" Available at: https://arxiv.org/pdf/0801.0246.pdf (last accessed August 26, 2016).

Pais, Abraham. 1986. *Inward Bound: Of Matter and Forces in the Physical World*. Oxford: Clarendon Press.

Plantinga, Alvin. 1993. *Warrant and Proper Function*. New York: Oxford University Press.

———. 2000. *Warranted Christian Belief*. New York: Oxford University Press.

———. 2011. *Where the Conflict Really Lies: Science, Religion, and Naturalism*. New York: Oxford University Press.

———. 2016. "Law, Cause, and Occasionalism." Michael Bergmann and Jeffrey E. Brower, eds. *Reason and Faith: Themes from Richard Swinburne*. Oxford: Oxford University Press, 126–144.

Polkinghorne, John. 2002. *Quantum Theory: A Very Short Introduction*. Oxford: Oxford University Press.

Pruss, Alexander. 2006. *The Principle of Sufficient Reason: A Reassessment*. Cambridge: Cambridge University Press.

———. 2009. "Leibnizian Cosmological Arguments." William L. Craig and J.P. Moreland, eds. *The Blackwell Companion to Natural Theology*. Oxford: Blackwell, 24–100.

Putnam, Hilary. 1974. "How to Think Quantum-Logically." *Synthese* 29: 55–61.

———. 1979. "The Logic of Quantum Mechanics." H. Putnam, *Matter and Method: Philosophical Papers, Volume 1*. Cambridge: Cambridge University Press, 174–197.

Quine, Willard V.O. 1951. "Two Dogmas of Empiricism," *The Philosophical Review* 60: 20–43.

Rae, Alistair. 2004. *Quantum Physics: Illusion or Reality?* (2nd edition). Cambridge: Cambridge University Press.

Ratzsch, Del. 1987. "Nomo(theo)logical Necessity." *Faith and Philosophy* 4, no. 4: 383–402.

Redhead, Michael. 1987. *Incompleteness, Nonlocality, and Realism: A Prolegomenon to the Philosophy of Quantum Mechanics*. Oxford: Clarendon Press.

———. 1995. *From Physics to Metaphysics*. Cambridge: Cambridge University Press.

Reichenbach, Hans. 1944. *Philosophic Foundations of Quantum Mechanics*. Berkeley: University of California Press, 144–166.

Rowe, M.A., D. Kielpinski, V. Meyer, C.A. Sackett, W.M. Itano, C. Monroe, and D.J. Wineland. 2001. "Experimental Violation of a Bell's Inequality with Efficient Detection." *Nature* 409: 791–794.

Ryckman, Thomas 2010 "Review of William Lane Craig and Quentin Smith, eds. *Einstein, Relativity and Absolute Simultaneity*" Available at: http://ndpr.nd.edu/news/24498-einstein-relativity-and-absolute-simultaneity/ (last accessed April 15, 2016).

Saunders, Simon. 1999. "The 'Beables' of Relativistic Pilot Wave Theory." Jeremy Butterfield and Constantine Pagonis, eds. *From Physics to Philosophy*. Cambridge: Cambridge University Press, 71–89.

———. 2014. "Physics." Martin Curd and Stathis Psillos, eds. *The Routledge Companion to Philosophy of Science*, 2nd edition. New York: Routledge, 645–658.

Saunders, S., J. Barrett, A. Kent, and D. Wallace, eds. 2010. *Many Worlds? Everett, Quantum Theory, & Reality*. Oxford: Oxford University Press.

Schlosshauer, Maximilian. 2007. *Decoherence and the Quantum-to-Classical Transition*. Berlin: Springer-Verlag.

Schrödinger, Erwin. 1935. "Die gegenwärtige Situation in der Quantenmechanik." *Naturwissenschaften* 23: 807–812, 823–828, and 844–849. Translated by John D. Trimmer as "The Present Situation in Quantum Mechanics: A Translation of Schrödinger's 'Cat Paradox' Paper" and reprinted in John A. Wheeler and Wojciech H. Zurek, eds. (1983), *Quantum Theory and Measurement*. Princeton, NJ: Princeton University Press, 152–167.

Shoemaker, Sydney. 1980. "Causality and Properties." Peter van Inwagen, ed. *Time and Cause*. Dordrecht: D. Reidel, 109–135.

Swoyer, Chris. 1982. "The Nature of Natural Laws." *Australian Journal of Philosophy* 60: 203–223.

Tooley, Michael. 1987. *Causation: A Realist Approach*. Oxford: Clarendon Press.

Tumulka, R. 2006a. "A Relativistic Version of the Ghirardi-Rimini-Weber Model." *Journal of Statistical Physics* 125: 821–840.

———. 2006b. "On Spontaneous Wave Function Collapse and Quantum Field Theory." *Proceedings of the Royal Society of London A* 462: 1897–1908.

Vaidman, Lev. 2014. "Many Worlds Interpretation of Quantum Mechanics." Available at: http://plato.stanford.edu/entries/qm-manyworlds/ (last accessed April 15, 2016).

Van Fraassen, Bas C. 1991. *Quantum Mechanics: An Empiricist View*. Oxford: Clarendon Press.

Von Neumann, John. 1932. *Mathematische Grundlagen der Quantenmechanik*, Berlin: Springer. Translated by R.T. Beyer as *Mathematical Foundations of Quantum Mechanics*. Princeton, NJ: Princeton University Press (1955).

Wallace, David. 2003. "Everettian Rationality." *Studies in History and Philosophy of Modern Physics* 34: 87–105.

Wheeler, John A. 1983. "Law without Law." John A. Wheeler and Wojciech H. Zurek, eds. (1983), *Quantum Theory and Measurement*. Princeton, NJ: Princeton University Press, 182–213.

Whitaker, Andrew. 1996. *Einstein, Bohr and the Quantum Dilemma*. Cambridge: Cambridge University Press.

Wigner, Eugene. 1961. "Remarks on the Mind-Body Question." I. J. Good, ed. *The Scientist Speculates*. London: Heinemann, 284–301. Reprinted in John A. Wheeler and Wojciech

H. Zurek, eds. (1983), *Quantum Theory and Measurement*. Princeton, NJ: Princeton University Press, 168–181.

Worrall, John. 1989. "Structural Realism: The Best of Both Worlds?" *Dialectica* 43: 99–124.

Zurek, W.H. 1991. "Decoherence and the Transition from Quantum to Classical—*Revisited*." Available at: http://arxiv.org/pdf/quant-ph/0306072 (last accessed April 5, 2016).

Afterword

TRENT DOUGHERTY AND ALVIN PLANTINGA: AN INTERVIEW ON FAITH AND REASON

⌒ ───

https://youtu.be/OxtyY2bp78E

TRENT DOUGHERTY: Right now we're just going to have a conversation with Alvin Plantinga about sort of . . . a little bit about the history of his thinking about theistic arguments and their roles, and maybe what he thinks about particular arguments. Al, thanks for coming.

ALVIN PLANTINGA: My pleasure.

TRENT: So, do you remember the first place you gave this lecture?

AL: I am sorry to say I don't. I don't remember that.

TRENT: Now Bill Craig said you gave it at Wheaton. What conference was that? A Wheaton philosophy conference. He said that might have been the first place.[1]

AL: Before we go into that I want to say first that I'm naturally very flattered and pleased that there should be such a conference, a conference of this sort. And I'd like to thank Jerry Walls and Brian Marshall who—as I understand it—first had the idea for such a conference.[2] I don't know if that's true or not, but that's what Jerry Walls told me. [*Laughter*] And of course I'd like to thank Trent who is an indefatigable worker along very many lines all at the same time. And I'd like to thank the Baylor . . . what is it? Program on the Study of Religion?

TRENT: The Institute for Studies of Religion and the Program for Philosophical Studies of Religion.

AL: Yeah, nobody could remember that. Right. [*Laughter*] Right, so. Back to the question I think maybe that's right, maybe it was a Wheaton conference many years ago. How long ago was that?

BILL [*in audience*]: Wheaton in the early 80s!

TRENT: Bill says it was in the early 80s.

AL: So maybe thirty years ago. And I haven't thought of a whole lot of arguments in addition to these. I thought I could find one in Richard Swinburne's paper because there was an argument from consciousness, and I didn't have an argument by that name, anyway. But then it turned out when we talked about it that it was the argument from colors and flavors of Bob Adams, maybe a special case of the argument from consciousness. So we're still stuck at about two dozen. [*Laughter*]

TRENT: Two dozen or so. So among these arguments is there a class of arguments that strike you as . . . that personally strike you as more compelling?

AL: I'm inclined to think the moral arguments the most compelling. I find it hard to see how there can be genuine moral obligation apart from a divine command. And since I think there really is genuine moral obligation—I'm wholeheartedly committed to that—that seems to me to be an argument with a very strong premise and a pretty good connection between premise and conclusion.

TRENT: And so that sort of argument has a more of a pull on you than either the a priori arguments or the more scientific based arguments.

AL: Right, I think so. With respect to most of these arguments I don't think they typically really *establish* their conclusion. They are evidence for the conclusion, maybe they raise the probability of the conclusions, maybe they make the conclusions more probable than not, but I don't think they actually establish it, so if a person believes in God in a wholehearted way that many of us on at least some occasions do, I don't think that sort of degree of certainty would be appropriate with respect to the conclusion of any of these arguments. And the other thing about the arguments is that they typically establish—if they establish anything—the existence of a being with, say, one or maybe two or three of God's attributes, but not all of them. So an argument for a creator, let's say, a first cause argument or something like that won't typically give us the conclusion that this being is wholly good, as the Christians think. So, in general I think the arguments are important and useful, but I don't think they are strong enough to bear the full weight of Christian, or even theistic conviction, let alone Christian conviction.

TRENT: So, there are two things you could mean by that. One is that for each individual argument, it's such that it does not establish the conclusion, that it doesn't bear the weight. What about taken jointly?

AL: Well, I think that's the strongest of the arguments, the argument from . . .I forgot what I called it. . . . . The argument from the proceeding ones . . .

TRENT: [The argument] 'from A to Y', I think it was.

AL: Something like that. The Argument from A to Y. I think that is the strongest one. Yeah, right.

TRENT: So you said you thought the arguments were nevertheless useful. What do you think they're useful for?

AL: They're useful along several different lines. I think they're useful for helping people who don't believe in God to come to belief in God. I think they very often serve that purpose. And I think they're also useful when it comes to shoring up one's own belief. I mean, Christians, believers in God, are often subject to doubt. One's spiritual life goes up and down, and so on. I think these arguments, in particular the moral argument, seems to me to be useful in that regard.

TRENT: This might seem like a really basic question, nevertheless such questions often uncover helpful information. You say it's useful for helping people who don't believe in God to come to believe in God. How does it help them come to believe in God when they don't believe in God?

AL: Well, if they may find that the argument is from premises they accept, and the may appear to be valid, or may actually be valid, it might lead them to move from a condition of not believing in God to believing in God. Or maybe to think it much more likely that there be such a person than they thought before.

TRENT: So that refers to their perspective. It draws them, it impels them, it seems to them to be truth indicative. That sort of thing.

AL: Yeah.

TRENT: So it affects them. Because that's different than in your. . . in the other aspect of reformed epistemology that the work of the Holy Spirit might be something that we don't necessarily see or feel in the same sort of way, whereas arguments we can sort of look at them, see their logical connections and feel that force directly.

AL: Yes. I think that's right. It could be also that the Holy Spirit on some occasions works via argument. It could be that on a given occasion the Holy Spirit takes that as an occasion for inducing or increasing credence.

TRENT: Okay, so I want to disambiguate there two things. I've recently written that the way to understand that sort of situation is that the Holy Spirit draws one's attention to logical relations in arguments, or maybe sort of prevents one from thinking of specious objections, that sort of thing. That's how I've modeled the application of arguments to the hearts of unbelievers by the Holy Spirit. Do you have a different way of thinking about that?

AL: That's one way, but it might be also that the Holy Spirit just induces increased credence, not by setting aside irrelevancies or anything like that, but just directly does so.

TRENT: Even if the individual doesn't get it, as it were?

AL: "Doesn't get it?"

TRENT: Doesn't see the logical connections, doesn't match . . . in other words, there's one reading of that where the arguments don't really play any role. A rock can hit my head and the Holy Spirit can . . .

AL: Right. Well, most of these arguments are not logically conclusive anyway, right? So, they are persuasive and—I don't mean they are merely psychologically persuasive; they can be very good arguments. But they are not logically conclusive arguments. And so it wouldn't be that the Holy Spirit would get somebody to see that it's logically conclusive, because they aren't. But it might be that the Holy Spirit makes or enables a person to find the argument more plausible, more convincing. And it could be also by setting aside distractions or setting aside someone's initial disinclination to accept the conclusion and the like.

TRENT: Suppose that some argument objectively supports the proposition that God exists to some finite degree—less than 1. Would the Holy Spirit, in your view, ever cause somebody to have more of a boost of credence than the degree of support that that argument actually gives that conclusion, in using that argument?

AL: You know, Trent originally told me that he was going to send me a list of the questions. . . . [*Laughter*]

TRENT: Now I'm just following the thoughts that come to my head! [*Laughter*] Anyway . . .

AL: Then a couple of times after he didn't do that, I emailed him and said, "well, okay, what about these questions you're going to ask me?" He never responded! And that leads me to be a little nervous here. [*Laughter*] With respect to your last question, I'd say the answer is "yes."

TRENT: Huh, okay.

AL: Do you remember what the question was?

TRENT: Uh, yeah. [*Laughter*] Does that seem untoward in any way at all, that he's almost deceptive?

AL: No, not at all. No, it's not the case that the only epistemically respectable way to believe in God is on the basis of arguments.

TRENT: That's true.

AL: Right.

TRENT: But he could make it. . . if the individual took that their boost of confidence was in virtue of this argument, it would just seem like they were . . . being led to misjudge the epistemic situation, if the Holy Spirit gave them a confidence boost through an argument more than that argument logically gave to the conclusion.

AL: Yeah, possibly, or it could be that the argument also creates a situation in which the internal testimony of the Holy Spirit—or the *sensus divinitatis*, depending on whether we're talking about Christian belief generally or about belief in God—works. Could go either way.

TRENT: Yeah. So, about . . . you said there are legitimate ways to believe other than through arguments. And I'm a committed evidentialist, and I certainly agree with that because I think that a lot of evidence doesn't consist in arguments but it consists in certain types of experience. And I think that you think that, too, right? That some evidence consists in just experiences.

AL: Sure.

TRENT: Yeah. So, in the body of believers there seems to be a division of labor . . . and I used to think that everybody needed to have arguments, or some serious religious experience . . . and I'm wondering if you think that, when the sorts of experiences that ground religious belief that's not grounded in discursive arguments . . . do you think it needs to be of any particular character, or needs to be dramatic in any way, or what?

AL: I don't think so. I mean, I think the internal testimony of the Holy Spirit can work in a wide variety of ways. It needn't be by virtue of some overwhelming, smashing, flashing experience or something like that at all. It could be a kind of quiet development of credence over a long period of time. Another way in which one often comes to believe is by virtue of testimony, in particular when you're young, the testimony of your parents and the community you are in. The Holy Spirit can also act under those conditions. So this can go, it seems to me, in very many different ways. It would be a mistake to corral the ways in which the Holy Spirit could teach us.

TRENT: Yeah, that sounds right. I mean I ask that in part because some people have portrayed . . . one objection I've read . . . in fact, a prominent objection I've read to the reformed epistemology is that, fine, there are plenty of people who have neither good arguments nor do they have these powerful religious experiences. And it seems to me that you just went between the horns of that dilemma.

AL: Right.

TRENT: "That's correct, indeed I did." [*Laughter*] So let's talk about the arguments that constitute the two dozen or so (a little bit more) . . . are there any on which your assessment has changed much in that thirty-year interval since you first made this list? Any that have. . . . For example, once upon a time I really thought that the ontological argument was just no good. Sorry, no offense! But then I became convinced that it's a very good argument. And so it really changed the way I think about that. I also used to think that the Leibnizian argument from the principle of sufficient reason was no good, then I read Alex Pruss's book and a few other things—Taylor. And I think the fine-tuning argument has gone up and down, up and down, in my estimation as various considerations have been raised. So I just wonder if you can give us a history of your thought on any of these.

AL: Well, on the fine-tuning argument, I think the argument Robin Collins is giving us is certainly something to further think about, and a really serious addition to the fine-tuning argument. So there's a very recent change, you know, in the last eight hours or something like that. [*Laughter*] With respect to the ontological argument, there was a time when I thought it was just a knock-down, drag-out, obviously correct argument. But I came to see, somewhat ruefully, that that was a bit of an overestimate. And then one argument I would really like somebody to work on—and I'd like to thank everybody here or the people who have so far worked on these arguments and saved me from all that hard work, which apparently I wasn't doing anyway—developed these arguments. But one argument I really sort of like is the argument from counterfactuals. I like it, not because I think it's a really good argument, but because it's intriguing, and I don't myself quite know what to say about it. So, let me read you just a bit here . . .

TRENT: Alvin Plantinga is going to quote Alvin Plantinga. [*Laughter*]

AL: I can't find that now.

TRENT: I can look for it while you . . .

AL: Well, let's move on from that one. I still don't understand it.

TRENT: A Baylor alumnus has found it for us [from the audience]. Thank you, Jonathan. Argument D.

AL: "Consider such a counterfactual as 'If Neal had gone into law [Neal is my brother] he would have been in jail by now.' [*Laughter*] It is plausible to suppose that such a counterfactual is true if and only if its consequent is true in the nearby (i.e., sufficiently similar) possible worlds in which its antecedent is true (Stalnaker, Lewis, Pollock, Nute). But of course for any pair of distinct possible worlds W and W*, there will be infinitely many respects in which they resemble each other, and infinitely many in which they differ. Given agreement on these respects and on the degree of difference within the respects, there can still be disagreement about the resultant total similarity of the two situations. What you think here—which possible worlds you take to be similar to which others *uberhaupt* will depend upon how you weight the various respects. . . . [I say at the end here . . .]. Now suppose you agree that such differences among respects of difference do in fact depend upon mind, but also think (as in fact most of us certainly do) that counterfactuals are objectively true or false: you can hold both of these if you think there is an unlimited mind such that the weightings it makes are then the objectively correct ones (its assignments of weights determine the correct weights). No human mind, clearly, could occupy this station. God's mind, however, could; what God sees as similar is similar." Well, I think that's an interesting argument, but also really puzzling and I don't really know quite what to make of it. But it's fun to think about it.

TRENT: It's interesting that you picked that one out, because I think that's the only one we ended up having two chapters on in the book. So we're doing double duty on that.

AL: Okay!

TRENT: I want to open it up to questions, to the whole audience, right now. And I want particularly to ask for questions from people outside the contributors who have been the principal discussants for the papers that are going to become chapters in the book. So, you guys be thinking about those questions. I'm going to ask Dr. Plantinga one more question, possibly a follow-up or two. So get those questions ready. I'm going to ask you, actually, to come up to the podium and state your question into that mic, if you will. So you can go ahead, if you know you have a question, and move up and form a queue at the podium. Thank you, Ben, leading the way! Mr. Ben Arbor. So, this is another one of those questions you may have wanted upfront, but it's really a harmless question! [*Laughter*] Just one I wonder about a lot and I don't remember if I ever remembered to ask you. A preliminary question: do you think that "God exists" is a proposition that you know?

AL: That I know? Yeah, I think so.

TRENT: Okay. Do you have any views about what the probability of that proposition is on your total evidence?

AL: I guess I take it to be part of my total evidence.

TRENT: Okay, take that one proposition and anything it entails and anything connected to it in the right sort of way . . . take that remaining body of evidence and consider, looking at that proposition, what do you think the probability of that proposition is on your remaining evidence.

AL: I guess I would say that it is considerably more probable than not.

TRENT: "Considerably more probable than not." Okay. And do you think there's a minimum threshold of probability required for knowing a proposition?

AL: Not a minimum threshold of probability for knowing it, with respect to what you know. I mean, I might know something that's not at all probable with respect to what I know. Not saying that this is an example, but that sort of thing can happen. So it's not the case that there has to be some minimum threshold, I would say.

TRENT: And with the normal way of there being . . . that being the case . . . for example, the deliverance of some faculty?

AL: Yeah, for example the deliverance of sense, it might be extremely unlikely that there should be a reindeer in the hall, but it could be that I go out there and see one. So it would be unlikely with respect to the rest of what I know but still might be something I know.

TRENT: Okay, so let's start taking some questions from the audience. Ben, go ahead and just state your question into the microphone.

QUEUE 1: Al, thanks for your work on ontological arguments. I'm really appreciative of it. I'm wondering if there's a way that you might talk to us about the way that what's been called the argument from A to Y might actually lend credence to the idea that possibly a maximally great being exists. If we have from other arguments reasons to think that a necessarily existent being exists, and from other arguments a morally perfect being, etc. Does that increase the evidence or the probability that the key premise in the modal ontological argument is true? And then can we see the argument from A to Y as giving us good reason to think that the ontological argument is stronger than it initially seems to be?

AL: Most of the rest of the arguments don't seem to lead to the existence of a necessarily existent being, right? I mean, at least I don't think that they mostly do. I can't think of any that does, really.

TRENT: Maybe some of the ones from abstracta might.

AL: Uh-huh. The argument from numbers . . . yeah. I guess so. That's a thing to think about. I mean, maybe the argument from numbers supports the idea that there is a necessarily existent intellect. It's still a step from that, though, to there being a greatest possible being. But I mean, it might sensibly be thought of as a step towards it, right?

QUEUE 2: Thank you, Alvin Plantinga. My question has to do with the role of Christian apologetics in these kinds of Christian arguments in evangelism. I've often wondered how significant they are. And I wonder based on the nature of human beings, whether human beings are the kinds of creatures that are significantly compelled by rational things, or whether they are not. Seems like a lot of these arguments should be more compelling to more people. So, my question to you is, I guess, if I can put it in a word, is "what is the role of Christian apologetics and evangelism?" is that what it's for?

AL: Now, if you're thinking about, say, missionary work and that sort of thing, I don't think it typically goes by way of arguments. I have a daughter who was a missionary in Cameroon and I don't think she and her confreres offer arguments. It's more by way of proclamation. You proclaim the word of God, and very often many people will find it compelling and accept it. That might be that they find it compelling and accept it because of the internal testimony of the Holy Spirit, or something like that. But it's probably not in general a very powerful means of evangelism to offer arguments. Especially not very complicated ones. I mean, people lose the thread of argument really quickly and stop paying attention, and they wonder why you're doing that, and so on. So I would say I don't think that's a very large role.

TRENT: As a follow-up to his question, I think you have noted in various places the differences relative to a population. If you're witnessing to a university professor or to a philosophy major, it's going to be maybe a different thing.

AL: Yes. Even there I think what actually brings someone around to believing typically isn't an argument. I say typically, I don't say it never happens. I'm sure it does happen. I've talked to people who say they were brought to believe in God by virtue of an argument, but I don't think that's the way it typically goes.

TRENT: But if you thought of evangelism broadly construed as stuff you do that bring it about that people believe the Gospel . . .

AL: That's how I was thinking we were thinking about it.

TRENT: Okay, it seems like in a lot of contexts that's one of the things you do, and one of the things you need to do, especially in today's day and age when people have a lot of exposure to objections to the existence of God and objections to Christianity.

AL: Yeah. I think there's a significant difference between arguments for the existence of God or arguments for the truth of Christianity on the one hand and showing the faults of arguments against the existence of God or the truths of Christianity on the other hand. I think the latter is very often important.

TRENT: That's often considered a part of apologetics, broadly construed.

AL: Right.

TRENT: Okay, we have a couple more people. Go ahead.

QUEUE 3: Mine is sort of a spin-off of the other one. First, thank you all; four or five of you I have used as major sources for papers I teach at a community college, a secular community college. And I have people who think they're Christians, find out they're not, they become Christians by the end of the course; proclaimed atheists that I guess "front-slide" by the end of the course. [*Laughter*] So that's been a great thing to be able to see the fruit of that. So thank you all, you are major contributors of that. I'll probably say this wrong, since I'm nervous . . . the sensus divinitatis . . . how would you say that interacts or inter-responds with one's personhood? Would it be more of a mechanism that can somehow or another . . . for lack of a better term . . . override one's personal yielding or personhood? Or, how would you describe the interaction there?

AL: I was thinking of the sensus divinitatis largely along the lines of John Calvin. Since I taught philosophy at Calvin College for many years, naturally enough, I think very highly of John Calvin. As John Calvin thinks of the sensus divinitatis, you can't really call it a "sense" like, say, sight or perception, that sort of thing. But a natural inclination on the parts of very many people—maybe most people, maybe nearly all people—a natural inclination to believe in such a person as God, to find it very plausible to think there is such a person. Children, when taught this by their parents, don't say "well, this is really wild" or "weird" or whatever. They sometimes do, when they get to be adolescents, and when they attain maturity. It's an idea, a thought, which has a great deal of natural resonance in human beings. That's how I was thinking of it.

QUEUE 3: So it wouldn't contradict one's personhood or override that, it would kind of work in tandem with . . . ?

AL: Right, it wouldn't in any way go against one's personhood, or be a kind of assault on it, or lead one in a different direction for which one was inclined to be led, or anything like that.

QUEUE 3: Thank you.

TRENT: We have another person in the queue.

QUEUE 4: Hey, thanks. I have a question about your evolutionary argument against naturalism.

TRENT: He's pulling up his sleeves, he's like 'I demand an answer!' [*Laughter*]

QUEUE 4: I'm a big fan of the argument but I think it's got a problem, so I'm hoping you can correct that for me. So, in the argument you ask the naturalist to evaluate what the probability is that they are reliable with respect to naturalism and evolution, but it seems though that the worry is that when you evaluate that you have to abide by an independence requirement on your total beliefs. So you can't rely on the beliefs that are in question in order to evaluate your reliability. But since, when you're evaluating your reliability, that's going to encompass all your beliefs. Then it seems like what you're left with is really a conclusion that shows that . . . not that . . . you get to the conclusion that you're unreliable because of your beliefs, but just that you don't have any beliefs left to evaluate how reliable you are, if you have to consider them independently. Then the argument just looks like a . . .

AL: I wasn't thinking in that argument of asking someone to start evaluating the reliability of their belief producing mechanisms, or whatever. I wasn't saying "first thing you do here is to see how reliable you think your belief-producing mechanisms are." I was rather trying to argue that if you accept naturalism and evolution, then you should suppose that that reliability is fairly low. That was the thought. So it wasn't a matter of trying to evaluate somehow what the reliability of your own belief-producing mechanisms is, or how many of your beliefs are true. That would be pretty hard, right? I mean, you'd wind up saying with respect to each belief that you accept it, that "yeah, well that one's true." You're not going to get anywhere that way, right?

QUEUE 4: So, it's just considering general populations, what the probability is with respect to this population given naturalism and evolution, that we think that population is likely to be reliable? And you're not evaluating your own?

AL: What I was suggesting was that if you accept naturalism and evolution then you've got a good reason for thinking that the reliability of one of your belief-producing processes is low.

TRENT: And so for every individual that's part of that class. Can we . . . you guys in the queue go ahead and get up a little closer.

QUEUE 5: Professor Plantinga, thanks for being here. I spit-balled this idea with my friend Jerry Walls about a year and a half ago in my front yard, so it's pretty fun to be here now with you. My question for you is this . . . it's a fairly broad on, but . . . so many of us here feel, whether rightly or wrongly, a debt of gratitude toward you and the work you've done as a Christian philosopher. I know Nicholas Wolterstorff a few years ago had that piece in *Faith and Philosophy*, "Then, Now, and Al," and talking about the changes that have come through your work, and so many others' over the last few decades. But I'm thinking towards the future, and thinking about people here, and thinking about as you think about . . . and not writing you off or pushing you . . .

AL: Off riding into the sunset? [*Laughter*]

QUEUE 5: But for some of us in the future just to think about what kind of charge did you have for Christian academics moving forward? Obviously it's a sort of different landscape than it was several decades ago. But if you had a word to say to those of us working in academia, what would be your charge to us as far as moving forward as Christians working in this field?

AL: I guess I wouldn't really have any specific advice, or any charge to give. I mean, I must say I'm really very much heartened by this conference and other events of this same sort. In my opinion, something like Christian philosophy, things of that general sort—don't really proceed or advance by some old guys saying "here's how it should go." Rather it sort of just develops on its own, it has its own momentum and takes its own direction. I think that's what's happening with respect to Christian philosophy, too. So I would rather just enjoy the results, enjoy seeing what's happening, rather than try to give anybody advice. I mean, I did give advice in that paper "Advice to Christian Philosophers" . . . [*Laughter*] I probably should take it back, what I just said.

QUEUE 6: In your book on science and religion you make the comment that you thought that the gospel story was the greatest possible story. I'm wondering if you could flesh that out in terms of, perhaps, its aesthetic value as a story. Maybe its epistemic value, such as the stuff that Timothy McGrew was talking about. Or other kinds of value. In what sense is that the greatest possible story?

AL: I guess it would be something like in an aesthetic sense. It's a magnificent story! I mean, here God creates human beings, and these human beings who are his children—and who know him and the like—turn their backs on him and reject him, get involved in their own projects, think of themselves more highly than of God. And then God's response is not to have them all beheaded or boiled in oil or something like that. His response is to send his son to suffer and die in order to make it possible for human beings once more to be in a right relationship with God. That seems to me to be an utterly magnificent story. I don't think it's merely a story, I think it's a true story. It's an utterly magnificent true story. Now, if you say "what kind of value does it have, what does its magnificence consist in?" I would say it's along the lines, broadly speaking, of aesthetics. I don't know what more to say about it than that. I've never thought about along what lines it's the most magnificent story, but it's surprising, it's dramatic, it involves the first being of the universe, it's a story of a display of enormous love. I don't know, what do you think? [*Laughter*]

QUEUE 6: I agree. [*Laughter*]

TRENT: Okay, so, we'll have this be the last question from the audience, I'll ask a few last questions, then I'll have an announcement.

QUEUE 7: My question has to do with the problem of evil. It seems to me that in the recent literature there has been a bit of an attempt to drive a wedge between a defense of moral evil and a defense of natural evil. I'm thinking, for example, of Nick Trakakis and his book *The God Beyond Belief.* And basically his thesis is that theists don't really have a good answer to the problem of natural evil. Now, of course, you're quite famous for providing a defense of natural evil in terms of moral evil, namely, the moral evil of Satan or disembodied agents and so forth. You've used the freewill defense to provide a possible explanation. I am curious—especially in light of this recent phenomenon of trying to separate those two—do you have any additional thought about natural evil per se?

AL: No, I don't really have any additional thoughts about that. I'd also hesitate to say that the freewill defense, either with respect to human beings or to Satan and his cohorts or other kinds of creatures, is a sort of conclusive solution to the argument from evil or to the problem of evil, or a resolution of it. I think this remains a kind of problem for Christians. Christians don't, nor do other believers in God as far as I know, really know why God permits evil. I can't really give a good reason, you know, "here's why God does it." You don't really know. But I guess that's all right. I mean, maybe one doesn't know why God permits evil. That in itself doesn't put one at a completely unsupportable position. There are lots of things we don't know, and I think that's one of them.

TRENT: So, to bring the interview towards a conclusion, an evidentialist like me and a reformed epistemologist like you can agree that robust Christian belief doesn't depend upon, doesn't need, doesn't require arguments for the existence of God. But we agree that there are various uses of the arguments—including to bolster faith, to help remove objections to the faith, to bring people closer to the faith. While there's the opposite side—arguments against, and doubts—and I'm wondering... this is kind of a personal question, you can always refuse to answer it ... but are there any kinds of experiences that you think God uses to bolster your faith in a non-argumentative way? Like, for me it might be every morning when I go in and wake up my kids, that sort of thing. Is there anything... In nature? I know you're a person who spends a lot of time in the mountains and you've used examples of sunsets and things like that. But are those experiences that actually you think God has used to bolter *your* faith?

AL: Yeah, I would certainly say so, even very mundane experiences, if you like, such as beautiful weather—as around here—

TRENT: You're welcome.

AL: —it seems to be as if God's smiling on us with this beautiful weather. And I don't mean that when it's thundering and lightning that God is angry with us, of course. That doesn't follow. But I think there are experiences of that kind.

Outside of my study window at home there is a kind of ravine with lots of beautiful trees in it and birds flying around and the like. Those things I think are used by God to sort of help us see his presence, and the like. God sometimes also comes to people—for example Jonathan Edwards, seemed often to have a very vivid appreciation of a very vivid sort of personal relationship with God. And people often talk about a personal relationship with God. I think for many people, though, there isn't a whole lot of that. It isn't that you just sort of do anything like perceive God—maybe under some relatively rare circumstances—but during much of one's life, it seems to me, you sort of coast on a kind momentum. You've got this strong inclination to believe in God, which is much stronger on some occasions than it is on others for many people, including myself. But there are these dry periods that many Christian saints have talked about. Periods when the heavens are as brass and when it seems God isn't present. And this shows up in the Psalms, "God, why are you so far from me?" and the like. It seems to me there's a kind of persistence that a believer in God needs, a kind of living on past capital, so to speak. I forgot what the question was. Did I answer it? [*Laughter*]

TRENT: Yeah, I mean you didn't necessarily apply it to yourself, but you talked about what the view from your porch—a view I've been privileged to experience as well—but you talked more about in general than you did yourself.

AL: Right—

TRENT: I mean, you don't have to.

AL: —The experience of reading the Bible is for me crucial. I mean, reading the Bible—maybe not every part, but many parts—is a powerful impetus to belief in God, to renew belief in God, and the like. And also going to church and listening to sermons. Sometimes sermons work in the wrong direction [*Laughter*]—but I go to a church in Grand Rapids—Church of the Servant—where there is regularly powerful worship of God and also excellent preaching. So I think that's another very important avenue.

TRENT: Last question about your own past. I'm just curious, have you ever presented a theistic argument to an unbelieving or doubting person?

AL: Sure.

TRENT: In any of those times, did you find that that was helpful, or that the person was moved a bit?

AL: Probably not. [*Laughter*]

TRENT: Never?

AL: Well, I mean, probably never an occasion where the person said, "Okay, well I guess I say, there really is such a person as God." But there might have been—even though I might not have been aware of it—a kind of movement in that direction.

TRENT: Because it seems that . . . what you said happens for the believer can also happen for the unbeliever: that they're moved in bits and pieces over a long period of time. Finally, you said that you didn't have any grand advice for the younger folks, didn't want to manage it from above. But I wonder if you could say what are some practices in your life that you have found helpful for connecting your work on the academic study of religion to the ultimate goal of those things, which is robust belief in the great things of the Gospel.

AL: I don't know about the connection, but I think such things as regular Bible reading, regular prayer, regular church attendance, regular talking if you can with other Christians and the like. I think that all of that is exceedingly important for Christian philosophers. And Christian philosophers also have to think of themselves, not as sort of above the Christian community, sitting in judgment on it—maybe approving of it, maybe disapproving of it, maybe approving of a part of it—Christian philosophers ought to be—indeed, are—part of the Christian community. And they have to think of themselves in that fashion. So, I would think one very important lesson—or, how can I put this—something that has seemed to me over many years to become increasingly important, is regular participation in the Christian community, and regular conversation with God, regular prayer even when—as it sometimes happens, the heavens seem as brass.

TRENT: All right, sage advice.

NOTES

This interview between Alvin Plantinga (Notre Dame/Calvin College) and Trent Dougherty (Baylor University) was held as a part of the "Two Dozen (or so) Theistic Arguments" Conference hosted by both the Baylor Institute for Studies of Religion and the Program for Philosophical Study of Religion at Baylor University on November 7, 2014.

1. The paper was actually first delivered in 1986 at the NEH Society for Christian Philosophers' summer seminar at Western Washington University, directed by William Alston. It was given that fall for the first time at a public event at the Wheaton College philosophy conference.

2. Brian Marshall first came up with the idea for the book, and proposed it to Jerry Walls. The idea for a conference was part of the early discussion about the book, and took concrete form when Trent Dougherty came on as co-editor, and secured funding for the conference from Baylor's Institute for Studies of Religion and the Program for Philosophical Studies of Religion.

PLANTINGA'S ORIGINAL "TWO DOZEN (OR SO)
THEISTIC ARGUMENTS"

Lecture Notes by Alvin Plantinga

I'VE BEEN ARGUING that theistic belief does not (in general) *need* argument either for deonto-logical justification, or for positive epistemic status, (or for Foley rationality or Alstonian justifi-cation)); belief in God is properly basic. But it doesn't follow, of course that there aren't any good arguments. Are there some? At least a couple of dozen or so.

Swinburne: good argument is one that has premises that everyone knows. Maybe aren't any such arguments: and if there are some, maybe none of them would be good arguments *for* anyone. (Note again the possibility that a person might, when confronted with an arg he sees to be valid for a conclusion he deeply disbelieves from premises he know to be true, give up (some of) those premises: in this way you can reduce someone from knowledge to ignorance by giving him an ar-gument he sees to be valid from premises he knows to be true.)

These arguments are not coercive in the sense that every person is obliged to accept their prem-ises on pain of irrationality. Maybe just that some or many sensible people do accept their prem-ises (oneself)

What are these arguments like, and what role do they play? They are probabilistic, either with respect to the premises, or with respect to the connection between the premises and con-clusion, or both. They can serve to bolster and confirm ('helps' a la John Calvin); perhaps to convince.

Distinguish two considerations here: (1) you or someone else might just *find yourself* with these beliefs; so using them as premises get an effective theistic arg for the person in question. (2) The other question has to do with warrant, with conditional probability in epistemic sense: perhaps in at least some of these cases if our faculties are functioning properly and we consider the premises we are inclined to accept them; and (under those conditions) the conclusion has considerable epistemic probability (in the explained sense) on the premises.

Add Aquinas' fifth way: this is really an argument from proper function, I think

I. HALF A DOZEN (OR SO) ONTOLOGICAL (OR METAPHYSICAL) ARGUMENTS

(A) The Argument from Intentionality (or Aboutness)

Consider propositions: the things that are true or false, that are capable of being believed, and that stand in logical relations to one another. They also have another property:

> aboutness or intentionality. (not intensionality, and not thinking of contexts in which co-referential terms are not substitutable *salva veritate*) *Represent* reality or some part of it *as being thus and so*. This is crucially connected with their being true or false. Diff from, e.g., sets, (which is the real reason a proposition would not be a set of possible worlds, or of any other objects.)

Many have thought it incredible that propositions should exist apart from the activity of minds. How could they just *be* there, if never thought of? (Sellars, Rescher, Husserl, many others; probably no real Platonists besides Plato before Frege, if indeed Plato and Frege were Platonists.) (and Frege, that alleged arch-Platonist, referred to propositions as *gedanken*.) Connected with intentionality. *Representing things as being thus and so*, being about something or other—this seems to be a property or activity of *minds* or perhaps *thoughts*. So extremely tempting to think of propositions as ontologically dependent upon mental or intellectual activity in such a way that either they just are thoughts, or else at any rate couldn't exist if not thought of. (According to the idealistic tradition beginning with Kant, propositions are essentially *judgments*.) But if we are thinking of human thinkers, then there are far too many propositions: at least, for example, one for every real number that is distinct from the Taj Mahal. On the other hand, if they were divine thoughts, no problem here. So perhaps we should think of propositions as divine thoughts. Then in our thinking we would literally be thinking God's thoughts after him.

(Aquinas, *De Veritate* "Even if there were no human intellects, there could be truths because of their relation to the divine intellect. But if, *per impossibile*, there were no intellects at all, but things continued to exist, then there would be no such reality as truth.")

This argument will appeal to those who think that intentionality is a characteristic of propositions, that there are a lot of propositions, and that intentionality or aboutness is dependent upon mind in such a way that there couldn't be something *p* about something where *p* had never been thought of.

(B) The Argument from Collections

Many think of sets as displaying the following characteristics (among others): (1) no set is a member of itself; (2) sets (unlike properties) have their extensions essentially; hence sets are contingent beings and no set could have existed if one of its members had not; (3) sets form an iterated structure: at the first level, sets whose members are nonsets, at the second, sets whose members are nonsets or first level sets, etc. Many (Cantor) also inclined to think of sets as *collections*—i.e., things whose existence depends upon a certain sort of intellectual activity—a collecting or "thinking together" (Cantor). If sets *were* collections, that would explain their having the first three features. But of course there are far too many sets for them to be a product of human thinking together; there are many sets such that no human being has ever thought their members together, many that are such that their members have not been thought together by any human being. That requires an infinite mind—one like God's.

A variant: perhaps a way to think together all the members of a set is to attend to a certain property and then consider all the things that have that property: e.g., all the natural numbers. Then many infinite sets are sets that could have been collected by human beings; but not nearly all—not, e.g., arbitrary collections of real numbers. (axiom of choice)

This argument will appeal to those who think there are lots of sets and either that sets have the above three properties or that sets are collections.

Charles Parsons, "What is the Iterative Conception of Set?" in *Mathematics in Philosophy* pp 268 ff.

Hao Wang *From Mathematics to Philosophy* chap. 6: iterative and constructivist (i.e., the basic idea is that sets are somehow constructed and are constructs) conception of set.

Note that on the iterative conception, the elements of a set are in an important sense prior to the set; that is why on this conception no set is a member of itself, and this disarms the Russell paradoxes in the set theoretical form, although of course it does nothing with respect to the property formulation of the paradoxes. (Does Chris Menzel's way of thinking about propositions as somehow *constructed* by God bear here?)

Cantor's definition of set (1895):

> By a "set" we understand any collection M into a whole of definite well-distinguished objects of our intuition or our thought (which will be called the "elements" of M) *Gesammelte Abhandlungen mathematischen und philosophischen*, ed. Ernst Zermelo, Berlin: Springer, 1932, 282.

Shoenfield (*Mathematical Logic*) 1967 writes:

> A closer examination of the (Russell) paradox shows that it does not really contradict the intuitive notion of a set. According to this notion, a set A is formed by gathering together certain objects to form a single object, which is the set A. Thus before the set A is formed, we must have available all of the objects which are to be members of A. (238)

Wang: "The set is a single object formed by collecting the members together." (238)
Wang: (182)

It is a basic feature of reality that there are many things. When a multitude of given objects can be collected together, we arrive at a set. For example, there are two tables in this room. We are ready to view them as given both separately and as a unity, and justify this by pointing to them or looking at them or thinking about them either one after the other or simultaneously. Somehow the viewing of certain objects together suggests a loose link which ties the objects together in our intuition.

(C) The Argument from (Natural) Numbers

(I once heard Tony Kenny attribute a particularly elegant version of this argument to Bob Adams.) It also seems plausible to think of *numbers* as dependent upon or even constituted by intellectual activity; indeed, students always seem to think of them as "ideas" or "concepts," as dependent, somehow, upon our intellectual activity. So if there were no minds, there would be no numbers. (According to Kroneker, God made the natural numbers and man made the rest—not quite right if the argument from sets is correct.) But again, there are too many of them for them to arise as a result of human intellectual activity. Consider, for example, the following series of functions: 2 lambda n is two to the second to the second . . . to the second n times. The second member is ##2 (n); the third 3#2(n), etc. (See *The Mathematical Gardener*, the essay by Knuth.) $6^{**}2(15)$, for example would be a number many times larger than any human being could grasp. We should therefore think of them as among God's ideas.

Perhaps, as Christopher Menzel suggests (special issue of *Faith and Philosophy*) they are properties of equinumerous sets, where properties are God's concepts.

There is also a similar argument re *properties*. Properties seem very similar to *concepts*. (Is there really a difference between thinking of the things that fall under the concept *horse* and considering the things that have the property of being a horse?) In fact many have found it natural to think of properties as reified concepts. But again, there are properties, one wants to say, that have never been entertained by any human being; and it also seems wrong to think that properties do not exist before human beings conceive them. But then (with respect to these considerations) it seems likely that properties are the concepts of an unlimited mind: a divine mind.

(D) The Argument from Counterfactuals

Consider such a counterfactual as

(1) If Neal had gone into law he would have been in jail by now.

It is plausible to suppose that such a counterfactual is true if and only if its consequent is true in the nearby (i.e., sufficiently similar) possible worlds in which its antecedent is true

(Stalnaker, Lewis, Pollock, Nute). But of course for any pair of distinct possible worlds **W** and **W***, there will be infinitely many respects in which they resemble each other, and infinitely many in which they differ. Given agreement on these respects and on the degree of difference within the respects, there can still be disagreement about the resultant total similarity of the two situations. What you think here—which possible worlds you take to be similar to which others *uberhaupt* will depend upon how you *weight* the various respects.

Illustrative interlude: *Chicago Tribune*, June 15, 1986:

> "When it comes to the relationship between man, gorilla and chimpanzee, Morris Goodman doesn't monkey around.
>
> "No matter where you look on the genetic chain the three of us are 98.3% identical" said Goodman, a Wayne State University professor in anatomy and cell biology.
>
> "Other than walking on two feet and not being so hairy, the main different between us and a chimp is our big brain" said the professor . . . the genetic difference between humans and chimps is about 1.7 %.
>
> "How can we be so close genetically if we look so different? There's only a .2 % difference between a dachshund and a Great Dane, yet both look quite different (sic)," Goodman said.
>
> "He explained that if you look at the anatomies of humans and chimps, chimps get along better in trees than people, but humans get along better on the ground. (Or in subways, libraries and submarines.)

How similar *uberhaupt* you think chimps and humans are will depend upon how you rate the various respects in which they differ: composition of genetic material, hairiness, brain size, walking on two legs, appreciation of Mozart, grasp of moral distinctions, ability to play chess, ability to do philosophy, awareness of God, etc. End of Illustrative interlude

Some philosophers as a result argue that counterfactuals contain an irreducibly *subjective* element. E.g., consider this from van Fraassen:

> Consider again statement (3) about the plant sprayed with defoliant. It is true in a given situation exactly if the 'all else' that is kept 'fixed' is such as to rule out the death of the plant for other reason. But who keeps what fixed? The speaker, in his mind. . . . Is there an objective right or wrong about keeping one thing rather than another firmly in mind when uttering the antecedent? (*The Scientific Image*, 116)

(This weighting of similarities) and therefore don't belong in serious, sober, objective science. The basic idea is that considerations as to which respects (of difference) are more important than which is not something that is given in *rerum natura,* but depends upon our interests and aims and plans. In nature apart from mind, there are no such differences in importance among respects of difference.

Now suppose you agree that such differences among respects of difference do in fact depend upon mind, but also think (as in fact most of us certainly do) that counterfactuals are objectively true or false: you can hold both of these if you think there is an unlimited mind such that the weightings it makes are then the objectively correct ones (its assignments of weights determine the correct weights). No human mind, clearly, could occupy this station. God's mind, however, could; what God sees as similar is similar.

Joseph Mondola, "The Indeterminacy of Options," *APQ* April 1987 argues for the indeterminacy of many counterfactuals on the grounds that I cite here, substantially.

(E) The Argument from Physical Constants

(Look at Barrow and Tipler *The Anthropic Cosmological Principle*)

Carr and Rees ("The Anthropic Principle and the Structure of the Physical World" (*Nature*, 1979)):

> The basic features of galaxies, stars, planets and the everyday world are essentially determined by a few microphysical constants and by the effects of gravitation. . . . [S]everal aspects of our Universe—some which seem to be prerequisites for the evolution of any form of life— depend rather delicately on apparent 'coincidences' among the physical constants" (605).

If the force of gravity were even slightly stronger, all stars would be blue giants; if even slightly weaker, all would be red dwarfs. (Brandon Carter, "Large Number Coincidences and the Anthropic Principle in Cosmology," in M.S. Longair, ed., *Confrontation of Cosmological Theories with Observational Data* 1979, 72 According to Carter, under these conditions there would probably be no life. So probably if the strength of gravity were even slightly different, habitable planets would not exist.

The existence of life also depends delicately upon the rate at which the universe is expanding. S.W. Hawking "The Anisotropy of the Universe at Large Times" in Longair, 285:

> "reduction of the rate of expansion by one part in 1012 at the time when the temperature of the Universe was 1010 K would have resulted in the Universe's starting to recollapse when its radius was only 1/3000 of the present value and the temperature was still 10,000 K"— much too warm for comfort. He concludes that life is only possible because the Universe is expanding at just the rate required to avoid recollapse".

If the strong nuclear forces were different by about 5% life would not have been able to evolve.

The same goes for the weak interaction force.

So if the weakness of the gravitational force relative to the electromagnetic force, or the strength of either the strong or weak forces were altered even slightly one way or the other, the universe would have been largely different, so different in fact that life could not exist. Pat Wilson, "The Anthropic Cosmological Principle" unpublished.

Similarly for the number of neutrinos, and for the mass of the neutrino

Before doing much of anything with this (and for Oxford, maybe only mention it and work harder with others) look again at: "The SAP also Rises:..." *American Philosophical Quarterly*, Oct. 1987

Davies, P.C.W., *The Accidental Universe*, 1982:

> All this prompts the question of why, from the infinite range of possible values that nature could
> have selected for the fundamental constants, and from the infinite variety of initial conditions
> that could have characterized the primeval universe, the actual values and conditions conspire
> to produce the particular range of very special features that we observe. For clearly the universe
> is a very special place: exceedingly uniform on a large scale, yet not so precisely uniform that
> galaxies could not form; ... an expansion rate tuned to the energy content to unbelievable ac-
> curacy; values for the strengths of its forces that permit nuclei to exist, yet do not burn up all
> the cosmic hydrogen, and many more apparent accidents of fortune. (111)

And what is impressive about all these coincidences is that they are apparently required
for the existence of life as we know it (as they say).

Some thinkers claim that none of this ought to be thought surprising or as requiring
explanation: no matter how things had been, it would have been exceedingly improbable.
(No matter what distribution of cards is dealt, the distribution dealt will be improbable.)
This is perhaps right, but how does it work? and how is it relevant? We are playing poker;
each time I deal I get all the aces; you get suspicious: I try to allay your suspicions by
pointing out that my getting all the aces each time I deal is no more improbable than any
other equally specific distribution over the relevant number of deals. Would that explanation play in Dodge City (or Tombstone)?

Others invoke the *Anthropic Principle*, which is exceedingly hard to understand but seems
to point out that a necessary condition of these values of the physical constants being observed
at all (by us or other living beings) is that they have very nearly the values they do have; we are
here to observe these constants only because they have the values they do have. Again, this
seems right, but how is it relevant? What does it explain? It still seems puzzling that these
constants should have just the values they do. Why weren't they something quite different?
This is not explained by pointing out that we are here. (a counterexample to Hempelian
claims about explanation) Like "explaining" the fact that God has decided to create me (instead of passing me over in favor of someone else) by pointing out that I am in fact here, and
that if God had not thus decided, I wouldn't have been here to raise the question.

Another approach: Abstract:

We examine the question of whether the present isotropic state of the universe could
have resulted from initial conditions which were "chaotic" in the sense of being arbitrary,
any anisotropy dying away as the universe expanded. We show that the set of spatially homogeneous cosmological models which approach isotropy at infinite times is of measure
zero in the space of all spatially homogenous models. This indicates that the isotropy of
the Robertson-Walker models is unstable to homogeneous and anisotropic perturbations.
It therefore seems that there is only a small set of initial conditions that would give rise to
universal models which would be isotropic to within the observed limits at the present
time. One possible way out of this difficulty is to suppose that there is an infinite number
of universes with all possible different initial conditions. Only those universes which are

expanding just fast enough to avoid recollapsing would contain galaxies, and hence intelligent life. However, it seems that this subclass of universes which have just the escape velocity would in general approach isotropy. On this view, the fact that we observe the universe to be isotropic would simply be a reflection of our own existence.

We shall now put forward an idea which offers a possible way out of this difficulty. This idea is based on the discovery that homogeneous cosmological models do in general tend toward isotropy if they have exactly the same escape velocity. Of course, such "parabolic" homogeneous models form a set of measure zero among all homogeneous models. However, we can justify their consideration by adopting a philosophy which has been suggested by R.H. Dicke, "Dirac's Cosmology and Mach's Principle," *Nature*, 192 (1961): 440–441 and B. Carter, "Global Structure of the Kerr Family of Gravitational Fields," *Physical Review*, 174 (1968): 1559–1571. In this approach one postulates that there is not one universe, but a whole infinite ensemble of universes with all possible initial conditions. From the existence of the unstable anisotropic model it follows that nearly all of the universes become highly anisotropic. However, these universes would not be expected to contain galaxies, since condensations can grow only in universes in which the rate of expansion is just sufficient to avoid recollapse. The existence of galaxies would seem to be a necessary precondition for the development of any form of intelligent life. Thus there will be life only in those universes which tend toward isotropy at large times. The fact that we have observed the universe to be isotropic therefore only a consequence of our own existence. (319)

Spatially homogeneous models can be divided into three classes: those which have less than the escape velocity (i.e., those whose rate of expansion is insufficient to prevent them from recollapsing), those which have just the escape velocity, and those which have more than the escape velocity. Models of the first class exist only for a finite time, and therefore do not approach arbitrarily near to isotropy. We have shown that models of the third class do in general tend to isotropy at arbitrarily large times. Those models of the second class which are sufficiently near to the Robertson-Walker models do in general tend to isotropy, but this class is of measure zero in the space of all homogeneous models. It therefore seems that one cannot explain the isotropy of the universe without postulating special initial conditions. . . .

The most attractive answer would seem to come from the Dickie-Carter idea that there is a very large number of universes, with all possible combinations of initial data and values of the fundamental constants. In those universes with less than the escape velocity small density perturbations will not have time to develop into galaxies and stars before the universe recollapses. In those universes with more than the escape velocity, small density perturbations would still have more than the escape velocity, and so would not form bound systems. It is only in those universes which have very nearly the escape velocity that one could expect galaxies to develop, and we have found that such universes will in general approach isotropy. Since it would seem that the existence of galaxies is a necessary condition for the development of intelligent life, the answer to the question "why is the universe isotropic?" is "because we are here". 334

C.B. Colling and S.W. Hawking, "Why is the Universe Isotropic?" *The Astrophysical Journal* (March 1, 1973)

Here you had better look up Alan Guth, "Inflationary Universes: A possible solution to the horizon and flatness problems, Physical Review D, 23, 1981 347–356, and some other pieces mentioned by John Earman, "The SAP also Rises: . . ." *American Philosophical Quarterly*, Oct. 1987

From a theistic point of view, however, no mystery at all and an easy explanation.

(F) The Naïve Teleological Argument

Swinburne:

The world is a complicated thing. There are lots and lots of different bits of matter, existing over endless time (or possibly beginning to exist at some finite time). The bits of it have finite and not particularly natural sizes, shapes, masses, etc; and they come together in finite, diverse and very far from natural conglomerations (viz. lumps of matter on planets and stars, and distributed throughout interstellar space). . . . Matter is inert and has no powers which it can choose to exercise; it does what it has to do. yet each bit of matter behaves in exactly the same way as similar bits of matter throughout time and space, the way codified in natural laws . . . all electrons throughout endless time and space have exactly the same powers and properties as all other electrons (properties of attracting, repelling, interacting, emitting radiation, etc.), all photons have the same powers and properties as all other photons etc., etc. Matter is complex, diverse, but regular in its behaviour. Its existence and behaviour need explaining in just the kind of way that regular chemical combinations needed explaining; or it needs explaining when we find all the cards of a pack arranged in order. EG 288

Newton: Whence arises all this order and beauty and structure?

Hume *Dialogues*: Cleanthes: Consider, anatomize the eye. Survey its structure and contrivance and tell me, from your own feeling, if the idea of a contriver does not immediately flow in upon you with a force like that of sensation. The most obvious conclusion, surely, is in favour of design, and it requires time, reflection and study to summon up those frivolous, though abstruse objections which can support infidelity.

The idea: the beauty, order and structure of the universe and the structure of its parts strongly suggest that it was designed; it seems absurd to think that such a universe should have just been there, that it wasn't designed and created but just happened. Contemplating these things can result in a strong impulse to believe that the universe was indeed designed—by God.

(Hume's version may be very close to a wholly different style of "argument": one where the arguer tries to help the arguee achieve the sort of situation in which the *Sensus Divinitatis* operates.)

(G) *Tony Kenny's Style of Teleological Argument*

(H) *The Ontological Argument*

(I) *Another argument thrown in for good measure*

Why is there anything at all? That is, why are there any *contingent* beings at all? (Isn't that passing strange, as S says?) An answer or an explanation that appealed to any contingent being would of course raise the same question again. A good explanation would have to appeal to a being that could not fail to exist, and (unlike numbers, propositions, sets, properties and other abstract necessary beings) is capable of explaining the existence of contingent beings (by, for example, being able to create them). The only viable candidate for this post seems to be God, thought of as the bulk of the theistic tradition has thought of him: that is, as a necessary being, but also as a concrete being, a being capable of causal activity. (Difference from S's Cosmo Arg: on his view God a contingent being, so no answer to the question "Why are there anything (contingent) at all?"

II. HALF A DOZEN EPISTEMOLOGICAL ARGUMENTS

(J) *The Argument from Positive Epistemic Status*

Clearly many of our beliefs do have positive epistemic status for us (at any rate most of us think so, most of us accept this premise). As we have seen, positive epistemic status is best thought of as a matter of a belief's being produced by cognitive faculties that are functioning properly in the sort of environment that is appropriate for them. The easiest and most natural way to think of proper functioning, however, is in terms of design: a machine or an organism is working properly when it is working in the way it was designed to work by the being that designed it. But clearly the best candidate for being the being who has designed our cognitive faculties would be God.

This premise of this argument is only a special case of a much broader premise: there are many natural (nonartifactual) things in the world besides our cognitive faculties such that they function properly or improperly: organs of our bodies and of other organisms, for example. (Tony Kenny's design argument)

Objection: perhaps there is indeed this initial tendency to see these things as the product of intelligent design; but there is a powerful defeater in evolutionary theory, which shows us a perfectly natural way in which all of these things might have come about without design.

Reply: (1) is it in fact plausible to think that human beings, for example, have arisen through the sorts of mechanisms (random genetic mutation and natural selection) in the time that according to contemporary science that has been available? The conference of biologists and mathematicians ("Mathematical Challenges to the NeoDarwinian Interpretation of Evolution," ed. Paul Morehead and Martin Kaplan, Philadelphia, Wistar Institute Press); the piece by Houston Smith. The chief problem: most of the paths one might think of from the condition of not having eyes, for example, to the condition of having them will not work; each mutation along the way has to be adaptive, or appropriately connected with something adaptive. (2) There does not appear to be any decent naturalistic account of the origin of life, or of language.

(K) The Argument from the Confluence of Proper Function and Reliability

We ordinarily think that when our faculties are functioning properly in the right sort of environment, they are reliable. Theism, with the idea that God has created us in his image and in such a way that we can acquire truth over a wide range of topics and subjects, provides an easy, natural explanation of that fact. The only real competitor here is nontheistic evolutionism; but nontheistic evolution would at best explain our faculties' being reliable with respect to propositions which are such that having a true belief with respect to them has survival value. That does not obviously include moral beliefs, beliefs of the kind involved in completeness proofs for axiomatizations of various first order systems, and the like. (More poignantly, beliefs of the sort involved in science, or in thinking evolution is a plausible explanation of the flora a fauna we see.) Still further, true beliefs *as such* don't have much by way of survival value; they have to be linked with the right kind of dispositions to behavior. What evolution requires is that our *behavior* have survival value, not necessarily that our beliefs be true. (Sufficient that we be programmed to act in adaptive ways.) But there are many ways in which our behavior could be adaptive, even if our beliefs were for the most part false. Our whole belief structure might (a) be a sort of byproduct or epiphenomenon, having no real connection with truth, and no real connection with our action. Or (b) our beliefs might be connected in a regular way with our actions, and with our environment, but not in such a way that the beliefs would be for the most part true.

Can we define a notion of natural plausibility, so that we can say with Salmon that belief in God is just implausible, and hence needs a powerful argument from what is plausible? This would make a good section in the book. Here could argue that what you take to be naturally plausible depends upon whether you are a theist or not. (It doesn't have to do only with what seems plausible to you, of course.) And here could put into this volume some of the stuff from the other one about these questions not being metaphysically or theologically neutral.

Patricia Churchland (JP LXXXIV Oct 87) argues that the most important thing about the human brain is that it has evolved; hence (548) its principle function is to enable the organism to move appropriately. "Boiled down to essentials, a nervous system enables the organism to succeed in the four F's: feeding fleeing, fighting and reproducing. The principle chore of nervous systems is to get the body parts where they should be in order that the organism may survive. . . . Truth, whatever that is, definitely takes the hindmost." (Self-referential problems loom here.) She also makes the point that we can't expect perfect engineering from evolution; it can't go back to redesign the basics.

Note that there is an interesting piece by Paul Horwich, "Three Forms of Realism," *Synthese*, 51 (1982): 181–201 where he argues that the very notion of mind independent truth implies that our claims to knowledge cannot be rationally justified. The difficulty "concerns the adequacy of the canons of justification implicit in scientific and ordinary linguistic practice—what reason is there to suppose that they guide us towards the truth? This question, given metaphysical realism, is substantial, and, I think, impossible to answer; and it is this gulf between truth and our ways of attempting to recognize it which constitutes the respect in which the facts are radically autonomous." Thus metaphysical realism involves to an unacceptable, indeed fatal, degree the autonomy of fact: there is from that perspective no reason to suppose that scientific practice provides even the slightest clue to what is true. (185 ff.)

(L) The Argument from Simplicity

According to Swinburne, simplicity is a prime determinant of *intrinsic probability*. That seems to me doubtful, mainly because there is probably no such thing in general as intrinsic (logical) probability. Still we certainly do favor simplicity; and we are inclined to think that simple explanations and hypotheses are more likely to be true than complicated epicyclic ones. So suppose you think that simplicity is a mark of truth (for hypotheses). If theism is true, then some reason to think the more simple has a better chance of being true than the less simple; for God has created both us and our theoretical preferences and the world; and it is reasonable to think that he would adapt the one to the other. (If he himself favored anti-simplicity, then no doubt he would have created us in such a way that we would too.) If theism is not true, however, there would seem to be no reason to think that the simple is more likely to be true than the complex.

(M) The Argument from Induction

Hume pointed out that human beings are inclined to accept inductive forms of reasoning and thus to take it for granted, in a way, that the future will relevantly resemble the past. (This may have been known even before Hume.) As Hume also pointed out, however, it is hard to think of a good (noncircular) reason for believing that indeed the future will be relevantly like the past. Theism, however, provides a reason: God has created us and our noetic capacities and has created the world; he has also created the former in such a way as to be adapted to the latter. It is likely, then, that he has created the world in such a way that in fact the future will indeed resemble the past in the relevant way. (And thus perhaps we do indeed have a priori knowledge of contingent truth: perhaps we know a priori that the future will resemble the past.) (Note here the piece by Aron Edidin: "Language Learning and A Priori Knowledge), *APQ* October 1986 (Vol. 23/ 4); Aron argues that in any case of language learning a priori knowledge is involved.)

This argument and the last argument could be thought of as exploiting the fact that according to theism God has created us in such a way as to be at home in the world (Wolterstorff.)

(N) *The Putnamian Argument (the Argument from the Rejection of Global Skepticism)*

Hilary Putnam (*Reason Truth and History*) and others argue that if metaphysical realism is true (if "the world consists of a fixed totality of mind independent objects," or if "there is one true and complete description of the 'the way the world is'") then various intractable skeptical problems arise. For example, on that account we do not know that we are not brains in a vat. But clearly we do know that we are not brains in a vat; hence metaphysical realism is not true. But of course the argument overlooks the theistic claim that we could perfectly well know that we are not brains in a vat even if metaphysical realism is true: we can know that God would not deceive us in such a disgustingly wholesale manner. So you might be inclined to accept (1) the Putnamian proposition that we do know that we are not brains in a vat (2) the anti-Putnamian claim that metaphysical realism is true and antirealism a mere Kantian galimatias, and (3) the quasi-Putnamian proposition that if metaphysical realism is true and there is no such person as God who has created us and our world, adapting the former to the latter, then we would not know that we are not brains in a vat; if so, then you have a theistic argument.

Variant: Putnam and others argue that if we think that there is no conceptual link between justification (conceived internalistically) and truth, then we should have to take global skepticism really seriously. If there is no connection between these two, then we have no reason to think that even our best theories are any more likely to be true than the worst theories we can think of. We do, however, know that our best theories are more likely to be true than our worst ones; hence. . . . You may be inclined to accept (1) the Putnamian thesis that it is false that we should take global skepticism with real seriousness, (2) the anti-Putnamian thesis that there is no *conceptual* link between justification and truth (at any rate if theism is false), and (3) the quasi-Putnamian thesis that if we think is no link between the two, then we should take global skepticism really seriously. Then you may conclude that there must be a link between the two, and you may see the link in the theistic idea that God has created us and the world in such a way that we can reflect something of his epistemic powers by virtue of being able to achieve knowledge, which we typically achieve when we hold justified beliefs.

Here in this neighborhood and in connection with anti-realist considerations of the Putnamian type, there is a splendid piece by Shelley Stillwell in the '89 *Synthese* entitled something like "Plantinga's Anti-realism" which nicely analyzes the situation and seems to contain the materials for a theistic argument.

(O) The Argument from Reference

Return to Putnam's brain in a vat. P argues that our thought has a certain *external* character: what we can think depends partly on what the world is like. Thus if there were no trees, we could not think the thought *there are no trees*; the word 'tree' would not mean what it does mean if in fact there were no trees (and the same for other natural kind terms—water, air, horse, bug, fire, lemon, human being, and the like, and perhaps also artifactual kind terms—house, chair, airplane, computer, barometer, vat, and the like.) But then, he says, we can discount brain in vat skepticism: it can't be right, because if we were brains in a vat, we would not have the sort of epistemic contact with vats that would permit our term 'vat' to mean what in fact it does. But then we could not so much as think the thought: we are brains in a vat. So if we were, we could not so much as think the thought that we were. But clearly we can think that thought (and if we couldn't we couldn't formulate brain in vat skepticism; so such skepticism must be mistaken).

But a different and more profound skepticism lurks in the neighborhood: we *think* we can think certain thoughts, where we can give general descriptions of the thoughts in question. Consider, for example, our thought that there are trees. We think there is a certain kind of large green living object, that grows and is related in a certain way to its environment; and we name this kind of thing 'tree'. But maybe as a matter of fact we are not in the sort of environment we think we are in. Maybe we are in a sort of environment of a totally different sort, of such a sort that in fact we can't form the sort of thoughts we think we can form. We think we can form thoughts of certain kind, but in fact we cannot. That could be the case. Then it isn't so much (or only) that our thoughts might be systematically and massively mistaken; instead it might be that we can't think the thoughts we think we can think. Now as a matter of fact we can't take this skepticism seriously; and, indeed, if we are created by God we need not take it seriously, for God would not permit us to be deceived in this massive way.

(P) The Kripke-Wittgenstein Argument from Plus and Quus (see Supplementary Handout)

(Q) The General Argument from Intuition

We have many kinds of intuitions: (1) logical (narrow sense and broad sense): the intuitions codified in propositional modal logic—if it could be the case that the moon is made of green cheese, then it is necessary that that could be so; moral, (2) arithmetical, set theoretical and mathematical generally, (3) moral, (4) philosophical (Leib's Law; there aren't any things that do not exist; sets don't have the property of representing things as being a certain way; neither trees nor numbers are neither true nor false; there are a great number of things that are either true or false; there is such a thing as positive epistemic status; there is such a property as being unpunctual; and so on.) You may be inclined to think that all or some of these ought to be taken with real seriousness, and give us real and important truth. It is much easier to see how this could be so on a theistic than on a nontheistic account of the nature of human beings.

At the Mississippi Philoso Association Meeting in Nov., l986, Robert Holyer read a paper nicely developing this argument, and referring to John Beversluis' book, who attacks the argument, but in a mean spirited way and not with much success. This argument along with Augustine's "Our hearts are restless til they rest in thee, O God."

A couple of more arguments: (1) the argument from the causal theory of knowledge: many philosophers think there is a problem with our alleged knowledge of abstract objects in that they think we can't know truths about an object with which we are not in the appropriate causal relation. They then point out that we are not in much of any causal relation with abstract objects, and conclude, some of them, that there is a real problem with our knowing anything about abstract objects. (e.g., Paul Benacerraf.) But if we think of abstract objects as God's thoughts, then he is in causal relation with them, and also with us, so that there should be no problem as to how it is that we could know something about them. (On the causal theory of knowledge, if you think of abstract objects as just *there*, and as not standing in causal relations, then the problem should really be that it is hard to see how even God could have any knowledge of them.)

There is another realism anti-realism argument lurking here somewhere, indicated or suggested by Wolterstorff's piece in the Tomberlin metaphysics volume. It has to do with whether there are really any joints in reality, or whether it might not be instead that reality doesn't have any joints, and there are no essential properties of objects. Instead, there is only de dicto reality (this could be the argument from de re modality) with all classifications somehow being done by us. Interesting. Also another topic for Christian philosophy.

Another argument, brought to my attention by Nick Wolterstorff: the Chomsky argument from language learning. look this up. Where does C say any such thing? And where exactly does it go? Does it go with the KW plus quus argument?

Another argument . . . Thomas Nagel, the view from nowhere 78ff. Thinks it amazing that there should be any such thing as the sort of objective thinking or objective point of view that we do in fact have. Perhaps it is really amazing only from a naturalist point of view. He says he has no explanation. Maybe you find it amazing, maybe you don't. (I'm not sure I see why it is amazing yet.) He argues cogently that there is no good evolutionary explanation of this: first, what needs to be explained is the very possibility of this, and second, supposed that is explained, he goes on to argue that evolution gives us no good explanation of our higher mental abilities. The question is whether the mental powers necessary for the making of stone axes, and hunter-gatherer success are sufficient for the construction of theories about sub atomic particles, proofs of Gödel's theorem, the invention of the compact disc, and so on. He thinks not. So he is really on to something else: not so much 'objective thinking' as higher mental powers involved in these striking intellectual accomplishments.

The evolutionary explanation would be that intellectual powers got started by going along for the ride, so to speak, and then turned out to be useful, and were such that improvements in them got selected when we came down from the trees. (At that point a bigger brain became useful (Don't whales have an even bigger one?). A sort of two part affair, the first part being accidental. So then the second part would be selected for survival value or advantage. But of course the question is whether this gives the slightest reason to think these theories have any truth to them at all. And he fails to mention the fact that all that really gets selected is behavior; there are various combinations of desire and belief that can lead to adaptive actions even if the belief is completely mistaken.

III. MORAL ARGUMENTS

(R) Moral Arguments (actually R1 to Rn)

There are many different versions of moral arguments, among the best being Bob Adams' favored version (in "Moral Arguments for Theistic Belief" in C. Delaney, *Rationality and Religious Belief* (Notre Dame). (1) One might find oneself utterly convinced (as I do) that morality is objective, not dependent upon what human beings know or think, and that it cannot be explained in terms of any "natural" facts about human beings or other things; that it can't ultimately be explained in terms of physical, chemical or biological facts. (2) One may also be convinced that there could not be such objective moral facts unless there were such a person as God who, in one way or another, legislates them.

Here consider George Mavrodes' argument that morality would be 'queer' in a Russellian or nontheistic universe (in "Religion and the Queerness of Morality" in *Rationality, Religious Belief and Moral Commitment*, ed. Audi and Wainwright.)

Other important arguments here: A.E Taylor's (*The Faith of a Moralist*) version, and Clem Dore's (and Sidgwick's) Kantian argument from the confluence of morality with true self-interest, some of the other arguments considered by Bob Adams in the above mentioned paper, and arguments by Hastings Rashdall in *The Theory of Good and Evil* and by W.R. Sorley, *Moral Values and the Idea of God* which we used to read in college.

(R*) The Argument from Evil

Many philosophers offer an anti-theistic argument from evil, and perhaps they have some force. But there is also a theistic argument from evil. There is real and genuine evil in the world: evil such that it isn't just a matter of personal opinion that the thing in question is abhorrent, and furthermore it doesn't matter if those who perpetrate it think it is good, and could not be convinced by anything we said. And it is plausible to think that in a nontheistic or at any rate a naturalistic universe, there could be no such thing. So perhaps you think there is such a thing as genuine and horrifying evil, and that in a nontheistic universe, there could not be; then you have another theistic argument.

How to make this argument more specific? "what Pascal later called the 'triple abyss' into which mankind has fallen: the libidinal enslavement to the egotistical self: the *libido dominandi*, or lust for power over others and over nature; the *libido sentiendi*, or lust for intense sensation; and the *libido sciendi*, or lust for manipulative knowledge, knowledge that is primarily used to increase our own power, profit and pleasure." Michael D. Aeschliman "Discovering the Fall," *This World* (Fall 1988): 93.

How think about utterly appalling and horrifying evil? The Christian understanding: it is indeed utterly appalling and horrifying; it is defying God, the source of all that is good and just. It has a sort of cosmic significance: in this way it is the other side of the coin from the argument from love. There we see that the deep significance of love can't be explained in terms of naturalistic categories; the same goes here. From a naturalistic perspective, there is nothing much more to evil—say the sheer horror of the holocaust, of Pol Pot, or a thousand other villains—than there is to the way in which animals savage each other. A natural outgrowth of natural processes.

Hostility, hatred, hostility towards outsiders or even towards one's family is to be understood in terms simply of the genes' efforts (Dawkins) to ensure its survival. Nothing perverted or unnatural about it. (Maybe can't even have these categories.) But from a theistic pint of view, deeply perverted, and deeply horrifying. And maybe this is the way we naturally see it. The point here is that it is objectively horrifying. We find it horrifying: and that is part of its very nature, as opposed to the naturalistic way of thinking about it where there really can't be much of anything like objective horrifyingness.

In Peter Berger, *A Rumor of Angels*, around page 53, there is an argument that certain kinds of human wickedness are so appalling that they require something like hell.

The thing to do here: take an example of some really horrifying evil—the Dostoyevsky thing from one of the visual aids.

On a naturalistic way of looking at the matter, it is hard to see how there can really be such a thing as evil: (though of course there could be things we don't like, prefer not to happen): how could there be something that was bad, worthy of disapproval, even if we and all other human beings were wildly enthusiastic about it? On naturalistic view, how make sense of (a) our intuition that what is right or wrong, good or evil does not depend upon what we like or think) and (b) our revulsion at evil—the story the prophet Nathan told David, at the sort of thing that went on in Argentina, Stalin's Russia, Hitler's Germany (*Sophie's Choice*); the case mention in Surin's book about the young child who was hanged and remained living for half an hour after he was hanged; the fact that the Nazis were purposely trying to be cruel, to induce despair, taunting their victims with the claim that no one would ever know of their fate and how they were treated; the thing from Dostoyevsky, who says that beasts wouldn't do this, they wouldn't be so artistic about it. Compare dying from cancer to the sort of horror the Germans did: the second is much worse than the first, somehow, but not because it causes more pain. It is because of the wickedness involved, a wickedness we don't see in the cancer. An appalling wickedness.

There seems to be a lot more to it than there could be on a naturalistic account of the matter. So the naturalist says: evil is a problem for you: why would a good God permit evil, or all that evil? But evil also a problem for him: There really isn't any evil, (or isn't any of a certain sort, a sort such that in fact we think there is some of that sort) on a naturalistic perspective. (This needs working out, but I think there is something to it.)

IV. OTHER ARGUMENTS

(S) The Argument from Colors and Flavors (Adams and Swinburne)

What is the explanation of the correlation between physical and psychical properties? Presumably there *is* an explanation of it; but also it will have to be, as Adams and Swinburne say, a personal, nonscientific explanation. The most plausible suggestion would involve our being created that way by God.

(T) The Argument from Love

Man-woman, parent-child, family, friendship, love of college, church, country—many different manifestations. Evolutionary explanation: these adaptive and have survival value. Evolutionarily useful for male and female human beings, like male and female hippopotami, to get together to have children colts) and stay together to raise them; and the same for the other manifestations of love. The theistic account: vastly more to it than that: reflects the basic structure and nature of reality; God himself is love.

(U) The Mozart Argument

On a naturalistic anthropology, our alleged grasp and appreciation of (alleged) beauty is to be explained in terms of evolution: somehow arose in the course of evolution, and something about its early manifestations had survival value. But miserable and disgusting cacophony (heavy metal rock?) could as well have been what we took to be beautiful. On the theistic view, God recognizes beauty; indeed, it is deeply involved in his very nature. To grasp the beauty of a Mozart's D Minor piano concerto is to grasp something that is objectively there; it is to appreciate what is objectively worthy of appreciation.

(V) The Argument from Play and Enjoyment

Fun, pleasure, humor, play, enjoyment. (Maybe not all to be thought of in the same way.) Playing: evolution: an adaptive means of preparing for adult life (so that engaging in this sort of thing as an adult suggests a case of arrested development). But surely there is more to it than that. The joy one can take in humor, art, poetry, mountaineering, exploring, adventuring (the problem is not to explain how it would come about that human beings enjoyed mountaineering: no doubt evolution can do so). The problem is with its significance. Is it really true that all there is to this is enjoyment? Or is there a deeper significance? The Westminster Shorter Catechism: the chief end of man is to glorify God and enjoy him (and his creation and gifts) forever.

(W) Arguments from Providence and from Miracles

(X) C.S. Lewis's Argument from Nostalgia

Lewis speaks of the *nostalgia* that often engulfs us upon beholding a splendid land or seascape; these somehow speak to us of their maker. Not sure just what the argument is; but suspect there is one there.

(Y) The Argument from the Meaning of Life

How does thought about the meaningfulness or meaninglessness of life fit in? Sartre, Camus, Nagel.

(Z) The Argument from (A) to (Y)

These arguments import a great deal of unity into the philosophic endeavor, and the idea of God helps with an astonishingly wide variety of cases: epistemological, ontological, ethical, having to do with meaning, and the like of that.

INDEX

Aaronson, Scott, 194
Adams, Marilyn McCord, 281–284, 287
Adams, Robert Merrihew, 60, 67, 71–72, 74,
    367n1, 368n2, 434, 447, 464, 478
  and the Euthyphro dilemma, 69
  and moral obligation, 274, 476
  and the principle of sufficient
    reason, 67
  and psychologism, 67
Albert, David, 191, 192–193, 419, 426–427
Alston, William, 461
  and divine command theory, 70, 274
  and moral obligation, 69
Anscombe, G.E.M., 269, 270, 274
Anselm of Canterbury
  and conceptions of God, 262
  and the ontological argument, 123–130,
    132–134
Aquinas, Saint Thomas, 103, 341, 343, 346,
    368n3, 462
  and the five ways, 24, 126, 416
  and the ontological argument, 129
  and the teleological argument, 112–113, 115
  and truth, 15

Aristotle, 233–234n8, 255, 269–270, 272, 360,
    368n3, 369n8
  and the teleological argument, 108
  and truth bearers, 15
Augustine, Saint, 11, 25n1, 223, 225–227, 241, 341,
    346, 368n3, 475

Babbage, Charles, 343
Balaguer, Mark, 73, 246
Balthasar, Hans Urs von, 321, 334
Barth, Karl, 322, 334
Basil the Great, 324
Bealer, George, 239, 250
Bell, John, 420–421, 425–426, 431, 437n3
Benardete, José, 391–392
Bergmann, Michael, 176, 251, 288n8
Berkeley, George, 64, 110, 116, 247, 434
Blackburn, Simon, 229–230
Boethius, 15, 233–234n8
Boghossian, Paul, 214, 216, 230, 234n12
Bohr, Niels, 418, 420–421, 423–424
Boolos, George, 32–33
Born, Max, 423
Bradley, Francis Herbert, 239

Brink, David, 268, 276n12
Brown, James, 73
Burns, Robert, 345

Callender, Craig, 192
Calvin, John, 114, 199, 454, 461
Cantor, Georg, 29, 403n12, 463
Carnap, Rudolf, 198
Carroll, Sean, 97–98, 194
Chalmers, David John, 142–143, 145
Chandler, Jake, 252
Cohen, Yishai, 392–395, 400, 403n14, 404n24
Cole, Thomas, 324
Collins, Francis, 119
Copan, Paul, 269, 274
Cosmides, Leda, 164
Craig, William Lane, 266–267, 446
Crane, Tim, 179–180

Dancy, Jonathan, 252, 253
Darwin, Charles Robert, 108–109, 118
    and Darwinian evolution, 109, 118, 209–210,
        239, 310
Davis, William, 324, 334
Dawkins, Richard, 109, 118, 184, 239, 310, 316, 477
Dennett, Daniel, 163, 165, 239
Descartes, René, 69, 110, 185, 218, 221, 343
Diller, Kevin, 281–284, 287
Djouadi, Abdelhak, 98
Dougherty, Trent, 383
Douglas, John, 348
Draper, Paul, 323
Durkheim, Émile, 114

Earman, John, 191, 343, 346, 469
Edwards, Jonathan, 434, 458
Einstein, Albert, 91, 418–421
Enoch, David, 265
Evans, C. Stephen, 3
    and divine command theory, 274
    and moral obligation, 269–270

Fakhry, Majid, 132, 133
Fales, Evan, 210, 431
al-Fârâbî, Abû Nsar, 132–134, 134–135n8
Feferman, Solomon, 391
Fendt, Gene, 130, 132
Fine, Arthur, 421, 431
Fitelson, Branden, 378

Flannagan, Matthew, 269, 274
Foot, Philippa, 272
Fraenkel, Abraham, 41
Freddoso, Alfred, 435
Frege, Gottlob, 15, 245, 462
Freud, Sigmund, 114
    and naïve set theory, 33–34
    and psychologism, 11, 67–68

Gaut, Berys, 333
Gettier, Edmund, 233n3, 249, 250
Gödel, Kurt, 64, 73, 475
    and number theory, 245
Goodman, Nelson, 198, 212n3
Grünbaum, Adolf, 390

Hackett, Stuart, 389
Hanks, Peter, 13, 16
Harman, Gilbert, 243
Hartle, James, 401
Hartshorne, Charles, 127, 367n1
Hawking, Stephen, 401, 469
Hedrick, Landon, 394
Heidegger, Martin, 306
Heisenberg, Werner, 419, 423
Holliday, Wesley, 218
Houston, Joseph, 346
Huemer, Michael, 195
    and phenomenal conservatism, 116
Huizinga, Johan, 336
Hume, David, 110, 185, 195
    and aesthetic value, 332–335
    argument against miracles, 342–346, 348
    and laws of nature, 432–433
    and the problem of induction, 185–187, 472
    and the supervenience thesis, 148, 432–433
    and the teleological argument, 108, 113, 469–470

Joyce, Richard, 268, 276n17
Jubien, Michael, 14, 17, 26n17
Justin Martyr, 227

Kant, Immanuel, 1, 219, 321, 327, 462
    and aesthetic value, 332–5, 338n9
    and categorical imperatives, 268
    and hypothetical imperatives, 268
    and kalam cosmological argument, 396–397
    and ontological argument, 127–128, 131–132
    and sense experience, 212n2

Kaplan, David, 32
Kelemen, Deborah, 165–168
Kenny, Sir Anthony John Patrick, 5, 60, 67, 464, 470
Keynes, John Maynard, 92, 383n3
King, Jeffrey, 13, 16–17, 25n14
Kitcher, Philip, 272–273
Koons, Robert, 390, 398, 400
Korman, Daniel, 246–247
Kreeft, Peter, 322
Kripke, Saul, 47–48, 214–215
    and the necessity of origin thesis, 144
    and rigid designators, 147
    and skepticism, 214–215, 221, 224–227, 229, 231
Kuhn, Thomas, 198, 418
Kvanvig, Jonathan, 251–252

Lactantius, Lucius, 214, 227, 233
Larsen, Timothy, 346
Law, Stephen, 131, 242, 248
Leibniz, Gottfried Wilhelm, 12, 66
    and divine command theory, 69
    and necessary truths, 66–69, 240–241
    and Platonism, 71–72
Leslie, Charles, 348–350
Lewis, Clive Staples, 346, 368n3, 479
    and aesthetic value, 326, 337
    and love, 316–317
    and the moral law, 268–269, 271, 332
Lewis, David, 77, 185, 241, 408
    and laws of nature, 432–433
    and modal realism, 187–189
    and possible worlds, 408–409, 413
Linnebo, Øystein, 44–48
Locke, John, 110, 209, 215, 346
Loke, Andrew, 394–396
Lowe, E.J., 61, 66, 71–72
    and the argument from *kinds*, 61–63
    and the modal ontological argument, 62
Lycan, William, 72, 179–180

Mackie, John Leslie, 269, 342–343, 351
Malcolm, Norman, 127–128, 135n9
Mavrodes, George, 269, 476
McGrew, Lydia, 104
McGrew, Timothy, 104, 262, 456
McKay, Ryan, 163

Meinong, Alexius, 408–409, 413
Menzel, Christopher, 60, 463, 464
Mill, John Stuart, 343
Mirza, Omar, 255
Miščević, Nenad, 242–243
Morriston, Wesley, 399
Murdoch, Iris, 123, 127–130, 132–134, 135n9

Nagel, Thomas, 307–309, 311–315, 369n7, 475, 479
Newton, Sir Isaac, 91, 469
Nietzsche, Friedrich Wilhelm, 311, 318, 321

O'Hear, Anthony, 323
Oppy, Graham, 146–147, 392
Otte, Richard, 343
Ouellette, Lauren, 194

Paley, William, 113, 350–351
Parfit, Derek, 265, 268–269
Pascal, Blaise, 477
    and knowledge of God, 111–112
Pauli, Wolfgang, 423
Philo of Alexandria, 241
Pierce, Charles Sanders, 378
Planck, Max, 418
Plato, 15, 130, 215, 217, 233–234n8, 462
    and moral obligation, 270
    and the ontological argument, 134n1
    and skepticism, 223–225, 227
    and the teleological argument, 108
Polkinghorne, John Charlton, 73, 119
Pollock, John, 77, 251–252, 451, 465
Price, Huw, 191–192
Pruss, Alexander, 82, 138, 139, 368n2, 370n17, 390, 398, 400, 425, 450
Puryear, Stephen, 398–399
Pust, Joel, 241, 250
Putnam, Hilary, 126, 198, 200, 208, 428, 473–474
    and the brain-in-a-vat puzzle, 200–201, 204–206, 214, 218–221
    and internal realism, 201–206
    and metaphysical realism, 200, 210, 223, 473

Quine, Willard Van Orman, 178, 198
    and plural quantification, 32, 52n12
    and quantum theory, 428
    and skepticism, 215, 225

Rasmussen, Joshua, 139, 141
Rea, Michael, 176, 246–247
Reid, Thomas, 110–111, 117
Ritchie, Angus, 264
Rorty, Richard, 203
Ross, James Francis, 139
Rowe, William, 123, 125–127, 130, 133, 139
Royall, Richard, 375–380, 383–384
Russell, Bertrand, 15, 19, 41, 305, 314, 370n16, 476
  and naïve set theory, 29, 34–37, 43, 45–46, 47,
    358–359, 365, 463
  and pragmatism, 234–235n15

Sartre, Jean-Paul, 305–308, 314–315, 479
Schaffer, Jonathan, 147
Schechter, Joshua, 242
Schrödinger, Erwin
  and the Schrödinger Equation, 94, 419
  and Schrödinger's Paradox, 422
Sellars, Wilfrid, 217–218, 225, 462
Shafer-Landau, Russ, 272
Shaw, Benjamin, 348
Skolem, Thoralf, 41
Soames, Scott, 13, 16–20, 23–24, 26n19,
    26n20, 26n28
Sober, Elliot, 104
Socrates, 19, 217, 270
Stalnaker, Robert, 25n6, 77
Steiner, Mark, 74, 91
Stillwell, Shelley, 231, 235n17, 473
Street, Sharon, 243
Suits, Bernard, 336
Swinburne, Richard, 5, 6n4, 175, 181n12, 184,
    240, 322, 379–380, 447, 461, 472, 478
  and beauty, 324–325

and the principle of credulity, 116
and the principle of dwindling
  probabilities, 344
and the rationality of belief in God, 2
and teleological argument, 109, 469

Tacelli, Ronald, 322
Taliaferro, Charles, 304
Tennant, Frederick Robert, 325
Tooley, Michael, 146, 368n2, 431

van Frassen, Bas, 423
van Inwagen, Peter, 59, 139, 368n2
Vestrup, Eric, 104
Vilenkin, Alexander, 400–401
Vitali, Giuseppe, 21–22
von Neumann, John, 423

Walls, Jerry, 271
Wang, Hao, 30, 52n5, 463–464
Weinberg, Steven, 246
Wielenberg, Erik, 82, 265, 267–268, 272
Wigner, Eugene, 74, 91, 423
Williams, Bernard, 370n15
Williamson, Timothy, 233n3, 239,
    242–244, 248
Wilson, Edward, 310
Wittgenstein, Ludwig, 214, 217–218, 231
Wolf, Susan, 370n15
Wolterstorff, Nicholas, 455, 473, 475
Wynn, Mark, 325–326, 330, 332

Zemach, Eddy, 327–329, 333
Zermelo, Ernst, 35–37, 41–43, 53n16, 53n21,
    54n29, 66

CPSIA information can be obtained
at www.ICGtesting.com
Printed in the USA
BVHW040552180519
548412BV00008B/6/P

9 780190 842222